Protestarchitektur
Barrikaden, Camps,
raumgreifende Taktiken
1830–2023

Protest Architecture
Barricades, Camps,
Spatial Tactics
1830–2023

T0283239

Hg. (Eds.)
Oliver Elser
Anna-Maria Mayerhofer
Sebastian Hackenschmidt
Jennifer Dyck
Lilli Hollein
Peter Cachola Schmal

 PARK BOOKS

Inhaltsverzeichnis

Contents

1830 Paris

1848 Paris

1848 Berlin

1848 Frankfurt am Main

1848 Wien (Vienna)

1849 Dresden

1830 Paris, Rue du Faubourg Saint-Antoine, 28. Juli 1830, Aquatinta, nach 1830. Bei den Barrikadenkämpfen während der → *Julirevolution* wurde – wie auf dieser Grafik eindrucksvoll (und sicherlich übertrieben) dargestellt – die Reiterei der königstreuen Truppen in Paris von den benachbarten Häusern herab mit Gegenständen beworfen. Engl.: During the barricade fights of the → *July Revolution* in Paris, the cavalry of the royalist troops was pelted with objects from neighboring houses — as is depicted impressively (albeit with some exaggeration) in this print. (SH)

1848 Paris, Charles-François Thibault: Barrikade Rue Saint-Maur, Daguerreotypie, 25. Juni 1848. Die wie ausgestorben wirkenden → *Barrikaden*, die auf dieser frühen Daguerreotypie zu erkennen sind, lassen nur düster erahnen, dass die Straßenkämpfe während des Juniaufstands in Folge der → *Februarrevolution* von 1848 insgesamt etwa 6500 Menschenleben forderten. Engl.: The seemingly deserted → *barricades* visible in this early daguerreotype are a somber indication of the approximately 6,500 lives the street fights claimed during the June Days Uprising in the wake of the → *February Revolution*. (SH)

1848 Berlin, Eduard Gaertner: Barrikade Breite Straße, Aquarell, 1848. Das Aquarell des renommierten Vedutenmalers Eduard Gaertner zeigt die → *Barrikade* in der auf das Stadtschloss zuführenden und deshalb während der → *Märzrevolution* 1848 besonders umkämpften Breiten Straße in Berlin. An der Hauswand am linken Bildrand hat der Künstler neben seinen Initialen das Datum der „Schreckensnacht" vom 18. auf den 19. März 1948 verewigt, in der die → *Straße* von den königlichen Truppen eingenommen wurde. Engl.: The aquarelle by the renowned veduta painter Eduard Gaertner shows the → *barricade* on Breite Straße in Berlin. As this street leads to the City Palace, it was especially embattled during the 1848 → *March Revolution*. On the building wall on the left, next to his own initials, the artist immortalized the date of the "night of terror" from March 18 to

19, 1848, during which the → *street* was seized by the royal troops. (SH)

1848 Frankfurt am Main, Barrikade Töngesgasse, 18. September 1848, kolorierte Lithografie, 1848. Obwohl die von den Bürger*innen während des → *Frankfurter Septemberaufstands* errichtete → *Barrikade* in der Töngesgasse bis an das zweite Stockwerk der angrenzenden Häuser reichte, konnte sie von den angeforderten österreichischen Truppen in der Nacht vom 18. auf den 19. September 1848 eingenommen werden. Engl.: Even though the → *barricade* citizens had erected on Töngesgasse during the → *Frankfurt September Uprising* reached up to the second story of the adjacent houses, the requested Austrian troops managed to seize it during the night of September 18, 1848. (SH)

1848 Wien (Vienna), Anton Ziegler: Revolutionäre auf der Barrikade am Stephansplatz am 25. Mai 1848, Öl auf Leinwand, 1848. Das Gemälde der großen → *Barrikade* am Stephansplatz, die im Rahmen des → *Wiener Oktoberaufstands* 1848 errichtet wurde, ist ein im wahrsten Sinne „überhöhtes" Idealbild, das mit seinem Menschenauflauf und den verschiedenen Landesflaggen eine über die Nationalitätsgrenzen hinausreichende Solidarität im Kampf gegen die herrschende Ordnung und die politische Repression zum Ausdruck bringt. Engl.: In the truest sense of the word, this painting presents an "elevated" idealization of the large → *barricade* that was set up on Stephansplatz during the → *Vienna Uprising* of 1848. The crowd as well as the variety of flags from different countries convey solidarity beyond the boundaries of nationality in the fight against the prevailing order and political repression. (SH)

1849 Dresden, Die Turnerin auf der Engelbarrikade zu Dresden, Druckgrafik, nach 1849. Die sich nähernden gegenrevolutionären Truppen wurden auf den → *Barrikaden* von 1848/1849 bisweilen von den in pro-demokratischen Vereinen organisierten Turner*innen empfangen – so auch beim → *Dresdner Maiaufstand* auf der sogenannten „Engelbarrikade" am Beginn der Wils-

1871 Paris

1891 Barcaldine

1919 Berlin

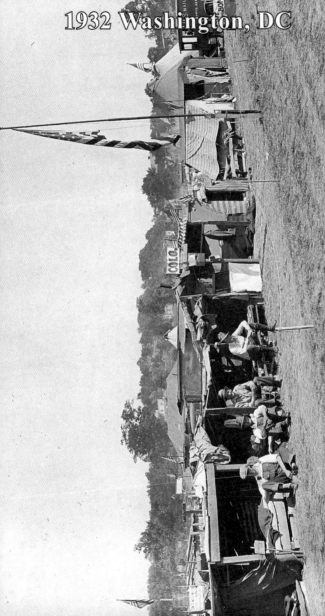

1932 Washington, DC

1936 Flint

1960 Greensboro

1960s Vancouver

druffer Gasse bei Engel's Restauration, die auch als → *Semper-Barrikade* in die Geschichte eingegangen ist. Engl.: Counterrevolutionary troops approaching the → *barricades* were sometimes met by gymnasts from pro-democratic associations—as was the case during the → *Dresden May Uprising* on the Engelbarrikade at the beginning of Wilsdruffer Gasse next to the tavern Engel's Restauration. The so-called "Angels' Barricade" also went down in history as the → *Semper barricade*. (SH)

1871 Paris, Alphonse Liébert: Barricade des Fédérés, Place de la Concorde, Fotografie, 1871. Bei der während der Revolution 1871 aus → *Ziegelsteinen* und Sandsäcken in zwei Ebenen errichteten Barricade des Fédérés scheint es sich um ein geradezu generalstabsmäßig geplantes Bauwerk gehandelt zu haben. Sie befand sich an der Einmündung der Rue de Rivoli auf die Place de la Concorde und ist nach den in Paris stationierten Nationalgardisten benannt, die sich der → *Pariser Kommune* angeschlossen hatten. Engl.: Made up of → *bricks* and sandbags, the two-tier "Barricade des Fédérés" appears to have been planned with almost military precision. The construction stood at the junction between Rue de Rivoli and Place de la Concorde and was named after the national guardsmen who were stationed in Paris and joined the → *Paris Commune*. (SII)

1891 Barcaldine, Chapman: Union Camp, Aquarell, 1891. Besser als die überlieferten Fotoaufnahmen zeigt diese künstlerische Darstellung die Struktur des → *Protestcamps* in Barcaldine. Der mehrere Monate andauernde → *Schafschererstreik* führte zur Gründung der sozialdemokratischen Australian Labor Party, die seit 2022 den Premierminister stellt. Engl.: This artistic representation provides a better insight into the structure of the → *protest camp* in Barcaldine than the surviving photographs. The → *Shearers' Strike* went on for several months and led to the founding of the social democratic Australian Labor Party, which won the federal election in 2022. (JD)

1919 Berlin, Willy Römer: Barrikade vor dem Berliner Tageblatt, Mossehaus, 11. Januar 1919. Die zahlreichen → *Barrikaden* aus Papier, die im Zeitungsviertel entstanden, sind durch die Aufnahmen mehrerer Fotojournalisten gut dokumentiert. Allerdings handelt es sich wohl um gestellte Szenen, angefertigt in den Kampfpausen. → *Januaraufstand / Spartakusaufstand* Engl.: The numerous paper → *barricades* that materialized in the newspaper district were well documented by several photojournalists. However, these scenes probably staged during breaks in the fighting. → *Spartacist Uprising* (JD)

1932 Washington, DC, Bonus Army Camp, Juli 1932. Der Großteil der → *Bonus Army* campierte auf einem sumpfigen Gebiet am Ufer des Anacostia River. Das Kapitol befindet sich auf der gegenüberliegenden Seite des Flusses. Engl.: The majority of the → *Bonus Army* camped on a marshy area on the bank of the Anacostia River opposite the Capitol. (JD)

1936 Flint, Sheldon Dick: General Motors Workers, 1937. Der → *Flint-Sitzstreik* gilt als Gründungsereignis der amerikanischen Gewerkschaft United Auto Workers. Die Protestform des Sitzstreiks breitete sich fortan auch auf andere Werke aus. Engl.: The → *Flint Sit-down Strike* is regarded as the founding event of the American United Auto Workers union. Subsequently, the sit-in as a form of protest also spread to other factories. (JD)

1960 Greensboro, Day 1, Woolworth lunch counter sit-in, 1. Februar 1960. Vier Studenten lösen die amerikanische Sit-in-Bewegung aus. → *Greensboro Sit-ins* Engl.: Four students initiated the American sit-in movement. → *Greensboro Sit-ins* (JD)

1960s Vancouver, Tony Westman: Filmstill „Mudflats Living", Vancouver, Sommer 1971. Die Pfahlbauten über dem Schlickwatt symbolisierten den Widerstand gegen den voranschreitenden urbanen Fortschritt. Sie wurden aus Treibholz und Abbruchmaterialien der Stadtentwicklungsprojekte von Vancouver gebaut. → *Maplewood Mudflats*

1965 Watts

1968 Washington, DC

1969 Nordirland
(Northern Ireland)

1970 Frankfurt am Main

1971 Kopenhagen
(Copenhagen)

1972 Canberra

Engl.: The pile structures over the mud-flats symbolize the resistance against advancing urban progress. They were composed of driftwood and demolition material from Vancouver's urban development projects. → *Maplewood Mud-flats* (JD)

1965 Watts, George R. Fry: Avalon Boulevard, Los Angeles, 15. August 1965. Die aus einem Hubschrauber fotografierte Luftaufnahme lässt zwei während der → *Watts-Unruhen* in Los Angeles in Brand gesetzte Gebäude-komplexe erkennen. Die Brandstiftungen beschränkten sich größtenteils auf Geschäfte von weißen Eigentümer*innen, deren Lohn- und Preisgestaltung den Unmut der überwiegend Schwarzen Bevölkerung hervorgerufen hatte (→ *Feuer*, → *Zerstörung*). Engl.: Taken from a helicopter, this aerial shot shows two building complexes that were set on fire during the → *Watts Riots*. The arson attacks mainly targeted the businesses of white owners, whose wages and pricing had sparked discontent among the predominantly Black population (→ *Fire*, → *Destruction*). (SH)

1968 Paris, Rue Gay-Lussac im Quartier Latin, 11. Mai 1968. Der Morgen nach der „Nacht der Barrikaden". Die Studierendenrevolte im → *Mai '68* brachte ein neues Fotomotiv hervor: Auf unzähligen Aufnahmen sind Einwohner*innen von Paris zu sehen, die durch das urbane Kampfgebiet laufen, als wären umgeworfene Autos (→ *Fahrzeuge*) und riesige Haufen von → *Pflasterstei-nen* ganz normal. Engl.: The morning after the "Night of the Barricades." The student revolt of → *May '68* gave rise to a new photographic motif: in countless photographs, the residents of Paris can be seen walking through the urban battle zone as if overturned cars (→ *Vehicles*) and huge piles of → *cobblestones* were quite normal. (OE)

1968 Washington, DC, Thomas O'Halloran: Resurrection City, 21. Mai 1968. Die → *Resurrection City* auf der National Mall wurde von Architekten als Planstadt entworfen. Die 650 A-Frame-Hütten waren in Höfen oder entlang der langen „Versorgungsachse" an-geordnet. Engl.: → *Resurrection City* on the National Mall was designed by architects according to a masterplan. The 650 A-frame huts were arranged in courtyards or flanking the long "supply axis." (AMM)

1969 Nordirland (Northern Ireland), Russel Boyce: Separation walls, Belfast, 13. Juli 1996. Ursprünglich als Provisorium gedacht, wurden die „Friedens-linien" später durch Mauern ersetzt. Heute ziehen sie viele Tourist*innen an. → *Nordirlandkonflikt* Engl.: Originally conceived as temporary, the "peace lines" were later replaced with walls. Today they attract many tourists. → *The Troubles* (JD)

1970 Frankfurt am Main, Hans Rem-pfer: VW-Käfer-Barrikade Bockenhei-mer Landstraße 111, Frankfurt am Main, 4. Oktober 1971. Mit dem → *Frankfur-ter Häuserkampf* beginnt ab 1970 die Hausbesetzer*innenbewegung in der Bundesrepublik (→ *Hausbesetzung*). Das Auto gehörte wohl einem der Beset-zer. Zeitzeug*innen erinnern sich, dass die Häuser mehrere Monate lang wie eine Festung gesichert waren. Engl.: In 1970, the → *Frankfurt Squatting Cam-paign* initiated the squatters' movement in West Germany (→ *Squatting*). The car probably belonged to one of the oc-cupiers. Contemporary witnesses recall that the houses were secured like for-tresses for several months. (JD)

1971 Kopenhagen (Copenhagen), Mini Wolff: Zaun an der Bådsmands-stræde-Kaserne, 4. September 1971. Alles begann 1971, als Anwohner*in-nen des Stadtteils Christianshavn den Zaun um die Bådsmandsstræde-Kaserne niederrissen, um ihren Kindern einen Spielplatz zu ermöglichen. → *Freistadt Christiania* Engl.: Everything started with residents from the district of Chris-tianhavn tearing down the fence of the Bådsmandsstræde Barracks so that their children could play there. → *Freetown Christiania* (JD)

1972 Canberra, Billy Craigie, Bert Williams, Michael Anderson, and Tony Coorey on the first day of protest in front of Parliament House, Canberra, 27. Ja-nuar 1972. Innerhalb weniger Tage ent-

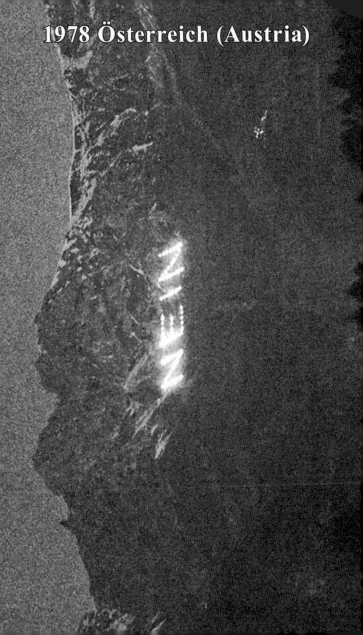

1978 Österreich (Austria)

1980 Gorleben

1980 Zürich (Zurich)

1980 Startbahn West
(Runway 18 West)

1981 Greenham

stand anstelle des Protestschirms ein Bürozelt mit Briefkasten, das bis heute als „Botschaft für Aborigines" fortbesteht (→ *Zelt*). → *Tent Embassy* Engl.: In the space of a few days, the protest parasol made way for an office tent with a mailbox which still exists today as an "embassy for Aborigines" (→ *Tent*). → *Tent Embassy* (JD)

1977 Buenos Aires, Plaza de Mayo, 1977. Am 30. April 1977 begann ein stiller Protest. Da es verboten war, sich stehend zu Kundgebungen zu versammeln, umrundeten die Mütter fortan jeden Donnerstag schweigend für eine halbe Stunde den Platz, um die Militärdiktatur für ihre verschleppten Angehörigen anzuklagen. → *Madres de Plaza de Mayo* Engl.: A silent protest began on April 30, 1977. Since it was forbidden to gather standing still for rallies, every Thursday, the mothers began to silently circle the square to denounce the military dictatorship's abduction of their relatives. → *Madres de Plaza de Mayo* (OE)

1978 Österreich (Austria), Bergfeuer bei Innsbruck, 4. November 1978. Am Vorabend der Volksabstimmung über die Zukunft des Atomkraftwerks → *Zwentendorf* wurde in der Tradition der Sonnwendfeuer, bei denen sonst eher religiöse Motive mit Fackeln umgesetzt werden, ein großes NEIN zum Leuchten gebracht. Engl.: On the eve of the referendum on the future of the nuclear power plant in → *Zwentendorf*, a big, glowing NO was created in the tradition of the solstice bonfires, at which torches are usually lit to convey more religious themes. (OE)

1980 Gorleben, Hans-Hermann Müller: Hüttendorf, 31. Mai 1980. Atomkraftgegner*innen errichteten ein Hüttendorf mit mehr als 100 Holzhäusern und fünf → *Türmen*. Der größte stand am Dorfplatz, dem sozialen Zentrum der Siedlung, und wurde vom eigenen Radiosender des → *Protestcamps* in → *Gorleben* genutzt. Engl.: Antinuclear activists set up a hut village with more than 100 wooden houses and five → *towers*. The largest was located on the village square, the social center of the settlement, and was used by the → *Gorleben* → *protest camp's* own radio station. (AMM)

1980 Zürich (Zurich), Patrick Lüthy, Comet Photo AG: Chaotendorf in der Sihl, Mai 1981. In unmittelbarer Nähe des besetzten Autonomen Jugendzentrums (AJZ) entstand 1981, im zweiten Jahr der bis 1982 andauernden Konflikte, ein → *Protestcamp* auf dem Platzspitz zwischen Limmat und Sihl. → *Züri brännt* Engl.: A → *protest camp* was set up on the Platzspitz in the immediate vicinity of the occupied Autonomous Youth Center (AJZ), between the Limmat and Sihl rivers in 1981, the second year of the conflicts that lasted until 1982. → *Zurich youth protests* (OE)

1980 Startbahn West (Runway 18 West), Manfred Prüfer: Hüttendorf, Frankfurt am Main, Sommer 1981. Die knapp vier Meter über dem Boden errichtete „F.A.G.-Baumhütte", benannt nach den Flughafen-Ausbaugegner*innen, ist eins der vielen → *Baumhäuser*, die im Hüttendorf gegen die → *Startbahn West* entstanden sind. FAG war zugleich der Name des Flughafenbetreibers, der verhassten Flughafen-Aktiengesellschaft. Von hier ließen sich der Dorfplatz sowie große Teile des „Westends" überblicken. Im Falle einer polizeilichen Räumung sollte eine Luke im Inneren verschlossen werden. Engl.: The "F.A.G.-Baumhütte" (F.A.G. tree hut), named after the Flughafen-Ausbaugegner*innen (airport expansion opponents) stood nearly four meters above the ground and is one of the many → *tree houses* that were constructed in the hut village to oppose → *Startbahn West*. FAG was also the name of the airport operator, the hated Flughafen-Aktiengesellschaft. The tree house afforded a view over the village square and large parts of the "Westend." In the event of the police trying to clear the camp, a hatch inside the tree house had to be closed to seal access from below. (AMM)

1981 Greenham, Sarah Booker: Dance on the Silos, United States Air Force Base Greenham Common, 1. Januar 1983. In der Silvesternacht 1982

1981 Hamburg

1984 Hainburger Au

1986 Manila

1989 Estland, Lettland, Litauen (Estonia, Latvia, Lithuania)

1994 London

1995 Istanbul

brachen die Frauen des → *Protestcamps* zum ersten Mal in den Militärstützpunkt ein. 44 Aktivistinnen kletterten über den Zaun und tanzten stundenlang auf den Atomwaffensilos. Alle Frauen wurden verhaftet, 36 von ihnen kamen ins Gefängnis. → *Greenham Common Friedenscamp* Engl.: On New Year's Eve 1982, the women from the → *protest camp* broke into the military base for the first time. Forty-four activists climbed over the fence and danced on top of the nuclear silos for hours. All women were arrested, thirty-six were put in prison. → *Greenham Common Peace Camp* (JD)

1981 Hamburg, Sven Simon: Barrikaden, Sankt Pauli Hafenstraße, 13. November 1987. Mit den → *Barrikaden* eskalierte der Konflikt um die besetzten Häuser. Sie bestanden etwa eine Woche. → *Hafenstraße* Engl.: The conflict surrounding the occupied houses escalated with the → *barricades*. They remained in place for about a week. → *Hafenstraße* (JD)

1984 Hainburger Au, Otto Bartel: Protestcamp, Dezember 1984. Die Bauplatzbesetzung in der → *Hainburger Au* begann am 8. Dezember 1984. Am 22. Dezember lenkte die Regierung ein – nach dem Ende des AKW in → *Zwentendorf* ein weiterer Sieg für die österreichische Umweltbewegung. Engl.: The construction site occupation in the → *Hainburger Au* began on Dec. 8, 1984. On Dec. 22, the government caved in—following the termination of the nuclear power plant in → *Zwentendorf*, it was another victory for the Austrian environmental movement. (OE)

1985 Bern, Andreas Blatter: Wohnsiedlung Zaffaraya, 8. September 2015. Die kuriose Lage von → *Zaffaraya* inmitten von Autobahnzufahrten entstand nach mehrmaligen Verschiebungen des alternativen Wohnprojekts. Engl.: The odd location of → *Zaffaraya* in the middle of highway on-ramps came about after the alternative housing project had been postponed several times. (OE)

1986 Manila, Pete Reyes: Philippine Revolution, 1986. Hände gegen Panzer – „People Power": Hier wird der → *Körpereinsatz* der Bevölkerung sichtbar. → *EDSA-Revolution* Engl.: Hands against tanks—"People Power": this picture manifests the people's → *body deployment*. → *EDSA Revolution* (JD)

1989 Estland, Lettland, Litauen (Estonia, Latvia, Lithuania), Vladimiras Gulevičius: Menschenkette, Vilnius, 23. August 1989. Die 600 Kilometer lange Menschenkette erstreckte sich über die drei Hauptstädte Vilnius (Litauen), Riga (Lettland) und Tallinn (Estland) entlang der „Via Baltica", einer Fernstraße, die das Baltikum durchquert. → *Baltischer Weg* Engl.: The 600-km-long human chain stretched across the three capitals of Vilnius (Lithuania), Riga (Latvia), and Tallinn (Estonia) along the "Via Baltica," a highway running through the Baltic states. → *Baltic Way* (JD)

1991 Riga, Agris Šiliņš: Riga, Januar 1991. Die behelfsmäßigen → *Barrikaden* wurden aus Baumstämmen, großen Steinblöcken, Mauern, Drahthindernissen und anderen Materialien errichtet. → *Barrikadentage (Riga)* Engl.: The makeshift → *barricades* were constructed from logs, large blocks of stone, wire obstacles, and other materials. → *The Barricades (Riga)* (JD)

1994 London, Andrew Wiard: Claremont Road, 28. November 1994. Ein 30 Meter hoher → *Turm* auf einem der Dächer krönte die → *Claremont Road*. Er wurde aus etlichen gefundenen Gerüststücken zusammengebaut. Die gespannten Netze dienten als Brücken zwischen Dächern und → *Baumhäusern*. Engl.: Made from scavenged pieces of scaffolding, the almost thirty-meter → *tower* on one of the roofs crowned → *Claremont Road*. The nets served as bridges between roofs and → *tree houses*. (JD)

1995 Istanbul, Osman Orsal: Cumartesi Anneleri, 28. Februar 2009. Nach dem Vorbild der → *Madres de Plaza de Mayo* kamen die → *Samstagsmütter (Cumartesi Anneleri)* einmal pro Woche für eine halbe Stunde zusammen, um auf das Schicksal ihrer verschleppten und zumeist ermordeten Angehö-

1999 Derbyshire

1999 Seattle

2007 Notre-Dame-des-Landes

2010 Westsahara (Western Sahara)

2011 Kairo (Cairo)

2011 Bahrain

rigen hinzuweisen. Engl.: Following the example of the → *Madres de Plaza de Mayo*, the → *Saturday Mothers (Cumartesi Anneleri)* met once a week for half an hour to draw attention to the fate of their abducted relatives, most of whom had been murdered. (OE)

1995 London, Adrian Fisk: Street Occupation, Sommer 1995. Eine der bekanntesten Aktionen von → *Reclaim the Streets* war die → *Besetzung* der Londoner Hauptverkehrsader A13 im Jahr 1996. Tausende blockierten die → *Straße* und verwandelten sie in eine große Partyzone. Engl.: One of the most famous actions of → *Reclaim the Streets* was the → *occupation* of the A13, London's main arterial, in 1996. Thousands blocked the → *street*, turning it into one big party zone. (JD)

1999 Derbyshire, Anna Badcock and Bob Johnston: Tree house with aerial rope walkway, 2008. Das Bild entstand während einer → *archäologischen Untersuchung* des → *Protestcamps*. Dabei konnte festgestellt werden, wie das Camp vor einer möglichen Räumung geschützt werden sollte. → *Endcliffe Protestcamp* Engl.: This picture was taken during an → *archaeological investigation* of the → *protest camp*, which helped to determine how the camp could be protected against a forced eviction. → *Endcliffe protest camp* (JD)

1999 Seattle, Paul Joseph Brown: Protesters in turtle costumes, WTO protests, 29. November 1999. Die Schildkröte wurde zum Symbol des Vorwurfs, die WTO stelle Unternehmensinteressen über soziale und ökologische Belange. → *Anti-Globalisierungs- / WTO-Proteste* Engl.: The turtle came to symbolize the accusation that the WTO was prioritizing corporate interests over social and ecological concerns. → *WTO Protests / Battle of Seattle* (JD)

2007 Notre-Dame-des-Landes, Immo Klink: ZAD, 4. Mai 2018. An der „route des chicanes" (deutsch: Straße der Schikanen), einer seit 2013 gesperrten → *Straße*, die das besetzte Gebiet der → *ZAD Notre-Dame-des-Landes* durchquerte, standen hütten, Wachtür-

me (→ *Turm*) und → *Barrikaden*. Die Forderung der Behörden, die Straße nach dem Ende der Flughafenplanungen 2018 freizuräumen, wurde in der Gemeinschaft der Protestierenden kontrovers diskutiert. Schließlich wurde die Straße freigegeben. Die ZAD besteht bis heute (2023). Engl.: Along the "route des chicanes" ("road of harassment"), a → *street* closed since 2013 that crossed the occupied area of the → *ZAD Notre-Dame-des-Landes*, huts, watchtowers (→ *Tower*), and → *barricades* were erected. The authorities' call for the street to be unblocked after plans to build an airport were scrapped in 2018 was the subject of heated discussions among the community of protesters. Eventually, the road was unblocked. The ZAD still exists today (2023). (AMM)

2010 Westsahara (Western Sahara), Antonio Velázquez: Protest camp with khaimas, 2010. Die Verwendung von traditionellen → *Zelten* wurde zum Protestsymbol und war Ausdruck der saharauischen Identität und Kultur, die durch die marokkanische Besetzung der Westsahara bedroht war – etwa durch die Expansion von marokkanischen Siedlungen in Form von Hochhäusern und moderner → *Infrastruktur*. → *Gdeim Izik Protestcamp* Engl.: Traditional → *tents* became a protest symbol and an expression of Sahrawi identity and culture, which was threatened by the Moroccan occupation of Western Sahara—e.g., through the expansion of Moroccan settlements in the shape of high-rise buildings and modern → *infrastructure*. → *Gdeim Izik protest camp* (AMM)

2011 Kairo (Cairo), Jonathan Rashad: Protestcamp, 9. Februar 2011. Während der „Revolution des 25. Januar" bauten Protestierende auf dem → *Tahrir-Platz* in Kairo eine labyrinthische Siedlung aus → *Zelten* und Planen. Engl.: During the "January 25 Revolution," protesters built a labyrinthine settlement consisting of → *tents* and tarpaulins on → *Tahrir Square* in Cairo. (AMM)

2011 Bahrain, bahrain.viewbook.com: Protestcamp, Bahrain, 13. März

2011 Madrid

LA CRISIS ES EL CAPITALISMO

2011 Athen (Athens)

2011 New York

2012 Hambacher Wald
(Hambach Forest)

2012 Berlin

2013 Istanbul

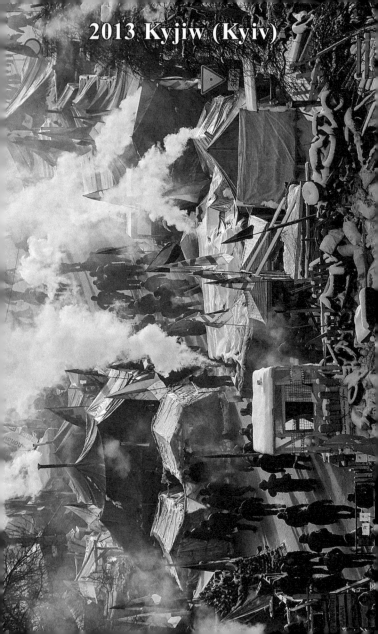

2013 Kyjiw (Kyiv)

2011. Auffällig ist die unterschiedliche → *Kleidung* der Besetzer∗innen auf dem → *Pearl Roundabout*: Frauen sind verschleiert und schwarz gekleidet. Engl.: The differences in → *clothing* of the occupiers on the → *Pearl Roundabout* is striking: the women are veiled and dressed in black. (OE)

2011 Madrid, Olmo Calvo: Protestcamp, 20. Mai 2011. Aktivist∗innen der → *Movimiento 15M* errichteten in Madrid ein → *Protestcamp* aus → *Seilen* und Planen, die zwischen Straßenlaternen und selbstgebauten Stützen gespannt wurden. Engl.: Activists of → *Movimiento 15M* set up a → *protest camp* in Madrid made of → *ropes* and tarpaulins tied between streetlamps and self-made supports. (AMM)

2011 Athen (Athens), linmtheu: Protestcamp, Athen, 12. Juni 2011. An den gepflasterten Wegen des → *Syntagma-Platzes* siedelten sich die Stände der aktivistischen Arbeitsgruppen an, während die individuellen Unterkünfte der Besetzer∗innen in den bepflanzten Grünbereichen aufgebaut wurden (→ *Siedlungsstruktur*). Zum → *Schutz gegen die Sonne* spannten die Besetzer∗innen zwischen den Bäumen große Planen. Engl.: The stands of the activist working groups were set up along the paved paths of → *Syntagma Square*, while the individual shelters of the occupiers were established in the green areas (→ *Settlement structure*). The occupiers suspended large tarpaulins between the trees to provide → *protection* from the sun. (AMM)

2011 New York, David Shankbone: Tag 43 der Besetzung, 29. Oktober 2011. An diesem Tag fiel in New York der erste Schnee. Bereits zuvor hatten die Aktivist∗innen von → *Occupy Wall Street* begonnen, sich über das anfängliche Verbot von → *Zelten* hinwegzusetzen. Engl.: The first snow fell in New York City that day. And even before that, the → *Occupy Wall Street* activists had started to ignore the initial ban on → *tents*. (AMM)

2012 Hambacher Wald (Hambach Forest), Tim Wagner: Baumhäuser „Stube" und „Mona", 26. Mai 2019. Im → *Barrio* „Oaktown" entstanden bei der Wiederbesetzung nach der Räumung des → *Hambacher Walds* im Jahr 2018 viele neue → *Baumhäuser*, die mit Hängebrücken verbunden sind. Engl.: In the "Oaktown" → *barrio*, many new → *tree houses* connected by suspension bridges were built during the re-occupation of the area after the eviction of the → *Hambach Forest* in 2018. (AMM)

2012 Berlin, Soeren Stache: Geflüchtetencamp auf dem Oranienplatz, Berlin, 4. Januar 2013. Zwei Jahre lang war der Platz soziales und politisches Zentrum, um die Forderungen der Geflüchteten an die Öffentlichkeit zu bringen. Die besetzte Gerhart-Hauptmann-Schule wurde zum Aufwärmen in den Wintermonaten genutzt und für Kinder und Kranke reserviert. → *Oranienplatz-Camp* Engl.: For two years, the square functioned as a social and political center where refugees' demands were made public. The occupied Gerhart Hauptmann School served as a refuge from the cold during the winter months and was reserved for children and sick people. → *Oranienplatz camp* (JD)

2013 Istanbul, Ian Usher: Protestcamp, Istanbul, 8. Juni 2013. Die Transformation des → *Gezi-Parks* in einen utopischen Raum ging einher mit der Errichtung informeller Strukturen: Matratzen, bunte Decken, an → *Seilen* gespannte Planen und hunderte → *Zelte* verbreiteten sich innerhalb kurzer Zeit. Engl.: The transformation of → *Gezi Park* into a utopian space was accompanied by the establishment of informal structures: mattresses, colorful blankets, tarpaulins stretched on → *ropes*, and hundreds of → *tents* spread within a short period of time. (AMM)

2013 Kyjiw (Kyiv), Gleb Garanich: Protestcamp, Kyjiw, 24. Januar 2014. Die Besetzer∗innen errichteten → *Barrikaden* aus Paletten, Sperrmüll, Autoreifen und Eis (→ *Baumaterial*), um das → *Protestcamp* auf dem → *Majdan* vor Angriffen der → *Polizei* zu schützen (→ *Schutz*). Engl.: The occupiers built → *barricades* from pallets, bulky waste, car tires, and ice (→ *Building*

2014 Caracas

2014 Hongkong (Hong Kong)

2014 Ouagadougou

MOUVEMENT

2015 Burundi

2016 Standing Rock Reservation

2017 Hamburg

*Selfie vor brennen-
den Barrikaden –
viele Schaulustige
machen sich so die
Arbeit der Polizei*
Getty Images

ie Stunde der Voyeure

Steinhagel, der den gerade vorrückenden
Räumpanzern aus Richtung Schulterblatt
empfängt, sind nur einige entfernt, Ausge-
zerrte Polizisten, das unter den Helmen
ben – soweit man das unter dem Helm
erkennen kann. Das scheint, dem Nach-
wuchsreporter von gegenüber zwei Me-
nicht aufzufallen, er geht, in der Hand hält er eine
ter weiter. In der einen Hand hält er eine
dreiviertelvolle Flasche Whisky. Mit
der anderen filmt er den Einsatz des
Panzers.

hartnäckig, sie erreicht, trägt sie sich in
Sicherheit.

Vier Junge, 14 oder 15 Jahr alt, in
Trainingsjacken und Jogginghosen, be-
gegnen einem immer wieder: An der
Helgoländer Allee, als von der Brücke
Steine auf Wasserwerfer fliegen; am Michel, als Demonstranten vor der Kirche
stehen und mit einem Wasserwerfer getrieben werden; am Grünen Jäger, als
eine Polizeieinheit einen Flaschenwerfer
festsetzt; am Polizeikommissariat 16 an

Vorbereitungen zum Einsatz ab. Hundertschaften stehen auf der Straße, Wasserwerfer blockieren die Eisenbahnbrü-
cke. Hinter ihnen ein Halbkreis von
Menschen, bestimmt 150 Personen. Ein
Pärchen drängelt sich nach vorn – ein
Selfie soll es sein, mit der Sondereinheit
im Hintergrund, die gleich in Richtung
Rote Flora vorrücken wird und dabei
ihre körperliche Unversehrtheit aufs
Spiel setzt.

Ein beliebtes Spiel unter Heran-
wachsenden und solchen, die maximal

nen! Wer traut sich auch noch kurz vor
Einrücken der Fahrzeuge, über die Straße zu laufen.

Schon am Sonnabendmorgen sind
sie wieder unterwegs: Die selbst ernann-
ten Berichterstatter, die ihre Version der
Wahrheit digital in die Welt posten.
Nicht differenziert, nicht die gründe,
sondern möglichst knallig: Beliebte Mo-
tive sind die geplünderten Barrikaden.
Überreste der herumziehenden Banden.
Wenn sie noch qualmen: umso besser.
Dass dort Menschen wohnen, die am

wo Feuerwehr, Straßenreinigung und
Anwohner verstehen, den kaum ein Kra-
walle zu beseitigen weiß! Nicht doch,
auch der Polizei: Auch während des Einsatzes im Schanzenviertel fordern die
Beamten per Lautsprecher und via Twitter wiederholt dazu auf, dass Unbeteiligte sich entfernen sollen, um nicht zwischen die Fronten aus Randalierern und
Einsatzkräften zu geraten. Mit wenig
Wirkung, es wird weiter gegafft und ge-
knipst. Schließlich kündigt die Polizei
an, dass ab sofort auch Schaulustige so

2017 São Paulo

material) to protect the → *protest camp* on → *Maidan* from attacks by the → *police* (→ *Protection*). (AMM)

2014 Caracas, Mariana Vincenti Urdaneta: A Barricade on the streets of Altamira, a neighborhood in Caracas, 28. Februar 2014. → *Barrikaden* wurden aus brennenden Reifen, Möbeln und Wellblechen errichtet (→ *Feuer*, → *Baumaterial*), wie hier in einem überwiegend von der Opposition bewohntem Viertel von Caracas. → *Venezuela-Proteste* Engl.: → *Barricades* were constructed from burning tires, furniture, and sheets of corrugated iron (→ *Fire*, → *Building materials*), as seen here in a district in Caracas mainly inhabited by the opposition. → *Venezuelan protests* (JD)

2014 Hongkong (Hong Kong), Vicky Chan: Protestcamp Harcourt Village, 12. November 2014. Auf einer achtspurigen → *Straße* im Central Business District errichteten Protestierende in → *Hongkong* während einer dreimonatigen → *Besetzung* ein → *Protestcamp* mit 2300 → *Zelten*. Engl.: Protesters set up a → *protest camp* with 2,300 → *tents* on an eight-lane road in the Central Business District of → *Hong Kong* in the course of a three-month → *occupation*. (AMM)

2014 Ouagadougou, Sophie Garcia: Bürger*innenbesen-Proteste. Besen (und Kochlöffel) wurden symbolisch in die Höhe gehalten, um das korrupte politische System „hinwegzufegen“. → *Bürger*innenbesen-Proteste* Engl.: In a symbolic gesture, brooms (and wooden spoons) were held up to "sweep away" the corrupt political system. → *Civic Broom protests* (JD)

2015 Burundi, Jerome Delay: Burundi-Proteste, 6. Mai 2015. Inszenatorischer → *Schutz* der Identität: Viele Demonstrierende verhüllten ihr Gesicht, mit einfachen Schals bis hin zu Masken aus Blättern und Zweigen. Andere begannen ihre Gesichter mit der Asche der → *Barrikaden* zu schwärzen. → *Burundi-Proteste* Engl.: More for dramatic effect than to protect their identity, many demonstrators covered their faces with anything from simple scarfs to masks made from leaves and twigs. Others

blackened their faces with ash from the → *barricades*. → *Burundi protests* (JD)

2016 Standing Rock Reservation, Scott Heins: Protestcamp, North Dakota, 25. November 2016. Die Bewohner∗innen des „Oceti Sakowin Camp“ bauten während der → *Dakota-Access-Pipeline-Proteste* → *Zelte*, Tipis und Jurten sowie ein großes Geodom für Versammlungen und Workshops. Engl.: The residents of the "Oceti Sakowin Camp" built → *tents*, tipis, and yurts as well as a large geodome for assemblies and workshops during the → *Dakota Access Pipeline protests*. (AMM)

2017 Hamburg, Jan Kahlcke: *Hamburger Abendblatt* vom 10. Juli 2017, in der *taz – die tageszeitung* vom 11. Juli 2017. Eine Demonstrantin machte während der → *G20-Proteste* ein Selfie vor einer brennenden → *Barrikade*, um ihre Schwester zu beruhigen (→ *Feuer*, → *Demonstration*). Das *Hamburger Abendblatt* und die *Frankfurter Allgemeine Sonntagszeitung* nutzten das Foto als Beleg für die angebliche Sensationsgier der Protestierenden. Die *taz* sprach daraufhin mit der abgebildeten Frau und rückte die Geschichte in ein anderes Licht. Engl.: A demonstrator at the → *G20 summit protests* took a selfie in front of a burning → *barricade* to reassure her worried sister (→ *Fire*, → *Demonstration*). The newspapers *Hamburger Abendblatt* and *Frankfurter Allgemeine Sonntagszeitung* used the photo as proof of the protesters' alleged sensationalism. Consequently, the newspaper *taz* spoke to the woman in the picture and showed another side of the story. (JD)

2017 São Paulo, Flavio Forner: Protestcamp, 25. November 2017. Die → *Besetzungen* der → *MTST* werden im Vorhinein geplant und sind sorgfältig organisiert. Ein „Architektursektor“ steckt lange Wege und dazwischen Bereiche für die Errichtung von Hütten ab. So kommt es zu der vergleichsweise regelmäßigen → *Siedlungsstruktur*. Engl.: The → *MTST* → *occupations* were planned in advance and meticulously organized. An "architectural sector" staked out long paths and areas for

2018 Frankreich (France)

2019 Brasília

2019 Hongkong (Hong Kong)

2019 Dannenröder Wald
(Dannenrod Forest)

2020 USA

2020 Lützerath

2020 Mexiko-Stadt (Mexico City)

2020 Delhi

the construction of huts in between. This is how the comparatively regular → *settlement structure* came to be. (AMM)

2018 Frankreich (France), Becker-Bredel: Autobahnabfahrt Forbach, 26. Januar 2019. Hier brennt keine → *Barrikade*, denn nichts wird blockiert. Trotzdem entsteht eine revolutionsromantische Stimmung. Die → *Gelbwesten* demonstrieren, wie bereits in den Monaten zuvor in ganz Frankreich, an unzähligen → *Kreisverkehren*. Engl.: No → *barricade* burns here because nothing is being blocked. Nevertheless, a romantic, revolutionary atmosphere emerges. The → *Yellow Vests* demonstrate at countless → *roundabouts*, as they have been doing throughout France for months. (OE)

2019 Brasília, Mídia Ninja: Free Land Camp, 24. April 2019. Seit 2004 jährlich ausgerichtetes → *Protestcamp*, auch ATL oder „Free Land Camp" genannt. Jedes Jahr wird das Camp anders gestaltet. Als es 2019 zum 15. Mal stattfand, wurden die → *Zelte* kreisförmig aufgestellt. → *Acampamento Terra Livre* Engl.: The ATL → *protest camp*, or "Free Land Camp," has been held annually since 2004. Every year the camp has a different layout. For its 15th congregation in 2019, the → *tents* were arranged in a circle. → *Acampamento Terra Livre* (JD)

2019 Hongkong (Hong Kong), Studio Incendo: Barrikaden, 15. November 2019. Protestierende bauten während der → *Hongkong-Proteste* auf den Zufahrtsstraßen zur Universität → *Barrikaden* aus drei übereinander gestapelten → *Ziegelsteinen*, sogenannte „Mini-Stonehenges", sodass → *Fahrzeuge* der → *Polizei* nicht zum besetzten Campus vordringen konnten. Engl.: Protesters built → *barricades* out of three → *bricks* stacked one out of another, so-called "mini Stonehenges," on the access roads to the university during the → *Hong Kong protests*, preventing → *police* → *vehicles* from getting through to the occupied campus. (AMM)

2019 Dannenröder Wald (Dannenrod Forest), Tim Wagner: Baumhäuser im Danni, 4. Oktober 2020. Das → *Bar-rio* „Nirgendwo" auf der geplanten Autobahnbaustelle war eines der größten → *Baumhausdörfer* im → *Dannenröder Wald*. Engl.: The "Nirgendwo" (nowhere) → *barrio* on the planned highway construction site was one of the largest → *tree house* villages in the → *Dannenrod Forest*. (JD)

2020 Seattle, Benjamin Morawek: Official concrete barricades, Capitol Hill Organized Protest (CHOP), 17. Juni 2020. Das → *Protestcamp* in Seattle war das einzig dauerhafte Camp der → *Black-Lives-Matter*-Bewegung und bestand zwischen dem 8. Juni und dem 1. Juli 2020. Engl.: The Seattle → *protest camp* was the only lasting protest camp organized by the → *Black Lives Matter* movement and existed from June 8 to July 1, 2020. (OE)

2020 Lützerath, Anna-Maria Mayerhofer: Protestcamp, 30. Mai 2022. Im → *Barrio* „Fantasialand" gab es neben vielen Pfahlbauten ein „Highpod" (→ *Turm*), das über → *Traversen* mit mehreren → *Baumhäusern* verbunden war (→ *Bautypen*). Die polizeiliche Räumung konnte so verzögert werden, da sich die Aktivist∗innen von → *Lützerath* über den Köpfen der → *Polizei* frei bewegen und immer wieder entwischen konnten. Engl.: In the "Fantasy Land" → *barrio*, alongside the many stilt structures there was a "highpod" (→ *Tower*), which was connected to several → *tree houses* by → *traverses* (→ *Building types*). This helped delay the camp's eviction because the activists at → *Lützerath* could move freely above the heads of the → *police* and evade them time and again. (OE)

2020 Mexiko-Stadt (Mexico City), Daniel Augusto: Zócalo, 3. Oktober 2020. → *Protestcamp*, das trotz der Corona-Maßnahmen stattfand. Die → *Zelte* wurden gemäß der Abstandsregeln aufgestellt. → *Anti-AMLO-Proteste* Engl.: → *Protest camp* that took place despite COVID measures. The → *tents* were set up according to the distancing rules. → *Anti-AMLO protests* (JD)

2020 Delhi, Rajat Gupta: Protestcamp, Singhu-Stadtgrenze, 14. Dezember 2020. Wo sonst reger Verkehr

2021 Washington, DC

2021 Myanmar

2021 Wien (Vienna)

2021 Fechenheimer Wald
(Fechenheim Forest)

2022 Ottawa

herrschte, befand sich während der → *Farmers-Proteste* in Delhi eine bis zu zehn Kilometer lange, dichte Siedlung (→ *Siedlungsstruktur*) aus → *Zelten*, Hütten und in Häuser umgebauten Traktoranhängern (→ *Bautypen*). Engl.: Where there was usually busy traffic, during the → *Farmers' protests* in Delhi, a dense settlement (→ *Settlement structure*) of → *tents*, huts, and tractor trailers converted into homes was formed, measuring up to ten kilometers in length (→ *Building types*). (AMM)

2021 Washington, DC, Jim Lo Scalzo: US-Kapitol, 6. Januar 2021. Die zeitweilige → *Besetzung* beider Kammern des Parlaments durch Trump-Unterstützer∗innen hatte kuriose Momente wie den Auftritt des QAnon-Schamanen Jake Angeli vor dem Senatssaal. Doch die Lage war bedrohlich. Die USA standen in den Stunden vor und während der → *Kapitol-Attacke* am Rande eines gewaltsamen Staatsstreichs. Engl.: The temporary → *occupation* of the House of Representatives and the Senate by Trump supporters had some strange moments, such as the appearance of QAnon shaman Jake Angeli outside the Senate chamber. However, in the hours before and during the → *Capitol attack*, the United States found itself on the verge of a violent coup. (OE)

2021 Myanmar, Aung Kyaw Htet: Blockade aus Frauenkleidern, 7. März 2021. Die Proteste gegen das Militär in Myanmar sind trotz großer staatlicher Brutalität häufig einfallsreich und bunt. Prodemokratische Protestierende hängten über eine blockierte → *Straße* in Yangon Frauenkleider auf Wäscheleinen. Die → *Barrikade*, die verhindern sollte, dass die Sicherheitskräfte die Straße durchquerten, spielt mit dem Tabubruch: Unter den Rock schaut man nicht. → *Myanmar-Proteste* Engl.: Protests against the military in Myanmar are often imaginative and colorful, despite significant state brutality. Pro-democracy protesters hung women's clothes on washing lines across a blocked → *street* in Yangon. The → *barricade*, which was intended to prevent security forces from crossing the street,

is a reference to breaking the local taboo that you shouldn't look under a woman's skirt. → *Myanmar protests* (AMM)

2021 Wien (Vienna), Tobias Steinmaurer: Räumung des Protestcamps, 1. Februar 2022. Die Pyramide in dem als Wüste bezeichneten → *Protestcamp* hatte sich in kürzester Zeit zu einer Art Signet der österreichischen „LobauBleibt"-Bewegung (→ *Ikone*, → *Lobau*) entwickelt. Am 1. Februar 2022 wurde sie von der → *Polizei* geräumt und abgerissen. Engl.: The pyramid in the → *protest camp* known as Wüste ("desert") had quickly become an → *icon* of the Austrian "LobauBleibt" movement (→ *Lobau*). On February 1, 2022, it was cleared by the → *police* and demolished. (SH)

2021 Fechenheimer Wald (Fechenheim Forest), Lucas Bäuml: Räumung des Protestcamps, Frankfurt am Main, 18. Januar 2023. Um die Räumung durch die → *Polizei* im Januar 2023 möglichst lange hinauszuzögern, besetzten Klimaaktivist∗innen im → *Fechenheimer Wald* die Bäume und alle von ihnen gebauten Strukturen (→ *Körpereinsatz*). Dazu zählte auch ein → *Monopod*, der etwa sieben Meter hoch und über eine Leiter begehbar war. Engl.: Climate activists occupied trees and all the structures they had built in order to delay the eviction of the → *Fechenheim Forest* camp by the → *police* in January 2023 for as long as possible (→ *Body deployment*). The structures included a → *monopod* that was about seven meters high and accessible via a ladder. (AMM/JD)

2022 Ottawa, Andre Pichette: Parliament Hill, Canada, 29. Januar 2022. Die LKW-Fahrer des → *„Freedom convoy"* nutzten die perfekte Protestmaschine: Trucks (→ *Fahrzeuge*) sind schwer abzuschleppen und darauf ausgelegt, dass ihre Fahrer∗innen eine Weile autark darin leben können. Durch Hupen können sie einen enormen → *Lärmpegel* erzeugen. Engl.: The truck drivers in the → *"Freedom convoy"* used the perfect protest machine: trucks (→ *Vehicles*) are difficult to tow away and are designed for their drivers to lead a self-sufficient life in them for a while. They can also

Abschütten. DB Publifoto: Um ihrer Forderung nach einer Erhöhung der Erzeugerpreise Nachdruck zu verleihen, schütten Bauern im Januar 1967 ihre Milch auf die Straßen von Mailand (Dumping. DB Publifoto: To emphasize their demands for an increase in producer prices, farmers pour their milk onto the streets of Milan in January 1967)

make an enormous amount of → *noise* by honking their horns. (OE)

Abschütten, engl. →*Dumping*. Eine vor allem im Rahmen von Protesten in der Landwirtschaft immer wieder verwendete Strategie besteht im Abschütten von Lebensmitteln auf öffentliche →*Straßen* und Plätze. (SH)

Abseilen. Matthias Balk (dpa): BlockIAA-Protest. Autobahn A9 bei München, 7. September 2021 (Rappelling. Matthias Balk (dpa): BlockIAA protest. Autobahn A9, Munich, September 7, 2021)

Abseilen, engl. →*Rappelling*. Proteststrategie der →*Blockade*. Durch den →*Körpereinsatz* beim Abseilen, etwa von Autobahnbrücken, bringen sich Protestierende in Gefahr, woraufhin der Verkehr gesperrt werden muss; darin dem →*Ankleben* vergleichbar. Bei den BlockIAA-Protesten fand es in Kombination mit dem Abseilen eine Aneignung der Typografie von deutschen Autobahnschildern für Protestbotschaften statt. (OE)

Absperrgitter, engl. →*Barrier*. 1987 schuf der Künstler Olaf Metzel für den Skulpturenboulevard anlässlich der 750-Jahr-Feier Berlins eine Installation, die überwiegend aus Absperrgittern bestand und damit eine häufig eingesetzte →*Anti-Protestmaßnahme* in die Sichtbarkeit rückte: Das provokante Kunstwerk bezog sich auf den Tag des 13. April 1981. An diesem Tag kam es auf dem Berliner Kurfürstendamm infolge der Meldung vom Tod des seit 1975 inhaftierten mutmaßlichen RAF-Terroristen Sigurd Debus zu heftigen Randalen und der →*Zerstörung* von rund 200 Schaufensterscheiben (tatsächlich starb Debus erst drei Tage später, nachdem er bereits im Februar in den Hungerstreik getreten war). Metzels Skulptur sorgte für stürmische Diskussionen, wurde mehrfach zum Zentrum von →*Demonstrationen* und musste daher selbst immer wieder von der →*Polizei* „abgesperrt" und vor einem →*Denkmalsturz* geschützt werden, wie hier beim Volkszählungsboykott 1987. (SH)

Absperrgitter. Hans Peter Stiebing: Olaf Metzels Installation *13.4.1981* auf dem Kurfürstendamm, Berlin, 1987 (Barrier. Hans Peter Stiebing: Olaf Metzel's installation *13.4.1981* on Kurfürstendamm, Berlin, 1987)

Acampamento Terra Livre, engl. →*Acampamento Terra Livre*. Größte Versammlung von Indigenen in Brasilien, bei der jährlich mehr als 4000 Teilnehmende in Brasília in einem →*Protestcamp* vor dem Parlament zusammenkommen, um ihren Widerstand zu vereinen und für ihre Rechte zu kämpfen. Das riesige Regierungsviertel ist ein beliebter Protestort in Brasilien. Im Jahr →*2019* richtete sich der Protest insbesondere gegen den rechtsextremen Präsidenten Jair Bolsonaro. (JD)

Acampamento Terra Livre, Ger. →*Acampamento Terra Livre*. The biggest assembly of Indigenous people in Brazil. Every year, over 4,000 participants come together at a →*protest camp* in front of the parliament building in Brasília to unite their resistance movements and fight for their rights. The expansive government district is a popular protest venue in Brazil. In →*2019*, the protest was mainly directed at the far-right President Jair Bolsonaro. (JD)

Acts of solidarity, Ger. →*Solidaritätsgeste*. Most protest movements receive help from the populace, from people who do not take to the →*streets* themselves and do not actively participate. Such acts of solidarity nevertheless receive significant attention in the press, as illustrated by the following example of the support of the street fights during the "Night of the Barricades" of May 10/11, 1968 in Paris (→*May '68*, →*Barricade*, →*Media*), which was reproduced on the front page of the *Neue Zürcher Zeitung* on May 13, 1968: "The residents of Rue Gay-Lussac sided with the students. They brought them water, biscuits, chocolate, and other food before the police attack; threw water down from the windows afterwards to disperse the gas clouds; gave the students wet cloths to protect their faces and respiratory system; and brought fugitives and the injured into their homes in a show of solidarity not common in Paris" (Frei 2008/2018, p. 18; →*Police*, →*Protection*). (OE)

Adobe hut, Ger. →*Lehmhütte*; →*Alternative architecture*, →*Building types*, →*Hambach Forest*, →*ZAD Notre-Dame-des-Landes*

A-Frame, engl. →*A-frame*; →*Bautypen*, →*Resurrection City*, →*Zelt*

A-frame, Ger. →*A-Frame*; →*Building types*, →*Resurrection City*, →*Tent*

Alternative architecture, Ger. →*Alternative Architektur*. Despite the important and serious political goals they express, the built structures and →*protest camps* of the protest movements presented in this publication usually appear very playful—at times they are reminiscent of allotment gardens, tent camps, or adventure playgrounds. The improvised, expandable, and sometimes movable structures of protest camps can be associated with alternative concepts that have had an impact on architectural history for centuries. In his *Ten Books* on *Architecture*, the ancient Roman architectural theorist Vitruvius referred to seemingly "archaic" practices in which he saw the origins of building: the simple constructions of wood and clay covered with reeds or leaves that he described and that could still be observed among "foreign peoples" (Vitruvius after 33 BCE/1964, pp. 79–81), stood out from the advanced architecture of his time and created the powerful counter-image of a supposedly primordial and nature-loving lifestyle. Especially since the Enlightenment in the mid-18th century, the various notions of a "primitive hut" combined the appeal of the foreign with the weariness with one's own, all-too-familiar culture—they served as models critical of civilization for a simple, unadulterated, and thus supposedly more authentic life (see Rykwert 1972).

In the nonconformist sub- and counter-culture of the 1960s, alternative architectural views took on a decidedly anti-capitalist and consumer-critical tone: under the motto "access to tools," the *Whole Earth Catalog*, which was regularly updated from 1968 until the 2000s, led the way in spreading the knowledge required for a decentralized, autonomous, and environmentally conscious product culture that extended to ephemeral dwellings. Subsequent publications such as *Domebooks*, published between 1970 and 1971, or the *Shelter* series, begun in 1973 (Kahn 1971; Kahn 1973), were also intended as reference works and manuals (→ *Handbücher / Online-Manuals*) for self-reliant living and promoted a lifestyle that was as independent of consumption as possible, for which mobile dwellings from all over the world served as inspiration. Accordingly, these publications repeatedly referred to the mobile and flexible tent structures of nomadic peoples—such as yurts and tipis (→ *Tent*)—as well as to vernacular building traditions without architects (see Kahn 1973; Rudofsky 1964). As well as this, contemporary architectural experiments, such as the geodesic domes and → *tensegrity* concepts of Richard Buckminster Fuller, the tensile constructions of Frei Otto

(→ *Ropes*), or widespread pneumatic structures, played an important role in the counterculture of the 1960s, serving as inspiration for particular → *building types*. The idea of not being perpetually defined as a consumer through do-it-yourself culture—not only DIY → *clothing* and furniture but also huts and houses—has not lost its appeal to this day. The desire to make things oneself is not only taken up by the current DIY culture but also plays a decisive role in the various constructions of protest movements—the → *tree houses*, stilt dwellings, adobe huts, and tent structures built from all kinds of → *building materials*. Alongside their strategic importance for achieving → *protest goals* (→ *Infrastructure*), the architecture of protest camps also demonstrates a playful creativity and desire to try out alternatives, however improvised and provisional they may initially be. (SH)

Alternative Architektur, engl. → *Alternative architecture*. Trotz der wichtigen und ernsten politischen Ziele, die sie zum Ausdruck bringen, wirken die Bauwerke und → *Protestcamps* der in dieser Publikation vorgestellten Protestbewegungen meist sehr spielerisch – bisweilen erinnern sie an Schrebergärten, Zeltlager oder Abenteuerspielplätze. Die improvisierten, erweiterbaren und teils beweglichen Bauwerke der Protestcamps können mit alternativen Konzepten in Verbindung gebracht werden, die sich seit Jahrhunderten auf die Architekturgeschichte ausgewirkt haben. Bereits der antike römische Architekturtheoretiker Vitruv hat in seinen *Zehn Büchern über Architektur* auf „altertümlich" anmutende Praktiken verwiesen, in denen er die Ursprünge des Bauens erblickte: Die von ihm geschilderten einfachen, mit Schilf oder Laub bedeckten Konstruktionen aus Holz und Lehm, die bei „auswärtigen Völkerschaften" noch zu beobachten seien (Vitruv ab 33 v. Chr./1964, S. 79–81), hoben sich von der avancierten Baukunst seiner Zeit ab und erzeugten das wirkmächtige Gegenbild eines vermeintlich ursprünglichen und naturverbundenen Lebensstils. Vor allem seit der Aufklärung Mitte des 18. Jahrhunderts verbanden die verschiedenen Vorstellungen einer „Urhütte" den Reiz des Fremden mit dem Überdruss an der eigenen, allzu vertrauten Kultur – sie dienten als zivilisationskritische Modelle für ein einfaches, unverfälschtes und damit angeblich authentischeres Leben (vgl. Rykwert 1972).

In der nonkonformistischen Sub- und Gegenkultur der 1960er Jahre erhielten die alternativen Architekturauffassungen eine dezidiert antikapitalistische und konsumkritische Note: Unter dem Motto „Access to tools" verbreitete allen voran der von 1968 bis in die 2000er regelmäßig aktualisierte *Whole Earth Catalog* das Know-how für eine dezentral organisierte, autonome und umweltbewusste Produktkultur, die sich bis zu nomadisch-ephemereren Behausungen erstreckte. Auch Folgepublikationen wie die zwischen 1970 und 1971 herausgegebenen *Domebooks* oder die 1973 begonnene *Shelter*-Serie (Kahn 1971; Kahn 1973) waren als Nachschlagewerke und →*Handbücher* für ein selbstständiges Leben intendiert und propagierten einen möglichst konsumunabhängigen Lebensstil, für den nomadische Behausungen aus aller Welt als Inspiration dienten. Entsprechend beriefen sich diese Publikationen immer wieder auf die mobilen und flexiblen Zeltbauten nomadischer Völker – etwa Jurten und Tipis (→*Zelte*) – sowie auf vernakulare Bautraditionen ohne Architekt*innen (vgl. Kahn 1973; Rudofsky 1964). Nicht zuletzt waren es aber auch die zeitgenössischen Architekturexperimente – etwa die geodätischen Kuppeln und →*Tensegrity*-Konzepte von Richard Buckminster Fuller, die Zugkonstruktionen von Frei Otto (→*Seile*) oder die weitverbreiteten pneumatischen Strukturen –, die in der Gegenkultur der 1960er Jahre als Inspiration für eigene →*Bautypen* eine wichtige Rolle spielten. Der Gedanke, sich durch das Selbermachen – nicht nur von →*Kleidung* und Möbeln, sondern auch von Hütten und Häusern – nicht fortwährend als Konsument definiert zu sehen, hat seinen Reiz bis heute nicht verloren. Die Lust am Selbermachen wird nicht nur von der gegenwärtigen Do-it-yourself-Kultur aufgegriffen, sondern spielt auch bei den verschiedenen Bauwerken der Protestbewegungen – den aus allen möglichen →*Baumaterialien* konstruierten ›*Baumhäusern*, Pfahlbauten, Lehmhütten und Zeltkonstruktionen – eine entscheidende Rolle: Neben ihrer strategischen Bedeutung für das Erreichen der →*Protestziele* (→*Infrastruktur*) zeugt die Architektur der Protestcamps auch von einer spielerischen Kreativität und der Lust, Alternativen zu erproben – wie improvisiert und provisorisch sie zunächst auch sein mögen. (SH)

Angriff, engl. →*Attack*. Zögermoment vor Ausübung der Gewalt / gegen Sachen / Der erfahrene Genosse, / Referent des vorhergehenden SDS-Vorstands, / registriert verblüfft / die Truppe von Genossen, die vor der Glastür / des Rektorats mehrere Minuten verharrt / Sie wollen die wertvolle / Dickglasscheibe nicht zerstören, / aber doch in das Rektorat / „zum Zwecke der Besetzung" / eindringen / Mehrere Genossen, die unmittelbar an die Rektoratstür / gedrängt stehen, haben / plötzlich ein Ramm-Mittel in der Hand / Die Scheibe der / Rektoratstür zersplittert /
(Alexander Kluge: *Angriff auf eine dicke Tür aus Glas*, Film, 01:52 Minuten, 2018; →*Besetzung*, →*Gewalt*, →*Waffen*, →*Zerstörung*)

Ankleben, engl. →*Super-gluing*. Aktionsform der 2020er Jahre. Das Ankleben ist wie das →*Abseilen* eine Form der →*Blockade*, bei der sich Aktivist*innen von →*Protestorganisationen* wie Letzte Generation und „Insulate Britain" mit Sekundenkleber oder Bauschaum auf stark befahrenen →*Straßen* festkleben. Mit den daraus resultierenden Sperrungen, Staus und Störungen des Alltags machen die Umweltschutzgruppen auf die Klimakrise aufmerksam. Anders als bei klassischen Sitzblockaden sind für die Anklebe-Aktionen nur wenige Menschen notwendig. Der →*Körpereinsatz* der Aktivist*innen ist jedoch erheblich größer, auch im Vergleich zu Blockaden und →*Besetzungen* mit →*Lock-on Devices*, denn durch das Festkleben ihrer

Hände und Füße auf der Straße riskieren sie irreversible gesundheitliche Schäden. Zum →*Schutz* gegen Übergriffe durch aufgebrachte Straßenteilnehmende (→*Gewalt*) kleben sich die Aktivist∗innen erst fest, wenn die →*Polizei* bereits eingetroffen ist. Mit den ersten Autobahnblockaden der Letzten Generation in Deutschland im Januar 2022 und der Ausweitung der Anklebe-Aktionen auf →*Museen*, →*Fahrzeuge* und Gebäude wie Flughäfen und Ölraffinerien entbrannte eine hitzige Mediendebatte über die wachsende Radikalisierung der Umweltbewegung. (AMM)

Ankleben. Stefan Müller: Blockade der Letzten Generation mit Markierungen der Polizei. Die Aktivist∗innen an Pos. 1 und 2 waren nicht festgeklebt, um eine Rettungsgasse bilden zu können. Berlin, 21. November 2022 (Super-gluing. Stefan Müller: Blockade by Letzte Generation with police markings. The activists at positions 1 and 2 were not glued in order to leave an emergency evacuation lane clear. Berlin, November 21, 2022)

Anti-AMLO-Proteste, engl. →*Anti-AMLO protests*. Anhänger∗innen der rechtspopulistischen Frena-Bewegung errichteten im Jahr →*2020* ein →*Protestcamp* auf dem symbolträchtigen Hauptplatz Zócalo vor dem mexikanischen Regierungspalast und forderten den Rücktritt des linken Präsidenten Andrés Manuel López Obrador (AMLO) (→*Platzbesetzung*, →*Rechte Proteste*). (JD)

Anti-AMLO protests, Ger. →*Anti-AMLO-Proteste*. In →*2020*, supporters of the right-wing populist Frena movement set up a →*protest camp* on Mexico

City's highly symbolic main square Zócalo, in front of the National Palace, and demanded the resignation of the leftist President Andrés Manuel López Obrador (AMLO) (→*Public square occupation*, →*Right-wing protests*). (JD)

Anti-Globalisierungs- / WTO-Proteste, engl. →*WTO Protests / Battle of Seattle*. „N30", wie das Ereignis auch genannt wird, gilt als erster Höhepunkt einer Phase von Anti-Globalisierungsprotesten. Anlass war die Ministerkonferenz der Welthandelsorganisation (WTO) in Seattle am 30. November →*1999*. Besonderes Merkmal waren Karnevalselemente wie die Schildkröten-Kostümierungen (→*Kostüm*). Schildkröten sind langsam und gutartig, das machte sie zu einem wirkungsvollen Symbol für einen friedlichen Protest. Neben friedlichen Straßenbesetzungen kam es in Seattle auch zu Vandalismus und Straßenschlachten (→*Straße*, →*Gewalt*). (JD)

Anti-Protestmaßnahmen. bahrain.viewbook .com: Zerstörung des Kreisverkehrs Pearl Roundabout nach der Niederschlagung der Proteste, Manama, Bahrain, 29. März 2011 (Anti-protest measures. bahrain.viewbook .com: Destruction of the Pearl Roundabout after the protests were crushed, Manama, Bahrain, March 29, 2011)

Anti-Protestmaßnahmen, engl. →*Anti-protest measures*. Der Einsatz von Wasserwerfern, Tränengas oder des gefürchteten →*Polizeikessels* – bei dem Polizist∗innen einen Ring um eine Gruppe von Protestierenden bilden und sie dadurch zwingen, an Ort und Stelle zu verbleiben – gehört auch in demokratischen Ländern zum gewohnten Bild bei → *Demonstrationen* und Besetzungen (→ *Platzbesetzung*, → *Bauplatzbesetzung*, → *Hausbesetzung*). Es handelt sich um Maßnahmen, die meist von der Staatsgewalt ergriffen werden, um Proteste zu unterbinden, aufzulösen oder wieder in die von ihr vorgesehenen Bahnen zu lenken (→ *Polizei*). Bisweilen, aber keineswegs immer, reagieren die Polizeikräfte dabei auf gewaltsame Ausschreitungen, Provokationen oder → *Blockaden* seitens der Protestierenden. Versammlungsfreiheit, Demonstrationsrecht und freie Meinungsäußerung sind in vielen demokratischen Ländern gültige Grundrechte (→ *Legalisierung*, → *Kommunikation*), denen jedoch behördliche Möglichkeiten entgegenstehen, Protestkundgebungen und Demonstrationen bereits im Vorfeld zu verhindern. So können Versammlungen verboten werden, wenn die öffentliche Sicherheit und Ordnung gefährdet erscheinen oder um der mutmaßlichen Ausübung von → *Gewalt* und → *Zerstörung* vorzubeugen. In vielen Ländern gilt zudem ein generelles Waffen- und Vermummungsverbot für Demonstrationsteilnehmer*innen, nicht jedoch für die Polizei. In ihrer Durchsetzungskraft ist die Staatsgewalt den Protestierenden daher fast immer überlegen und sie setzt diese Dominanz auch psychologisch ein, etwa wenn → *Fahrzeuge* wie Hubschrauber, Lautsprecherkraftwagen und Wasserwerfer zur Einschüchterung aufgefahren werden und → *Waffen* wie Schlagstöcke, Pfefferspray oder Pistolen mit Gummigeschossen als Drohgebärde zum Einsatz kommen. In Ländern, in denen die Menschenrechte weniger geachtet werden, besitzt die Obrigkeit meist weniger Skrupel, gewaltsam ein- und durchzugreifen; dabei werden die Verletzung und der Tod vieler Menschen oft billigend in Kauf genommen. Doch auch in Westeuropa und Nordamerika kommt es immer wieder zu Menschenrechtsverletzungen durch Polizeigewalt – nicht zuletzt, wenn es darum geht, Eigentum und Grundstücke vor Übergriffen zu schützen (→ *Guerillataktiken*):

Es handelt sich um ein gesellschaftlich sanktioniertes Missverhältnis zwischen Menschen- und Eigentumsrechten, das sich in der „ständigen Gleichsetzung von Gewalt und Sachbeschädigung" in der Protestberichterstattung der → *Medien* spiegelt (Fisher 2020, S. 398).

Anti-Protestmaßnahmen erfolgen allerdings nicht nur in unmittelbarer operativer Reaktion auf aktuelle Proteste, sondern auch als präventive Maßnahmen im Stadtraum. Schon der radikale Umbau von Paris Mitte des 19. Jahrhunderts durch breit angelegte Boulevards nach Entwurf des Baron Georges-Eugène Haussmann sollte nach der Revolution von → *1848* nicht zuletzt künftigen Aufständen vorbeugen: Die neuen → *Straßen* erlaubten nicht nur, Truppen schnell und effizient durch die Stadt zu manövrieren, sie boten auch ein freies Schussfeld und machten improvisierte Straßensperren aufgrund ihrer Breite fast unmöglich. In diesem Zusammenhang können die seinerzeit eingeführten Straßenbeläge Makadam – ein gewalzter Schotterbelag – und Asphalt als geradezu konterrevolutionäre Materialien aufgefasst werden: Sie wurden nicht zuletzt deshalb eingesetzt, um dem revolutionären Brauch Einhalt zu gebieten, das Pflaster der Straßen herauszureißen und als → *Baumaterial* für → *Barrikaden* und Wurfgeschosse zu verwenden. Einem → *Denkmalsturz* kam die Umgestaltung des → *Pearl Roundabout* in Manama nach dem Arabischen Frühling → *2011* in Bahrain gleich: Das Monument in der Mitte des Platzes wurde abgetragen und der → *Kreisverkehr* wurde zu einer Straßenkreuzung zurückgebaut, deren Verkehrsführung diesen Ort für künftige Proteste unwahrscheinlich werden lässt. Um den Protestierenden den Zugang zu bestimmten privaten oder öffentlichen Räumen zu verwehren, kommen neben den im Stadtraum längst allgegenwärtigen Pfosten, Pfeilern und Pollern – die als „stumme Polizisten" (Höge 2010, S. 12) das Abstellen bzw. die Zufahrt von Fahrzeugen in den Konsum- und Geschäftszentren kontrollieren – vor allem → *Absperrgitter* und Bauzäune, bisweilen auch Barrieren aus

Stacheldraht oder Beton zum Einsatz. Wenn dagegen bereits besetzte Areale geräumt werden sollen, muss die Staatsgewalt oft mit speziell ausgebildeten Einsatzgruppen operieren, um keine Personen zu verletzten oder zu gefährden, etwa wenn sich Menschen mit → *Lock-on Devices* oder Sekundenkleber stationär befestigt oder in Baumwipfeln oder → *Baumhäusern* verschanzt haben (→ *Ankleben*, → *Körpereinsatz*). (SH)

Anti-protest measures, Ger. → *Anti-Protestmaßnahmen (fig.)*. The use of water cannons, tear gas, or the dreaded → *kettling*—in which police officers form a ring around a group of protesters, forcing them to remain in place— is a common sight in → *demonstrations* and squats, even in democratic countries (→ *Public square occupation*, → *Building site occupation*, → *Squatting*). These are measures that are usually taken by the state to stop protests, to break them up, or to steer them back onto their intended course (→ *Police*). Sometimes— but by no means always—police are reacting to violent riots, provocations, or → *blockades* by protesters. Freedom of assembly, the right to demonstrate, and freedom of expression are fundamental rights in many democratic countries (→ *Legalization*, → *Communication*), however these rights are counterbalanced by legislation allowing authorities to preemptively ban rallies and demonstrations. For example, assemblics can be banned if public safety and order appear to be at risk or in order to prevent the alleged perpetration of → *violence* and → *destruction*. In many countries, there is also a general ban on → *weapons* and wearing face coverings at demonstrations, which does not apply to the police. In its enforceability, state authority is therefore almost always superior to the protesters, while it also uses this dominance psychologically, for example when → *vehicles* such as helicopters, trucks with loudspeakers, and water cannons are brought in for intimidation, and weapons such as batons, pepper spray, or pistols with rubber bullets are used as threatening gestures. In countries where human rights are less

respected, the authorities usually have fewer qualms about intervening and using force, often accepting the injury and death of many people. However, even in Western Europe and North America, human rights violations due to police violence occur time and again—not least when it is a matter of protecting property and land from encroachment (→ *Guerrilla tactics*): reflecting a socially sanctioned mismatch between human and property rights, which can be seen in the way the → *media* "constantly equates violence and property damage" in its coverage of protests (Fisher 2020, p. 398).

Anti-protest measures, however, occur not only as immediate operational responses to protests but also as preventive measures in urban space. The radical reconstruction of Paris in the mid-19th century by means of wide boulevards designed by Baron Georges-Eugène Haussmann was intended not least to prevent future uprisings after the revolution of → *1848*: the new → *streets* not only allowed troops to maneuver quickly and efficiently through the city, they also provided a clear field of fire and made improvised roadblocks almost impossible due to their width. In this context, the road surfaces introduced at the time, macadam—a rolled gravel surface—and asphalt, can be seen as downright counterrevolutionary materials: they were used not least to put a stop to the revolutionary custom of tearing out the cobblestones and using them as → *building material* for → *barricades* and projectiles. The re-design of the → *Pearl Roundabout* in Manama after the Arab Spring in Bahrain in → *2011* was tantamount to → *toppling monuments*: the monument in the center of the square was demolished and the → *roundabout* was turned into an intersection, whose traffic routing makes this location unlikely for future protests. In order to deny protesters access to certain private or public spaces, the posts, pillars, and bollards that have long been ubiquitous in urban space and act as "silent policemen" (Höge 2010, p. 12), controlling the parking or access of vehicles in consumer and business centers, are primarily supplemented by → *barriers* and construction fences, sometimes also including barriers made of barbed wire or concrete. If, on the other hand, occupied areas are to be cleared, the authorities often have to operate with specially trained task forces in order to avoid injuring or endangering people, for example if people have fastened themselves to something using → *lock-on devices* or superglue, or have entrenched themselves in treetops or → *tree houses* (→ *Body deployment*, → *Super-gluing*). (SH)

a. Archäologische Untersuchung. Attila Dézsi: Grabungsschnitt auf dem Gelände des Hüttendorfs in Gorleben, 16. Oktober 2017
b. Archäologische Untersuchung. Attila Dézsi: Fundobjekte auf dem Gelände des Hüttendorfs in Gorleben, 19. August 2020 (a. Archaeological investigations. Attila Dézsi: Section of the excavation at the Hüttendorf site in Gorleben, October 16, 2017; b. Archaeological investigations. Attila Dézsi: Finds from the Hüttendorf site in Gorleben, August 19, 2020)

Archaeological investigations, Ger. → *Archäologische Untersuchungen*.

Within the field of contemporary archaeology, investigations are sometimes conducted at the sites of → *protest camps*, e.g., in order to gain new insights into the buildings erected there or if a decision is to be made on declaring the material remains a cultural monument (→ *Heritage protection*). In → *Gorleben*, it was above all the clearing strategy pursued by the → *police* that ensured the settlement was well preserved, as following the destruction by the bulldozers, structures and their contents were buried under about a meter of sand. For a research project, archaeologist Attila Dézsi conducted archaeological investigations at the site, and having made nine precise excavation trenches, he uncovered traces of several huts as well as items left behind by both the occupiers and the police. In total, 3,043 artifacts were recovered, including kitchen utensils and crockery → *building materials*, tools, musical instruments, and clothing. After the village was cleared, the police used the remains of a storage cabin dug into the ground as a waste pit. There are immense differences in what was found: here, instead of kitchen utensils, there were cans of food and plastic cutlery. (Material provided by Attila Dézsi)

Archäologische Untersuchungen, engl. → *Archaeological investigations*, werden in der Gegenwartsarchäologie manchmal an Orten von → *Protestcamps* durchgeführt, z.B. um neue Erkenntnisse über die dort entstandenen Bauten zu gewinnen oder wenn über die Deklaration der materiellen Überreste zum Kulturdenkmal (→ *Denkmalschutz*) entschieden wird. In → *Gorleben* hat vor allem die Räumungsstrategie der → *Polizei* zur guten Konservierung der Siedlung beigetragen, denn die Bauten wurden nach ihrer → *Zerstörung* bei Planierungsarbeiten mitsamt ihrer Inneneinrichtung von einer ca. ein Meter dicken Sandschicht begraben. Der Archäologe Attila Dézsi führte für ein Forschungsprojekt archäologische Untersuchungen auf dem Gelände durch und fand bei insgesamt neun präzise gesetzten Grabungsschnitten Spuren von mehreren Hütten sowie von Hinterlassenschaften der Besetzer∗innen und der Polizei. Insgesamt wurden 3043 Artefakte geborgen, darunter → *Küchen-* und Essgeschirr, → *Baumaterialien*, Werkzeuge, Musikinstrumente und → *Kleidung*. Die Überreste einer in den Boden versenkten Lagerhütte wurden nach der Räumung des Dorfes von den Polizeikräften als Abfallgrube weitergenutzt. Der Unterschied im Fundspektrum ist enorm: Statt Kochutensilien gab es hier Konservendosen und Plastikbesteck. (Material: Attila Dézsi)

Archiv, engl. → *Archive.* Unabhängige Archive, die sich speziell der Dokumentation und Archivierung von Protestbewegungen widmen, entstanden erstmals mit den Friedens- und Umweltbewegungen der 1980er Jahre (→ *Greenham Common Friedenscamp,* → *Hainburger Au*). Während → *Protestschilder*, Plakate und → *Banner* weiterhin in analogen Archiven gesammelt werden, wächst seit dem 21. Jahrhundert die Zahl der digitalen Bewegungsarchive, die Fotos und Videos meist frei zugänglich zur Verfügung stellen, z.B. das 2018 gegründete Digitale Deutsche Frauenarchiv. Auch bei Protesten mit räumlichen Manifestationen wie → *Protestcamps* und → *Barrikaden* liegt der Sammlungsschwerpunkt mangels Lagermöglichkeiten oft auf zweidimensionalem Material. Eingang in die Protestarchive finden aber auch → *Schutzschilde* und ausgebrannte → *Fahrzeuge*, etwa vom → *Majdan* in Kyijw von → *2013*, sowie → *Zelte* und Teile von Barrikaden der → *Hongkong-Proteste* von → *2014*. Ziel der Bewegungsarchive ist nicht nur die Bewahrung von bedeutsamen Dokumenten der oft kurzlebigen Proteste für die Nachwelt, sondern auch, die Kontrolle darüber zu behalten, wo und wie die Bewegung in → *Medien* und → *Museen* präsentiert wird. Bei den → *Occupy-Wall-Street*-Protesten → *2011* in New York City schickten etablierte Museen und Organisationen wie die Smithsonian Institution und die New-York Historical Society ihre Mitarbeitenden zum Protestcamp, um Objekte für ihre Sammlungen zu besorgen. Die Aktivist∗innen gründeten daraufhin eine Archiv-Arbeitsgruppe und sicherten Material von den Protesten in eigenen Lagern. Das Museo Reina Sofía in Madrid ging sensibler vor: Es beauftragte die Kunsthistorikerin und Aktivistin Julia Ramírez Blanco mit der Gestaltung eines Raums in seiner Dauerausstellung aus dem Archiv der → *Movimiento 15M*. Bei den Majdan-Protesten in Kyijw wurde nach einer von Kulturschaffenden und Aktivist∗innen gestarteten Initiative gar ein internationaler Architekturwettbewerb für den Bau des Majdan-Museums ausgeschrieben. (AMM)

Archive, Ger. → *Archiv.* Independent archives specifically dedicated to documenting and archiving protest movements first emerged with the peace and environmental movements of the 1980s (→ *Greenham Common Peace Camp,* → *Hainburger Au*). While → *protest placards*, posters, and → *banners* continue to be collected in analog archives, in the 21st century, a growing number of digital archives related to social movements have emerged, most of which make photos and videos freely available, such as the Digitales Deutsches Frauenarchiv (Digital German Women's Archive), founded in 2018. Even in protests with spatial manifestations, such as → *protest camps* and → *barricades*, the focus of collections is often on two-dimensional material due to a lack of storage facilities. However, → *protective shields* and burned-out → *vehicles*, for example from the → *Maidan* in Kyiv in → *2013*, as well as → *tents* and parts of barricades from the → *Hong Kong protests* in → *2014*, have also found their way into protest archives. The objective of these movement archives is not only to preserve important documents of the often short-lived protests for posterity but also to maintain control over where and how a particular movement is presented in the → *media* and → *museums*. During the → *Occupy Wall Street* protests in New York City in → *2011*, established museums and organizations such as the Smithsonian Institution and the New-York Historical Society sent their staff to the pro-

Art

test camp to obtain objects for their collections. The activists then formed an archival working group and secured material from the protests in their own storage facilities. The Museo Reina Sofía in Madrid took a more sensitive approach: it commissioned the art historian and activist Julia Ramírez Blanco to design a room in its permanent exhibition from the archive of → *Movimiento 15M*. During the Maidan protests in Kyiv, an initiative launched by cultural professionals and activists led to an international architectural competition for the design of the Maidan Museum. (AMM)

Art, Ger. → *Kunst*; → *Barrier*, → *Graffiti*, → *Guerrilla tactics*, → *Icon*, → *Light projection*, → *Media*, → *Television set*, → *Toppling monuments*

Asphalt, engl. → *Asphalt*; → *Anti-Protestmaßnahmen*

Asphalt, Ger. → *Asphalt*; → *Anti-protest measures*

Attack, Ger. → *Angriff*. Moment of hesitation before the use of force / against objects / The experienced comrade, / aide to the previous SDS board, / is perplexed by / the group of comrades / lingering in front of the rectorate's / glass door for several minutes / Though reluctant to destroy / the valuable plate glass, / they want to enter the rectorate / "for the purpose of occupation"/ Clustered together by the door, / several comrades are suddenly armed with a ramming device / The pane of the / rectorate door shatters / (Alexander Kluge: *Attack on a Thick Glass Door*, film, 1 min. 52 sec., 2018; → *Destruction*, → *Occupation*, → *Violence*, → *Weapons*)

Authors, Ger. → *Autor∗innen*.

Andreia Barbosa (→ *MTST*) joined MTST in 2014 as a homeless person and was the main coordinator of the Povo Sem Medo occupation in 2017/2018. Today, she is a member of the MTST leadership in the state of São Paulo, as well as the head of the PSOL party in Santo André.

Aron Boks (→ *Lützerath*) was born in Wernigerode in 1997. He lives and works as an author and slam poet in Berlin and writes, among other things, the *taz.FUTURZWEI* column "Stimme meiner Generation." In 2023, he released the book *Nackt in die DDR. Mein Urgroßonkel Willi Sitte und was die ganze Geschichte mit mir zu tun hat.*

Larissa Denk (→ *Clothing*) received her PhD in anthropology from the University of Hamburg. She contributed as an author to the book *Kommt herunter, reiht euch ein... Eine kleine Geschichte der Protestformen sozialer Bewegungen*, which was based on a multi-semester research project.

Attila Dézsi (→ *Archaeological investigations*) is a modern archaeologist researching protest sites and utopian settlements from the 19th to the 21st century. Working for the State Office for the Preservation of Historic Monuments, he is responsible for the inventorying of concentration camps in Baden-Württemberg.

Jennifer Dyck (JD) is an architectural and art historian. She works as a scientific trainee at the Deutsches Architekturmuseum (DAM).

Beka Economopolous and Jason Jones (→ *Occupy Wall Street*) are co-founders of Not An Alternative, a collective that works at the intersections of art, activism, and critical theory. The group's work has been widely exhibited nationally and internationally. Their latest project, The Natural History Museum, is a mobile and pop-up museum that highlights the sociopolitical forces that shape nature, yet are excluded from traditional natural history museums.

Oliver Elser (OE) is a curator at the Deutsches Architekturmuseum (DAM) in Frankfurt am Main. He was the curator of *Making Heimat*, the German Pavilion at the 2016 Venice Architecture Biennale. In 2017, he co-founded the Center for Critical Studies in Architecture (CCSA).

Anna Feigenbaum (→ *Camp Studies*, → *Protest camp*) is a professor in digital storytelling at Bournemouth University in England, where she is co-director of the Centre for Science, Health and Data Communication Research. She is the co-author of the book *Protest*

Camps (2013) and the author of *Tear Gas* (2017).

Fabian Frenzel (→ *Camp Studies*, → *Protest camp*) is a reader in mobility and organization at Oxford Brookes Business School. He has written on protest camps and the mobilities of social movement activists, as well as on tourism in low income neighbourhoods.

Jesse Goldstein (→ *Occupy Wall Street*) is an associate professor of sociology at Virginia Commonwealth University. His work explores conflicts between capital, colonialism, and creativity as manifested in constructs such as entrepreneurship and the green economy. He is currently engaged in community-based research on minority-led urban agriculture and food sovereignty in Richmond, VA (USA).

Sebastian Hackenschmidt (SH) is a curator at the Museum of Applied Arts (MAK) in Vienna. He has curated numerous exhibitions, most recently in 2022 on the Viennese architects' group Missing Link.

Sonja Hildebrand (→ *Semper barricade*) is a tenured professor of architectural history at the Università della Svizzera italiana. She is (co-)editor of several books on Gottfried Semper, and her biography of the architect was published in 2020.

Petra Lange-Berndt (→ *Squatting*, → *Tree house*) is a professor of modern and contemporary art at the University of Hamburg. Her current research examines Monte Verità as a center of the *Lebensreform* movement and the concept of communes in 1970s art.

Anna-Maria Mayerhofer (AMM) is a curatorial assistant at the Deutsches Architekturmuseum (DAM) in Frankfurt am Main. Previously, she worked for the Berlin architecture magazine *ARCH+* and the TU Munich's Architekturmuseum. In 2021, she graduated from TU Munich with a master's degree in architecture.

Norbert Mayr (→ *Lobau*) lives and works in Vienna. Since 1993 he has worked as a freelance architectural historian, urban researcher, and author, conducting research on Austrian and international architectural history, architectural theory, urban and regional development, and monument preservation.

Patrick McCurdy (→ *Camp Studies*, → *Protest camp*) is an associate professor in the Department of Communication at the University of Ottawa, Canada, and co-author of *Protest Camps* (2013). His research views media as a site and source of social struggle.

Roland Meyer (→ *Digital media*) is a media theorist who works on virtual image archives at the DFG's Collaborative Research Center 1567 "Virtual Environments" at the Ruhr University Bochum. His most recent publication is *Gesichtserkennung*, Berlin 2021.

Stephan Mörsch (→ *Hambach Forest*) is an artist who builds exact 1:10 scale models of mainly self-organized architectural configurations, such as the "Jungle of Calais" or the tree house settlements in the Hambach Forest.

Larissa Napoli (→ *MTST*) is an architect and urbanist with a bachelor's degree from Universidade de São Paulo. Since 2020, she has been a member of the MTST leadership in the State of São Paulo and of the movement's architecture and urbanism sector.

Monika Ottermann (→ *MTST*), German religious studies scholar, in Brazil since 1989, is an MTST activist in the sectors of organization and international relations. She writes regularly for the *BrasilienNachrichten* (brasilieninitiative freiburg e.V.).

Ihor Poshyvailo (→ *Maidan*) is the director general of the Maidan Museum in Kyiv. He holds a PhD in history and was a Fulbright scholar at the Smithsonian Institution. Poshyvailo is the author of the award-winning *Phenomenology of Pottery* and articles about civic protests, conflicted history, traumatic memory, and the protection of heritage in times of war.

Julia Ramírez Blanco (→ *Movimiento 15M*) is a senior researcher (Ramón y Cajal program) at Madrid's Complutense University. Her interdisciplinary work connects art history, utopian studies, and activist movements. She is the author of *Artistic Utopias of Revolt*

(2018), *15M. El tiempo de las plazas* (2021), und *Amigos, disfraces y comunas* (2022), und *La ciudad del Sol: Le mouvement 15M entre formes et performances* (2023).

Annika Reiß (→ *Lützerath*) is an editor for climate issues at the *taz*. For several weeks, she lived in Lützerath to report on the eviction of the protest camp.

Julia Riedel (→ *Hambach Forest*) is an activist for climate justice. She quit her job as a doctor to join others in seeking ways to avert the destruction of the world by capitalist, colonial economics. She found allies from the Global South who can build on 500 years of resistance.

Kathrin Rottmann (→ *Cobblestone*) is an assistant professor at the Institute of Art History at the Ruhr University Bochum. After finishing her dissertation on *Aesthetik von unten. Pflaster und Asphalt in der bildenden Kunst der Moderne*, she has worked on industrial modes of production in 20th- and 21st-century art.

Anders Rubing (→ *Tent*) is an architect, critic, and researcher. His interest in protest, architecture, and public space has resulted in numerous publications and projects, including the book *The City between Freedom and Security*, which he co-edited.

Dietmar Rübel (→ *Music*) is an author, curator, and a professor of art history at the Academy of Fine Arts in Munich. His focus is on art since 1800, especially contemporary art.

Klaus Schönberger (→ *Communication*, → *Protest goals*) is a professor of cultural anthropology at the University of Klagenfurt. He works on the past and present of the protest forms of social movements.

Friederike Sigler (→ *Street*) is an assistant professor at the Institute of Art History at the Ruhr University Bochum. She works on labor relations and (new) nationalisms in contemporary art.

Aatika Singh (→ *Farmers' protests*) is a Delhi-based artist, activist, and scolar. She is currently a writing fellow with TwoCircles and a PhD research scholar in the School of Arts and Aesthetics at Jawaharlal Nehru University, Delhi.

Her research is on the philosophical and political connections of aesthetics in the Indian subcontinent with respect to Dalit cultural history and assertion.

Tom Ullrich (→ *Barricade*) is a postdoctoral researcher at the Department of Media and Cultural Studies and the Collaborative Research Center "Studies in Human Categorization" at the Johannes Gutenberg University Mainz. He works on the history of Parisian barricades, urban infrastructure, and surveillance.

Tim Wagner (→ *Hambach Forest*) is a freelance photojournalist who previously studied sociology in Leipzig. Since 2015, he has been observing the movements for climate justice in Germany with his camera.

Ahmed Zaazaa (→ *Tahrir Square*) is a researcher and urban planner, focusing on social justice in housing and planning. Recently, Zaazaa co-founded two entities, the latest of which was 10 Tooba: Applied Research on the Built Environment. Through 10 Tooba, Zaazaa is leading participatory projects with deprived and marginalized communities in different informal settlements in Cairo.

Ronni Zepplin (→ *Hambach Forest*) is an activist in the climate justice movement who is working to build combative commons to overcome capitalism

Autohupe, engl. → *Car horn*; → *Fahrzeuge*, → *Lärm*

Autonome Zone, engl. → *Autonomous zone*. Der Begriff Temporäre Autonome Zone (T.A.Z.) wurde von dem US-amerikanischen Schriftsteller und Philosophen Hakim Bey (Peter Lamborn Wilson) geprägt und etabliert. Gemeint sind die bei gewaltfreien Aktionen wie Flashmobs oder → *Hausbesetzungen* entstehenden Freiräume, in denen geltende Gesetze und Ordnungen vorübergehend außer Kraft gesetzt werden. Bey erweiterte später seine Theorie um die sogenannte Permanente Autonome Zone (P.A.Z.). Mehrere solcher dauerhaft besetzten Gebiete entstanden in den 2010er Jahren nach der gescheiterten Räumung der ersten *zone à défendre* („zu verteidigende Zone"), der → *ZAD Notre-Dame-des-Landes*, in ganz Frankreich, der Schweiz und in Deutschland, um Großprojekte für Flughäfen, Einkaufszentren oder Tagebaugebiete (ZAD Rheinland in → *Lützerath*) zu blockieren. Manchmal kommt es bei lange bestehenden Besetzungen zur → *Legalisierung* der Projekte (→ *Protestziele*). Als Autonome Zentren (AZ) werden selbstverwaltete soziokulturelle Einrichtungen in dauerhaft besetzten Häusern wie die Rote Flora in Hamburg und die „Køpi" in Berlin bezeichnet. Die Einflussnahme staatlicher oder städtischer Institutionen auf die basisdemokratisch organisierten Kulturzentren wird zwar abgelehnt, jedoch rufen die Besetzer∗innen anders als bei aktivistisch motivierten Fantasiestaaten wie der „Republik Freies Wendland" in → *Gorleben* → *1980* keine eigenen Staatsgebiete aus. „Wir müssen draußen bleiben", stand unter der karikaturhaften Zeichnung von zwei Polizeibeamten auf einem → *Hinweisschild* an der Passstelle des Protestdorfs in Gorleben. Weniger spielerisch im Umgang mit alternativen staatlichen Autoritäten sind → *Rechte Proteste* wie die Reichsbürgerbewegung, welche die Illegitimität der Bundesrepublik mit dem Fortbestehen des Deutschen Kaiserreichs begründet. (AMM)

Autonomous zone, Ger. → *Autonome Zone*. The term Temporary Autonomous Zone (T.A.Z.) was coined and established by the writer and philosopher Hakim Bey (Peter Lamborn Wilson). It refers to the free spaces created by nonviolent actions such as flash mobs or → *squatting*, in which existing laws and regulations are temporarily suspended. Bey later expanded his theory to include what he calls Permanent Autonomous Zones (P.A.Z.). Several such permanently occupied zones emerged throughout France, Switzerland, and Germany in the 2010s following the failed eviction of the first *zone à défendre* (zone to defend), the → *ZAD Notre-Dame-des-Landes*, to block major projects for airports, shopping centers, or open-pit mining (ZAD Rheinland in → *Lützerath*). Sometimes, long-standing occupations result in their → *legalization* (→ *Protest goals*). Autonomous

social centers are self-managed sociocultural institutions in permanently occupied buildings, such as the Rote Flora in Hamburg and the Køpi in Berlin. The influence of government or municipal institutions on the direct-democratically organized cultural centers is rejected, but unlike activist-motivated fantasy states such as the Republik Freies Wendland (Republic of Free Wendland) in → *Gorleben* in → *1980*, the squatters do not proclaim their own state territories. The slogan "Wir müssen draußen bleiben" ("We have to stay outside") was written under the cartoon-like drawing of two police officers on an → *information sign* at the passport office of the protest village in Gorleben. The alternative state apparatuses of movements such as the → *right-wing* Reichsbürger in Germany—which claims that the Federal Republic of Germany is an illegitimate institution because of the continued existence of the German Empire—are markedly less playful. (AMM)

Autoreifen, engl. → *Tires*; → *Barrikade*, → *Baumaterial*, → *Majdan*

Autor∗innen, engl. → *Authors*.
Andreia Barbosa (→ *MTST*) kam 2014 als Wohnungslose zu MTST und war 2017/2018 die Hauptkoordinatorin der Povo-Sem-Medo-Besetzung. Heute ist sie Mitglied der MTST-Leitung im Staat São Paulo sowie die Vorsitzende der Partei PSOL in Santo André.

Aron Boks (→ *Lützerath*) wurde 1997 in Wernigerode geboren. Er lebt und arbeitet als Autor und Slam Poet in Berlin und schreibt unter anderem die *taz.FUTURZWEI*-Kolumne „Stimme meiner Generation". 2023 erschien sein letztes Buch *Nackt in der DDR. Mein Urgroßonkel Willi Sitte und was die ganze Geschichte mit mir zu tun hat*.

Larissa Denk (→ *Kleidung*) promovierte im Fach Ethnologie an der Universität Hamburg. Sie hat als Autorin am Buch *Kommt herunter, reiht euch ein... Eine kleine Geschichte der Protestformen sozialer Bewegungen* mitgewirkt, welches im Rahmen eines mehrsemestrigen Studienprojektes entstanden ist.

Attila Dézsi (→ *Archäologische Untersuchungen*) forscht als Neuzeitarchäologe zu Protestorten und utopischen Siedlungen des 19. bis 21. Jahrhunderts. Für das Landesamt für Denkmalpflege ist er für die denkmalfachliche Erfassung von KZ-Außenlagern in Baden-Württemberg tätig.

Jennifer Dyck (JD) ist Architektur- und Kunsthistorikerin. Sie arbeitet als wissenschaftliche Volontärin am Deutschen Architekturmuseum (DAM).

Beka Economopolous und Jason Jones (→ Occupy Wall Street) sind Mitbegründer∗innen von „Not An Alternative", einem Kollektiv, das an der Schnittstelle von Kunst, Aktivismus und kritischer Theorie arbeitet. Die Werke der Gruppe wurden in den USA und international ausgestellt. Ihr neuestes Projekt, The Natural History Museum, ist ein mobiles Pop-up-Museum, das die sozio-politischen Kräfte beleuchtet, die die Natur formen, aber von den traditionellen Naturkundemuseen ausgeblendet werden.

Oliver Elser (OE) ist Kurator am Deutschen Architekturmuseum (DAM) in Frankfurt am Main. 2016 war er Kurator von *Making Heimat*, dem Deutschen Pavillon auf der Architekturbiennale von Venedig. Er zählt zu den Gründungsmitgliedern des seit 2017 bestehenden Center for Critical Studies in Architecture (CCSA).

Anna Feigenbaum (→ *Camp Studies*, → *Protestcamp*) ist Professorin für Digital Storytelling an der Universität Bournemouth in England, wo sie Co-Direktorin des Centre for Science, Health and Data Communication Research ist. Sie ist Mitautorin des Buches *Protest Camps* (2013) und Autorin von *Tear Gas* (2017).

Fabian Frenzel (→ *Camp Studies*, → *Protestcamp*) ist Dozent für Mobilität und Organisation an der Oxford Brookes Business School. Er hat über Protestcamps und die Mobilität von Aktivist∗innen sozialer Bewegungen sowie über Tourismus in einkommensschwachen Vierteln geschrieben.

Jesse Goldstein (→ *Occupy Wall Street*) ist außerordentlicher Professor für Soziologie an der Virginia Commonwealth University. In seiner Arbeit untersucht er die Konflikte zwischen Kapital, Kolonialismus und Kreativität, die sich in Konstrukten wie dem grünen Unternehmertum manifestieren. Derzeit betreibt er gemeinschaftsbasierte Forschung über die von Minderheiten geführte urbane Landwirtschaft in Richmond, VA (USA).

Sebastian Hackenschmidt (SH) ist seit 2005 Kustos am Museum für angewandte Kunst (MAK) in Wien, wo er zahlreiche Ausstellungen kuratiert hat, zuletzt 2022 über die Wiener Architekt∗innengruppe Missing Link.

Sonja Hildebrand (→ *Semper-Barrikade*) ist ordentliche Professorin für Architekturgeschichte der Moderne an der Università della Svizzera italiana. Sie ist (Co-)Herausgeberin mehrerer Bücher über Gottfried Semper; 2020 erschien ihre Biografie des Architekten.

Petra Lange-Berndt (→ *Baumhaus*, → *Hausbesetzung*) ist Professorin für Moderne und Gegenwartskunst an der Universität Hamburg. Ihre gegenwärtige Forschung untersucht den Monte Verità als Zentrum der Lebensreformbewegung sowie das Konzept Kommune in der Kunst der 1970er Jahre.

Anna-Maria Mayerhofer (AMM) ist kuratorische Assistentin am Deutschen Architekturmuseum (DAM) in Frankfurt am Main. Zuvor arbeitete sie für das Berliner Architekturmagazin *ARCH+* und das Architekturmuseum der TUM in München. 2021 schloss sie an der TU München ihr Architekturstudium ab.

Norbert Mayr (→ *Lobau*) lebt und arbeitet in Wien. Seit 1993 ist er als freier Architekturhistoriker, Stadtforscher sowie Autor tätig und forscht zur österreichischen und internationalen Architekturgeschichte, Architekturtheorie, Stadt- und Regionalentwicklung sowie Denkmalpflege.

Patrick McCurdy (→ *Camp Studies*, → *Protestcamp*) ist außerordentlicher Professor in der Abteilung für Kommunikation an der University of Ottawa, Kanada, und Co-Autor von *Protest Camps* (2013). Er forscht über Medien als Ort und Quelle sozialer Kämpfe.

Roland Meyer (→ *Digitale Medien*) forscht als Bild- und Medienwissenschaftler am DFG-Sonderforschungsbereich 1567 „Virtuelle Lebenswelten" der Ruhr-Universität Bochum zu virtuellen Bildarchiven. Seine jüngste Veröffentlichung: *Gesichtserkennung*, Berlin 2021.

Stephan Mörsch (→ *Hambacher Wald*) ist Künstler und baut exakte Modelle im Maßstab 1:10, vor allem von selbstorganisierten Architekturen, wie zum Beispiel dem sogenannten „Dschungel von Calais" oder den Baumhaussiedlungen im Hambacher Wald.

Larissa Napoli (→ *MTST*) ist Architektin und Stadtplanerin mit einem Bachelor-Abschluss von der Universidade de São Paulo. Seit 2020 ist sie Mitglied der MTST-Leitung im Staat São Paulo und des MTST-Sektors für Architektur und Urbanistik.

Monika Ottermann (→ *MTST*), deutsche Theologin, seit 1989 in Brasilien, ist MTST-Aktivistin in den Sektoren Organisation und Internationale Beziehungen. Sie schreibt regelmäßig für die *BrasilienNachrichten* (brasilieninitiative freiburg e.V.).

Ihor Poshyvailo (→ *Majdan*) ist Generaldirektor des Majdan-Museums in Kyjiw. Er ist promovierter Historiker und war Fulbright-Stipendiat an der Smithsonian Institution. Poshyvailo ist Autor von *Phenomenology of Pottery* und von Artikeln über Bürger∗innenproteste, konfliktreiche Geschichte, traumatische Erinnerung und den Schutz des Kulturerbes in Kriegszeiten.

Julia Ramírez Blanco (→ *Movimiento 15M*) ist Wissenschaftlerin (Ramón-y-Cajal-Programm) an der Universidad Complutense in Madrid. Ihre interdisziplinäre Arbeit verbindet Kunstgeschichte, Utopieforschung und aktivistische Bewegungen. Sie ist die Autorin der folgenden Bücher: *Artistic Utopias of Revolt* (2018), *15M. El tiempo de las plazas* (2021), *Amigos, disfraces y comunas* (2022), *La ciudad del Sol. Le mouvement 15M entre formes et performances* (2023).

Annika Reiß (→ *Lützerath*) ist Redakteurin für Klimathemen bei der *taz*. Für die Berichterstattung über die Räumung Lützeraths lebte sie mehrere Wochen vor Ort.

Julia Riedel (→ *Hambacher Wald*) ist

Aktivistin für Klimagerechtigkeit. Sie ließ die Betätigung als Ärztin links liegen, um gemeinsam mit anderen nach Auswegen im Angesicht der Zerstörung der Welt durch die kapitalistische, koloniale Wirtschaftsweise zu suchen. Sie fand Verbündete aus dem Globalen Süden, die an 500 Jahre Widerstand anknüpfen können.

Kathrin Rottmann (→ *Pflasterstein*) ist wissenschaftliche Mitarbeiterin am Kunstgeschichtlichen Institut der Ruhr-Universität Bochum. Sie arbeitet nach ihrer Dissertation über die *Aesthetik von unten. Pflaster und Asphalt in der bildenden Kunst der Moderne* über industrielle Produktionsweisen in der Kunst des 20. und 21. Jahrhunderts.

Anders Rubing (→ *Zelt*) ist Architekt, Kritiker und Forscher. Sein Interesse an Protest, Architektur und öffentlichem Raum hat u.a. zu dem Buch *The City between Freedom and Security* geführt, dessen Co-Herausgeber er ist.

Dietmar Rübel (→ *Musik*) ist Autor, Kurator und Professor für Kunstgeschichte an der Akademie der Bildenden Künste München. Seine Schwerpunkte liegen auf der Kunst seit 1800, insbesondere der zeitgenössischen Kunst.

Klaus Schönberger (→ *Kommunikation*, → *Protestziele*) ist Professor für Kulturanthropologie an der Alpen-Adria-Universität Klagenfurt / Celovec. Einer seiner Themenschwerpunkte ist die Geschichte und Gegenwart von Protestformen sozialer Bewegungen.

Friederike Sigler (→ *Straße*) ist wissenschaftliche Mitarbeiterin am Kunstgeschichtlichen Institut der Ruhr-Universität Bochum. Sie befasst sich mit Arbeitsverhältnissen und (Neuen) Nationalismen in der Kunst der Gegenwart.

Aatika Singh (→ *Farmers-Proteste*) ist eine in Delhi lebende Künstlerin, Aktivistin und Wissenschaftlerin. Derzeit ist sie Stipendiatin von TwoCircles und Doktorandin an der School of Arts and Aesthetics der Jawaharlal Nehru University, Delhi. Ihre Forschungsarbeit befasst sich mit philosophischen und politischen Fragen der Ästhetik im Hinblick auf die Kulturgeschichte der Dalits auf dem indischen Subkontinent.

Tom Ullrich (→ *Barrikade*) ist wissenschaftlicher Mitarbeiter (Postdoc) der Professur Medienkulturwissenschaft am Sonderforschungsbereich „Humandifferenzierung" der Johannes Gutenberg-Universität Mainz. Er forscht zu Pariser Barrikaden, urbanen Infrastrukturen und Überwachungsdiskursen.

Tim Wagner (→ *Hambacher Wald*) ist freiberuflicher Fotojournalist und hat zuvor Soziologie in Leipzig studiert. Seit 2015 begleitet er die Bewegungen für Klimagerechtigkeit in Deutschland fotografisch.

Ahmed Zaazaa (→ *Tahrir-Platz*) ist Forscher und Stadtplaner, der sich auf Fragen der sozialen Gerechtigkeit im Wohnungs- und Städtebau konzentriert. Er ist Mitbegründer von zwei Initiativen, zuletzt von „10 Tooba: Applied Research on the Built Environment". Im Rahmen von 10 Tooba leitet Zaazaa partizipative Projekte mit benachteiligten und marginalisierten Gemeinschaften in verschiedenen informellen Gebieten in Kairo.

Ronni Zepplin (→ *Hambacher Wald*) ist Aktivistin in der Klimagerechtigkeitsbewegung und baut dort kämpfende Commons auf, um den Kapitalismus zu überwinden.

Badewanne. David Klammer: Protestcamp, Hambacher Wald, 2018 (Bathtub. David Klammer: Protest camp, Hambach Forest, 2018)

Badewanne, engl. → *Bathtub*. Ein Wannenbad im → *Protestcamp*, also ohne die Möglichkeit, heißes Wasser einfach aus einer Leitung zu beziehen – das ist Luxus. So viel Aufwand zu betreiben, macht aus dem Bad eine symbolische Handlung: Das demonstrativ entspannte Inbesitznehmen des Geländes wird zelebriert, ob in → *Gorleben* 1980 oder im → *Hambacher Wald* 2018. (OE)

Baltic Way, Ger. → *Baltischer Weg*. On August 23, → *1989*, hundreds of thousands of Balts formed an approximately 600-kilometer-long human chain across Estonia, Latvia, and Lithuania to protest for freedom and independence from the Soviet Union. The protest made reference to the Hitler-Stalin Pact, which had led to the annexation of these states fifty years prior. With the collapse of the Soviet Union in 1991 and successful referendums, the three Baltic states finally regained their independence. (JD)

Baltischer Weg, engl. → *Baltic Way*. Mit einer rund 600 Kilometer langen Menschenkette durch Estland, Lettland und Litauen haben am 23. August → *1989* hunderttausende Balt∗innen für ihre Freiheit und Unabhängigkeit von der Sowjetunion protestiert. Sie erinnerten damit an den Hitler-Stalin-Pakt, der 50 Jahre zuvor zur Annexion dieser Staaten führte. Mit dem Zusammenbruch der Sowjetunion im Jahr 1991 und erfolgreichen Volksabstimmungen erlangten schließlich alle der drei baltischen Staaten ihre Unabhängigkeit zurück. (JD)

Banner, engl. → *Banner*. Räumliche Steigerungsform des → *Protestschilds*, da ein Banner immer von mehreren Personen getragen wird oder eine Fläche von mehr als zwei Armlängen überspannt. Banner bestehen aus flexiblen, leichten Materialien. Bei → *Demonstrationen* verkünden Banner oft als Leittransparente das zentrale Anliegen oder können zur Abschirmung des Demonstrationszuges dienen (→ *Schutz*). Das Banner mit dem Musil-Zitat ist dem *Handbuch der Kommunikationsguerilla* (→ *Handbücher / Online-Manuals*) entnommen, wo es im Kapitel zum Verfremdungsprinzip konsequenterweise ohne weitere Erläuterung und ohne Bildnachweis abgedruckt wurde. (OE)

Banner, Ger. → *Banner (fig.)*. An expanded form of the → *protest placard*, as a banner always has to be carried by more than one person or is stretched across an area wider than two arms' lengths. Banners are made of flexible, light materials. At → *demonstrations*, banners often act as the leading statement conveying the main issue, or can be used to shield the line of marchers (→ *Protection*). The banner with the quote from Robert Musil stems from the *Handbuch der Kommunikationsguerilla* (→ *Handbücher / Online-Manuals*), where it was reprinted in the chapter on the principle of alienation—logically without any further explanation or image credit. (OE)

Banner auf einer Berliner 1. Mai-Demonstration 1996 mit Zitat aus Robert Musil: *Der Mann ohne Eigenschaften*, Band 1, 1930 (Banner at a May Day demonstration in Berlin, 1996, with a quote from Robert Musil's *The Man without Qualities*, vol. 1, 1930)

Barbed wire, Ger. → *Stacheldraht*; → *Anti-protest measures*, → *Barricade*, → *Building materials*

Barrel, Ger. → *Fass (fig.)*. This presumably staged image shows British soldiers who have gone to ground behind a wall of beer barrels during the so-called Easter Uprising in Dublin at the end of April 1916. It incisively brings to mind the possible derivation of the word → *barricade* from the French word *barrique* (wooden barrel). The uprising against British rule instigated by Irish Republicans was one of the most important events in the Irish revolutionary period and also marked the first instance of armed conflict since the Irish Rebellion of 1798. (SH)

Barricade, Ger. → *Barrikade (fig.)*. The classic barricade is a French invention. In his encyclopedia, Larousse dates its origin to the so-called "Day of the Barricades" of May 12, 1588, a Pa-

risian uprising at the time of the wars of religion (Larousse 1866, p. 262). Opinions differ, however, about the word's origin. Some derive it from the French verb *barrer* (to block). Others refer to misappropriated *barriques* (→ *Barrel*) which were filled with earth and stones, and reinforced with iron chains. With them, the Parisians successfully resisted the royal troops in 1588. The very term *barricade* thus points to its hybrid character: it is both a popular practice of resistance in → *public space* and the material interim result of this effort, i.e. an ephemeral structure assembled from the diverse items in the → *street* (→ *Blockade*).

In the 19th century, the modern barricade embarks on its stellar career by adding a third important dimension: it becomes a revolutionary symbol of the oppressed and an → *icon* of protest, for example in Eugène Delacroix's famous painting of 1830 or in Victor Hugo's novel *Les Misérables* of 1862. This is accompanied by a decisive further development: on the one hand, the barricade merges with the myth of revolutionary Paris. In the tradition of 1789, it now stands symbolically for a violent upheaval of political and social conditions (see Corbin, Mayeur 1997). On the other, it simultaneously detaches itself from Paris, becomes more pluralistic, and circulates far beyond the French capital, until around 1848 it becomes first a European and then, in the 20th and 21st centuries, a worldwide affair. The barricades of all places and all times are thus always characterized by the respective specific relationship of practical, material, and symbolic conditions. What constitutes a barricade as an intuitive practice, an unwieldy artifact, or an effective image cannot be discussed universally but only in concrete cases.

The successful Paris revolutions of July → *1830* and February → *1848* provide the founding myth of the modern barricade. Protest against royal despotism takes place in the streets, or more precisely, under the conditions and with the means of the street: when any public gathering is broken up by force of arms, barricades provide → *protection* and disrupt opposing movements (→ *Weapons*, → *Violence*). Building together promotes solidarity and creates a tangible provocation that can no longer be ignored (see Traugott 2010).

This is also due to the brazen repurposing of all kinds of urban items that can be mobilized and combined for barricade construction (→ *Misappropriation*). → *Cobblestones*, → *barrels*, furniture, building materials, and means of transport (→ *Building materials*, → *Vehicles*) were especially popular. Thus, each barricade is dependent on the material environment typical of its time: carriages and omnibuses in the 19th century, Citroën 2CVs and traffic signs in Paris in → *May '68*, e-scooters and rental bikes during the → *Yellow Vests movement* in → *2018*.

What, by contrast, seems unchanging is a universally shared "desire for definiteness": those who speak of barricades or erect them insist on "concrete friend-foe relationships" coming to a head. "The barricade is a fascinating projection surface. In practice, it was and is a grandiosely functioning wishing machine" (Briese 2011, p. 447).

This may explain why barricades became the means of choice in the uprisings and revolutions in many European cities around 1848. Gottfried Semper's architectural consulting on the construction of barricades in Dresden or the establishment of a "barricade commission" in Rome in May 1849 document the professionalization of this protest technique (→ *Semper barricade*).

However, barricades seem to multiply not only in the streets but also on paper. Specially created → *barricade plans* serve as a reminder or analysis of the events. In 1868, the revolutionary Auguste Blanqui wrote a clandestine manual for organized street fighting, including a schematic design for a "regular barricade." The opposing side also systematizes its barricade knowledge: after 1848, military officers published manuals on how to fight insurrections, while architects have presented the invention of "movable counter-barricades."

The obsessive and increasingly imaginary preoccupation with barricades reaches its climax in the debate about the Haussmannization of Paris, when contemporary critics such as Friedrich Engels reduce the road openings for the construction of the new boulevards to counterrevolutionary motifs (see Ullrich 2020). Nevertheless, some photogenic fortifications were built on the boulevards during the Paris Commune in May 1871, which were supposed to follow the tradition of the revolutionary barricades but ultimately failed as elements of a military city defense.

Throughout the 20th century and into our present day, barricading streets remains a common and widespread practice, even if it has long been supplemented or replaced by other forms of protest. Barricades are also increasingly a means of (urban) warfare. They are erected locally and disseminated globally (→ *Digital media*), though the materials used and their ambiguous symbolism can vary widely: newspaper rolls in the Berlin street fighting of → *1919*, car tires on the → *Maidan* in Kyiv in → *2013/2014*, bamboo poles in → *Hong Kong* in → *2014* and → *2019*, or the burning piles of garbage in Paris in 2023 after the municipal sanitation department also went on strike in protest against French pension reforms. (Tom Ullrich)

Barricade plan, Ger. → *Barrikadenplan (fig.)*. Plans of barricades were important → *media* of orientation, historicization, and → *communication* in 19th-century protest culture. They featured city maps charting the position of the barricades and of troops, along with other strategically important information. One of the most impressive maps relating to the → *1830* → *July Revolution* in Paris was Charles Motte's *Plan figuratif des barricades*, outlining the three-day-long street fighting between the government troops and the revolutionaries, with the barricades marked in yellow and the gun salvoes in red. (SH)

Barrier, Ger. → *Absperrgitter (fig.)*. For the sculpture boulevard that formed part of Berlin's 750th anniversary celebrations, artist Olaf Metzel created

Barrikade. Albert Robida: *Construction des barricades* (Barrikadenbau), aus dem Zukunfts-
roman *Le Vingtième Siècle* (Das zwanzigste Jahrhundert), 1883 (Barricade. Albert Robida:
Construction des barricades (building the barricades), from the novel about the future entitled
Le Vingtième Siècle (The Twentieth Century), 1883)

an installation that primarily consisted
of barriers and thus gave great visibility to a frequently used →*anti-protest
measure*. The provocative artwork referred to April 13, 1981, the day when
there was substantial rioting on Berlin's
Kurfürstendamm, along with the →*destruction* of about 200 shop windows,
after the news broke that Sigurd Debus,
accused of being a Red Army Faction
terrorist and in prison since 1975, had
died. (In actual fact, Debus died three
days later, having started a hunger strike
in February). Metzel's sculpture caused
fierce debate and was itself on several
occasions the target of →*demonstrations*, leading the police to erect barriers
around it, too, to protect it (→*Toppling
monuments*), as in the image above from
the Census Boycott of 1987. (SH)

Barrikade, engl. →*Barricade*. Die
klassische Barrikade ist eine französische Erfindung. In seiner Enzyklopädie
datiert Larousse ihren Ursprung auf den
sogenannten „Tag der Barrikaden" vom

12. Mai 1588, einen Pariser Aufstand
zur Zeit der Religionskriege (Larousse
1866, S. 262). Über die Wortherkunft
gehen die Meinungen allerdings ausei-
nander. Manche leiten sie vom französischen Verb „versperren" (*barrer*) ab.
Andere verweisen auf die Zweckentfremdung von Barriquefässern, die mit
Erde und Steinen gefüllt und Eisenket-
ten verstärkt wurden. Mit ihnen gelang
es den Pariser∗innen 1588, Widerstand
gegen die königlichen Truppen zu leisten. Bereits der Begriff *barricade* ver-
weist also auf ihren hybriden Charakter:
Sie ist sowohl eine populäre Praxis des
Widerstands im →*öffentlichen Raum*,
als auch das materielle Zwischenergeb-
nis dieser Anstrengung, d.h. ein aus den
diversen Dingen der →*Straße* montier-
tes ephemeres Bauwerk (→*Blockade*).
Im 19. Jahrhundert beginnt die steile
Karriere der modernen Barrikade, indem eine dritte wichtige Dimension
hinzukommt: Die Barrikade wird zum
revolutionären Symbol der Unterdrück-

ten und zur → *Ikone* des Protests, etwa in Eugène Delacroix' berühmtem Gemälde von 1830 oder in Victor Hugos Roman *Les Misérables* von 1862. Damit einher geht eine entscheidende Weiterentwicklung: Einerseits verschmilzt die Barrikade mit dem Mythos des revolutionären Paris. In der Tradition von 1789 steht sie nunmehr sinnbildlich für die gewaltsame Umwälzung der politischen und sozialen Verhältnisse (vgl. Corbin, Mayeur 1997). Andererseits löst sie sich zugleich von Paris, wird pluraler und zirkuliert weit über die französische Hauptstadt hinaus, bis sie um 1848 zunächst zu einer europäischen und dann im 20. und 21. Jahrhundert zu einer weltweiten Angelegenheit wird. Die Barrikaden sind also überall und zu jeder Zeit gekennzeichnet durch das jeweils spezifische Verhältnis von praktischen, materiellen und symbolischen Bedingungen. Was demnach eine Barrikade als intuitive Praxis, sperriges Artefakt oder wirkungsvolles Bild ausmacht, lässt sich nicht universell, sondern immer nur am konkreten Fall diskutieren.

Die erfolgreichen Pariser Revolutionen vom Juli → *1830* und Februar → *1848* liefern den Gründungsmythos der modernen Barrikade. Der Protest gegen königliche Willkür findet in den Straßen statt, genauer gesagt unter den Bedingungen und mit den Mitteln der Straße: Wenn jede öffentliche Versammlung mit Waffengewalt aufgelöst wird, bieten Barrikaden → *Schutz* und stören gegnerische Bewegungen (→ *Waffen*, → *Gewalt*). Das gemeinsame Bauen befördert Solidarisierung und schafft eine handfeste Provokation, die nicht mehr ignoriert werden kann (vgl. Traugott 2010).

Das liegt auch an der dreisten Umnutzung aller möglichen urbanen Dinge, die sich für den Barrikadenbau mobilisieren und kombinieren lassen (→ *Zweckentfremdung*). Beliebt waren vor allem → *Pflastersteine*, → *Fässer*, Möbel, Baustoffe und Verkehrsmittel (→ *Baumaterial*, → *Fahrzeuge*). So ist jede Barrikade abhängig von ihrer zeittypischen materiellen Umgebung: Kut-

schen und Omnibusse im 19. Jahrhundert, Citroën 2CV und Verkehrsschilder im Pariser → *Mai '68*, E-Scooter und Leihräder während der → *Gelbwestenbewegung* → *2018*.

Unveränderlich dagegen scheint ein allseits geteiltes „Begehren nach Eindeutigkeit": Wer von Barrikaden spricht oder sie errichtet, dringt auf die Zuspitzung „konkreter Freund-Feind-Verhältnisse [...]. Die Barrikade ist eine faszinierende Projektionsfläche. In praxi war und ist sie eine grandios funktionierende Wunschmaschine" (Briese 2011, S. 447).

Das mag erklären, warum Barrikaden zum Mittel der Wahl in den Aufständen und Revolutionen in vielen europäischen Städten um 1848 werden. Die fachmännische Beteiligung Gottfried Sempers am Barrikadenbau in Dresden oder die Einrichtung einer „Barrikadenkommission" in Rom im Mai 1849 dokumentieren die Professionalisierung einer Protesttechnik (→ *Semper-Barrikade*).

Jedoch scheinen sich die Barrikaden nicht nur in den Straßen, sondern auch auf dem Papier zu vermehren. Eigens erstellte → *Barrikadenpläne* dienen zur Erinnerung oder Analyse der Ereignisse. Der Revolutionär Auguste Blanqui verfasst 1868 eine klandestine Anleitung zum organisierten Straßenkampf samt schematischem Entwurf einer „regulären Barrikade". Aber auch die Gegenseite systematisiert ihr Barrikadenwissen: Nach 1848 veröffentlichen Militärs Handbücher zur Bekämpfung von Aufständen, während Architekten die Erfindung „beweglicher Gegen-Barrikaden" präsentieren.

Ihren Höhepunkt erreicht die obsessive und zunehmend imaginäre Beschäftigung mit Barrikaden in der Debatte um die Haussmannisierung von Paris, wenn zeitgenössische Kritiker wie Friedrich Engels die Straßendurchbrüche zum Bau der neuen Boulevards auf konterrevolutionäre Motive reduzieren (vgl. Ullrich 2020). Trotzdem entstehen auf den Boulevards während der Pariser Kommune im Mai 1871 einige fotogene Fortifikationsanlagen, die an die Tradition der revolutionären Barrikaden anschließen sollten, als Elemente einer militärischen Stadtverteidigung aber letztlich scheiterten.

Das 20. Jahrhundert hindurch und bis in unsere Gegenwart hinein bleibt das Verbarrikadieren von Straßen eine gängige und weit verbreitete Praxis, auch wenn es längst durch andere Protestformen ergänzt oder ersetzt wird. Auch sind Barrikaden zunehmend ein Mittel der Kriegsführung und von *Urban Warfare*. Sie werden lokal errichtet und global verbreitet (→ *Digitale Medien*), wobei die verwendeten Materialien und ihre ambivalente Symbolik sich sehr unterscheiden können: Zeitungsrollen bei den Berliner Straßenkämpfen → *1919*, Autoreifen auf dem → *Majdan* in Kyjiw → *2013/2014*, Bambusstäbe in → *Hongkong* → *2014* und → *2019*, oder die brennenden Müllhaufen in Paris 2023, nachdem auch die Stadtreinigung aus Protest gegen die französische Rentenreform in den Streik getreten ist. (Tom Ullrich)

Barrikadenplan. Charles Motte: *Plan figuratif des barricades*, handkolorierter Druck, 1830 (Barricade plan. Charles Motte: *Plan figuratif des barricades*, hand-colored print, 1830)

Barrikadenplan, engl. → *Barricade plan*. Barrikadenpläne waren wichtige → *Medien* der Orientierung, Historisierung und → *Kommunikation* in der Protestkultur des 19. Jahrhunderts. Dabei handelte es sich um Stadtpläne, auf denen die Position der → *Barrikaden* und Stellung der Truppen sowie andere strategische Informationen kartografiert waren. Als eine der eindrucksvollsten Karten zur → *Julirevolution* in Paris → *1830* verzeichnete Charles Mottes *Plan figuratif des barricades* die drei Tage während Straßenkämpfe zwischen den Regierungstruppen und den Revolutionär∗innen, wobei die Barrikaden gelb und das Geschützfeuer rot markiert waren. (SH)

Barrikadentage (Riga), engl. → *The Barricades (Riga)*. Nach dem → *Baltischen Weg* und vor dem Zerfall der Sowjetunion hatte es während der „Barrikadentage" im Januar → *1991* in Litauen schwere Auseinandersetzungen mit sowjetischen Einheiten gegeben. Trotz *Glasnost* (Offenheit) und *Perestroika* (Umgestaltung) starben 14 Menschen. In Litauen und im lettischen Riga entstanden daraufhin präventive → *Barrikaden* zum Schutz der Regierungsgebäude vor weiteren Angriffen. (JD)

Barrio, engl. → *Barrio*. Spanisch für „Stadtteil". Begriff für Vorstädte von lateinamerikanischen Metropolen, häufig auch romantisierende Selbstbezeichnung der lebendigen Arbeiter∗innenvororte in bewusster Abgrenzung zu elitären Stadtvierteln. In den → *Protestcamps* der gegenwärtigen deutschen Klimagerechtigkeitsbewegung bezeichnen Barrios Nachbar∗innenschaften, in denen sich die dort lebenden Aktivist∗innen organisieren. Je nach → *Siedlungsstruktur* und Größe sind → *Besetzungen* häufig in Viertel mit bis zu zwanzig → *Baumhäusern* (in Waldbesetzungen) und Bodenstrukturen eingeteilt. Sie versorgen sich über eigene → *Infrastrukturen* teils autark und treffen im Fall einer Räumung durch die → *Polizei* ihre Entscheidungen unabhängig von anderen Barrios. Für die Bewohner∗innen der Besetzung sind Barrios zugleich bedürfnisorientierte → *Schutz*- und Freiräume. Im → *Dannenröder Wald* gab es beispielsweise ein FLINTA∗-Barrio („Die Zukunft"), ein veganes Barrio („Nirgendwo"), ein Laissez-faire-Barrio („Drüben"), in dem Alkohol konsumiert werden durfte, sowie mehrere Barrios, in denen die gemeinsame Sprache Englisch war. Barrios gibt es auch bei zeitlich begrenzten Protestcamps, etwa bei den → *Klimacamps* im Rheinland oder im → *Hambacher Wald*. Hier gestalten antirassistische, herrschaftskritische oder queerfeministische Barrios jeweils eigene Veranstaltungsprogramme. (AMM)

Barrio, Ger. → *Barrio*. Spanish, "urban quarter." The term refers to areas on the outskirts of Latin American metropolises, which often also includes a romanticizing self-designation of lively working-class suburbs in deliberate distinction from elitist urban quarters. In the → *protest camps* of the current German climate justice movement, barrios refer to neighborhoods where resident activists organize themselves. Depending on the → *settlement structure* and size, the → *occupation* is often divided into areas with up to twenty → *tree houses* and ground-based structures. They are partly self-sufficient through their own → *infrastructures* and make their decisions independently from other barrios in case of eviction by the → *police*. For the residents of the occupation, barrios are at the same time needs-oriented spaces of → *protection* and freedom. In the → *Dannenrod Forest*, for example, there was a FLINTA∗ barrio (reserved for women, lesbians, non-binary, trans, and agender people), called "Die Zukunft" (The Future), a vegan barrio, called "Nirgendwo" (Nowhere), a laissez-faire barrio called "Drüben" (Over There), where alcohol could be consumed, and several barrios where the common language was English. Barrios also exist at temporary protest camps, such as the → *Camps for Climate Action* in the Rhineland or in the → *Hambach Forest*. Here, anti-racist, counter-hegemonic, or queer-feminist barrios each create their own event programs. (AMM)

Bathtub, Ger. → *Badewanne (fig.)*. Having a bathtub in a → *protest camp*, with no access to running hot water is a real luxury. Making such an effort turns the tub into a symbolic act: The

demonstratively relaxed act of occupation is celebrated, be it in → *Gorleben* in → *1980* or in the → *Hambach Forest* in 2018. (OE)

Baumaterial, engl. → *Building materials*. Unter dem Titel *La protesta dei giovani* wurde im Sommer 1968 auf der XIV. Triennale di Milano eine → *Barrikade* inszeniert, deren Bestandteile charakteristisch für die damaligen Protestbewegungen waren: Auf einem großen Haufen aus → *Pflastersteinen* waren gut sichtbar mehrere ausrangierte → *Waschmaschinen*, Kühlschränke und → *Fernseher*, einige zerstörte Teile von Straßenabsperrungen, ein altes Fahrrad und zwei umgestürzte Autos arrangiert. Während die kaputten Elektrogeräte als Zeichen der Ablehnung bürgerlicher Werte gelesen werden konnten, verwiesen die umgekippten → *Fahrzeuge* auf die realen Barrikaden, mit denen erst kurz zuvor – im → *Mai '68* – Protestierende das Quartier latin in Paris vor der Polizei abgeriegelt hatten. Die Pflastersteine der unter Anleitung des Architekten Giancarlo di Carlo errichteten Barrikaden-Attrappe riefen nicht nur die → *Straße* als den eigentlichen Ort der aktuellen Proteste auf, sondern auch eine alte revolutionäre Tradition: Seit der → *Julirevolution* → *1830* galten Pflastersteine „als bestens geeignet, um sich damit politisch aufzulehnen" (Rottmann 2016, S. 24).

Der Bau von Barrikaden hat etwas Adhocistisches: Als Baumaterial dient, was gerade zur Hand ist. Wie schriftliche und bildliche Dokumente nahelegen, können alle möglichen Dinge für Barrikaden verwendet werden – von Straßenpflaster, Erdaushub und Sandsäcken über Fässer, Bottiche, Möbel, Paletten, Holzlatten und Bambusstangen bis zu Mülleimern und alten Autoreifen. Weil die Barrikaden meist öffentliche Straßen oder Plätze versperren (→ *Blockade*, → *Platzbesetzung*), wird oft auf Fahrzeuge und Stadtmobiliar zurückgegriffen, ebenso wie auf eventuell vorhandene → *Absperrgitter*, Bauzäune und Beton-Barrieren (→ *Anti-Protestmaßnahmen*). Die umfunktionierten Gegenstände werden dabei überwiegend zerstört oder beschädigt und im Zuge von Straßenkämpfen bisweilen auch in Brand gesetzt (→ *Feuer*, → *Zerstörung*).

Mitte des 19. Jahrhunderts hatte der Dichter Heinrich Heine noch süffisant vorgeschlagen, endlich den „rechten Gebrauch" von den deutschen Eichenwäldern zu machen – „nämlich zu Barrikaden für die Befreiung der Welt" (Heine 1840/1976, S. 58). Zu Beginn des 21. Jahrhunderts geht es aber – im Gegenteil – zunehmend darum, Waldbestände vor der Rodung zu schützen und gegen Umweltzerstörung, Bodenversiegelung und Klimaerwärmung anzukämpfen. Genau das haben sich in den letzten Jahren viele der → *Protestcamps*, → *Bauplatzbesetzungen* und → *Baumhäuser* zur Aufgabe gemacht. Die verschiedenen → *Bautypen* wirken meist sehr improvisiert und machen sich eine Vielzahl unterschiedlicher Materialien zunutze. Selbst mehrstöckige Konstruktionen kommen zwar fast immer ohne wirkliches Fundament aus Steinen oder Beton aus, besitzen aber stabile Gerüste, die überwiegend aus Holzlatten und Brettern oder auch Baumstämmen und Ästen zusammengefügt und mit Pappe, wetterfesten Planen, Wellblech oder Sperrholzpaneelen verkleidet und abgedeckt werden (→ *Alternative Architektur*). Professioneller ausgeführte Bauwerke können zusätzlich über Glasfenster, offene Feuerstellen oder Öfen, Schlafstätten und winterfeste Isolierungen – etwa aus → *Stroh* oder Textilien – verfügen oder spezielle Funktionen als Großküchen, Duschen oder Toiletten erfüllen (→ *Infrastruktur*). Zur Ausstattung kommen neben alten und ausrangierten Möbeln und Gegenständen mit Sperrmüllcharakter auch viele Produkte und Halbfabrikate aus dem Baumarkt zum Einsatz – nicht zuletzt bei der Installation von temporären Strom- oder Wasserleitungen.

In klimatisch wärmeren Regionen bestehen die Architekturen der Protestbewegungen überwiegend aus leichteren und weicheren Baustoffen; häufig – wie etwa bei den Protesten in Kairo und Madrid – sind sie fast gänzlich aus

mit → *Seilen* und Schnüren verspannten Planen und Tüchern gebaut (→ *Tahrir-Platz*, → *Movimiento 15M*). Seile eignen sich zudem für großräumige Abspannungen und regelrechte Netzkonstruktionen, die es den Protestierenden ermöglichen, sich hoch über dem Boden – etwa zwischen verschiedenen Baumhäusern – räumlich flexibel zu bewegen und sich bei Bedarf dem Zugriff der → *Polizei* zu entziehen (→ *Schutz*). Der Charakter der Protestcamps ist in den letzten Jahrzehnten aber vor allem von → *Zelten* und zeltähnlichen Strukturen geprägt worden: Während manche Camps – insbesondere in der globalen Occupy-Bewegung (→ *Occupy Wall Street*) – von normalen Camping-Zelten dominiert wurden, ließen sich vielerorts neben professionell ausgeführten Jurten und Tipis auch selbstgemachte Zelte – sogenannte → *Bender* – beobachten, bei denen in den Boden gesteckte und gebogene Zweige mit vorhandenen Planen oder Textilien abgedeckt werden. (SH)

Baumhaus, engl. → *Tree house*. Baumhäuser kommen als → *Bautypen* in vielen → *Protestcamps* vor, also in Kontexten, in denen einzelne Bäume oder Wälder vor der Abholzung für Bauprojekte oder zur Gewinnung von Rohstoffen geschützt werden sollen, etwa im → *Hambacher Wald* und → *Dannenröder Wald*, in → *Lützerath* oder bei den Protesten gegen die → *Startbahn West*. Darüber hinaus spielen Baumhäuser in den → *alternativen Architekturen* der Countercultures sowie in der Kunst eine Rolle. In bestimmten Regionen werden Baumhäuser zudem als reguläre Wohngebäude genutzt.

Für diesen Aktivismus stellt die Zeit um 1970 einen wichtigen Bezugspunkt dar. So kam es 1969 zu einer frühen Baumbesetzung auf dem Campus der University of Texas, Austin (Battle of Waller Creek). Und Lloyd Kahns zentrale Publikation *Shelter* aus dem Jahr 1973 benennt neben Domes, → *Zelten* oder Jurten Baumhäuser als geeignete Architekturen für die Etablierung einer Counterculture (Kahn 1973/2013, S. 94 f.; Lange-Berndt 2021). Diese entrückten Schlupfwinkel über dem Erdboden verheißen Intimität sowie ein Leben wie in einer von Vitruv beschriebenen Urhütte, also in einem von lebendiger Natur mitbestimmten Haus (Rykwert 1972). Und sie waren für diese Zwecke auch geeignet, weil Bäume in Europa und Nordamerika schon seit längerer Zeit mit Revolution, einer Rhetorik der Freiheit und Protest verbunden waren. Nach der Französischen Revolution spielten sie eine wichtige Rolle für das Bürger∗innentum. Alleine im Mai 1792 wurden in Frankreich um die 60 000 Freiheitsbäume in Dörfern und Gemeinden gepflanzt. Es galt, die ganze Republik in einen Garten zu verwandeln; so wurden etwa die Pflanzen der königlichen Orangerien aus der „Knechtschaft der Kästen" befreit. Innerhalb dieser Utopie sollte die Gesellschaft in eine übergreifende natürliche Ordnung überführt werden. Bäume verkörperten Harmonie, soziale Eintracht und demonstrierten politische Freiheit (Harten, Harten 1989, S. 23 ff., 64, 110 ff., 113 f.). Mit der Romantik sowie unter Bezug auf die Schriften des Philosophen und Naturforschers Jean-Jacques Rousseau entstand ab dem 18. Jahrhundert eine Vielzahl von Baumhäusern (Henderson, Mornement ²2006, S. 30 ff.). Eine zentrale Publikation für diesen Kontext ist der Roman *Die Schweizer Familie Robinson* des Dichters und Philosophen Johann David Wyss aus dem Jahr 1813 (Wyss 1813). Das Buch berichtet davon, wie sich die nach einem Schiffbruch auf einer Insel bei Neuguinea gestrandete Familie Robinson ihr Haus in einem Baum baut: Mit Architekturen wie L'Île de Robinson in Paris etablierte sich in Europa auch das problematische Konzept der edlen Wilden, vermeintlich von der Zivilisation unverdorbene „Naturmenschen", welche in paradiesischer Unschuld leben (Ellingson 2001).

Die Nester der „Woodstock Nation" sowie der auf ihr beruhende gegenwärtige Aktivismus trägt all diese Geschichten im Gepäck. Ein Leben ohne Möbel auf dem Baum verheißt eine Befreiung von den Zurichtungsmaßnahmen der Zivilisation sowie einer konsumorientierten Gesellschaft. Dieser Blick der Indus-

trienationen kann jedoch diejenigen ausblenden, die auf existenziellere Art und Weise von Bäumen abhängig waren und sind. So bezieht sich die Narration von Wyss, geschrieben in Zeiten kolonialer Expansion, auch auf die realen Wohnungen der in Neuguinea lebenden Koiari; der Stamm verwendete Baumhäuser als Wachtposten und Zufluchtsort bei Angriffen (Hackenschmidt 2009, S. 143). Mitglieder der späteren Counterculture haben diese Zusammenhänge nicht immer kritisch reflektiert, sie waren teilweise ebenfalls daran interessiert, sich als Stammesgemeinschaft zu inszenieren. Viele glaubten daran, dass vermeintlich primitive Völker die Tendenz dazu besäßen, sich existierende Ressourcen sensibel anzueignen und neu zu organisieren (Lévi-Strauss 1962/1966).

Diese „Outlaw Nation", die schnell zur Mediensensation avancierte, markiert jedoch auch die Selbstdarstellung in einer wachsenden globalen Medienwelt (→ *Medien*). So werden kommerzielle Baumhäuser gegenwärtig als Wellness-Oasen genutzt. (Petra Lange-Berndt)

Bauplatzbesetzung, engl. → *Building site occupation*. Bei Bauplatzbesetzungen gibt es keine freie Standortwahl: Im Unterschied zu → *Platzbesetzungen*, die sich vor allem aus Gründen der Sichtbarkeit an zentralen oder symbolisch wichtigen Stellen im → *öffentlichen Raum* festsetzen, oder → *Barrikaden*, die an strategisch günstigen Punkten errichtet werden, geht es darum, den Fortschritt von Bauarbeiten an ganz spezifischen Orten zu verzögern oder zu verhindern (→ *Blockade*). Dabei kann es sich um den vorgesehenen Abriss eines Gebäudes (→ *Denkmalschutz*, → *Hausbesetzung*) handeln, aber auch um die geplante Bebauung von Parkanlagen wie bei den → *Gezi-Park*-Protesten in Istanbul → *2013*. Wenn sich die besetzten Bauplätze im urbanen Umfeld befinden, profitieren die Proteste meist von der günstigen Lage: Nicht nur verfügen sie in den Innenstädten automatisch über eine viel größere Aufmerksamkeit, sondern auch oft über eine bessere Versorgung hinsichtlich Energie, Trinkwasser,

Nahrung und Hygiene. Oft liegen die Plätze, an denen es Baumaßnahmen zu verhindern gilt, abseits der städtischen Zentren – etwa die Rodung von Waldbeständen in der → *Lobau*, die Errichtung eines atomaren Endlagers wie in → *Gorleben* oder die Zerstörung ganzer Ortschaften durch den Tagebau wie in → *Lützerath* → *2020*. Um sich dauerhaft und wirkungsvoll an diesen teils sehr entlegenen Orten einrichten zu können, muss nicht nur für → *Schutz*, Logistik und eine funktionierende → *Infrastruktur* gesorgt, sondern auch die öffentliche Aufmerksamkeit auf die besetzten Orte gelenkt werden: Neben den → *Medien* gilt es dafür auch möglichst viele Menschen zu mobilisieren: Können diese nicht vor Ort mitwirken, entfalten mitunter auch → *Solidaritätsgesten* aus der Ferne die angestrebte Wirkung – etwa durch → *Demonstrationen* oder Ausstellungen (→ *Archiv*, → *Museum*) in den Stadtzentren. (SH)

Bautypen, engl. → *Building types*. Ähnlich wie in permanenten Siedlungen lassen sich auch in → *Protestcamps* unterschiedliche Bautypen identifizieren. Die Kategorisierung dieser Bautypen nach Funktionen und Formen bietet sich an, um die technischen, sozialen, politischen und kulturellen Eigenschaften von → *Protestarchitektur* zu verstehen.
1. Funktionstypen: Die Mehrzahl der gebauten Strukturen eines Protestcamps dienen der Unterbringung von Aktivist*innen und bieten ihnen → *Schutz* vor Kälte und Regen sowie einen Rückzugsort. Individuelle Unterkünfte werden von einzelnen Personen oder Kleingruppen gebaut und bewohnt. Gemeinschaftsunterkünfte wie auf dem → *Majdan* in Kyjiw oder im → *Hambacher Wald* entstehen im Kollektiv und beherbergen mehrere Menschen, teils in wechselnder Besetzung. → *Küchen*, Medienzelte, Informationsstände, Bibliotheken, Toilettenhäuschen und Versammlungsgebäude zählen zur gemeinschaftlich genutzten → *Infrastruktur*, die der Versorgung, der Organisation des Zusammenlebens, → *Kommunikation* und Unterhaltung dient. → *Barrikaden*, Überwachungstürme (→ *Turm*)

und Räumungsarchitekturen wie → *Tripods* und Baumschaukeln schützen Protestcamps vor Angriffen oder verzögern Räumungsversuche durch die → *Polizei*.
1a. Größe: Protestcamp-Bauten reichen von winzigen Baumhütten (→ *Fechenheimer Wald*) bis zu weite Plätze überspannenden Dachkonstruktionen (→ *Movimiento 15M*). Je nach Funktion sind sie für unterschiedlich viele Menschen angelegt. Das „Freundschaftshaus" in → *Gorleben* → *1980* hatte bei Versammlungen Platz für 400 Personen und war so konstruiert, dass sich bei einer Räumung auf dem Dach bis zu 100 Menschen aufhalten konnten. Viele Strukturen in Protestcamps sind Einraumbauten. Mehrgeschossige Strukturen werden wie im Hambacher Wald oft über außenliegende Leitern erschlossen.
1b. Standort: Ebenerdige → *Zelte* und Hütten sind für alle zugänglich, daher befinden sich hier meist die Gemeinschaftsräume, während in → *Baumhäusern*, z.B. im → *Dannenröder Wald*, Aktivist*innen mit Klettererfahrung unterkommen. Bewohner*innen von Erdhäusern wie im Hüttendorf gegen die → *Startbahn West* → *1980* demonstrieren ihre Naturverbundenheit und suchen im Erdreich Schutz vor Hitze und Kälte. Aufwendige Tunnelbauten (→ *Tunnel*) wurden im Hambacher Wald und in → *Lützerath* über Monate geplant und erst während der Räumung von Protestcamps bezogen. Sie sind wie Baumhäuser Verzögerungsarchitekturen, die nur von Spezialeinheiten der Polizei geräumt werden dürfen und die Räumung dadurch erschweren.
1c. Dauerhaftigkeit: Trotz ihres ephemeren Charakters gibt es auch in der Protestarchitektur große Unterschiede dahingehend, wie lange gebaute Strukturen genutzt werden. Räumungsarchitekturen wie Tripods und → *Monopods* sind meist nur während einer Räumung in Gebrauch. Bei den Grundstücksbesetzungen der → *MTST* in Brasilien stehen die provisorischen Hütten, die in der ersten Nacht zur Sicherung der → *Besetzung* rasch aufgestellt werden, maximal zwölf Stunden und werden am

Baut

Bautypen. 1 Turm, Lützerath 2 Tripod, Lützerath 3 Steilwandzelt, Occupy Wall Street 4 Überwachungsturm, Occupy Wall Street 5 Bambushütte, MTST 6 A-Frame, Resurrection City 7 Traktorwagen, Farmers-Proteste 8 Freundschaftshaus, Gorleben 9 Zelt, Tahrir-Platz 10 Pyramide, Lobau 11 Beobachtungsturm, Majdan 12 Bambushütte, MTST 13 Kuppelzelt 14 Pfahlbau, Lützerath 15 Baumhaus, Hambacher Wald 16 Turm, Gorleben 17 Steilwandzelt, Majdan 18 Erdhütte, Startbahn West 19 Zelt, Tahrir-Platz 20 Rundhütte, Gorleben (Building types. 1 Tower, Lützerath 2 Tripod, Lützerath 3 Wall tent, Occupy Wall Street 4 Surveillance tower, Occupy Wall Street 5 Bamboo hut, MTST 6 A-frame, Resurrection City 7 Tractor trailer, Farmers' protests 8 Friendship house, Gorleben 9 Tent, Tahrir Square 10 Pyramid, Lobau 11 Observation tower, Maidan 12 Bamboo hut, MTST 13 Dome tent 14 Pile house, Lützerath 15 Tree house, Hambach Forest 16 Tower, Gorleben 17 Wall tent, Maidan 18 Earth hut, Startbahn West 19 Tent, Tahrir Square 20 Round hut, Gorleben)

nächsten Tag durch sorgfältig gebaute „Baracken" ersetzt. Mobile Architekturen wie Wohn- und Bauwagen oder Traktoren bei den Protesten der → *Farmers* in Indien dienen je nach Bedarf als Unterkunft oder Fortbewegungsmittel (→ *Fahrzeuge*). Viele Häuser der seit → *2007* besetzten → *ZAD Notre-Dame-des-Landes* werden hingegen dauerhaft bewohnt (→ *Legalisierung*).

2. Formtypen: Die häufigste Bauform in Protestcamps ist das Kuppelzelt. Weltweit gibt es heute kaum noch Protestdörfer ohne die leicht zu errichtenden und überall verfügbaren Readymades. Typische Bautypen sind außerdem selbstgebaute Hütten mit Flach-, Pult- und Satteldächern (MTST, Lützerath), Steilwandzelte (→ *Pearl Roundabout*, → *Majdan*) und offene Pavillonzelte (→ *Gezi-Park*, → *Hongkong-Proteste*). Rundhütten (Gorleben), Bauten mit Nurdächern (→ *Resurrection City*, Startbahn West) sowie First- und Kegelzelte (→ *Schafschererstreik*, → *Bonus Army*) sind dagegen heute kaum noch zu finden. Sonderformen wie Pyramiden (→ *Lobau*) oder Zirkuszelte erzielen genau wie Turmbauten oft vergleichsweise viel mediale Aufmerksamkeit (→ *Ikone*, → *Medien*).

2a. Bauweise: Viele Zelte und Hütten in Protestcamps sind einfache Rahmen- und Stangenbauten, die je nach verfügbaren → *Baumaterialien* mit Textilien, oft Planen oder Stoffen, Holzplatten, Brettern oder Ästen verkleidet bzw. beplankt werden. In Washington bewohnten die Aktivist∗innen der Resurrection City → *1968* vorfabrizierte A-Frames aus Holzlatten und Brettsperrholzplatten, die von Architekten entworfen und von Freiwilligen errichtet wurden. Turmartige Bauformen in Waldbesetzungen (Gorleben, Hambacher Wald) sind meist Pfahlbauten an langen Baumstämmen. Auf Pfählen steht auch der in Lützerath entwickelte Hüttentyp, der durch seine Höhe die Räumung der Polizei effizient verzögert, weil nur Spezialeinheiten mit Hebebühnen und Seilsicherungen das Betreten von Strukturen ab einer Höhe von 2,5 Metern erlaubt ist. Auch Biegedächer und -zelte,

sogenannte → *Bender*, entstehen bei Besetzungen außerhalb der Großstädte, z.B. im Friedenscamp vor → *Greenham Common* → *1981* oder im Hambacher Wald. Dabei werden kuppelartige Skelette aus gebogenen und im Boden fixierten Ästen mit (oft durchsichtigen) Planen bezogen. In der ZAD Notre-Dame-des-Landes und im Hambacher Wald bauten Aktivist∗innen aus Ästen und schmalen Baumstämmen außerdem Geodome, Gittertragwerke und Exoskelette sowie Lehmhütten mit aufwendigen Kegeldächern. Seilkonstruktionen werden genutzt, um zum Schutz vor Sonne und Regen Dächer zwischen Bäumen (→ *Syntagma-Platz*, Gezi-Park), Straßenmobiliar (→ *Tahrir-Platz*, Movimiento 15M) und Gebäuden zu spannen. Auch für den Bau von Räumungsstrukturen wie → *Traversen*, Monopods und → *Tensegrities* sowie für die Befestigung von hängenden Baumhäusern werden → *Seile* verwendet. Nicht nur bei Protesten von Indigenen wie in North Dakota gegen die → *Dakota Access Pipeline* → *2016* leben Aktivist∗innen in traditionellen Tipis. Bei der Errichtung von Zelten und zeltähnlichen Strukturen – etwa den kegelförmigen, mit Textil bezogenen Hütten aus Baumstämmen in Gorleben oder im seit → *1985* bestehenden Schweizer Hüttendorf → *Zaffaraya* – kann über die kulturelle Aneignung traditioneller Bautypen wie Jurten, Wigwams und „Nomadenzelte" diskutiert werden.

2b. Formensprache: Protestarchitekturen entstehen meist aus der Notwendigkeit und aus einem Mangel an Mitteln heraus. Viele der in diesem Kontext entwickelten Strukturen sind durch eine einfache Bauweise charakterisiert, die oft als Rückkehr zu den „Urformen des Bauens" bzw. einer vermeintlichen „Urhütte" (Rykwert 1972) gelesen wird. Funktionalität und Einfachheit sind für viele Klimaaktivist∗innen ein Ausdruck der Verweigerung eines Lebensstils, der auf der kapitalistischen Ausbeutung von Mensch und Natur basiert und zu Umweltzerstörung führt. Frei nach Georg Büchners Parole „Friede den Hütten! Krieg den Palästen!" setzen sie

Bend

Bender. Paula Allen: Greenham Common Friedenscamp, zwischen 1981 und 1984 (Bender. Paula Allen: Greenham Common Peace Camp, between 1981 and 1984)

mit ihren bescheidenen Behausungen ein Zeichen gegen Reichtum und Verschwendung. Die funktionale Bauweise der Protestbauten lässt jedoch nicht auf ihre reduzierte Ästhetik schließen: Buntes Textil, Planen, →Protestschilder, →Banner, →Fahnen und →Graffiti prägen die heterogene Erscheinung heutiger Protestcamps – anders als noch in der ersten Hälfte des 20. Jahrhunderts (Schafscherer-Streik, Bonus Army). Je nachdem, wie lange sich eine Besetzung hinzieht, wie verfügbar Baumaterialien sind und wie viel Zeit und Energie die Aktivist∗innen in die Errichtung der Bauten stecken können, entstehen in Protestcamps Architekturen voller Fantasie und Einfallsreichtum. Formenvielfalt ist dabei nicht nur eine Folge kreativer Do-it-yourself-Strategien, sondern eine bewusste Entscheidung gegen Einheitlichkeit und Konformität von Konsumgesellschaft und Mainstream-Architektur. (AMM)

Bender, engl. →Bender. Die im deutschen auch „Biegezelt" genannten Konstruktionen wurden von den Besetzerinnen des →Greenham Common Friedenscamp errichtet, weil das Aufstellen von →Zelten vorher durch die →Polizei verboten worden war. Die Fotografin Paula Allen lebte drei Jahre lang selbst in diesem →Protestcamp, natürlich ebenfalls in einem Bender. Das Konstruktionsprinzip dieses →Bautypus wird bisweilen auch bei den Dächern von →Baumhäusern verwendet. (OE)

Bender, Ger. →Bender (fig.). These bended structures were erected by the occupiers of the →Greenham Common Peace Camp because the →police had forbidden them to erect →tents. Photographer Paula Allen herself lived for three years in the →protest camp, in precisely this kind of bender tent. The structural principle underlying this →building type is sometimes also used for the roofs of →tree houses. (OE)

Beobachtungsturm, engl. →Watchtower; →Bautypen, →Hongkong-Proteste, →Majdan, →Occupy Wall Street, →Turm

Bergfeuer →Feuer, →Zwentendorf

Besetzung, engl. →Occupation, wird im vorliegenden Buch als →Bauplatzbesetzung, →Hausbesetzung oder →Platzbesetzung behandelt.

Betonpyramide, engl. →Concrete pyramid. Variante eines →Lock-on Device für den →Körpereinsatz bei einer →Blockade von Atommüll auf dem Weg nach →Gorleben. Die in mehreren Ausführungen zum Einsatz gebrachten Betonpyramiden waren aus unterschiedlichen Materialschichten so konstruiert, dass die →Polizei möglichst lange dafür benötigt, die Arme der Aktivist∗innen aus den grabkammerartigen Kanälen im Inneren der Pyramiden zu befreien. (OE)

Betonpyramide. Wolfgang Rattay: Mitglieder der Bäuerlichen Notgemeinschaft blockieren mit ihrem Lock-on Device die Bahnstrecke des Castor-Transports ins atomare Zwischenlager Gorleben, Hitzacker, 27. November 2011 (Concrete pyramid. Wolfgang Rattay: Members of Bäuerliche Notgemeinschaft used their lock-on device to block the rail tracks used to transport the Castor units to the interim nuclear dump at Gorleben, Hitzacker, November 27, 2011)

Bibliography →Literaturverzeichnis
Black Lives Matter, engl. →Black Lives Matter. Gegründet wurde Black Lives Matter (BLM) bereits 2013. Weltweite Bekanntheit erlangte die Bewegung im Jahr →2020, nachdem in Minneapolis George Floyd durch vier Polizisten getötet wurde. Die Proteste eskalierten über Monate. Zum ersten Mal seit dem Civil Rights Movement der 1960er Jahre hatte es den Anschein, dass seither grundlegende Änderungen bewirkt werden konnten: Stellenbesetzungen, Lehrpläne und das Programm von Kulturinstitutionen entwickelten sich in eine diversere Richtung, es entstand ein erweitertes Bewusstsein für rassistische Diskriminierung, auch in Europa.

Im Zuge der Proteste entstand in Seattle für circa drei Wochen eine →Autonome Zone, die meist als Capitol Hill Organized Protest (CHOP) bezeichnet wird. Im Zentrum stand ein zeitweise von der lokalen →Polizei aus Sorge vor Angriffen aufgegebenes Wachgebäude. Zunächst entstanden →Barrikaden, danach verhandelte die Stadtverwaltung eine Reduzierung des autonomen Gebiets im Austausch gegen Betonabsperrungen. Nach gewalttätigen Auseinandersetzungen (→Gewalt) innerhalb der Zone räumten die Ordnungskräfte das Gebiet und kehrten in die Polizeistation zurück. (OE)

Black Lives Matter, Ger. →Black Lives Matter. Black Lives Matter (BLM) was founded back in 2013. The movement became known internationally in →2020 in the wake of four police officers killing George Floyd in Minneapolis. As the months passed, the protests escalated, and for the first time since the 1960s civil rights movement, it seemed as if fundamental changes might be brought about. Since then, staffing policies, educational curricula, and the programs of cultural institutions have started to become more diverse, and a greater awareness of racial discrimination has arisen, not just in the US but also in Europe.

In the course of the protests, for some three weeks, an →autonomous zone came into being in Seattle that that was widely known as the Capitol Hill Organized Protest (CHOP). At its center was a precinct which, for a while, was abandoned by the local →police for fear of attacks. Initially →barricades went up, and then the municipal authorities negotiated to reduce the size of the autonomous zone in exchange for concrete barriers. After violent conflict (→Violence) within the zone, the authorities had it cleared and returned to their offices in the police precinct. (OE)

Blockade, engl. →Blockade. Begriff

aus dem militärischen Sprachgebrauch (z.B. Seeblockade, Berlin-Blockade). Eine Blockade zielt darauf ab, einen Zugang zu sperren oder eine Durchfahrt für andere komplett zu unterbinden, im Protestkontext etwa durch →*Barrikaden*, →*Abschüttungen*, →*Fahrzeuge*, Menschenmengen oder auch einzelne, exponierte Personen, die sich dabei durch →*Körpereinsatz* in Gefahr bringen. Ein Streik ist im Gegensatz dazu eine weniger physisch wirksame Blockade, obwohl das Resultat ähnlich ausfällt. Er kann Wirtschaftsunternehmen – als Generalstreik: ganze Staaten – durch Arbeitsverweigerung blockieren. Bei lokal begrenzten Streiks kommt eine wiederum physische Blockade durch Streikposten oft unterstützend hinzu, um Streikbrecher∗innen abzuwehren.

Im Protestzusammenhang wurde der Begriff Blockade zuerst ab den 1950er Jahren als Sitzblockade etabliert. Diese wird oft verwechselt mit dem →*Sit-in*. Das Sit-in entstand bereits in den 1940er Jahren in den USA im Zuge des Civil Rights Movement als Widerstandsgeste gegen rassistische Diskriminierung. Zu den medial erfolgreichsten Aktionen der deutschen Friedensbewegung zählte die „Prominentenblockade" vor einem US-Atomwaffenstützpunkt in Mutlangen 1983, an der u.a. die Schriftsteller Heinrich Böll und Günter Grass sowie die Bundestagsabgeordnete Petra Kelly (Die Grünen) teilnahmen. Sie blieben straffrei, obwohl die Rechtsprechung in Deutschland den Straftatbestand der Nötigung vorsah.

Blockaden durch Menschenmengen können auch als →*Die-in*, als kollektives Niederknien oder bei →*Demonstrationen* gebildet werden. Eine Blockade kann jedoch auch durch den Körpereinsatz von nur wenigen Menschen entstehen. Zunächst begannen professionelle →*Protestorganisationen* wie Greenpeace mit Abseilaktionen, die darauf abzielen, die Tätigkeiten großer Konzerne zum Stillstand zu bringen. Seit den Klimaprotesten der 2010er Jahre seilen sich Einzelpersonen von Autobahnbrücken ab, blockieren den Verkehr und somit eine zufällig zusammengesetzte, große und quasi „unschuldige" Menschenmenge (→*Abseilen*). Je weniger Personen allerdings an Blockaden aktiv teilnehmen, desto größer, so scheint es, ist die öffentliche Debatte über die Angemessenheit dieser Protestform. Eine Blockade, die nur von Einzelnen ausgeführt wird, gerät schnell in den Verdacht der unzureichenden Legitimation. So wurde in Deutschland seit 2022 intensiv über die Anklebe-Aktionen der Letzten Generation auf →*Straßen* und in Museen debattiert (→*Ankleben*). In Großbritannien führten vergleichbare Diskussionen zu der am 1. Januar 2023 verlautbarten Erklärung „We Quit" von Extinction Rebellion, womit der vorläufige Verzicht auf konfrontative Blockaden gemeint war. (OE)

Blockade, Ger. →*Blockade*. Term from military usage (e.g. sea blockade, Berlin Blockade). A blockade aims to block access or completely prevent passage for others, in the context of protest, for example, through →*barricades*, →*dumping*, →*vehicles*, crowds, or even exposed individuals who thereby put themselves in danger through →*body deployment*. A strike, in contrast, is a less physically effective blockade, although the result is similar. It can block businesses or even entire states in the case of a general strike—by refusal to work. In the case of localized strikes, a physical blockade by pickets is often added to ward off strikebreakers.

In the context of protest, the term blockade was first established in the 1950s in the form of a sit-in-like blockade. This is often conflated with the classic →*sit-in*. The sit-in originated as early as the 1940s in the USA in the course of the civil rights movement as a gesture of resistance against racist discrimination. In terms of media coverage, one of the most successful actions of the German peace movement was the "celebrity blockade" in front of a US nuclear weapons base in Mutlangen in 1983, in which, among others, the writers Heinrich Böll and Günter Grass, and the politician Petra Kelly (The Greens) took part. They escaped prosecution, though under German law they could have been charged with the criminal offense of coercion.

Blockades by crowds can also be formed as →*die-ins*, collective kneeling, or at →*demonstrations*. However, a blockade can also be created by the body deployment of just a few people. Initially, professional →*protest organizations* such as Greenpeace began with rappelling actions aimed at bringing the activities of large corporations to a halt. Since the climate protests of the 2010s, individuals have been rappelling from highway bridges, blocking traffic and thus a randomly assembled, large, and quasi "innocent" crowd (→*Rappelling*). However, the fewer the individuals who actively participate in blockades, the greater, it seems, is the public debate about the appropriateness of this form of protest. A blockade that is only carried out by a small number of individuals is quickly accused of lacking legitimacy. In Germany, for example, there has been intense debate about the Letzte Generation's super-gluing actions on →*streets* and in museums since 2022 (→*Super-gluing*). In the United Kingdom, comparable discussions led to Extinction Rebellion's "We Quit" declaration, announced on January 1, 2023, declaring the temporary renunciation of confrontational blockades. (OE)

Body deployment, Ger. →*Körpereinsatz*. Every →*demonstration*, every →*blockade*, every →*sit-in* (or comparable forms of action) require body deployment and involve the risk of being injured, arrested, or subjected to psychological →*violence*. When individuals dare to confront injustice, iconic images (→*Icon*) often result. The "Tank Man" became famous when he stood alone in front of a row of tanks the day after the Tiananmen Square protests in Beijing were suppressed in 1989. The image of nurse Ieshia Evans, who in a light summer dress faced off against police officers in massive riot gear in 2016, became a symbol of the protests against police violence in the USA (→*Black Lives Matter*). The dancer Erdem Gündüz became known as the "Standing Man" (Turkish: *Duran Adam*) when he demonstrated against the ban on demonstrations following the eviction of →*Gezi Park* by standing silently in the crowd for about eight hours and staring at an Atatürk monument. The fact that individuals expose themselves in such a way, whether accompanied by the →*media* or, as in the case of the "Tank Man," observed only by chance by journalists, has shaped the image of protests since the French Revolution. It is, however, not only a—sometimes staged—media phenomenon. The activists of →*Claremont Road* in London in →*1994* climbed on daringly stretched nets, which were at the same time large, hedonistically utilizable hammocks—difficult to clear for the police and an excellent motif for photographers. In the →*tree house* protests of the climate movement, which began in Germany around 2000, the structures erected high above the ground no longer stand alone, unlike earlier tree houses. They are connected to each other by →*ropes*, bridges, or nets (→*Hambach Forest*, →*Dannenrod Forest*, →*Lützerath*, →*Fechenheim Forest*). Those who stay there must not only be able to climb professionally but also deliberately put themselves in danger through their body deployment. The activists risk falling if certain supporting ropes are cut by the police. In the Dannenrod Forest, the "Suicide Box" was used, a kind of free-floating →*lock-on device*, to delay eviction using this device with its macabre title. To ward off police attacks during high-altitude evictions, skin is sometimes greased with margarine, and fingertips are coated with superglue to make them anonymous. Even the provision of supplies and support at protests, coordination activities, as well as acts of perseverance can require extreme levels of psychological strength and body deployment. (OE)

Bonus Army, engl. →*Bonus Army*. Während der „Great Depression" strömten →*1932* tausende arbeitslose Veteranen des Ersten Weltkriegs aus dem ganzen Land nach Washington, DC, um von der Regierung unter Hoover die sofortige Auszahlung einer versprochenen

Prämie zu fordern. Der Protest wurde als „Bonus Army" bekannt und dauerte etwa drei Monate. Die → *Protestcamps* glichen den allgegenwärtigen „Hoovervilles", wie die neuen Elendsquartiere während der Weltwirtschaftskrise genannt wurden, und waren gut organisiert: Es wurden → *Straßen* angelegt und Latrinen gegraben. Neuankömmlinge mussten sich ausweisen und registrieren. (JD)

Bonus Army, Ger. → *Bonus Army*. In → *1932*, during the Great Depression, thousands of unemployed World War I veterans flocked from all over the country to Washington, DC, to demand the immediate payout of the promised bonuses from the Hoover government. The protest became known as the "Bonus Army" and lasted about three months. Similar in appearance to the ubiquitous "Hoovervilles," as the new slums were called during the Great Depression, the → *protest* camps were well organized. They had → *streets* and latrines. New arrivals had to identify themselves and enroll. (JD)

Branded Protest, engl. → *Branded protest*; → *Erkennungszeichen*

Branded protest, Ger. → *Branded Protest*; → *Identifier*

Brick, Ger. → *Ziegelstein*. In contrast to the → *cobblestone*, which—at least in Europe—forms the ubiquitous bedrock of protest culture, as it were, the use of bricks as a revolutionary material is primarily associated with the anti-government protests in → *Hong Kong* in → *2019*. Protesters of the democracy movement had blocked → *streets* with hundreds of small archways, each made of three ordinary bricks, with two placed upright and a third one as a roof. In larger groups, these ankle-high formations, using mostly the paving stones of sidewalks and pedestrian zones, formed effective roadblocks that paralyzed rush hour traffic in places and slowed down police emergency vehicles. When one of the structures was touched by the wheel of a → *vehicle*, the falling top brick buttressed the other two and impeded or prevented further travel. However, the bricks in Hong Kong were also used quite conventionally as projectiles (→ *Weapons*) and walled up to form → *barricades*. (SH)

Bridge, Ger. → *Brücke*; → *Hambach Forest*, → *Lützerath*, → *Rappelling*, → *Ropes*, → *Traverse*

Brücke, engl. → *Bridge*; → *Abseilen*, → *Hambacher Wald*, → *Lützerath*, → *Seile*, → *Traverse*

Building materials, Ger. → *Baumaterial*. Under the title *La protesta dei giovani*, a → *barricade* was staged at the Milan Triennial XIV in the summer of 1968, whose features were characteristic of the protest movements of the time: several discarded → *washing machines*, refrigerators, and → *television sets*, some destroyed parts of road barriers, an old bicycle, and two overturned cars were arranged on a large pile of → *cobblestones* in plain sight. While the broken electrical appliances could be read as a sign of the rejection of bourgeois values, the overturned → *vehicles* referred to the real barricades with which only a short while earlier, in → *May '68*, protesters had sealed off the Latin Quarter in Paris from the police. The cobblestones of the dummy barricades, erected under the guidance of architect Giancarlo di Carlo, not only invoked the → *street* as the actual site of the current protests but also an old revolutionary tradition: since the → *July Revolution* in → *1830*, cobblestones were "considered ideally suited for political revolt" (Rottmann 2016, p. 24).

There is something ad hoc about the construction of barricades: whatever is at hand serves as building material. As written and pictorial documents suggest, all sorts of things can be used for barricades—from paving stones, excavated soil, and sandbags to → *barrels*, vats, furniture, pallets, wooden laths, and bamboo poles to trash cans and old car tires. Since the barricades usually block public streets or squares (→ *Blockade*, → *Public square occupation*), vehicles and street furniture are often used, as well as any existing → *barriers*, construction fences, and concrete barriers (→ *Anti-protest measures*). In doing so, the converted objects are mostly destroyed or damaged and sometimes set on fire in the course of street fighting (→ *Fire*, → *Destruction*).

In the mid-19th century, the poet Heinrich Heine was still smugly suggesting that German oak forests should finally be put to "right use"—"namely, as barricades for the liberation of the world" (Heine 1840/1976, p. 58). At the beginning of the 21st century, however, it is—on the contrary—increasingly a matter of protecting forests from clearing and fighting against environmental destruction, soil sealing, and global warming. This is exactly what many of the → *protest camps*, → *building site occupations*, and → *tree houses* have made their mission in recent years. The various → *building types* usually appear very improvised and make use of a variety of different materials. Even multi-story structures almost always manage without a real foundation of stones or concrete but have sturdy frames that are mainly assembled from wooden slats and boards, or even tree trunks and branches, and covered with cardboard, weatherproof tarpaulins, corrugated iron, or plywood panels (→ *Alternative architecture*). More professionally constructed structures may additionally have glass windows, open fireplaces, or stoves, sleeping quarters, and winter-proof insulation—for example, made of → *straw* or textiles—or fulfill special functions such as collective kitchens, showers, or toilets (→ *Infrastructure*). In addition to old and discarded furniture and other bulky-waste-like objects, many products and semi-finished items from the hardware store are used for furnishing—not least for the installation of temporary power or water lines.

In regions with warmer climates, the architecture of the protest movement is predominantly made of lighter and softer building materials; often—as in the protests in Cairo and Madrid—it almost entirely consists of tarpaulins and cloths braced with → *ropes* and cords (→ *Tahrir Square*, → *Movimiento 15M*). Ropes also lend themselves to large-scale suspensions and veritable net

structures that allow protesters to move flexibly in space and high above the ground—between different tree houses, for example—and to escape the grasp of the → *police* if necessary (→ *Protection*). In recent decades, however, the character of protest camps has been shaped primarily by → *tents* and tent-like structures: while some camps, especially in the global Occupy movement (→ *Occupy Wall Street*), were dominated by normal camping tents, in many places, professionally fabricated yurts and tipis, as well as homemade tents, so-called → *benders*, could also be observed, in which branches are inserted into the ground and then bent, before being covered with existing tarpaulins or textiles. (SH)

Building site occupation, Ger. → *Bauplatzbesetzung*. In the case of a building site occupations, there is no free site selection: in contrast to a → *public square occupation*, which takes places at central or symbolically important locations in public space to enhance visibility, or → *barricades*, which are erected at strategically favorable points, the aim here is to delay or prevent the progress of construction work at very specific locations (→ *Blockade*). This can include the planned demolition of a building (→ *Heritage protection*, → *Squatting*) but also the planned development of parks, as in the → *Gezi Park* protests in Istanbul in → *2013*. If the occupied building sites are located in an urban environment, the protests usually benefit from the favorable location: not only do they automatically attract much greater attention in the inner cities but they also often have a better supply situation in terms of energy, drinking water, food, and hygiene. The places where construction measures need to be prevented are frequently located away from urban centers—for example, the clearing of forests in the → *Lobau*, the construction of a permanent nuclear waste disposal site as in → *Gorleben*, or the destruction of entire villages by open-pit mining as in → *Lützerath*. In order to allow for a permanent and effective set-up in these sometimes very remote places, it is not only necessary to provide →*protection*, logistics, and a functioning →*infrastructure* but also to draw public attention to the occupied places: in addition to the →*media*, this also requires mobilizing as many people as possible: if they cannot participate on site, →*acts of solidarity* from afar can sometimes have the desired effect for example, through →*demonstrations* or exhibitions (→*Archive*, →*Museum*) in the city centers. (SH)

Building types, Ger. →*Bautypen (fig.)*. Similar to permanent settlements, different building types can be identified in →*protest camps*. The categorization of these building types according to functions and forms helps to understand the technical, social, political, and cultural characteristics of →*protest architecture*.

1. Functional types: The majority of built structures in a protest camp serve to house activists and provide them →*protection* from the elements, as well as a place to retreat. Individual shelters are built and inhabited by individuals or small groups. Community shelters, such as those on the →*Maidan* in Kyiv or in the →*Hambach Forest*, are created collectively and house several people, often with shifting groups of occupants. →*Kitchens*, media tents, information booths, libraries, toilet huts, and assembly buildings are part of the communally used →*infrastructure*, which serves the functions of supply, the organization of cohabitation, →*communication*, and entertainment. →*Barricades*, surveillance towers (→*Tower*), and eviction architecture such as →*tripods* and tree swings protect protest camps from attack or delay eviction attempts by the →*police*.

1a. Size: Protest camp buildings range from tiny tree huts (→*Fechenheim Forest*) to roof structures spanning wide spaces (→*Movimiento 15M*). Depending on their function, they are designed to accommodate different numbers of people. The "Freundschaftshaus" ("Friendship House") at →*Gorleben* in →*1980* had room for 400 people at gatherings and was constructed so that up to 100 people could be on the roof during an eviction. Many structures in protest camps are single-room buildings. Multi-story buildings are often accessed via external ladders, as in Hambach Forest.

1b. Location: Ground-level tents and huts are accessible to all, so the community rooms are usually located here, while →*tree houses*, for example in the →*Dannenrod Forest*, accommodate activists with climbing experience. Inhabitants of earth shelters, such as in the hut village during the protest against →*Startbahn West* in →*1980*, demonstrate their closeness to nature and seek protection from heat and cold in the soil. Elaborate tunnel constructions (→*Tunnel*) were planned for months in the Hambach Forest and at →*Lützerath* and were only occupied during the eviction of protest camps. Like tree houses, they act as delaying architectures that may only be cleared by special police units, thus complicating the eviction.

1c. Durability: Despite its ephemeral nature, protest architecture also varies greatly in terms of how long built structures are used. Eviction architectures such as →*tripods* and →*monopods* are usually only in use during evictions. In the →*MTST* land occupations in Brazil, the temporary huts that are quickly erected on the first night to secure the →*occupation* stand for a maximum of twelve hours and are replaced by carefully constructed "barracks" the next day. Mobile architectures such as residential and construction trailers or tractors at the protests of the →*farmers* in India serve as either shelter or means of transportation (→*Vehicles*) as needed. Many houses of the →*ZAD Notre-Dame-des-Landes*, which has been occupied since →*2007*, on the other hand, are permanently inhabited (→*Legalization*).

2. Form types: The most common form of construction in protest camps is the dome tent. Worldwide, there are hardly any protest villages without these ready-made shelters today, which are easy to erect and available everywhere. Typical construction types also include

self-built huts with flat, shed, and gabled roofs (MTST, Lützerath), wall tents (→*Pearl Roundabout*, →*Maidan*), and gazebo tents (→*Gezi Park*, →*Hong Kong protests*). Round huts (Gorleben), A-frame structures (→*Resurrection City*, Startbahn West), as well as ridge and conical tents (→*Shearers' Strike*, →*Bonus Army*), on the other hand, are hardly to be found today. Special forms such as pyramids (→*Lobau*) or circus tents, just like tower structures, often attract comparatively high levels of media attention (→*Icon*, → *Media*).

2a. Construction methods: Many tents and huts in protest camps are simple frame and pole structures that are covered or cladded with textiles, often tarpaulins or fabrics, wood panels, boards, or branches, depending on available →*building materials*. In Washington, DC, in →*1968*, Resurrection City activists inhabited prefabricated A-frames made of wooden slats and cross-laminated timber, designed by architects and erected by volunteers. Tower-like constructions in forest occupations (Gorleben, Hambach Forest) are mostly pile structures made of long tree trunks. The type of hut developed in Lützerath likewise stands on stilts, with its height efficiently delaying police evictions, since only special units with lifting platforms and rope safety devices are allowed to enter structures above a height of 2.5 meters. Bending roofs and tents, so-called →*benders*, are also set up during occupations outside major cities, for example in the →*Greenham Common Peace Camp* in →*1981* and in the Hambach Forest. These structures consist of dome-like frames made of bent branches that are fixed in the ground and covered with (often transparent) tarpaulins. At the ZAD Notre-Dame-des-Landes and in the Hambach Forest, activists also built geodomes, lattice structures, and exoskeletons out of branches and narrow tree trunks, as well as adobe huts with elaborate conical roofs. Rope structures are used to stretch roofs between trees (→*Syntagma Square*, Gezi Park), street furniture (→*Tahrir Square*, Movimiento 15M),

and buildings to protect them from sun and rain. →*Ropes* are also used to build eviction structures such as →*traverses*, monopods, and →*tensegrities*, as well as to attach hanging tree houses. It is not only during protests by Indigenous peoples like in North Dakota against the →*Dakota Access Pipeline* in →*2016* that activists live in traditional tipis. In the construction of tents and tent-like structures—such as the cone-shaped, textile-covered huts made of tree trunks in Gorleben or in the Swiss hut village →*Zaffaraya*, which has existed since →*1985*—it is also possible to enter into debates about the cultural appropriation of traditional building types such as yurts, wigwams, and "nomad tents."

2b. Design vocabulary: Protest architecture usually emerges out of necessity and a lack of resources. Many of the structures developed in this context are characterized by a simplicity of construction, often read as a return to the "archetypes of building" or a supposed "primitive hut" (Rykwert 1972). For many climate activists, functionality and simplicity are an expression of the refusal of a lifestyle based on the capitalist exploitation of people and nature that leads to environmental destruction. Loosely based on Georg Büchner's slogan "Peace to the huts! War on the palaces!," they set an example against wealth and waste with their modest dwellings. The functional construction of the protest buildings, however, does not mean that their aesthetic range is restrictive: colorful textiles, tarpaulins, →*protest placards*, →*banners*, →*flags*, and →*graffiti* characterize the heterogeneous appearance of today's protest camps—unlike in the first half of the 20th century (Shearers' Strike, Bonus Army). Depending on how long an occupation lasts, how available building materials are, and how much time and energy the activists can invest in the construction of the buildings, architectural constructions full of fantasy and ingenuity are created in protest camps. In this respect, diversity of form is not only a consequence of creative do-it-yourself strategies but a conscious decision against the homogeneity and conformity of consumer society and mainstream architecture. (AMM)

Bürger∗innenbesen-Proteste, engl. → *Civic Broom protests.* Mehrtägige → *Demonstrationen* im Jahr → *2014* auf den → *Straßen* der Hauptstadt von Burkina Faso. Sie richteten sich gegen die 27-jährige Diktatur von Blaise Compaoré, der das Land in Armut, Korruption und Günstlingswirtschaft geführt hatte. Hunderttausende Demonstrierende trugen Besen als Symbol für die Reinigung des politischen Systems. Die Proteste führten zum Sturz der Regierung und zum Rücktritt von Compaoré. (JD)

Burundi-Proteste, engl. → *Burundi protests.* Die erneute Kandidatur von Präsident Pierre Nkurunziza führte von April bis Juni → *2015* zu gewaltvollen Protesten in Burundi und zu einem blutigen Putschversuch (→ *Demonstration,* → *Gewalt*). Die → *Polizei* und regierungsnahe Milizen gingen brutal mit Tränengas, → *Wasserwerfern* und scharfer Munition (→ *Waffen*) gegen Demonstrierende vor, es kam zu zahlreichen Verhaftungen und Todesfällen. Seitdem hat sich die politische Situation in Burundi nicht verbessert, es gibt weiterhin Menschenrechtsverletzungen und politische Unterdrückung. (JD)

Burundi protests, Ger. → *Burundi-Proteste.* From April to June → *2015,* the renewed candidacy of President Pierre Nkurunziza led to violent protests in Burundi and a bloody coup attempt (→ *Demonstration,* → *Violence*). The → *police* and the pro-government militia took brutal action against the demonstrators with teargas, → *water cannons,* and live ammunition (→ *Weapons*), with numerous arrests and casualties. Since then, the political situation has not improved, with human rights violations and political oppression still common. (JD)

Cake, Ger. → *Torte;* → *Weapons,* → *Protest goals*

Camps for Climate Action, Ger. → *Klimacamps,* are → *protest camps* focusing on climate-policy issues which are located in big cities or in places of environmental damage, such as power stations or airports. The first Camp for Climate Action was organized in 2006 at the Drax Power Station in North Yorkshire, England. Others followed in the course of the noughties in West Europe, Canada, and Australia. From 2010 onwards, in the two largest German lignite mining regions the "Lausitzcamp" and the "Klimacamp im Rheinland" were held annually. Among other things, they served → *protest organizations* such as Ende Gelände as the basis for occupying open-pit mines (→ *Finger*). Since 2020, the Fridays for Future movement has been co-organizing many Camps for Climate Action. The protest camps are planned in advance like a construction project (→ *Master plan*), usually approved by the authorities, and have a fixed events program. As venues for low-threshold participation and networking, they have a different target group than do → *blockades* or → *occupations.* Camps for Climate Action are often intended to last only a few days; in some cases, however, they run far longer. The Camp for Climate Action in Augsburg celebrated its first 1,000 days on March 27, 2023. (AMM)

Camp Studies, engl. → *Camp Studies.* Von den → *Straßen* von → *Hongkong* bis zum → *Tahrir-Platz* in Kairo, vom New Yorker Zuccotti Park (→ *Occupy Wall Street*) bis zum Istanbuler Taksim-Platz (→ *Gezi-Park*), von der National Mall in Washington, DC (→ *Resurrection City*), bis zum → *Majdan* in Kyjiw: → *Protestcamps* sind bedeutende Schauplätze von politischen Auseinandersetzungen. Sie sind Katalysatoren für Identitätsbildung und Inkubatoren für soziale Prozesse. Protestcamps sind „eine ortsbasierte Strategie sozialer Bewegungen mit zwei Komponenten: Sie sind die Ausgangsbasis für Protestaktionen und dienen zugleich dazu, den Alltag in solchen Ausnahmesituationen erträglich zu gestalten" (Feigenbaum, Frenzel, McCurdy 2013). Protestcamps können ein breites Spektrum sozialer Bewegungen integrieren und einer Vielzahl von Forderungen nach sozialem Wandel Ausdruck verleihen. Ihre → *Infrastrukturen* und Praktiken sind inspiriert von Zeltstädten, Festivalkulturen, Hausbesetzer*innengemeinschaften, Kommunen, indigenen Strategien und nicht zuletzt auch von anderen Protestcamps.

Obwohl Protestcamps schon seit einiger Zeit erforscht werden (Doherty 1998; Feigenbaum, Frenzel, McCurdy 2013; Roseneil 1995; Krasniewicz 1992; Seel 1997), haben sie im letzten Jahrzehnt aufgrund ihrer Bedeutung bei großen Protestereignissen wie dem Arabischen Frühling → *2011* und den Occupy-Bewegungen (Brown, Feigenbaum, Frenzel, McCurdy 2017; Feigenbaum, Frenzel, McCurdy 2013; Halvorsen 2012, 2015; Ramadan 2013; Reinecke 2018) verstärkte wissenschaftliche Aufmerksamkeit erfahren. Protestcamps wurden hinsichtlich ihrer räumlichen und territorialen Fragestellungen (Halvorsen 2013; Frenzel 2011, 2020), ihrer Organisationsformen und -politik (Eschle 2017; Feigenbaum, Frenzel, McCurdy 2013; Maestri, Hughes 2017; Sörensen 2018; Reinecke 2018; Tominaga 2017), ihrer Care-Aspekte (English 2017; Kavada 2023; Rollmann, Frenzel 2017) und ihrer Medienpraktiken (Feigenbaum, McCurdy 2015; Gerbaudo 2017; Kavada, Dimitriou 2018; Feigenbaum, Frenzel, McCurdy 2013; → *Medien*) untersucht. Schließlich zeigt eine kürzlich herausgegebene Aufsatzsammlung von Cathrine Eschle und Alison Bartlett (2023) eine feministische Perspektive auf Protestcamps als Schauplatz von Geschlechterverhältnissen und feministischem Aktivismus.

Um Protestcamps zu analysieren, müssen wir sie als lebendige Orte des Konflikts verstehen, an denen Menschen und Ideen innerhalb bestimmter historisch einmaliger Situationen, Kontexte, Umgebungen, Politiken und Zeiträume aufeinandertreffen. Sie sind gleichzeitig der Ausgangspunkt, von dem aus Proteste in Aktionen münden, und setzen, durch ihre bloße Existenz, wiederum selber Protestsignale. Sie sind sowohl Orte des täglichen Lebens als auch Räume der politischen Vision, wo die erträumten neuen Formen von Gesellschaften in die Praxis umgesetzt werden. Sie sind auch Orte des Medieninteresses, sie sind Bühnen, um Errungenschaften zu präsentieren und von dort in die sozialen Medien zu tragen. Angesichts dieser sich überschneidenden und miteinander verflochtenen Elemente erfordert die Untersuchung von Protestcamps ein Gespür für ihre vielfältigen Infrastrukturen.

In der Soziologie bezieht sich der Begriff Infrastrukturen auf die Summe aller Dienstleistungen und Angebote, die zur Aufrechterhaltung einer Gesellschaft oder Gemeinschaft notwendig sind. Wir schlagen hier einen infrastrukturellen Ansatz für die Untersuchung von Protestcamps vor, um zu erfassen, wie Bewohner*innen eines Camps miteinander verknüpfte, funktionsfähige Strukturen für das tägliche Leben in vier Bereichen aufbauen:

1. Medien- und → *Kommunikationsinfrastrukturen* befassen sich mit Medienstrategien, Verbreitungsnetzen und Produktionstechniken sowohl für die vom Camp (und seinen Bewohner*innen) produzierten und gesendeten Inhalte als auch für den Umgang mit der Darstellung des Camps durch die Mainstream-Medien.

2. Aktionsinfrastrukturen und -praktiken ermöglichen wirkungsvolle Protestaktionen, bieten Schulungen für Verhandlungen mit der → *Polizei*, bieten Rechtshilfe, medizinische Dienste und Transportnetze an.

3. Leitungsinfrastrukturen und -praktiken umfassen die formellen und informellen Entscheidungsprozesse, Regeln und Verfahren, aber auch deren räumliche Gestaltung.

4. Versorgungsinfrastrukturen und -praktiken unterstützen die Besetzer*innen mit Lebensmitteln (→ *Küche*), Unterkünften und sanitären Anlagen. Dazu zählt auch die Instandhaltung von Gemeinschafts- und Privaträumen sowie die Betreuung und Sicherheit der Bewohner*innen und Besucher*innen von Protestcamps.

Diese Infrastrukturen und die mit ihnen verbundenen Praktiken wirken zusammen, um Miniaturgesellschaften zu schaffen, die in der Lage sind, Informa-

Camp

tionen zu verbreiten, Güter zu verteilen und Dienstleistungen anzubieten (z.B. Schulungen zur Gewaltfreiheit, medizinische Versorgung und juristische Beratung). Der von uns vorgeschlagene Fokus auf Materialitäten und Infrastrukturen ist weder endgültig noch normativ, sondern dient hier vielmehr als Ausgangspunkt.

In der Vergangenheit hat sich die Forschung auf westliche Camps konzentriert. Protestcamps sind jedoch ein globales Phänomen. Inzwischen gibt es eine breite Palette von Forschungsergebnissen, die den Vergleich der erstaunlichen Vielfalt auf weltweiter Ebene möglich macht (Brown, Feigenbaum, Frenzel, McCurdy 2017). Das Faszinierendste an Camps ist vielleicht, wie sie sich gegenseitig inspirieren. Vorbilder verbreiten sich, Ideen reisen herum. Die Menschen in Madrid und Athen waren im Jahr → *2011* von den Geschehnissen an den südlichen Ufern des Mittelmeers elektrisiert, und was in Tunis und Kairo passiert ist, hat danach New Yorker Aktivist*innen dazu angeregt, zur Einrichtung von Occupy-Camps in der ganzen Welt aufzurufen. Die Dynamik und der politische Verlauf eines Protestcamps ergeben sich aus den Wechselwirkungen von materiellen Objekten (→ *Zelte*, Straßen, Fahrräder, Holzpaletten, Planen und Tische), physischen Geografien (Umgebungen, gebaute Architekturen, Klima), medialen Repräsentationen (von den Mainstream-Medien bis hin zu Livestreams und Social-Media-Posts; → *Digitale Medien*) sowie aus den lokalen, regionalen und nationalen Gesetzen. Fragen zur kulturellen Identität und zu den Nachwirkungen des Kolonialismus, so etwa der indigene Kampf um Selbstbestimmung, haben einige Protestcamps hervorgebracht. Aus Verflechtungen und Adaptionen sind die Symbole von Protestcamps hervorgegangen – vom „People's Mic" von Occupy Wall Street bis zu den ikonischen Regenschirmen der Studierendenproteste in Hongkong.

Camp Studies müssen sich auch mit den Spannungen zwischen Utopie und Dystopie auseinandersetzen, zwischen der Entschlossenheit, dass eine andere Welt möglich sein soll, und den praktischen Einschränkungen des Lebens im Freien, das oft zugleich mit täglicher → *Gewalt* durch die Polizei konfrontiert ist. Fragen der Autonomie und des Zwangs spielen eine große Rolle: Protestcamps sind keine freien und radikal demokratischen Räume – Muster der Ungleichheit spiegeln sich auch in den „offen" entstandenen Strukturen wider. Umgekehrt sind feste Strukturen und ein geregelter Ablauf nicht per se ausschließlich und repressiv: Selbst von Behörden aufgebaute Camps, wie z.B. Flüchtlingslager, können zu Orten der politischen Organisation und des autonomen Überlebens werden. Die Erforschung von Protestcamps darf nicht versuchen, diese Widersprüche auszublenden oder sie zu leugnen. Denn: Wie die Menschen, die sie bauen und in ihnen leben, sind auch die Protestcamps chaotisch und umstritten, schön und beschädigt, voller Hoffnungen und Ängste. (Anna Feigenbaum, Fabian Frenzel, Patrick McCurdy)

Camp Studies, Ger. → *Camp Studies*. From the streets of → *Hong Kong* to Cairo's → *Tahrir Square*, from New York's Zuccotti Park (→ *Occupy Wall Street*) to Istanbul's Taksim Square (→ *Gezi Park*), from the National Mall in Washington, DC (→ *Resurrection City*), to the → *Maidan* in Kyiv, → *protest camps* are important sites and catalysts for political contention and expression of identity, as well as incubators for social change. Protest camps are "a place-based social movement strategy that involves both acts of ongoing protest and acts of social reproduction needed to sustain daily life" (Feigenbaum, Frenzel, McCurdy 2013). They occur across a wide range of social movements, encompass a diversity of demands for social change and adapt → *infrastructures* and practices from → *tent* cities, festival cultures, squatting communities, land-based autonomous movements, Indigenous occupations and, indeed, other protest camps.

Although protest camps have been studied for some time (Doherty 1998;

118

Feigenbaum, Frenzel, McCurdy 2013; Roseneil 1995; Krasniewicz 1992; Seel 1997), they have seen increased academic attention in the last decade due to their significance at large protest events such as the → *2011* Arab Spring and Occupy Movements (Brown, Feigenbaum, Frenzel, McCurdy 2017; Feigenbaum, Frenzel, McCurdy 2013; Halvorsen 2012, 2015; Ramadan 2013; Reinecke 2018). Protest camps have been studied for their relation to space and territory (Halvorsen 2012; Frenzel 2011, 2020), their modes and politics of organizing (Eschle 2017; Feigenbaum, Frenzel, McCurdy 2013; Maestri, Hughes 2017; Sörensen 2018; Reinecke 2018; Tominaga 2017), their methods of caring for participants (English 2017; Kavada 2023; Rollmann, Frenzel 2017), and their → *media* practices (Feigenbaum, McCurdy 2015; Gerbaudo 2017; Kavada, Dimitriou 2018; Feigenbaum, Frenzel, McCurdy 2013). A recently edited collection of essays by Catherine Eschle and Alison Bartlett (2023) applies a feminist theoretical and methodological lens to protest camps as sites of gendered relations and feminist activism.

To study protest camps, we must see them as active sites of struggle where people and ideas converge within specific histories, contexts, environments, politics, and temporalities. They are simultaneously base camps for protest and protests in themselves. They are sites for daily living and spaces of prefigurative politics where the imagined possibilities of daily life are put into practice. They are also sites of media interest and stages for legacy and social media representation. Bearing in mind these overlapping and entangled elements, the study of protest camps requires sensitivity to their multiple infrastructures.

In sociological research, infrastructures refer to the organized services and facilities necessary for supporting a society or community. Here we put forward an infrastructural approach to the study of protest camps in order to capture how protest campers build interrelated, operational structures for daily living across four areas:

1. Media and → *communication* infrastructures are concerned with the media strategies, distribution networks, and production techniques for media produced by the camp (and its campers), as well as practices for dealing with the camp's representation in mainstream media.

2. Action infrastructures and practices comprised of direct action tactics, education, → *police* negotiations, legal aid, medical support, and transportation networks.

3. Governance infrastructures and practices are the formal and informal decision-making processes, rules, and procedures, which also involve their spatial organization.

4. Recreation infrastructures and practices which provide food (→ *Kitchen*), shelter, and sanitation to camps and campers, the maintenance of communal and private spaces, as well as for the care and safety of those living in and visiting protest camps.

These infrastructures and the practices attached to them function together to create miniature societies that are able to disseminate information, distribute goods, and provide services (such as non-violence training, medical care, and legal support). Our proposed focus on materialities and infrastructures is neither conclusive nor prescriptive but, instead, serves as a starting point.

Historically, much empirical work has focused on Western camps. But protest camps are a truly global phenomenon, and a wide range of research is now available to compare and contrast this amazing phenomenon (Brown, Feigenbaum, Frenzel, McCurdy 2017). Perhaps one of the most fascinating things about camps is how they inspire each other with lineages of transmission. They are contagious, and they travel well, as shown by how people in Madrid and Athens were inspired by what had happened on the southern shores of the Mediterranean, in Tunis and Cairo, during the winter of 2011, as well as how New York activists took inspiration from these places when they called for the establishment of Occupy camps and ignited a fire across the globe. The dynamics and political trajectories of a protest camp are formed from the entanglements and interactions of material objects (canvas tents, city roads, bicycles, wooden pallets, tarps, and tables), physical geographies (environments, built architectures, climate), mediated representations (from mainstream media to livestreams and social media posts; → *Digital media*), as well as local, provincial and national laws that shape how these conditions are navigated. The ongoing legacy and consequences of colonialism and Indigenous struggles for sovereignty over unceded territory also underly the politics of some protest camps. It is these entanglements and adaptations that give rise to the emblematic symbols of protest camps—from Occupy Wall Street's people's mic to the iconic umbrellas of the Hong Kong student protests.

Camp studies must also navigate the tensions between utopia and dystopia, between the determination that another world is possible and the practicalities of living outside—often facing daily acts of → *violence* from the police. Questions of autonomy and force loom large: autonomously created camps are not free and radically democratic spaces—patterns of inequality are mirrored in the "open" structures that emerge. But likewise, planned camps with structures and systems are not closed: even those erected by authorities, such as refugee camps, are open to becoming places of political organization and autonomous survival. Protest camp studies cannot seek to resist or deny these contradictions. Rather, like the people who build them and live in them, protest camps are messy and contentious, beautiful and damaged, bursting with hopes and fears. (Anna Feigenbaum, Fabian Frenzel, Patrick McCurdy)

Capitol attack, Ger. → *Kapitol-Attacke*. On January 6, → *2021*, Donald Trump, who had been voted out as US President, called on his followers to come to the Capitol in order to prevent the confirmation of the election victory of his successor Joe Biden by the House of Representatives and the Senate at the very last minute. The attack on Congress sought to conquer the architectural symbol of US democracy (→ *Right-wing protests*). A coup likewise starts with the violent conquest of the symbolic and real centers of power (→ *Violence*). Only after hours of indecisive inaction did the security forces clear the buildings of protesters. (OE)

Cazerolazo, engl. → *Cazerolazo*; → *Kochtopf*, → *Lärm*

Cazerolazo, Ger. → *Cazerolazo*; → *Cooking pot*, → *Noise*

Children, Ger. → *Kinder*; → *Gorleben*, → *Infrastructure*, → *Protection*, → *Tahrir Square*

Civic Broom protests, Ger. → *Bürger∗innenbesen-Proteste*. Several days of → *demonstrations* on the → *streets* of Burkina Faso's capital, Ouagadougou, in → *2014*. They were directed against the twenty-seven-year dictatorship of Blaise Compaoré, who had brought poverty, corruption, and cronyism to the country. Hundreds of thousands of demonstrators carried brooms to symbolize cleaning up the political system. The protests led to the overthrow of the government and to Compaoré's resignation. (JD)

Civil disobedience, Ger. → *Ziviler Ungehorsam*. "Civil disobedience is a morally *justified* protest which may not be founded only on private convictions or individual self-interests; it is a *public* act which, as a rule, is announced in advance and which the police can control as it occurs; it includes the *premeditated transgression* of individual legal norms without calling into question obedience to the rule of law as a whole; it demands the readiness to *accept* the legal *consequences* of the transgression of those norms; the infraction by which civil disobedience is expressed has an exclusively *symbolic character*—hence is derived the restriction to *nonviolent* means of protest." (Habermas 1983/1985, p. 100)

Claremont Road, engl. → *Claremont Road*. Die achtmonatige Besetzung der Claremont Road und angrenzender Häuser im Jahr → *1994* in London war Teil des britischen Anti-Roads-Movement der 1990er. Die →*Blockade* und temporäre Umgestaltung der →*Straße* war eine direkte Widerstandsaktion gegen den Bau der Verbindungsstraße M11, der 35 Reihenhäuser weichen sollten. Es wurden verschiedene Strukturen (→*Bautypen*) errichtet: →*Baumhäuser*, →*Barrikaden*, kunstvolle Skulpturen aus Abfall, Fassadenbemalungen, ein großer →*Turm* und verbindende Stege und Netze über den Dächern. Die Proteste verwandelten die Straße in ein Experiment für unkonventionelle Lebensweisen. Die Häuser wurden durch eine ausgedehnte Untertunnelung miteinander verbunden, indem in jede einzelne Wand einer Häuserreihe ein Loch geschnitten wurde. Im Inneren wurden Bunker, Schleusen und →*Tunnel* mithilfe von Schutt getarnt. Die Räumung dauerte fünf Tage. (JD)

Claremont Road, Ger. →*Claremont Road.* The eight-month occupation of Claremont Road and the adjacent houses in →*1994* in London was part of the British anti-roads movement in the 1990s. The →*blockade* and the temporary transformation of the →*street* was a direct act of resistance against the construction of the M11 motorway for which thirty-five row houses were to make way. Various structures (→*Building types*) were installed: →*tree houses*, →*barricades*, artistic trash sculptures, facade paintings, a big →*tower*, and connecting bridges and nets spanned across the roofs. The protests turned the street into an experiment for unconventional ways of living. An extensive tunnel system joined the buildings, for which a hole was cut into each wall of a row of houses. Inside, rubble was used to conceal bunkers, locks, and →*tunnels*. The eviction took five days. (JD)

Clothing, Ger. →*Kleidung.* In various social movements, clothing expresses a political position; its meaning is emblematic and only understandable in the respective cultural and historical context where it is subject to constant change. Combined with make-up, tattoos, beards, or hairstyles, individual pieces of clothing and accessories make up an ensemble. Together with facial expression, gestures,

and postures, the "language of clothing" becomes a form of nonverbal →*communication* within social interaction (Hoffmann 1985). Clothing as a form of protest is either temporarily relevant for the duration of a political action or it can express dissent when worn permanently as an everyday outfit. The absence of clothing is also used as a form of protest, since →*nakedness* in public generates a high level of attention.

The members of the climate-activist alliance Ende Gelände (literally: end of the terrain, used to call a stop to something, as in "this far and no further") not only use their mass appearances in white overalls and face masks to gain attention. According to their *Activist Guide*, the masks and overalls protect their wearers from dirt, mud, and the potential health risks posed by inhaling dust. The fact that uniform clothing and masks impede detection by the →*police* and security personnel is a welcome by-effect (*Shut Shit Down!* 2020). The white suits are also supposed to present a friendlier, almost innocent image in contrast to the homogenous mass of the black bloc. The activists draw on the history of →*civil disobedience* and its movements, such as the German anti-nuclear protests and the Italian Tute Bianche, who stood out due to their expansive repertoire of protective clothing. The Tute Bianche were a critical reaction to the Autonomia Operaia in Italy in the 1970s. In Germany similarly militant forms of protest, such as the Frankfurt Spontis' "Putztruppe" ("cleaning crew," the term *Sponti* refers to a preference for spontaneity instead of dogmatism) in the 1970s, defined street demonstrations (→*Street*, →*Demonstration*). However, the police did not perceive their protective clothing as defensive →*protection*, but as an expression of their readiness to use violence and as "aggressiveness" (Grob 1985, p. 280; →*Violence*). In 1985, the "anti-mask law" as well as the ban on so-called "passive arming" was introduced in Germany. The law was criticized, not only because it insinuated a latent propensity toward violence, but also for fear of its arbitrary interpretation (Meyn 1988, p. 93f.; Grob 1985, p. 279).

As a means of impeding identification through the police or political opponents, disguise is an important function of protective clothing in the context of confrontative forms of protest. The balaclava, a symbol of militant protest, became an integral part of the autonomists' clothing repertoire. Together with the uniform black outfit it is part of the black bloc's performative form of protest at street demonstrations. In 1985, the "anti-mask law" placed considerable constraints on face coverings (Haunss 2004, p. 169f.). The mask mandate introduced in connection with the Covid safety precautions turned the anti-mask law into a mask requirement. Since the lifting of the measures in winter 2022/2023, the police have had to decide case-by-case whether a nose and mouth covering is a protection against infection or against identification. Despite the ban, disguises and protective clothing are part of the repertoire of political forms of action. The leather gear and helmets worn during the militant district and house-to-house fights in the 1980s have thus been replaced by fashionable but functional streetwear. Costumes and disguises often manifest simultaneously in protest events, as was the case at carnival processions in the 17th and 18th century, where marginalized groups used ritualized tumults to express their discontent with the political conditions (Denk, Spille 2009, p. 221). The aristocracy responded with the first ban on face coverings (Carl, Kessler 1989, p. 183). In the wake of the antiauthoritarian movement of the 1960s, costuming was used to expose and denounce political opponents and—to quote cultural theorist Mikhail Bakhtin—as an expression of a "carnivalization of awareness" (Bachtin 1995, p. 101). Accordingly, the proclamation "a revolution without fun isn't a revolution" (Carl, Kessler 1989, p. 192) circulated in the sphere of the Situationist artists' group SPUR and the group Subversive Aktion (subversive action).

Likewise, the new social movements of the 1990s appropriated the use of masquerades in the context of anti-globalization protests with carnivalesque forms of action such as "Pink & Silver" or "Rebel Clown Army." The expression of provocative fun subverts gender role expectations and binarism as well as the negative stereotype of the police as militant "tough guys." Absurd costumes create confusion in paradoxical contexts, thus generating new possibilities for protest situations (Amann 2005, p. 128), such as the humorous appearance of the "monk of → *Lützerath*," who who went viral after the occupation had been evicted to make way for a brown coal mine in 2023.

Uniformization in the context of protest actions can evolve in reference to actual uniforms worn by authorities, through professional uniforms (e.g., in the context of union demonstrations) or through matching and uniform clothing without any connection to existing uniforms. In → *2018* and 2019 participants in the mass protests in France triggered by the government's reform plans wore neon-yellow high-visibility vests (→ *Yellow Vests movement*). On the one hand, the "gilets jaunes" were an expression of the "protest reaction of specific class positions" (Rackwitz 2022, p. 112). On the other hand, they unified a politically heterogenous protest, which mostly took place as a spontaneous, decentralized, predominantly local occurrence organized via social media. Initially the protesters were only linked by their → *identifier* and the fact that they met at → *roundabouts*. Uniform clothing also attracts the attention of the police, the → *media*, and other demonstrators, as in the case of the black bloc or—more subtly—when samba groups perform in concert outfits during anti-nuclear protests (→ *Music*).
(Larissa Denk)

Cobblestone, Ger. → *Pflasterstein (fig.).* In Western Europe, torn out cobblestones or other kinds of pavers have been regarded as the epitome of political revolt and → *violence* in the → *streets* ever since they were first ripped out of the ground, stacked to form →*barricades*, and repurposed as →*weapons* against the royal troops during the three-day street fights of the →*July Revolution* in Paris in →*1830*. Previously laid in neat rows, the cuboid stones were so big and heavy in Paris that the revolutionaries, unable to throw them at the military in the streets, hurled them out of windows from which they apparently rained down like "hail" (Anonym 1831, p. 55) alongside furniture and other household items. They earned the "citizen king" Louis Philippe, who ascended the throne after the revolution, the nickname "Pavement King" (Börne 1832/1964, p. 439). The act of tearing them out was regarded as so subversive that the journalist Ludwig Börne, when asked by his editor to write texts for lithographs depicting the July Revolution, decided he "wanted to contribute to *de-paving* Germany" (Börne 1830/1968, p. 1208). In France the street surface was known as *pavé du Roi*, the "king's paving" (Birk 1934/1971, p. 292) ever since Louis XIV had had the military and trade road from Paris to Orléans plastered in this fashion. While the perfect alignment of the firmly joined stones on the ground, which had been cut and laid out by serfs, was regarded as a "monument" of the monarchy (Patte 1765, p. 9), the flying cobblestones aptly symbolized the toppling of the established vertical hierarchies.

This revolutionary application, which has become prevalent almost all over Europe since the revolution of →*1848*, attached itself to the stones and has survived despite efforts to quickly repave the streets after the revolutions to ensure, as Heinrich Heine surmised, that "no outward trace of the revolution remain" (Heine 1832/1976 p. 110)—even when the stones were replaced with gravel, and then with asphalt after 1968 to prevent future riots, as "deterrence against barricades" (Archives de Paris), hence the title of the respective files of the municipal administration in Paris. Since then, cobblestones have been purposefully collected and used by various groups: by the →*Yellow Vests* move-

ment demonstrating against the financing of the overdue energy transition, by residents of the banlieues fighting back against systemic exclusion and discrimination, at protests against the outcome of French presidential elections on the Place de la Bastille, which is famous for left-wing →*demonstrations*, and in Berlin-Kreuzberg on May 1 since the 1980s. Especially in →*May '68* the protesting students in Paris used them as a "historical reference" (Gilcher-Holtey 1995, p. 240) when they occupied the Sorbonne, broke apart the paving in the Latin Quarter, threw cobblestones at the →*police* and the riot police, and blocked the streets with barricades made up of cobblestones, thus giving their protest the appearance of a revolution, even though Friedrich Engels had declared this "old-style rebellion" (Engels 1895/1972, p. 519)—which may have experienced its first renewal with the →*brick* barricades in the →*Hong Kong protests* in →*2019*—obsolete a long time ago. The students' slogan "sous les pavés, la plage" (beneath the pavement, the beach) promised an original state without the paving, with every step a reminder of the erstwhile royal power that had degraded anyone walking across it as a mere subject. The extracted and thrown cobblestones of 1968, which no longer visualized the king's exercise of power but that of the rioters and their disruption of rigid social, political, and formal conventions, were supposed to stir the imagination and thereby trigger the realization that other conditions are possible, as in Jo Schnapp's photomontage of the Parisian May: "L'imagination au pouvoir" (Power to the imagination)! According to a poster by the Atelier Populaire, an activist collective that produced placards at the occupied art academy, this would bring beauty to the streets instead of domination.

The cobblestones have long since found their way into →*museums*. After 1968 artists such as Robert Filliou marked the "fetishization of the revolt" (Lebel, Brau, Merlhès 1969, p. 460) with cobblestone multiples in boxes,

Comm

while Joseph Beuys tried to capture the stones' inherent subversive possibilities in his own multiples which he distributed via art shipments in the hope of spreading this quality. And yet, objects in museums, mostly displayed in showcases, no longer trigger revolutions. The same applies to all the cobblestones that were taken home as personal souvenirs or wound up in historical museums or as exhibits in the evidence rooms of the police—the latter are probably running a secret cobblestone museum with stones from all the important street fights, as frequently surmised in urban legends. And yet the "magic" (Sarrans 1832, p. 311) of the loose cobble stones in the street still seems to work. How else to explain that demonstration announcements are constantly followed by targeted false reports in → *digital media* with photographs of ordinary construction sites and warnings that "the left" have prepared themselves by laying out cobblestones they cunningly disguised with hoarding, construction-site signs, and barrier tape? (Kathrin Rottmann)

Communication, Ger. → *Kommunikation*. Protest movements need to make themselves and their causes heard. However, they often struggle to be seen. To communicate their → *protest goals*, they must overcome various (spatial, but also cognitive) obstacles. This applies not only to indirect communication (via mass → *media* and technology) and direct (face-to-face) external communication, but also to internal communication (Schönberger, Sutter 2009, p. 19). After all, the protest activists also need to communicate to coordinate and to discuss the matters at hand.

Protest movements are also regarded as "laboratories of democracy" (Teune 2012; Ullrich 2015, p. 19). They not only react to the much-lamented crisis of political representation in modern institutions (see Vester 2003), but also develop new "democratic forms for a different, better democracy." "Democratic innovations" evolve in the process, for instance, "in the shape of certain hand gestures that simplify coordination processes", such as the "human micro-phone" (Ullrich 2015, p. 19; → *Hand signals*). In → *2011* the *human microphone* or *people's microphone* became a symbol of the → *Occupy Wall Street* movement. It was an invention by the General Assembly. The city of New York had enacted a law according to which the use of amplifiers in → *public spaces* without a permit was to be punished with up to thirty days in jail. In response, Occupy Wall Street invented the simple and communicative assembly technique of the *human mic*. In this form of communication, a sentence is repeated verbatim and in chorus by those standing closest to the speaker. The process continues until those farthest away from the speaker have repeated the sentence. This unplugged assembly technique helped bridge the space between the participants and promoted democratic communication. It was defined by slowness. Charisma and virtuosity made way for a communal performative act. The *human mic* has become a symbol of the Occupy movement. It requires simple language as well as a low-threshold choice of words (Kim 2011).

A performative, distinctly expansive, albeit silent form of protest communication was developed during the → *Gezi Park* demonstrations on Istanbul's Taksim Square in → *2013* by the Turkish artist Erdem Gündüz. For his "Standing Man" performance, Gündüz stood in front of a portrait of modern Turkey's founder Mustafa Kemal Atatürk and did no more than look at the picture (Gündüz 2014, p. 134f.). He thereby opposed the Turkish president Erdogan's Islamization efforts and contradicted the assertions about allegedly violent protests. Global visual communication played a part in transcending the spatial limits of the local protest communication.

The participants in current protest movements have become regular experts in the use of symbols. Their actual impotence in the face of governments and corporations forces them to opt for symbolic acts of defiance or symbolic politics. In society as a whole, the production of signs, images, and symbols in general, has become an increasingly important aspect of value creation in an aesthetically inclined manifestation of capitalism. The current protests thus not only reflect contemporary developments but also the status quo of productive forces (autonome a.f.r.i.k.a.-gruppe 1997/2012, p. 238f.).

In "Towards a Seismological Guerrilla Warfare," Umberto Eco described the "variability of interpretation" as "the constant law of mass communications". He rejected the simple sender-receiver model of communication theory which equates the sent content with the received content. According to him, the only way to control the content of a message would be to extend the communication chain spatially. Namely by occupying the first row in front of the listeners (Eco 1967/1985, p. 152).

And then there is an additional problem: What if nobody wants to listen? This question led the autonomous group a.f.r.i.k.a. to develop the concept of guerrilla communication, which is not about sabotage as an interruption of the communication channel in a technical sense. Guerrilla communication does not seek to convince or persuade, but rather to help unsettle ideologically deluded certainties. In *Handbuch der Kommunikationsguerilla* ($\rightarrow$ *Handbücher / Online-Manuals*), the authors analyze the problem of political communication as a counter public. In keeping with Roland Barthes (1971, p. 141), their aim is not to destroy the codes, but rather to distort them. Furthermore, the handbook's fake theory explains why people believe conspiracy theories and alternative facts. Apparently, they do not owe their power of persuasion to the plausibility of the communicated content but to what the consumers want to hear and see. A sobering realization for any informative project, since this means that the current problem in political communication is not so much the dominance of social media but rather the structure of the subjects' wishes ($\rightarrow$ *Digital media*).

The aim of guerrilla communication is to spread false information to create real events ($\rightarrow$ *Guerrilla tactics*). One example is the Yes Men's concept of "image pollution" (Bichlbaum, Bonanno, Spunkmeyer 2004). They borrow their adversaries' names (corporations of ill repute) and pose as their spokespeople to spread facts the companies would prefer not to address. In 2004, the Bhopal fake reached fame when the Yes Men, posing as the spokespeople of the Dow Chemical Company, were able to announce on the BBC that, on the occasion of the twentieth anniversary of one of the world's worst chemical disasters in the Indian city of Bhopal, the corporation was finally going to compensate the victims of the lethal gas accident. The corporation was forced to deny the false announcement, and this was the message the Yes Men wanted to spread.

Generating publicity and creating an order of knowledge that lends urgency to change is the key element in all protest communication. However, what or whom people believe has to be renegotiated every time. (Klaus Schönberger)

Concrete pyramid, Ger. $\rightarrow$ *Betonpyramide (fig.)*. Special case of a $\rightarrow$ *lock-on device* used for $\rightarrow$ *body deployment* for a $\rightarrow$ *blockade* of nuclear waste being transported to $\rightarrow$ *Gorleben*. The concrete pyramids were used in several versions and were made of different layers of materials so that it took the $\rightarrow$ *police* as long as possible to extricate the activists' arms from the tomb-chamber-like channels inside them. (OE)

Converging protest marches, Ger. $\rightarrow$ *Sternmarsch*; $\rightarrow$ *Demonstration*

Cooking pot, Ger. $\rightarrow$ *Kochtopf (fig.)*. You can make a lot of $\rightarrow$ *noise* using pots and pans. This form of protest is called a *cazerolazo* in South America, derived from *cacerola* (Spanish for pot). Pots and pans and sieves or plastic bowls were worn as head protection during the $\rightarrow$ *Maidan* protests after government anti-protest legislation made it illegal, among other things, to wear a helmet ($\rightarrow$ *Protection*). (OE)

Costume, Ger. $\rightarrow$ *Kostüm (fig.)*. At the "Animals' Press Conference" in May $\rightarrow$ *1984*, several prominent environmentalists dressed up as red floodplain deer, purple herons, black cormorants, black storks, and ground beetles—animals that were directly threatened by the construction of the power plant in the → *Hainburger Au*. Since the 1980s, costumes have often been used in protest actions, including the → *Greenham Common Peace Camp* and the → *WTO Protests* in Seattle. (AMM)

Counter-construction, Ger. → *Gegenbau (fig.)*. In a defamatory diatribe during the Pegida demonstrations (→ *Demonstration*, → *Right-wing protests*) in Dresden in January 2017, the far-right German AfD politician Björn Höcke had called the Memorial to the Murdered Jews of Europe in Berlin a "monument of shame" and demanded a "180-degree turnaround in remembrance policies" (see Frank 2017; → *Toppling monuments*). In response, the artists' group Center for Political Beauty (ZPS) purchased a plot of land in the immediate vicinity of Höcke's home in the Thuringian village of Bornhagen and erected a scaled-down replica of the Berlin Holocaust Memorial there. The redesign of the site by the ZPS can be described using a term from the art historian Martin Warnke as "counter-construction" (*Gegenbau*, Warnke 1996). Across from Höcke's private domicile, an old wood-clad parish house, a structure was erected along the lines of the cuboid concrete stelae designed by the architect Peter Eisenman, which the politician had to perceive as an ideological attack. With reference to the specific context of this protest architecture dictionary, counter-construction presents itself as a polemical construction that gains its ideological persuasiveness from direct confrontation with the architecture of political opponents, using this manifestation to attempt to achieve a media echo (→ *Tent Embassy*, → *Media*). (SH)

Critical Mass, engl. → *Critical Mass*; → *Demonstration*, → *Fahrzeuge*
Critical Mass, Ger. → *Critical Mass*; → *Demonstration*, → *Vehicles*
Dagegensein, engl. → *Opposition*. „Stärker noch als das Bekenntnis zur sozialen Marktwirtschaft und zu ihrer demokratischen Dividende hat die Gewohnheit zu protestieren einen festen Platz in der Geschichte der Bundesrepublik. Und damit treten wir auch weltweit hervor. Die Themen haben gewechselt, und zwar so schnell, daß biographische Brüche in der Protestiergeneration unvermeidlich gewesen wären, hätte es nicht die Möglichkeit gegeben, von Protest zu Protest überzuziehen. Auf Proteste gegen Remilitarisierung und Atombewaffnung folgen Ostermarschierer und Notstandsopposition, Studentenbewegung und Neomarxismus, Bürgerinitiativen-Initiativen, Antiberufsverbot-Kampagnen, Friedensbewegung, Frauenbewegung, Selbsthilfegruppen und – mit besten Ergebnissen – die Ökologiebewegung. Neue soziale Bewegungen formieren sich unter dem Zeichen des ‚Wertewandels' und nehmen Übersiedler aus den marxistischen Lagern auf, die nur noch an ihrem Akzent zu erkennen sind. Verteilungsthemen werden durch Risikothemen ergänzt, nicht ersetzt. Man bleibt alternativ. Dagegensein verpflichtet." (Luhmann 1990/2016, S. 159)

Dakota-Access-Pipeline-Proteste, engl. → *Dakota Access Pipeline protests*. In North Dakota, USA, protestierten indigene Aktivist∗innen gegen den Bau einer umstrittenen Erdölpipeline, um das Gebiet der Standing Rock Reservation vor Boden- und Wasserverschmutzungen zu schützen. 6000 Menschen aus 300 indigenen Stämmen lebten → *2016* mehrere Monate lang in bis zu drei → *Protestcamps* – es war die größte Zusammenkunft von Native Americans seit knapp 100 Jahren. Viele nutzten die Proteste, um ihre indigenen Wurzeln wieder zu entdecken: Zeremonien bestimmten den Alltag im Camp, es gab traditionelle Gerichte, junge Männer patrouillierten auf Pferden. Tipis und Jurten standen zwischen → *Zelten* und Wohnwagen (→ *Bautypen*). Im „Oceti Sakowin Camp", dem Hauptcamp, fanden täglich Infoveranstaltungen, Dekolonialisierungstrainings und Workshops zum gewaltfreien Widerstand statt; das kleinere „Sacred Stone Camp" war dichter gebaut und lag direkt am Flussbett des

Cannonball River; das „Red Warrior Camp" diente als Kommandozentrale und Basislager, u.a. für Sabotageaktionen an bereits gebauten Pipelineteilstücken. Sicherheit spielte eine wichtige Rolle, denn das Camp wurde von der → *Polizei* immer wieder angegriffen. Es gab Wachen an den Eingängen, Neuankömmlinge wurden befragt und auf → *Waffen* untersucht. Für eine aktivistische Performance entwarf der Künstler Cannupa Hanska Luger → *Schutzschilde* aus → *Spiegeln*, sogenannte „Mirrored Shields", die neben ihrem praktischen Nutzen die Sicherheitskräfte zur Reflexion über ihre eigene Rolle anregen sollten. Große Aufmerksamkeit in den → *Medien* erregte der Einsatz von → *Wasserwerfern* bei Minustemperaturen im November 2016. Von Standing Rock aus entstand eine nationale Protestbewegung für Umweltschutz und die Rechte von Native Americans. (AMM)

Dakota Access Pipeline protests, Ger. → *Dakota-Access-Pipeline-Proteste*. In North Dakota, USA, Indigenous activists protested against the construction of a controversial oil pipeline in order to protect the Standing Rock Reservation against soil and water pollution. In → *2016*, 6,000 people from 300 Indigenous tribes lived for several months in up to three → *protest camps*—it was the largest gathering of Native Americans in almost a century. Many used the protests to rediscover their Indigenous roots: with ceremonies defining everyday life in the camp, traditional meals, and young men patrolling on horses. Tipis and yurts stood between the → *tents* and trailer homes (→ *Building types*). In the central "Oceti Sakowin Camp," information events and workshops on decolonization and nonviolent resistance were held on a daily basis. The smaller "Sacred Stone Camp" was more densely built and was located directly at the bed of the Cannonball River, while the "Red Warrior Camp" served as command center and base camp, e.g. for acts of sabotage on parts of the pipeline that had already been built. Security played a major role, as the camp was repeatedly attacked by the → *police*. There were guards at the entrances, and new arrivals were questioned and searched for → *weapons*. For an activist performance, artist Cannupa Hanska Luger designed → *protective shields* made of → *mirrors*, the "Mirrored Shields," which, in addition to their practical use, were also intended to encourage the security forces to reflect on their own role. The deployment of → *water cannons* in sub-zero temperatures in November 2016 attracted great attention in the → *media*. Standing Rock gave birth to a national protest movement for environmental protection and the rights of Native Americans. (AMM)

Dannenröder Wald, engl. → *Dannenrod Forest*. In → *2019* besetzten Klimaaktivist∗innen einen Wald zwischen Kassel und Gießen, um Rodungen im Zusammenhang mit dem Ausbau der A49 zu verhindern. Innerhalb kürzester Zeit wurde ein → *Protestcamp* aus rund 100 → *Baumhäusern* und rund 400 → *Barrikaden* entlang der geplanten Autobahntrasse gebaut. Die Zahl der Aktivist∗innen wuchs zwischenzeitlich auf etwa 100 an. Ende 2020 wurde die → *Besetzung* durch einen der größten Polizeieinsätze Hessens nach 69 Tagen beendet. Dabei wurden mehrere Personen teils schwer verletzt – u.a. stürzte ein Aktivist von einem → *Tripod*, weil die → *Polizei* ein → *Seil* durchtrennte, obwohl es mit einem Warnschild versehen war. (JD)

Dannenrod Forest, Ger. → *Dannenröder Wald*. In → *2019*, climate activists occupied a forest between Kassel and Gießen to prevent clearings in connection with the expansion of the A49 highway. In next to no time, a → *protest camp* with about 100 → *tree houses* and around 400 → *barricades* was set up along the planned highway section. The number of activists grew to about 100. In late 2020, after sixty-nine days, one of the biggest police operations ever to be carried out in Hesse ended the → *occupation*. In the process, many people were injured, some severely—one activist fell from a → *tripod* because the → *police* cut through a → *rope* despite a warning sign. (JD)

Demonstration, engl. → *Demonstration*. Meist sind Demonstrationen rasch vorüberziehende Ereignisse. Eine Demonstration dauert selten länger als einen Tag. Wenn sie im Zusammenhang einer Protestbewegung stehen, dann können sie sich regelmäßig oder in dichter Folge wiederholen (z.B. die Montagsdemonstrationen in der DDR 1989; die → *Samstagsmütter*, türkisch „Cumartesi Anneleri", seit → *1995* in Istanbul; 2022/2023 die Proteste im Iran; 2023 die Proteste in Israel). Manchmal entstehen aus Demonstrationen heraus → *Protestcamps*; dann kommt es zu einer Art von „Sesshaftwerdung" der Protestierenden wie in Kairo, als sich aus mehreren Demonstrationszügen die Besetzung des → *Tahrir-Platzes* entwickelte. Wenn also Demonstrationen zumeist eher mobile und zeitlich begrenzte Gebilde sind, was haben sie dann überhaupt mit Protestarchitektur zu tun?

Antworten sind auf zwei unterschiedlichen Ebenen der Betrachtung zu finden: einerseits in der Analyse des Raums, also der Fläche, auf der eine Demonstration stattfindet. Protestarchitekturen sind raumgreifend; Demonstrationen beanspruchen ebenfalls ein auffälliges Maß an → *öffentlichem Raum*, sonst würde sie niemand bemerken. Raumfragen sind zudem Machtfragen: Wer kann wie viel Raum einnehmen? Der zweite Aspekt, warum Demonstrationen auch eine architektonische Komponente haben können, ist auf der Ebene der bisweilen mitgeführten Objekte und Kleinarchitekturen nachweisbar.

Zuerst zum Raum: Demonstrationen nehmen eine bestimmte Fläche in Anspruch, meist auf öffentlichen Plätzen und → *Straßen*. Es gibt ein Innen und ein Außen: Beteiligte bilden den Demonstrationsraum, dem die Zuschauer∗innen, Gegendemonstrant∗innen oder die → *Polizei* gegenüberstehen. Doch es geht nicht immer um Massenereignisse. Demonstrationen können sehr klein sein, auch wenn ihre Wirksamkeit häufig danach bemessen wird, wie viele Personen daran teilnehmen. Greta Thunberg stand mit ihrem „Skolstrejk för klimatet"-Schild in der ersten Woche ganz allein vor dem schwedischen Parlament, doch daraus entwickelte sich, angefacht durch Medienberichte, die weltweite Fridays-for-Future-Bewegung. In den ersten Tagen nach dem Angriff russischer Truppen auf die Ukraine im Februar 2022 waren die Schlagzeilen weniger davon bestimmt, wie viele Menschen in den russischen Städten dagegen demonstriert haben, sondern ob überhaupt Proteste stattfanden und wie lange es dauerte, bis diese von den Sicherheitskräften unterdrückt wurden. Mitte März 2022 wurden Menschen in Russland verhaftet, obwohl sie lediglich alleine mit leeren weißen Papierbögen auf der Straße standen. In China brachte diese Protestform des vermeintlichen Nicht-Protests mit weißen Blättern Ende November 2022 die Regierung dazu, binnen weniger Tage den restriktiven Zero-Covid-Kurs zu beenden. Diese Demonstrationen wurden selbst auf dem Höhepunkt nur von wenigen tausend Menschen getragen, waren zeitgleich jedoch über das ganze Land verteilt. Die räumliche Ausdehnung und zahlenmäßige Größe einer Demonstration sagt also nicht unbedingt etwas über den Rückhalt in der Bevölkerung aus, sondern kann auch ein Anhaltspunkt dafür sein, wie repressiv oder gut organisiert die Gegenseite ist (→ *Anti-Protestmaßnahmen*). Im Mai 1968 war die Zahl derer, die in Paris für Ruhe und Ordnung demonstrierten, also den Kurs der Regierung stützten, sogar größer als die der regierungskritischen Demonstrierenden, die den Rücktritt von Staatspräsident Charles de Gaulle forderten und auf der Seite der aufständischen Studierenden standen (Frei 2008/2018, S. 26; → *Mai '68*). In Österreich protestierten → *1984* mehr Menschen für den Bau eines Donaukraftwerks als dagegen (Rosenberger 2014, S. 6; → *Hainburger Au*). Die Umweltbewegung musste sich erst formieren, die gut organisierten Gewerkschaften hingegen sorgten sich um den Verlust von Arbeitsplätzen, sollte das Kraftwerksprojekt scheitern. Im öffentlichen Bewusstsein hingegen sind diese Gegendemonstrationen häufig nicht mehr präsent. Die Menge der Teilnehmenden ist nicht immer ein Gradmesser für den Erfolg von Demonstrationen und Protestbewegungen.

Ebenso vielfältig kann die räumliche Ausrichtung einer Demonstration organisiert sein. Oft gruppiert sich die Menge der Demonstrierenden dicht zueinander, seltener ist sie aufgereiht zu einer Menschenkette (→ *Greenham Common* → *1981*, → *Baltischer Weg* → *1989*) oder bedient sich beim Sternmarsch der Metapher des Zusammenfließens vieler Demonstrationszüge zu einem breiten Strom. Ist die Menschenkette als → *Blockade* formiert, kann sie eine Strategie vor Gegendemonstrationen sein, so beispielsweise seit 2010 jährlich in Dresden bei der symbolischen Abriegelung der Innenstadt gegen rechte Gedenkveranstaltungen zum Jahrestag der Bombardierung im Zweiten Weltkrieg. In solchen Fällen stehen sich zwei Demonstrationen gegenüber, die meist durch die Polizei getrennt gehalten werden (→ *Rechte Proteste*).

Dass der öffentliche Raum für Demonstrationen genutzt werden kann, ist in demokratischen Staaten durch die Versammlungsfreiheit geschützt. In Deutschland bestimmt das Grundgesetz, Art. 8, „das Recht, sich ohne Anmeldung oder Erlaubnis friedlich und ohne Waffen zu versammeln". Das nachrangige Versammlungsgesetz regelt zwar eine Anmeldepflicht gegenüber der Polizei, doch eine Demonstration braucht keine Genehmigung. Sie kann aber verboten werden, wobei hierzu der „Brokdorf-Beschluss" des Bundesverfassungsgerichts aus dem Jahr 1985 hohe Hürden gesetzt hat. Der Verlauf der Demonstrationsroute und damit die Sichtbarkeit oder auch Blockadewirkung von Demonstrationen sind häufig Gegenstand von Auseinandersetzungen mit der Polizei. Während der Corona-Pandemie mussten zudem Hygieneauflagen eingehalten werden, was aber durch die Deklarierung von unangemeldeten Demonstrationen als „Spaziergang" ausgehebelt wurde.

1985 wurde in Deutschland das Vermummungsverbot bei Demonstrationen eingeführt. Außerdem ist selbst die sogenannte passive Bewaffnung (etwa durch Säcke aus → *Stroh*) ein Straftatbestand. An bestimmten Orten sind in Deutschland Demonstrationen generell nicht erlaubt, hierzu zählen die Bannmeilen um den Bundestag, den Bundesrat, die Länderparlamente und um das Bundesverfassungsgericht sowie das Verbot der Beeinflussung in der Nähe von Wahllokalen.

Demonstrationen finden bisweilen selbst in Staaten, in denen Versammlungsfreiheit herrscht, spontan statt, da eine vorherige Ankündigung die Wirksamkeit einschränken würde. So etwa bei der Aktionsform der Critical Mass (z.B. indem viele Radfahrer sich verabreden, um Autos auszubremsen) oder bei Flashmobs (Personen finden ebenso schnell zu einer Aktion zusammen, wie sie danach wieder verschwinden). Veranstaltungen wie die Love Parade in Berlin oder der Christopher Street Day sind Sonderformen der Demonstration: Ursprünglich politisch motiviert, erinnern sie inzwischen eher an Umzüge. Auch die britischen Proteste unter dem Slogan → *Reclaim the Streets* ab → *1995* nutzten den öffentlichen Raum als Partyzone und blockierten den Autoverkehr, waren aber meist nicht als offizielle Demonstration angekündigt oder genehmigt. Der bunte, wild kostümierte Protest dieser Bewegung prägte zugleich die → *Anti-Globalisierungsbewegung*. Das Ziel, den öffentlichen Raum hedonistisch in Besitz zu nehmen und somit ein Gegenmodell zum passiven Konsum- oder reinen Verkehrsraum entstehen zu lassen, bringt die Partystimmung dieser Proteste in die Nähe der „konkreten Utopie" (Ernst Bloch). Es entsteht eine euphorisierte Atmosphäre, wie sie auch für viele Protestcamps prägend ist.

Wenn Demonstrationen verboten sind, aber dennoch stattfinden, können sie – wie im Falle der → *Madres de Plaza de Mayo* – einen jeweils spezifischen Umgang mit dem öffentlichen Raum entwickeln. Im Jahr 1989 beispielsweise boten die Kirchen wichtige Rückzugsräume für die Straßenproteste in der DDR. Private Nutzungsrechte an öffent-

Demo

lichen Flächen können verblüffenderweise Sicherheit gegenüber staatlichen Maßnahmen gewähren. So konnte sich beispielsweise → *Occupy Wall Street* nur deswegen als Protestcamp festsetzen, weil der Zuccotti Park dem Unternehmen Brookfield Properties gehört und damit dem Zugriff der Polizei zunächst entzogen war.

Die Fragen der Nutzung, Aneignung oder Verteidigung von Demonstrationsräumen können genauso vielfältig anhand der konkreten Objekte oder Verhaltensweisen diskutiert werden, die bei Demonstrationen zu finden sind. Das übliche Zubehör von Demonstrationen, sofern sie grundsätzlich erlaubt sind, umfasst → *Banner*, → *Protestschilder*, → *Fahnen* sowie Lautsprecher oder Megaphone zur Erzeugung eines akustischen Raums (→ *Musik*, → *Lärm*). Sind Demonstrationen dagegen verboten oder ist mit → *Gewalt* zu rechnen, so reagieren Demonstrierende mit bisweilen paradoxen Taktiken, z.B. mit → *Nacktheit* – einer Form des → *Körpereinsatzes* mit entwaffnender Wirkung. Auch → *Spiegel* können der Deeskalation dienen, denn sie sind fragil und sollen der Polizei ihr Auftreten buchstäblich vor Augen führen. Am anderen Ende des Spektrums stehen Maßnahmen zum → *Schutz* der Versammlung vor Gewalt durch Mittel der Gegenwehr (→ *Barrikade*, → *Schutzschild*, → *Kochtopf*). Ihre Wirkung ist architektonisch, weil sie der Schutz- oder Blockadefunktion von gebauten Strukturen entspricht. Dies alles als Protestarchitektur zu bezeichnen, da schwingt etwas Metaphorik mit, denn natürlich ist ein Helm etwas anderes als ein Dach über dem Kopf. Doch es finden sich bei Demonstrationen auch echte, nicht bloß metaphorische Kleinarchitekturen. Diese können durch → *Zweckentfremdung* von Mobilien zu Immobilien werden (→ *Fahrzeuge* bei den → *Farmers-Protesten* in Indien oder der → *„Freedom Convoy"* in Kanada). Objekte mit architektonischer Wirkung können auch eigens als demotaugliche „fliegende Bauten" hergestellt werden. Hierzu zählen → *Tripods* oder → *Tensegrity*-Strukturen. (OE)

Demonstration, Ger. → *Demonstration*. Most of the time, demonstrations are rapidly passing events. A demonstration rarely lasts longer than a day. If they are linked to a protest movement, they may be repeated regularly or in close succession (for example, like the Monday demonstrations in the GDR in 1989; the → *Saturday Mothers, Cumartesi Anneleri* in Turkish, since → *1995* in Istanbul; the 2022/2023 protests in Iran; or the 2023 protests in Israel). Sometimes → *protest camps* emerge from demonstrations, leading to a kind of "settling down" of previously wandering protesters, as in Cairo, when the occupation of → *Tahrir Square* developed from several demonstration marches. So if demonstrations are primarily mobile and temporary entities, what do they have to do with protest architecture at all?

Answers can be found on two different levels of consideration: on the one hand, in the analysis of space, i.e. the area where a demonstration takes place. Protest architecture is space-consuming; demonstrations also claim a conspicuous amount of → *public space*, otherwise no one would notice them. Moreover, questions of space are also questions of power: Who can occupy how much space? The second aspect of why demonstrations can also have an architectural component is demonstrable at the level of the objects and small-scale architecture that are sometimes carried along.

Let us first turn to the question of space: demonstrations take up a certain amount of space, usually on public squares and → *streets*. There is an inside and an outside: participants form the demonstration space, facing the spectators, counterdemonstrators, or the → *police*. However, it is not always about mass events. Demonstrations can be very small, even if their effectiveness is often measured by how many people participate. Greta Thunberg stood alone with her "Skolstrejk för klimatet" placard in front of the Swedish parliament for the first week, but it grew into the worldwide Fridays for Future movement, fueled by media reports. In the first days after Russian troops attacked Ukraine in

February 2022, the headlines were determined less by how many people demonstrated against this in Russian cities than by whether protests took place at all and how long it took for them to be suppressed by security forces. In mid-March 2022, people were arrested in Russia despite merely standing alone in the street with blank sheets of white paper. In late November 2022 in China, this form of protest by supposedly not protesting and holding white sheets of paper led the government to end its restrictive Zero Covid policy within a few days. Even at their peak, these demonstrations were supported by only a few thousand people, yet they were also spread across the entire country. The spatial extent and numerical size of a demonstration thus does not necessarily say anything about its popular support but can also be an indication of how repressive or well-organized the opposing side is ($\rightarrow$ *Anti-protest measures*). In May 1968, the number of people demonstrating for peace and order in Paris—that is, supporting the government's policy—was even larger than that of the anti-government demonstrators demanding the resignation of President Charles de Gaulle and siding with the rebellious students (Frei 2008/2018, p. 26; $\rightarrow$ *May '68*). In Austria, more people protested for the construction of a Danube power plant than against it in $\rightarrow$ *1984* (Rosenberger 2014, p. 6; $\rightarrow$ *Hainburger Au*). The environmental movement had to be formed first, while well-organized trade unions worry about job losses if, as in the above case, the power plant project fails. In the public consciousness, however, such counter-demonstrations are often no longer present. The number of participants is not always a measure of the success of demonstrations and protest movements.

The spatial orientation of a demonstration can be organized just as diversely. Often the crowd of demonstrators is grouped close to each other, more rarely it is lined up to form a human chain ($\rightarrow$ *Greenham Common Peace Camp* in $\rightarrow$ *1981*, $\rightarrow$ *Baltic Way* in $\rightarrow$ *1989*) or, in the case of demonstration marches from different starting points, converg-

es to form a broad stream. If the human chain is formed as a $\rightarrow$ *blockade*, it can be a strategy of counterdemonstrations, as for example in Dresden in the symbolic blockade of the city center against right-wing commemoration events on the anniversary of the bombing in World War II, which has taken place every year since 2010. In such cases, two demonstrations confront each other, usually kept apart by the police ($\rightarrow$ *Right-wing protests*).

The use of public space for demonstrations is protected in democratic states by the freedom of assembly. In Germany, the Basic Law, Article 8, stipulates that "all Germans shall have the right to assemble peacefully and unarmed without prior notification or permission." While the subordinate Public Meetings Act does regulate an obligation to register with the police, a demonstration does not require a permit. It can, however, be banned, though the Federal Constitutional Court's "Brokdorf Decision" of 1985 has set high hurdles in this regard. Demonstration routes and thus the visibility or even blocking effect of demonstrations is often the subject of disputes with the police. During the COVID-19 pandemic, health regulations also had to be observed, but this was undermined by declaring unannounced demonstrations to be "walks."

In 1985, the ban on face coverings at demonstrations was introduced in Germany. In addition, even so-called passive arming (for example, with bags of $\rightarrow$ *straw*) is a criminal offense. Demonstrations are generally not permitted in certain places in Germany, including the no-protest zones around the Bundestag, the Bundesrat, the state parliaments, and the Federal Constitutional Court, while there is also a ban on influencing near polling stations.

Demonstrations sometimes take place spontaneously, even in countries where there is freedom of assembly, because prior announcement would limit their effectiveness. This is the case, for example, with the Critical Mass form of action (where large groups of cyclists arrange to slow down cars) or with flash mobs (people coming together for an action just as quickly as they disappear again afterwards). Events such as the Love Parade in Berlin or Christopher Street Day are special forms of demonstration: originally politically motivated, they are now more reminiscent of parades. The British protests under the slogan → *Reclaim the Streets* from → *1995* also used public space as a party zone and blocked car traffic, but they were usually not announced or approved as official demonstrations. The colorful, wildly costumed protest of this movement simultaneously shaped the anti-globalization movement. The goal of taking hedonistic possession of public space, thus creating a counter-model to passive consumption or pure traffic spaces, brings the party atmosphere of these protests close to a "concrete utopia" (Ernst Bloch). A euphoric atmosphere is created, which is also characteristic of many protest camps.

When demonstrations are banned but still take place, they can—as in the case of the → *Madres de Plaza de Mayo*—each develop a specific way of dealing with public space. In 1989, for example, churches provided important spaces of retreat for street protests in the GDR. Private rights to use public spaces can, amazingly, provide security against state action. For example, → *Occupy Wall Street* was only able to establish its protest camp because Zuccotti Park belongs to the Brookfield Properties company and was thus initially withdrawn from police access.

The issues of using, appropriating, or defending demonstration spaces can be discussed in just as many ways based on the specific objects or behaviors found at demonstrations. The usual accessories of demonstrations, if they are allowed in principle, include → *banners*, → *protest placards*, → *flags*, and loudspeakers or megaphones to create an acoustic space (→ *Music*, → *Noise*). If, on the other hand, demonstrations are banned or if → *violence* is to be expected, demonstrators sometimes react with paradoxical tactics, such as with → *nakedness*, a form of → *body deployment* with dis-

arming effect. → *Mirrors*, too, can serve de-escalation due to their fragility and intended ability to literally show the police their appearance before their own eyes. At the other end of the spectrum are measures for the → *protection* of the assembly from violence by means of counter-defense (→ *Barricades*, → *Protective shield*, → *Cooking pot*). Their effect is architectural because they correspond to the protective or blocking function of built structures. To call all of this protest architecture involves a bit of metaphor—of course a helmet is different than a roof over one's head. However, there is also real and not merely metaphorical small-scale architecture in demonstrations. Through the → *misappropriation* of movables, this can turn into immovables (→ *Vehicles*, → *Farmers' protests* in India, or the → *"Freedom convoy"* in Canada). Objects with an architectural impact can also be specially produced for demonstrations, including → *tripods* or → *tensegrity* structures. (OE)

Denkmalschutz, engl. → *Heritage protection*, bezieht sich in erster Linie auf den Schutz von Kulturgütern wie historischen Gebäuden, Kunstwerken und Orten. Viele Länder haben spezielle Gesetze, die den Denkmalschutz regeln und die Erhaltung von kulturellem Erbe sicherstellen sollen. In einigen Fällen wurden identitätsstiftende Ereignisorte und Bauwerke, die mit Protesten zusammenhängen, zu Denkmälern. So zählt seit 1992 der natürlich belassene Ort, an dem das → *Protestcamp* des → *Schafschererstreiks* am Ufer des Lagoon Creek gestanden hatte, zum Kulturerbe von Queensland. In der Nähe des Frankfurter Flughafens erinnern die wieder aufgebaute Hüttenkirche und die von ihrem ursprünglichen Standort verschobenen Originalteile der berühmten Betonmauer an den Widerstand gegen die → *Startbahn West*. Diese wurden 2019 auf Initiative des Stadtmuseums Mörfelden-Walldorf und in Zusammenarbeit mit der Fraport AG wieder aufgestellt.

An Orten des Protests werden bisweilen → *archäologische Untersuchungen* durchgeführt, um Erkenntnisse darüber zu gewinnen, wie Protestcamps in der jüngeren Vergangenheit organisiert waren – so z.B. auf den Arealen des Schafschererstreiks (Egloff, O'Sullivan, Ramsay 1991), des → *Greenham Common Friedenscamps* (Schofield, Beck, Drollinger 2008) und des → *Endcliffe Protestcamps* (Badcock, Johnston 2009). Das Forschungsinteresse besteht darin herauszufinden, wo die genauen Standorte waren, welche → *Bautypen* und → *Siedlungsstrukturen* die Camps hatten und wie Raum genutzt und Landschaft – insbesondere bei langjährigen Camps – verändert wurde. Archäologische Untersuchungen von Protestcamps gewinnen in der deutschsprachigen Archäologie erst seit wenigen Jahren an Bedeutung. Sie gehören zum Forschungsfeld der Gegenwartsarchäologie, die nicht selten kritischer Bewertung und der Frage nach ihrer Sinnhaftigkeit ausgesetzt ist – wie im Fall der Ausgrabung in → *Gorleben* durch den Archäologen Attila Dézsi, der das entsprechende Areal als Kulturdenkmal diskutieren wollte (Dézsi 2018). 2019 lehnte das zuständige Landesamt für Denkmalpflege eine Eintragung in die Denkmalliste jedoch ab, da ein Bodendenkmal aus einer vergangenen Zeitepoche stammen müsse und die Ausgrabungsstätte außerdem nicht gefährdet sei. Bereits 1980 hatten Aktivist∗innen eine Ad-hoc-Unterschutzstellung des noch bestehenden Hüttendorfes in Gorleben als lebendes „Kulturdenkmal 1004" beantragt, was das Oberverwaltungsgericht allerdings ablehnte.

Um den jeweiligen Forderungen einen besonderen Ausdruck zu verleihen, findet bei Protesten nicht selten eine Aneignung oder → *Besetzung* von Plätzen und Bauwerken statt, die bereits Kulturdenkmäler sind oder solche beherbergen, wie z.B. der → *Tahrir-Platz* beim Arabischen Frühling oder die geschichtsträchtige Puerta del Sol bei → *Movimiento 15M*. Der Platz in Madrid hat durch die 15M-Bewegung eine Erweiterung seiner Bedeutung erhalten, an die seit 2021 auch eine Plakette erinnert. „El pueblo de Madrid, en reconocimiento al movimiento 15M que tuvo su

origen en esta Puerta del Sol. Dormíamos, despertamos" („Die Bevölkerung von Madrid, in Anerkennung der 15M-Bewegung, die an dieser Puerta del Sol ihren Ursprung hatte. Wir schliefen, wir wachten auf"), heißt es auf der Tafel, auf der auch das Wappen der Stadtverwaltung Madrid abgebildet ist.

Proteste können auch dazu beitragen, den Wert und die Bedeutung eines Bauwerks in das öffentliche Bewusstsein zu rücken und den Denkmalschutz zu fordern, wie im Mai 1968 in Wien, als gegen den Abriss der Stadtbahnstationen von Otto Wagner demonstriert wurde. Eine kritische Hinterfragung von Denkmälern hingegen kann zum → *Denkmalsturz* führen, so etwa bei Protesten von → *Black Lives Matter* in Bristol (UK) und Richmond (USA). (JD)

Denkmalsturz. Fortune Méaull (nach einer Zeichnung von Daniel Vierge): Sturz der Vendôme-Säule in Paris am 16. Mai 1871, Holzstich, Paris 1874 (Toppling monuments. Fortune Méaull (after a drawing by Daniel Vierge): Toppling the Vendôme Column in Paris on May 16, 1871, wood engraving, Paris 1874)

Denkmalsturz, engl. → *Toppling monuments*. Im Zuge der wachsenden Sensibilität für Fragen des kolonialistischen

Dest

Erbes und der Anerkennung bislang marginalisierter Kulturen wurden in den letzten Jahren viele Denkmäler zu Fall gebracht. In Bristol (UK) und Richmond (USA) stieß die transnationale Bürger∗innenrechtsbewegung → *Black Lives Matter* → *2020* etwa die Monumente für den englischen Kaufmann Edward Colston, der seinen Reichtum durch Sklav∗innenhandel erworben hatte, und den amerikanischen Präsidenten Jefferson Davis, der die Sklaverei befürwortet hatte, vom Sockel. Die → *Zerstörung* von Statuen und Denkmälern ist allerdings kein neues Phänomen: Politischer Ikonoklasmus und Bildersturm wurden schon in der Antike betrieben, um den Verlust von Macht und Bedeutung symbolisch sichtbar zu machen oder um eine vergangene Herrschaft – im Sinne einer *Damnatio memoriae* – dauerhaft aus der Erinnerung zu tilgen. In der Neuzeit verbanden sich Denkmalstürze vermehrt mit Revolutionen und Aufständen. So wurde während der → *Pariser Kommune* am 16. Mai → *1871* die *Colonne Vendôme* gestürzt: Für die Kommunard∗innen verkörperte die zwischen 1806 und 1810 errichtete und von einer Statue Napoleons gekrönte Siegessäule die Tyrannei des Kaisertums und den Verrat an den revolutionären Idealen. Neben Denkmälern mit Herrscherbildern und anderen Insignien der Macht wurden immer wieder auch Bauwerke eingenommen, besetzt, beschädigt und teilweise zerstört, die – wie die Bastille in Paris während der Französischen Revolution 1789 oder die Berliner Mauer 1989 – mit politischen Systemen in Verbindung gebracht wurden. Ein Sonderfall ist die → *Kapitol-Attacke* → *2021*. Umgekehrt ist allerdings auch immer wieder für den Erhalt von Bauwerken und Denkmälern protestiert worden (→ *Frankfurter Häuserkampf*, → *Denkmalschutz*). Um eine gleichsam diskursiv betreuten Denkmalsturz handelt es sich bei der Umgestaltung des seit langem in der Kritik stehenden Ehrenmals für Karl Lueger, dem antisemitischen Bürgermeister der Stadt Wien von 1897 bis 1910: Nach der temporären Überschreibung durch → *Graffitis* soll in einem mehrstufigen Verfahren eine dauerhafte „künstlerische Kontextualisierung" für das Denkmal gefunden werden. (SH)

Destruction, Ger. → *Zerstörung*. Protests and → *demonstrations* sometimes leave the impression of destruction and devastation. However, what is often sweepingly referred to in the news as vandalism can have completely different causes. Random damage to building facades, shop windows, street furniture, and vehicles often occurs when peaceful protests escalate into violent clashes. During armed street clashes (→ *Violence*, → *Street*), protesters have repeatedly taken refuge behind → *barricades* (→ *Protection*), which were usually erected at short notice and consisted of a wide variety of objects, most of which were destroyed in the process. In the past, the pavement was often torn up and turned into → *building materials* for the barricades or used as a projectile (→ *Cobblestone*, → *Weapons*). The supposedly blind and predominantly illegal destruction of things—for example, by setting a → *fire*—can, however, also appear as a proven means of creating meaning: in a society in which hardly anything is protected as well as property, it can represent an intended provocation. The destruction of images of rulers, emblems of sovereignty, and memorials constitutes a targeted attack on the symbols of power that must inevitably be seen as an affront. The toppling of monuments (→ *Toppling monuments*) and the burning of → *flags* are deliberately chosen strategies that are usually staged to serve the → *media* and guarantee the protests special attention. (SH)

Die-in, engl. → *Die-in*. Während sich Demonstrierende bei einem → *Sit-in* hinsetzen, legen sie sich bei einem Die-in so, als wären sie tot, auf den Boden (→ *Körpereinsatz*). Bei den → *Black-Lives-Matter*-Protesten blieben Aktivist∗innen acht Minuten und sechsundvierzig Sekunden lang liegen – so lange drückte im Mai 2020 ein Polizist sein Knie auf den Hals von George Floyd, bis er starb. (JD)

Die-in, Ger. → *Die-in (fig.)*. While demonstrators sit down at a → *sit-in*, at

134

a die-in they lie down demonstratively on the public ground as if dead (→ *Body deployment*). As part of → *Black Lives Matter*, activists lay down for eight minutes and forty-six seconds—the amount of time a police officer pressed his knee on George Floyd's neck until he died in May 2020. (JD)

Die-in. Fibonacci Blue: Protest gegen die Misshandlung von Marcus Abrams durch die Polizei, St. Paul, Minnesota, 20. September 2015 (Die-in. Fibonacci Blue: Protest against the police's physical mistreatment of Marcus Abrams, St. Paul, Minnesota, September 20, 2015)

Digitale Medien, engl. → *Digital media.* „Die jahrtausendealte Distanz zwischen Tat und Rede, Geschehen und Zeugnis ist geschrumpft", so hat Roland Barthes jene Medienrevolution beschrieben, die er in den Barrikadennächten des → *Mai '68* in Paris beobachten konnte (→ *Medien,* → *Barrikade*). In deren Zentrum stand das Transistorradio, das, mit gesenktem Blick ans Ohr gepresst, für die Protestierenden auf den → *Straßen* „zum Körperfortsatz, zur Hörprothese, zum neuen Sciencefiction-Organ" geworden war (Barthes 1968/2006, S. 174). Bereits im Moment des Geschehens informierte sie der Rundfunk über die Effekte ihrer Aktionen wie über die Reaktionen der Sicherheitskräfte – eine instantane Medialisierung des Protests, die Ereignis und Berichterstattung in einer Rückkopplungsschleife kurzschloss (→ *Fernseher*).

Proteste sind Medienereignisse: Sie lassen sich nicht trennen von den Nachrichten, die über sie zirkulieren und die sowohl ihre Wahrnehmung als auch ihren Verlauf mitbestimmen. Was im Pariser Mai 1968 das Transistorradio war, ist heute das Smartphone, und Videos und Kurzmitteilungen auf dem Display haben die Stimme aus dem Äther ersetzt. Doch wo im Pariser Mai nur Botschaften empfangen werden konnten, die das Massenmedium Radio an alle aussandte, sind heute nahezu alle Teilnehmenden eines Protestgeschehens zugleich miteinander vernetzte Sender: Knotenpunkte digitaler Informationsströme, die sie teilen, kommentieren und mit weiteren Informationen anreichern. Digitale Medien stellen so nicht allein eine Etappe jenes fortschreitenden Distanzverlusts zwischen Geschehen und Zeugnis dar, die Barthes so faszinierte, sie haben in den letzten gut zwei Jahrzehnten die Dynamiken und Formen politischen Protests fundamental verändert.

Mit einigem Recht hat man den Arabischen Frühling von 2010 / → *2011* auch als „Facebook-Revolution" bezeichnet: In Facebookgruppen mit Zehntausenden von Mitgliedern konnten Demonstrationsaufrufe (→ *Demonstration*) mit zuvor unbekannter Geschwindigkeit und Reichweite zirkulieren, und auch bei der Koordination der Massenproteste spielten soziale Medien, E-Mail und SMS eine zentrale Rolle. Nicht zuletzt zeigten die Aufstände die neue Rolle der Bilder unter digital vernetzten Bedingungen: Bei den Straßenprotesten etwa auf dem Kairoer → *Tahrir-Platz* waren Digitalkameras und Mobiltelefone allgegenwärtig, und über Facebook, Twitter und YouTube verbreiteten sich Aufnahmen der Demonstrationen wie der gewalttätigen Reaktionen der Sicherheitskräfte in Windeseile weit über Ägypten hinaus.

Protestkulturen im digitalen Zeitalter, so hat es Kerstin Schankweiler beschrieben, werden wesentlich durch digitale Bilder mobilisiert und konstituiert: Handyaufnahmen, die in sozialen Medien zirkulieren, bezeugen die Stärke und Mobilisierungskraft einer Bewegung wie die Brutalität ihrer Gegner, sie erzeugen Sichtbarkeit für das, was in den Massenmedien ansonsten unsichtbar bliebe, und stiften global vernetzte „Affektgemeinschaften", aus denen heraus neue Formen der Solidarität erwachsen können. Hashtags wie #BlackLivesMatter oder jüngst #MahsaAmini, der Name der jungen Kurdin, deren gewaltsamer Tod in Polizeigewahrsam 2022 die Proteste im Iran auslöste, dienen dabei als digitale Anker, die verteilte Bilderströme bündeln und verstreute Akteur∗innen vernetzen. Als hybride „Bildproteste" lassen sich die Ereignisse auf der Straße und ihr visuelles Echo in den sozialen Medien kaum mehr voneinander trennen: „Digitale und analoge Formen des Protests stehen also nicht nebeneinander, sie durchdringen einander" (Schankweiler 2019, S. 57).

Kaum ein Ereignis hat diese Durchdringung von physischen und virtuellen Räumen so eindrücklich vor Augen geführt wie die Ereignisse vom 6. Januar → *2021*. Der sogenannte „Sturm aufs Kapitol" war nicht zuletzt ein „digitales Bildereignis" (Pratschke 2022; → *Kapitol-Attacke*). Tatsächlich wirkte es so, als sei die Echtzeit-Dokumentation des Vordringens der Trump-Anhänger∗innen in die Zentren der Macht das eigentliche Ziel ihres Aufstands. Wolfgang Ullrich hat davon gesprochen, hier fände ein „Re-Enactment von Plots und Phantasien" statt (Ullrich 2021), die zuvor bereits in Chatgruppen und auf Messageboards kollektiv entworfen worden waren. Am 6. Januar brachen diese virtuell gezüchteten faschistischen Umsturzimaginationen in den physischen Raum ein, und wie zur Bestätigung der hybriden Realität des Ereignisses wurden die dabei produzierten Bilder in unzähligen Livestreams instantan wieder in digitale Kommunikationsnetze eingespeist (→ *Kommunikation*).

Als Bildereignis wird ein Aufstands- oder Protestgeschehen aber auch in neuartiger Weise digital kontrollierbar. Nicht zuletzt angesichts des zunehmenden Einsatzes automatisierter Gesichtserkennung erscheint Sichtbarkeit in sozialen Medien überaus riskant (vgl. Meyer 2021). Bereits bei den Massenprotesten in → *Hongkong* → *2019* setzten sich die Protestierenden mittels Masken, Regenschirmen, Laserpointern

und Farbspray (→ *Erkennungszeichen*) gegen Überwachungskameras zur Wehr oder brachten sie mit Sägen und → *Seilen* zu Fall. Doch mittlerweile kann jede Smartphone-Kamera zur unfreiwilligen Zeugin der Anklage werden, sobald Behörden Zugriff auf die Bilder erhalten, die sie aufgenommen hat und die im Netz zirkulieren. Den Demonstrierenden der → *Black-Lives-Matter*-Proteste → *2020* war diese Gefahr überaus bewusst, und speziell für sie stellte die Messenger-App Signal im Jahr 2020 eine neue Funktion vor: „Blur faces" erlaubt es seitdem, auf jedem Bild, das mit der App verschickt wird, automatisch alle Gesichter mit einem Unschärfefilter zu maskieren. Die Maske, vielleicht eines der ältesten Medien subversiven Protests, erlebte damit ihr digitales Update. (Roland Meyer)

Digitale Medien. Werbung für die Anonymisierungssoftware des Messenger-Dienstes Signal, USA 2020 (Digital media. Ad for anonymization software by the Signal messenger app, USA 2020)

Digital media, Ger. → *Digitale Medien (fig.)*. "The age-old distance between act and discourse, event and testimony, was reduced," Roland Barthes wrote of the media revolution he witnessed in Paris during the nights of the barricades in → *May '68* (→ *Media*, → *Barricade*). At its center was the transistor radio, which for the protesters in the → *streets*, their eyes down, their ears glued to the device, "became the bodily appendage, the auditory prosthesis, the new science-fiction organ" (Barthes 1968/1989, p. 150). As the events unfolded, the radio informed them about the effects of their actions and the security forces' reactions, thereby fusing the incident and its coverage in a feedback loop through this instantaneous media coverage (→ *Television set*).

Protests are media events: they cannot be separated from the news circulating about them, which has a defining impact not only on their perception but also on their progress. What the transistor radio was to the Parisian May of 1968 the smartphone is to modern-day protests, and the voice from the ether has been replaced by videos and text messages on displays. But while the protesters in Paris were only able to receive the messages the mass medium of radio sent to all its listeners, virtually all participants in contemporary → *demonstrations* are also interconnected transmitters: hubs of digital streams of information they share, comment on, and supplement with further information. Digital media are thus not only a stage in the ongoing reduction between act and discourse that was so fascinating to Barthes, but have also fundamentally changed the dynamics and forms of political protest over the past two decades.

With some justification, the Arab Spring of 2010 / → *2011* has also been described as a "Facebook revolution": Facebook groups with tens of thousands of members enabled calls for demonstration to circulate with previously unknown speed and outreach. Likewise, social media, email, and text messaging played a key role in the coordination of the mass protests. Notably, the uprisings manifested the new role of images under interconnected circumstances: during street protests at sites such as → *Tahrir Square* in Cairo, digital cameras and mobile phones were ubiquitous, and via Facebook, Twitter, and YouTube shots of the demonstrations, as well as the security forces' violent reactions, spread beyond Egypt in next to no time.

Protest cultures in the digital age are largely mobilized and constituted through digital images, as Kerstin Schankweiler has explained: mobile shots circulating in social media testify to the strength and mobilizing power of a movement, but also to the brutality of its opponents, they reveal details that would otherwise remain invisible in the mass media and generate globally connected "affect communities" from which new forms of solidarity can grow. Hashtags such as #BlackLivesMatter, or more recently, #MahsaAmini, the name of the young Kurdish woman whose violent death in police custody triggered the 2022 protests in Iran, serve as digital anchors which bundle shared image streams and connect scattered activists. As hybrid "image protests" the events on the streets and their visual echoes are almost inseparable in social media: "digital and analog forms of protest are thus not parallel occurrences, they permeate each other" (Schankweiler 2019, p. 57).

Practically no other incident has encapsulated this permeation of physical and virtual spaces as profoundly as the events of January 6, → *2021*. The so-called "storm on the Capitol" was not least a "digital image event" (Pratschke 2022; → *Capitol attack*). By all appearances, the advance on the centers of power in real time seemed to be the Trump supporters' true aim. Wolfgang Ullrich spoke of a "re-enactment of plots and fantasies" (Ullrich 2021) previously conceived as collective efforts in chat groups and on message boards. On January 6, these virtually spawned visions of a fascist coup broke into physical space, and like a confirmation of the hybrid reality of the event, the images produced in the process were instantly fed into digital communication networks via numerous livestreams (→ *Communication*).

However, as an image event, an uprising or a protest also encompasses novel means of digital control. Not least because of the increasing use of automatic facial recognition, visibility in social media seems especially risky (see Meyer 2021). During the mass protests in

→ *Hong Kong* in → *2019*, protesters resisted surveillance cameras with masks, umbrellas, laser pointers, and spray paint (→ *Identifier*), or took them down with saws and → *ropes*. At this point, however, any smartphone camera can become an involuntary witness for the prosecution once authorities gain access to the images taken with it and circulated on the internet. The demonstrators of the → *Black Lives Matter* protests of → *2020* were aware of this danger, and for them, the messenger app Signal provided a new function in the same year: since then, the "blur tool" has enabled the automatic masking of faces on every image sent with the app. The mask, perhaps one of the oldest instruments of subversive protest, has thus undergone a digital update. (Roland Meyer)

Dresden May Uprising, Ger. → *Dresdner Maiaufstand*. Democratically motivated protests had already erupted in Saxony during the → *March Revolution* of 1848. However, it was not until May → *1849* that Dresden also became the site of a popular revolt, in which not only the Russian revolutionary Mikhail Bakunin but also the court music director Richard Wagner and the director of the Dresden Building Academy, the architect Gottfried Semper, were involved. The latter made a significant contribution to the cause with his conception of the defensive → *barricade* in the city center, the so-called → *Semper barricade*. (SH)

Dresdner Maiaufstand, engl. → *Dresden May Uprising*. Schon im Rahmen der → *Märzrevolution* von 1848 hatte es in Sachsen demokratisch motivierte Proteste gegeben, aber erst im Mai → *1849* brach auch in Dresden ein Volksaufstand aus, an dem neben dem russischen Revolutionär Michail Bakunin auch der damalige Hofkapellmeister Richard Wagner sowie der Direktor der Dresdener Bauschule – der Architekt Gottfried Semper – beteiligt waren. Letzterer engagierte sich nicht zuletzt durch die Konzeption einer wehrhaften → *Barrikade* im Stadtzentrum, der so-genannten → *Semper-Barrikade*. (SH)

Dumping, Ger. → *Abschütten (fig.)*. A

strategy repeatedly seen in the context of farmers' protests is to dump food on public → *streets* and squares. (SH)

Dying water, Ger. → *Wasser einfärben (fig.)*. Dying lakes, rivers, brooks, canals, and fountains is a → *guerrilla tactic* that is increasingly popular during protests and → *demonstrations*. In Vienna, Austria, to coincide with the 16th European Gas Conference in March 2023, the tactic was used when the Danube Canal and several fountains downtown were dyed green using a chemical die called uranine as part of a protest action. The protests were triggered by the greenwashing tactics of the politicians, financial experts, and businesspeople at the conference with regards to the continued use of fossil fuels. (SH)

Earth shelter, Ger. → *Erdhaus*; → *Building types*, → *Gorleben*, → *Startbahn West*

EDSA-Revolution, engl. → *EDSA Revolution*. Komplett gewaltlose politische Bewegung auf den Philippinen, die innerhalb von nur vier Tagen zum Sturz des Diktators Ferdinand Marcos führte, der seit 1965 Präsident war. Der Name bezieht sich auf die „Epifanio de los Santos Avenue" (EDSA), eine der Hauptverkehrsadern von Manila, Hauptstadt der Philippinen. Am 22. Februar → *1986* strömten Hunderttausende als menschliche Schilde auf die → *Straßen* und blockierten auf der EDSA Marcos' Truppen (→ *Blockade*, → *Demonstration*, → *Körpereinsatz*): Es kam zum Stillstand, der vor Ort als „People Power" in die Geschichte einging. (JD)

EDSA Revolution, Ger. → *EDSA-Revolution*. In only four days, this completely nonviolent political movement in the Philippines led to the overthrow of dictator Ferdinand Marcos, who had been president since 1965. The name refers to Epifanio de los Santos Avenue (EDSA), one of the Philippine capital Manila's major arterials. On February 22, → *1986*, hundreds of thousands flocked to the → *streets* as human shields and blocked Marcos's troops on the EDSA (→ *Blockade*, → *Demonstration*, → *Body deployment*). The action led to a standstill which went down in local history as "People Power." (JD)

Eis, engl. → *Ice*; → *Majdan*

Endcliffe Protestcamp, engl. → *Endcliffe protest camp*. Eine bis zu 80 Menschen umfassende Gruppe besetzte → *1999* in Derbyshire, Großbritannien, ein 13 Hektar großes Waldgebiet, um den Sandsteinabbau zu verhindern. Das → *Protestcamp* bestand aus verschiedenen Bodenstrukturen und Brücken, welche → *Baumhäuser* miteinander verbanden. Mit der Zeit verstetigte sich die → *Siedlungsstruktur* mit eigener → *Infrastruktur* und offizieller Postleitzahl. Es bestand zehn Jahre, damit war es eines der langlebigsten Protestcamps in Europa (Badcock, Johnston 2009). (JD)

Endcliffe protest camp, Ger. → *Endcliffe Protestcamp*. In → *1999* a group of close on 80 people occupied a 32-acre piece of forest in Derbyshire, Great Britain, to prevent sandstone quarrying. The → *protest camp* consisted of various ground structures and bridges that connected → *tree houses*. Over time, the → *settlement structure* became increasingly established with its own → *infrastructure* and an official zip code. It lasted ten years and was thus one of the most enduring protest camps in Europe (Badcock, Johnston 2009). (JD)

Erdhaus, engl. → *Earthshelter*; → *Bautypen*, → *Gorleben*, → *Startbahn West*

Erkennungszeichen, engl. → *Identifier*, dienen dazu, sich als Teilnehmer*in oder Unterstützer*in einer Protestbewegung zu erkennen zu geben. In den unterschiedlichen Kontexten von Alltag, Massenmedien und den Protesten selbst können dabei jeweils eine Vielzahl verschiedener Dinge als Zeichen dienen: von den klassischen Insignien der Gegenkultur wie Plakaten, Buttons, Aufklebern, → *Graffitis* und Aufnähern (→ *Medien*, → *Ikone*) über teils selbstgemachte, teils professionell beauftragte → *Fahnen*, Flaggen, → *Banner* und → *Protestschilder* bis zu bedruckten T-Shirts, Taschen und anderen, bisweilen auch modischen Accessoires, etwa der im Zuge des Nahostkonflikts im deutschen Sprachraum als Palästinensertuch bekannt gewordenen Kufiya oder Kefije (→ *Kleidung*). Oft wird dieses materielle Zubehör zum Symbol der Protestbewegungen wie die Guy-Fawkes-Maske für die → *Occupy-Wall-Street*-Bewegung → *2011*, die Regenschirme für die → *Hongkong-Proteste* → *2014* oder die für Autofahrer*innen seit 2008 verpflichtenden Warnwesten für die französische → *Gelbwestenbewegung* → *2018/2019*. Durch einheitliche Kleidungsstücke wie weiße → *Overalls* und → *Kostüme* – oder auch kollektive → *Nacktheit* – werden oft besonders medienwirksame Bilder von → *Demonstrationen* oder → *Platzbesetzungen* erzielt. Auch jenseits der realen, physischen Anwesenheit bei Protesten (→ *Körpereinsatz*) signalisieren bestimmte Gesten, → *Handzeichen*, Choreografien oder das Singen von Protestsongs (→ *Musik*) die Zugehörigkeit oder Zustimmung zu den → *Protestzielen* (→ *Kommunikation*). (SH)

Erkennungszeichen. Guy-Fawkes-Maske (nach David Lloyds Illustrationen für die Graphic Novel *V for Vendetta*), um 2010
(Identifier. Guy Fawkes mask (after David Lloyd's illustrations for the graphic novel *V for Vendetta*), around 2010)

Fahne, engl. → *Flag*. Fahnen markieren Territorien, tatsächlich oder metaphorisch. Daher sind die an sich diskreten Textilien ein eminent räumliches Protestwerkzeug. Bei → *Demonstrationen* dienen Fahnen der Lufthoheit: Ein

Meer von gleichen Fahnen signalisiert Einstimmigkeit. Im teils militant mit der → *Polizei* ausgefochtenen Kampf gegen Mietwucher, Gebäudeleerstand und Immobilienspekulation wurde von der Hausbesetzer∗innenszene häufig die schwarz-rote Fahne gehisst, wie etwa in den 1980ern im Hamburger Schanzenviertel. Diese Fahne ist ein → *Erkennungszeichen* autonomer linker Gruppierungen und wird politisch mit sozialrevolutionären und anarcho-kommunistischen Einstellungen verbunden. (SH)

Fahne. Mike Schröder: Besetzung im Schanzenviertel, Hamburg, 9. August 1987 (Flag. Mike Schröder: Squat in Schanzenviertel, Hamburg, August 9, 1987)

Fahrzeuge, engl. → *Vehicles*, spielen als sich bewegende oder stillstehende Objekte bei ganz unterschiedlichen Protestformen eine wichtige Rolle. Bei → *Demonstrationen* sind Autos, Paradewagen und Showtrucks gleichzeitig Träger von Botschaften (→ *Medien*) und Hilfsmittel für den Transport von Soundanlage und Verpflegung. Ein Protestfloß mit der Aufschrift „Schiff & Bahn statt Straßenwahn" hatte 1996 bei Protesten gegen den Bau der Bundesstraße 31 in Breisach eine ähnliche Vorbildwirkung wie das Fahrrad bei Fahrraddemonstrationen. Aufgrund der großen Masse von Fahrzeugen sind Traktorendemonstrationen (→ *Zwentendorf*, → *Farmers-Proteste*) und → *Flotillas*, Rallyes mit Booten oder „Kayaktivists" (Aktivist∗innen in Kajaks), besonders wirkungsvoll. Bei → *Blockaden* wie dem → *„Freedom Convoy"* → *2022* in Kanada stören Trucks nicht nur den Verkehr, sondern

erregen durch die exzessive Benutzung von Autohupen zusätzlich Aufmerksamkeit (→ *Lärm*). Traktoren boten den Farmer∗innen in Delhi eine Unterkunft innerhalb der Blockade und versorgten die Bewegung mit dem mitgebrachten Transportgut. Auch Wagenburgen bestehen aus mobilen Elementen wie Wohnwagen oder Anhängern, die jedoch im Normalfall nur selten bewegt werden. Geparkte Autos werden bei Protesten im → *öffentlichen Raum* nicht nur beschmiert (→ *Graffiti*), beschädigt (→ *Zerstörung*), verbrannt (→ *Feuer*) oder in triumphaler Geste eingenommen (→ *G20-Proteste* → *2017* in Hamburg), sie können auch als → *Baumaterial* für → *Barrikaden* dienen, ähnlich wie Kutschen und Wagen bei Protesten im 19. Jahrhundert (Revolutionen von → *1848*). Aktivist∗innen der → *Protestorganisation* Extinction Rebellion protestierten 2022 bei einer Automesse in Paris gegen Greenwashing in der Autoindustrie, indem sie sich an den neuesten Sportwagen festklebten (→ *Ankleben*). Auch die → *Polizei* nutzt Fahrzeuge bei Protesten, z.B. → *Wasserwerfer* oder den mobilen „Skywatch"-Überwachungsturm bei → *Occupy Wall Street*. (AMM)

Fahrzeuge. Siggi Held: Floß bei Protesten gegen Bau der Bundesstraße 31, Breisach, 1996 (Vehicles. Siggi Held: Raft during protests against the construction of Bundesstraße 31, Breisach, 1996)

Farmers-Proteste, engl. → *Farmers' protests*. Im November → *2020* entstanden auf drei wichtigen Zufahrtstraßen von Delhi kilometerlange → *Protestcamps*. Zehntausende Farmer∗innen aus verschiedenen Regionen des Landes fuhren mit ihren Traktoren in die Hauptstadt (→*Fahrzeuge*), um gegen drei umstrittene Agrargesetze zu protestieren, deren Einführung die garantierten Mindestpreise für Getreide abschaffen und den Handel liberalisieren würde. Als die Traktorenkonvoys die Grenzen von Delhi erreichten, kam es zu gewaltsamen Zusammenstößen mit der →*Polizei* (→*Gewalt*). Diese setzte →*Wasserwerfer* ein und installierte →*Barrikaden*, um zu verhindern, dass die Farmer*innen in die Hauptstadt vordringen. Daraufhin blockierten die Protestierenden die sonst vielbefahrenen Autobahnen (→*Blockade*). Sie stellten →*Zelte* auf und bauten ihre Anhänger und LKWs in Unterkünfte um. Nach mehr als einem Jahr beendeten die Farmer*innen die Proteste und kehrten in ihre Heimatdörfer zurück, nachdem der indische Premierminister Narendra Modi im November 2021 die Gesetzesvorlage zurückgezogen hatte.

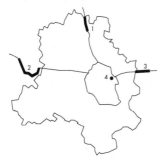

Farmers-Proteste. 1 Protestcamp Singhu-Grenze 2 Protestcamp Tikri-Grenze 3 Protestcamp Ghazipur-Grenze 4 Rotes Fort (Farmers' protests. 1 Singhu border protest camp 2 Tikri border protest camp 3 Ghazipur border protest camp 4 Red Fort)

Die Politikwissenschaftlerin Natasha Behl beschäftigt sich seit Jahren mit der indischen Politik und forscht an der Arizona State University u.a. zur Frage von *Race*, Gender und sozialen Bewegungen. Sie beobachtete die Proteste aus der Ferne und veröffentlichte 2022 einen Artikel in der *American Political Science Review*, in dem sie die Hintergründe beleuchtet:

*Im September 2020 verabschiedete das indische Parlament drei Gesetze zur Agrarreform, die die Preisgestaltung, den Verkauf und die Lagerung von landwirtschaftlichen Erzeugnissen betreffen. [...] Viele Farmer*innen befürchteten, dass die Reformen die Preise für ihre Produkte senken, Anreize für die gezielte Verknappung lebenswichtiger Güter schaffen und ein wichtiges soziales Sicherungsnetz beseitigen würden. [...] Als Reaktion darauf forderten die protestierenden Farmer*innen, dass die Zentralregierung die drei Landwirtschaftsgesetze aufhebt und einen nationalen MSP-Index [Mindestpreisindex] für landwirtschaftliche Produkte einführt. [...] Am 26. November 2020 starteten die Proteste landesweit mit zwei unterschiedlichen Organisationstaktiken. Zum einen schlossen sich die Farmer*innen mit den Gewerkschaften zu einem massiven landesweiten eintägigen Streikbündnis zusammen, an dem sich 250 Millionen Menschen beteiligten (Joy 2020). Außerdem nahmen Zehntausende von Farmer*innen aus Punjab, Haryana, Uttar Pradesh, Madhya Pradesh und Rajasthan an dem Marsch „Delhi chalo" („Auf nach Delhi") teil. Die überwiegend friedlichen Demonstrant*innen sahen sich einer schwer bewaffneten Polizei gegenüber, die sie an den Grenzen zwischen Punjab und Haryana sowie zwischen Haryana und Delhi mit Tränengas, Schlagstöcken und Wasserwerfern attackierte (Slater 2020). [...]*

*Dennoch marschierten die Farmer*innen nach zwei Tagen in Delhi ein und errichteten Protestcamps um Rande der Stadt. Mehr als ein Jahr lang organisierten die Farmer*innen Sit-ins mit etwa 300 000 Beteiligten, die sich außerhalb Delhis an den Grenzen von Tikri, Singhu und Ghazipur versammelten (Sandhu 2021). Die Farmer*innen konfrontierten die Regierung auch mit gewaltfreien Aktionen, indem sie unter anderem die Häuser von Politiker*in-*

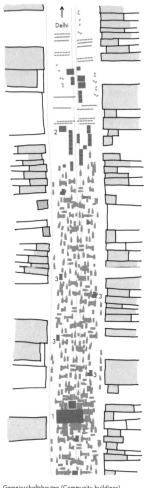

■ Gemeinschaftsbauten (Community buildings)
■ Individuelle Unterkünfte (Individual shelters)
■ Polizeibarrieren (Police barriers)

Farmers-Proteste. 1 Versammlungshalle
2 Bühne 3 Essensstand (Farmers' protests.
1 Assembly hall 2 Stage 3 Food stand)

nen umstellten, Regierungsgebäude blockierten, Mautstellen lahmlegten und Eisenbahnlinien unterbrachen (Dubal, Gill 2020). [...] Die BJP-Regierung reagierte auf die anhaltenden Proteste, indem sie militärisch gesicherte Grenzen um die Protestcamps errichtete und Hunderte von Demonstrant∗innen verhaftete (BBC 2021). [...]

Obwohl die Mehrheit der protestierenden Farmer∗innen Sikhs sind, schlossen sich auch Hindus, Muslim∗innen, Christ∗innen und Buddhist∗innen an (Mander 2021), und ihre Protestformen spiegeln diese Vielfalt wider. Die Farmer∗innen haben sich an Mahatma Gandhis Prinzipien der Gewaltlosigkeit [...] und an Sikh-Traditionen [...] orientiert, insbesondere an Langar (Gemeinschaftsküche), Shahidi (Märtyrertum) und Seva (Dienst) (Singh 2014). Zum Beispiel [...] versorgte mindestens ein Sikh-Tempel nach Zusammenstößen mit der Polizei trotzdem die Beamten, die noch immer in Einsatzkleidung gekleidet waren (Ghazali 2020). [...]

Der Protest der Farmer∗innen hat, wenn auch nur für kurze Zeit, eine integrative Demokratie geschaffen, zu der die Protestcamps ebenso wie ihre ländlichen Unterstützungsnetzwerke gehörten. In den Camps wurden grundlegende öffentliche Dienstleistungen wie Schulen und Bibliotheken, Kunst und Musik sowie medizinische und zahnärztliche Versorgung für alle zugänglich gemacht (Economic Times 2020). Die Gemeinschaftsküchen verpflegten Hunderttausende von Menschen unabhängig von Religion, Klasse, Kaste oder Geschlecht, wodurch die Kastenregeln untergraben und heterogene Koalitionen gebildet wurden. Wenn möglich, wurden Entscheidungen kollektiv von einer gemeinsamen Leitung getroffen, die von verschiedenen Mitgliedsgewerkschaften repräsentiert wurde (Sharma 2020). Über die Protestcamps hinaus haben Dörfer in ganz Punjab und Haryana die Demonstrant∗innen unterstützt, indem sie lebenswichtige Güter lieferten und rotierende Gruppen von Protestteilnehmer∗innen organisierten (Sethi 2021). Und Familien haben sich bereit erklärt, ihre Zeit zwischen der Arbeit auf den Feldern und der Teilnahme an den Protestcamps aufzuteilen (Mander 2021). [...]

Der Beitrag der Frauen zum Farmer*innenprotest wurde mit Schlagzeilen gefeiert, die verkündeten, dass Frauen „Indiens Farmer*innenprotest anführen" (Bhowmick, Sonthalia 2021). [...] Dennoch mussten Frauen im Farmer*innenprotest [...] mit Drohungen geschlechtsspezifischer Gewalt zurechtkommen. [...] Als Reaktion darauf schlossen sich einige von ihnen zu einem landesweiten Netzwerk zusammen [...] und forderten die Anführer*innen der Farmer*innen auf, die Bewegung für Frauen sicherer zu machen, indem sie interne Beschwerdeausschüsse für Vorwürfe sexuellen Fehlverhaltens einrichten, Opfer anhören und mögliches Vergehen untersuchen (WSS 2021). (Behl 2022)

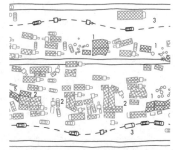

■ Gemeinschaftsbauten (Community buildings)
■ Individuelle Unterkünfte (Individual shelters)

Farmers-Proteste. 1 Gemeinschaftsküche 2 Überspannter Innenhof 3 Durchfahrtsweg (Farmers' protests. 1 Community kitchen 2 Covered courtyard 3 Drive-through pathway)

Die Künstlerin, Aktivistin und Wissenschaftlerin Aatika Singh lebte drei Monate lang im Protestcamp an der Singhu-Grenze und widmete sich Kunst- und Medienprojekten. Sie schlief in Zelten, umgebauten Traktorwagen oder kam bei Bewohner*innen der angrenzenden Dörfer unter (→Solidaritätsgeste).

Im Online-Magazin The Wire schrieb sie über die Architektur der „Trolley Towns":

Durch einfache Anpassungen und die Verwendung von vor Ort verfügbaren Materialien wie Eisengittern, Holzleitern, Plastikflaschen und mit Pflanzenstoppeln gefüllten Steppdecken wurden die Anhänger zu lustigen Minihäusern mit viel Sonnenlicht und Platz ausgebaut. Dachstützen wurden hinzugefügt und Polyethylenplanen machten die Wagen wind- und regenfest. Ladestationen wurden mit einer verzinkten Eisenkette an einer bereits vorhandenen LKW-Struktur angebracht, um Mobiltelefone und andere Geräte mit Strom zu versorgen. Die festen Aufbauten der Anhänger dienten zur Anbringung von Solidaritätsbekundungen und politischen Plakaten. Außerdem wurden Kühlboxen, Wechselrichter und Schaltschränke eingebaut. An einigen Zeltplanen wurden Leinen für die Kleidung gespannt und auf Zwischenebenen wurden Kuhfladen, Decken, Musikanlagen, Lebensmittel und Wasser gelagert. [...]

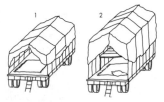

Farmers-Proteste. Umgebauter Traktorwagen 1 Einstöckig 2 Zweistöckig (Farmers' protests. Converted tractor trolley 1 Single deck 2 Double deck)

Ein zentrales Merkmal der zum Wohnen umfunktionierten Fahrzeuge war die Erfahrung von Komfort und Wärme. Einige Wagen hatten exklusive Kabinen für Frauen mit an Schnüren hängenden Vorhängen und Trennwänden aus vertikalen Holzböden. [...] Die Wagen wurden auch in Museen, Gurughars, Fitnessstudios, Bibliotheken und Gemeindezentren umgewandelt, indem sie auf unterschiedliche Weise vertikal und

Harp Farmer Pictures: Singhu border, 8. Dezember 2020

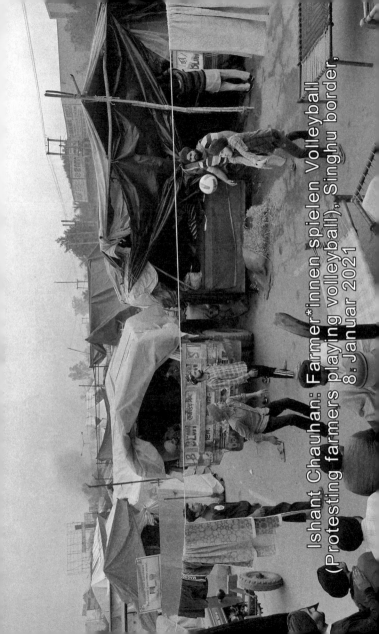

Ishant Chauhan: Farmer*innen spielen Volleyball (Protesting farmers playing volleyball), Singhu border, 8. Januar 2021

Ajay Pal Singh: Kundgebung (Rally), Singhu border, 25. Dezember 2020

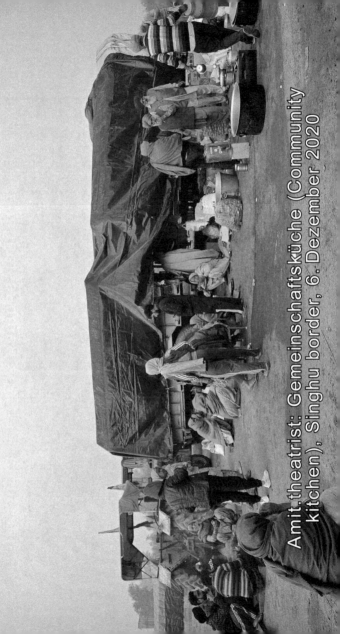

Amit.theatrist: Gemeinschaftsküche (Community kitchen), Singhu border, 6. Dezember 2020

Rajat Gupta: Zelt aus Bambusstangen (Tent made of bamboo poles), Ghazipur border, 29. Dezember 2020

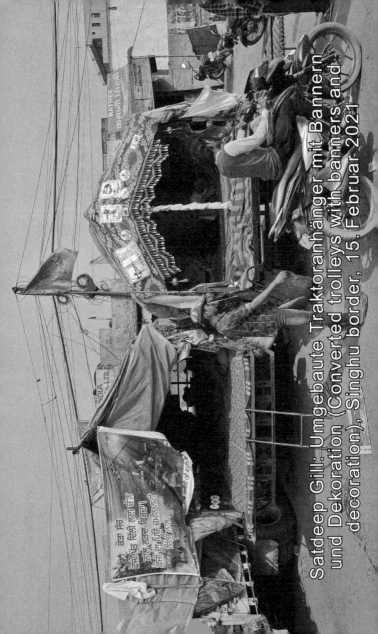

Satdeep Gill: Umgebaute Traktoranhänger mit Bannern und Dekoration (Converted trolleys with banners and decoration), Singhu border, 15. Februar 2021

Aatika Singh: Zweigeschossige Unterkunft in umgebautem Traktoranhänger (Two-story shelter in converted trolley), Singhu border, 22. Dezember 2020

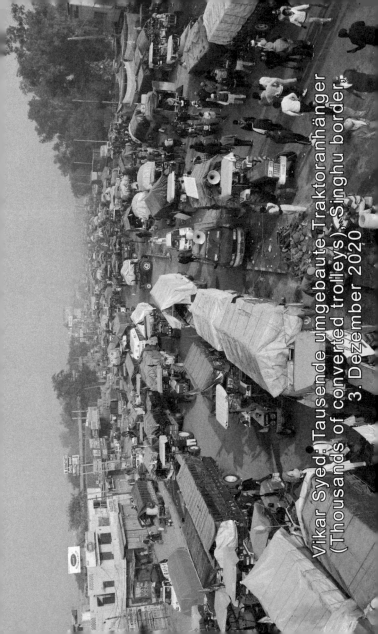

Vikar Syed: Tausende umgebaute Traktoranhänger
(Thousands of converted trolleys), Singhu border,
3. Dezember 2020

Vijay Pandey: Barrikaden der Polizei (Barricades installed by the police), Ghazipur border, 2. Februar 2021

horizontal überspannt wurden. [...] Solange der Protest anhielt, glich die gesamte provisorische Stadt einem Bauprojekt, das jeden Tag erweitert wurde, gebaut von den Farmer*innen und den angelernten Arbeiter*innen der angrenzenden peripheren Dörfer, die das Hinterland von Delhi bilden. [...] Die Aufteilung wurde von den Gewerkschaften festgelegt und die Flächen für die Wagen entsprechend zugewiesen [...]. Dieser Prozess schuf Raum für die Vermischung verschiedener Gruppen und die Bewegungsfreiheit von Frauen. Diese Gendersensibilität stand im Widerspruch zum weit verbreiteten Bild der LKW fahrenden Machos, die auf ihren Fahrzeugen posieren oder in Gruppen herumlungern und anzügliche Lieder grölen. (Singh 2022)

Im April 2023 fand ein Zoom-Gespräch mit Aatika Singh über die Entstehung, Entwicklung und Organisation der Trolley-Siedlungen statt:

Anna-Maria Mayerhofer: Die Protestcamps an den Grenzen von Delhi waren mehrere Kilometer lang und bestanden aus tausenden Trolleys und Zelten. Wie lange dauerte es, die Siedlungen zu errichten?

Aatika Singh: Ungefähr ein bis zwei Wochen. Um mit ihren Traktoren nach Delhi zu gelangen, waren viele der Farmer*innen mehrere Tage unterwegs. Als sie an den Stadtgrenzen ankamen, brauchten sie schnell eine Unterkunft. Geld zum Aufbau der Zelte und zum Umbau der Traktoranhänger in überdachte Wohn- und Schlafbereiche bekamen sie von den Gewerkschaften. Der Rest wurde zusammengelegt. In den Baumärkten der Umgebung konnten sie → Baumaterialien zu vergünstigten Preisen kaufen. Häufig wurden mehrere Trolleys so zusammengestellt, dass sich kleine Höfe bildeten. Die Zwischenräume wurden mit Bambusstangen, → Seilen und Planen überdacht. Mitglieder der Gewerkschaften erstellten zusammen mit Farmer*innen, die sich in der Region gut auskannten, Pläne für die Camps und teilten die Trolley-Siedlung in kleinere Zonen ein, die sich teils autonom versorgten. Menschen aus einer Region, manchmal sogar demselben Dorf, wohnten auch in den Protestcamps in der gleichen Nachbar*innenschaft und halfen sich gegenseitig. In jedem der Protestcamps gab es außerdem eine große Halle mit einer Bühne, wo Vorträge gehalten, Gedichte und Performances präsentiert, zu Spenden aufgerufen und Abstimmungen durchgeführt wurden.*

AMM: Wie war das Zusammenleben im Protestcamp organisiert? Wie wurden hier Entscheidungen getroffen?

AS: Jede Zone entsendete eine Vertreter*in ins Komitee, wo alle wichtigen Entscheidungen gefällt wurden. Diese Person war häufig auch Mitglied einer Gewerkschaft. Zwischen den Gewerkschaften und den „normalen" Protestierenden gab es ein Machtgefälle: Die Gewerkschaften trafen die Entscheidungen und delegierten Aufgaben an die Protestierenden, die den Gewerkschaften sehr verbunden waren. Auch die Beziehungen zu den Bewohner*innen der umgebenden Dörfer war gut. Viele Gewerkschaften hatten dort Büros. Übrigens nahmen nicht nur Farmer*innen an den Protesten teil. Studierende, Aktivist*innen, Akademiker*innen und Medienvertreter*innen schlossen sich an, auch weil viele Menschen in Delhi Verbindungen zu den Dörfern in Punjab und Haryana haben.

AMM: Damit sich die Farmer*innen auch um ihre Betriebe zu Hause kümmern konnten, gab es eine Art Rotationssystem zwischen den Protestcamps und den Heimatdörfern. Die Proteste wurden so zudem mit neuen Vorräten aus den „Kornkammern des Landes" versorgt, wie die Regionen Punjab und Haryana häufig bezeichnet werden. Manche Traktoren waren dauerhaft in die Siedlungen integriert, andere pendelten zwischen den Heimatdörfern und den Protestcamps. Wie funktionierte das, wenn die → Straßen durch die Trolleys und Zelte blockiert waren?

AS: Die Highways waren nie ganz blockiert. Protestierende und Anwohner*innen konnten sich auch weiterhin frei durchbewegen, auch wenn sie natürlich viel länger für die Strecken brauchten. Häufig wurde eine Richtung des

Highways frei gelassen oder es gab Bereiche innerhalb der Siedlungen, die als Durchfahrtswege genutzt wurden, meist an den Straßenrändern oder in der Mitte des Highways. Nur die Polizei betrat den Protestort meist nicht ohne Weiteres, da sie erwartete, dass es zu einem Eklat kommen würde. Seit dem 26. Januar 2021, als hunderte Demonstrierende ins Stadtzentrum eingedrungen waren und das Rote Fort gestürmt hatten, hatten sich die Spannungen zwischen der Polizei und den Protestierenden noch mal verschärft. Professionelle Betonbarrikaden mit Stacheldraht wurden errichtet, die Protestcamps wurden überwacht und es gab Internetsperren.

AMM: In den → Platzbesetzungen von → Occupy Wall Street und der → Movimiento 15M änderte sich nach einigen Wochen der Euphorie die Stimmung in den Protestcamps. Viele Protestierende waren müde, denn die Selbstverwaltung und die Organisation des Alltags kosteten viel Kraft. Die Protestcamps der Farmer∗innen existierten mehr als ein Jahr. Wie entwickelte sich hier die Stimmung über die Monate der → Besetzung?

AS: Je stärker sich die Protestcamps vergrößerten, desto mehr wurde in den → Medien darüber berichtet, desto schneller wuchsen die Camps. Niemand wollte dieses Ereignis verpassen. Gerade für die jungen Farmer∗innen war es spannend, dort zu wohnen. Alle hatten genug zu essen, die Protestcamps wurden immer besser ausgebaut, es gab sogar Massagemaschinen. Als die Unterkünfte fertig aufgebaut waren, holten viele Männer ihre Frauen und Kinder nach und lebten dort mit ihren Familien. Einige Protestierende nutzten die Möglichkeit, auch die Innenstadt von Delhi zu sehen. Gleichzeitig war die Angst groß, dass die neuen Agrargesetze tatsächlich umgesetzt werden würden. Gerade in der Region Punjab gibt es seit der grünen Revolution in den 1960er Jahren hohe Arbeitslosigkeit. Strukturelle Armut ist ein großes Problem. Für die Menschen stand also auch viel auf dem Spiel. (Texte von Natasha Behl, Aatika Singh; Gesprächspartnerin: Aatika

Singh; Einleitung, Recherche und Interview-Redaktion: AMM)

Farmers' protests, Ger. → *Farmers-Proteste*. In November 2020, kilometers-long → *protest camps* materialized on three important access roads to Delhi. Tens of thousands of farmers from different regions in the country drove to the capital with their tractors (→ *Vehicles*) to protest the three contested agriculture reform bills which sought to liberalize trade and to abolish the guaranteed minimum prices for grain. When the convoys of tractors reached the outskirts of Delhi, violent clashes with the → *police* occurred (→ *Violence*). The latter employed → *water cannons* and installed → *barricades* to keep the farmers from entering the capital. The protesters responded by blocking the otherwise busy highways (→ *Blockade*). They set up → *tents* and converted their trolleys and trucks into accommodations. Over a year later, the farmers ended their protests and returned to their villages after Indian prime minister Narendra Modi withdrew the bill in November 2021.

Political scientist Natasha Behl has been following Indian politics for some years and has dedicated her research at Arizona State University to questions of race, gender, and social movements. She watched the protests from afar and shed light on the background in an article published in the *American Political Science Review* in 2022.

In September 2020, the Indian Parliament passed three agriculture reform bills concerning the pricing, sale, and storage of farm products. [...] Many farmers feared that the reforms would lower prices for their products, incentivize the hording of essential goods, and remove an essential safety net. [...] In response, protesting farmers have demanded that the central government repeal the three farm laws and legalize a national MSP [Minimum support price] index for farm produce. [...] On November 26, 2020, the movement emerged nationally through two distinct organizational tactics. First, farmers joined trade unions in a massive nationwide one-day strike, with 250 million participants (Joy

2020). Second, tens of thousands of farmers from Punjab, Haryana, Uttar Pradesh, Madhya Pradesh, and Rajasthan participated in the Delhi chalo (Let's go to Delhi) march. Predominantly peaceful protesters confronted a militarized police force that attacked them with tear gas, batons, and water cannons at the Punjab-Haryana and Haryana-Delhi borders (Slater 2020). [...]

Nevertheless, after two days of marching, the farmers entered Delhi and established protest camps on the outskirts of the city. For more than a year, farmers organized sit-ins with some 300,000 supporters gathered outside Delhi at the Tikri, Singhu, and Ghazipur borders (Sandhu 2021). Farmers also confronted the government through nonviolent actions, including surrounding the homes of politicians, closing down government buildings, opening up toll plazas, and stopping railway lines (Dubal, Gill 2020). [...] The BJP government reacted to the ongoing protest by erecting militarized borders around the protest camps and arresting hundreds of protesters (BBC 2021). [...]

Although a majority of the protesting farmers have been Sikh, their membership includes Hindus, Muslims, Christians, and Buddhists (Mander 2021), and their practices reflect this diversity. The farmers have engaged in forms of protest based both in Gandhian practices of nonviolence [...] and in Sikh practices [...], especially langar (communal kitchen), shahidi (martyrdom), and seva (service) (Singh 2014). For example, [...] after clashes with police officers, at least one Sikh temple fed officers who were still dressed in riot gear (Ghazali 2020). [...]

If only for a short time, the farmers' protest has created an inclusive democracy, which includes the protest camps and rural support networks. At the camps, basic public services including schools and libraries, arts and music, and medical and dental camps, have been made available to everyone (Economic Times 2020). Communal kitchens have fed hundreds of thousands of people, regardless of religion, class, caste, or gender, thus undermining caste rules regarding interdining and building heterogenous coalitions. When possible, decisions have been made collectively with shared leadership that ensures representation of multiple member unions (Sharma 2020). Beyond the camps, villages across Punjab and Haryana have supported the protesters by sending essential supplies and organizing rotating batches of protesters (Sethi 2021). And families have agreed to divide their time between working in the fields and participating in the protest camps (Mander 2021). [...]

Women's contribution to the farmers' protest has been celebrated with headlines proclaiming that women have been "leading India's farmers' protest" (Bhowmick, Sonthalia 2021). [...] Nevertheless, women in the farmers' protest [...] have had to navigate threats of gendered violence. [...] In response, some women in the protest joined forces with the nationwide network [...] and called on farmer leaders to make the movement safer for women by creating internal complaint committees for accusations of sexual misconduct, listening to survivors, and investigating potential offenses (WSS 2021). (Behl 2022)

The artist, activist, and scholar Aatika Singh lived in the protest camp on the Singhu border for three months and worked on art and media projects. She slept in tents, converted tractor trolleys, or found accommodation with residents in neighboring villages (→ Acts of solidarity). In the online magazine The Wire, she wrote about the architecture of the "trolley towns":

Basic modifications and the use of local material like iron mesh, wooden ladders, plastic bottles and quilts filled with crop stubble helped develop the trolleys into amusing mini homes with ample sunlight and space. Roof supports were added and polyethylene tarpaulin made the trolleys wind and rain resistant. Charging points were attached through a galvanised iron chain to an already existing truck structure, providing power to mobile phones and other devices. The exterior iron surface of the trolleys was used to display solidarity statements and political posters, while coolers, inverters, switchboards were fitted in, ropes were stretched on one side of the tarp for clothes and raised platforms helped store cow dung cakes, blankets, music systems, groceries, water and food. [...]

A central feature of the trolley home was the experience of comfort and warmth. A few trolleys had exclusive cabins for women, with curtains hanging from string or vertical wooden flooring as partitions. [...] Trolleys were also converted into museums, gurughar, gyms, libraries and community centres by different means of vertical and horizontal spanning. [...] As long as the protest continued, the entire makeshift town resembled a construction project under expansion every day, being built by the farmers and the semi-skilled labourers of the adjacent peripheral villages that form the afterlife of Delhi. [...] The plans were demarcated by the unions and the areas accordingly allocated for the trolleys [...]. The process made room for the intermingling of different groups and the free movement of women. This gender functionality became significant due to the common projected image of the trolley's machismo, with groups of men standing outside and blaring bawdy music. (Singh 2022)

In April 2023, there was a Zoom conversation with Aatika Singh about the formation, development, and organization of the trolley settlements:

Anna-Maria Mayerhofer: The protest camps on Delhi's borders were several kilometers long and consisted of thousands of trolleys and tents. How long did it take to set up the settlements?

Aatika Singh: About one to two weeks. To get to Delhi with their tractors, many of the farmers had been on the road for several days. When they arrived at the city's borders, they needed instant accommodation. Money to set up tents and to convert their tractor trolleys into roofed living and sleeping areas was provided by the unions. The rest was collectively pooled. Protesters were able to buy → building materials at a discount at local hardware stores. Often several

trolleys were moved together so that little courtyards formed. The gaps between them were covered with bamboo poles, →ropes, and tarpaulins. Together with farmers who knew the region, union members drew plans and divided the trolley settlement into smaller, partly self-sufficient zones. People from a particular region, sometimes even the same village, also lived in the same neighborhood in the protest camps and helped each other. Each of the protest camps had a large hangar with a stage where lectures were held, poems and performances were presented, donations appeals were made, and votes were taken.

AMM: How was communal life in the protest camp organized? How were decisions made?

AS: Every zone sent a representative to the committee where all the important decisions were made. In many cases, this person was also a union member. There was a power hierarchy between the "normal" protesters and the unions. The unions made decisions and delegated tasks to protesters who were strongly attached to the unions. Relations with the people living in the surrounding villages were also good. Many unions had offices there. Not only farmers took part in the protests. Students, activists, academics, and media representatives joined them, also because many people in Delhi have ties to the villages in Punjab and Haryana.

AMM: A kind of rotation system between the protest camps and the villages allowed the farmers to take care of their businesses at home. This also meant that the protests received new supplies from the "country's breadbaskets," as the Punjab and Haryana regions are often called. Some of the tractors were permanently integrated into the settlements, some commuted between the home villages and the protest camps. How was this possible when the →streets were blocked with trolleys and tents?

AS: The highways were never completely blocked. Protesters and residents could still pass through freely, even though it naturally took them a lot longer. Often one direction on the highway was left open, or areas within the settlements were used as passage routes, usually at the roadsides or in the middle of the highway. The police, however, refrained from simply showing up at the site of the protest as they feared this would cause an uproar. Since January 26, 2021, when hundreds of demonstrators had entered the city center and stormed the Red Fort, tensions between the police and the protesters had further intensified. Professional concrete barricades with barbed wire were set up, the protest camps were surveilled, and there were internet blockades.

AMM: After several weeks of euphoria, the mood at the protest camps of the → Occupy Wall Street and → Movimiento 15M → occupations changed. Many protesters were tired because the self-management and organization of everyday life was very taxing. The farmers' protest camps lasted over a year. How did the mood evolve during the months of occupation?

AS: As the protest camps expanded, they gained even more media attention and grew even faster. Nobody wanted to miss this event. Especially for younger farmers it was exciting to live there. Everybody had enough food, and the protest camps became increasingly sophisticated, there were even massage machines. Once the shelters had been set up, many men got their wives and children to join them and lived there as families. Some protesters also used the opportunity to visit Delhi's city center. At the same time people were very anxious that the new agriculture bills really would be implemented. Especially in the Punjab region, unemployment has been high ever since the Green Revolution in the 1960s. Structural poverty is a big problem. There was so much at stake for the people. (Texts by Natasha Dehl and Aatika Sıngh; conversation with Aatika Singh; introduction, research, and interview editing: AMM)

Fass, engl. → *Barrel*. Diese vermutlich gestellte Aufnahme zeigt britische Soldaten, die sich während des sogenannten Osteraufstands in Dublin Ende April 1916 hinter einer Wand aus Bierfässern

verschanzt haben – und erinnert damit eindringlich an die mögliche Herleitung des Wortes → *Barrikade* vom französischen Wort *barrique* (Holzfass). Der von irischen Republikaner*innen gegen die britische Herrschaft angezettelte Aufstand bildete eines der wichtigsten Ereignisse der irischen Revolutionszeit und zugleich den ersten bewaffneten Konflikt seit der irischen Rebellion von 1798. (SH)

Fass. Britische Soldaten gehen beim Osteraufstand von 1916 hinter einer Barrikade aus Bierfässern in Deckung, Dublin, 24. April 1916 (Barrel. British soldiers duck behind a barricade made of beer barrels during the 1916 Easter Uprising, Dublin, April 24, 1916)

Februarrevolution / Juniaufstand, engl. → *February Revolution / June Days Uprising*. Nach der Februarrevolution → *1848*, die zunächst erfolgreich gegen die zunehmend restaurative Politik des Bürgerkönigs Louis-Philippe aufbegehrt hatte, wurden die aufständischen Kräfte im Juni desselben Jahres blutig niedergeschlagen. Die Kämpfe auf den Pariser → *Barrikaden* von 1848 mündeten damit in einer reaktionären Konterrevolution, die letztlich auch das Schicksal der demokratischen Erhebungen in anderen europäischen Ländern besiegelte. (SH)

February Revolution / June Days Uprising, Ger. → *Februarrevolution / Juniaufstand*. After the February Revolution of → *1848*, which had started off as a successful rebellion against the increasingly retrograde politics of the "citizen king" Louis Philippe, the insurgents were violently beaten down in June that same year. The fights on the

Paris →*barricades* in 1848 led to a reactionary counterrevolution which also sealed the fate of democratic uprisings in other European countries. (SH)

Fechenheimer Wald, engl. →*Fechenheim Forest*. Im September →*2021* besetzten Klimaaktivist∗innen des Bündnisses „Wald statt Asphalt" ein Waldstück in Frankfurt am Main, das für den Bau eines Autobahntunnels gerodet werden sollte. Ein →*Protestcamp* vergleichbar mit der →*Besetzung* des 100 Kilometer entfernten →*Dannenröder Waldes* →*2019* entstand, nahm jedoch weder die Ausmaße an noch wurden ähnlich viele Menschen mobilisiert. Knapp zwanzig →*Baumhäuser* wurden innerhalb von eineinhalb Jahren errichtet: winzige Hütten hoch oben in den Baumkronen; größere Strukturen, die mehrere Meter über der Erde zwischen Baumstämmen eingebunden wurden; hängende Häuser, die auf dem Boden gebaut und anschließend mit →*Seilen* hochgezogen wurden. Als die polizeiliche Räumung Ende 2022 näher rückte (→*Polizei*), kamen zahlreiche →*Traversen*, Schaukeln, ein →*Monopod* und ein 40 Meter hoher „Skypod" hinzu (→*Bautypen*). Angesichts des Standorts am Rande der Großstadt konnten die Besetzer∗innen auf viele Angebote und Ressourcen zurückgreifen, z.B. wurden von der Ada Kantine, einer solidarischen Nachbar∗innenschaftsküche, regelmäßig warme Mahlzeiten in den Wald geliefert (→*Solidaritätsgeste*). (AMM, JD)

Fechenheim Forest, Ger. →*Fechenheimer Wald*. In September →*2021*, climate activists from the alliance Wald statt Asphalt (Forest not Asphalt) occupied a piece of the woods in Frankfurt that was to be cleared for the construction of a highway tunnel. A →*protest camp* was established comparable to the →*2019* →*occupation* of the →*Dannenrod Forest* 100 kilometers away, albeit without the same scale or a similar number of supporters mobilized. Almost twenty →*tree houses* were built within the space of one and a half years: tiny huts high up in the crowns of the trees; larger structures tied between tree trunks several meters above the ground;

and hanging houses that were built on the ground and then pulled up into place using →*ropes*. At the end of 2022, as the date the →*police* had set to clear the camp approached, numerous →*traverses*, swings, a →*monopod*, and a forty-meter-high "skypod" were added (→*Building types*). Given the location on the edge of a large city, the occupiers were able to rely on various forms of support and resources, such as regular meals being delivered to the forest by the Ada canteen, a solidarity-based neighborhood kitchen (→*Acts of solidarity*). (AMM, JD)

Fernseher, engl. →*Television set*. Neben Elektrogeräten wie der →*Waschmaschine* und dem Kühlschrank entwickelte sich der Fernseher in der zweiten Hälfte des 20. Jahrhunderts zum Inbegriff der Wohlstandsgesellschaft und der Konsumgüterindustrie. Durch die symbolische Zerstörung von Fernsehgeräten durch Künstler∗innen im Rahmen der Gegenkultur seit den 1960er Jahren (z.B. Fluxus, Ant Farm) wurde den bürgerlichen Lebensentwürfen der Nachkriegszeit jedoch häufig eine klare Absage erteilt. Zugleich sind Protestbewegungen aber bis heute auf das Massenmedium des Fernsehens angewiesen (→*Medien*): Ziel der Proteste war und ist es ja meist, möglichst große Aufmerksamkeit zu erregen und in die Nachrichten zu kommen (→*Kommunikation*). Immer wieder konnte auch das Fernsehprogramm selbst für Proteste genutzt werden, etwa als →*1984* Umweltaktivist∗innen in der Unterhaltungssendung *Wetten, dass...?* ein Transparent mit der Aufschrift „Nicht wetten – Donauauen retten" enthüllten und dadurch auf die Besetzung der →*Hainburger Au* in Österreich aufmerksam machen konnten. Eine regelrechte Fernsehbarrikade (→*Barrikade*) wurde dagegen im November 1981 auf Initiative des späteren Filmregisseurs Samir Jamal Aldin in Zürich errichtet: In Fortsetzung der seit →*1980* andauernden Jugendunruhen sperrten Aktivist∗innen vor dem von ihnen besetzten Autonomen Jugendzentrum die Limmatstraße mit einer Installation aus Fernsehgeräten ab

Fernseher. Olivia Heussler: Barrikade aus eingeschalteten Fernsehgeräten vor dem besetzten Jugendzentrum, Zürich, November 1981 (Television set. Olivia Heussler: Barricade made of switched-on TV sets in front of the occupied Youth Center, Zurich, November 1981)

(→ *Blockade,* → *Züri brännt*). Um kurz vor acht Uhr wurden auf den Geräten die Nachrichten eingeschaltet, wodurch die Logik der Medienberichterstattung gewissermaßen umgekehrt wurde: Bevor das Ereignis als Straßenkrawall in den Nachrichten gezeigt werden konnte, wurde die Nachrichtensendung auf der → *Straße* im wahrsten Sinne des Wortes vorgeführt. (SH)

Feuer, engl. → *Fire.* Brennende Autos, Müllcontainer und → *Barrikaden* werden vor allem mit linksradikalen Protesten in Verbindung gebracht und als Ausdruck eines → *Gewalt*-Potenzials gedeutet, dessen bevorzugte → *Waffe* der als Molotowcocktail bezeichnete Wurfbrandsatz ist. Werden Dinge oder gar Häuser in Brand gesetzt – wie bei den Straßenkämpfen um den → *Majdan* in der Ukraine im Winter → *2013/2014* oder anlässlich des → *G20-Gipfels* in Hamburg → *2017* –, berichten die → *Medien* meist davon, dass die Proteste außer Kontrolle geraten seien. Die → *Zerstörung* durch Feuer im Rahmen der Protestbewegungen bedeutet aber nicht nur Eskalation und Provokation, sie kann auch konkrete Botschaften übermitteln

(→ *Kommunikation*). So zielt die weit verbreitete symbolische Verbrennung von Geld, heiligen Schriften oder Nationalflaggen auf die öffentliche Diskussion über Besitz und Eigentum oder die machtpolitische Rolle von Staaten, Institutionen und Religionsgemeinschaften. Das deutliche „Nein" aus Bergfeuern der Atomkraftgegner*innen bei Innsbruck am Vorabend der Volksabstimmung über das geplante österreichische Atomkraftwerk → *Zwentendorf* im November → *1978* transformierte ein Element der Brauchtumspflege in ein aktuelles Statement. Die *Ultima Ratio* des → *Körpereinsatzes* ist die Selbstverbrennung: „Aus schierer Verzweiflung macht man sich selbst zu einer einzigen, letzten Botschaft. Nicht immer, aber meistens geschehen Selbstverbrennungen im Dienste eines höheren politischen oder religiösen kollektiven Interesses" (Wenger 2018). (SH)

Finger, engl. → *Finger.* Bei → *Blockaden* teilt sich ein zunächst geschlossener Demonstrationszug (→ *Demonstration*) häufig in kleinere Gruppen, sogenannte „Finger", auf, um Polizeiketten (→ *Polizei*) ohne Einsatz von → *Gewalt* effektiv zu durchbrechen. Wie die Finger einer Hand fächern sich die einzelnen Züge auf, um hinter einer Absperrung oder am Ziel der Blockade (z.B. einem Kohlebagger) wieder zusammenzufinden. An der Spitze läuft eine Gruppe mit → *Fahnen* in der Erkennungsfarbe („roter Finger", „blauer Finger", „silberner Finger"). Innerhalb des Fingers, der meist aus mehreren hundert Aktivist∗innen besteht, bilden je 5 bis 15 Menschen eine Bezugsgruppe, die während der Blockade autonom handelt, indem sie z.B. selbst entscheidet, ob sie eine Eskalation in Kauf nimmt oder die Aktion abbricht. Auch das „Delegiertenplenum" eines Fingers trifft teilweise vor Ort unabhängig von anderen Fingern Entscheidungen. Die vom Netzwerk „X-tausendmal quer" entwickelte „Fünf-Finger-Taktik" wurde zum ersten Mal bei einer Sitzblockade gegen die Castor-Transporte im Jahr 2001 in der Nähe von → *Gorleben* angewendet. Später kam sie beim G8-Gipfel in Heiligendamm 2007 und bei den Tagebaubesetzungen der → *Protestorganisation* Ende Gelände zum Einsatz. (AMM)

Finger. Tim Wagner: Aktivist∗innen von Ende Gelände am Tagebau Hambach, 5. November 2017 (Finger. Tim Wagner: Activists from the Ende Gelände group at the Hambach open-pit mine, November 5, 2017)

Finger, Ger. → *Finger (fig.)*. During → *blockades* an initially closed-rank protest march frequently divides up into smaller groups, so-called fingers, in order to breach police lines effectively (→ *Police*) without resorting to → *violence*. Like the fingers of a hand, the individual groups fan out in order to regroup behind the barriers or at the target of the blockade (e.g., a coal excavator). At the front, a group moves with → *flags* in the respective finger color ("red finger," "blue finger," "silver finger"). Within each finger, which usually consists of several hundred activists, sets of five to fifteen people form a social peer group that acts independently during the blockade by, for example, deciding for itself whether to accept escalation or to discontinue the action. The "delegation committee" of a finger is also able to make its own decisions on site, independent of the other fingers. The "five-finger tactic" developed by the X-tausendmal quer network was deployed for the first time during a → *sit-in* against the Castor transports in 2001 near → *Gorleben*. It was later used again at the G8 summit in Heiligendamm in 2007 and during the occupation of open-pit mines by the → *protest organization* Ende Gelände. (AMM)

Fire, Ger. → *Feuer*. Burning cars, garbage containers, and → *barricades* are primarily associated with radical left-wing protests and interpreted as an expression of a potential for → *violence*, whose preferred → *weapon* is the hand-thrown incendiary device known as a Molotov cocktail. If things or even houses are set on fire and—as in the case of the street fighting around the → *Maidan* in Ukraine in the winter of → *2013/2014* or on the occasion of the → *G20 summit protests* in Hamburg in → *2017*—the → *media* usually report that the protests have gotten out of control. However, → *destruction* by fire in the context of protest movements does not only mean escalation and provocation, it can also convey concrete messages (→ *Communication*). For example, the widespread symbolic burning of money, sacred scriptures, or national flags is aimed at sparking public discussion about property and ownership or the political role of states, institutions, and religious communities. The clear "Nein" (No) conveyed through fires arranged on a mountainside by anti-nuclear activists near Innsbruck on the eve of the referendum on the planned Austrian nuclear power plant at → *Zwentendorf* in November → *1978* transformed an element of custom into a topical statement. The last resort of → *body deployment* is self-immolation: "Out of sheer desperation, people turn themselves into a single, final message. Not always, but usually self-immolations happen in the service of a higher political or religious collective interest" (Wenger 2018). (SH)

Flag, Ger. → *Fahne (fig.)*. Flags define territories, literally or metaphorically. Therefore, these textiles, discrete in themselves, are an eminently spatial protest tool. In → *demonstrations*, flags serve to establish air sovereignty: a sea of identical flags signals uniformity. In the sometimes militant struggle with the → *police* against exorbitant rents, vacant buildings and real estate speculation, the squatter scene often hoisted the black-and-red flag, as in Hamburg's Schanzenviertel in the 1980s. The flag is a distinctive sign of autonomist groups groups and is politically associated with revolutionary and anarcho-communist attitudes (→ *Identifier*). (SH)

Flashmob, engl. → *Flash mob*; → *Demonstration*, → *Myanmar-Proteste*, → *Öffentlicher Raum*, → *Reclaim the Streets*

Flash mob, Ger. → *Flashmob*; → *Demonstration*, → *Myanmar protests*, → *Public space*, → *Reclaim the Streets*

Flint Sit-down Strike, Ger. → *Flint-Sitzstreik*. In the winter of → *1936/1937* about 2,000 workers at General Motors refused to work and fought for higher wages by occupying the entire plant in Flint, Michigan for forty days. Organizational structures and departments were established to manage daily needs and there were leisure activities and courses. A so-called kangaroo court was supposed to mediate disputes. By remaining in the factory, the workers blocked operations as well as the employment of substitute workers (→ *Blockade*, → *Sit-in*) and ultimately succeeded in forcing General Motors to react. (JD)

Flint-Sitzstreik, engl. → *Flint Sit-down Strike*. Im Winter → *1936/1937* verweigerten rund 2000 Arbeiter von General Motors ihre Arbeit und besetzten für 40 Tage eine komplette Fabrik in Flint, Michigan, um für höhere Löhne zu kämpfen. Es wurden Organisationsstrukturen und Abteilungen für den täglichen Bedarf aufgebaut und es gab Freizeit- und Lehrangebote. Ein sogenanntes „Känguru-Gericht" sollte Streitfälle schlichten. Indem die Arbeiter innerhalb der Fabrik blieben, blockierten sie den Betrieb sowie den Einsatz von Ersatzarbeitern (→ *Blockade*, → *Sit-in*) und zwangen General Motors schließlich erfolgreich zum Handeln. (JD)

Flotilla. Marcus Donner: „Shell no"-Aktivist∗innen in Seattle, 16. Mai 2015 (Flotilla. Marcus Donner: "Shell no" activists in Seattle, May 16, 2015)

Flotilla, engl. → *Flotilla*, eine als Bootsversammlung angelegte → *Demonstration* auf dem Wasser, die verschiedene Formen annehmen kann. Flotilla-Proteste werden oft von Umweltschutzorganisationen veranstaltet, um öffentliche Aufmerksamkeit zu erlangen oder eine → *Blockade* bestimmter Schifffahrtsrouten zu erreichen. 2015 blockierten am Hafen von Seattle hunderte Aktivist∗innen mit ihren Kajaks die Reparatur einer riesigen Bohrinsel von Shell Oil und deren Transport in die Arktis. Die „Kajakaktivist∗innen" erreichten eine Verlangsamung der Arbeiten und sorgten für viel schlechte Publicity, die letztlich das gesamte 7-Milliarden-Dollar-Projekt stoppte. (JD)

Flotilla, Ger. → *Flotilla (fig.)*. A → *demonstration* on the water created by a gathering of small boats; it can take various different forms. Environmental organizations often protest by using a flotilla in order to attract public attention or to → *blockade* a specific shipping route. In 2015, in the Port of Seattle, hundreds of people in kayaks blocked the repair of a huge Shell oil rig, preventing it being transported on to the Arctic Ocean. These "kayaktivists" managed to slow work down and trigger a lot of poor publicity that ultimately brought the entire US$7 billion project to a halt. (JD)

Foreword, Ger. → *Grußwort*. Commonly a paratext on the first pages of a publication which combines references to the cultural policies and funding enabling the project's existence with programmatic gestures of affirmation (often from the funders' perspective). In the case of the volume at hand, a lexical, and thus conceptually faithful, expression of acknowledgement by the German Federal Cultural Foundation to the Deutsches Architekturmuseum in Frankfurt and the Museum für angewandte Kunst in Vienna, and especially to the whole curatorial team, consisting of Oliver Elser, Anna-Maria Mayerhofer, Sebastian Hackenschmidt, Jennifer Dyck, Lilli Hollein, and Peter Cachola Schmal, combined with the wish that this thematically relevant and formally most original exhibition and publication project receive both broad and positive recognition (signed by the board of the German Federal Cultural Foundation, Katarzyna Wielga-Skolimowska and Kirsten Haß)

Frankfurter Häuserkampf, engl. → *Frankfurt Squatting Campaign*. Diverse Akteur∗innen, darunter Bürger∗innen der Initiative AG Westend, linksgerichtete Jugendliche und migrantische Familien, waren ab → *1970* an Mieter∗innenstreiks, → *Demonstrationen* und → *Hausbesetzungen* beteiligt. Das Westend, ein bürgerliches Wohnviertel, das von Vernachlässigung, Abriss und Immobilienspekulation bedroht war, bildete das Zentrum der Aktionen, innerhalb dessen der sogenannte „Block" – vier besetzte Häuser an der Ecke Bockenheimer Landstraße/ Schumannstraße – als Ort des Wider-

stands und der alternativen Lebensmodelle von besonderer Bedeutung war. Bis zur Räumung am 21. Februar 1974 lebten dort rund 80 Besetzer∗innen, die zu unterschiedlichen Gruppierungen der radikalen Frankfurter Linken zählten. Im Block war auch ein Mieter∗innenzentrum untergebracht und hier traf sich der Häuserrat, das Plenum der Szene. In Frankfurt entstand das *Handbuch für Hausbesetzer* (1972) (→ *Handbücher / Online-Manuals*). Die Schwerpunkte der Hausbesetzer∗innenbewegung verlagerten sich später nach West-Berlin und nach Hamburg (→ *Hafenstraße*; vgl. Ausst.-Kat *Dieses Haus ist besetzt!* 2020). (JD)

Frankfurter Septemberaufstand, engl. → *Frankfurt September Uprising*. Die Entscheidung der Frankfurter Nationalversammlung, den Schleswig-Holsteinischen Krieg gegen Dänemark nicht fortzusetzen, wurde von der anti-preußisch eingestellten Bevölkerung als Missachtung national-deutscher Interessen empfunden – sie führte im September → *1848* zu einem spontanen Volksaufstand und der Errichtung zahlreicher → *Barrikaden* in Frankfurt. (SH)

Frankfurt September Uprising, Ger. → *Frankfurter Septemberaufstand*. The Frankfurt Parliament's decision not to continue the Schleswig-Holstein War against Denmark was perceived by the anti-Prussian population as disregarding German nationalist interests—in September → *1848*, it led to a spontaneous popular uprising and the erection of numerous → *barricades* in Frankfurt. (SH)

Frankfurt Squatting Campaign, Ger. → *Frankfurter Häuserkampf*. A diverse range of people, including citizens of the association AG Westend, left-leaning youths, and migrant families, took part in the → *demonstrations* and → *squatting* from → *1970* onward. The Westend, a middle-class residential district threatened by neglect, demolition, and real estate speculation, was at the heart of the actions. In this context, four occupied houses on the corner of Bockenheimer Landstraße/Schumannstraße—the so-called "Block"—were especially significant as sites of resistance and alternative ways of living. Until the eviction on February 21, 1974, about eighty occupiers from different groups within Frankfurt's radical left lived there. The Block also had a tenants' center where the plenum of the scene, the "Häuserrat" (house council), met. A squatters' manual (*Handbuch für Hausbesetzer* 1972; → *Handbücher / Online-Manuals*) was developed in Frankfurt. Subsequently, the focus of the squatters' movement shifted to West Berlin and Hamburg (→ *Hafenstraße*, → *1981*; see exh. cat. *Dieses Haus ist besetzt!* 2020). (JD)

„Freedom Convoy", engl. → *"Freedom convoy"*. Als Protest gegen die Corona-Maßnahmen gegenüber LKW-Fahrer∗innen blockierten → *2022* hunderte Trucks die Innenstadt von Ottawa (→ *Fahrzeuge*, → *Blockade*). Zahlreiche Bürger∗innen solidarisierten sich (→ *Solidaritätsgeste*). Die Trucker∗innen kaperten ähnlich wie bei den Anti-Corona-Maßnahmen in Europa den Begriff „Freiheit" für ihren Widerstand gegen staatliche Auflagen zur Eindämmung der Pandemie (→ *Rechte Proteste*). Die architektonische Seite des Protests bestand darin, mit den → *Infrastrukturen* der LKW eine „Stadt in der Stadt" zu erzeugen, die für polizeiliche Maßnahmen (→ *Polizei*) viel zu widerstandsfähig war. (OE)

"Freedom convoy," Ger. → *"Freedom Convoy"*. By way of protest against the COVID-19 measures imposed on truck drivers, in → *2022,* hundreds of trucks blocked downtown Ottawa (→ *Vehicles*, → *Blockade*). Countless citizens expressed their solidarity (→ *Acts of solidarity*). Similar to anti-COVID-19 measures in Europe, the truckers hijacked the term "freedom" for their opposition to government stipulations to contain the pandemic (→ *Right-wing protests*). The architectural side of the protest involved using the truck → *infrastructures* to create a "city inside the city" that was far too resolute to be defeated by police measures (→ *Police*). (OE)

Freetown Christiania, Ger. → *Freistadt Christiania*, is an autonomous self-governed community in the Danish capital Copenhagen on an approximately 84-acre former military area. The town was founded in → *1971* by a group of activists who occupied the deserted premises and transformed it into an alternative housing and culture project. Today about 1,000 people live in Christiania in the former barracks and self-built accommodations (→ *Building types*). The inhabitants run their own stores, restaurants, and bars, and put on artistic and cultural events, as well as organizing ecological initiatives. (JD)

Freistadt Christiania, engl. → *Freetown Christiania*. Die Freistadt Christiania ist eine autonome, selbstverwaltete Gemeinde in der dänischen Hauptstadt Kopenhagen auf einem rund 34 Hektar großen ehemaligen Militärareal. Gegründet wurde sie → *1971* von einer Gruppe von Aktivist∗innen, die das verlassene Gelände besetzten und zu einem alternativen Wohn- und Kulturprojekt umgestalteten. Heute leben rund 1000 Menschen in Christiania in den früheren Kasernen und selbstgebauten Behausungen (→ *Bautypen*). Die Bewohner∗innen betreiben eigene Geschäfte, Restaurants und Bars, und es gibt zahlreiche Kunst- und Kulturveranstaltungen und ökologische Initiativen. (JD)

Furniture, Ger. → *Möbel*; → *Barricade*, → *Building materials*, → *Gezi Park*, → *Infrastructure*

G20-Proteste, engl. → *G20 summit protests*. Um einen reibungslosen Ablauf des G20-Gipfels in Hamburg (→ *2017*) und die Sicherheit der Staatsgäste zu gewährleisten, setzte die → *Polizei* polarisierende Maßnahmen um – u.a. die Einrichtung von polizeilichen Sonderrechtszonen. Kritiker∗innen bezeichneten das abgesperrte Innenstadtareal, in dem → *Demonstrationen* verboten waren, als „demokratiefreie Zone". Auch das Verbot von → *Protestcamps* war hart umstritten und wurde 2022 vom Hamburger Verwaltungsgericht als rechtswidrig eingestuft. Die konfliktgeladene Stimmung führte zu Straßenkämpfen rund um das Schanzenviertel (→ *Straße*). (JD)

G20 summit protests, Ger. → *G20-Proteste*. To guarantee the smooth running of the G20 Summit in Hamburg in → *2017* as well as the safety of the guests of the state, the → *police* implemented polarizing measures—such as zones in which the police possessed special rights. Critics referred to the closed-off inner city area where → *demonstrations* were not permitted as a "democracy-free zone." The ban on → *protest camps* was also strongly contested and classified as unlawful by the Hamburg administrative court in 2022. The contentious atmosphere erupted in street fights all around the Schanzenviertel district (→ S*treet*). (JD)

Garbage can, Ger. → *Mülltonne (fig.)*. Barricades are erected from street furniture. This also includes garbage cans that are especially suitable for creating → *blockades*, given their size and their mobility. The tactic can be intensified by setting them on fire. Often by way of a symbolic act, a → *fire* is lit that seems dangerous but only (unlike real arson) speeds up the fate of the garbage by a few hours, which would be incinerated anyway. In Paris in → *May '68*, students used the lids of garbage cans as → *protective shields*. The Frankfurt garbage-can barricade arose shortly after "Bloody Wednesday" in 1973, one of the highpoints in the → *Frankfurt Squatting Campaign*. (OE)

Gdeim Izik Protestcamp, engl. → *Gdeim Izik protest camp*. Das → *Protestcamp* war Teil des Westsaharakonflikts und Ausdruck des saharauischen Widerstands gegen die marokkanische Kontrolle. Es beherbergte schätzungsweise fünfzehntausend Saharauis, die indigenen Bewohner∗innen der Westsahara, in traditionellen → *Zelten* (Khaimas). Das Camp war autark und hatte seine eigene → *Infrastruktur*, was die Unabhängigkeit von Marokko und die Fähigkeit zur Selbstversorgung beweisen sollte. Es bestand etwa einen Monat und wurde am 8. November → *2010* gewaltsam durch die marokkanischen Behörden aufgelöst (→ *Gewalt*). (JD)

Gdeim Izik protest camp, Ger. → *Gdeim Izik Protestcamp*. This → *protest camp* was part of the Western Sahara conflict and an expression of the

Sahrawi resistance against Moroccan control. It housed approximately 15,000 Sahrawis, the Indigenous people of Western Sahara, in traditional → *tents* (khaimas). The camp was autonomous and had its own → *infrastructure*, which was supposed to demonstrate independence from Morocco as well as self-sufficiency. On November 8, → *2010*, after about a month, it was forcefully removed by the Moroccan authorities (→ *Violence*). (JD)

Gegenbau. Zentrum für Politische Schönheit: Holocaust-Mahnmal neben dem Grundstück des deutschen rechtsextremen AfD-Politikers Björn Höcke, Bornhagen, 2017 (Counter-construction. Zentrum für Politische Schönheit (Center for Political Beauty): Holocaust monument next to the home of German far-right politician Björn Höcke, Bornhagen, 2017)

Gegenbau, engl. → *Counter-construction*. In einer diffamierenden Hetzrede im Rahmen der Pegida-Demonstrationen (→ *Demonstration*, → *Rechte Proteste*) in Dresden im Januar 2017 hatte der rechtsextreme deutsche AfD-Politiker Björn Höcke das *Denkmal für die ermordeten Juden Europas* in Berlin als „Denkmal der Schande" bezeichnet und eine „erinnerungspolitische Wende um 180 Grad" gefordert (vgl. Frank 2017; → *Denkmalsturz*). In Reaktion darauf erwarb die Künstler∗innengruppe „Zentrum für politische Schönheit" (ZPS) ein Grundstück in unmittelbarer Nachbar∗innenschaft zu Höckes Wohnhaus in der thüringischen Ortschaft Bornhagen und errichtete dort einen verkleinerten Nachbau des Berliner Holocaustmahnmals. Die Umgestaltung des

Grundstücks durch das ZPS lässt sich mit einem Begriff des Kunsthistorikers Martin Warnke als „Gegenbau" beschreiben (Warnke 1996). Vis-à-vis von Höckes privatem Domizil – einem alten holzverkleideten Pfarrhaus – entstand nach dem Vorbild der von dem Architekten Peter Eisenman entworfenen quaderförmigen Beton-Stelen ein Bauwerk, das der Politiker als einen weltanschaulichen Angriff begreifen musste. Auf den spezifischen Kontext dieses Protestarchitekturlexikons bezogen, stellt sich der Gegenbau als ein polemisches Bauwerk dar, das seine ideologische Überzeugungskraft aus der direkten Konfrontation mit der Architektur der politischen Gegner*innen gewinnt – und aus dieser Manifestation einen medialen Widerhall zu erzielen versucht (→ *Tent Embassy*, → *Medien*). (SH)

Gelbwestenbewegung, engl. → *Yellow Vests movement*. Startpunkt der Bewegung der „Gilets jaunes" war die Ankündigung der französischen Regierung, zur Finanzierung der Energiewende die Kraftstoffpreise zu erhöhen. Daher fanden die im Jahr → *2018* beginnenden Proteste zunächst an den → *Kreisverkehren* an den Stadträndern statt, da dort eine Solidarisierung der Autofahrer*innen zu erwarten war. Es war somit die erste suburbane Protestbewegung, die zudem mit dem sozialen Stadt-Land-Gefälle kodiert war. Kurz darauf fanden in Paris große → *Demonstrationen* mit gewaltsamen Ausschreitungen statt (→ *Gewalt*). Der Versuch missglückte, die Bewegung danach wieder auf die lokale Ebene von Bürgerräten zurückzubringen. (OE)

General Assembly, engl. → *General Assembly*; → *Handzeichen*, → *Kommunikation*, → *Majdan*, → *Movimiento 15M*, → *Occupy Wall Street*

General Assembly, Ger. → *General Assembly*; → *Communication*, → *Hand signals*, → *Maidan*, → *Movimiento 15M*, → *Occupy Wall Street*

Gewalt, engl. → *Violence*. In der ein oder anderen Form spielt Gewalt bei fast allen Protesten eine Rolle, die hier im Zusammenhang mit ihrer Protestarchitektur untersucht wurden. Gewalt-same Eskalationen zwischen Protestierenden und Sicherheitskräften führen oft dazu, dass eine sich neu formierende Protestbewegung einen größeren Zulauf aus der Bevölkerung erhält, als dies vorher abzusehen war (→ *Solidaritätsgeste*). Gewalt kann von drei Seiten ausgehen: von den Demonstrierenden, von den Vertreter*innen des staatlichen „Gewaltmonopols" oder von dritter Seite. In diesem Fall kann der → *Polizei* die Aufgabe zukommen, Gewalt zwischen Protesten und Gegenprotesten zu verhindern.

Wie aber wird die Protestarchitektur durch Gewalt geformt? Bei den → *Barrikaden* ist dies offensichtlich, denn sie sollen → *Schutz* vor Gewalt bieten, bisweilen aber auch Gegen-Gewalt ermöglichen. Ob überhaupt Barrikaden entstehen sollen, wird innerhalb von Protestbewegungen immer wieder diskutiert. In → *Gorleben* wurde gestritten, ob die → *Türme* nicht bloß die Räumung erschweren, sondern auch dazu genutzt werden sollten, Gülle oder Farbe auf die Polizei hinunterzuwerfen (ein Konsensbeschluss sprach sich letztlich dagegen aus). Das → *Protestcamp* auf dem → *Majdan* in Kyjiw war dagegen in Erwartung gewaltvoller Auseinandersetzungen zu einer regelrechten Festung ausgebaut worden.

Gewalt wird oft als Drohkulisse verwendet: Proteste könnten gewaltsam verlaufen, deswegen werden sie im Ansatz unterbunden. Dinge wie → *Strohsäcke* könnten als → *Waffe* dienen, weswegen sie zur passiven Bewaffnung zählen und in Deutschland verboten sind, ebenso wie andere Mittel zum Schutz vor Polizeigewalt.

Ob ein Protest gewaltfrei verläuft – und wenn nicht, wer für eine Eskalation verantwortlich war – zählt zu den meistdiskutierten Fragen nahezu jeder Protestbewegung. Der Gewaltbegriff ist ein weites Feld: Wird bei einer → *Blockade* schon Gewalt ausgeübt? Und wie verhält es sich mit Aktionen des → *zivilen Ungehorsams*? Andere Länder haben andere Traditionen. So zählen in Frankreich brennende Barrikaden und Sachbeschädigungen bis heute zur re-

Gezi

volutionären Folklore von Protesten und Streiks. Der Staat wird zwar eingreifen, wenn derlei passiert, die gesellschaftliche Toleranzschwelle ist dort jedoch vor dem Hintergrund mehrerer erfolgreicher Aufstände (Französische Revolution von 1789, →Julirevolution →1830, →Märzrevolution →1848) deutlich höher als anderswo. (OE)

Gezi-Park, engl. → *Gezi Park*. Die Proteste gegen den Bau einer Shopping Mall auf dem Grundstück des Gezi-Parks in Istanbul führten nach der Eskalation eines Polizeieinsatzes am 1. Juni → *2013* zur Errichtung eines → *Protestcamps*. Tausende Besetzer∗innen bewohnten vorübergehend den bewaldeten Stadtpark, abends beteiligten sich an → *Demonstrationen* gegen die autoritäre Politik unter Recep Tayyip Erdoğan bis zu 100 000 Menschen. → *Infrastrukturen* wie → *Küchen*, sanitäre Anlagen, Erste-Hilfe-Stationen, Pressezelte (→ *Medien*) und Orte für Versammlungen entstanden spontan, das Wissen erfahrener Aktivist∗innen war jedoch essenziell für die Organisation des gemeinschaftlichen Zusammenlebens. Der kurze Zeitraum von zwei Wochen und die große Anzahl der Beteiligten verhinderte Burnout-Gefühle, starre Rollen und eine rigide Arbeitsteilung. Aus gefundenen Materialien bauten die Besetzer∗innen Möbel, z.B. Bänke mit Schachfiguren als Füße, eine Bücherei aus → *Ziegelsteinen* und einen Essensstand aus umfunktionierten Straßenbrüstungen (→ *Zweckentfremdung*, → *Baumaterial*). Fasziniert von der Kreativität fertigte die Gruppe Herkes İçin Mimarlık („Architektur für alle") Zeichnungen von den Architekturen an (Herkes İçin Mimarlık 2013). Der Aktivist und Blogger Oscar Ten Houten dokumentierte auf einem → *Lageplan* die Aufteilung des Parks in Nachbar∗innenschaften verschiedener sozio-religiös-politischer Gruppen. Er bezeichnete es als „Wunder vom Gezi-Park", dass die Proteste Kommunist∗innen, Sozialist∗innen, Nationalist∗innen, Muslim∗innen, Kurd∗innen, Anarchist∗innen, Grüne, Queere, und Fußballfans verschiedener (!) Vereine zusammenbringen konnten. Auf dem

benachbarten Taksim-Platz und in der Umgebung kam es während der Proteste immer wieder zu gewaltsamen Konfrontationen (→ *Gewalt*) mit der → *Polizei*. Die Fassade des Kulturzentrums Atatürk wurde mit → *Fahnen* aller beteiligten Gruppen behängt. → *Barrikaden* aus Straßenmobiliar und Schrott (alte Waschmaschinen, ausrangierte → *Fahrzeuge*) erschwerten der Polizei den Zugang zum besetzten Gebiet, funktionierten jedoch vor allem als Treffpunkt der Protestierenden und symbolische Grenze der → *Besetzung*. Nach der gewaltsamen Räumung des Camps am 12. Juni 2013 weiteten sich die Proteste über die gesamte Türkei aus. (AMM)

Gezi Park, Ger. → *Gezi-Park*. The protests against the construction of a shopping mall on the grounds of Gezi Park in Istanbul led to a police operation escalating, and on June 1, → *2013*, to a → *protest camp* being set up. Thousands of occupiers resided temporarily in the wooded urban park, and in the evening as many as 100,000 people took part in the → *demonstrations* against the authoritarian policies under Recep Tayyip Erdoğan. → *Infrastructure* such as → *kitchens*, sanitary facilities, first-aid stations, press tents (→ *media*), and spaces for assemblies arose spontaneously, whereby the knowledge of experienced activists was crucial to the organization of communal life. The short period of two weeks and the large number of participants prevented feelings of burnout, rigid roles, or stringent divisions of labor. The occupiers used found materials to build furniture, such as benches with oversized chess figures as legs, a library made from → *bricks*, and a food dispensing counter made from repurposed street → *barriers* (→ *Misappropriation*, → *Building materials*). Fascinated by the creativity, the group Herkes İçin Mimarlık (Architecture for Everyone) made drawings of the architectural structures (Herkes İçin Mimarlık 2013). Activist and blogger Oscar Ten Houten documented on a → *site plan* the subdivision of the park into neighborhoods for different socioreligious and political groups. He termed it the "miracle of

Gezi Park" that the protests succeeded in bringing together communists, socialists, nationalists, Muslims, Kurds, anarchists, environmentalists, queers, and football fans from different (!) clubs. In and around the adjacent Taksim Square, during the protests there were repeatedly violent confrontations (→ *Violence*) with the → *police*. The frontage of the Atatürk Cultural Center was festooned with → *flags* of all the groups involved. → *Barricades* made from street furniture and scrap (old washing machines, discarded → *vehicles*) made it harder for the police to access the occupied zone, but above all functioned as a meeting point for the protesters and as the symbolic border of the → *occupation*. After the camp was violently cleared on June 12, 2013, the protests spread throughout Turkey. (AMM)

Glue, Ger. → *Klebstoff*; → *Blockade*, → *Body deployment*, → *Guerrilla tactics*, → *Hong Kong protests*, → *Super-gluing*, → *Vehicles*

Gorleben, engl. → *Gorleben. Am Dorfeingang steht ein großes Schild: „Herzlich willkommen im freien Wendland!" [...] Der rot-grüne Schlagbaum steht offen, Info-Haus (eine Art Kiosk) und „Paßstelle" sind verwaist. Dafür gibt es Hinweistafeln: Eine zeigt zwei finster dreinblickende Polizisten mit der Unterschrift „Wir müssen draußen bleiben". Auf der Rückseite die Warnung für „Wenden": „Halt! Hier BRD. Vorsicht, Schußwaffen." Eine Grenze ähnlich der „Zonengrenze", die nur ein paar Kilometer weit weg ist. [...] Auf der freien Fläche stehen etwa 120 Holzhütten, nach altwendischer Sitte in Rundlingsform um einen Dorfplatz gruppiert. Da, wo vermutlich der Bohrmeißel [...] 2000 Meter tief in den Gorlebener Salzstock fahren soll, um dessen Eignung als Atommüll-Lager zu erkunden, ist ein klobiger Findling in den Heidesand gegraben. Beschriftung (was ist hier eigentlich nicht beschriftet?): „Wendische Kultstätte aus dem Jahr 1004." (Rosenblatt 1981)*

Im Mai → *1980* besetzten 5000 Atomkraftgegner∗innen ein Gelände in der Nähe von Gorleben, auf dem Tiefenbohrungen für ein geplantes Atommüll-Endlager durchgeführt werden sollten. Sie errichteten die „Republik Freies Wendland", ein → *Protestcamp* mit 800 Menschen, die für 33 Tage in einer utopischen Alternativ-Enklave zusammenlebten. Seit dem Beschluss der niedersächsischen Landesregierung im Jahr 1977, das dünn besiedelte Wendland an der Grenze zur DDR als Standort für die Lagerung von Atommüll zu erkunden, organisierten Vereinigungen wie die „Bürgerinitiative Lüchow-Dannenberg" und die „Bäuerliche Notgemeinschaft" zahlreiche Kundgebungen, → *Demonstrationen* und → *Blockaden* gegen das Vorhaben. Der sechstägige Gorleben-Treck im März 1979, der im Wendland begann, war mit 100 000 Protestierenden und 350 Traktoren die bis dahin größte Anti-Atom-Demonstration in Deutschland. Das „Hüttendorf 1004", benannt nach der besetzten „Bohrstelle 1004", wurde in bundesweiten Vorbereitungstreffen drei Monate lang geplant. Eine spontane → *Besetzung* im April durch militante Aktivist∗innen, die sich mit den Planungen der übrigen Atomkraftgegner∗innen nicht identifizierten, führte beinahe zum Abbruch der Aktion.

Bereits in der Vorbereitungsphase drehten sich viele Diskussionen um die Frage, wie bei einer Konfrontation mit der → *Polizei* zu handeln sei. Die Spaltung der Bewegung in „Gewaltfreie" oder „Militante" war während der Besetzung Kernthema vieler Gesprächsrunden, u.a. als es um den Bau von → *Barrikaden* und die Verteidigung der → *Türme* ging. In Planspielen wurde das Verhalten bei der polizeilichen Räumung gemeinsam geprobt. Alarmketten wurden eingerichtet, damit Menschen außerhalb des Hüttendorfs kurzfristig zur Räumung kommen konnten. Die Siedlung wurde nach einem → *Lageplan* als Runddorf mit zentralem Dorfplatz errichtet, auf dem im Falle einer Räumung 5000 Menschen passen sollten.

Der Hüttenbau und die Gestaltung des Dorfalltags hatten für die Platzbesetzer∗innen einen hohen Stellenwert. Eine fantasievolle Siedlung entstand,

Gorleben / Case Study

die an den Wochenenden viele Besucher*innen aus der gesamten Region anzog. Gemeinschaftseinrichtungen wurden errichtet, u.a. eine →Küche, Badeanstalt, Radiostation, Sauna, ein Frisiersalon, Kinderhaus und eine Ponyreitanlage für Tourist*innen. Wasser wurde mit einer Solar-Warmwasseranlage erwärmt.

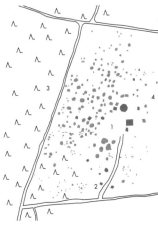

■ Gemeinschaftsbauten (Community buildings)
■ Individuelle Unterkünfte (Individual shelters)

Gorleben. 1 Dorfplatz 2 Passstelle 3 Wald 4 Gerodete Fläche (Gorleben. 1 Village square 2 Passport office 3 Forest 4 Cleared area)

Die Journalistin Sabine Rosenbladt lebte damals fünf Tage im Hüttendorf und schrieb in einem 1981 veröffentlichten Bericht über den Alltag während der letzten Tage vor der Räumung:

Wir kommen am Freundschaftshaus vorbei, „Das einzige Haus, das aus zurechtgesägten Brettern und nach Plan gebaut wurde", erläuterte Kuddel, „sonst ist fürs Dorf kein einziger Baum gefällt worden." Das Freundschaftshaus ist ein achteckiges Gebilde aus hellem Kiefernholz, mit schrägem Dach und einem Türmchen über dem Licht- und Luftschacht in der Mitte. Entworfen haben es Hamburger Architekturstudenten. Neben den Krüppel-Hogans, Sperrmüll-Hütten und Erd-Wigwams rundherum sieht das Profi-Haus ein bißchen aus wie die feine Tante aus der Stadt. [...]

Die Häuser – „die hauen einen doch um, was?" schreit Kuddel begeistert. Und tatsächlich sind sie schön, die wendischen Hütten und Paläste. Fürs erste Sightseeing brauchen wir drei Stunden. Und auch dann haben wir erst ein Bruchteil gesehen von der Dorfarchitektur, die zudem noch ständig wächst: Trotz Wochenende wird an allen Ecken und Enden wild gebaut. Da steht das Heartbreak-Hotel und das Meditationshaus („Kommt zur Yin-Yang-Fahne"). [...] Ein Strobo (von den Hamburger Stromboykotteuren) zeigt uns die einzigartige Türkonstruktion der Strobohütte: Man zieht an einem Knüppel, und die Drehtür schwingt auf. Das Haus des Akrobaten daneben besteht fast ausschließlich aus Glastüren und -fenstern vom Sperrmüll. Es wirkt äußerst zierlich und elegant, ganz im Gegenteil zur „Matthias-Knetssl-Alm" [eine Art bayerischer Robin Hood]: Vierschrötig, duckt sie sich tief in den Boden, so daß nur das solide Schindeldach zu sehen ist. [...]

Die Bauwut hat die bizarrsten Formen hervorgebracht: Dachterrassen und Loggien, Emporen, Flach-, Spitz- und Runddächer. Sogar einen Kirchturm gibt es, erbaut von der „Initiative Kirche für Gorleben – Beten statt Bohren". Am Nordrhein-Westfalen-Haus – eigentlich eine Reihenhausanlage aus fünfeckigen, wabenförmig zusammenhängenden Hütten mit kleinen Innenhöfen – klebt das Schild „Wüstenrot-Musterhaus". [...]

Vor dem Haus Bochum sitzt ein Typ in der Sonne. Daneben stillt eine Frau mit langem Zopf ihr Baby. Wir hocken uns dazu und lassen uns ein wenig Dorfklatsch berichten. „Gestern", grinst er, „hat jemand ein Bad genommen. [...] Sie haben ein riesiges Feuer gemacht, und dann hat der sich reingelegt. Im Freien." Wochentags, meint er, sind jetzt ungefähr 200 bis 300 Leute auf dem Platz. Die Stimmung angesichts der drohenden Räumung schwankt: „Es gibt solche Panik-Minuten. Dann hämmert plötzlich niemand mehr. [...] Erst um fünf Uhr, wenn alle denken, jetzt ist es zu spät für eine Räumung, geht das Leben wieder los." [...]

Am Vorgartenzaun – auch Zäune gibt es schon im Dorf, na und? Die schützen die frisch angepflanzten Bäumchen – bleiben Wochenendausflügler stehen, holen verschämt den Fotoapparat aus der Handtasche. „Eben hat mich ein Tourist am Info-Haus gefragt, ob es Eintritt kostet", grinst Kuddel. Die Freie Republik lockt Tausende von Neugierigen an, die das alternative Leben hautnah bestaunen möchten. [...]

Ich hab Hunger. Also schlendern wir zur Küchenhütte rüber. Hinter der Theke wirbeln fünf Leute, schmieren Quarkbrote, das Stück 30 Pfennig. Daneben gibt's Tee, von der „Gruppe volle Kanne – ohne Dampf kein Kampf!" Warum heißt das Frauenhaus eigentlich so, frage ich, braucht ihr schon einen Zufluchtsort für geschlagene Frauen? „Nee, natürlich nicht, das haben die Frauen eben allein gebaut." [...] Mir klingt das alles ein bißchen zu perfekt, um wahr zu sein. Wie funktioniert dieses Dorf? Die Bewohner sind zusammengewürfelt aus der ganzen Bundesrepublik, sind Studenten und Arbeitslose, Bürgerinitiativler und Anarchos, militante Chaoten sollen doch auch dabei sein. Bis zu 4000 Leute leben und arbeiten auf diesem Platz. Die Atmosphäre, das fühle ich, ist ungewöhnlich freundschaftlich, geradezu zärtlich. Wer koordiniert das hinter den Kulissen? Wer organisiert die Verpflegung, weist „Bauplätze" zu, vermittelt, schlichtet?

„Im Sprecherrat", berichtet der Bochumer, „herrscht Chaos. Die diskutieren ständig, was gewaltfrei ist und was nicht. Und ob man sich im Sitzen oder im Knien räumen läßt ..." [...] Vorn am Info-Haus klebt ein Erklärungsversuch: „Der Sprecherrat, ist keine Regierung, Staat etc., sondern ein Modell von basisdemokratischer Entscheidungsfindung auf'm Platz." Jede Bezugsgruppe, so sollte es eigentlich ablaufen, schickt jeden Tag einen Abgeordneten in den Sprecherrat. Außerdem kann jeder an den Sitzungen teilnehmen, der Lust hat.

Es gibt keine Mehrheitsentscheidungen oder Abstimmungen, sondern es wird so lange diskutiert, bis ein „Konsens" gefunden ist. Eine mühsame Prozedur. Ob es klappt, weiß niemand so recht. Jedenfalls scheint über das Verhalten während der Räumung noch viel Unklarheit zu herrschen. [...]

„Nach dem Konsens im Sprecherrat werden wir uns absolut gewaltfrei verhalten, nur passiven Widerstand leisten." Ein „Neuer" will diskutieren. „Was heißt denn überhaupt Gewalt?" ruft er dazwischen. Neben mir murmelt jemand: „O Gott, nein, bitte nicht schon wieder!" [...]

Gabi Jäger, Literaturstudentin aus Hamburg mit zweitem Wohnsitz im Landkreis, sagt mir: „[...] Grob gesprochen, gibt es im Dorf diese drei Fraktionen: Ein sehr kleiner ‚harter Kern' von teilweise sehr jungen Leuten, die ihr ganzes Leben lang Außenseiter waren und irrsinnige Aggressionen haben gegen alles, was sie bevormunden will. Sie wollen das Dorf natürlich nicht kampflos aufgeben, werden aber als Minderheit unterdrückt. Dann gibt es die Fraktion der linken Studenten aus den Städten, die mit ihrem Liberalismus hier keine klare Linie vertreten. Die größte Fraktion sind die, die die Aktion als Unterstützung des Widerstands im Landkreis betrachten." [...]

Die Gewaltfrage ist der große Konfliktstoff im Dorf 1004. Ständig brechen die Gegensätze wieder auf, ständig gibt es Auseinandersetzungen, ständig laufen auch Aktionen, die dem gewaltfreien Konsenspapier widersprechen. Zum Beispiel die Barrikaden. Am Sonntagmorgen erscheint im Sprecherrat der Bürgermeister von Trebel. Er weist darauf hin, daß von den gemeindeeigenen Wegen im Gartower Forst die von den Platzbesetzern aus Baumstämmen gebauten Barrikaden entfernt werden müssen. [...] Der Sprecherrat sagt ihm zu: Bis Montag sind die Barrikaden weggeräumt. [...] Am Montag sind die Barrikaden aber nicht weggeräumt, es stehen sogar noch mehr da. „Der Unsicherheitsfaktor im Dorf", so Gabi, „ist, daß manche Leute hier einfach

169

Gorleben / Case Study

keinen Bock auf Sitzungen haben. Die machen dann Aktionen, ohne sich abzustimmen." Deshalb wird im Sprecherrat am Montag noch mal drei geschlagene Stunden über das Barrikaden-Problem diskutiert. [...] Schließlich setzen die zahlenmäßig stärkeren Barrikadengegner sich durch. [...]

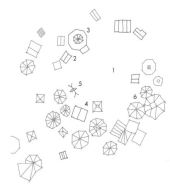

■ Gemeinschaftsbauten (Community buildings)
■ Individuelle Unterkünfte (Individual shelters)

Gorleben. 1 Dorfplatz 2 Küche 3 Freundschaftshaus 4 Turm 5 Schaukel 6 „Reihenhausanlage" (Gorleben. 1 Village square 2 Kitchen 3 Friendship House 4 Tower 5 Swing 6 "Terraced house estate")

Krieg. Panzer. Messerscharfe NATO-Drahthaue. Hubschrauber, die donnernd landen, Truppen entladen. Bulldozer. Helme, Schilde, dahinter unbewegte Gesichter. Uniformierte bis zum Horizont. Berittene Einheiten. Einheiten mit schwarzgefärbten Gesichtern. Noch mehr Hubschrauber. Krieg. [...] 5000 Polizei- und Bundesgrenzschutzbeamte entfernten am Mittwoch, dem 4. Juni 1980, 2500 Atomkraftgegner vom Flurstück 89/7 der Gemarkung Trebel, das sie aus Protest gegen die geplante Tiefbohrung 1004 illegal besetzt hielten. Nach Abschluß des Einsatzes bedankte sich der Einsatzführer bei den Demonstranten für ihr friedliches Verhalten. [...] Nach „polizeitaktischen

Maßstäben" ist die Räumung glimpflich abgelaufen. Und auch manche Atomkraftgegner haben sich hinterher darüber lustig gemacht, daß Besetzer sich in die Horrorszenerie von „Apocalypse Now" versetzt fühlten, Parallelen zu My Lai und anderen Massakern zogen. [...]

Mit Schlagstöcken wurden die Platzbesetzer aus ihrer Freien Republik in die rauhe Wirklichkeit der Bundesrepublik zurückgeholt. Und da war alles beim alten: Im Juli gibt das Kabinett Albrecht grünes Licht für ein Zwischenlager mit einer Kapazität von 1500 Tonnen Uran in Form abgebrannter Kernbrennstäbe bei Gorleben. (Rosenblatt 1981)

Auch nach der Räumung des Hüttendorfs, einer der größten Polizeieinsätze der deutschen Nachkriegsgeschichte, bleibt Gorleben ein zentraler Ort für die Anti-AKW-Proteste. Zwischen 1996 und 2011 finden regelmäßig Castor-Transporte ins Zwischenlager in Gorleben statt. Protestaktionen wie Sabotagen und Blockaden, auch unter dem Einsatz von →*Lock-on Devices* (u.a. der →*Betonpyramide* der „Bäuerlichen Notgemeinschaft") führen immer wieder zu großen Polizeieinsätzen. Als 2020 * der Salzstock Gorleben von einer Expert*innenkommission als Endlager ausgeschlossen wird, finden vier Jahrzehnte Protest ein erfolgreiches Ende.

Die Architektur des Hüttendorfs wurde Motiv vieler Fotos und Protestplakate sowie Gegenstand zahlreicher Zeitungsartikel und Filme (→ *Medien*). In seinem Aufsatz „Besetzerarchitektur" beschreibt der Architekt Andreas Orth verschiedene →*Bautypen*, die er in den Anti-Atom-Protestdörfern der 1970er und 1980er Jahre vorfand. Vorbild für das Freundschaftshaus in Gorleben war eine Hütte im Anti-AKW-Protestdorf im Whyler Wald. Die „runden Holzhäuser" seien dann zum „Erkennungsmerkmal für besetzte Bauplätze" geworden (Orth 1980). Auch der Zimmermann Dieter Schaarschmidt erinnert sich an die besonderen Bauten, die in den Hüttendörfern als Versammlungs- und Veranstaltungsorte genutzt wurden:

Bei meiner ersten Platzbesetzung im baden-württembergischen Wyhl am

Kaiserstuhl lernte ich, wie wichtig so ein festes, schützendes Gebäude eines Freundschaftshauses für den dauerhaften Erfolg einer Protestbewegung ist. [...] Als wir die Platzbesetzung der Atomkraftwerksbaustelle Brokdorf planten, habe ich das Baumaterial für ein Freundschaftshaus nach dem Vorbild Wyhl [...] auf einem LKW bereitgehalten. Leider kam es wegen der massiven Polizeieinsätze nie zu einer baulichen Umsetzung. Später, als ich bereits im Wendland lebte, haben wir ebenfalls auf diese Erfahrungen aufgebaut. (Persönliche Kommunikation, Dieter Schaarschmidt 2022)

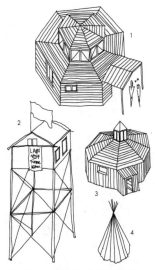

Gorleben. 1 Freundschaftshaus 2 Turm 3 Rundhütte 4 Tipi (Gorleben. 1 Friendship House 2 Tower 3 Round hut 4 Tipi)

Ein weiterer Typ der „Besetzerarchitektur" ist das Tipi – es erfordert den geringsten Zeitaufwand: Mit Hilfe einiger langer Stangen ist es ohne umständliches Sägen und Nageln schnell zu errichten. [...] Das Rundhaus auf vier Stützen, mit mannshohen Seitenwänden

und Kegeldach ist sicherlich der meistgebaute Typ in dem vielgestaltigen Sammelsurium von Hütten gewesen. (Orth 1980)

In den letzten Wochen vor der Räumung entstand im Hüttendorf ein 12 Meter hoher Turm-Pfahlbau. Dass dieser → Turm im Dorf eine Sonderrolle hatte, legten nicht nur die Sprüche auf den am Turm befestigten → Bannern nahe, die eine Differenzierung der Besetzung in „Dorf" und „Turm" vornahmen: „Turm und Dorf könnt ihr zerstören, aber nicht die Kraft, die es schuf" und „Auf Platz + Turm: Den Kampf der Wenden könnt ihr hier nicht beenden". Auch die Verteidigung des Turms bei der kurzbevorstehenden Räumung wurde im Sprecherrat unabhängig von der Besetzung des Dorfplatzes und des Freundschaftshauses diskutiert. Sie machte die Spaltung der Bewegung in „Gewaltfreie" und „Militante" besonders sichtbar.

Im Juli 2020 sprach Sigurd Elert, der im Hüttendorf lebte und den Turm geplant hatte, mit Andreas Conradt von der *Gorleben Rundschau* über die Entstehung des Baus:

„Ich habe mir damals angeschaut, was Zimmerleute, Bauern und Widerständler da aus Bäumen, Bohlen und Brettern aufbauen. Es waren großartige Hütten und Häuser, phantasievoll und mit lauter alternativen Ideen, aber dem täglich erwarteten, gewaltigen Polizeieinsatz konnten sie nicht standhalten. Mir schwebte etwas vor, das die Polizei vor Schwierigkeiten bei der Räumung von Demonstranten stellen würde. Ein Turm zum Beispiel, der hoch und stabil sein musste." [...] Am Ende war der Turm gut zwölf Meter hoch; trotz Höhenangst zimmerten Sigurd und seine Kumpel ganz oben noch eine geschlossene Hütte. In ihr war später die Sendetechnik von Radio Freies Wendland untergebracht.

[...] „Wenn alle auf dem Boden sitzen, geht so eine Räumung ratzfatz. Mit einem Turm kann man's der Polizei schwerer machen. Das war die Idee. [...] Den Turm zu stürmen hat genauso viel Zeit gebraucht, wie alles andere." Als er schließlich umfiel, war die Republik

171

Günter Zint: Hüttendorf und Turm mit Radiostation (Hut village and tower with radio station), Mai 1980

Günter Zint: Versammlung im Freundschaftshaus
(Assembly at the Friendship House), Mai 1980

Günter Zint: Erstellung von Passbildern in der Passstelle (Passport photo production in the passport office), Mai 1980

Günter Zint: Selbstgebaute Warmwasseranlage mit Solarpaneelen (Self-made hot-water system with solar panels), Mai 1980

Burckhard Kretschmann: Sonntagsbesucher*innen (Sunday visitors), Mai 1980

Hans-Hermann Müller: Badewanne (Bathtub), Mai 1980

Räumung mit eingekesseltem Dorfplatz (Eviction, police kettling the square), 4. Juni 1980

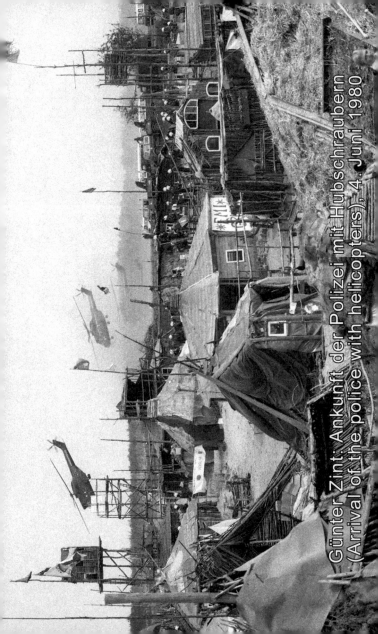

Günter Zint: Ankunft der Polizei mit Hubschraubern (Arrival of the police with helicopters), 4. Juni 1980

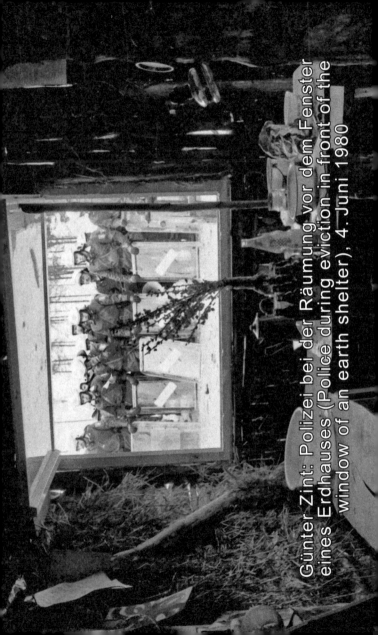

Günter Zint: Polizei bei der Räumung vor dem Fenster eines Erdhauses (Police during eviction in front of the window of an earth shelter), 4. Juni 1980

Günter Zint: Panzer des Bundesgrenzschutzes, dahinter das besetzte Dach des Freundschaftshauses (Tanks of the Federal Border Guard, in the background the occupied roof of the Friendship House), 4. Juni 1980

Gorleben / Case Study

Freies Wendland Geschichte. Die Bilder aber blieben im kollektiven Gedächtnis: Das Meer aus Hütten, die Passstelle und eben der Turm. (Conradt 2020) (Texte von Sabine Rosenblatt, Andreas Orth, Andreas Conradt; Gesprächspartner: Dieter Schaarschmidt; Einleitung und Recherche: AMM)

Gorleben, Ger. → *Gorleben. At the entrance to the village, a big sign reads: "Welcome to the free Wendland!" [...] The red and green barrier is open, the information house (a kind of kiosk) and the "passport office" are deserted. But there are sign-boards: one shows two frowning policemen with the label "We have to stay outside". On the back, a warning for "Wends": "Stop! FRG starts here. Caution, firearms." A border similar to the one between West and East Germany just a few kilometers away. [...] In the open area, there are about 120 wooden huts arranged around a village square like a Rundling according to old Wendish custom. There, where presumably the drill bit [...] is to drive 2,000 meters deep into the Gorleben salt dome to explore its suitability as a nuclear waste repository, a chunky boulder is dug into the heather sand, labeled (what is not labeled here?): "Wendish cultic site from the year 1004."* (Rosenblatt 1981)

In May → 1980, 5,000 opponents of nuclear power occupied a site near Gorleben where deep drilling for a planned nuclear waste repository was to be carried out. They set up the "Free Republic of Wendland," a → *protest camp* with 800 people who lived together in a utopian alternative enclave for thirty-three days. Following the Lower Saxony state government's decision in 1977 to explore the sparsely populated Wendland region on the border with East Germany as a site for storing nuclear waste, associations such as the Bürgerinitiative Lüchow-Dannenberg (Lüchow-Dannenberg Citizens' Initiative) and the Bäuerliche Notgemeinschaft (Rural Emergency Association) organized numerous rallies, → *demonstrations*, and → *blockades* against the project. The six-day Gorleben trek in March 1979, which began in the Wendland region, was the largest anti-nuclear demonstration in Germany up to that time, with 100,000 protesters and 350 tractors. The "Hüttendorf 1004" (Hut Village 1004), named after the occupied "Bohrstelle 1004" (Drilling Site 1004), was planned for three months in nationwide preparatory meetings. A spontaneous → *occupation* in April by militant activists, who did not identify with the plans of the other anti-nuclear activists, almost led to the cancellation of the campaign.

Right from the preparation phase, many discussions revolved around the question of how to act in a confrontation with the → *police*. The division of the movement into "nonviolent" and "militant" factions was the core issue of numerous discussion rounds during the occupation, including when it came to building → *barricades* and defending the → *towers*. Simulation games were used to collectively rehearse how to behave during a police eviction. Alarm chains were set up so that people outside the hut village could come to the eviction on short notice. The settlement was built according to a → *site plan* as a circular village with a central village square that could accommodate 5,000 people in the event of an eviction.

The construction of huts and the organization of everyday life in the village were of great importance to the occupiers. An imaginative settlement was created, which attracted many visitors from the entire region on weekends. Community facilities were built, including a → *kitchen*, bathhouse, radio station, sauna, hairdressing salon, children's house, and a pony-riding facility for tourists. Water was heated with a solar hot water system.

The journalist Sabine Rosenblatt lived in the hut village for five days and wrote about everyday life during the last days before the eviction in a report published in 1981:

We pass the Friendship House, "the only house built from sawn boards and according to plan," Kuddel explained, "otherwise not a single tree has been felled for the village." The Friendship

House is an octagonal structure made of light pine, with a sloping roof, and a turret above the light and air shaft in the center. Architecture students from Hamburg designed it. Next to the slapdash hogans, bulky-waste huts, and earthen wigwams all around, the professional house looks a bit like the posh aunt from the city. [...]

The houses—"they're mind-blowing, aren't they?" cries Kuddel enthusiastically. Indeed, they are beautiful, the Wendish huts and palaces. For the first sightseeing we need three hours. And even then, we've only seen a fraction of the village architecture, which is, moreover, constantly growing: despite the fact that it's the weekend, frenzied construction is going on everywhere. There is the Heartbreak Hotel and the Meditation House ("Come to the yin-yang flag"). [...] A strobo (from Hamburg's electricity [Strom] boycotters) shows us the unique door construction of the strobo hut: you pull a stick and the revolving door swings open. The acrobat's house next to it consists almost entirely of glass doors and windows from bulky waste. It looks extremely delicate and elegant, quite the opposite of the "Matthias Kneissl Alp" [a kind of Bavarian Robin Hood]: stocky, it ducks deep into the ground so that only the solid shingle roof is visible. [...]

The building mania has produced the most bizarre shapes: roof terraces and loggias, galleries, flat, pointed, and round roofs. There is even a church tower, built by the "Initiative Kirche für Gorleben–Beten statt Bohren" (Church for Gorleben Initiative—Praying instead of Drilling). On the North Rhine-Westphalia House, which is actually a row house complex consisting of pentagonal cottages linked in a honeycomb pattern with small inner courtyards, a sign reads "Wüstenrot model home." [...]

A guy is sitting in the sun in front of the Bochum House. Next to him, a woman with a long braid is breastfeeding her baby. We squat down and listen to a bit of village gossip. "Yesterday," he recounts with a grin, "someone took a

bath. [...] They built a huge fire, and then he got in. Out in the open." Weekdays, he says, there are now about 200 to 300 people in the square. The mood fluctuates in the face of the impending eviction: "There are such minutes of panic. Then suddenly no one is hammering. [...] It's not until five o'clock, when everyone thinks it's now too late for an eviction, that life starts again." [...]

At the front garden fence—fences also already exist in the village, so what? They protect the freshly planted trees—weekenders pause and bashfully take their cameras out of their handbags. "Just now, a tourist at the information house asked me if there was an entrance fee," Kuddel announces with a smirk. The Free Republic attracts thousands of curious visitors who want to marvel at alternative life up close. [...]

I'm hungry. So we stroll over to the kitchen hut. Behind the counter, five people are scurrying around making quark sandwiches, 30 pfennigs each. Next to them, there is tea from the "Gruppe volle Kanne – ohne Dampf kein Kampf!" (Balls-to-the-Wall Group [lit. "full pot group"]—No Steam No Fight!). Why is the Women's House actually called that, I ask. Do they already need a refuge for women who have been beaten? "Nah, of course not, the women just built it on their own." [...] It all sounds a bit too perfect to be true. How does this village work? The inhabitants are thrown together from all over West Germany, including students and unemployed people, citizens' initiative activists and anarchists, while violent radicals are also supposed to be there. Up to 4,000 people live and work in this square. I feel that the atmosphere is unusually friendly, almost tender. Who is coordinating behind the scenes? Who organizes the catering, assigns "building sites," mediates, arbitrates?

"Chaos reigns in the Speaker's Council," reports the Bochum native. "They are constantly discussing what is nonviolent and what is not. And whether to be evicted sitting down or kneeling down ..." [...] An attempted explanation sticks on the front of the info house: "The

Speaker's Council is not a government, state, etc., but a model of grassroots decision-making in the square." Each social peer group sends a delegate to the Speaker's Council every day—at least this is how it is meant to work. In addition, anyone who wants to can attend the meetings. There are no majority decisions or votes, but discussions are held until a "consensus" is reached. A laborious procedure. Whether it works or not, nobody really knows. In any case, there still seems to be a lot of confusion about how to behave during the eviction. [...]

"According to the consensus in the Speaker's Council, we will be absolutely nonviolent and only offer passive resistance." A "newcomer" is keen to discuss. "What does violence mean anyway?" he shouts in between. Next to me someone murmurs, "Oh God, no, please not again!" [...]

Gabi Jäger, a literature student from Hamburg with a second residence in the district, tells me: "[...] Roughly speaking, there are three factions in the village: a very small 'hard core' of partly very young people who have been outsiders all their lives and have an insane aggression against everything that seeks to patronize them. Of course, they don't want to give up the village without a fight, but they are suppressed as a minority. Then there is the faction of left-wing students from the cities, whose liberalism does not represent a clearcut course here. The largest faction is made up of those who see the campaign as support for the resistance in the district." [...]

The question of violence is the greatest source of conflict in the Village 1004. Contrasting opinions constantly come to a head, there are perpetual confrontations, as well as constant actions that contradict the non-violent consensus paper. As in the case of the barricades, for example. On Sunday morning, the mayor of Trebel appears at the Speaker's Council. He points out that the barricades built by the occupiers from tree trunks must be removed from the communal paths in the Gartow Forest. [...]

The Speaker's Council promises him that by Monday the barricades will be cleared away. [...] But on Monday the barricades are still there, and there are even more. "The insecurity factor in the village," says Gabi, "is that some people here just don't want to go to meetings. They then take actions without coordinating." That's why the Speaker's Council will discuss the barricade problem for another three full hours on Monday. [...] Finally, the numerically stronger barricade opponents prevail. [...]

War. Tanks. Razor wire. Helicopters landing thunderously, unloading troops. Bulldozers. Helmets, shields, behind them motionless faces. Uniformed men all the way to the horizon. Mounted units. Units with blackened faces. More helicopters. War. [...] On Wednesday, June 4, 1980, 5,000 police and federal border guard officers removed 2,500 opponents of nuclear power from parcel 89/7 of the Trebel district, which they were illegally occupying in protest against the planned deep borehole 1004. At the end of the operation, the commander thanked the demonstrators for their peaceful behavior. [...] According to "police tactical standards," the eviction went off smoothly. Some opponents of nuclear power even made fun afterwards that occupants felt transported into the horror scene of "Apocalypse Now," drawing parallels to My Lai and other massacres. [...]

With batons, the squatters were brought back from their Free Republic to the harsh reality of the Federal Republic of West Germany. And there, everything remained the same: in July, Albrecht's cabinet gave the green light for an interim storage facility with a capacity of 1,500 tons of uranium in the form of spent nuclear fuel rods near Gorleben. (Rosenbladt 1981)

Even after the eviction of the hut village, which was one of the largest police operations in German postwar history, Gorleben remains a hub for anti-nuclear protests. Castor transports to the interim storage facility in Gorleben took place regularly between 1996 and 2011. Protest actions such as sabotage and blockades, also using →*lock-on devices* (including the →*concrete pyramid* of the "Bäuerliche Notgemeinschaft") repeatedly lead to large police deployments. When the Gorleben salt dome was ruled out as a final repository by a commission of experts in 2020, four decades of protest came to a successful end.

The architecture of the hut village became the motif of many photographs and protest posters as well as the subject of numerous newspaper articles and films (→ *Media*). In his essay "Besetzerarchitektur" (Occupier's Architecture), the architect Andreas Orth describes various →*building types* he found in the anti-nuclear protest villages of the 1970s and 1980s. The model for the Friendship House in Gorleben was a hut in the anti-nuclear protest village in Whyl Forest. The "round wooden houses" then became the "distinguishing feature of occupied building sites" (Orth 1980). The carpenter Dieter Schaarschmidt also remembers the special buildings that were used as meeting and event locations in the hut villages:

During my first site occupation in Wyhl in Baden-Württemberg, I learned how important such a solid, protective building of a friendship house is for the lasting success of a protest movement. [...] When we planned the occupation of the Brokdorf nuclear power plant construction site, I kept the building material for a friendship house based on the Wyhl model [...] ready on a truck. Unfortunately, I never got the chance to construct it because of the massive police operations. Later, when I was already living in the Wendland, we also built on these experiences. (Personal communication, Dieter Schaarschmidt 2022)

Another type of "occupier's architecture" is the tipi—it requires the least amount of time: with the help of a few long poles, it can be erected quickly without cumbersome sawing and nailing. [...] The round house on four supports, with head-high side walls and a conical roof, has certainly been the most built type in the multiform hodgepodge of huts. (Orth 1980)

In the last weeks before the eviction,

a twelve-meter-high pile construction was set up in the hut village. This → *tower* played a special role in the village, as was highlighted not only by the slogans on the → *banners* attached to the tower, which differentiated the occupation into the "village" and the "tower": "You can destroy tower and village but not the power that created it" and "In the square + tower: you cannot end the struggle of the Wends here." The defense of the tower during the imminent eviction was also discussed independently of the occupation of the village square and the Friendship House in the Speaker's Council. It made the division of the movement into "non-violent" and "militant" factions all the more visible.

In July 2020, Sigurd Elert, who lived in the hut village and planned the tower, spoke with Andreas Conradt of the *Gorleben Rundschau* about the building's development:

"At that time, I looked at what carpenters, farmers, and resisters were building out of trees, planks, and boards. There were great huts and houses, imaginative and full of alternative ideas, but they could not withstand the huge police deployment that was expected every day. I had something in mind that would present the police with difficulties in clearing demonstrators. A tower, for example, that had to be tall and sturdy." [...] In the end, the tower was a good twelve meters high; despite a fear of heights, Sigurd and his buddies even built a closed hut at the top. It later housed the broadcasting equipment for Radio Freies Wendland.

[...] *"If everyone sits on the ground, such an eviction is over in no time. With a tower, you can make it harder for the police. That was the idea. [...] Clearing the tower took as much time as everything else." When it finally fell, the Free Republic of Wendland was history. But the images remained in the collective memory: the sea of huts, the passport office, and the tower.* (Conradt 2020) (Texts by Sabine Rosenbladt, Andreas Orth; conversation with Dieter Schaarschmidt; introduction and research: AMM)

Graf

Graffiti, engl. → *Graffiti*. Während sich bestimmte Ausprägungen von Graffiti heute längst als eigenständige Kunstform etabliert haben (z.B. bei Banksy oder Keith Haring), werden die im öffentlichen Raum oder auf privatem Eigentum angebrachten Bilder, Schriftzüge, Tags, Symbole und Zeichen (→ *Erkennungszeichen*) überwiegend als Vandalismus und Provokation wahrgenommen: Sie werden meist ohne Genehmigung und anonym auf Mauern und Hauswände, Brücken, Unterführungen, Stromkästen, Verkehrsschilder, Züge, Straßenbahnen und Busse gemalt oder gesprayt. Solche illegalen Graffitis werden in vielen westlichen Ländern strafrechtlich als Sachbeschädigung verfolgt (→ *Zerstörung*). Dies gilt auch für die Übermalung von Wahlkampf- oder Werbeplakaten, wobei insbesondere die künstlerische → *Guerillataktik* des *Adbusting* einen konsum- bzw. gesellschaftskritischen Anspruch stellt (→ *Medien*). Für den Kontext dieses Lexikons sind indes eher die explizit politischen Graffitis von Belang, die sich zu Themen wie Religion, Menschenrechten, Rassismus, Antisemitismus und Diskriminierung positionieren oder sich – vor allem in totalitären Staaten – gegen die bestehenden Herrschaftsverhältnisse wenden (→ *Kommunikation*). Beispielsweise waren im Rahmen der Proteste auf dem → *Tahrir-Platz* in Kairo → *2011* während des Arabischen Frühlings zahlreiche Graffitis zu lesen, die sich gegen den ägyptischen Präsidenten Muhammad Husni Mubarak und seine Familie richteten. (SH)

Graffiti, Ger. → *Graffiti (fig.)*. While certain forms of graffiti have long since established themselves as an art form in their own right (e.g. Banksy or Keith Haring), the images, lettering, tags, symbols, and signs (→ *Identifier*) applied in public spaces or on private property are predominantly perceived as vandalism and provocation: they are usually painted or sprayed without permission and anonymously on various types of walls, bridges, underpasses, junction boxes, traffic signs, trains, streetcars, and buses. Such illegal graffiti is prosecuted in many Western countries as damage to property (→ *Destruction*). This also applies to painting over election campaign or advertising posters, whereby the artistic → *guerrilla tactic* of adbusting in particular seeks to express a critique of consumption or society (→ *Media*). In the context of this dictionary, however, it is more the explicitly political graffiti that is relevant, which takes a stand on topics such as religion, human rights, racism, antisemitism, and discrimination, or—especially in totalitarian states—against existing power relations (→ *Communication*). For example, as part of the protests in Cairo's → *Tahrir Square* in → *2011* during the Arab Spring, a great deal of graffiti could be found denouncing President Muhammad Hosni Mubarak and his family. (SH)

Graffiti. Statue von General Robert E. Lee (errichtet 1890) mit Reaktionen auf die Ermordung von George Floyd durch Polizisten in Minneapolis, Richmond, VA, 2020 (Graffiti. Statue of General Robert E. Lee (erected in 1890) with responses to the police murder of George Floyd in Minneapolis, Richmond, VA, 2020)

Greenham Common Friedenscamp, engl. → *Greenham Common Peace Camp*. Im Jahr → *1981* ausschließlich von Frauen gegründet und organisiert, um friedlich gegen die Stationierung von Atomwaffen in Großbritannien zu protestieren. Es entwickelte sich durch verschiedene kreative Aktionen, u.a. in →*Kostümen*, zu einem Symbol des gewaltfreien Widerstands und des Feminismus. Bei der Aktion „Embrace the Base" versammelten sich 30000 Frauen am Zaun, hielten sich an den Händen und bildeten eine Menschenkette. Das →*Protestcamp* bestand neunzehn Jahre. Kleinere Camps säumten die Base, jedes nach einer Farbe des Regenbogens benannt und mit unterschiedlichen Eigenschaften, z.B. das Yellow Gate, in dem die Presse betreut wurde und anfangs auch Männer zugelassen waren; das Blue Gate, das einen New-Age-Schwerpunkt hatte; oder das Green Gate für Frauen mit Kindern. Charakteristische Unterkünfte waren selbstgebaute →*Bender*. (JD)

Greenham Common Peace Camp, Ger. →*Greenham Common Friedenscamp*. This camp was founded and organized solely by women in →*1981* as a peaceful protest against the storage of nuclear weapons in the UK. Through various creative actions, sometimes in →*costume*, it became a symbol of peaceful resistance and feminism. During the action "Embrace the Base," 30,000 women gathered at the fence and held hands to form a human chain. The protest camp survived for nineteen years. Smaller camps fringed the base, each one was named after a color in the rainbow and had a different theme, such as the Yellow Gate, which took care of the press and initially also admitted men; the Blue Gate, which had a New Age focus, or the Green Gate for women with children. Self-built →*benders* were characteristic forms of accommodation. (JD)

Greensboro Sit-ins, engl. →*Greensboro Sit-ins*. Wichtiges Ereignis der US-amerikanischen Bürger∗innenrechtsbewegung. Die Proteste begannen am 1. Februar →*1960* als vier Schwarze Studenten in North Carolina einen „Whites only"-Woolworth-Lunch-Counter besetzten und sich weigerten zu gehen, obwohl ihnen die Bedienung verweigert wurde (→*Blockade*, →*Demonstration*). Weitere →*Sit-ins* breiteten sich im College-Städte im gesamten Süden der USA aus. Obwohl viele der Demonstrierenden wegen unbefugten Betretens verhaftet wurden, hatten ihre Aktionen eine unmittelbare und dauerhafte Wirkung und zwangen Woolworth und andere Einrichtungen, ihre rassistische Segregationspraktik zu ändern. (JD)

Greensboro Sit-ins, Ger. →*Greensboro Sit-ins*. An important event in the American civil rights movement. The protests started on February 1, →*1960*, when four Black students in North Carolina occupied a "whites only" Woolworth's lunch counter and would not leave, even though they were refused service (→*Blockade*, →*Demonstration*). Further →*sit-ins* spread to college cities throughout the Southern United States. While many demonstrators were arrested on charges of trespassing, their actions had an immediate and lasting effect and forced Woolworth's and other establishments to change their racist segregation practices. (JD)

Grußwort, engl. →*Foreword*. Üblicherweise auf den allerersten Buchseiten verorteter Paratext, der Hinweise auf kulturpolitische bzw. ökonomische Existenzbedingungen eines Publikationsprojektes mit programmatischen Affirmationsgesten (oft aus Fördererperspektive) kombiniert. Im Fall des vorliegenden Lexikons konzeptionsgetreu ebenfalls in Form eines Lexikoneintrags realisierte Dankesbotschaft der Kulturstiftung des Bundes an das Deutsche Architekturmuseum in Frankfurt am Main und das Museum für angewandte Kunst in Wien, insbesondere an das gesamte kuratorische Team, bestehend aus Oliver Elser, Anna-Maria Mayerhofer, Sebastian Hackenschmidt, Jennifer Dyck, Lilli Hollein und Peter Cachola Schmal, verbunden mit den besten Wünschen für eine ebenso breite wie positive Resonanz auf dieses gleichermaßen inhaltlich relevante wie formal höchst originelle Ausstellungs- und Publikationsprojekt. (gezeichnet vom Vorstand der Kulturstiftung des Bundes, Katarzyna Wielga-Skolimowska und Kirsten Haß)

Guerillataktiken, engl. → *Guerrilla tactics*, der sub- und gegenkulturellen Urban Art und des sogenannten *Urban Hacking* operieren nicht selten hart an den Grenzen zur Illegalität. Bisweilen müssen sie sich auch den Vorwurf des Vandalismus und der Sabotage gefallen lassen, etwa bei Farbbeutelanschlägen auf Fassaden, Firmensignets, Billboards und öffentliche Verkehrsmittel (→ *Fahrzeuge*), der → *Blockade* von → *Straßen* und Plätzen oder der → *Zerstörung* von Überwachungskameras, Telefonzellen und Abfallbehältern. Das illegale Übersprayen, Übermalen, Überkleben und Umgestalten von Werbetafeln, Ladenfronten, Schaufenstern, Verkehrsschildern, Stromkästen oder Denkmälern (→ *Denkmalsturz*) geht nicht selten mit dem direkten Aufruf zu Konsumverweigerung, → *zivilem Ungehorsam* oder politischem Aktivismus einher, und auch viele → *Graffiti*-Sprayer∗innen fassen ihre Arbeit in der Tat als Systemkritik auf. Verstanden werden diese Formen der → *Kommunikation* allerdings vorwiegend als „Sachbeschädigung", vor der sich Firmen und Behörden, Verkehrsunternehmen und Hauseigentümer∗innen mit speziellen Industrielacken und Anti-Graffiti-Beschichtungen zu schützen versuchen (→ *Anti-Protestmaßnahmen*).

Das hauptsächliche Ziel der Bilder und Schriftzüge, Installationen und Aktionen der urbanen Spaßguerillas scheinen die Standardisierung, Homogenisierung, Kommodifizierung, Gentrifizierung und oft auch Touristifizierung großstädtischer Räume zu sein. Die meist temporären Interventionen, die sich auch Strategien wie *Détournement* und *Culture Jamming* zunutze machen, bilden dabei → *Medien* des Widerstands und des Protests, mit denen sich die kapitalistisch glatt polierten Oberflächen des öffentlichen Raums aufrauen, untergraben oder umfunktionieren lassen (→ *Zweckentfremdung*). Zugegeben: Banner, Plakate, Sticker und das sogenannte *Adbusting* operieren in erster Linie über bildliche und linguistische Codes (→ *Erkennungszeichen*), und viele der urbanen Interventionen – etwa im Bereich von *Guerilla Knitting* und *Guerilla Gardening* – kommen weniger aufständisch als vielmehr beiläufig daher. Aber gerade die zarten und bunten, um Parkbänke, Laternenmasten oder Brückengeländer gestrickten Textilien und die in Mauerritzen, Mülleimer oder schadhaftes Straßenpflaster (→ *Pflastersteine*) eingesetzten Pflanzen demonstrieren, dass hier den harten, kalten und glatten Oberflächen aus Asphalt, Stein, Stahl, Glas und Beton im Sinne von Umweltschutz, → *Denkmalschutz* und Friedensbewegung das Nachgiebige, Weiche, Lebendige und Pflegebedürftige entgegengesetzt wird. Bei den Eingriffen in den Stadtraum geht es folglich nicht nur um alternative Formen von Raumnutzung und Öffentlichkeit, sondern auch um ein subversives Spiel mit den Codes der gesellschaftlichen Oberflächen: So machen abgelegte → *Kleidung*, Gummipuppen oder Abgüsse von Körperteilen – etwa John Ahearns Büsten von Leuten aus dem New Yorker Stadtteil Bronx Mitte der 1980er Jahre – auf die An- beziehungsweise Abwesenheit von Menschen an bestimmten Plätzen aufmerksam und thematisieren → *Gewalt* und soziale Ausgrenzung. Und wenn Installationen aus Erde, alten Teppichen oder Pappkartons – man denke an die Arbeiten des Künstlers Thomas Hirschhorn – eine unheimliche Materialität gewinnen, die den öffentlichen Raum der vermeintlich „sauberen" Geschäftsviertel zu kontaminieren droht, dann verdeutlichen diese Eingriffe nicht zuletzt, dass Legitimität eine Frage des sozialen Kontextes und die Einstufung von etwas als Abfall oder Schmutz von der Umgebung abhängig ist (vgl. Seno 2010; Ausst.-Kat. *In die Stadt* 2018). (SH)

Guerrilla tactics, Ger. → *Guerillataktiken* (fig.), of sub- and counter-cultural urban art and so-called urban hacking frequently operate on the verge of illegality; sometimes they are also branded as acts of vandalism and sabotage, for example in the case of paint bomb attacks on facades, company signs, billboards, and public transportation (→ *Vehicles*), the → *blockade* of → *streets* and squares, or the → *destruction* of surveillance cameras, telephone booths, and trash cans. The illegal over-spraying, over-painting, over-sticking, and redesigning of billboards, store fronts, shop windows, traffic signs, junction boxes, or monuments (→ *Toppling monuments*) is often accompanied by a direct call for anti-consumerism, → *civil disobedience*, or political activism, and many → *graffiti* artists do indeed see their work as criticism of the system. However, these forms of → *communication* are predominantly understood as "damage to property," from which firms and authorities, transportation companies and property owners try to protect themselves with special industrial paints and anti-graffiti coatings (→ *Anti-protest measures*).

With their images and writing, installations and actions, these urban fun guerrillas mainly seem to target the standardization, homogenization, commodification, gentrification, and often also "touristification" of metropolitan spaces. These mostly temporary interventions, which also make use of strategies such as *détournement* and culture jamming, thereby form → *media* of resistance and protest with which the capitalistically smoothly polished surfaces in public space can be roughened, undermined, or repurposed (→ *Misappropriation*). Admittedly, banners, posters, stickers, and so-called adbusting operate primarily through pictorial and linguistic codes (→ *Identifiers*), and many of the urban interventions—for example, in the realm of guerrilla knitting and guerrilla gardening—come across as less rebellious and more casual. However, it is precisely the delicate and colorful textiles knitted around park benches, lampposts, or bridge railings, and the plants inserted into wall cracks, trash cans, or damaged pavements (→ *Cobblestone*) that demonstrate how the hard, cold, smooth surfaces of asphalt, stone, steel, glass, and concrete are counteracted here by what is pliable, soft, living, and in need of care, for the cause of environmental protection, → *heritage protection*, and the peace movement. The interventions in urban space are thus not only about alternative forms of space use and public life but also about a subversive play with the codes of societal surfaces: thus, discarded → *clothing*, rubber dolls, or casts of body parts—for example, John Ahearn's busts of people from the Bronx borough of New York in the mid-1980s—call attention to the presence or absence of people in certain places and address → *violence* and social exclusion. When installations made of earth, old carpets, or cardboard boxes, as in the works of the artist Thomas Hirschhorn, acquire an uncanny materiality that threatens to contaminate the public space of supposedly "clean" business districts, these interventions not least illustrate that legitimacy is a question of social context and that classifying something as waste or dirt depends on its surroundings (see Seno 2010; exh. cat. *In die Stadt* 2018). (SH)

Guerillataktiken. Rocco und seine Brüder: *Begräbnis bezahlbarer Mieten*, Berlin 2016 (Guerrilla tactics. Rocco und seine Brüder: *Funeral for Affordable Rents*, Berlin 2016)

Hafenstraße, engl. → *Hafenstraße*. Um die jahrelangen Auseinandersetzungen um die → *Hausbesetzungen* an der Hamburger Hafenstraße möglichst gewaltfrei zu beenden, machte der damalige Bürgermeister Dohnanyi (SPD) den Besetzer*innen im November 1987 ein Angebot, nachdem die Situation zuvor eskaliert war: „Baut die → *Barrikaden* ab, dann bekommt ihr einen Pachtvertrag." Der seit → *1981* bestehende Konflikt beruhigte sich, eine endgültige Lösung wurde aber erst 1995 gefunden. (JD)

Hafenstraße, Ger. → *Hafenstraße*. To put a preferably peaceful end to the yearslong contentions surrounding the → *squatting* on Hamburg's Hafenstraße (since → *1981*), the then mayor Dohnanyi (SPD) made the occupiers an offer after the situation had escalated: "take down the → *barricades* and you'll get a lease." Although the conflict relaxed, a definitive solution was only reached in 1995. (JD)

Hainburger Au, engl. → *Hainburger Au*. Die Proteste gegen den Bau eines Wasserkraftwerks in den Donauauen östlich von Wien sind, neben dem Widerstand gegen das AKW in → *Zwentendorf*, das zweite wesentliche Protest-Ereignis in Österreich. Wesentlich für den Erfolg der Bewegung im Jahr → *1984* waren nicht nur die kreativen Protestformate wie die „Pressekonferenz der Tiere" oder eine Aktion in der Fernsehshow „Wetten, dass...?". Auch das kurzzeitige → *Protestcamp* in Form einer → *Bauplatzbesetzung* und eine Großdemonstration waren wohl nicht alleine ausschlaggebend für den von der Regierung als „Weihnachtsfrieden" verkündeten Baustopp. Wichtiger war mutmaßlich ein von der *Kronen Zeitung* – der relativ zur Einwohnerzahl weltweit reichweitenstärksten Boulevardzeitung – begleiteter Umschwung in der öffentlichen Meinung: Die Ökologiebewegung war plötzlich in der gesellschaftlichen Mitte angelangt. Darin schwingt auch eine gewisse Ambivalenz mit. Umweltschutz war in den 1980er Jahren keineswegs ein ausschließlich linkes Anliegen, sondern wurde auch vom konservativen bis rechten politischen Spektrum als neues Thema entdeckt. (OE)

Hainburger Au, Ger. → *Hainburger Au*. The protests against the construction of a hydropower plant on the floodplains along the Danube east of Vienna was, alongside the opposition to the nuclear power station in → *Zwentendorf*, the second major protest event in postwar Austria. Key to the movement's success in → *1984* were not only the creative protest formats such as an "Animals Press Conference" or an action during the popular *Wetten, dass...?* TV show. The short-lived → *protest camp* in the form of a → *building site occupation* and a large-scale → *demonstration* were in themselves reason enough for the government to declare a halt to construction by way of a "Christmas truce." Presumably what was more important was the shift in public opinion, partly driven by the *Kronen Zeitung,* which has the highest readership relative to the size of the population of any tabloid paper in the world. Suddenly, the ecological movement was an establishment matter. This also attests to a certain ambivalence. In the 1980s, environmental protection was by no means exclusively a leftist matter, with conservative and right-wing groups also discovering it as a political issue. (OE)

Hambacher Wald, engl. → *Hambach Forest*. Für den Braunkohleabbau werden in Deutschland seit Jahrzehnten Wälder gerodet und Dörfer abgerissen. Im Hambacher Wald errichteten Klimaaktivist∗innen seit → *2012* mehrere Generationen von Baumhaussiedlungen, um die Abholzung des Waldes zur Erweiterung des Tagebaus Hambach zu blockieren (→ *Blockade*). Die Waldbesetzung in „Hambi" wurde zum Symbol des Widerstands gegen die Umweltzerstörung durch Braunkohleverbrennung. Selten zuvor bestanden → *Protestcamps* aus derartig vielen und großen → *Baumhäusern*, die auf so komplexe Weise durch → *Traversen*, Brücken und Netze miteinander verbunden waren. Zusätzlich entstand auf einem Grundstück am Waldrand, das einem privaten Unterstützer der Waldbesetzung gehört, das „Wiesencamp" mit Wohnwagen, Lehmbauten und einem „Museum" genannten Gebäude für Ausstellungen und kulturelle Veranstaltungen (→ *Bautypen*).

Die Räumung im Oktober 2018 war nicht der erste, aber der umfassendste Versuch, die Waldbesetzung zu beenden, und der bis dahin größte Polizeieinsatz in der Geschichte Nordrhein-Westfalens (→ *Polizei*). Die Ordnungsbehörden hatten argumentiert, dass die Baumhäuser „bauliche Anlagen" seien, bei denen durch die teils eingebauten → *Küchen* und Elektroleitungen akute Brandgefahr bestehe. Das Verwaltungsgericht Köln urteilte zwar 2021, dass diese Begründung nur vorgeschoben sei. Im Juni 2023 widersprach jedoch das Oberverwaltungsgericht Nordrhein-Westfalen der Vorinstanz: die Räumung von 2018 sei rechtmäßig erfolgt.

genannten Kohlekommission im Jahr 2019 wurde der Erhalt des Hambacher Waldes gesichert. Die verbliebenen 200 Hektar des ursprünglich 4100 Hektar großen Naturdenkmals sind trotzdem stark gefährdet, denn wegen des Tagebaus wurde der Grundwasserspiegel abgesenkt, sodass die Vegetation immer mehr austrocknet.

Im Sommer 2020 wurde im 40 Kilometer entfernten Weiler →*Lützerath*, der von RWE für den Tagebau Garzweiler abgebaggert werden sollte, mit dem Abriss erster Straßen und Gebäude begonnen. Viele Aktivist*innen schlossen sich der neuen →*Besetzung* dort an, die Anzahl der Bewohner*innen im Hambacher Wald ging dagegen über die letzten Jahre stark zurück.

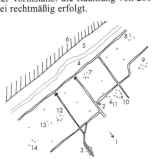

■ Barrikade der Protestierenden (Protesters' barricade)
▨ Erdwall von RWE (Earth wall of RWE)

Hambacher Wald, Januar 2019. 1 Mahnwache 2 Jesus Point 3 Wiesencamp 4 Wall 5 Vorfeld 6 Kante 7–14 Barrios: 7 „Winkel" 8 „Krähennest" 9 „Endor" 10 „Oaktown" 11 „Lluna" 12 „Hazelnut" 13 „Beechtown" 14 „Anmarsch" (Hambach Forest, January 2019. 1 Protest vigil 2 Jesus Point 3 Meadow Camp 4 Wall 5 Run-up 6 Edge 7–14 Barrios: 7 "Angle" 8 "Crow's Nest" 9 "Endor" 10 "Oaktown" 11 "Lluna" 12 "Hazelnut" 13 "Beechtown" 14 "Approach")

Als Reaktion auf die →*Zerstörung* der Baumhaussiedlung demonstrierten im Oktober 2018 über 50 000 Menschen am Hambacher Wald (→*Demonstration*) – eine →*Solidaritätsgeste*, die zeigte, wie gut die vergleichsweise kleine Gruppe von Waldbesetzer*innen in der lokalen Bevölkerung und darüber hinaus verankert war. Nach einer Eilentscheidung des Oberverwaltungsgerichts Münster, die zum sofortigen Rodungsstopp führte, begann noch im gleichen Monat der Wiederbesetzung des Waldes und der Bau neuer →*Türme* und Baumhäuser, die bis heute (Stand 2023) bewohnt sind.

Im Rahmen der Verhandlungen der so-

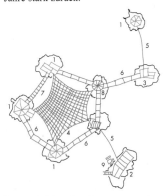

■ Gemeinschaftliche Strukturen (Community structures)
▨ Individuelle Strukturen (Individual structures)

Hambacher Wald. 1 Baumhaus 2 Turm 3 Plattform 4 Netz 5 Traverse 6 Holzbrücke 7 Strickleiter 8 Spindeltreppe 9 Versammlungsort (Hambach Forest. 1 Tree house 2 Tower 3 Platform 4 Net 5 Traverse 6 Wooden bridge 7 Rope ladder 8 Spiral staircase 9 Meeting area)

Der Hambacher Wald wird gelegentlich auch als Hambacher Forst bezeichnet, was viele Aktivist*innen jedoch ablehnen, weil diese Bezeichnung die ökonomische, d.h. forstwirtschaftliche

Perspektive betone. Der Hambacher Wald gehört größtenteils dem Energiekonzern RWE. Die Besetzung war dennoch möglich, weil durch das in Deutschland geltende Waldbetretungsrecht eine öffentliche Nutzung gewährleistet werden musste. Es konnten keine Zäune errichtet werden.

Die Klimaaktivist∗innen Julia Riedel und Ronni Zepplin engagierten sich sowohl im Hambacher Wald als auch im Anschluss daran bei der Besetzung in Lützerath. Sie verfassten für diesen Beitrag einen Text, in dem sie vom kollektiven Bauen im Wald erzählen:

Wir sehen ein riesiges Loch. Es ist nicht nur groß, es reicht bis zum Horizont. Wir sehen die Farben der verschiedenen Erdschichten und ganz unten, hunderte Meter in der Tiefe, schwarze Kohle. Von den eisernen Schaufelradbaggern heraufbefördert, verbrannt, zu Energie verwandelt. Energie, die uns das Leben nimmt. Den Boden vertrocknet, das Meer zum Überlaufen bringt, die Jahreszeiten aus dem Ruder wirft. An der Abbruchkante gerodetes Gebiet, dann beginnt Wald. Wir laufen auf einem kleinen Pfad hinein und es eröffnet sich eine Welt, die unterschiedlicher als der Tagebau nicht sein könnte.

Viele kleine verschachtelte Gebäude hoch in den Kronen der Bäume, verbunden durch →Seile und Hängebrücken, trotzen der Zerstörung und locken ein beflügelndes Gefühl hervor. Wir bauen Baumhäuser, Hütten, Türme und viel mehr, um den Tagebau zu blockieren und zu lernen, uns kollektiv zu organisieren. Was gebaut wird, entscheidet das Plenum nach Bedarf: neue Schlaf- und Rückzugsorte, ein Büro für Pressearbeit (→Medien), ein Materiallager. In regelmäßigen Versammlungen bringen wir Vorschläge ein und priorisieren: Wofür ist genug →Baumaterial da? Wer hat Lust und Zeit mitzuwirken? Wer hat welche Fähigkeiten, die einzelnen Schritte zu übernehmen? Gibt es noch andere Projekte, die erst mal fertiggestellt werden sollen? Oft ist die Motivation groß, etwas Neues zu schaffen, ohne daran zu denken, wie lange es dauert. Um Bauprojekte zu beenden, an denen

wir nicht weiterkamen oder in die es immer wieder reinregnet, muss sich mehr aufgerafft werden. Oft laufen mehrere parallel und wir können uns aufteilen: Hier muss ein Baum erschlossen werden, dort ein Dach gebaut, woanders die Inneneinrichtung der Küche finalisiert werden. Noch nie einen Akkuschrauber bedient oder einen komplexen Knoten gemacht zu haben ist kein Problem. Die Erfahreneren tun sich zusammen mit den Neuen und geben die Fähigkeiten im Bauprozess weiter. Dabei lernt man sich kennen, spricht über den Ort und die Motivation, da zu sein. Manche Baustellen sind besondere Lernräume, z.B. ausschließlich für FLINTA∗ (Frauen, Lesben, intergeschlechtliche, nichtbinäre, trans und agender Personen), um einen geschützteren Raum zu schaffen, sich auszuprobieren und Fähigkeiten zu entwickeln, ohne sich von Cis-Männern ausbremsen zu lassen, wenn sie denken, sie wissen es besser.

Wie ein Baumhaus aussehen wird, wissen wir zu Beginn noch nicht. Das kommt darauf an, wie weit sich die Äste in der Krone auseinanderstrecken und ob sie noch stabil genug sind, eine Plattform zu tragen. Wir beurteilen, ob ein Baum geeignet ist, auch hinsichtlich seiner Gesundheit. Manchmal ziehen wir dabei Baumpfleger∗innen zu Rate. Oben in der Krone wird der Grundriss für die Plattform gelegt und bestimmt, an welcher Stelle die zwei Hauptbalken befestigt werden. Jetzt brauchen wir viele Leute, die die schweren Balken zu unserer Baustelle tragen und zusammen am Flaschenzug ziehen, bis sie in der richtigen Position sind. „Ziehen! Sperre rein! Stopp! Und weiter!", hallt es durch den Wald. Dieser Teil ist der nervenaufreibendste, in der Luft hängend den schweren Balken durch die Krone zu bugsieren, bis wir ihn festmachen. Doch danach haben wir den ersten festen Stand unter den Füßen und wir können mit dem Bau der Plattform beginnen. Das geht schnell, wenn wir gute Platten haben, dauert lange, wenn wir erst noch Paletten auseinandernehmen müssen, um die Bretter als Bodenplanken zu benutzen. Ist die Plattform fertig, sehen wir nicht dauernd den viele Meter entfernten Boden unter uns. Das Bauen geht weniger zittrig von der Hand. Jetzt kommt das Haus, dessen Außenwände in etwa dort stehen, wo die Plattform endet, bei genug Platz mit einer Aussparung für den Balkon. Mindestens für die Länge von einem Bett müssen wir an einer Stelle genug Platz einplanen. Ansonsten läuft der Hausbau ziemlich frei. Es stehen immer andere Baumaterialien in der Besetzung zur Verfügung, die die Konstruktionsweise mitbestimmen. Haben wir viele Kanthölzer, können wir ein Gerüst mit einem Spitz- oder Schrägdach bauen. Gibt es vor allem Paletten, können diese direkt als Wand verwendet werden.

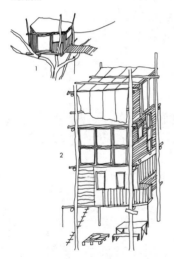

Hambacher Wald. 1 Baumhaus in der Baumkrone 2 Tower (Hambach Forest. 1 Tree house in the treetop 2 Tower)

Über die genaue Gestaltung, Stabilisierung und Durchführung diskutieren wir immer wieder während dem Bauen und da die Zusammensetzung der Baugruppe manchmal wechselt, gehen Ideen verloren und ein Fenster wird zur Tür

oder ein Ast aus Versehen mit eingebaut. Bauen wir im Sommer, ist die Freude, wenn vier Wände stehen, meist schon so groß, dass gleich der Einzug erfolgt und Möbel gebaut werden. Wenn dann im Winter noch keine Räumung passiert ist, braucht das Haus noch eine Dämmung. Dafür eignen sich Palettenwände sehr gut. Die noch offene Innenseite der gedämmten Wand kann auch nur mit Stoff verkleidet werden, falls kein Holz da ist und es schnell gehen muss. In den Zwischenraum kommt, was an Material da ist: → Stroh von Ende Gelände, Styropor, → Kleidung, Seegras, etc. Kaum ein Gebäude trägt nicht auch eine Botschaft, die es in einen größeren Zusammenhang einordnet: weltweite Solidarität mit den Kämpfen von links und unten.

Stephan Mörsch ist Künstler und Aktivist. Er baute 2021 ein Architekturmodell der Siedlung Beechtown im Hambacher Wald, das als Skulptur bei zahlreichen Kunstausstellungen zu sehen war. Dafür führte er viele Gespräche mit den Bewohner*innen des → Barrios und beschäftigte sich intensiv mit den baulichen Strukturen. Im Frühjahr 2023 fand ein Interview statt:

Anna-Maria Mayerhofer: Du bist in der Tagebauregion in Nordrhein-Westfalen aufgewachsen und hast die Proteste im Hambacher Wald seit ihrem Beginn 2012 beobachtet. Wie hat die Besetzung angefangen und wie hat sie sich über die Jahre entwickelt?

Stephan Mörsch: Jedes Jahr gab es eine Rodungsperiode, in der RWE den Tagebau Richtung Süden erweitern durfte. Beim Waldfest „Wald statt Kohle" im April 2012 besetzten einige Menschen zum ersten Mal ein Stück des Waldes. Weil sie auf dem Boden der RWE-Security schutzlos ausgesetzt waren, die ihr Betriebsgelände oft mit → Gewalt verteidigte, verlagerten sie die Besetzung in die Bäume. Der Wald war damals eine Art rechtsfreie Zone. In den ersten Jahren haben sich die Menschen dort daher sehr strategisch bewegt. Sie haben jeweils nur die Bäume besetzt, die in diesem Jahr gerodet werden sollten, und sie mit dem eigenen Körper und dem Bau von ein-

Tim Wagner: Baumhaus, wahrscheinlich „Wilde 13", im Barrio „Lorien" (Tree house, probably "Wild 13," in the barrio "Lorien"), 30. August 2018

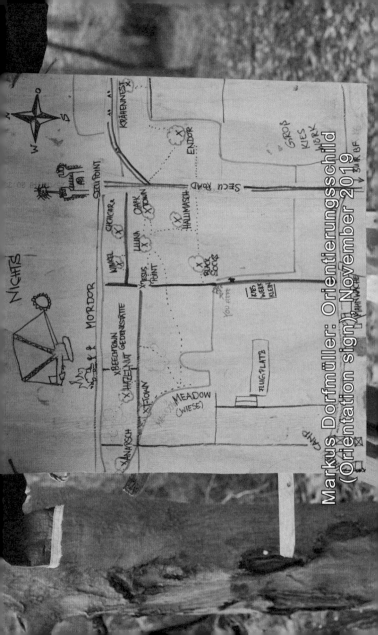

Markus Dorfmüller: Orientierungsschild (Orientation sign), November 2019

David Klammer: Einbindung der Hauptbalken eines neuen Baumhauses (Tying the main beams of a new tree house), 27. Februar 2019

Markus Dorfmüller: Zwischen mehreren Bäumen eingebundenes Baumhaus (Tree house tied between several trees), September 2018

Tim Wagner: Verbindungsbrücken im Barrio „Beechtown"
(Connecting bridges in the barrio "Beechtown").
31. August 2018

Angie: „Airbase Camp", *Outtake*
2017–2023, 25. April 2018

Markus Dorfmüller: Tower „Luftschloss" (Tower "Castle in the Air"), September 2018

Tim Wagner: „Lluna-Tower“,
9. Februar 2019

Markus Dorfmüller: Hänge-Baumhaus in der Nähe von „Cozy Town" (Suspended tree house near "Cozy Town"), September 2018

David Klammer: Baumhaus „ABC" zwischen Barrio „Endor" und „Krähennest" (Tree house "ABC" between barrio "Endor" and "Crow's Nest"), 25. März 2023

Tim Wagner: Lehmhütte „Teestube" im Wiesencamp
(Adobe hut "tea room" in the Meadow Camp),
29. August 2018

Anna-Maria Mayerhofer: „Museum" im Wiesencamp
("Museum" in the Meadow Camp), 30. Mai 2022

Markus Dorfmüller: Barrikade am Waldeingang (Barricade at forest entrance), September 2018

Daniel Chatard: Räumung eines Tripods (Eviction of a tripod), 26. September 2018

Peter Hinschläger: Modell des Barrios „Beechtown" von
Stephan Mörsch im Leopold-Hoesch-Museum (Model
of the barrio "Beechtown" by Stephan Mörsch in the
Leopold-Hoesch-Museum), 4. Dezember 2021

fachen Plattformen beschützt. Die Besetzung wurde zur Dauerpräsenz, aber die Bauten waren prekär und kurzfristig. Durch die seit 2014 stattfindenden monatlichen Waldspaziergänge von Eva Töller und Michael Zobel kamen immer mehr bisher unbeteiligte Menschen in Kontakt mit den Besetzer*innen und ihren Bauten. Die nationale und internationale Presse wurde aufmerksam und die überregionale Vernetzung der Bewegung begann. Als die ersten Pressefotos erschienen, ging es plötzlich nicht mehr nur darum, die Rodung der Bäume zu verhindern, sondern auch ein medienwirksames Bild vom Hambacher Wald zu erzeugen. Manche Aktivist*innen sorgten sich um die ästhetische Erscheinung der Siedlung. Sie sahen Fotos von den Strukturen in der Zeitung und waren unzufrieden. Statt simpler Holzhütten entwarfen die Besetzer*innen nun Baumhäuser mit gestalterischem Anspruch: Glasfassaden und sorgfältig durchdachte Grundrisse wurden realisiert, auf Plastik als Baumaterial sollte verzichtet werden. Mit der Zeit veränderte sich auch die Strategie für polizeiliche Räumungen. Statt den →Lock-on Devices, die aus der Anti-Atomkraft-Bewegung kamen, setzten die Besetzer*innen jetzt darauf, der Polizei zu entkommen, indem sie über Seilverbindungen wegkletterten.

AMM: Wie hat diese neue Räumungsstrategie das Protestcamp im Hambacher Wald verändert?

SM: Das Barrio, das diese Strategie als Erstes und vielleicht auch am erfolgreichsten umsetzte, war Beechtown. 2018 brauchte die Polizei vier Versuche, um die Siedlung zu räumen. Es war ein sehr hohes Barrio, denn die Buchen (engl. beech) dort gehören zu den höchsten Bäumen im Hambacher Wald. Die Küche begann auf 18 Metern Höhe, das achteckiges Baumhaus lag auf 21 Metern, die „Bushaltestelle", die höchste Hütte im Hambacher Wald, saß 26 Meter hoch in den Bäumen. Ein begehbarer Ausguck mit →Fahne war mit 36 Metern der höchste Punkt im Protestcamp und endete mehrere Meter über dem Wald. Alle Baumhäuser und Plattfor-

men in Beechtown waren mit Brücken, Strickleitern oder Traversen verbunden. Die Polizei kam bei der Räumung 2018 zwar mit mehreren Hebebühnen, aber das reichte nicht, denn die Aktivist*innen konnten sich dank der vielen Verbindungen über den Köpfen der Polizei von einem Barrio ins nächste bewegen.

AMM: Wie sind diese Verbindungen in Beechtown entstanden? Gab es Menschen, die sich mit solchen Konstruktionen auskannten?

SM: Frodo, ein Mathematiker und langjähriger Bewohner des Barrios, der jeden Baum im Barrio gut kannte, beschäftigte sich mit der Statik vieler Hängebrücken und der Kräfteverteilung im Baum. Die Kräfte mussten über die gesamte Krone verteilt und in den Stamm oder die nächste Brücke abgeleitet werden. Der Wald war zu dem Zeitpunkt schon in einem sehr schlechten Zustand, weil ihm durch den Kohleabbau das ganze Grundwasser entzogen wurde. Durch die Brücken und Traversen stützen sich die Bäume aber auch gegenseitig, und stürzten bei Wind nicht mehr um.

AMM: Die Benutzung der Brücken war für die Aktivist*innen aber auch mit Risiken verbunden. Bei der Räumung 2018 stürzte der Journalist Steffen Meyn in Beechtown von einer Hängebrücke und verunglückte tödlich.

SM: Die gefährlichsten Stellen waren bekanntermaßen die Verbindungspunkte zwischen den Brücken und den Baumhäusern. Denn die Plattformen in den Baumkronen waren relativ statisch, die Hängebrücken bewegten sich dagegen viel mehr. Der Sturz von Steffen Meyn ereignete sich an so einer Stelle, an einer der ersten Brücken, die im Hambacher Wald überhaupt gebaut wurden. In der Hektik der Räumung eines benachbarten Barrios achtete der sonst sehr vorsichtige Steffen nicht mehr auf seine Eigensicherung. Es ging ihm um die Aufzeichnung der [...] Räumung. Der Bau der Brücken war ein ständiger Lernprozess. Am Anfang bauten die Aktivist*innen die Brücken direkt im Baum, später gingen sie dazu über, sie auf dem Boden vorzubauen und sie dann *nur noch in die Bäume einzuhängen. In den ersten Jahren war das Material oft knapp und kam hauptsächlich aus Zufallsfunden, bald wurden Paletten in großem Stil organisiert. Und das Wissen für den Bau solcher Brücken verbreitete sich von Beechtown ausgehend im ganzen Wald. In Oaktown, heute das Barrio mit den meisten Verbindungen, gab es diese Art von Brücken erst später.*

AMM: Warum hast Du Dich entschlossen, Beechtown im Modell nachzubauen? War das für Dich eine Möglichkeit, das Wissen für den Bau solcher Strukturen zu verbreiten?

SM: Aktivismus und Kunst bedingen sich für mich oft, das stimmt. Und natürlich lässt sich aus dem Modell etwas lernen. Jeder Knoten ist im Modell zum Beispiel genau so gewickelt wie im 1:1. Im Prinzip ist das Modell ein dreidimensionales Knotenlehrbuch. Aber für mich war es vor allem wichtig, mit meiner Arbeit die Gesellschaft zu erreichen und zu vermitteln, was in der Presse manchmal nicht durchkam: Das waren nicht irgendwelche durchgeknallten Leute, die diese fantastischen Strukturen gebaut haben. Sondern hier sind wirklich durchdachte Architekturen entstanden, die es wert sind, im Museum betrachtet zu werden. (Beitrag von Julia Riedel und Ronni Zepplin; Gesprächspartner: Stephan Mörsch; Interview-Protokoll: Uta Winterhager; Einleitung und Recherche: AMM)

Hambach Forest, Ger. →*Hambacher Wald*. For decades, forests have been cleared and villages demolished for lignite mining in Germany. In the Hambach Forest, climate activists have built several generations of tree house settlements since 2012 to block the logging of the forest for the expansion of the Hambach open-pit mine (→*Blockade*). The forest occupation in the "Hambi" became a symbol of resistance against environmental destruction through lignite combustion. Rarely before have →*protest camps* consisted of such large and numerous →*tree houses* connected in such complex ways by →*traverses*, bridges, and nets. In addition, on a plot of land at the edge of the forest, owned

by a private supporter of the forest occupation, the "Meadow Camp" was built with travel trailers, mud houses, and a building called the "museum" for exhibitions and cultural events (→*Building types*).

The eviction in October 2018 was not the first but the most comprehensive attempt to end the forest occupation and the largest police operation in the history of North Rhine-Westphalia to date (→*Police*). The regulatory authorities had argued that the tree houses were "physical facilities" in which there was an acute fire risk due to the partly installed →*kitchens* and electrical lines. The Administrative Court of Cologne ruled in 2021 that this justification was only pretextual. In June 2023, however, the Higher Administrative Court of North Rhine-Westphalia overruled the finding of the lower court: the eviction of 2018 was deemed legal.

In response to the →*destruction* of the tree house settlement, over 50,000 people →*demonstrated* at Hambach Forest in October 2018—an →*act of solidarity* that showed just how firmly established the comparatively small group of forest occupiers was in the local population and beyond. After an urgent decision by the Higher Administrative Court of Münster, which led to an immediate stop of the woodland clearing, the reoccupation of the forest and the construction of new →*towers* and tree houses began in the same month, which are inhabited to this day (as of 2023).

As part of the negotiations of the so-called Coal Commission in 2019, the preservation of Hambach Forest was secured. The remaining 200 hectares of the originally 4,100-hectare natural landmark are nevertheless severely endangered, since the groundwater level has been lowered due to open-pit mining, resulting in the vegetation drying out more and more.

In the summer of 2020, the demolition of the first roads and buildings began in the hamlet of →*Lützerath*, forty kilometers away, which was to be mined by RWE for the Garzweiler open-pit mine. Many activists joined the new →*occu-*

pation there, while the number of residents in Hambach Forest, by contrast, declined sharply over the last few years.

Hambach Forest (Hambacher Wald) is sometimes also referred to as "Hambacher Forst" (denoting a managed forest or timberland), though many activists reject this term because it emphasizes the economic—that is, forestry-related—dimension. Hambach Forest is largely owned by the energy company RWE. An occupation was nevertheless possible because the forest access law applicable in Germany guarantees public use. Meaning no fences could be erected.

The climate activists Julia Riedel and Ronni Zepplin were involved both in Hambach Forest and subsequently in the occupation at Lützerath. They wrote a text for this case study where they talk about collectively building in the forest:

We see a huge hole. It's not just big, it reaches all the way to the horizon. We see the colors of the different layers of earth and at the very bottom, hundreds of meters down, black coal. Carried up by iron bucket-wheel excavators, burned, and turned into energy. Energy that takes our lives away; dries up the soil; causes the sea to overflow; throws the seasons out of whack. On the edge of the mine the land has been cleared, then the forest begins. We walk into it on a small path, revealing a world that could not be more different from the open-pit mine.

Many small, nested buildings high in the treetops, connected by → ropes and suspension bridges, defy destruction and elicit an empowering feeling. We build tree houses, huts, towers, and much more to block open-pit mining and learn how to organize ourselves collectively. What gets built is decided in the plenary assemblies as needed: new places to sleep and retreat, an office for press work (→ Media), a materials store. In regular meetings, we make proposals and prioritize: What can be built with the → building materials at hand? Who is willing and has time to contribute? Who has what skills to take on the individual steps? Are there other projects

that need to be completed first? Often there is great motivation to create something new without thinking about how long it will take. In order to finish construction projects that we got stuck on or where the rain keeps getting in, more effort is needed. Often there are several running in parallel and we can divide the work: a tree needs to be accessed in one place, a roof needs to be built in another, while somewhere else the interior design of the kitchen needs to be finalized. Never having operated a cordless screwdriver or tied a complex knot is no problem. Those who have more experience team up with the newcomers and pass on the skills in the building process. In doing so, people get to know each other, talk about the site and their motivation for being there. Some building sites are special learning spaces, for example exclusively for FLINTA* (women, lesbians, intersexual, non-binary, trans, and agender persons), to create a more protected space for trying out and developing skills without being thwarted by cis men when they think they know better.

We don't know what a tree house will look like at the beginning. That depends on how far apart the branches in the crown stretch and whether they are still stable enough to support a platform. We assess whether a tree is suitable, also in terms of its health. Sometimes we consult arborists. At the top of the crown, we lay the ground plan for the platform and determine where the two main beams will be attached. At this point, we need many people to carry the heavy beams to our construction site and jointly pull on the pulley until they are in the right position. "Pull! Lock in! Stop! Go on!" it echoes through the forest. This part is the most nerve-wracking, hanging in the air to maneuver the heavy beam through the crown until we tie it in. After this is accomplished, we have the first firm footing under our feet and we can start building the platform. This goes quickly if we have large boards and takes a long time if we first have to take apart pallets to use the boards as floor planks. Once the platform is finished, we can't constantly see the ground many meters below us and construction proceeds less shakily. Now comes the house, whose outer walls stand roughly where the platform ends, with a recess for the balcony if space permits. We need to plan enough room to at least accommodate the length of a bed. Other than that, the construction of the house proceeds rather freely. There are always different building materials available during the occupation, which help determine the method of construction. If we have a lot of squared timber, we can build a frame with a pointed or sloped roof. If there are mainly pallets, they can be used directly as a wall.

We discuss the exact design, stabilization, and implementation again and again during construction, and since the composition of the building group sometimes changes, ideas get lost, a window becomes a door, or a branch is installed by mistake. If we build in the summer, the joy of having erected four walls is usually so great that we move in right away and start building furniture. If by the onset of winter an eviction has not yet taken place, the house also needs insulation. For this purpose, pallet walls are very suitable. The still open interior side of the insulated wall can also be covered only with fabric, if there is no wood and little time. The interstitial space is filled by whatever material is available: → straw from Ende Gelände, polystyrene, → clothing, seaweed, etc. Almost every building also carries a message that places it in a larger context: worldwide solidarity with the struggles of the left and the downtrodden.

Stephan Mörsch is an artist and activist. In 2021, he built an architectural model of the Beechtown settlement in Hambach Forest, which was shown as a sculpture at numerous art exhibitions. For this purpose, he had many conversations with the residents of the → barrio and dealt intensively with the built structures. He was interviewed in the spring of 2023:

*Anna-Maria Mayerhofer: You grew up in the open-pit mining region in North Rhine-Westphalia and have observed the protests in Hambach Forest since they began in 2012. How did the occu-*pation start and how did it develop over the years? *Stephan Mörsch:* Every year there was a clearing period in which RWE was allowed to expand the open-pit mine further south. At the forest festival "Wald statt Kohle" (Forest Not Coal) in April 2012, some people occupied a piece of the forest for the first time. As they were defenselessly exposed on the ground to RWE security, which often defended its premises with → violence, they moved their occupation into the trees. At that time, the forest was a kind of lawless zone. In the first years, people therefore moved there very strategically. They occupied only those trees that were to be cleared in a given year, protecting them with their own bodies and by building simple platforms. The occupation became a permanent presence, but the structures were precarious and short-term. Through the monthly forest walks by Eva Töller and Michael Zobel, which have been taking place since 2014, more and more previously uninvolved people came into contact with the occupiers and their constructions. The national and international press took notice and the movement's cross-regional networking began. When the first press photos appeared, it was suddenly no longer just about preventing the clearing of the trees but also about creating a media-savvy image of the Hambach Forest. Some activists worried about the aesthetic appearance of the settlement. They saw photos of the structures in the newspaper and were unhappy. Instead of simple wooden huts, the occupiers subsequently designed tree houses with a creative approach: glass facades and carefully thought-out floor plans were realized, while plastic as a building material was to be dispensed with. Over time, the strategy for police evictions also changed. Instead of the → lock-on devices that came from the anti-nuclear movement, the occupiers now relied on evading the police by climbing away via rope connections.

AMM: How has this new eviction strategy changed the protest camp in Hambach Forest?

SM: The barrio that implemented this strategy first, and perhaps most successfully, was Beechtown. In 2018, it took the police four attempts to evict the settlement. It was a very high barrio because the beech trees there are among the tallest trees in the Hambach Forest. The kitchen started at a height of eighteen meters; an octagonal tree house was at twenty-one meters; and the "bus stop," the highest hut in Hambach Forest, sat twenty-six meters up in the trees. A walkable lookout with a →flag was the highest point in the protest camp at thirty-six meters, ending several meters above the forest. All tree houses and platforms in Beechtown were connected by bridges, rope ladders, or traverses. Although the police arrived with several lifting platforms during the 2018 eviction, it was not enough, as the many connections allowed the activists to move from one barrio to the next above the heads of the police.

AMM: How did these connections come about in Beechtown? Were there people who were familiar with such constructions? SM: Frodo, a mathematician and long-time resident of the barrio who knew every tree in the barrio well, worked on the structural engineering of many suspension bridges and the distribution of forces in the tree. The forces had to be distributed throughout the crown and diverted into the tree trunk or the next bridge. The forest was already in a very poor condition at that time because all the groundwater had been removed from it by coal mining. But the bridges and traverses also meant that the trees supported each other and no longer toppled over in windy conditions.

AMM: The use of the bridges was, however, also associated with risks for the activists. During the 2018 eviction, the journalist Steffen Meyn fell from a suspension bridge in Beechtown and was fatally injured.

SM: The most dangerous spots were known to be the connection points between the bridges and the tree houses. This was because the platforms in the treetops remained relatively static, whereas the suspension bridges moved much more. Steffen Meyn's fall occurred at such a spot, at one of the first bridges ever built in Hambach Forest. In the hectic rush to clear a neighboring barrio, Steffen, who was usually very careful, neglected his own safety. He was concerned with documenting the eviction […]. The construction of the bridges was a constant learning process. In the beginning, the activists built the bridges directly in the tree, later they moved on to prefabricating them on the ground and then just hanging them in the trees. In the early years, materials were often scarce and came mainly from chance finds, but soon pallets were organized on a large scale. The know-how for building such bridges spread from Beechtown throughout the forest. In Oaktown, which was later the barrio with the most connections, this type of bridge did not exist until later.

AMM: Why did you decide to build a model of Beechtown? Was it also a way for you to spread the knowledge of building such structures?

SM: Activism and art are often interdependent for me, that's true. And of course something can be learned from the model. For example, every knot is tied exactly the same way in the model as in a 1:1 scale. In principle, the model is a three-dimensional knot textbook. But for me, the most important thing was to connect with society through my work and to convey what sometimes didn't come through in the press: these weren't just some wacky people who built these fantastic structures. Instead, what we have here are really well-thought-out architectural designs that are worth looking at in a museum. (Contribution by Julia Riedel and Ronni Zepplin; conversation with Stephan Mörsch; interview transcript: Uta Winterhager; introduction and research: AMM)

Handbücher / Online-Manuals, engl. Manuals.

Autonome a.f.r.i.k.a.-gruppe, Luther Blissett, Sonja Brünzels: Handbuch der Kommunikationsguerilla (1997), Hamburg / Berlin ⁵2012

Andrew Boyd, Dave Oswald Mitchell (Hg.): Beautiful Trouble, New York /

Hand

London 2012. Online: https://www.creativityandchange.ie/wp-content/uploads/2017/06/beautiful-trouble.pdf (Zugriff: 25. Juni 2023)

Earth First! Direct Action Manual (1997), ³2015. Online: https://archive.org/details/direct_action_manual_3/page/n3/mode/2up (Zugriff: 25. Juni 2023)

Handbuch für Hausbesetzer, hg. von Verlagskollektiv Rote Klinke, Bad Godesberg ca. 1972

Keith: *Disco Dave's Tunnel Guide*, 2013. Online: https://underminers.files.wordpress.com/2013/01/disco_daves_tunnelling_guide_pdf_version_kf.pdf (Zugriff: 25. Juni 2023)

Redaktionskollektiv „Autokorrektur", Clara Thompson, Tobi Rosswog, Jutta Sundermann, Jörg Bergstedt (Hg.): *Aktionsbuch Verkehrswende. Acker, Wiese & Wald statt Asphalt*, München 2021

Road Alert: *Road Raging. Top Tips for Wrecking Roadbuilding*, Newbury 1997. Online: http://www.networkforclimateaction.org.uk/toolkit/action_resources/guides_to_taking_action/road_raging/index.html (Zugriff: 25. Juni 2023)

The HK19 Manual, Part 1: The Roles. Online: https://docs.google.com/document/d/1ZrIiXypVUvPIRs9JG8AsU55FkLsz81pqZstKQcbsAHc/edit# (Zugriff: 25. Juni 2023); Part 2: How To Guides. Online: https://docs.google.com/document/d/1UROUN37gUqrDd-4FYDFYXQAmYuXtsBAfaDLo47Im-Kk/edit#heading=h.55068nn22s5m (Zugriff: 25. Juni 2023)

Trees are friends. A Zine on Building Tree houses, 2022. Online: https://archive.org/details/treesarefriends (Zugriff: 25. Juni 2023)

x-tausendmal quer: Blockadefibel. Anleitung zum Sitzenbleiben, Hamburg ²2010. Online: https://www.kommunikationskollektiv.org/wp-content/uploads/2013/04/Blockadefibel.pdf (Zugriff: 25. Juni 2023)

Hand signals, Ger. → *Handzeichen* (fig.). At → *Occupy Wall Street*, choreographed hand signals were used instead of traditional acoustic signals for → *communication* within the General Assembly and to form consent within a large crowd. They were first introduced in → *2011* by → *Movimiento 15M* and subsequently appeared at many other protest sites. (JD)

Handy, engl. → *Mobile phone*; → *Digitale Medien*, → *Hongkong-Proteste*

Handzeichen. Ape Lad: *Illustrated Guide of Occupy Wall Street Hand Signals*, 2011 (Hand signals. Ape Lad: *Illustrated Guide to Occupy Wall Street Hand Signals*, 2011)

Handzeichen, engl. → *Hand signals.* Bei → *Occupy Wall Street* dienten, anstelle von herkömmlichen akustischen Signalen, choreografierte Handzeichen der → *Kommunikation* innerhalb der General Assembly. Eingeführt wurden sie erstmals → *2011* bei → *Movimiento 15M* und tauchten danach auch an vielen anderen Protestorten auf. (JD)

Hausbesetzung, engl. → *Squatting.* Hausbesetzungen zielen darauf ab, leerstehende Gebäude langfristig gegen den Willen der Eigentümer*innen zu bewohnen. In Europa und Nordamerika entsteht seit den 1970er Jahren eine der Anarchismus- und Autonomenbewegung nahestehende Hausbesetzer*innenszene, die sich bewusst von gesellschaftlichen Normen abgrenzt und mit dauerhaften alternativen Formen des Zusammenlebens und selbstverwalteten Räumen experimentiert. Hier kommen der Aktivismus obdachloser oder notdürftig wohnender Menschen, Forderungen nach bezahlbarem Wohnraum, der Protest gegen spekulativen Leerstand und hohe Mieten oder auch der Wunsch zusammen, Architekturen vor dem Abriss zu retten. Dieses Protestwohnen findet sich in urbanen wie ländlichen Bereichen; es grenzt sich von der kurzfristigen, politisch motivierten In-besitznahme öffentlicher Gebäude wie Parlamenten, Radiostationen oder Elek-trizitätswerken ab.

Der anarchistische Schriftsteller und Sozialhistoriker Colin Ward sieht den Vorgang des urbanen *Squatting* im Zu-sammenhang mit bis ins Mittelalter zu-rückreichenden Beispielen, in denen Menschen Land besetzten, um dort ohne Erlaubnis der Regierenden über Nacht ein neues Haus zu bauen (Ward 2002/2009). Ein bekanntes Beispiel der Frühen Neuzeit stellen die *Digger* dar, die sich Mitte des 17. Jahrhunderts gegen Ende des Englischen Bürger*innen-kriegs bemerkbar machten. Diese christ-lich-frühkommunistische Bewegung, die Privateigentum ablehnte, besetzte einige Jahre lang Land und errichte-te Hütten, um das Gebiet als Teil einer umfassenden Reform gemeinschaftlich zu bearbeiten. Solche Landnahme kann jedoch auch im Zeichen der Regieren-den geschehen: Zeitgleich zu den *Dig-gern* bereiteten europäische Siedler*in-nen die spätere Kolonisation der USA vor. Hausbesetzungen sind historisch schwierig zu fassen, denn nicht immer wollten *Squatter* ihre Anwesenheit be-kannt geben. Eine entscheidende struk-turelle Änderung der Moderne ist, dass ab dem 20. Jahrhundert öffentliche wie private Eigentümer*innen die Entschei-dung treffen, bewohnbare Häuser lang-fristig leer stehen zu lassen, anstatt sie zu vermieten (Ward 1980, S. 109). Hausbe-setzungen existieren weltweit, doch sind je nach geografischem Kontext unter-schiedliche Dynamiken zu verzeichnen, denn nicht überall existieren → *Infra-strukturen*, die besetzt werden können. In Südafrika etwa stehen großflächige Slums – *Squatter Camps* und Townships – für Segregationspolitik; das indische Mumbai besteht zur Hälfte aus *Squat-tings* und in Brasilien existieren mit Fa-velas wie Rocinha, Rio de Janeiro, eben-falls großflächige, informelle urbane Strukturen, bewohnt von den Ärmsten der Gesellschaft.

Fahrt nahmen Hausbesetzungen als so-ziale Bewegung in Europa und Nord-amerika im Umfeld der niederländischen Provo-Bewegung und in der Folge von 1968 auf. So hatte der marxistische So-ziologe und Philosoph Henri Lefebvre im Angesicht von Urbanisierungsprozes-sen wie dem Massenwohnungsbau der Nachkriegszeit das kollektive „Recht auf Stadt" gefordert (Lefebvre 1968/2016). Im Mittelpunkt dieses Aktivismus, der sich in lokalen Strukturen engagiert, ste-hen neben einer basisdemokratischen oder anarchistischen Organisation oft gemeinschaftliches Leben als Alterna-tive zur bürgerlichen Kernfamilie sowie die Etablierung von Gegenkulturen. Be-setzte Häuser können in ein überregiona-les Netzwerk eingebunden sein und als urbane *Crash Pads* mit Landkommunen oder weiteren Projekten im Kontakt ste-hen (Gordon 2008, S. 61 ff.); Projekte wie die → *1971* gegründete → *Freistadt Christiania* in Kopenhagen haben sich teilweise auf größeren Gebieten ausge-breitet. Werden diese Tätigkeiten öffent-lich sichtbar durchgeführt, finden Trans-parente, → *Graffitis* oder Wandgemälde Einsatz, um politische Forderungen zu kommunizieren und um eine Differenz zur Umgebung zu formulieren. Teilwei-se wurden besetzte Häuser nach erfolg-reichem Häuserkampf in legale Wohnge-noss*innenschaften überführt. Dabei ist die Hausbesetzung nicht ausschließlich ein Phänomen kapitalistischer Gesell-schaften. In sozialistischen und kommu-nistischen Staaten wurden Hausbeset-zungen offiziell nicht toleriert. Trotzdem waren beispielsweise in der DDR ab den 1970er Jahren Wohnungsbesetzungen in Altbauten etwa im Prenzlauer Berg zu verzeichnen, welche das staatssozia-listische Monopol umgingen (Grashoff 2011). (Petra Lange-Berndt)

Heritage protection, Ger. → *Denkmal-schutz*, primarily refers to the protection of cultural assets such as historic sites, buildings, and works of art. Many coun-tries have specific laws that regulate heritage protection and are intended to ensure the preservation of cultural her-itage. In some cases, identity-building event sites and structures related to pro-tests have become memorials. For exam-ple, the site where the → *protest camp* of the →*Shearers' Strike* had stood on the banks of Lagoon Creek, left in its natural state, has been a Queensland heritage site since 1992. Near Frankfurt Airport, the rebuilt hut church and original parts of the famous concrete wall, moved from their original location, commemorate the resistance to the →*Startbahn West*. These were reinstalled in 2019 on the initiative of the Stadtmuseum Mörfelden-Walldorf and in cooperation with Fraport AG.

→*Archaeological investigations* are also conducted at sites of protest to gain insights into how protest camps were organized in the recent past—for example, at the sites of the Shearers' Strike (Egloff, O'Sullivan, Ramsay 1991), the →*Greenham Common Peace Camp* (Schofield, Beck, Drollinger 2008), and the →*Endcliffe protest camp* (Badcock, Johnston 2009). The research interest is to find out where the exact sites were, what →*building types* and →*settlement structures* the camps had, and how space was used and the landscape changed, particularly in the case of long-standing camps. Protest camps have only recently begun to become recognized as sites of significant archaeological interest in the German-speaking world. They belong to the research field of contemporary archaeology, a field which is often viewed critically and whose meaningfulness has been called into question, as in the case of the excavation in →*Gorleben* by the archaeologist Attila Dézsi, who wanted to discuss the corresponding area as a cultural monument (Dézsi 2018). In 2019, however, the responsible state office for the preservation of historical monuments rejected an entry in the list of monuments, since an archaeological monument would have to originate from a past era and, moreover, the excavation site was not endangered. As early as 1980, activists had applied for ad hoc protection of the still existing hut village in Gorleben as the living "Cultural Monument 1004," which the Higher Administrative Court, however, rejected.

In order to give special expression to their respective demands, it is not uncommon for protests to include the appropriation or →*occupation* of squares and buildings that are already cultural monuments or which house monuments, such as →*Tahrir Square* during the Arab Spring or the historic Puerta del Sol at →*Movimiento 15M*. The square in Madrid has received an extension to its meaning through the 15M movement, which has also been commemorated by a plaque since 2021. The plaque reads: "El pueblo de Madrid, en reconocimiento al movimiento 15M que tuvo su origen en esta Puerta del Sol. Dormíamos, despertamos" (The people of Madrid, in recognition of the 15M Movement that originated at the Puerta del Sol. We were asleep, but we have awoken), and also features the coat of arms of the City Council of Madrid.

Protests can also help to raise public awareness of the value and significance of a building and demand monument protection, as in Vienna in May 1968, when demonstrations were held against the demolition of Otto Wagner's urban rail stations. Critical questioning of monuments, on the other hand, can lead to →*toppling monuments*, as in protests by →*Black Lives Matter* in Bristol (UK) and Richmond (USA). (JD)

Hinweisschild. Günter Zint: Vorsicht Schild!, Gorleben 1980 (Information sign. Günter Zint: Caution Sign!, Gorleben 1980)

Hinweisschild, engl. →*Information sign*. Die meisten →*Protestcamps* sind voller Hinweisschilder, die der internen →*Kommunikation* der Besetzer∗innen dienen sollen oder an Besucher∗innen sowie an die →*Polizei* gerichtet sein können. Sie verbreiten – im Unterschied zu →*Bannern* oder →*Protestschildern* – zumeist alltägliche, organisatorische

Botschaften. Oft hat es den Eindruck, dass interne Konflikte über Hinweisschilder geregelt werden sollen, vergleichbar zu den schriftlich fixierten Mahnhinweisen in Wohngemeinschaftsküchen. So entsteht ein dichter Schilderwald, ironisch auf die Spitze getrieben durch dieses Hinweisschild aus → *Gorleben*, das darauf hinzuweisen scheint, dass schon wieder ein neues Hinweisschild zu beachten ist. (OE)

Hongkong-Proteste, engl. → *Hong Kong protests*. In Hongkong kam es → *2014* und → *2019* zu zwei Protestwellen, die sich gegen den stark zunehmenden Einfluss Chinas richteten. 2014 sollte das allgemeine Wahlrecht der Hongkonger*innen eingeschränkt werden, 2019 plante die Peking-nahe Stadtregierung ein Auslieferungsgesetz von Straftäter*innen nach China. Beide Protestbewegungen profitierten vom dichten Angebot der modernen Großstadt (WLAN, Restaurants, Zugang zu sanitären Einrichtungen, öffentliche Verkehrsmittel). Sie nutzten den Stadtraum allerdings auf ganz unterschiedliche Weise, da sich zwischen 2014 und 2019 die repressive Politik in Hongkong massiv verschärft hatte.

Aktivist*innen des Umbrella Movement (benannt nach dem Protestsymbol, einem gelben Regenschirm) errichteten im September 2014, nachdem es bei → *Demonstrationen* im Regierungsviertel zu Ausschreitungen gekommen war, mehrere → *Protestcamps*, die wichtige Verkehrsadern in verschiedenen Stadtvierteln für drei Monate → *blockierten*. → *Besetzungen* mit tausenden → *Zelten* entstanden, die je nach Standort unterschiedliche Charaktere entwickelten: Im größten der Protestcamps im Admiralty-Distrikt lebten hauptsächlich Studierende und Mitglieder der OCLP-Gruppe (Occupy Central with Love and Peace). In Mong Kok hingegen entstand ein Camp von Arbeiter*innen und Frachtfahrer*innen, wo es immer wieder zu Auseinandersetzungen mit der → *Polizei* sowie zwischen Befürworter*innen und Gegner*innen der Bewegung kam. → *Barrikaden* aus Straßenbrüstungen, Mülleimern und alltäglichen Objekten

wie Schaufensterpuppen (→ *Baumaterial*) wurden anfangs zum → *Schutz* der Besetzungen errichtet, funktionierten später aber vor allem als sichtbare Grenzen des besetzten Gebiets. Zusammen mit den langen Zeltreihen trugen die Barrikaden dazu bei, ein medienwirksames Bild der Besetzung zu erzeugen (→ *Medien*), wie es die Protestierenden von den großen → *Platzbesetzungen* in Kairo (→ *Tahrir-Platz*) und Kyjiw (→ *Majdan*) kannten. Nach dem Abklingen der anfänglichen Begeisterung, mit der viele Protestierende in den ersten Wochen in den Camps lebten, dienten diese bald nur noch als Treffpunkt für Veranstaltungen und Aktionen. Über die Monate verlor die Bewegung an Unterstützung. Die Protestcamps waren oft menschenleer und wurden schließlich weitgehend ohne Widerstand von der Polizei geräumt.

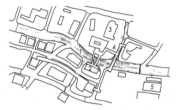

■ Barrikade der Protestierenden (Protesters' barricade)
▢ Polizeibarriere (Police barrier)

Hongkong-Proteste. 1 Protestcamp, Admiralty-Distrikt 2 Admiralty Centre 3 Regierungsbüros 4 Civic Square 5 Polizeipräsidium (Hong Kong protests. 1 Protest camp, Admiralty district 2 Admiralty Centre 3 Government offices 4 Civic Square 5 Police headquarters)

Die Protesttaktik von 2019 war inspiriert von einem Zitat des Hongkonger Martial-Arts-Künstlers Bruce Lee. „Be water, my friend!", stand im Kontrast zur ortsbezogenen Strategie von 2014: dezentralisierte Führung, spontane Aktionen und Vermeidung von Konfrontationen mit der Polizei. Die Protestierenden organisierten sich über anonyme Online-Plattformen, den Nachrichtendienst Telegram und das Online-Forum LIHKG (→ *Digitale Medien*). Über Bluetooth-Ketten konnten, ohne das Internet zu nutzen, anonym und schnell Informationen wie Karten von Versorgungs- und Erste-Hilfe-Stationen ausgetauscht werden. Die Grenzen zwischen Online- und Offline-Organisation waren oft verschwommen: → *Handzeichen* für die Übermittlung von Botschaften durch große Menschenmassen, z.B. welche Hilfsmittel in Konflikten mit der Polizei akut benötigt werden (Regenschirme, Atemmasken, Frischhaltefolie gegen Tränengaseinsätze), wurden in schnellen Handskizzen aufgezeichnet und digital verbreitet. Während das Umbrella Movement von 2014 den Regenschirm als eher defensives Protestsymbol hervorbrachte, waren die → *Erkennungszeichen* der 2019er-Bewegung der aggressivere Laserpointer und die Minibarrikaden aus einzelnen → *Ziegelsteinen*. Die Laserpointer, oft in Kombination mit Schirmen eingesetzt, dienten anfangs dazu, Überwachungskameras der Polizei zu blenden, wurden bald aber auch in gemeinschaftsbildenden Aktionen verwendet, vergleichbar mit Pop-Konzerten. Die Ziegelsteine, arrangiert als „brick henge" in einer an Stonehenge erinnernden Form, sollten Polizeifahrzeuge an der Durchfahrt hindern. In einigen Berichten hieß es, sie seien mit Sekundenkleber an der → *Straße* fixiert – was sich jedoch durch Aktivist∗innen nicht bestätigen ließ. Größere Barrikaden bestanden aus Absperrelementen, Bambusstangen, Holzleitern, Paletten, Stühlen und Mülltonnen. Schaumstoff-Schwimmbretter und Schranktüren dienten als → *Schutzschilde* gegen Gummigeschosse (→ *Waffen*). Beobachtungstürme (→ *Turm*) wurden aus zusammengebunden Bambusstäben und Autoteilen gebaut.

Ein in Hongkong lebender Aktivist vergleicht in einem für die Ausstellung *Protest/Architektur* verfassten Textbeitrag die Strategien beider Bewegungen: *Früher galten die Menschen in Hongkong als fleißige Arbeitstiere. Damals war das unerbittliche Streben nach Reichtum und materiellem Erfolg ihr ultimatives Ziel, während die Schwierig-* *keiten der politischen Verhältnisse gern in den Hintergrund gedrängt wurden. Die bloße Erwähnung von Hongkong beschwört Bilder herauf von einer „kapitalistischen Utopie" – einem Paradies für die wohlhabenden transnationalen Eliten sowie für große multinationale Unternehmen. Mit ihren niedrigen Steuersätzen und dem reibungslosen Waren- und Arbeitsmarkt wurde die Stadt zu einem pulsierenden Zentrum mit hoch aufragenden Bürogebäuden und weitläufigen Einkaufszentren. Hongkong wurde zum Inbegriff einer modernen Metropole. Für die einfachen Leute jedoch gilt dieses Sinnbild eines urbanen Paradieses als Produkt einer „Immobilienhegemonie", einem System, das die Interessen der Reichen und Mächtigen begünstigt, während es die Kreativität und die demokratischen Bestrebungen der Basis unterdrückt.*

Doch der Mythos der „kapitalistischen" Utopie wurde durch die Umbrella Movement im Jahr 2014 und die Anti-Auslieferungs-Bewegung 2019/2020 erschüttert. Dies waren zwei entscheidende Momente des politischen Erwachens für die Menschen in Hongkong, die in Scharen auf die Straße gingen, um ihren demokratischen Forderungen Ausdruck zu verleihen. Während sie marschierten und Slogans riefen, begannen sie, ihr Verhältnis zu ihrer Umgebung und ihren Platz in der Gesellschaft grundlegend zu hinterfragen. Sie gaben sich nicht länger damit zufrieden, nur Zuschauer∗innen zu sein, sondern ergriffen mutige Maßnahmen, um ihre Stadt zurückzuerobern und ihre Rechte als Bürger∗innen einzufordern. Diese beiden Protestbewegungen waren mehr als nur ein Plädoyer für die Demokratisierung der Wahlen – sie waren ein Aufruf für ein neues Verständnis des städtischen Lebens, ein Leben, das den Bürger∗innen Hongkongs ermöglichen sollte, dort in Würde zuhause zu sein. Obwohl beide Protestbewegungen unterschiedliche Ansätze verfolgten, handelte es sich um kühne urbane Experimente, die versuchten, die Struktur ihrer Stadt auf einzigartige, aber dennoch korrespondierende Weise umzugestalten.

Während der Umbrella-Bewegung besetzten die Bürger∗innen von Hongkong die pulsierenden Geschäftsviertel und gründeten drei utopische Protestcamps, in denen die Bürger∗innen sich für politische Alternativen einsetzten und sowohl die „Unvermeidlichkeit, als auch die Richtigkeit der herrschenden Modelle" in Frage stellten (Peterson 2005, S. 3). Von diesen drei Camps war „Harcourt Village" das bekannteste und einzigartigste. Das Camp befand sich in Admiralty, dem politischen und wirtschaftlichen Zentrum von Hongkong. Dort stehen die bedeutendsten Gebäude der Stadt – der Central Government Complex, das High Court Building, die Hongkong-Dependance der chinesischen Volksbefreiungsarmee sowie bemerkenswerte Geschäftshochhäuser wie der Bank of America Tower und der CITIC Tower. Vom 28. September bis zum 11. Dezember 2014 übernahmen die Protestierenden die Kontrolle über die Hauptstraßen von Admiralty. Die Mehrheit der Besetzer∗innen zog zur Harcourt Road, und bald wurde die Gegend als „Harcourt Village" bekannt, ein Symbol für den Widerstand und die Entschlossenheit der Menschen.

Der Prozess des Zusammenlebens erzeugte eine neue Art von kreativen urbanen Experimenten, da die Protestierenden es sich zur Aufgabe gemacht hatten, ihr Lebensumfeld von Grund auf selbst zu gestalten. In den ersten Nächten, als der harte Boden das Schlafen fast unmöglich machte, initiierten einige Leute eine „One Man, One Tent"-Kampagne und riefen zur Spende von Zelten auf. In der 12. Nacht der Besetzung waren bereits mehr als 2000 Zelte in Admiralty aufgestellt. Um die Grundbedürfnisse der Menschen zu befriedigen, gab es etwa 30 Versorgungsstationen in verschiedenen Bereichen von Harcourt Village. An den Vormittagen kochte eine ältere Frau namens Wong im Dorf oft gedämpfte Reisrollen, ein traditionelles kantonesisches Gericht, weil sie wollte, dass die jungen Leute „mehr Abwechslung beim Essen haben und gesund bleiben". Abends verteilten viele Freiwillige hausgemachte Geträn-

ke wie Ingwer- und Kräuterblütentee sowie rote Bohnensuppe. Eine engagierte Gruppe von Freiwilligen richtete außerdem den „Chater Study Room" ein, einen bescheidenen, aber wichtigen Raum, der aus Bambusstäben und Holzbrettern gebaut wurde, damit die Schüler∗innen und Student∗innen in dem Protestcamp einen Platz zum Lernen hatten. Später errichteten wiederum andere ein Windkraftwerk. Drei Fahrraddynamos dienten zur Stromerzeugung. Der Chater Study Room konnte daraufhin Licht, Wärmflaschen, heiße Getränke und kostenloses WLAN anbieten, damit die Nutzer∗innen auch nachts weiterarbeiten konnten. Zu den sonstigen Einrichtungen gehörten u.a. ein Briefkasten, eine Raucherecke, Batteriestationen und die berühmte „Lennon Wall", auf der man Nachrichten auf bunten Post-It-Zetteln hinterlassen konnte. Der symbolträchtigste Veranstaltungsort war die „Hauptbühne" (Dai Toi), die sich unter den beiden Brücken befand, die das Admiralty Centre und die zentralen Regierungsbüros miteinander verbinden. 40 Student∗innen der Hong Kong Baptist University schufen dort ein riesiges Kunstwerk. Sie nähten die zerstörten Regenschirme, mit denen sich die Demonstrant∗innen gegen Tränengasgranaten gewehrt hatten, zu einem Schutzraum zusammen. Die Protestierenden nannten diesen speziellen Bereich „Umbrella Square" (Platz der Regenschirme), auf dem verschiedene Gruppen wie HKFS und Scholarism, zwei der Studierendenorganisationen, die die Bewegung anführten, täglich Versammlungen abhielten, um Informationen zu verbreiten und die Besetzer∗innen zu unterstützen.

Eine der entscheidenden Maßnahmen im Harcourt Village war die Montage von Treppenstufen. Bevor diese Treppen entstanden, war das Camp durch die hohen Verkehrsbarrieren zwischen den Fahrbahnen und Gegenfahrbahnen getrennt, was es den Menschen fast unmöglich machte, quer hindurchzugehen. Eine Gruppe von Freiwilligen, darunter Schreiner∗innen und einfache Bürger∗innen, baute daraufhin Dut-

219

zende von Treppen, die die verschiedenen Straßen miteinander verbanden und Kindern und älteren Menschen die Fortbewegung im Camp erleichterten. Sie wurden aus Holz- und Kunststoffbrettern, Rohren und wiederverwendeten Wassertanks zusammengeschustert und von den Schreiner*innen jeden Tag verstärkt und auf ihre Sicherheit hin überprüft. Ein Demonstrant berichtet: „Die Freiwilligen patrouillieren durch das Dorf, um die Treppen zu überprüfen und zu reparieren. Ihre Struktur wurde immer ausgefeilter. Die Entwicklung der Treppen ist ein Beleg dafür, dass sich die besetzte Zone zu einer Gemeinschaft entwickelt hat. Widerstand ist jetzt Teil des täglichen Lebens der Menschen. Harcourt Village ist ein neues Hongkong." (Chow 2015)

Auch wenn die Zelte, die selbstgebauten Kraftwerke, der Lernraum und die Treppen im Vergleich zu den glitzernden Wolkenkratzern des Regierungskomplexes und den hochwertigen Büros primitiv wirken mögen, erzählen sie doch alle von der fundamentalen Wirkung der Architektur und der Substanz sozialer Bewegungen sowie davon, wie diese Elemente zusammenkommen können, um eine mächtige Triebfeder für Veränderungen zu sein.

In den Jahren zwischen 2015 und 2019 wurde immer wieder über den generellen Ansatz und die Strategie der Umbrella-Bewegung nachgedacht. Eine wichtige Diskussion war die Frage, ob ähnliche Proteste noch einmal durchgeführt werden sollten. Der Wunsch nach einem radikaleren Protest, der das Funktionieren der Stadt behindert, beruht in gewisser Weise auf dem Gedanken, dass sich die Ereignisse von 2014 nicht wiederholen sollten.

Wenn die Umbrella-Bewegung von 2014 ein lebendiges Beispiel dafür ist, wie Bewohner*innen ein bestimmtes Gebiet besetzen und einen Do-it-yourself-Ansatz nutzen, um eine utopische Gemeinschaft zu verwirklichen, dann zeigen die Proteste gegen die Auslieferungsgesetze 2019/2020 eine ganz andere Strategie. Das Erfordernis, dezentral zu protestieren, musste mit der

Notwendigkeit zusammengedacht werden, sich post-digital untereinander abzustimmen.

Mit dem Einsatz von Tränengas, →Wasserwerfern und anderen polizeilichen Maßnahmen gegen die protestierenden Bürger*innen waren Protestcamps obsolet geworden. 2019 erschien die Anwendung einer Strategie wie von 2014 unmöglich und irrelevant. Fluidität – charakterisiert durch den ikonischen Slogan „Be Water" – definierte fortan während dieser neuen Protestbewegung die Beziehung zwischen den Bürger*innen und der Stadt. Von wilden Streiks bis hin zu Menschenketten entwickelten sie eine Vielzahl von räumlichen Taktiken, die die Proteste auf verschiedene Ecken der Stadt verteilten. Die Beziehung zwischen der Architektur und den Menschen wurde schnell politisiert: Einkaufszentren, Universitätsgebäude und Wohnsiedlungen wurden zu Schlachtfeldern, und die materielle Beschaffenheit dieser Strukturen wurde verstärkt und als Waffe eingesetzt. Manche Auseinandersetzungen waren körperlicher und gewalttätiger als andere (→ Gewalt). Ein solches Beispiel war die Belagerung der Chinesischen Universität Hongkong, wo Demonstrant*innen die strategisch günstige Position der Brücke Nr. 2 besetzten und Gegenstände auf die Bahngleise warfen, wodurch der Verkehr in der gesamten Stadt gestört wurde. Zugleich wurden die Eingänge zum Campus zu Barrikaden ausgebaut und Sportplätze in Krankenstationen umgewandelt. Ein Teil des Campus stand während der Kämpfe in Flammen, und mindestens 119 Studierende wurden verletzt. Die Belagerung eines anderen Campus, der Polytechnischen Universität Hongkong, war hingegen ein neuer Höhepunkt der politischen Gewalt. Die Demonstrant*innen, zumeist Studierende, bauten Mauern aus Ziegelsteinen und schossen Molotowcocktails und brennende Pfeile von den Bastionen des Campus in die Stadt hinein (→ Feuer). Doch ihre selbstgebauten Strukturen und Taktiken schienen sinnlos angesichts der Wasserwerfer, gepanzerten

Fahrzeuge und Schallkanonen, die von der Polizei eingesetzt wurden.

Zu den auffälligsten Konstruktionen, die bei den Protesten errichtet wurden, gehörten die Ziegelbarrikaden. Die „Mini-Stonehenges" aus drei auf der Straße gestapelten Ziegelsteinen sollten Polizeifahrzeuge aufhalten. Sie waren ein wichtiges Beispiel dafür, wie die Demonstrant∗innen die Materialressourcen der Stadt für vielfältige Zwecke einsetzten. Auch wenn nicht alle von ihnen als echte Barrikaden funktionierten, spiegelten sie den „Be Water"-Charakter der Proteste wider: Wenn die Polizei die verbarrikadierten Bereiche erreichte, zogen sich die Demonstrant∗innen zurück, während die Ziegelbarrikaden ihre vorherige Dominanz symbolisch zum Ausdruck brachten.

Während und nach den Anti-Auslieferungs-Protesten wurden Architektur und städtischer Raum nicht nur materiell, sondern auch symbolisch durch kollektive Praktiken umgewidmet. Ein solches Beispiel ereignete sich am 19. Juni 2019, als Leung Ling-Kit, der einen gelben Regenmantel und ein → Protestschild trug, auf tragische Weise am Pacific Place in Admiralty verstarb. Nach seinem Tod verwandelte sich eines der luxuriöses-ten Einkaufszentren der Stadt in einen Ort der Trauer, wo die Menschen Blumen hinterließen und eine Schweigeminute einlegten. Ähnliche Trauerszenen gab es an der Prince-Edward-MTR-Station, wo Online-Gerüchten zufolge am 31. August 2019 Menschen von der Polizei zu Tode geprügelt worden waren, und am Sheung-Tak-Parkplatz, wo ein 22-jähriger studentischer Aktivist nach einem Sturz aus dem dritten Stock tragisch ums Leben kam. Als die Bürger∗innen die Gehwege, Überführungen und Tunnel mit Post-it-Zetteln und anderen Kunstwerken schmückten – eine Praxis, die als „Lennon Walls" bekannt wurde –, verwandelten sich Nicht-Orte in lebendige Street-Art-Galerien, wo Kontakte zwischen den Leuten geknüpft wurden. Das Konzept des „Yellow Economy Circle" verwandelte Läden und Bürogebäude in einen Raum der politischen Meinungsäußerung und Auseinandersetzung. → Graffitis und Aufkleber tauchten in unerwarteten Ecken der Stadt auf, eine subtile und doch kraftvolle Form des visuellen Widerstands. Pro-demokratische „gelbe Geschäfte" zeigten ihre Solidarität mit der Bewegung, indem sie ihre Inneneinrichtung mit Bannern und Maskottchen wie dem

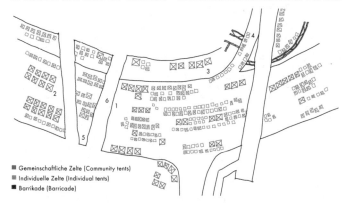

■ Gemeinschaftliche Zelte (Community tents)
■ Individuelle Zelte (Individual tents)
■ Barrikade (Barricade)

Hongkong-Proteste, September 2014. 1 Bühne 2 Study Room 3 Gemüsegarten 4 Lennon Wall 5 Handyaufladestation 6 Medien (Hong Kong protests, September 2014. 1 Stage 2 Study room 3 Vegetable garden 4 Lennon Wall 5 Charging station 6 Media)

LIHKG-Schwein schmückten. Die Läden sind einige der wenigen verbliebenen Spuren der Bewegung von 2019, auch wenn die Haltung ihnen gegenüber durchaus zwiespältig ist, da viele Hongkonger∗innen zum normalen Leben zurückgekehrt sind und ihre Konsumentscheidungen nicht mehr von der politischen Ausrichtung der Geschäfte abhängig machen. Neben den Geschäften und Büros wurden auf dem Höhepunkt der politischen Polarisierung auch viele andere alltägliche Räume mobilisiert, vom privaten Schlafzimmer bis hin zu den öffentlichen Sportplätzen an Spieltagen.

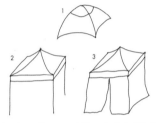

Hongkong-Proteste. 1 Kuppelzelt 2–3 Pavillonzelt (Hong Kong protests. 1 Dome tent 2–3 Gazebo tent)

Genau durch diesen Politisierungsprozess wurde die Anti-Auslieferungs-Bewegung zu einem seltenen Moment, an dem politisch motivierte Bürger∗innen lernten, ihre Stadtviertel selbst zu verwalten und ihre umgebende Architektur zu demokratischen Treffpunkten zu gestalten. Zwar wird die Anti-Auslieferungs-Bewegung oft als „dezentraler Protest" dargestellt, doch können Dezentralisierung und Zentralisierung als ineinander verschränkt gedacht werden. Da die traditionellen Modelle der städtischen Verwaltung und der Bereitstellung von Ressourcen zusammenbrachen, wurden die Aufgaben der räumlichen Organisation von der Bevölkerung übernommen. Freiwillige Teams, die für die Verwaltung der Lennon Walls und der versteckten Netzwerke von Materialstationen verantwortlich waren, wurden

über Telegram und andere bereits bestehende soziale Netzwerke rekrutiert. Die Freiwilligen nutzten angepasste digitale Stadtpläne, um Geschäftsräume nach ihrer politischen Einstellung zu klassifizieren, sodass die Bürger∗innen leicht erkennen konnten, welche Unternehmen ihre Anliegen unterstützten. Während die Protestierenden durch die Stadt zogen, organisierten einige Autobesitzer∗innen „Autoteams", um Vorräte zu verteilen und Transportmöglichkeiten zu schaffen. Dies war der Moment, in dem die Menschen lernten, digitale Karten zu nutzen, um jede enge Gasse zu studieren, sich mit den örtlichen Geschäften vertraut zu machen und ein tieferes Verständnis für ihre Stadt zu erlangen.

Inmitten der turbulenten Ereignisse dieser Zeit entwickelten die Menschen in Hongkong ein neues Zugehörigkeitsgefühl, das durch körperliche Erfahrungen im städtischen Raum zum Ausdruck kam. Am 1. Juli 2020 tauchte inmitten eines massiven Protests ein fünf Meter langes Banner aus der Menge auf, auf dem eine einfache, aber kraftvolle Botschaft stand: „we just really f∗∗∗ing love Hong Kong."

Nachdem die Anti-Auslieferungs-Bewegung mit staatlicher Repression zum Schweigen gebracht wurde, sind die physischen Spuren des Widerstands der Menschen systematisch ausgelöscht worden. Graffitis hat man weggeschrubbt und Banner verschwanden in Mülldeponien. Einige Veränderungen werden jedoch von Dauer sein. Wann immer die Menschen an den Orten des Protests wie dem Pacific Palace, einigen MTR-Stationen oder dem Hongkonger Berufungsgericht vorbeigehen, können sie nicht anders, als diese Orte durch andere Augen zu sehen; mit einem Blick, der von den Kämpfen und Opfern der Bewegung geprägt ist. (Einleitung und Recherche: AMM)

Hong Kong protests, Ger. → *Hongkong-Proteste*. In Hong Kong in → *2014* and → *2019*, there were two waves of protests against China's ever greater influence. In 2014, Beijing sought to restrict Hong Kong citizens' universal suffrage, and in 2019, the Hong Kong government, with its close ties to Beijing, planned a law enabling offenders to be extradited to China. Both protest movements benefited from the dense web of services the big city offers (WiFi, restaurants, access to sanitary facilities, public transportation). However, they used the urban space in very different ways, as between 2014 and 2019, policies in Hong Kong had become substantially more repressive.

Activists in the Umbrella Movement (named after the protest symbol, a yellow umbrella) in September 2014 erected several → *protest camps* after there had been rioting at → *demonstrations* in the government quarter, → *blocking* important traffic arteries in different districts over the course of three months. → *Occupations* with thousands of → *tents* were formed, which developed different characteristics depending on the location: The largest of the protest camps in the Admiralty district was mainly inhabited by students and members of the OCLP group (Occupy Central with Love and Peace). In Mong Kok, by contrast, a camp arose inhabited by workers and haulage drivers, and where there were repeatedly conflicts with the → *police* as well as between supporters and opponents of the movement. → *Barricades* erected using street railings, trash cans, and everyday objects such as shop window mannequins (→ *Building materials*) were initially put in place to provide → *protection* for the occupations, and later functioned primarily as visible borders of the occupied areas. Together with long rows of tents, the barricades helped create a media-savvy image of the occupation (→ *Media*), similar to what the protesters knew from the large → *public square occupation* in Cairo (→ *Tahrir Square*) and Kyiv (→ *Maidan*). After the initial enthusiasm felt by many protesters living in the camps during the first few weeks waned, the latter soon served only as a meeting point for events and actions. Over the months, the movement lost support. The protest camps were often deserted and eventually cleared by the police, largely without any resistance.

The protest tactics in 2019 were inspired by a quote from Hong Kong's martial arts superstar Bruce Lee. "Be water, my friend!" contrasted starkly with the site-specific 2014 strategy and instead emphasized decentralized leadership, spontaneous actions, and avoiding confrontations with the police. The protesters organized via anonymous online platforms, the Telegram messenger app, and the LIHKG online forum (→ *Digital media*). By means of Bluetooth chains, information such as maps of supply stations and first-aid stations could be swapped anonymously and swiftly. The lines dividing online and offline organization were often blurred: → *Hand signals* for conveying messages through large groups of people, such as stating what resources were urgently needed in conflicts with the police (umbrellas, breathing masks, clingfilm against teargas attacks) were recorded by swift sketches produced by hand and spread digitally. While the 2014 Umbrella Movement had created the umbrella as a more defensive protest symbol, the → *identifiers* of the 2019 movement were more aggressive laser pointers and mini-barricades erected from individual → *bricks*. The laser pointers were often deployed in combination with umbrellas, serving initially to dazzle the police surveillance cameras, but were soon also being used in community-building actions, comparable with pop concerts. The bricks, arranged as a "brick henge" reminiscent of the shape of Stonehenge, were intended to prevent police vehicles from being able to pass. Some reports suggested that they were attached to the → *street* surface using superglue—something that activists did not, however, confirm. Larger barricades were built using → *barriers*, sticks of bamboo, wooden ladders, pallets, chairs, and trash cans. Foam kickboards for swimming and cupboard doors served as → *protective shields* against rubber bullets (→ *Weapons*). Watchtowers (→ *Towers*) were built out of bamboo poles and parts of automobiles tied together.

In an essay written specially for the

Vicky Chan: Holzbrücke aus Paletten zur Überquerung
der Mittelleitplanke (Wooden-bridge made of pallets for
crossing the central guardrail), 12. November 2014

Vicky Chan: Zelte auf einem achtspurigen Highway im Admiralty-Distrikt (Tents on an eight-lane highway in the Admiralty district), 12. November 2014

Vicky Chan: Protestcamp im Mong-Kok-Distrikt (Protest camp in the Mong Kok district), 6. November 2014

Vicky Chan: Überdachte Zelte im Causeway-Bay-Distrikt
(Covered tents in the Causeway Bay district),
15. November 2014

Vicky Chan: Fernsehkameras im Mong-Kok-Distrikt (Television cameras in the Mong Kok district), 6. November 2014

鬥戰旅月來出身挺

Olaf Schülke: Auf Seilen gespannte Dachkonstruktion mit selbstgebauter Stütze (Roof structure on ropes with improvised support), 8. Oktober 2014

Studio Incendo: Demonstration im Causeway-Bay-Distrikt (Demonstration in Causeway Bay district)
18. August 2019

Kin Cheung: Protestaktion mit Laserpointern vor dem Hong Kong Space Museum (Protest action with laser pointers in front of the Hong Kong Space Museum), 7. August 2019

Studio Incendo: Menschenmenge kommuniziert über Handzeichen, um Krankenwagen durchfahren zu lassen (Crowd communicates via hand signals to make way for ambulances), 16. Juni 2019

Studio Incendo: Raumgreifende Barrikaden aus Ziegeln und Bambusstangen (Spatial barricades made of bricks and bamboo poles), 13. November 2019

Studio Incendo: Barrikade aus Straßenbrüstungen und langen Bambusstangen (Barricade made of street barriers and long bamboo poles), 24 August 2019

Studio Incendo: Polizei-Wasserwerfer versprühen blau eingefärbtes Wasser, um die an Straßenkämpfen beteiligten Protestierenden zu identifizieren (Police water cannons spray water dyed blue to identify protesters involved in street fights), 29. September 2019

Kin Cheung: Barrikaden aus Ziegelsteinen nahe der Polytechnischen Universität Hongkong (Brick barricades near the Hong Kong Polytechnic University), 14. November 2019

Studio Incendo: Ziegelbarrikaden zwischen Wohnhochhäusern (Brick barricades between high-rise residential buildings), 14. November 2019

Studio Incendo: Protestierende mit Schutzausrüstung und Regenschirmen im Straßenkampf (Protesters with protective gear and umbrellas in street fight), 18. November 2019

Protest/Architecture exhibition, an activist who lived in Hong Kong compares the strategies of the two movements:

Long ago, the people of Hong Kong were often portrayed as economic animals. There was a time when the relentless pursuit of wealth and material success was seen as the ultimate goal, while the intricacies of political discourse were relegated to a backseat. The mere mention of Hong Kong conjures up images of a "capitalist utopia"—a paradise for the affluent and transnational elites, as well as large multinational corporations. With its low tax rates and smooth movement of goods and labor, the city is a bustling hub of towering office buildings and sprawling shopping malls, painting a vivid picture of a modern metropolis. However, for the common people, this very image of the urban paradise represents a "real estate hegemony," a system that favors the interests of the wealthy and powerful, while stifling the creativity and democratic aspirations of the grassroots.

Yet, the myth of this "capitalist utopia" was shattered by the Umbrella Movement in 2014 and the Anti-Extradition Movement in 2019/2020. These were two pivotal moments of political awakening for the people of Hong Kong, who took to the streets in droves to express their democratic aspirations. As they marched and protested, they began to fundamentally rethink their relationship with their surroundings and their place in society. No longer content to be mere spectators, they took bold action to reclaim their cities and assert their rights as citizens. These movements were more than just a plea for electoral democratization—they were a call for a new approach to urban life, one that would allow the citizens of Hong Kong to live with dignity in the place they called home. Though differing in approach, the two movements were bold urban experiments, attempting to reshape the very fabric of their cities in unique but interrelated ways.

During the Umbrella Movement, the citizens of Hong Kong occupied the bustling business districts and establishing three utopian communities in which people embody alternatives and challenge both the "inevitability and the rightness of dominant models" (Peterson 2005, p. 3). Of these communities, "Harcourt Village" was the most established and unique. The village was nestled in the Admiralty district, figuratively the political and economic center of Hong Kong. It is there that the most significant buildings of the city are all located: the Central Government Complex, the High Court Building, the Chinese People's Liberation Army Forces Hong Kong Building, as well as notable commercial towers like Bank of America Tower and CITIC Tower. From September 28 to December 11, 2014, the protesters took control of the main roads of Admiralty. The majority of the demonstrators made their homes along Harcourt Road, and soon the area became known as Harcourt Village, a symbol of the people's resistance and determination.

The process of co-habitation unfolds different kind of creative urban experiments, as the protesters took it upon themselves to build their living environment from the scratch. At the first few nights, when the hard ground made sleep nearly impossible, some people initiated a "One Man, One Tent" campaign, calling for the donation of tents. By the 12th night of the occupation, there were more than 2,000 tents pitched at Admiralty. There were approximately 30 supply stations in different corners of Harcourt Village to provide for the basic needs of people. On many mornings, an elderly woman named Wong cooked steamed rice rolls, a traditional Cantonese dish, in the village because she wanted the young participants to "have more food choices and stay healthy." At night, many volunteers would hand out home-made drinks like ginger tea and mixed flowers herbal tea and red bean soup. In addition, a dedicated group of volunteers came together to establish the "Chater Study Room," a humble yet vital space constructed with bamboo sticks and wooden boards, so the students could do revision in the occupied area. Later, volunteers established a wind power plant and three bicycle dynamos to generate electricity. The Chater Study Room was then able to provide lighting service, warmers, hot drinks and free Wi-Fi services to users so they could study at night. Other facilities included, but were not limited to, a mailbox, a smoking corner, battery stations and the famous "Lennon Wall," on which people could write messages on colorful Post-It notes. The most symbolic venue was the "Main Stage" (Dai Toi), located beneath the two bridges connecting Admiralty Centre and Central Government Offices. Forty students from Hong Kong Baptist University created a huge installation artwork at the two bridges. The students sewed the broken umbrellas used by protesters to resist tear gas grenades together to create a shelter. The protesters called this specific area "Umbrella Square," in which different groups, such as HKFS and Scholarism, two of the student organizations that were leading the movement, would hold assemblies to release information and maintain the morale of the occupants every day.

One of the defining moments of Harcourt Village was the establishment of staircases. Prior to their construction, the occupied zone was divided by tall main road arteries, making it nearly impossible for people to traverse the area. In response, a group of volunteers, including carpenters and ordinary citizens, came together to build dozens of staircases, linking different main roads and making it easier for children and the elderly to move around the district. These staircases were crafted using wooden and plastic boards, pipes, and re-purposed water barriers, and were reinforced and safety-checked every day by the carpenters. As one protester notes:

"The volunteers patrol around the village to check and repair the staircases. The structure of staircases became more and more sophisticated. The evolution of staircases is witness to the fact that the occupation zone has developed into a community. Resistance is part of

the everyday life of people now. Harcourt Village is a new Hong Kong." (Chow 2015)

The staircases not only eradicated physical barriers but also turned the occupied zone into a cohesive community. Although the tent-homes, DIY power stations, study rooms, and staircases may appear primitive when compared to the gleaming skyscrapers of the government complex and grade A offices, they all speak to the fundamental meaning of architecture and the materiality of social movements, and how these elements can come together to create a powerful force for change.

In the years between 2015 and 2019, there was constant reflection on the overall style and strategy employed in the Umbrella Movement. A prominent topic of discussion was whether similar kind of protests should be staged again. In a way, the sentiment that there should be a more radical protest to obstruct the city's functioning is captured in the idea that what happened in 2014 should not be repeated.

If the Umbrella Movement is a living tale of how residents occupied a defined area of land and used a DIY approach to materialize a utopian community, then the Anti-Extradition protests present a very distinctive approach, one that is embedded in the connective logics of decentralized protests in a post-digital context.

As tear gas, → water cannons, and other police weapons were unleashed upon the progressive citizens, the limits of the physical body and settlements were crushed, rendering the notion of fixity both impossible and irrelevant. Liquidity—best characterized by the iconic slogan "Be Water"—defined the relationship between citizens and the city through movement. From wildcat strikes to human chains, citizens innovated a multitude of spatial tactics that diffused the protests towards different city corners. The relationships between architecture and the people were rapidly politicized; as shopping malls, university buildings, and residential estates all became battlegrounds, and the material nature of these structures was fortified and weaponized. Some confrontations were more bodily and physical than others (→ Violence). One such instance was the siege of the Chinese University of Hong Kong, where protesters occupied the strategically advantageous position of No. 2 Bridge and threw objects onto the railway tracks, disrupting the city's transport. Meanwhile, the campus entrances were consolidated into barricades, and sports grounds were transformed into medical stations. Some of the campus was set on fire during the fighting, and at least 119 students were injured. The siege of the more central Hong Kong Polytechnic University marked a new height of political violence. While protesters, mostly students, constructed and built brick walls, and shot firebombs (→ fire) and bows from campus podiums, their DIY structures and tactics seemed futile in the face of the modern weapons employed by the police, such as water cannons, armored vans, and sonic weapons.

One of the most visible structures when the protests became widespread in the city were the brick barricades. The "mini Stonehenges" of three bricks stacked on the road were intended to slow police vehicles down. They were a key example of how protesters made use of the city's material resources. While not all of them functioned as real barricades, they reflected the "Be Water" nature of the protests: When the police reached the barricaded areas, the protesters would retreat, while the brick barricades denoted their presence by serving a symbolic function.

During and after the Anti-Extradition protests, architecture and urban space were repurposed not only materially but also symbolically through collective practices. One such example occurred on June 19, 2019, when Leung Ling-Kit, wearing a yellow raincoat and carrying a → protest placard, tragically passed away at Pacific Place in Admiralty. In the aftermath of his death, one of the city's most luxurious shopping malls was transformed into a space of mourning, as people left flowers and observed moments of silence. Similar scenes of mourning took place at the Prince Edward MTR Station, where online rumors alleged that people had been beaten to death by the police on August 31, 2019, and at the Sheung Tak car park, where a 22-year-old student activist tragically died after falling from the third floor. On the other hand, when citizens adorned walkways, sky bridges, and tunnels with Post-It notes and other forms of artwork, a practice hailed as the "Lennon Walls," non-places were transformed into vibrant street art galleries, where relationships between people were forged. The concept of the "Yellow Economy Circle" turned shops and office buildings into a space of political manifestation and contestation. → Graffiti and stickers sprang up in unexpected corners of the city, a subtle yet powerful form of visual resistance. Pro-democracy "yellow shops" vividly displayed their solidarity with the movement by adorning their interior designs with banners and mascots, such as the LIHKG Pig. The shops are some of the few remaining traces of the 2019 movement, even though the attitude towards them is ambivalent as many Hong Kongers returned to normal life and ceased making their consumption choices based on the shops' political orientation. In addition to shops and offices, a wide range of everyday spaces were mobilized during the height of political polarization, from the most private of bedrooms to the most public of sports grounds on matchdays.

However, it was precisely through this politicization process that the Anti-Extradition movement became a rare moment in which politically engaged citizens learned to self-govern their neighborhoods and mold their surrounding architecture into democratic venues. While the Anti-Extradition movement was often portrayed as a matter of "decentralized protests," decentralization and centralization can be viewed through a geographic lens, as they refer to the distribution of power, resources, and decision-making across geographic space. As traditional mod-

241

els of leadership and resource mobilization collapsed, spatial management tasks were crowdsourced. Volunteer teams responsible for managing Lennon walls and hidden networks of material stations were recruited through Telegram and other pre-existing social networks. Volunteers utilized customized digital maps and mobile phone maps to classify commercial spaces according to their political stance, allowing citizens to easily identify which businesses were supportive of their cause. As protesters navigated through the city, some car owners organized "car teams" to distribute supplies and provide transportation. This was one moment when people learned to utilize digital maps to study every narrow alley, become familiar with local shops, and gain a deeper comprehension of their city.

Amid the tumultuous events of the time, the people of Hong Kong developed a new sense of belonging that was expressed through bodily experiences in urban spaces. On July 1, 2020, in the middle of a massive protest, a five-meter-long fabric banner emerged from the crowd, emblazoned with a simple yet powerful message: "we just really f***ing love Hong Kong." While the Anti-Extradition movements ended with state repression, the physical traces of people's resistance were systematically erased, as graffiti was scrubbed off walls and posters were condemned to landfills. However, some changes will be long-lasting, as people walked past landmarks such as the Pacific Palace, certain MTR stations, and the Hong Kong Court of Final Appeal, they could not help but see these spaces through a new lens, one that was shaped by the struggles and sacrifices of the movement. (Introduction and research: AMM)

Human chain, Ger. → *Menschenkette*; → *Baltic Way*, → *Body deployment*, → *Demonstration*, → *Greenham Common Peace Camp*, → *Hong Kong protests*

Ice, Ger. → *Eis*; → *Maidan*

Icon, Ger. → *Ikone (fig.)*. Eugène Delacroix's monumental history painting *Liberty Leading the People* has in-

scribed itself as an icon in our collective visual memory: not only is it considered an artistic masterpiece, but with its depiction of Marianne crossing the → *barricade*—as the symbolic figure of freedom—it is one of the most copied and reproduced images of the modern era (→ *Media*). In the course of more recent protests too, particularly poignant images, usually photographs of specific people or events, have repeatedly been declared icons: the image sequence of the "Lady in Red," a woman in a red dress who was attacked by police with pepper spray at the → *Gezi Park* protests in Istanbul on May 28, 2013 (→ *Weapons*, → *Anti-protest measures*), went viral in the → *digital media*, as did the photograph of the Black "superheroine" from the → *Black Lives Matter* movement who confronted police officers in Baton Rouge on July 9, 2016, with full → *body deployment*. However, the buildings of the protest movements can also have an iconic effect: although the large tower of the protests against the nuclear waste disposal center at → *Gorleben* in → *1980* and the pyramid of the Austrian → *Lobau* movement in Vienna are not necessarily "architectural icons," they are associated with these movements as unmistakable structures in certain sociotopes and are used as a kind of emblem (→ *Identifier*). (SH)

Identifier, Ger. → *Erkennungszeichen (fig.)*. An identifier is something that makes people recognizable as a participant or supporter of a protest movement. identify oneself as a participant or supporter of a protest movement. In the varied contexts of everyday life, mass media, and the protests themselves, a variety of different things can serve as identifiers: from the classic insignia of counterculture such as posters, buttons, stickers, → *graffiti* and patches (→ *Media*, → *Icon*) to homemade or professionally commissioned → *flags*, banners, and → *protest placards*, to printed T-shirts, bags, and other, sometimes fashionable accessories, such as the *keffiyeh* (→ *Clothing*), which is known as a symbol of support for Palestine in the Arab-Israeli conflict. Often, these material accessories become the symbol of protest movements, such as the Guy Fawkes mask for the →*Occupy Wall Street* movement in →*2011*, the umbrellas for the →*Hong Kong protests* in →*2014*, or the high-visibility vests—obligatory for drivers in France since 2008—for the French →*Yellow Vests* movement in →*2018/2019*. Uniform items of clothing such as white →*overalls* and →*costumes*—or even collective →*nakedness*—are often used to achieve particularly effective media images of →*demonstrations* or →*public square occupations*. Also, beyond a real, physical presence at protests (→*Body deployment*), certain gestures, →*hand signals*, choreographies, or the singing of protest songs (→*Music*) serve to indicate approval of, or affiliation with, the →*protest goals* (→*Communication*). (SH)

Ikone, engl. →*Icon*. Eugène Delacroix' monumentales Historienbild *Die Freiheit führt das Volk* hat sich als Ikone in das kollektive Bildgedächtnis eingeschrieben: Es gilt nicht nur als künstlerisches Meisterwerk, sondern ist mit seiner Darstellung der die →*Barrikade* überschreitenden Marianne – der Symbolgestalt der Freiheit – eines der am meisten kopierten und vervielfältigten Bilder der Moderne (→*Medien*). Auch im Zuge jüngerer Proteste sind besonders ergreifende Bilder, meist Fotografien bestimmter Personen oder Ereignisse, immer wieder zu Ikonen erklärt worden: Die Bildsequenz der „Lady in Red", einer Frau mit rotem Kleid, die am 28. Mai →*2013* bei den →*Gezi-Park*-Protesten in Istanbul von der Polizei mit Pfefferspray angegriffen wurde (→*Waffen*, →*Anti-Protestmaßnahmen*), ging in den →*Digitalen Medien* ebenso viral wie die Fotografie der Schwarzen „Superheldin" aus der →*Black-Lives-Matter*-Bewegung, die sich am 9. Juli 2016 in Baton Rouge mit vollem →*Körpereinsatz* den Polizisten entgegenstellte. Ikonische Wirkung können aber auch die Bauwerke der Protestbewegungen entfalten: Zwar sind der große Turm der Proteste gegen das nukleare Entsorgungszentrum →*Gorleben* →*1980* und die Pyramide der österreichischen →*Lobau-bleibt*-Bewegung in Wien nicht unbedingt „Architekturikonen", doch werden sie als unverkennbare Konstruktionen in bestimmten Soziotopen mit diesen Bewegungen in Verbindung gebracht und als eine Art Signet verwendet (→*Erkennungszeichen*). (SH)

Ikone. Eugène Delacroix: *Die Freiheit führt das Volk*, Öl auf Leinwand, 1830 (Icon. Eugène Delacroix: *Liberty Leading the People*, oil on canvas, 1830)

Information sign, Ger. →*Hinweisschild (fig.)*. Most →*protest camps* are full of information signs intended for internal communication among the occupiers and/or the police. Unlike →*banners* or →*protest placards*, they usually spread everyday organizational messages. Often, the impression is that the intention is to solve internal conflicts using information signs, comparable with the notorious passive-aggressive notes in flat-share kitchens. The result is a dense wall of signs, as is ironically exaggerated by this information sign from →*Gorleben* that seems to point out that yet another new information sign bears heeding. (OE)

Infrastructure, Ger. →*Infrastruktur*. When people settle in places to protest, they require built structures that enable them to organize and meet their basic needs for food and drink, shelter, hygiene, and medical care. How much effort it takes to build and maintain these infrastructures depends on the location and the resources available. When

→ *squatting*, protesters can make use of the → *protection* a building provides and sometimes even access existing utilities such as water, electricity, and gas. → *Public square occupations* in large cities often benefit from existing food-service businesses and public toilets, they can be supplied with energy around the clock via tapped streetlights and use nearby buildings to accommodate protesters. By contrast, in order to be able to reach areas of → *building site occupations* in forests or in remote villages at all, activists today organize carpools and shuttle buses for large-scale demonstrations increasingly via messenger services (→ *Digital media*). → *Building materials* and food to be prepared in self-managed → *kitchens* are bought with donated money or brought by local residents as friendly → *acts of solidarity*. With do-it-yourself strategies, methods of creative → *misappropriation,* and great improvisational talent, protesters appropriate the occupied sites and build infrastructures for supply, assembly, security, → *communication*, and individual self-expression. In → *Gezi Park* in → *2013*, activists built furniture such as lecterns, tables, and food stalls out of the → *barriers* that the → *police* used to seal off the → *protest camp*. At the → *Hong Kong protests* in → *2014*, homemade stairs made of wooden pallets and painter's drop sheets bridged the median guardrail on the occupied highway, making it accessible to all. On → *Tahrir Square* in Cairo, a fast-food restaurant became a clinic for the injured (→ *Violence*). Instead of radio stations like those that still existed in the protest settlements of the 1980s in → *Gorleben* and in the hut village against → *Startbahn West*, huge media centers (with camping tables full of cable drums and laptops) characterize the image of today's protest camps (→ *Occupy Wall Street*, → *Movimiento 15M*, → *Media*). Childcare services such as pony rides and kindergartens ensure that families can also participate in the protests. Solar energy systems and exercise bikes have been used to generate energy at → *Lützerath* and Gorle-

ben, e.g. to heat water for → *bathtubs* and showers. (AMM)

Infrastruktur, engl. → *Infrastructure*. Wenn Menschen sich an Orten niederlassen, um zu protestieren, braucht es gebaute Strukturen, die es ihnen möglich machen, sich zu organisieren und ihre Grundbedürfnisse nach Essen und Trinken, Unterkunft, Hygiene und medizinischer Versorgung zu erfüllen. Wie aufwendig die Herstellung und Aufrechterhaltung dieser Infrastrukturen ist, hängt vom Standort und den zur Verfügung stehenden Ressourcen ab. Bei → *Hausbesetzungen* können sich Protestierende im → *Schutz* eines Gebäudes einrichten und manchmal sogar auf die bestehende Versorgung mit Wasser, Strom und Gas zugreifen. → *Platzbesetzungen* in Großstädten profitieren oft von bereits vorhandenen gastronomischen Angeboten und öffentlichen Toiletten, lassen sich über angezapfte Straßenlaternen rund um die Uhr mit Energie versorgen und können nahe Gebäude für die Unterbringung von Protestierenden nutzen. Um dagegen Areale von → *Bauplatzbesetzungen* in Wäldern oder abgelegenen Dörfern überhaupt erreichen zu können, organisieren Aktivist∗innen heute Mitfahrgelegenheiten und Shuttlebusse für Großdemonstrationen vermehrt über Messengerdienste (→ *Digitale Medien*). → *Baumaterialien* und Lebensmittel für die Weiterverarbeitung in selbstverwalteten → *Küchen* werden von gespendetem Geld gekauft oder von Anwohner∗innen als freundliche → *Solidaritätsgeste* vorbeigebracht. Mit Do-it-yourself-Strategien, Methoden der kreativen → *Zweckentfremdung* und großem Improvisationstalent eignen sich Protestierende die besetzten Orte an und errichten Infrastrukturen für die Versorgung, Versammlung, Sicherheit, → *Kommunikation* und persönliche Selbstentfaltung: Im → *Gezi-Park* bauten Aktivist∗innen → *2013* Möbel wie Redner∗innenpulte, Tische und Essensstände aus den → *Absperrgittern*, welche die → *Polizei* zur Abriegelung des → *Protestcamps* verwendete. Bei den → *Hongkong-Protesten* von → *2014* überbrückten selbstgebaute Treppen aus Holzpaletten und

Malerteppichen die Mittelleitplanken auf dem besetzten Highway und machten ihn so für alle zugänglich. Auf dem → *Tahrir-Platz* in Kairo wurde ein Schnellrestaurant zur Klinik für Verletzte (→ *Gewalt*). Statt Radiostationen, wie es sie in den Protestsiedlungen der 1980er Jahre in → *Gorleben* und im Hüttendorf gegen die → *Startbahn West* gab, prägen riesige Medienzentren mit Campingtischen voll Kabeltrommeln und Laptops das Bild heutiger Protestcamps (→ *Occupy Wall Street*, → *Movimiento 15M*, → *Medien*). Betreuungsangebote für Kinder wie Ponyreitanlagen und Kindergärten sorgen dafür, dass sich auch Familien an den Protesten beteiligen können. Solaranlagen und Heimtrainer wurden in → *Lützerath* und Gorleben zur Energiegewinnung genutzt, u.a. um Wasser für → *Badewannen* und Duschen zu erhitzen. (AMM)

Internet, engl. → *Internet*; → *Digitale Medien*

Internet, Ger. → *Internet*; → *Digital media*

Intervention, engl. → *Intervention*; → *Guerillataktiken*

Intervention, Ger. → *Intervention*; → *Guerrilla tactics*

Januaraufstand / Spartakusaufstand, engl. → *Spartacist Uprising*. Im Januar → *1919* kam es in Berlin zu Straßenkämpfen, die auch als „Spartakusaufstand" bezeichnet werden (→ *Straße*, → *Barrikade*). Anhänger∗innen der USPD und KPD kämpften gegen Truppen, die sich loyal zur Regierung verhielten. Da zu diesem Zeitpunkt die provisorische Reichsregierung unter Friedrich Ebert aus Sozialdemokrat∗innen der MSPD gebildet wurde, standen sich also zwei linke Fraktionen gegenüber. Ziel war es ursprünglich, das Regierungsviertel zu besetzen. Mutmaßlich durch Polizeispitzel wurde der Protest dann aber in das Zeitungsviertel umgelenkt (→ *Polizei*). Dort hatten sozialdemokratische Zeitungen immer wieder kritisch bis feindselig über die konkurrierenden Kommunist∗innen berichtet. Die Arbeit der Zeitungen kam zum Erliegen (vgl. Ausst.-Kat. *Berlin in der Revolution 1918/1919* 2018). (JD)

Julirevolution, engl. → *July Revolution*. In Reaktion auf die reaktionäre Politik des Königs Karl X. kam es → *1830* in Paris zur sogenannten Julirevolution, die das Ende der Bourbonen in Frankreich besiegelte und in einer erneuten Machtergreifung des Bürger∗innentums resultierte. Bei den vom 27. bis 29. Juli 1830 andauernden Barrikadenkämpfen unterstützten die Bewohner∗innen der umliegenden Häuser die auf der → *Straße* kämpfenden Bürger∗innen, indem sie die königstreuen Truppen aus den Fenstern der Häuser heraus mit siedendem Wasser begossen und mit verschiedenen Gegenständen bewarfen (→ *Barrikade*, → *Waffen*). (SH)

July Revolution, Ger. → *Julirevolution*. In → *1830*, the reactionary politics of King Charles X triggered the socalled July Revolution in Paris, which put an end to the rule of the Bourbons in France and resulted in a renewed attempt by the bourgeoisie to seize power. During the barricade battles from July 27 to 29, 1830, residents in the surrounding buildings supported the citizens fighting in the → *streets* by pouring boiling water and throwing various objects onto the royalist troops from their windows (→ *Barricade*, → *Weapons*). (SH)

Jurte, engl. → *Yurt*; → *Alternative Architektur*, → *Bautypen*, → *Dakota-Access-Pipeline-Proteste*, → *Lobau*, → *Majdan*, → *Zelt*

Kapitol-Attacke, engl. *Capitol attack*. Am 6. Januar → *2021* rief Donald Trump, der abgewählte Präsident der USA, seine Anhänger*innen dazu auf, zum Kapitol zu kommen, um die formelle Bestätigung des Wahlerfolges seines Nachfolgers Joe Biden durch den Kongress in letzter Minute zu verhindern. Die Attacke auf das Parlamentsgebäude zielte auf die Eroberung des architektonischen Symbols der amerikanischen Demokratie (→ *Rechte Proteste*). Auch ein Staatsstreich beginnt mit der gewaltsamen Eroberung der symbolischen und tatsächlichen Zentren der Macht (→ *Gewalt*). Erst nach Stunden der Erstarrung gelang den Sicherheitskräften die Räumung. (OE)

Kett

Kettling, Ger. → *Polizeikessel (fig.)*. Extended encirclement and thus blocking of protesters' movement by the → *police* (→ *Blockade*). The "Hamburg Kettling" in 1986 saw people who wished to protest against police obstruction of an anti-nuclear-power demonstration detained for up to thirteen hours on an open street by a second police action. The measure was later declared illegal by the Hamburg Administrative Court. The kettling of about 1,000 protesters in Frankfurt in 2013 for about five hours during the Blockupy protests was, by contrast, judged by the Federal Constitutional Court to be legal (→ *Street*). (OE)

Kinder, engl. → *Children*; → *Gorleben*, → *Infrastruktur*, → *Schutz*, → *Tahrir-Platz*

Kitchen, Ger. → *Küche*. As places for food preparation, kitchens are an integral part of the → *infrastructure* in many → *protest camps*. Beyond their function of storing food and preparing meals, kitchens strengthen social cohesion by organizing communal catering for protesters. Since sharing meals fosters a sense of community that goes beyond the protesters' political interest (→ *Protest goals*), the establishment of kitchens can also be understood as → *acts of solidarity*. In the course of the → *squatting* in Germany in the 1980s, the so-called "Volxküche" or "Küfa" (kitchen for all) emerged in the autonomist scene, which is still used today time and again at protest camps and → *demonstrations*. If the protests take place in the centers of large cities (→ *Public square occupation*), there is often no need to have one's own kitchen: firstly because there may be enough restaurants, food stalls, cookshops, or mobile vendors to cover the food needs; and secondly because the protestors are often also supplied by sympathizers from the neighborhood, as was the case, for example, in the → *Gezi Park* protests in Istanbul in → *2013*. The protests in Cairo's → *Tahrir Square* during the Arab Spring in → *2011* attracted a large number of mobile vendors, many of whom remained around the square after the protests ended. (SH)

Klebstoff, engl. → *Glue*; → *Ankleben*, → *Blockade*, → *Fahrzeuge*, → *Guerillataktiken*, → *Hongkong-Proteste*, → *Körpereinsatz*

Kleidung, engl. → *Clothing*. In verschiedenen sozialen Bewegungen dient Kleidung als Ausdruck politischer Haltung; ihre Bedeutung ist zeichenhaft und kann nur in ihrem jeweiligen kulturellen und historischen Kontext verstanden werden, wo sie einem ständigen Wandel unterliegt. Dabei bilden einzelne Kleidungsstücke und Accessoires in Kombination mit Make-up, Tätowierungen, Bart oder Frisur ein Ensemble. Zusammen mit Mimik, Gestik und Körperhaltung wird die „Kleidersprache" zu nonverbaler → *Kommunikation* in der sozialen Interaktion (Hoffmann 1985). Kleidung als Protestform ist entweder temporär für die Dauer einer politischen Aktion relevant oder sie kann dauerhaft im Alltag getragen Protest artikulieren. Auch das Weglassen von Kleidung wird als Protest eingesetzt, da → *Nacktheit* in der Öffentlichkeit einen hohen Grad an Aufmerksamkeit generiert.

Das klimaaktivistische Bündnis Ende Gelände macht durch sein massenhaftes Auftreten in weißen Overalls und Atemschutzmasken nicht nur auf sich aufmerksam. Laut ihrem *Activist Guide* schützen Maske und Overall vor Schmutz und Matsch und vor möglichen gesundheitlichen Folgen des eingeatmeten Staubes. Die Nebenwirkung, die das Tragen einheitlicher Kleidung und Masken mit sich bringt – schlechter von → *Polizei* und Sicherheitspersonal erkannt zu werden –, wird dabei gern in Kauf genommen (*Shut Shit Down!* 2020). Auch freundlicher, nahezu unschuldig sollen die weißen Anzüge wirken, im Gegensatz zur homogen schwarz gekleideten Masse des Schwarzen Blocks. Die Aktivist∗innen beziehen sich auf die Geschichte des → *zivilen Ungehorsams* und ihrer Bewegungen, wie die deutsche Anti-Atomkraft-Bewegung und die italienischen Tute Bianche, die durch ihr umfangreiches Repertoire an Schutzkleidung auffielen. Die Tute Bianche waren eine kritische Reaktion auf die Autonomia Operaia der 1970er Jahre in Italien. Auch in Deutschland prägten ähnliche militante Protestformen, wie die „Putztruppe" der Frankfurter Spontis der 1970er Jahre, Straßendemonstrationen (→ *Straße*, → *Demonstration*). Ihre Schutzkleidung wurde jedoch von der Polizei nicht als defensiver → *Schutz* wahrgenommen, sondern als Ausdruck von Gewaltbereitschaft und „Aggressivität" (Grob 1985, S. 280; → *Gewalt*). 1985 wurde in der Bundesrepublik Deutschland das „Vermummungsverbot" sowie das Verbot der sogenannten „passiven Bewaffnung" durchgesetzt. Daran kritisiert wurde nicht nur die den Protestierenden unterstellte latente Gewaltbereitschaft, sondern auch die befürchtete Willkür bei der Auslegung dieses Gesetzes (Meyn 1988, S. 93 f.; Grob 1985, S. 279).

Vermummung ist eine wichtige Funktion von Schutzkleidung im Kontext konfrontativer Protestformen, um die Identitätsfeststellung durch Polizei oder politische Gegner*innen zu erschweren. Die Sturmhaube, Symbol militanten Protests, wurde wesentlicher Bestandteil des Kleidungsrepertoires der Autonomen. Zusammen mit der einheitlichen schwarzen Kleidung ist sie Teil der performativen Protestform des Schwarzen Blocks auf Straßendemonstrationen. Das sogenannte „Vermummungsverbot" schränkte das Verhüllen erheblich ein (Haunss 2004, S. 169 f.). Mit der Maskenpflicht im Rahmen der Corona-Schutzmaßnahmen wurde aus dem Verbot ein Vermummungsgebot. Nach Aufhebung der Maßnahmen im Winter 2022/2023 obliegt es der Polizei, jeweils im Einzelfall zu entscheiden, ob der Mund- und Nasenschutz vor Infektion oder vor der Identitätsfeststellung schützt. Trotz des Verbots gehört das Verhüllen sowie die Schutzkleidung zum Repertoire politischer Aktionsformen. Die behelmte Lederkluft, wie sie beispielsweise im Rahmen der militanten Stadtteil- und Häuserkämpfe der 1980er Jahre Verwendung fand, wurde mittlerweile durch modische, aber funktionale Streetwear abgelöst.

Kostümierung und Vermummung tritt im Protestgeschehen oft gleichzeitig auf, wie etwa bei den Fastnachtsumzügen des 17. bis 18. Jahrhunderts: Marginalisierte Gruppen brachten durch ritualisierte Tumulte ihren Unmut über die politischen Verhältnisse zum Ausdruck (Denk, Spille 2009, S. 221). Der Adel reagierte darauf mit den ersten Vermummungsverboten (Carl, Kessler 1989, S. 183). In Folge der antiautoritären Bewegung der 1960er Jahre diente Verkleidung der Entlarvung und Bloßstellung politischer Gegner*innen und – mit den Worten des Kulturtheoretikers Michail Bachtin gesprochen – als Ausdruck einer „Karnevalisierung des Bewusstseins" (Bachtin 1995, S. 101). So wurde im Umfeld der situationistischen Künstler*innengruppe SPUR und der Subversiven Aktion proklamiert: „Eine Revolution ohne Gaudi ist keine Revolution" (Carl, Kessler 1989, S. 192). Auch die neuen sozialen Bewegungen der 1990er Jahre nahmen den Gebrauch von Maskerade im Kontext globalisierungskritischer Proteste mit karnevalistischen Aktionsformen, wie „Pink & Silver" oder „Rebel Clown Army", auf. Der Ausdruck provokanten Spaßes bricht mit Geschlechterrollenerwartungen, zweigeschlechtlicher Ordnung und dem typischen polizeilichen Feindbild des militanten „Mackers". Absurde Kostüme stiften in paradoxen Kontexten Verwirrung, sodass neue Möglichkeiten für Protestsituationen entstehen (Amann 2005, S. 128 ff.; Harvie, Milburn, Trott, Watts 2005, S. 243 ff.), wie im Fall des clownesken Auftritts des „Mönchs von → *Lützerath*", der 2023 nach der Besetzung des für ein Braunkohlerevier geräumten Dorfes virale Berühmtheit erlangte.

Uniformierung im Kontext von Protestaktionen kann in Anlehnung an tatsächliche Uniformen der Obrigkeit, durch Berufsuniformen (z.B. im Rahmen von Gewerkschaftsdemonstrationen) oder auch ohne Bezug auf vorherrschende Uniformbilder durch übereinstimmende und gleichförmige Kleidung entstehen. → *2018* und 2019 trugen Teilnehmende der Massenproteste in Frankreich, die sich an den Reformplänen der Regierung entfachten, neongelbe Warnschutzwesten (→ *Gelbwestenbewegung*). Zum einen waren die „Gilets jaunes" Ausdruck einer „Protestreaktion spezifischer Klassenlagen" (Rackwitz 2022, S. 112). Zum anderen einten sie einen Protest, der meist spontan, über die sozialen Medien organisiert, dezentralisiert, hauptsächlich lokal stattfand und politisch heterogen war. Die Protestierenden vereinte zunächst nur ihr → *Erkennungszeichen* und dass sie sich an → *Kreisverkehren* versammelten. Zudem zieht gleichförmige Kleidung große Aufmerksamkeit von Polizei, → *Medien* und anderen Demonstrierenden auf sich, wie im Fall des Schwarzen Blocks, oder – in subtilerer Form – wenn beispielsweise Sambagruppen während Anti-Atom-Protesten in Konzertkleidung spielen (→ *Musik*). (Larissa Denk)

Klimacamps, engl. → *Camps for Climate Action*, sind → *Protestcamps* mit Fokus auf klimapolitische Themen, die in Großstädten oder an Orten der Umweltschädigung, etwa bei Kraftwerken oder Flughäfen stattfinden. Das erste Klimacamp wurde 2006 bei der Drax Power Station in North Yorkshire, England ausgerichtet. Weitere folgten in den 2000er Jahren in Westeuropa, Kanada und Australien. Ab 2010 fand in den zwei größten deutschen Braunkohlerevieren jährlich das „Lausitzcamp" und das „Klimacamp im Rheinland" statt. Sie dienten unter anderem für → *Protestorganisationen* wie Ende Gelände als Basis für Tagebaubesetzungen (→ *Finger*). Seit 2020 ist die Gruppe Fridays for Future Mitorganisatorin vieler Klimacamps. Die Protestcamps werden im Vorhinein wie ein Bauvorhaben geplant (→ *Masterplan*), sind meist von Behörden genehmigt und haben ein festes Veranstaltungsprogramm. Als Orte der niedrigschwelligen Beteiligung und Vernetzung haben sie eine andere Zielgruppe als → *Blockaden* oder → *Besetzungen*. Klimacamps sind häufig nur für wenige Tage angesetzt, in einigen Fällen dauern sie jedoch auch wesentlich länger: Das Klimacamp in Augsburg feierte am 27. März 2023 sein 1000-tägiges Bestehen. (AMM)

Klimakleber → *Ankleben*, → *Blockade*, → *Dagegensein*, → *Fahrzeuge*, → *Gewalt*, → *Körpereinsatz*, → *Ziviler Ungehorsam*

Kochtopf. Hi sashi: Cazerolazo bei den chilenischen Studierendenprotesten, 13. Juni 2013 (Cooking pot. Hi sashi: Cazerolazo at the Chilean student protests, June 13, 2013)

Kochtopf, engl. → *Cooking pot*. Mit Kochtöpfen kann → *Lärm* erzeugt werden. Diese Protestform wird in Südamerika „Cazerolazo" (von „Cacerola", spanisch für Topf) genannt. Kochtöpfe sowie Küchensiebe oder Plastikschüsseln wurden bei den → *Majdan*-Protesten als Kopfschutz getragen, nachdem die Regierung in einem restriktiven Anti-Protest-Gesetzespaket u.a. das Aufsetzen von Helmen verboten hatte (→ *Schutz*). (OE)

Kommunikation, engl. → *Communication*. Protestbewegungen müssen sich für ihre Anliegen Gehör verschaffen. Sie haben aber zumeist Schwierigkeiten, sichtbar zu werden. Um ihre → *Protestziele* zu kommunizieren, müssen sie verschiedene (räumliche, aber auch kognitive) Hindernisse überwinden. Dies gilt nicht nur für die indirekte (massenmediale, technisch vermittelte) wie die direkte (face-to-face) externe Kommunikation, sondern auch für die interne Kommunikation (Schönberger, Sutter 2009, S. 19; → *Medien*). Denn Protestaktivist∗innen müssen auch kommunizieren, um sich abzustimmen und zu diskutieren.

Protestbewegungen werden auch als „Laboratorien der Demokratie" (Teune

2012; Ullrich 2015, S. 19) angesehen. Sie reagieren nicht nur auf die vielbeklagte Krise der Repräsentation des Politischen in den modernen Institutionen (vgl. z.B. Vester 2003), sie entwickeln zugleich neue „demokratische Formen für eine andere, bessere Demokratie". Dabei entstehen „demokratische Innovationen", etwa „in Gestalt von bestimmten Handzeichen, die Abstimmungsprozesse vereinfachen" wie das „Human Microphone" (Ullrich 2015, S. 19; → *Handzeichen*). Das *Human Microphone* oder *People's Microphone* wurde → *2011* zum Symbol von → *Occupy Wall Street*. Es war eine Erfindung der General Assembly. Die Stadt New York hatte ein Gesetz erlassen, wonach die Nutzung von Verstärkeranlagen im → *öffentlichen Raum* ohne Genehmigung mit bis zu 30 Tagen Haft geahndet werden sollte. Als Reaktion darauf erfand Occupy Wall Street die schlichte wie kommunikationsfördernde Versammlungstechnik des *Human Mic*. Sie ist eine Form der Kommunikation, bei der ein von den Redner∗innen gesprochener Satz anschließend Wort für Wort von den Nächststehenden im Chor wiederholt wird. Dies wiederholt sich, bis die räumlich am weitesten entfernt Umstehenden diesen Satz wiederholt haben. Diese Unplugged-Versammlungstechnik half den Raum zwischen den Teilnehmer∗innen zu überwinden und beförderte die demokratische Kommunikation. Sie zeichnete sich durch Langsamkeit aus. Charisma oder Virtuosität traten hinter einen performativen Akt des Gemeinsamen zurück. Das *Human Mic* gilt inzwischen als das Symbol für die Occupy-Bewegung. Es erfordert zugleich eine einfache Sprache und eine niederschwellige Wortwahl (Kim 2011).

Eine performative, durchaus raumgreifende, stille Form der Protestkommunikation entwickelte der türkische Künstler Erdem Gündüz → *2013* auf dem Istanbuler Taksim-Platz bei den → *Gezi-Park*-Protesten. In seiner „Standing Man"-Performance stand Gündüz vor einem Portrait des Begründers der modernen Türkei, Mustafa Kemal Atatürk, und machte nichts anderes als

auf das Bild zu blicken (Gündüz 2014, S. 134 f.). Auf diese Weise wandte er sich gegen die Islamierungsbestrebungen des türkischen Präsidenten Erdogan und er konterkarierte die Behauptungen über die angeblich gewalttätigen Proteste. Die globale Bildkommunikation trug dazu bei, die räumliche Begrenzung der lokalen Protestkommunikation zu überschreiten.

Die gegenwärtigen Protestbewegungen haben sich inzwischen zu regelrechten Spezialist∗innen der Symbolverwendung entwickelt. Ihre reale Ohnmacht gegenüber Regierungen oder Konzernen zwingt sie zum symbolischen Protesthandeln beziehungsweise zu symbolischer Politik. Gesamtgesellschaftlich rückt die Produktion von Zeichen, Bildern, also Symbolen ganz allgemein, immer mehr in das Zentrum der Wertschöpfung eines ästhetischen Kapitalismus, sodass sich der gegenwärtige Protest durchaus auf der Höhe der Zeit beziehungsweise auch auf dem neuesten Stand der Produktivkräfte bewegt (autonome a.f.r.i.k.a.-gruppe 1997/2012, S. 238 f.).

Umberto Eco bezeichnete in seinem Text „Für eine semiologische Guerilla" die Interpretationsvariabilität als „das Grundgesetz der Massenkommunikation". Er verwarf das schlichte Sender-Empfänger-Modell der Kommunikationstheorie, wonach der gesendete Inhalt auch der rezipierte Inhalt sei. Er zeigte, dass die Kontrolle des Inhalts einer Botschaft nur über eine räumliche Erweiterung der Kommunikationskette möglich sein würde. Nämlich durch das Besetzen der ersten Reihe vor den Zuhörenden (Eco 1967/1985, S. 152).

Zu diesem Problem gesellt sich ein weiteres: Was ist, wenn einem niemand zuhören will? Daher entwickelte die autonome a.f.r.i.k.a.-gruppe das Konzept der Kommunikationsguerilla, das nicht die Sabotage als Unterbrechung des Kommunikationskanals im einem technischen Sinn meint. Die Kommunikationsguerilla möchte weniger überzeugen oder überreden, als vielmehr ideologisch verblendete Gewissheiten erschüttern helfen. Im *Handbuch der*

Kommunikationsguerilla (→ *Handbücher / Online-Manuals*) analysieren die Autor∗innen die Problematik politischer Kommunikation als Gegenöffentlichkeit. Ihnen geht es dabei – im Sinne von Roland Barthes (1971, S. 141) – nicht darum, die Codes zu zerstören, sondern sie zu entstellen. Die Fake-theorie des Handbuchs erklärt zudem, warum Verschwörungstheorien und alternative Fakten geglaubt werden. Deren Überzeugungskraft resultiere nicht aus der Plausibilität eines Kommunikationsinhaltes, sondern vielmehr daraus, was die Konsument∗innen zu hören und zu sehen begehren. Eine ernüchternde Erkenntnis für jedes aufklärerische Projekt, weil es bedeutet, dass das gegenwärtige Problem politischer Kommunikation weniger die mediale Dominanz von Social Media darstellt, als vielmehr die Begehrensstruktur der Subjekte (→ *Digitale Medien*).

Kommunikationsguerilla zielt auf die Verbreitung falscher Informationen zur Herstellung wahrer Ereignisse (→ *Guerillataktiken*). Ein Beispiel hierfür ist das Imagebeschmutzungskonzept der Yes Men (Bichlbaum, Bonanno, Spunkmeyer 2004). Sie leihen sich den Namen ihrer Gegner (schlecht beleumundete Konzerne) aus und verbreiten als ihre vermeintlichen Sprecher Sachverhalte, die diese nicht thematisiert sehen möchten. Berühmt wurde 2004 der Bhopal-Fake, als es den Yes Men gelang, als vermeintliche Sprecher der Dow Chemical Company in der britischen BBC zu verkünden, dass anlässlich des 20. Jahrestages von einem der schlimmsten Chemieunfälle im indischen Bhopal der Konzern endlich die Opfer des Giftgas-Unfalls entschädigen würde. Der Konzern musste die Falschmeldung dementieren und das war die Nachricht, die die Yes Men verbreiten wollten.

Die Erzeugung von Öffentlichkeit und die Herstellung einer Wissensordnung, die Veränderung dringlich erscheinen lässt, bilden das zentrale Moment einer jeden Protestkommunikation. Was und wem am Ende geglaubt wird, das muss aber jedes Mal von Neuem ausgehandelt werden. (Klaus Schönberger)

Körpereinsatz, engl. → *Body deployment*. Jede → *Demonstration*, jede → *Blockade*, jedes → *Sit-in* (oder vergleichbare Aktionsformen) erfordern Körpereinsatz und beinhalten das Risiko, verletzt, festgenommen oder psychischer → *Gewalt* ausgesetzt zu werden. Wenn es einzelne Menschen wagen, sich der Ungerechtigkeit entgegenzustellen, resultieren daraus häufig ikonische Bilder (→ *Ikone*). Berühmt wurde der „Tank Man", der sich 1989 am Tag nach der Niederschlagung der Proteste auf dem Tian'anmen-Platz in Peking ganz allein einer Kolonne Panzer entgegenstellte. Zum Symbol der Proteste gegen Polizeigewalt in den USA (→ *Black Lives Matter*) avancierte das Bild der Krankenschwester Ieshia Evans, die 2016 in einem leichten Sommerkleid auf Polizisten in massiver *Riot Gear* traf. Der Tänzer Erdem Gündüz wurde als „Standing Man" (türkisch „Duran Adam") bekannt, als er gegen das Demonstrationsverbot nach der Räumung des → *Gezi-Parks* demonstrierte, indem er etwa acht Stunden still in der Menge stand und auf ein Atatürk-Denkmal starrte. Dass sich einzelne Personen derart exponieren, ob in Begleitung von → *Medien* oder, wie im Falle des „Tank Man", nur zufällig durch Journalist∗innen beobachtet, prägt das Bild von Protesten seit der Französischen Revolution. Doch es ist nicht nur ein – mitunter inszeniertes – Medienphänomen. Die Aktivist∗innen der → *Claremont Road* in London kletterten → *1994* auf waghalsig gespannte Netze, die zugleich große, hedonistisch bespielbare Hängematten waren – schwer zu räumen für die Polizei und ein hervorragendes Motiv für Fotograf∗innen. Bei den → *Baumhaus*-Protesten der Klimabewegung, die in Deutschland ab etwa 2000 einsetzten, stehen die hoch über dem Boden errichteten Bauten im Gegensatz zu früheren Baumhäusern nicht mehr jeweils für sich allein. Sie sind durch → *Seile*, Brücken oder Netze miteinander verbunden (→ *Hambacher Wald*, → *Dannenröder Wald*, → *Lützerath*, → *Fechenheimer Wald*). Wer sich dort aufhält, muss nicht nur professionell klettern können, sondern bringt sich durch Körpereinsatz bewusst in Gefahr. Die Aktivist∗innen drohen damit abzustürzen, wenn bestimmte Halteseile von der Polizei durchtrennt werden. Im Dannenröder Wald wurde die „Suicide-Box" eingesetzt, eine Art freischwebendes →*Lock-on Device*, um mit dieser makaber betitelten Vorrichtung die Räumung hinauszuzögern. Zur Abwehr von Polizeigriffen bei Höhenräumungen wird mitunter die Haut mit Margarine eingefettet und zur Anonymisierung werden Fingerkuppen mit Sekundenkleber bestrichen. Auch die Versorgung und Betreuung, das Ausharren und Koordinieren bei Protesten erfordert bisweilen höchsten physischen und psychischen Körpereinsatz. (OE)

Kostüm. Hubert Kluger: „Pressekonferenz der Tiere", Wien, 7. Mai 1984 (Costume. Hubert Kluger: "Animals' Press Conference," Vienna, May 7, 1984)

Kostüm, engl. →*Costume*. Bei der „Pressekonferenz der Tiere" verkleideten sich im Mai →*1984* mehrere prominente Umweltschützer∗innen als Roter Auhirsch, Purpurreiher, schwarzer Komoran, Schwarzstorch und Laufkäfer – jene Tiere, die durch den Bau des Kraftwerks in der →*Hainburger Au* unmittelbar bedroht waren. Seit den 1980er Jahren wurden Kostüme häufig bei Protestaktionen eingesetzt, u.a. im →*Greenham Common Friedenscamp* sowie bei den →*Anti-Globalisierungs- / WTO-Proteste* in Seattle. (AMM)

Kreisverkehr, engl. →*Roundabout*. Zahlreiche →*Platzbesetzungen* fanden auf Kreisverkehren statt. Der Architekt, Kurator und Gründer von Forensic Architecture, Eyal Weizman, hat den Zusammenhang von Protesten und Kreisverkehren in seinem Buch *The Roundabout Revolutions* ausführlich dargestellt (vgl. Weizman 2015; →*Tahrir-Platz*, →*Pearl Roundabout*, →*Gezi-Park*). (OE)

Kreisverkehr. Na Gyeong-taek: Aufstand in Gwangju, Südkorea, 26. Mai 1980 (Roundabout. Na Gyeong-taek: Uprising in Gwangju, South Korea, May 26, 1980)

Küche, engl. →*Kitchen*. Als Orte der Nahrungszubereitung sind Küchen in vielen →*Protestcamps* ein integraler Bestandteil der →*Infrastruktur*. Über ihre Funktion zur Lagerung von Nahrungsmitteln und zur Zubereitung von Speisen hinaus stärken Küchen den sozialen Zusammenhalt, indem sie die gemeinschaftliche Verpflegung der Protestierenden organisieren. Da das Teilen von Mahlzeiten ein über das politische Interesse der Protestierenden (→*Protestziele*) hinausgehendes Gemeinschaftsgefühl befördert, lässt sich die Einrichtung von Küchen auch als →*Solidaritätsgeste* verstehen. Im Zuge der →*Hausbesetzungen* im Deutschland der 1980er Jahre entstand in der autonomen Szene die sogenannte Volxküche bzw. die Küfa (Küche für alle), die bis heute immer wieder bei Protestcamps und →*Demonstrationen* zum Einsatz kommt. Finden die Proteste in den Zentren großer Städte statt (→*Platzbesetzung*), erübrigen sich eigene Küchen aber auch oft: Zum einen können ausreichend Restaurants, Imbissstände,

Garküchen oder fliegende Händler vorhanden sein, die den Nahrungsmittelbedarf abdecken; zum anderen werden die Protestierenden häufig auch von Sympathisant∗innen aus der Nachbar∗innenschaft versorgt, wie dies etwa bei den → *Gezi-Park*-Protesten in Istanbul → *2013* der Fall war. Die Proteste auf dem → *Tahrir-Platz* in Kairo während des Arabischen Frühlings → *2011* lockten eine große Anzahl an fliegenden Händler∗innen an, von denen viele auch nach dem Ende der Proteste im Umfeld des Platzes verblieben. (SH)

Kunst, engl. → *Art*; → *Absperrgitter*, → *Denkmalstsur*, → *Fernseher*, → *Graffiti*, → *Guerillataktiken*, → *Ikone*, → *Lichtprojektion*, → *Medien*

Lageplan, engl. → *Site plan*. Dass Lagepläne bei Protesten eine Rolle spielen, scheint auf den ersten Blick paradox, haben die spontan organisierten Aktionen von Graswurzelbewegungen doch eher wenig gemeinsam mit den langwierigen Baugenehmigungsverfahren, bei denen diese normalerweise zum Einsatz kommen. Doch genau an der Schnittstelle von Protest und Bauplanung haben Lagepläne eine wichtige Bedeutung. Für die → *Resurrection City* in Washington, DC, entwarfen Architekten vor dem Beginn der Proteste einen funktionalistischen → *Masterplan*, der die Wiese auf der National Mall, auf der ein Protestcamp errichtet werden sollte, in Organisationseinheiten und Nachbar∗innenschaften einteilte. Den → *Klimacamps* in Deutschland gehen z.T. lange Genehmigungsprozesse voraus, in denen die Nutzung von genau definierten Grundstücksflächen als Ruhe-, Versorgungs- oder Versammlungsräume mit den Behörden abgesprochen werden muss. Manchmal werden auch während Protesten noch Lagepläne gezeichnet, wenn wie bei der → *Movimiento 15M* in Madrid das → *Protestcamp* im Laufe der Zeit so stark erweitert wird, dass sich Protestierende darin nicht mehr zurechtfinden. Als Versuch, den Überblick zu behalten, zeichneten sie ständig neue Karten, die aber aufgrund der kontinuierlichen Veränderung des Camps rasch veralteten. Daher wurden zusätzlich → *Hinweisschilder* produziert, um sich in der → *Platzbesetzung* zurechtzufinden. Beide Systeme, der Lageplan und das Hinweisschild, koexistierten, trugen jedoch am Ende weniger zur Orientierung als vielmehr zur Dokumentation der überraschend komplexen Struktur der Siedlung bei. Bei den Protesten von → *Occupy Wall Street* und auf dem → *Majdan* in Kyjiw wurden Lagepläne der Camps zudem von begeisterten Architekt∗innen angefertigt, um die ephemeren Architekturen für die Nachwelt festzuhalten. Eine ganz andere Strategie, sich in einer unübersichtlichen Besetzung zu orientieren, verfolgen dagegen die Besetzer∗innen der → *MTST* in São Paulo: Jede Hütte bekommt hier eine Adresse, die sich aus der Zone, in der sie steht, sowie einer zwei- oder dreistelligen Nummer zusammensetzt. (AMM)

Lärm, engl. → *Noise*, kann genauso wie → *Musik* auf beiden Seiten eines Protestereignisses auftreten. Die Sicherheitskräfte können durch Lärm (oder Musik) einschüchtern und die Proteste stören. Bei den → *Majdan*-Protesten → *2013/2014* haben die Sondereinheiten der *Berkut* mit Schlagstöcken rhythmisch auf ihre Schilde getrommelt, um ihr martialisches Auftreten auch akustisch zu unterstreichen. Hubschraubertiefflüge wurden gegen die → *Demonstrationen* in → *Gorleben* → *1980* und Brokdorf 1981 eingesetzt. Mit einer dröhnend lauten „playlist from hell" versuchte die Regierung von Neuseeland im Februar 2022, Demonstrationen gegen die strengen Corona-Regeln vor dem Parlament zu zerstreuen.

Weitaus üblicher ist die Erzeugung von Lärm aufseiten der Protestierenden. *Cazerolazo* bezeichnet das lautstarke Schlagen von → *Kochtöpfen* und Topfdeckeln, eine vor allem in Südamerika verbreitete Protestform. Viele Demonstrationen erweitern den tatsächlich eingenommenen Raum um eine akustische Sphäre. Besonders effektiv war bei den kanadischen Trucker-Protesten des Jahres → *2022* die Kombination aus schwer zu räumenden LKWs und dem Lärmpegel ihrer durchdringenden Hornsignale

(→ „*Freedom Convoy*", →*Fahrzeuge*). Sprechchöre auf Demonstrationen verschmelzen Lärm und Musik zu einem akustischen Raumereignis. (OE)

Laserpointer, engl. →*Laser pointer*; →*Hongkong-Proteste*, →*Schutz*

Laser pointer, Ger. →*Laserpointer*; →*Hong Kong protests*, →*Protection*

Legalisierung, engl. →*Legalization*. Viele der seit den 1970er Jahren durchgeführten eigentlich rechtswidrigen →*Hausbesetzungen* sind heute legalisiert und die Besetzer*innen haben Duldungs-, Miet- oder Nutzungsverträge mit den Eigentümer*innen abgeschlossen. Auch lange bestehende →*Protestcamps* und →*Autonome Zonen* durchlaufen manchmal Legalisierungsprozesse, die nicht selten zu einer Spaltung der Bewegung führen: in „Radikale", die den Autonomie-Status der Besetzung beibehalten möchten, und „Konstruktive", die sich eine langfristige Perspektive für ihr Zuhause wünschen. In der →*ZAD Notre-Dame-des-Landes* verhandelten die Bewohner*innen inmitten einer Räumungsaktion 2018 die Anerkennung von 28 Häusern auf dem Areal mit dem erklärten Ziel, dort neue Formen des Zusammenlebens und alternative Bauweisen zu testen (→*Alternative Architektur*). Nach staatlicher Prüfung bekamen 15 Projekte Pachtverträge, viele weitere Strukturen wurden bei der wieder aufgenommenen Räumung abgerissen. (AMM)

Legalization, Ger. →*Legalisierung*. Many of the actually illegal →*squats* that have been carried out since the 1970s have since been legalized and the squatters have signed acquiescence, tenancy, or user agreements with the owners. Also long-standing →*protest camps* and →*autonomous zones* sometimes go through legalization processes, which not infrequently lead to a split in the movement: into "radicals" who want to maintain the autonomous status of the occupation, and "constructives" who want long-term prospects for their home. At →*ZAD Notre-Dame-des-Landes*, in the midst of an eviction operation in 2018, residents negotiated the recognition of twenty-eight houses on the site with the stated goal of testing new forms of cohabitation and alternative construction methods there (→*Alternative architecture*). Following a state review, fifteen projects received rental agreements, while many more structures were demolished during the resumed eviction. (AMM)

Lehmhütte, engl. →*Adobe hut*; →*Alternative Architektur*, →*Bautypen*, →*Hambacher Wald*, →*ZAD Notre-Dame-des-Landes*

Lichtprojektion. Tim Wagner: Laserprojektion des Künstlers Joanie Lemercier auf das Kohlekraftwerk bei Lützerath, 2. November 2021 (Light projection. Tim Wagner: Laser projection by artist Joanie Lemercier onto the coal-fired power station at Lützerath, November 2, 2021)

Lichtprojektion, engl. →*Light projection*. Form des Protests im →*öffentlichen Raum*, bei der Botschaften und Forderungen durch visuelle Darstellungen und Effekte über große Entfernungen meist mithilfe von Laserstrahlen sichtbar gemacht und vermittelt werden (→*Kommunikation*). Kunst, Technologie und Aktivismus werden kombiniert, um Aufmerksamkeit zu erregen und die Öffentlichkeit für wichtige Themen zu sensibilisieren. Dabei werden im Stadtraum oder an Orten, die umkämpft sind, beispielsweise Gebäudefassaden oder öffentliche Plätze mit leuchtenden Botschaften, Symbolen oder Grafiken angeeignet. Das projizierte „X" auf dem Kohlekraftwerk bei →*Lützerath* ist das Symbol für den Widerstand gegen die Förderung fossiler Brennstoffe. (JD)

Light projection, Ger. →*Lichtprojek-*

tion (fig.). Form of protest in →*public space* in which messages and demands are visualized and conveyed by means of impressive visual displays and laser effects (→*Communication*). Art, technology, and activism are combined in order to attract attention and raise awareness among the general public for important issues. In the process, within the urban space or at sites of struggle, illuminated messages, symbols, or graphics are used to appropriate structures such as building facades or public squares. The "X" projected onto the coal-fired power station at →*Lützerath* is the symbol for opposition to the extraction of fossil fuels. (JD)

Literaturverzeichnis, engl. *Bibliography.*

S. = Seite/*page*
Hg. = Herausgeber∗in/*editor*
hg. von = herausgegeben von/*edited by*
Jg. = Jahrgang/*volume*
H. = Heft/*number*
Bd. = Band/*volume*
Ausst.-Kat. = Ausstellungskatalog/*exhibition catalog*
Diss. = Dissertation/*dissertation*
Dies., Ders. = Dieselbe, Derselbe/*idem*
Zugriff = *access date*

Marc Amann: Pink & Silver. Sich taktisch frivol immer wieder neu entwerfen, in: Ders. (Hg.): *go.stop.act! Die Kunst des kreativen Straßenprotests. Geschichten, Aktionen, Ideen,* Frankfurt am Main 2005, S. 124–136

Anonym (Franz Servatius August Gathy): *Briefe aus Paris, geschrieben während der großen Volkswoche im Juli 1830 von einem deutschen Augenzeugen an seinen Freund in Deutschland,* Hamburg 1831

Archives de Paris, Département de la Seine, Ville de Paris, Modèle No. 25–Art. 24 de l'Instruction, Ponts et chaussées, Service municipal, 2ème division–5ème section Chemise de dossier, Insurrection de Février, Suppression des barricades, 1848, und ebd., Insurrection de Juin, Suppression des Barricades, 1848

Hannah Arendt: *The Human Condition,* Chicago 1958

Ausst.-Kat. *Berlin in der Revolution 1918/1919. Fotografie, Film, Unterhaltungskultur,* hg. von Ludger Derenthal, Evelin Förster, Enno Kaufhold (Kunstbibliothek – Staatliche Museen zu Berlin), Dortmund 2018

Ausst.-Kat. *Dieses Haus ist besetzt! Frankfurter Häuserkampf 1970–1974,* hg. von Frankfurter Archiv der Revolte e.V., Offenes Haus der Kulturen e.V., Institut für Selbstorganisation e.V. (Studierendenhaus, Universitätscampus Bockenheim), Frankfurt am Main 2020

Ausst.-Kat. *In die Stadt,* hg. von Christine Wetzlinger-Grundnig (Museum Moderner Kunst Kärnten), Klagenfurt 2018

autonome a.f.r.i.k.a.-gruppe, Luther Blissett, Sonja Brünzels: *Handbuch der Kommunikationsguerilla* (1997), Hamburg / Berlin ⁵2012

Michail Bachtin: *Rabelais und seine Welt. Volkskultur als Gegenkultur,* Frankfurt am Main 1995

Anna Badcock, Robert Johnston: Placemaking Through Protest. An Archaeology of the Lees Cross and Endcliffe Protest Camp, Derbyshire, England, in: *Archaeologies. Journal of the World Archaeological Congress,* Jg. 5, H. 2, August 2009, S. 306–322

Roland Barthes: Das Schreiben des Geschehens (1968), in: Ders.: *Das Rauschen der Sprache,* Frankfurt am Main 2006, S. 173–179

Roland Barthes: *Sade. Fourier. Loyola,* Paris 1971

Jean Baudrillard: *KOOL KILLER oder Der Aufstand der Zeichen,* Berlin 1978

BBC: India Farmer Protests. 'War-Like Fortification' to Protect Delhi, 3. Februar 2021. Online: https://www.bbc.com/news/world-asia-india-55899754# (Zugriff: 21. Juni 2023)

Natasha Behl: India's Farmers' Protest. An Inclusive Vision of Indian Democracy, in: *American Political Science Review,* Jg. 116, H. 3, August 2022, S. 1141–1146

Hakim Bey (Peter Lamborn Wilson): *T.A.Z. The Temporary Autonomous Zone,* New York 1991

Nilanjana Bhowmick, Kanishka Sonthalia: 'I Cannot Be Intimidated. I Cannot Be Bought.' The Women Leading

India's Farmers' Protests, in: *Time*, 4. März 2021. Online: https://time.com/5942125/women-india-farmers-protests/ (Zugriff: 22. Juni 2023)

Andy Bichlbaum, Mike Bonanno, Bob Spunkmeyer: *The Yes Men. The True Story of the End of the World Trade Organization*, New York 2004

Alfred Birk: *Die Strasse. Ihre verkehrs- und bautechnische Entwicklung im Rahmen der Menschheitsgeschichte* (1934), Aalen 1971

Ludwig Börne: Briefe aus Paris (1832–1834), in: Ders.: *Sämtliche Schriften*, hg. von Inge Rippmann, Walter Rippmann, Bd. 3, Düsseldorf 1964

Ludwig Börne: Brief Nr. 29, Paris, Mittwoch, d. 24. Nov. 1830, in: Ders.: *Sämtliche Schriften*, hg. von Inge Rippmann, Walter Rippmann, Bd. 4, Darmstadt 1968, S. 1207–1212

Olaf Briese: Moment-Architektur. Die Kunst der Barrikade und die Kunst ihrer medialen Mythisierung, in: Roland Berbig, Iwan-Michelangelo D'Aprile, Helmut Peitsch, Erhard Schütz (Hg.): *Berlins 19. Jahrhundert. Ein Metropolen-Kompendium*, Berlin 2011, S. 433–447

Gavin Brown, Anna Feigenbaum, Fabian Frenzel, Patrick McCurdy (Hg.): *Protest Camps in International Context. Spaces, Infrastructures and Media of Resistance*, Bristol 2017

Herbert Carl, Doris Kessler: Eine Revolution ohne Gaudi ist keine Revolution, in: Ludwig-Uhland-Institut für empirische Kulturwissenschaft (Hg.): *Wilde Masken. Ein anderer Blick auf die Fasnacht*, Tübingen 1989, S. 181–194

Isolde Charim: Die Freiheitlichen in Fantasie, in: *FALTER* 06/23, 8. Februar 2023

Irene Cheng, Charles L. Davis II, Mabel O. Wilson (Hg.): *Race and Modern Architecture. A Critical History from the Enlightenment to the Present*, Pittsburgh, PA, 2020

Simon Chow: *Umbrella Chronicle*, Hongkong 2015

Andreas Conradt: Der Turmbauer zu 1004, in: *Gorleben Rundschau*, Juli 2020, S. 28–29

Alain Corbin, Jean-Marie Mayeur (Hg.): *La barricade*, Paris 1997

Gregory Cowan: Nomadic Resistance. Tent Embassies and Collapsible Architecture. Illegal Architecture and Protest, in: *The Koori History Website*. Online: http://www.kooriweb.org/foley/images/history/1970s/emb72/embarchit.htm (Zugriff: 11. April 2023)

Ulrich Cremer: *Bauen als Urerfahrung. Dargestellt am Beispiel des Hüttendorfes gegen die Startbahn West*, hg. von Prof. Helmut Striffler, TH Darmstadt, Fachgebiet Entwerfen und Gebäudekunde, München 1982

Larissa Denk, Jan Spille: Kleidsamer Protest. Medium und Moden des Protestes, in: Klaus Schönberger, Ove Sutter (Hg.): *Kommt herunter, reiht euch ein... Eine kleine Geschichte der Protestformen sozialer Bewegungen*, Berlin / Hamburg 2009, S. 210–234

Attila Dézsi: Zeitgeschichtliche Archäologie des 20. Jahrhunderts an Orten des Protests und der „Freien Republik Wendland", in: Frank Nikulka, Daniela Hofmann, Robert Schumann (Hg.): *Menschen – Dinge – Orte. Aktuelle Forschungen des Instituts für Vor- und Frühgeschichtliche Archäologie der Universität Hamburg*, Hamburg 2018, S. 195–202

Paul Dobraszczyk: *Architecture and Anarchism. Building Without Authority*, London 2021

Brian Doherty: Opposition to Road-Building, in: *Parliamentary Affairs*, Jg. 51, H. 3, Juli 1998, S. 370–383

Veena Dubal, Navyug Gill: "Long Live Farmer-Laborer Unity". Contextualizing the Massive Resistance Going On in India, in: *The Law and Political Economy Project* (Blog), 28. Dezember 2020. Online: https://lpeproject.org/blog/long-live-farmer-laborer-unity-contextualizing-the-massive-resistance-going-on-in-india/ (Zugriff: 21. Juni 2023)

Umberto Eco: Für eine semiologische Guerilla (1967), in: Ders.: *Über Gott und die Welt. Essays und Glossen*, München 1985, S. 146–156

Economic Times: Over 50 Medical Camps Set Up for Farmers at Singhu Border, 10. December 2020. Online: https://economictimes.indiatimes.com/

news/politics-and-nation/over-50-me-dical-camps-set-up-for-farmers-at-singhu-border/articleshow/79655538.cms?from=mdr# (Zugriff: 21. Juni 2023)

Lukas Eberle: „Deeskalation bedeutet nicht, dass es keine Räumung gibt", in: *Spiegel Online*, 13. Januar 2023. Online: https://www.spiegel.de/panorama/luetzerath-deeskalation-bedeutet-nicht-dass-es-keine-raeumung-gibt-a-6edc944b-5afb-40b2-83d5-942776656e61 (Zugriff: 23. Mai 2023)

Brian J. Egloff, Michael O'Sullivan, Juliet Ramsay: Archaeology of the 1891 Shearers' War. The Main Strike Camp at Barcaldine, Queensland, in: *Australian Journal of Historical Archaeology*, Jg. 9, 1991, S. 63–75

Ter Ellingson: *The Myth of the Noble Savage*, Berkeley / Los Angeles / London 2001

Günter Emberger: *Erreichbarkeit der Wiener Stadterweiterungsgebiete in Aspern bei Verzicht auf die Donauquerung der S1. Executive Summary der beiden durchgeführten Studien*, hg. von Bundesministerium für Klimaschutz, Umwelt, Energie, Mobilität, Innovation und Technologie, 3. Oktober 2022. Online: www.bmk.gv.at/dam/jcr:8df2c6dd-984a-409d-8ce0-c38b9c84bee2/22_BMK_Executive-Summary-Studie-Emberger.pdf (Zugriff: 8. Mai 2023)

Friedrich Engels: Einleitung [zu Karl Marx" „Klassenkämpfe in Frankreich 1848 bis 1850"] (1895), in: Karl Marx, Friedrich Engels: *Werke*, hg. vom Institut für Marxismus-Leninismus beim ZK der SED, Bd. 22, Berlin ³1972, S. 509–527

Claire English: Security Is No Accident. Considering Safe(r) Spaces in the Transnational Migrant Solidarity Camps of Calais, in: Gavin Brown, Anna Feigenbaum, Fabian Frenzel, Patrick McCurdy (Hg.): *Protest Camps in International Context. Spaces, Infrastructures and Media of Resistance*, Bristol 2017, S. 353–370

Catherine Eschle: Beyond Greenham Woman? Gender Identities and Anti-nuclear Activism in Peace Camps, in: *International Feminist Journal of Politics*, Jg. 19, H. 4, 2017, S. 471–90

Catherine Eschle, Alison Bartlett (Hg.): *Feminism and Protest Camps. Entanglements, Critiques and Re-Imaginings*, Bristol 2023

Anna Feigenbaum, Fabian Frenzel, Patrick McCurdy: *Protest Camps*, London 2013

Anna Feigenbaum, Patrick McCurdy: Protest Camps as Media Stages. A Case Study of Activist Media Practices Across Three British Social Movements, in: Rita Figueiras, Paula do Espírito Santo (Hg.): *Beyond the Internet. Unplugging the Protest Movement Wave*, London 2015, S. 31–52

Anna Feigenbaum: Occupy Architecture, in: *Icon Magazine*, 2. April 2015. Online: https://www.iconeye.com/architecture/occupy-architecture (Zugriff: 11. April 2023)

Matthias Feyerabend: Das Dorf im Flörsheimer Wald. Ein Jahr Widerstand gegen die Startbahn-West, in: *ARCH+*, Jg. 14, H. 61, 1982, S. 11–13

Martina Fineder, Thomas Geisler, Sebastian Hackenschmidt: *Nomadic Furniture 3.0. Neues befreites Wohnen?* (= MAK Studies, Bd. 23), Zürich 2017

Mark Fisher: Der Winter der Unzufriedenheit 2.0. Notizen über einen Monat der Militanz (2010), in: Ders.: *K-Punk. Ausgewählte Schriften (2004–2016)*, Berlin 2020, S. 386–399

Rudolf Förster: Die bürgerlich-demokratische Revolution – Gottfried Semper im Dresdner Maiaufstand 1849, in: Ausst.-Kat. *Gottfried Semper zum 100. Todestag. Ausstellung im Albertinum zu Dresden vom 15. Mai bis 29. August 1979* (Staatliche Kunstsammlungen Dresden), Dresden ²1980, S. 53–56

Michel Foucault: Of Other Spaces (1967), in: *Diacritics*, Jg. 16, H. 1, Frühling 1986, S. 22–27

Michel Foucault: Andere Räume (1967), in: Karlheinz Barck (Hg.): *Aisthesis. Wahrnehmung heute oder Perspektiven einer anderen Ästhetik*, Leipzig ⁵1993, S. 34–46

Arno Frank: Aktion des Zentrums für politische Schönheit. Ein Holocaust-Mahnmal – bei Björn Höcke vor der

Haustür, in: *Spiegel Online*, 22. November 2017. Online: https://www.spiegel.de/kultur/gesellschaft/zentrum-fuer-politische-schoenheit-bjoern-hoecke-und-das-denkmal-der-schande-a-1179515.html (Zugriff: 29. März 2023)

Norbert Frei: *1968. Jugendrevolte und globaler Protest* (2008), München ²2018

Fabian Frenzel: Entlegene Orte in der Mitte der Gesellschaft. Zur Geschichte der britischen Klimacamps, in: Achim Brunnengräber (Hg.): *Zivilisierung des Klimaregimes. NGOs und soziale Bewegungen in der nationalen, europäischen und internationalen Klimapolitik*, Wiesbaden 2011, S. 163–186

Fabian Frenzel: The Role of Spatial Organization in Resurrection City and Other Protest Camps, in: *Contention*, Jg. 8, H. 1, Juni 2020, S. 28–48

Dario Gamboni: *Zerstörte Kunst. Bildersturm und Vandalismus im 20. Jahrhundert*, Köln 1998

Paolo Gerbaudo: Feeds from the Square. Live Streaming, Live Tweeting and the Self-Representation of Protest Camps, in: Gavin Brown, Anna Feigenbaum, Fabian Frenzel, Patrick McCurdy (Hg.): *Protest Camps in International Context. Spaces, Infrastructures and Media of Resistance*, Bristol 2017, S. 91–108

Mohammad Ghazali: As Farmers, Police Face Off in Delhi, Haryana Religious Centre Feeds Cops, in: *NDTV*, 28. November 2020. Online: https://www.ndtv.com/india-news/farmers-protest-as-farmers-police-clash-in-delhi-gurudwara-in-haryanas-karnal-feeds-cops-2331391 (Zugriff: 21. Juni 2023)

Ingrid Gilcher-Holtey: *„Die Phantasie an die Macht". Mai 68 in Frankreich*, Frankfurt am Main 1995

Alastair Gordon: *Spaced Out. Radical Environments of the Psychedelic Sixties*, New York 2008

Viktoria Graf: Wellness und Theater. Besetzte Baustelle. Protestcamp oder Disneyland?, in: *Kronen Zeitung*, 28. Dezember 2021. Online: https://www.krone.at/2590625 (Zugriff: 27. April 2023)

Udo Grashoff: *Schwarzwohnen. Die Unterwanderung der staatlichen Wohnraumlenkung in der DDR*, Göttingen 2011

Marion Grob: *Das Kleidungsverhalten jugendlicher Protestgruppen in Deutschland im 20. Jahrhundert. Am Beispiel des Wandervogels und der Studentenbewegung*, Münster 1985

R(einer) Gr(oß): Aufruf des Vaterlandsvereins Dresden (2.5.1849), in: Ausst.-Kat. *Gottfried Semper zum 100. Todestag. Ausstellung im Albertinum zu Dresden vom 15. Mai bis 29. August 1979* (Staatliche Kunstsammlungen Dresden), Dresden ²1980a, S. 59

R(einer) Gr(oß): Barrikadenanordnung der Provisorischen Regierung Dresden (5.5.1849), in: Ausst.-Kat. *Gottfried Semper zum 100. Todestag. Ausstellung im Albertinum zu Dresden vom 15. Mai bis 29. August 1979* (Staatliche Kunstsammlungen Dresden), Dresden ²1980b, S. 60

R(einer) Gr(oß): Barrikaden-Plan von Dresden (3.–9.5.1849), in: Ausst.-Kat. *Gottfried Semper zum 100. Todestag. Ausstellung im Albertinum zu Dresden vom 15. Mai bis 29. August 1979* (Staatliche Kunstsammlungen Dresden), Dresden ²1980c, S. 60

Erdem Gündüz: Standing Still, in: Steirischer Herbst, Florian Malzacher (Hg.): *Truth Is Concrete. A Handbook for Artistic Strategies in Real Politics*, Berlin 2014, S. 134–135

Jürgen Habermas: Ziviler Ungehorsam. Testfall für den demokratischen Rechtsstaat, in: Peter Glotz (Hg.): *Ziviler Ungehorsam im Rechtsstaat*, Frankfurt am Main 1983, S. 29–53

Jürgen Habermas: Civil Disobedience. Litmus Test for the Democratic Constitutional State (1983), in: *Berkeley Journal of Sociology*, Jg. 30, 1985, S. 95–116

Sebastian Hackenschmidt: Baumhaus. Die Fabrikation der Fiktionen, in: Petra Lange-Berndt, Dietmar Rübel (Hg.): *Sigmar Polke. Wir Kleinbürger! Zeitgenossen und Zeitgenossinnen. Die 1970er Jahre*, Köln 2009, S. 138–145

Nicos Hadjinicolaou: *Die Freiheit führt das Volk von Eugène Delacroix. Sinn und Gegensinn*, Dresden 1991

Sam Halvorsen: Beyond the Network? Occupy London and the Global Movement, in: *Social Movement Studies*, Jg. 11, H. 3–4, August 2012, S. 427–433

Sam Halvorsen: Taking Space. Moments of Rupture and Everyday Life in Occupy London, in: *Antipode*, Jg. 47, H. 2, Januar 2015, S. 401–417

Handbuch für Hausbesetzer, hg. von Verlagskollektiv Rote Klinke, Bad Godesberg ca. 1972

Phineas Harper: „Extinction Rebellion's Tensegrity Structures Have Rekindled the Spirit of Early High-Tech", in: *Dezeen*, 16. September 2020. Online: https://www.dezeen.com/2020/09/16/extinction-rebellions-high-tech-stirling-prize/ (Zugriff: 19. Juni 2023)

Hans-Christian Harten, Elke Harten: *Die Versöhnung mit der Natur. Gärten, Freiheitsbäume, republikanische Wälder, heilige Berge und Tugendparks in der Französischen Revolution,* Reinbek bei Hamburg 1989

David Harvie, Keir Milburn, Ben Trott, David Watts: *Shut Them Down! The G8, Gleneagles 2005 and the Movement of the Movements*, Leeds / New York 2005

Wolf Dieter Hasler: *Das Dorf am Damm und die neue B8*, Kelkheim 1982. Online: http://www.bund-koenigstein-glashuetten.de/fileadmin/bundgruppen/bcmsovkoenigstein/Das_Dorf_am_Damm.pdf (Zugriff: 23. Mai 2023)

Sebastian Haunss: *Identität in Bewegung. Prozesse kollektiver Identität bei den Autonomen und in der Schwulenbewegung*, Wiesbaden 2004

Heinrich Heine: Französische Zustände (1832), in: Ders.: *Sämtliche Schriften in zwölf Bänden*, hg. von Klaus Briegleb, Bd. 5: Schriften 1831–1837, München 1976, S. 89–279

Heinrich Heine: Ludwig Börne (1840), in: Ders.: *Sämtliche Schriften in zwölf Bänden*, hg. von Klaus Briegleb, Bd. 7: Schriften 1837–1844, München 1976, S. 7–148

Marius Helten, Leonard Wertgen (Lehrstuhl für Wohnbau, RWTH Aachen): *Feldforschung im Rahmen des Unabhängigen Studios im Oktober 2022*, unveröffentlicht, Publikation in Vorbereitung

Paula Henderson, Adam Mornement: *Die Welt der Baumhäuser*, München ²2006

Klaus Herding, Rolf Reichardt: *Die Bildpublizistik der Französischen Revolution*, Frankfurt am Main 1989

Sonja Hildebrand: *Gottfried Semper. Architekt und Revolutionär*, Darmstadt 2020

Helmut Höge: *Pollerforschung* (= Massenmedien und Kommunikation, Bd. 179/180), hg. von Philipp Goll, Siegen 2010

Hans-Joachim Hoffmann: Kleidersprache. Eine Psychologie der Illusionen in Kleidung, Mode und Maskerade, Frankfurt am Main / Berlin / Wien 1985

Shemin Joy: At Least 25 Crore Workers Participated in General Strike, in: *Deccan Herald*, 26. November 2020. Online: https://www.deccanherald.com/national/at-least-25-crore-workers-participated-in-general-strike-some-states-saw-complete-shutdown-trade-unions-920200.html# (Zugriff: 21. Juni 2023)

Lloyd Kahn: *Domebook 1 & 2*, Bolinas, CA 1970–1971

Lloyd Kahn: *Shelter*, Bolinas, CA 1973

Friederike Kamann, Eberhard Kögel (Hg.): *Ruhestörung. Eine moderne Heimatgeschichte*, 2 Bde., Grafenau 1993 u. 1994

Horst Karasek: *Das Dorf im Flörsheimer Wald. Eine Chronik vom alltäglichen Widerstand gegen die Startbahn-West*, Darmstadt / Neuwied ²1981

Jürgen Kaube: Empfindliche Revolutionäre, in: *Frankfurter Allgemeine Zeitung*, 19. Januar 2023, S. 9

Anastasia Kavada, Orsalia Dimitriou: Protest Spaces Online and Offline. The Indignant Movement in Syntagma Square, in: Gavin Brown, Anna Feigenbaum, Fabian Frenzel, Patrick McCurdy (Hg.): *Protest Camps in International Context. Spaces, Infrastructures and Media of Resistance*, Bristol ²2018, S. 71–90

Anastasia Kavada: Project Democracy in Protest Camps. Caring, the Commons and Feminist Democratic Theory, in: Catherine Eschle, Alison Bartlett (Hg.): *Feminism and Protest Camps. Entan-*

glements, Critiques and Re-Imaginings, Bristol 2023, S. 176–194

Richard Kim: We Are All Human Microphones Now, in: *The Nation*, 3. Oktober 2011. Online: https://www.thenation.com/article/archive/we-are-all-human-microphones-now/ (Zugriff: 30. März 2023)

Seongcheol Kim, Martin Nonhoff: Bewegungsparteien und Volksparteien neuen Typs. Konturen einer Forschungsagenda, in: *Mittelweg 36*, H. 4, August/September 2022, S. 5–16

Louise Krasniewicz: *Nuclear Summer. The Clash of Communities at the Seneca Women's Peace Encampment*, Ithaca, NY 1992

Petra Lange-Berndt: Treehugging. Kontaktzonen von Kunst und Ökologie, in: Annika Schlitte, Markus Verne, Gregor Wedekind (Hg.): *Die Handlungsmacht ästhetischer Objekte*, Berlin / Boston 2021, S. 143–165

Pierre Larousse: Barricade, in: Ders.: *Grand dictionnaire universel du XIXe siècle*, Bd. 2, Paris 1866, S. 262–264

Emily Laquer [@EmilyLaquer]: „Der Polizeichef wusste, dass das Architektur-Museum den historischen Turm in #Lützerath als Stück Zeitgeschichte haben wollte. Es war ihm egal." [Tweet] [Video enthalten], *Twitter*, 16. Januar 2023, 10:31 Uhr. Online: https://twitter.com/EmilyLaquer/status/1614918198691827712 (Zugriff: 23. Mai 2023)

Tunney Lee, Lawrence Vale: Resurrection City. Washington DC, 1968, in: *Thresholds*, H. 41, Frühling 2013, S. 112–121

Jean-Jacques Lebel, Jean-Louis Brau, Philippe Merlhès: Nachwort, in: Dies. (Hg.): *La Chienlit. Dokumente zur französischen Mai-Revolte*, hg. im Auftrag eines Komitees der Bewegung des 22. März, Darmstadt 1969, S. 450–461

Henri Lefebvre: *Le droit à la ville*, Paris 1968

Henri Lefebvre: *Das Recht auf Stadt* (1968), Hamburg 2016

Le Nouvel Observateur, Nr. 334, 5. April 1971

Claude Lévi-Strauss: *The Savage Mind* (1962), Chicago 1966

Niklas Luhmann: Dabeisein und Dagegensein. Anregungen zu einem Nachruf auf die Bundesrepublik (1990), in: Kai-Uwe Hellmann (Hg.): *Niklas Luhmann. Protest. Systemtheorie und soziale Bewegungen*, Frankfurt am Main ⁵2016, S. 156–159

Gaja Maestri, Sarah M. Hughes: Contested Spaces of Citizenship. Camps, Borders and Urban Encounters, in: *Citizenship Studies*, Jg. 21, H. 6, 2017, S. 625–639

Harry Francis Mallgrave: *Gottfried Semper. Ein Architekt des 19. Jahrhunderts*, Zürich 2001

Harsh Mander: Six Months On, India's Protesting Farmers Are Creating History, in: *Scroll.in*, 31. Mai 2021. Online: https://scroll.in/article/995971/harsh-mander-six-months-on-indias-protesting-farmers-are-creating-history (Zugriff: 21. Juni 2023)

Miguel Ángel Martínez: El Movimiento de Okupaciones: Contracultura Urbana y Dinámicas Alter-Globalización, in: *Revista de Estudios de Juventud*, Jg. 76, März 2007, S. 225–243

Roland Meyer: *Gesichtserkennung*, Berlin 2021

Jörn-Henrik Meyn: *Die sogenannte Vermummung und passive Bewaffnung. Verfassungs- und verwaltungsrechtliche Probleme unter besonderer Berücksichtigung der Änderung des Versammlungsgesetzes von 1985*, Diss. Universität Hamburg 1988, Frankfurt am Main / Bern / New York / Paris 1988

Herkes İçin Mimarlık: *#occupygezi architecture*, 2013. Online: https://occupygeziarchitecture.tumblr.com/ (Zugriff: 12. Juni 2023)

Linda Norris: If I Ran a Museum in Kyiv, Right Now, in: *the uncatalogued museum*, 1. Dezember 2013. Online: http://uncatalogedmuseum.blogspot.com/2013/12/if-i-ran-museum-in-kyiv-right-now.html (Zugriff: 31. Mai 2023)

Martina Nußbaumer, Peter Stuiber: Protestbewegungen dokumentieren und ausstellen, in: *Wien Museum Magazin*, 20. Dezember 2021. Online: https://magazin.wienmuseum.at/protestbewegungen-dokumentieren-und-ausstellen (Zugriff: 30. März 2023)

Lite

Andreas Orth: Besetzerarchitektur, in: Günter Zint (Hg.): *Republik Freies Wendland. Eine Dokumentation*, Frankfurt am Main 1980, S. 132–133

Frei Otto: *Das hängende Dach. Gestalt und Struktur*, Berlin 1954

Pierre Patte: *Monumens érigés en France à la gloire de Louis XV.*, Paris 1765

Roland Peball, Klaus Schönberger: „Letzte Generation". Klimaprotest, der aufregt, aber durchaus legitim ist. Ziel sollte sein, Bündnisse zu schließen und eine selbstreflexive Radikalität zu entwickeln, in: *Der Standard* (Blog: Kulturanalyse des Alltags), 15. Dezember 2022. Online: https://www.derstandard.at/story/2000141666130/letzte-generation-klimaprotest-der-aufregt-aber-durchaus-legitim-ist (Zugriff: 6. April 2023)

Friedrich Pecht: *Aus meiner Zeit*, München 1894

Anna L. Peterson: *Seeds of the Kingdom. Utopian Communities in the Americas*, New York 2005

Polizeiliche Maßnahmen aus Anlass des Baues der Startbahn 18-West. Dokumentation, Erfahrungen, hg. durch den Polizeipräsidenten in Frankfurt am Main, 1984

Margarete Pratschke: „Aufruhr. Über den Sturm auf das Kapitol als digitales Bildereignis", Vortrag, TU Dresden, 15. November 2022

Carrie Quinlan: Revealed. The Vatican's Favourite Bands, in: *The Guardian*, 15. Februar 2010. Online: www.theguardian.com/commentisfree/belief/2010/feb/15/pope-top-10-albums-vatican (Zugriff: 15. März 2023)

Hans Rackwitz: Der ökologische Gesellschaftskonflikt als Klassenfrage. Konvergenzen, Divergenzen und Wechselwirkungen von Klassen- und Naturverhältnissen, in: Jakob Graf, Kim Lucht, John Lütten (Hg.): *Wiederkehr der Klassen. Theorien, Analysen, Kontroversen*, Frankfurt am Main 2022, S. 91–122

Adam Ramadan: From Tahrir to the World. The Camp as a Political Public Space, in: *European Urban and Regional Studies*, Jg. 20, H. 1, Januar 2013, S. 145–149

Julia Ramírez Blanco: Disobedience as an Urban Form. The Acampadasol in Madrid, in: Dies.: *Artistic Utopias of Revolt. Claremont Road, Reclaim the Streets, and the City of Sol*, Cham 2018

Juliane Reinecke: Social Movements and Prefigurative Organizing. Confronting Entrenched Inequalities in Occupy London, in: *Organization Studies*, Jg. 39, H. 9, März 2018, S. 1299–1321

Niko Rollmann, Fabian Frenzel: From Protest Camp to Tent City. The 'Free Cuvry' Camp in Berlin-Kreuzberg, in: Gavin Brown, Anna Feigenbaum, Fabian Frenzel, Patrick McCurdy (Hg.): *Protest Camps in International Context. Spaces, Infrastructures and Media of Resistance*, Bristol 2017

Manfred Rosenberger: *Geschichte des Nationalpark Donau-Auen. Die Phase vor der Au-Besetzung*. Chronologie, 2014. Online: https://infothek.donau-auen.at/files/PDF/NPDAChronVorphaseAubesetzung_Rosenberger2014.pdf (Zugriff: 11. Mai 2023)

Sabine Rosenbladt: Die Hoffnung und die Angst. Eindrücke aus der „Freien Republik Wendland", in: Ingrid Müller-Münch, u.a.: *Besetzung – weil das Wünschen nicht geholfen hat. Köln, Freiburg, Gorleben, Zürich und Berlin*, Reinbek 1981, S. 142–175

Sasha Roseneil: Disarming Patriarchy. Feminism and Political Action at Greenham, Buckingham 1995

Kathrin Rottmann: „*Aesthetik von unten". Pflaster und Asphalt in der bildenden Kunst der Moderne*, München 2016

Anders Rubing: Textile Geographies, Plasticity as Protest, in: Gavin Brown, Anna Feigenbaum, Fabian Frenzel, Patrick McCurdy (Hg.): *Protest Camps in International Context. Spaces, Infrastructures and Media of Resistance*, Bristol [2]2018, S. 35–52

Bernard Rudofsky: *Architecture Without Architects. A Short Introduction to Non-Pedigreed Architecture*, New York 1964

Luigi Russolo: *Die Kunst der Geräusche* (1913), hg. von Johannes Ullmaier, Mainz 2000

Joseph Rykwert: *On Adam's House in Paradise. The Idea of the Primitive Hut in Architectural History*, New York 1972

Amandeep Sandhu: Dispatch from India's Farmers Protest, in: *Zócalo Public Square*, 19. April 2021. Online: https://www.zocalopublicsquare.org/2021/04/19/dispatch-from-indias-farmers-protest/ideas/dispatches/ (Zugriff: 21. Juni 2023)

Bernard Sarrans: *Lafayette und die Revolution von 1830*, Bd. 1, Hamburg 1832

Kerstin Schankweiler: *Bildproteste*, Berlin 2019

Rainer Schoch: Michels Revolution. Zur deutschen Bildpublizistik der Revolution von 1848/49, in: Ausst.-Kat. *1848. Das Europa der Bilder*, 2 Bde., Bd. 1: *Der Völker Frühling* (Germanisches Nationalmuseum, Nürnberg), Nürnberg 1998, S. 89–101

Klaus Schönberger, Ove Sutter (Hg.): *Kommt herunter, reiht euch ein... Eine kleine Geschichte der Protestformen sozialer Bewegungen*, Berlin / Hamburg 2009

Klaus Schönberger: Protest-Selfies als Artikulation des Gemeinsamen, in: *Fotogeschichte. Beiträge zur Geschichte und Ästhetik der Fotografie*, Jg. 39, H. 154, 2019, S. 47–52

John Schofield, Colleen Beck, Harold Drollinger: Alternative Archaeologies of the Cold War. The Preliminary Results of Fieldwork at the Greenham and Nevada Peace Camps, in: Ludomir R. Lozny (Hg.): *Landscapes Under Pressure. Theory and Practice of Cultural Heritage Research and Preservation*, New York 2008, S. 149–162

Scientists for Future Wien: Stellungnahme. Wer die Stadtstraße baut, bedroht die Zukunft unserer Kinder, in: *°Celsius. Der Klimablog von Scientists for Future Österreich*, 11. Dezember 2021. Online: https://at.scientists4future.org/2021/12/11/stellungnahme-von-scientists-for-future-wien-wer-die-stadtstrasse-baut-bedroht-die-zukunft-unserer-kinder/ (Zugriff: 8. Mai 2023)

Ben Seel: Strategies of Resistance at the Pollok Free State Road Protest Camp, in: *Environmental Politics,* Jg. 6, H. 4, 1997, S. 108–139

Gottfried Semper: Vorläufige Bemerkungen über bemalte Architectur und Plastik bei den Alten (1834a), in: Gottfried Semper: *Gesammelte Schriften*, Bd. 1.1, hg. von Henrik Karge, Hildesheim / Zürich / New York 2014, S. 63–125

Gottfried Semper, Brief an seine Mutter, 1.11.1834b, Nachlass Gottfried Semper, gta Archiv, ETH Zürich, 20-K-1834-11-01(S)

Gottfried Semper, Brief an seinen Bruder Carl, 14.5.1849 (= Datum Poststempel, Brief von Semper falsch datiert auf den 15.5.1848), Nachlass Gottfried Semper, gta Archiv, ETH Zürich, 20-K-1849-05-14(S)

Ethel Seno (Hg.): *Trespass. Die Geschichte der Urbanen Kunst*, Berlin 2010

Chitleen Sethi: 5 Reasons Why Farmers Won the Farm Laws Battle against Modi Govt, in: *The Print*, 19. November 2021. Online: https://theprint.in/india/5-reasons-why-farmers-won-the-farm-laws-battle-against-modi-govt/768424/ (Zugriff: 22. Juni 2023)

Puroshotam Sharma: A New Leap of Struggle. The Farmers Siege of Delhi, in: *Trolley Times*, 18. Dezember 2020, S. 3

Maryna Shevtsova: Euromaidan and the Echoes of the Orange Revolution, in: Gavin Brown, Anna Feigenbaum, Fabian Frenzel, Patrick McCurdy (Hg.): *Protest Camps in International Context. Spaces, Infrastructures and Media of Resistance*, Bristol 2017, S. 243–260

Shut Shit Down! An Activist's Guide to Ende Gelände, Berlin 2020. Online: https://www.ende-gelaende.org/wp-content/uploads/2021/02/Basics-Ende-Gelaende-online-version.pdf (Zugriff: 5. April 2023)

Martin Siegler: Unter Tunneln. Zur Aktualität und Geschichte des terrestrischen Protests, in: *Geschichte der Gegenwart*, 29. März 2023. Online: https://geschichtedergegenwart.ch/unter-tunneln-zur-aktualitaet-und-geschichte-des-terrestrischen-protests/ (Zugriff: 5. Mai 2023)

Aatika Singh: How the Architecture of Trolley Towns of the Farmers' Movement Was a Protest in Itself, in: *The*

Lite

Wire, Februar 2022. Online: https://the-wire.in/politics/how-the-architecture-of-trolley-towns-of-the-farmers-move-ment-was-a-protest-in-itself (Zugriff: 29. Mai 2023)

Pashaura Singh: An Overview of Sikh History, in: Pashaura Singh, Louis Fenech (Hg.): *The Oxford Handbook of Sikh Studies*, Oxford 2014, S. 19–34

Joanna Slater: Why India's Farmers Are in Revolt in the Middle of a Pandemic, in: *The Washington Post*, 4. Dezember 2020. Online: https://www.washingtonpost.com/world/asia_pacific/india-farmers-protest-delhi-reforms/2020/12/04/98db8634-3414-11eb-9699-00d311f13d2d_story.html (Zugriff: 21. Juni 2023)

Paul Sörensen: »Zeugung« oder »Geburt« – Zeitlichkeiten politischer Transformation oder: Ist Schlafen politisch?, in: *Leviathan*, Jg. 46, H. 2, 2018, S. 232–254

stern, 6. Juni 1971, Titelseite und S. 16–23: „Wir haben abgetrieben"

Simone Teune: Das produktive Moment der Krise. Platzbesetzungen als Laboratorien der Demokratie, in: *WZB Mitteilungen*, H. 137, September 2012, S. 32–34

Kyoko Tominaga: Social Reproduction and the Limitations of Protest Camps. Openness and Exclusion of Social Movements in Japan, in: *Social Movement Studies*, Jg. 16, H. 3, 2017, S. 269–282

Mark Traugott: *The Insurgent Barricade*, Berkeley, CA 2010

Stephan Trüby: *Rechte Räume. Politische Essays und Gespräche* (= Bauwelt Fundamente Bd. 169), Basel 2021

Peter Ullrich: *Postdemokratische Empörung. Ein Versuch über Demokratie, soziale Bewegungen und gegenwärtige Protestforschung*, Berlin 2015

Tom Ullrich: Working on Barricades and Boulevards. Cultural Techniques of Revolution in Nineteenth-Century Paris, in: Jörg Dünne, Kathrin Fehringer, Kristina Kuhn, Wolfgang Struck (Hg.): *Cultural Techniques. Assembling Spaces, Texts & Collectives*, Berlin / Boston 2020, S. 23–45

Wolfgang Ullrich: „Was uns die Bilder von der Erstürmung des Kapitols erzählen", Radiointerview, *BR24*, 8. Januar 2021

...ums Ganze!: *Nichts ist unmöglich. Über den automobilen Kapitalismus und sein Ende*, Berlin 2021

Michael Vester: Die Krise der politischen Repräsentation. Spannungsfelder und Brüche zwischen politischen Eliten, oberen Milieus und Volksmilieus, in: Stefan Hradil, Peter Imbusch (Hg.): *Oberschichten – Eliten – Herrschende Klassen*, Wiesbaden 2003, S. 237–270

Vitruv (Marcus Vitruvius Pollio): *Zehn Bücher über Architektur* (ab 33 v. Chr.), Darmstadt 1964

Richard Wagner: *Mein Leben*, Bd. 1, München 1911

Colin Ward: *Housing. An Anarchist Approach*, London 1976

Colin Ward: The Early Squatters. Six Centuries of Squatting, in: Nick Wates, Christian Wolmar (Hg.): *Squatting. The Real Story*, London 1980, S. 104–109

Colin Ward: *Cotters and Squatters. Housing's Hidden History* (2002), Nottingham 2009

Martin Warnke: Bau und Gegenbau, in: Hermann Hipp, Ernst Seidel (Hg.): *Architektur als politische Kultur. Philosophia Practica*, Berlin 1996, S. 11–18

Nick Wates, Christian Wolmar (Hg.): *Squatting. The Real Story*, London 1980

Laura Weber: HISTORY OF THE NOW—A Museum for Maidan. An Interview With Ihor Poshyvailo, in: *novinki-Blog*, 14. Februar 2016. Online: https://novinkiblog.wordpress.com/2016/02/14/history-of-the-now-a-museum-for-maidan-an-interview-with-ihor-poshyvailo/ (Zugriff: 15. Mai 2023)

Eyal Weizman: *Sperrzonen. Israels Architektur der Besatzung*, Hamburg 2009

Eyal Weizman: *The Roundabout Revolutions*, Berlin 2015

Marius Wenger: Brandopfer. Zur Symbolik des Feuers im Protest, in: Ausst.-Kat. *Protest. Eine Zukunftspraxis*, hg. von Basil Rogger, Jonas Voegeli, Ruedi Widmer (Museum für Gestaltung Zürich), Zürich 2018, S. 122–125

Whole Earth Catalog, hg. von Stewart Brand, 1968–2003

John Wiebenson: Planner's Notebook.

Planning and Using Resurrection City, in: *Journal of the American Institute of Planners*, Jg. 35, H. 6, November 1969, S. 405–411

Wiener Klimafahrplan, hg. von Stadt Wien, 2022. Online: https://www.wien. gv.at/spezial/klimafahrplan/klima-schutz-wien-wird-klimaneutral/mobili-tat/ (Zugriff: 8. Mai 2023)

Mabel O. Wilson: Lessons from Resurrection City, in: Beatriz Colomina, Ignacio G. Galán, Evangelos Kotsioris, Anna-Maria Meister (Hg.): *Radical Pedagogies*, Cambridge, MA, 2022, S. 168–172

WSS (Women against Sexual Violence and State Repression): *Statement on Making Movements Spaces Safe for Women*, 4. Mai 2021. Online: https://wssnet.org/2021/05/04/wss-statement-on-making-movement-spaces-save-for-women/ (Zugriff: 22. Juni 2023)

Johann David Wyss: *Die Schweizer Familie Robinson*, Zürich 1813

(→ *Handbücher / Online-Manuals*)

Lobau, engl. → *Lobau*. Die Lobau – ein als schützenswert ausgewiesenes Auengebiet, das sich am nördlichen Ufer der Donau von Wien flussabwärts bis zur Grenze der Slowakei erstreckt – wird seit langem von den Plänen der österreichischen Verkehrspolitik bedroht. Konkret geht es um die fehlenden Bauabschnitte der Nordostumfahrung Wiens, die den großräumigen Autobahnring um die österreichische Hauptstadt schließen sollen. Erste → *Demonstrationen* gegen die sogenannte Lobau-Autobahn, die eine Untertunnelung des Naturschutzgebietes vorsieht, reichen bis in das Jahr 1999 zurück; in letzter Instanz genehmigt wurde das Bauprojekt allerdings erst 2018. Nachdem im August → *2021* mit dem Bau eines Autobahnzubringers im Stadtteil Hirschstetten begonnen worden war, kam es zur → *Besetzung* von verschiedenen strategisch wichtigen Orten durch → *Protestcamps* der „LobauBleibt"-Bewegung.

Anfänglich bestanden die Protestcamps lediglich aus Camping-Zelten (→ *Zelt*), wurden aber schon bald mit aufwendigeren Bauwerken und Gemeinschaftseinrichtungen ausgebaut

(→ *Bautypen*, → *Infrastruktur*). Ein wichtiges → *Protestziel* wurde im Dezember 2021 erreicht, als Leonore Gewessler, die zuständige Bundesministerin für Klimaschutz, Umwelt, Energie, Mobilität, Innovation und Technologie, offiziell das Aus für den Lobau-Tunnel erklärte. Dennoch setzte die Stadt Wien ihre Verkehrspolitik unbeirrt fort und ließ im Februar und April 2022 zwei der Camps gewaltsam von der → *Polizei* räumen und abreißen (→ *Zerstörung*).

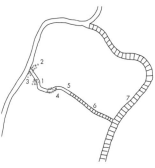

Lobau. 1 Basiscamp 2 „Grätzl 1" 3 „Grätzl 2" 4 „Wüste" 5 Autobahnzubringer „Stadtstraße", 2023: im Bau 6 Autobahnzubringer „Spange Aspern", 2023: in Planung 7 Außenring-Schnellstraße, 2023: in Planung (Lobau. 1 Base camp 2 „Grätzl 1" 3 „Grätzl 2" 4 „Desert" 5 Feeder road "Stadtstraße," 2023: under construction 6 Feeder road "Spange Aspern," 2023: planning stage 7 Outer ring highway, 2023: planning stage)

Der Architekt, Architekturhistoriker und Stadtforscher Norbert Mayr war als Aktivist selbst an den Protesten beteiligt und hat die Wanderausstellung *LOBAU BLEIBT* zusammengestellt, die an verschiedenen Orten in Wien sowie an der ETH Zürich gezeigt wurde. In seinem Beitrag für diese Publikation mit dem Titel „LOBAU BLEIBT – Von der Besetzung zum gebauten Widerstand" gibt er einen Überblick über die → *Protestarchitektur* der Bewegung und zeichnet die Chronologie der Ereignisse von 2021/2022 noch einmal nach:

→ 1984 konnte die österreichische Umweltbewegung mit der legendären Besetzung der → Hainburger Au ein Wasserkraftwerk an der Donau östlich von Wien verhindern und die Saat dafür legen, dass der Nationalpark Donau-Auen seit 1996 unter Naturschutz steht. Heute bedroht der Bau eines 8,2 Kilometer langen Tunnels als Teil der unzeitgemäß autozentrischen Planung eines Autobahnnetzes an Wiens Stadtrand den Nationalpark Lobau, intensiv thematisiert von der Protest- und Klimagerechtigkeitsbewegung „LobauBleibt". Ende 2021 sagte die grüne Klimaschutz- und Verkehrsministerin Leonore Gewessler das Lobautunnel- bzw. Autobahnprojekt ab, eine Neuaufnahme ist damit aber nicht abgewandt: Genehmigungsverfahren für die umwelt- und klimaschädliche Verkehrsschneise laufen weiter. Nicht allein die (Transit-)Wirtschaft, konservative und rechte Parteien lobbyieren intensiv, auch das sozialdemokratische Wien verweigert sich der Analyse der Wissenschaft (Scientists for Future Wien 2021; Emberger 2022, S. 2 f.). Statt den öffentlichen Verkehr im dynamisch wachsenden Nordosten offensiver auszubauen, konterkariert die Stadt ihre eigenen Verkehrsreduktionsziele, bis 2030 den Autoanteil annähernd zu halbieren (Wiener Klimafahrplan 2022). Wien baut zu der von ihr und dem Nachbarbundesland sowie der Wirtschaftskammer etc. forcierten Lobauautobahn seit Frühjahr 2022 die städtische Zubringerautobahn – verzögert durch zwei Besetzungen 2021/2022, die versucht haben, das zu verhindern – und demonstriert, wie fruchtbare landwirtschaftliche Flächen, wertvolle Grünräume, alte Ortskerne und Wohnquartiere zerstört bzw. massiv belastet werden.

Im Sommer 2021 besetzte „LobauBleibt" – ein breites Bündnis aus Fridays for Future, Jugendrat, „System Change Not Climate Change" und Extinction Rebellion, den lokalen Bürger*innen-Initiativen „Hirschstetten retten", „Rettet die Lobau – Natur statt Beton" und unterstützt von Greenpeace und Global 2000 – spontan einige der gerade begonnenen Baustellen. Das Ende August offiziell angemeldete Basiscamp Anfanggasse wurde unter Bäumen in einem kleinen Park in Hirschstetten direkt an der Zubringer-Autobahn-Trasse aufgeschlagen (es bestand schließlich ein Jahr). Wenige Tage später besetzten Aktivist*innen spontan weitere Baustellen in der Nähe – und wurden nicht geräumt. So beherbergten das „Grätzl 1" westlich und die „Wüste" östlich vom Basiscamp gut sieben bzw. fünf Monate lang friedlich gelebten und gebauten Widerstand bis ins Frühjahr 2022. Dann stürmte jeweils eine Übermacht an Polizeikräften die beiden Baustellenbesetzungen, sie wurden umgehend dem Boden gleichgemacht, hunderte Bäume wurden für die Autotrasse gefällt.

Im Sommer 2021 besiedelten kleine Zelte alle drei Orte – das Basiscamp, das Grätzl 1 und die Wüste –, teilweise wurden sie winterfest eingehaust. Eine mit Holz und Stroh als Dämmstoff möglichst ökologische DIY-Architektur war neben (gespendeten) Zelten aller Art die Grundlage dafür, das Camps weiter- und auszubauen (→ Baumaterial). Das Basiscamp hatte bald einen Info-Stand, eine beheizbare Jurte, Zelte unterschiedlicher Größe für einen Kost-Nix-Laden, für Aufenthalt, Wohnen und Schlafen, eine Bühne und andere Orte für die zahlreichen Workshops, Kunst- und Kulturveranstaltungen, eine → Küche, die von „Robin Foods" gerettete Lebensmittel verarbeitete; eigene Küchen entstanden später in allen Camps.

Der unwirtlichste Ort war das Grätzl 1 direkt bei der Autobahnanbindung zur A23 mit belastenden Emissionen und ohrenbetäubendem Lärm, einem akustischen Vorgeschmack auf die neue Stadtautobahn. Die hölzerne Tor- bzw. Info-Plattform des Camps wurde zum kompakten Turm mit Schlafgeschoß ausgebaut. Ein nächtlicher, bis heute unaufgeklärter Brandanschlag am 30. Dezember 2021 brachte acht schlafende Aktivist*innen in Lebensgefahr und zerstörte den Holzturm. Unmittelbar darauf, im Jänner 2022, entstanden im Grätzl 1 neue Strukturen, nun etwas weiter von den Verkehrsbelastungen abgerückt. Das bauliche Spektrum reichte von informell-temporären Gebilden wie einem „Lützerath-Denkmal" aus Andreas-Kreuzen bis zu einem durchgeplanten Cube, einem zweistöckigen Holzturm.

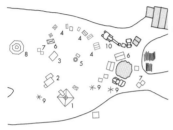

■ Gemeinschaftsbauten (Community buildings)
■ Individuelle Unterkünfte (Individual shelters)

Lobau, Protestcamp „Wüste", Januar 2022. 1 Pyramide 2 Bauhütte und Küche 3 „Wohnzimmer" 4 Schlafkoje 5 Feuerstelle 6 Materiallager 7 „Türme" 8 Permakultur-Garten 9 Tripod 10 Besetzte Baufahrzeuge (Lobau, Protest camp "Desert," January 2022. 1 Pyramid 2 Builder's hut and kitchen 3 "Living room" 4 Sleeping bunk 5 Fire pit 6 Material storage 7 "Towers" 8 Permaculture garden 9 Tripod 10 Occupied construction vehicles)

Die hölzerne Pyramide, die das Wüste-Camp dominierte, war bereits ab Herbst 2021 nach einem klaren baulichen Konzept entstanden; sie avancierte rasch zum Signet von „LobauBleibt". Nachdem fruchtbare Äcker zu einem riesigen Schotterfeld planiert worden waren, „erblühte" die Wüste zu einem offen-kommunikativen „Stadtteil", wie auch das Massenblatt Kronen Zeitung konstatierte (Graf 2021). Die von einer Landschaftsarchitektin konzipierte und gespendete „Widerstandshecke" – ein lockerer Kranz aus Dutzenden angepflanzten Sträuchern mit essbaren Früchten – umsäumte das Areal einladend, ein roter Teppich deutete einen abgestellten Bagger zum Eingangstor um. Gemüsebeete und nachgenutzte Photovoltaik-Paneele erhöhten die Au-

tonomie dieser demokratisch-alternativen Stadtproduktion zwischen Aktivismus und Fachexpertise.

Der Bausektor, als Großemittent und Ressourcenzerstörer auch für die eskalierende Klimakrise maßgeblich verantwortlich, im Schlepptau die Architektur als baukulturelles Dekor, kann nur radikal reformiert zur klimagerechten Transformation beitragen. Baulich klimafittes Gestalten muss intelligent und sparsam weiterbauen und wieder an der vorfossilen Praxis „form follows availability" anschließen. Diesen anspruchsvollen Geist der Selbstbeschränkung vermittelten auch die sogenannten „Bautage" in den drei Camps, die gemeinsam mit Anrainer*innen und Aktivist*innen aus der Stadtregion durchgeführt wurden.

Auch die Anstrengungen gegen die polizeilichen Räumungen waren kollektiv. Das soziale Fundament der Protestarchitektur bildeten basisdemokratische Entscheidungen in periodischen oder anlassbezogenen Plena: Sie reichten vom Camp-Alltag, dem verbindlichen Rahmen inklusiven Zusammenlebens („Grätzlkonsens") bis zur Vorbereitung auf Räumungen, die durch →Lock-on Devices und hohe Plattformen aus Holz verzögert wurden. Neben den gewaltfreien Baustellenbesetzungen in Transdanubien wurden auch die Aktionen, (Groß-)Demonstrationen und Straßenproteste in Wiens Zentrum (Ring, SPÖ-Zentrale, Rathauspark, Naschmarkt etc.) als friedlicher Widerstand mit →Bannern und mobilen Kunst- und Architekturelementen durchgeführt. Besonders markant war Mitte Mai 2022 die Straßenblockade (→Straße, →Blockade) nahe der Secession und über →Tensegrity-Struktur. Ein solches stabiles Stabwerk aus Bambus lässt sich rasch aufbauen und erschwert die Räumung der Aktivist*innen. Der von tension und integrity abgeleitete Name spiegelt die Spannung und gewaltfreie Entschiedenheit wider, aber auch die Hierarchiefreiheit, die Integrität und den Zusammenhalt der (Bezugs-)Gruppen während der Straßenblockade.

Der Information, dem Diskurs und der Dokumentation der Bewegung diente *die an der Eidgenössischen Technischen Hochschule Zürich gestartete Ausstellung „LOBAU BLEIBT – Dokumente des Widerstandes gegen eine zukunftsfeindliche Stadtentwicklungspolitik", die an vier Orten in Wien gezeigt wurde. Banner und Objekte (→ Medien) wechselten dabei als „Exponate in Aktion" zwischen Ausstellungsraum und öffentlichem Raum. „LobauBleibt" wurde Anfang 2023 im Volkskundemuseum Wien als vorläufig letzte Station in der Ausstellung „VON ZWENTENDORF ZU CO₂ – Kämpfe der Umweltbewegung in Österreich" präsentiert (→ Museum). Von einer Musealisierung kann aber keine Rede sein: „Eine Mehrheit unserer Gesellschaft, und mit ihr die Großparteien, wollen möglichst nichts ändern, einfach so weitermachen wie bisher. Dass ihnen das langfristig auf den Kopf fallen wird, glauben sie nicht. Ein wenig Verleugnung und Verharmlosung, garniert mit Wissenschaftsskepsis – Problem gelöst, zumindest im Kopf", analysiert Reinhard Steurer, Professor für Klimapolitik an der Universität für Bodenkultur Wien (persönliche E-Mail-Korrespondenz vom 7. April 2023). Deshalb bleiben Klimagerechtigkeitsbewegungen weiterhin wichtig – und „LobauBleibt" für die Mobilitätswende in Österreich aktiv.*

Mit dem Bau der Pyramide ist den „LobauBleibt"-Protesten eine gleichsam ikonische Protestarchitektur geglückt (→Ikone), durch deren gewaltsame Zerstörung sich die Wiener Stadtregierung viele Sympathien verspielt hat. Über die Konzeption, Entstehung und Bedeutung der Pyramide haben wir mit ihrem Planer – der namentlich hier nicht benannt werden will – ein kurzes Interview geführt:

Sebastian Hackenschmidt: Am 1. Februar 2022 wurde die Pyramide, die Du entworfen hast, unter dem Schutz von Einsatzkräften der Wiener Polizei abgerissen. Sie stand nur knapp drei Monate, ist aber zu so etwas wie dem Markenzeichen der Lobau-Proteste geworden. Wie bist Du darauf gekommen, dem Bauwerk die Form einer Pyramide zu geben? Wer hat entschieden, wo sie

positioniert werden würde? Und welche praktischen und strategischen Zwecke sollte sie erfüllen?

Lobau. 1 Kuppelzelt 2 Pyramide 3 „Türme"
(Lobau. 1 Dome tent 2 Pyramid 3 "Towers")

Antwort: In Vorbereitung für den Tunnel, der hier rauskommen sollte, hatten die Bagger das fruchtbare Wiener Ackerland schon in eine große Schotterpiste verwandelt. Durch die vorhandenen Pläne von NGOs, die sich bereits seit Jahren gegen die Bauvorhaben eingesetzt haben, konnten wir ermitteln, wo genau die Öffnung des Tunnels geplant war. Die Menschen, die mit ihren Zelten im Herbst 2021 die Bagger besetzt hatten, sind von der Polizei nicht gleich geräumt worden; offenbar wollte man taktisch erst mal abwarten, wie viele Menschen die Besetzung unterstützen und welche Gruppierungen sich da beteiligen. Die haben wohl gedacht, dass sich das Ganze im Winter von selbst auflöst. Wir mussten die Zeit vor dem Kälteeinbruch also nutzen, um ein gedämmtes und beheizbares Gebäude zu schaffen, groß genug, damit 30 bis 40 Leute das Areal dauerhaft besetzen können. Und wir wollten ein sichtbares Zeichen setzen, ein Mahnmal, das daran erinnert, dass dieses Bauprojekt nicht vereinbar ist mit den Klimazielen. Die Pyramide war deshalb ein gutes Symbol für die „Wüste", wie wir diese riesige, öde Schotterfläche inzwischen genannt haben.

SH: Die Pyramide erschien Dir als passende Architekturform für die neue Wüstenregion, die in Wien entstanden ist?

A: Ja, auch die 1,5-Grad-Flagge auf dem Turm oben sollte eine Warnung vor der Verwüstung durch Klimaerwärmung, Bodenversiegelung und Naturzerstörung sein. Die Form der Pyramide hatte aber nicht zuletzt damit zu tun, dass es hier um eine Gemeinschaft von vielen und um einen langen Winter ging. Es ist ja die einfachste Form der Zufluchtssuche, schnell einige Hölzer wie ein Zelt übereinander zu legen, um darunter → Schutz zu finden. Die Maße haben sich nach dem gerichtet, was wir bekommen haben: Glasscheiben von einer Gebäude-Sanierung, Holzbalken als Spenden von verschiedenen Personen, Werkzeuge und so weiter. Man baut mit dem, was verfügbar ist und was man sich leisten kann, aber eben ökologisch und größtenteils recycelt, mit Holz und Stroh gegen Beton und Asphalt. Unser Ziel war nicht, ein ewiges Bauwerk zu schaffen, sonst wäre Holz, Stroh und Glas wohl kaum die richtige Wahl gewesen. Wir müssen vielmehr Symbole des Widerstands, des Umdenkens und des Wandels schaffen. Die → Baumhäuser vom → Hambacher Wald oder die Pyramide in der Wüste des Lobau-Tunnelprojektes sind Bilder, die hoffentlich einmal genauso den Weg zu einem gelungenen gesellschaftlichen Wandel dokumentieren, wie dies weltweit auch schon tausende andere Leuchtturmprojekte der ökologisch-sozialen Neuorientierung tun.

SH: Ausgeführt wurde die Pyramide dann von vielen verschiedenen Leuten bzw. Gruppen – wie ist das abgelaufen?
A: Nachdem wir die Wüste im September 2021 mit Zelten besetzt hatten, wurde erst mal eine Bauhütte errichtet, in der wir das Werkzeug unterbringen und in der auch schon ein paar Leute schlafen konnten. Die Hütte war schon gedämmt und mit einem kleinen Ofen beheizbar, wie es die Pyramide sind später auch sein sollte. Ich habe dann das Material für die Pyramide kalkuliert, Stücklisten angelegt und sogar ein kleines Modell gebaut. Das Baumaterial wurde uns größtenteils überlassen; durch Gelder von Unterstützer*innen konnten wir die Holzplatten aber zukaufen. Für die Mitarbeit am Bau der Pyramide haben sich ganz verschiedene Leute zusammengefunden, auf die mehr oder weniger Verlass war, einige davon haben die WhatsApp-Gruppe „Winterfest" gebildet. Und irgendwann war dann Joe da, der meinte, er könnte die Bauleitung übernehmen; er und andere haben das Ganze dann koordiniert und die Arbeiten verteilt. Es gab aber auch eine FLINTA-Gruppe [Anmerkung: Die Abkürzung FLINTA steht für Frauen, Lesben, intergeschlechtliche, nichtbinäre, trans und agender Personen], die dafür gesorgt hat, dass das Bauen, das sonst meist Männerdomäne ist, gendermäßig bei uns etwas anders lief. Im Dezember war die Pyramide dann fertig und winterfest; leider stand sie nur bis Anfang Februar, dann wurde sie unter Polizeischutz abgerissen. Ich freu mich aber darüber, dass sie als Symbol für die Lobau-Proteste nach wie vor Gültigkeit hat und sich die Menschen an sie erinnern. Genau deswegen haben wir ja auch nicht einfach eine normale Hütte gebaut. (Beitrag von Norbert Mayr; Gesprächspartner: Anonym; Einleitung, Recherche und Interview-Redaktion: SH)

Lobau, Ger. → Lobau. The Lobau are meadows earmarked as worthy of protection and located on the northern banks of the River Danube in Vienna, extending downstream as far as the border with Slovakia. The meadows have long been at risk owing to Austrian transportation policy plans, specifically the sections of the Vienna northeast bypass that are still lacking and would complete the large-scale highway ring-road round the Austrian capital. The first → demonstrations against the so-called Lobau highway, which involves building a tunnel under the nature reserve, took place as long ago as 1999; in the final instance, the construction project was not actually officially approved until 2018. In August → 2021, construction started in Vienna's Hirschstetten district on a feeder road for the highway, and this prompted the → occupation of various strategically important locations in the form of → protest camps by the "LobauBleibt" (Lobau Stays) movement.

Oliver Ressler: Drohnenaufnahme *Die Wüste lebt,*
wenige Tage vor der Räumung (Drone shot *The Desert
Lives a few days before eviction*), 27. Januar 2022

Merle: Bau der Pyramide im Protestcamp „Wüste", mit Modell (Construction of the pyramid in the "Desert" protest camp, with scale model), 24. November 2021

Helga Herzog: Bau der Pyramide (Construction of the pyramid), November 2021

Merle: Unterer Raum der Pyramide (Lower room of the pyramid), 12. Januar 2022

Merle: Abgestellter Bagger, eine Art Eingangstor zum Protestcamp „Wüste" (Parked excavator, a kind of entrance gate to the "Desert" protest camp), 23. November 2021

Merle: Pyramide und Bauhütte (Pyramid and builder's hut), 9. Dezember 2021

Norbert Mayr: Zelte im Protestcamp „Grätzl" (Tents in the "Grätzl" protest camp), 21. September 2021

Norbert Mayr: Nach einem Brandanschlag neu entstandene Bauten im Protestcamp „Grätzl" (Newly constructed buildings in the "Grätzl" protest camp after an arson attack), 25. Februar 2022

Basiscamp (Base camp), Herbst 2021

Merle: Basiscamp, im Hintergrund eine Jurte (Base camp, with a yurt in the background), 3. Juli 2022

Räumung des Protestcamps „Wüste" (Eviction of the "Desert" protest camp), 1. Februar 2022

Initially, the protest camps consisted simply of camping tents (→ *Tent*) but were soon expanded to include more elaborate structures and community facilities (→ *Building types*, → *Infrastructure*). An important → *protest goal* was achieved in December 2021, when Leonore Gewessler, the Federal Minister for Climate Protection, the Environment, Energy, Mobility, Innovation, and Technology officially declared the Lobau tunnel project terminated. The City of Vienna nevertheless continued undeterred with its transportation policy plans and in February and April 2022 had the → *police* clear two of the camps by force and then demolish them (→ *Destruction*).

Architect, architectural historian, and urban researcher Norbert Mayr took part in the protests himself as an activist and compiled the traveling exhibition *LOBAU BLEIBT* which went on show at various venues in Vienna and at ETH Zurich, Switzerland. In his contribution for the present publication, entitled "Lobau Stays—From Occupation to the Construction of Resistance," he provides a synopsis of the movement's → *protest architecture* and outlines the exact chronology of the events of 2021/2022:

In → *1984*, the Austrian environmental movement's legendary occupation of the → *Hainburger Au* prevented the construction of a power plant on the Danube to the east of Vienna and paved the way for the declaration of the Donau-Auen National Park as a protected area in 1996. Today the construction of an 8.2-kilometer tunnel as part of the antiquated car-centric plan for a highway network on Vienna's outskirts is threatening the Lobau National Park, an issue the protest and climate justice movement LobauBleibt has addressed extensively. In late 2021 the Minister of Climate Protection and Transport, Leonore Gewessler (Greens), canceled the Lobau tunnel and highway project, and yet, a resumption of these plans cannot be ruled out. Authorization processes for the traffic route, which poses a hazard for both the environment and the climate, are still underway. It is not only (transit) economists and conservative and right-wing parties that are involved in intense lobbying. Social-democratic Vienna has also chosen to ignore scientific analysis (Scientists for Future Wien 2021; Emberger 2022, p. 2f.). Instead of pushing to expand public transport in the dynamically growing northeast, the city is thwarting its own plans to roughly halve the number of cars by 2030 (Wiener Klimafahrplan 2022). Vienna as well as its neighbor state and the Federal Economic Chamber etc. are adamant about the Lobau Highway, and since the spring of 2022 the city has been building a municipal access highway. The endeavor, which was delayed by two occupations aimed at preventing it in 2021/2022, manifests the massive burden on fertile agricultural land, valuable green spaces, old town centers, and residential quarters.

In the summer of 2021, LobauBleibt—a broad alliance made up of Fridays for Future, the youth council, "System Change Not Climate Change," and Extinction Rebellion, along with the local citizens' initiatives "Hirschstetten retten" (Saving Hirschstetten) and "Rettet die Lobau—Natur statt Beton" (Save Lobau—Nature instead of Concrete), and supported by Greenpeace and Global 2000—spontaneously occupied some of the newly started construction sites. Officially registered in late August, the base camp Anfanggasse was set up under trees in a small park in Hirschstetten, right next to the access highway route (it ultimately lasted a year). A few days later, activists spontaneously occupied further construction sites in the vicinity—and were not removed. Thus, Grätzl 1 to the west and Wüste to the east of the base camp harbored peacefully lived and built resistance for over seven months and five months respectively until the spring of 2022. After which, disproportionately large → *police* forces stormed both occupied construction sites. They were instantly razed to the ground, and hundreds of trees were felled for the roadway.

In the summer of 2021, small →tents populated all three sites—the base camp, Grätzl 1, and Wüste—some of them with winterproof encasements. Besides (donated) tents of all kinds, preferably ecological DIY architecture featuring straw and wood as insulation served as the basis for extending and expanding the camps (→building materials). The base camp soon had an information booth, a heatable yurt, tents in different sizes for a give-away shop, a lounge area, living and sleeping spaces, a stage, and other places for the many workshops and art and cultural events, and a →kitchen that prepared food saved by "Robin Foods"; and kitchens were subsequently established in all camps.

The least hospitable site was Grätzl 1 next to the highway connection to the A23 with its harmful emissions and deafening noise, an acoustic foretaste of the new city highway. The camp's wooden gate and information platform was converted into a compact tower with a floor for sleeping accommodation. An as yet unsolved arson attack on the night of December 30, 2021, put eight sleeping activists in mortal danger and destroyed the wooden tower. In January 2022, not long after the incident, new structures developed at Grätzl 1 which were further away from the impacting traffic. The constructional spectrum ranged from informal and temporary objects, such as the "Lützerath Monument" made up of St. Andrew's crosses, to the meticulously planned Cube, a two-story wooden tower.

The wooden pyramid that dominated the Wüste camp was built in autumn 2021 according to a precise constructional concept, and soon became the emblem of LobauBleibt. After fertile fields had been bulldozed into a giant gravel plain, the Wüste (desert) site "blossomed" into an open and communicative "district," as the popular paper Kronen Zeitung also stated (Graf 2021). Conceived and donated by a landscape architect, the "Widerstandshecke" (resistance hedge)—a loose ring made up of a dozen shrubs with edible berries—framed the area invitingly, and a red carpet reinterpreted a parked excavator as a gateway. Vegetable beds and re-used photovoltaic panels enhanced the autonomy of this democratic-alternative municipal production between activism and expertise.

As a major emitter and destroyer of resources, the building industry, with architecture in tow to provide the cultural embellishments, is largely responsible for the escalating climate crisis and can only contribute to a climate-conscious transformation after radical reforms have taken place. Structurally climate-conscious design must continue building with a smart and economical approach and return to the pre-fossil practice of "form follows availability." This ambitious spirit of self-restraint was also conveyed during the so-called "Bautage" (building days) in the three camps, which were carried out together with residents and activists in the urban region.

Likewise, the resistance against the police evictions was a collective effort. The social foundation of the protest architecture grew from decisions reached through a grassroots approach during periodical or occasion-related assemblies: ranging from everyday camp-life to the binding framework of inclusive communal life ("Grätzlkonsens" [The Grätzl Agreement]) to preparations for evictions which were delayed with the aid of →lock-on devices and high wooden platforms. In addition to the nonviolent occupations of construction sites in Transdanubia, the actions, (large-scale) demonstrations, and street protests in Vienna's center (Ring, SPÖ headquarters, Rathauspark, Naschmarkt etc.) were implemented as peaceful resistance with →banners, and mobile art and architectural elements. In mid-May 2022, a street blockade (→street, →blockade) near the Secession with a →tensegrity structure was especially powerful. While easy to set up, a stable bamboo construction of this kind hampers efforts to remove activists. Derived from tension and integrity, the name conveys the suspense and nonviolent determination, but also the nonhierarchical integrity and solidarity among the (peer) groups during the street blockade.

The exhibition "LobauBleibt—Dokumente des Widerstandes gegen eine zukunftsfeindliche Stadtentwicklungspolitik" (Lobau Stays—Documents of Resistance against Reactionary City Development Policies), which started at ETH Zurich and was shown at four venues in Vienna, provided information about the movement and promoted its discourse and documentation. As "exhibits in action" banners and objects switched between the exhibition space and public space (→ Media). In early 2023, LobauBleibt reached its final venue at the Austrian Museum of Folk Life and Folk Art as part of the exhibition "Von Zwentendorf zu CO₂—Kämpfe der Umweltbewegung in Österreich" (From Zwentendorf to CO₂—The Battles of Austria's Environmental Movement; → Museum). However, this was a far cry from a musealization: "Most people in our society, alongside the main parties, would prefer to change as little as possible and to simply continue as before. They do not believe that this approach will eventually blow up in their faces. A bit of denial paired with some downplaying, garnished with science skepticism—problem solved, at least in their minds," Reinhard Steurer, professor of climate politics at the University of Natural Resources and Life Sciences, Vienna, explains (personal email correspondence from April 7, 2023). That is why climate justice movements continue to matter—and why LobauBleibt will continue to play an active part in Austria's mobility transformation.

With the construction of the pyramid, the LobauBleibt protests succeeded in creating a truly iconic piece of protest architecture (→ Icon), the forcible destruction of which caused the City Government of Vienna City to lose a great deal of sympathy. We conducted a short interview with its planner (who wishes to remain nameless here) on the concept for the pyramid, how the edifice came about, and its significance:

Sebastian Hackenschmidt: On February 1, 2022, the pyramid you designed was torn down under guard by the Vienna police force. It had stood in place for almost three months and became something like the landmark or trademark of the Lobau protests. How did you come up with the idea of giving the structure the shape of a pyramid? Who decided where to position it? And what practical and strategic purposes was it expected to fulfill?

Answer: When doing preparatory works for the tunnel that was supposed to be built here, the bulldozers had already turned fertile Vienna farmland into a large site covered in gravel. On the basis of plans drawn up by the NGOs who had already been opposing the construction project for years, we ascertained where exactly the tunnel was supposed to emerge. The people who occupied the dozers with their tents back in the fall of 2021 were not forced out immediately by the police; evidently back then the tactic was to wait and see how many people would actually support the occupation and which groups were involved. The powers that be no doubt thought that it would all dwindle away in the course of the winter. So we had to use the time before temperatures really dropped to make an insulated building that could be heated and was large enough to enable thirty or forty people to permanently occupy the site. And we wanted to create a visible symbol, a monument that reminded everyone that this construction project is not compatible with the climate protection goals. The pyramid was therefore a good symbol for the "desert," which is what we had since nicknamed the huge, barren expanse of gravel.

SH: To your mind, the pyramid was the fitting architectural shape for the new desert region that had arisen in Vienna?

A: Yes, and the 1.5°C flag on the top was meant as a warning against desertification as a result of global warming, the ground being sealed, and nature being destroyed. The shape of the pyramid derived not least from the fact that here, a community of many had raised their voices and were about to face a

Lock

long winter. After all, the simplest form of making a shelter is to swiftly bang together a few slats of wood in the shape of a tent in order to enjoy →protection underneath. The measurements reflect the materials we were able to lay our hands on: panes of glass from a building modernization project, wooden beams donated by various individuals, tools, and so on. We built with what was available and what we could afford, but we did so in an ecologically sound manner and largely using recycled materials, using wood and straw to oppose the tunnel of concrete and asphalt. Our objective was not to create an edifice for all eternity, as otherwise wood, straw, and glass would hardly have been our preferred choices. Rather we must construct symbols of resistance, of how to rethink and change things. The →tree houses in the →Hambach Forest, or the pyramid in the Lobau tunnel project desert—now they are images that will hopefully at some point document the path to successful social change as thousands of other flagship projects for a new ecological-social trajectory have already done the world over.

SH: The pyramid was then realized by many different people and groups. How did that take place?

A: We used tents to occupy the desert in September 2021 and first set about erecting a construction site shed where we could store our tools and where a few people could already sleep. The shed was itself insulated and there was a small stove to heat it, just as was to be the case later in the pyramid. I then calculated what material we would need for the pyramid, compiled lists of items, and even made a small model of it. We were largely gifted the construction material; and we were able to buy additional wooden panels with the money donated by supporters. All manner of different people chose to help build the pyramid and we were more or less able to rely on them; some of them formed the "Winterfest" (Ready for Winter) WhatsApp group. And at some point, Joe popped up; he said he could handle site management and he and oth-

ers then coordinated the whole thing and assigned tasks to people. There was also a FLINTA group [NB: FLINTA stands for women, lesbians, as well as intersex, non-binary, trans, and agender people] who ensured that the construction effort, which is otherwise typically a male domain, was somewhat different in gender terms when it came to the pyramid. The structure was finished and ready for winter by December; sadly, it only stood there until early February, when it was torn down by a construction gang protected by the police. I'm so happy it remains a valid symbol of the Lobau protests, and that people remember it. That is precisely why we did not choose to simply build a normal hut. (Contribution by Norbert Mayr; conversation with: anonymous; introduction, research, and interview editing: SH)

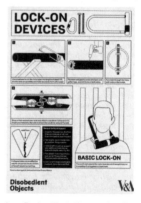

Lock-on Device. Illustration aus dem Katalog *Disobedient Objects*, Victoria and Albert Museum, 2014 (Lock-on device. Illustration from the catalog *Disobedient Objects*, Victoria and Albert Museum, 2014)

Lock-on Device, engl. →*Lock-on device*. Vorrichtung, die dazu dient, sich durch →*Körpereinsatz* an etwas festzuketten mit dem Ziel, eine →*Blockade* zu bilden. Meist sind Lock-on Devices als Röhren konstruiert. Die Aktivist∗innen strecken ihre Arme tief hinein und sichern ihre Hände mit einer Art Handschelle. Die Ordnungskräfte können zur Handschelle im Innern des Rohrs (oder der → *Betonpyramid*e von → *Gorleben*) nur vordringen, indem sie das Lock-on Device gewaltsam öffnen und damit die Verletzung der Aktivist∗innen riskieren. Diese können sich aber, im Unterschied zur Blockadestrategie des → *Anklebens*, in einer Notlage relativ schnell selbst daraus befreien. (OE)

Lock-on device, Ger. → *Lock-on Device (fig.)*. Device used to chain yourself to something, as a form of → *body deployment,* with the goal of creating a → *blockade*. Usually, lock-on devices are designed as tubes. The activists stick their arms deep into the tube and secure their hands with a kind of handcuff. The authorities can only reach the handcuffs inside the tube (or the → *concrete pyramid* at → *Gorleben*) by using force to open the lock-on device, which risks harming the activists. Unlike the strategy of creating a blockade by → *super-gluing*, however, in an emergency, activists using these devices can free themselves relatively quickly. (OE)

Lützerath, engl. → *Lützerath*. Nachdem der letzte verbliebene Rest des → *Hambacher Waldes* durch die Proteste der Klimaaktivist∗innen von der Rodung verschont werden konnte, entwickelte sich in Lützerath ein neues → *Protestcamp*. Das etwa 40 Kilometer vom Tagebau Hambach entfernte Lützerath zählt zu einer Reihe von Dörfern, die zum Abriss vorgesehen sind, um den Braunkohleabbau am Standort Garzweiler II auszuweiten – bevor dann ab 2038 endgültig keine Kohleverstromung in Deutschland mehr stattfinden soll.

Könnte nicht die → *Blockade* einer Tagebauerweiterung, die im „Hambi" nach jahrelangen Konflikten zum Erfolg geführt hatte, in Lützerath ein zweites Mal gelingen? Den Ausgangspunkt des zwischen Sommer → *2020* und Januar 2023 bestehenden Protestcamps bildete der Bauernhof von Eckardt Heukamp mit seinen Neben- und Nachbargebäuden, die zuletzt nur etwa 200 Meter von der Hangkante des Tagebaus Garzweiler II entfernt waren. Heukamp, dem letz-

ten Bewohner von Lützerath, der nicht an RWE verkaufen wollte, drohte die Enteignung. Er erlaubte den Klimaaktivist∗innen, auf seinem Grundstück ihr Camp aufzubauen. Als weitere Proteststrategie verkaufte er in der Hoffnung, damit eine weitere juristische Hürde gegen die → *Zerstörung* von Lützerath errichten zu können, eine Wiese an den Steuerberater Kurt Claßen, der zugleich der Grundeigentümer des „Wiesencamps" am Hambacher Wald ist.

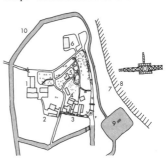

Angeeignetes Gebäude (Appropriated building)
■ Barrikade (Barricade)
▨ Infrastruktur Polizei (Police infrastructure)

Lützerath, Januar 2023. 1 Küfa (Küche für alle) 2 Paulas Hof 3 Eckardts Hof 4 „Wilde 8" 5 Villa 6 Skatehalle 7 Vorfeld 8 Tagebaukante 9 Polizeiparkplatz 10 Polizeiringstraße (Lützerath, January 2023. 1 Küfa (community kitchen) 2 Paula's Farm 3 Eckardt's Farm 4 "Wild 8" 5 Villa 6 Skate hall 7 Forefield 8 Open-pit edge 9 Police parking lot 10 Police ring road)

Charakteristisch für das Protestcamp Lützerath ist die Kombination aus → *Baumhäusern* und Bodenstrukturen. Da der Platz in Lützerath begrenzt war und bereits nach kurzer Zeit nahezu alle geeigneten Bäume mit Baumhäusern belegt waren, wurde mit den Bodenstrukturen ein neuer → *Bautypus* der Verzögerungsarchitektur erfunden. Diese am Boden stehenden, aber auf Stelzen oder Pfählen errichteten „Baumhäuser ohne Bäume" waren mindestens 2,50 Meter hoch und hatten ein betretbares Dach. Denn für alle Räumungseinsätze in einer Höhe von mehr als 2,50 Metern muss die → *Polizei* Spezialkräfte aufbieten, die im Jargon der Aktivist∗innen „Kletter-Cops" genannt werden. Da Höheninterventionsteams nur begrenzt zur Verfügung stehen, so kalkulierten die Besetzer∗innen, wird der Räumungseinsatz in die Länge gezogen. Der Zeitgewinn kann für Solidaritätsdemonstrationen genutzt werden – oder dafür, durch die Medienberichterstattung über eine lange und sehr wahrscheinlich konfliktreiche Räumung einen Meinungsumschwung zu erreichen (→ *Demonstration*, → *Medien*). Oft, das zeigen viele Beispiele, solidarisieren sich bei gewaltvollen Polizeieinsätzen viele bisher Unbeteiligte und eine Protestbewegung vergrößert sich (→ *Solidaritätsgeste*, → *Gewalt*).

Auffällig ist, dass es zwar verschiedene, dicht gedrängte Siedlungsbereiche für Baumhäuser und Bodenstrukturen in Lützerath gab (etwa die „Reihenhaussiedlung", „Fantasialand" auf „Kurts Wiese" oder das „Wäldchen"), diese aber, so der Eindruck bei zwei Besuchen im Mai 2022 und Januar 2023, im Vergleich zu den → *Barrios* im Hambacher Wald einen weniger starken inneren Zusammenhalt haben. Viele der Bodenstrukturen wirkten im Januar 2023 – zwei Tage vor dem angekündigten Räumungstermin – gar nicht dauerhaft bewohnt, sondern wurden offenbar mit dem Ziel errichtet, sie erst im Falle der Räumung zu beziehen. Diese Vermutung stützt sich auf die Beobachtung, dass an einigen Bauten Formulare hingen, auf denen abgefragt wurde, ob sich dort jemand dauerhaft aufhalte und wie hoch die maximalen Kapazitäten zur Unterbringung waren.

Die Vielzahl der augenscheinlich für den Bedarfsfall auf Vorrat (so die These) errichteten Verzögerungsarchitekturen hängt wohl auch damit zusammen, dass viele Besetzer∗innen bis zur Räumung in den zahlreichen Bestandsbauten in Lützerath unterkommen konnten. Neben „Eckardts Hof" gab es noch „Paulas Hof", die „Villa", „Die wilde 8"

(ein „U40-Bereich – Safe Space für junge Menschen") sowie mit Stroh gefüllte Scheunen (Helten, Wertgen 2022).

Der Außenbereich war in Zonen mit jeweils speziellen Gebäuden gegliedert: Auf einer Wiese stand der etwa 15 Meter hohe Tower (→ *Turm*), das höchste Gebäude von Lützerath, unter dessen weit aufgespannten Planen Plenumssitzungen stattfanden. Neben dem Tower entstand die Fahrradwerkstatt, das „brennende Jobcenter" (eine Art Info-Pavillon), ein Zelt mit Klavier sowie mehrere Bodenstrukturen als Kleinstwohnbauten. Die Küfa (Küche für alle) befand sich in den großen Blechscheunen. Eine andere Scheune diente als Atelier oder als Skatehalle, die auch für Klettertrainings genutzt wurde.

Wichtiger Anlaufpunkt und rechtlich abgesicherter Anker war die „Mahnwache", ein Wohnwagen an der Straße, die zwischen Lützerath und der Hangkante des Tagebaus lag. Eine Bauaufnahme der RWTH Aachen (Helten, Wertgen 2022) aus dem Oktober 2022 verzeichnet zusätzlich zu den 29 Baumhäusern und 11 Bodenstrukturen noch eine Vielzahl von Kleinarchitekturen: First Aid Zelt, „Awareness Kiosk", Badezimmer, Müll-Station, COVID-Room, Corona-Testcenter, „Hock-Piss-Klo", Gemeinschaftswaschbecken.

Im Januar 2023 war eine Reihe weiterer Bauten hinzugekommen. Am Sonntag, den 8. Januar, fand der zweite Besuch des Teams der *Protest/Architektur*-Ausstellung in Lützerath statt. Diesmal ging es darum, in Gesprächen mit Aktivist∗innen zu klären, unter welchen Umständen eine Bodenstruktur namens „Rotkœlchen" als Exponat für die Ausstellung gerettet werden könnte. An diesem Tag, knapp 48 Stunden bevor mit der Räumung zu rechnen war, prägte die Errichtung von → *Barrikaden* und → *Tripods* die Eindrücke. Lützerath wurde quasi von innen nach außen gestülpt, indem überall die befestigten Wege zwischen den Höfen entpflastert und aus den Beton-Knochensteinen (Doppel-T-Verbundpflaster) barrikadenartige Befestigungen aufgetürmt wurden. Die bestehenden → *Traversen*, also Brücken aus Kletterseilen (→ *Seile*), wurden durch mehrere Tripods ergänzt, in denen sich jeweils Menschen einhängen konnten. Es wäre möglich gewesen, von Tripod zu Tripod zu gelangen, ohne den Boden zu berühren.

■ Gemeinschaftsbauten (Community buildings)
■ Individuelle Unterkünfte (Individual shelters)
■ Barrikade (Barricade)
  Angeeignetes Gebäude (Appropriated building)

Lützerath, Januar 2023. 1 Mahnwache 2 Tower 3 „Reihenhaussiedlung" 4 Fantasialand 5 Rotkœlchen 6 Wäldchen 7 Zeltwiese (Lützerath, January 2023. 1 Protest vigil 2 Tower 3 "Terraced house settlement" 4 Fantasy Land 5 Rotkœlchen 6 Little forest 7 Tent meadow)

Die Polizei hatte unterdessen ein effektives System von Straßen und Aufstellflächen rund um das Dorf geschaffen, um mit Einsatz- und Räumungsfahrzeugen zügig anrücken zu können: eine geschotterte Polizei-Ringstraße zur Einkreisung von Lützerath.

Die Räumung fand unter großer medialer Aufmerksamkeit statt. Die Anzahl der Live-Reportagen, Features und Sonderberichte dürfte das mediale Echo der Räumungsaktion im Hambacher Wald übertroffen haben. Der Polizeieinsatz selbst kann an dieser Stelle nur aus der Distanzperspektive intensiver Mediennutzung wiedergegeben werden. Bei aller Vorsicht, aus einer bequemen Warte zu Urteilen zu gelangen, sei doch festgestellt, was auch durch Auskünfte von Aktivist∗innen bestätigt wird: Die Räumung konnte viel zu schnell abgeschlossen werden. Sie begann am Dienstagmorgen und war am Samstag weitgehend beendet. Die diversen Verzögerungsstrategien hatten sich angesichts des großen Polizeiaufgebots als relativ uneffektiv erwiesen. Ein erst während der Räumung entdeckter → *Tunnel*, aus dem sich die beiden Aktivist∗innen Pinky und Brain per Video meldeten, sorgte für den längsten Aufschub.

Als die Räumung begann, startete der Versuch, das Rotkœlchen zu retten. Die Bodenstruktur stand in Fantasialand, hatte eine Grundfläche von ca. 6 Quadratmetern und eine Höhe von ca. 5 Metern. Zwischen den Aktivist∗innen und dem DAM war ein Leihvertrag geschlossen worden, der erst dann gegenüber der Polizei zum Einsatz gebracht werden sollte, wenn die Besetzer∗innen bereit für die Übergabe sind. Am Rotkœlchen wurde ein Denkmalschild angebracht, mit einer Handynummer und der Bitte an die Polizei, das DAM zu verständigen.

Am Mittwochnachmittag, 11. Januar, klingelte im Architekturmuseum das Telefon: Die Polizei sei jetzt im Fantasialand, meinte ein Aktivist, unser Leihvertrag könnte die Räumung verzögern. Also wird ein Amtshilfeersuchen per Telefax an die zuständige Polizei in Aachen abgeschickt. Am Donnerstag bekommt der Polizeipräsident von Aachen das Amtshilfeersuchen vorgelegt, der daraufhin meint: „Wollen die mich verarschen?" (Eberle 2023). Es wird viel telefoniert: mit Aktivist∗innen, die sich noch im Rotkœlchen aufhalten und mit einem freien Journalisten, der einen Kommunikationsbeamten der Polizei mit dem Museumsteam verbindet. Später ruft die Polizei zurück: Das Rotkœlchen sei jetzt leer, ein Absperrband zur Sicherung wolle man aber nicht anbringen, zuständig sei nun der Eigentümer, also der RWE-Konzern. Darauf ein Anruf bei der Leiterin der Konzernkommunikation, Stephanie Schunck, die kein Interesse zeigt, sich für den Erhalt der Bodenstruktur zu engagieren. Am Freitagnachmittag schreibt der Leiter der RWE-Rechtsabteilung, Elmar Schweers, er könne „zum derzeitigen Zeitpunkt weder nachvollziehen, mit wem Sie einen etwaigen Leihvertrag am vergangenen Sonntag haben abschließen können, noch, ob die jeweiligen Personen berechtigt waren, über die von Ihnen beschriebene Behausung zu verfügen." Zu diesem Zeitpunkt stand das Rotkœlchen noch unversehrt auf der Wiese, versichern Journalist∗innen vor Ort. Andere Bodenstrukturen hingegen wurden teils durch die Polizei, teils durch RWE sofort zerstört.

Damit war die Rotkœlchen-Aktion eigentlich gescheitert. Am Samstagnachmittag klingelt jedoch wieder das Telefon. Eine Gruppe aus dem Umfeld des Towers, der zu diesem Zeitpunkt noch besetzt ist, meldet sich: Ob das DAM vielleicht versuchen könnte, den Tower zu retten? Dieser ist zwar wegen seiner vielen Abspannungen bautechnisch sogar noch interessanter, würde aber in jeder Hinsicht jeden Rahmen sprengen: Für die Ausstellung in Frankfurt wäre er zu groß, zu kompliziert, zu teuer in der Handhabung. Die Verzweiflung in Lützerath ist groß, jeder Aufschub ist ein Strohhalm. Schließlich wird vereinbart, dass das DAM sich per Social Media an die Öffentlichkeit wendet und die Rettung von Rotkœlchen und Tower fordert. Stunden später sind beide zerstört, ein Video vom Abriss des Towers wird auf Twitter 1,2 Millionen Mal angeschaut (Laquer 2023). Am Montag läuft die Meldung über dpa: „Architekturmuseum wollte Hütte aus Lützerath für Ausstellung". DLF Kultur bittet zum Interview. Am Donnerstag, 19. Januar, mokiert sich der FAZ-Herausgeber Jürgen Kaube über die Rotkœlchen-Aktion: „Kulturgüter, hieß es, darf man nicht kaputt schlagen. Nur mit Erbsensuppe übergießen, müsste ergänzt werden, darf man sie schon" (Kaube 2023).

Am selben Tag gelingt es, diesmal mit Unterstützung der Polizei, in Frankfurt ein Relikt aus der → Besetzung des → Fechenheimer Waldes zu bergen: Die Spitze eines → Monopods wandert ins Museum. In den folgenden Monaten wird versucht, mit den Aktivist∗innen abzustimmen, wie ihr Protestgerät in der

Ausstellung gezeigt werden kann. Es soll nicht der Eindruck entstehen, dass das DAM nun eine Art Trophäe zeigen oder sich ohne Anerkennung der unendlich mühevollen Besetzungsarbeit auf relativ einfache Weise mit einem Objekt schmücken kann, das in einem Museum notwendigerweise aus dem Zusammenhang seiner Entstehung herausgerissen wird.

In einer E-Mail schildert Morsch, einer der Besetzer des Rotkœlchens, seine Geschichte:

Am Donnerstagmorgen kam ein Kommunikations-Cop auf uns zu und wollte mit uns reden. Der Cop wollte wissen, ob die Struktur, auf der wir saßen, das Rotkœlchen ist. Wir haben ihn dann auf das Schild und den Kontakt hingewiesen und er meinte es sähe danach aus, dass das Rotkœlchen stehen bleiben könnte. Was soll ich sagen, eine halbe Stunde später haben sie uns die Tür eingetreten und mit Brechstangen die hintere Fassade gelöst. Wir waren natürlich längst über dem 2,50 m bzw. im oberen Stockwerk und hatten die Klappe dazwischen vernagelt.

Wir haben immer wieder auf das Schild im Fenster und die Aussage des Kommunikations-Cops hingewiesen, aber stur wurde weiter abgerissen. Ein Cop sagte, als er das Schild dann doch mal anguckte, dass Kunst ja Ansichtssache wäre. Kommunikation wie mit einer Wand. Irgendwann war es denen dann offensichtlich genug und sie haben unsere Sachen im unteren Stockwerk durchwühlt und Teile mitgenommen. Aber immerhin die Struktur nicht weiter angegriffen.

Abends haben wir dann die Segel gestrichen. Als Bedingung fürs freiwillige Absteigen haben wir verlangt, nochmal mit den Kommunikations-Cops sprechen zu können. Diese zu besorgen hat bestimmt eine Stunde gedauert. Als sie dann da waren, wurde uns gesagt, dass die E-Mail bzw. dein Kontakt als Fake entlarvt wurde und niemand wüsste, welcher Kommunikations-Cop mit uns morgens gesprochen hätte. Daraufhin hab' ich die Visitenkarte [des DAM] weitergegeben, und ich denke, ihr habt dann telefoniert. Auf jeden Fall ging das ziemlich lange hin und her, und einige Menschen wurden angerufen. Das Ganze wurde auch von einem solidarischen Presse-Menschen begleitet und unterstützt. Am Ende hieß es, RWE sei in der Verantwortung, aber dass es gut aussehe für das Rotkælchen. Dann sind wir gegangen.

Um weitere Stimmen aus Lützerath wiederzugeben, wurden Annika Reiß und Aron Boks zu kurzen Texten eingeladen, die sich für eine *taz*-Kolumne zwei Wochen im Protestcamp aufhielten und täglich von dort berichtet haben. Zuerst schreibt Annika Reiß, Journalistin und Klimaaktivistin:

Wie besetzt man ein Dorf? Ein ganzes Dorf mit Häusern, Straßen, Scheunen und Äckern? Ich bin langjährige Klimaaktivistin und berichtete aus der Besetzung Lützeraths als Journalistin. Beide Rollen haben gemein, sich sehr detailliert mit der Umgebung auseinanderzusetzen, entweder um über sie berichten zu können oder um einen erfolgreichen Protest zu organisieren. Waldbesetzungen habe ich in den letzten Jahren viele erlebt und einige der zentralen Elemente dieser Besetzungen – besetzte Plattformen, Baumhäuser, Barrios (kleine „Dörfer" mit ein paar besetzten Strukturen) und →Banner, die immer und überall an diesen und weitere Proteste erinnern – waren auch in Lützerath zu finden. Die Baumhäuser, die in einer Höhe von fünf bis zehn Metern gebaut wurden, haben für mich einen Konflikt illustriert, der in Lützerath oft auftrat. Sie stehen für manche Menschen in erster Linie für ein bestimmtes Lebensgefühl. Die Vorstellung, auf kleinem Raum in der Höhe zu leben, wirkt auf den ersten Blick wie ein cooler Ausdruck von Freiheit und vom Abwenden von gesellschaftlichen Konventionen, was dazu einlädt, es zu romantisieren. Klar, ich wünschte mir auch, dass das die ganze Wahrheit wäre. Dabei ist die Besetzung einer Struktur in der Höhe ein zentrales Element des Protests. Sie ist schwierig zu räumen und bedarf rein rechtlich viel mehr Sicherheitsvorkehrungen als eine Räumung am Boden. In Wirklichkeit hat das nichts mit Romantik zutun.

Die kleinen Hüttenansammlungen auf Äckern und Wiesen in Lützerath waren fast alle viele Meter in die Höhe gebaut. Während der Räumung harrten Menschen auf Dächern, an Traversen und auf Plattformen in den riesigen Hangars und Scheunen aus. Im Regen. Stundenlang.

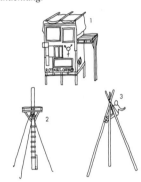

Lützerath. 1 Rotkælchen, Pfahlbau 2 Monopod 3 Tripod (Lützerath. 1 Rotkælchen, pile dwelling 2 Monopod 3 Tripod)

Es ist leicht zu vergessen, welch strategisch wichtige Rolle es spielt, wie und wo man baut, wie man das sehr begrenzte →Baumaterial nutzt, das für eine Besetzung zur Verfügung steht. Es ist wichtig zu betonen, dass das Leben bei einer Besetzung nicht ausschließlich aufregend und lustig ist und dass wir als Besetzer*innen nicht einfach nur unser inneres Kind ausleben. Das ist der Konflikt. Wir müssen rational vorgehen und befinden uns in einer ernsten, manchmal sogar gefährlichen Situation. Warum sonst schlug mein Herz so stark, dass ich dachte es muss jemand hören, als ich das Dorf – an zwanzig Polizeitransportern, Polizeipferden und Räumpanzern vorbei – zum letzten Mal verließ.

Aron Boks, Journalist und Autor, blieb noch einige Stunden länger:

Ich weiß nicht, ob Sie vorhaben, bald mal ein Haus zu besetzen (→Hausbesetzung), aber ich möchte Ihnen von

287

einem Erlebnis erzählen. Über zwei Wochen habe ich mit Klimaaktivist∗innen in einem Haus in einem besetzten Dorf gelebt. Ich habe dort in Zivil für eine Zeitung Tagebuch geschrieben, weil mich vor allem dieses aufregende Leben dort interessierte. Besetzungen kannte ich nur aus Jörg Fausers Gedichten oder Ton-Steine-Scherben-Songs (→ Musik). Es war alles weniger romantisch. Aber etwas, das in dem Haus daran erinnerte, war ein obligatorisches Zitat an einer Wand im Badezimmer: „Das ist unser Haus". Einer von tausend Sprüchen, der sich mit anderen Kurzmitteilungen wie „Ich liebe es, wie Lützi lebt" oder Dringlichkeiten wie „Räumt auf ihr Arschkrampen!" an allen Ecken des besetzten Bauernhauses zu einem riesigen Notizbuch verwebte.

Und jeden Morgen habe ich darüber nachgedacht, ob ich diese Wand auch mit einem Spruch versehen sollte und es auf später verschoben. Es fühlte sich seltsam an. Vielleicht weil die Wand doch eh zerstört würde, dachte ich dann und fühlte mich einmal mehr als Gast. So lief das auch am letzten Morgen vor der Räumung ab. Dann ging ein Alarm los und wenig später sah ich am besetzten Haus schwarz gekleidete Leute mit Helmen und Schilden auf andere schwarz gekleidete Leute einknüppeln. Ich sah Steine, Flaschen und noch mehr Knüppelschläge und was weiß ich noch alles – eigentlich habe ich das nur aus dem Augenwinkel beobachten können, da ich vor lauter Angst keine einzige Sekunde das Haus verteidigen wollte und einfach weggerannt bin. Zuflucht fand ich in einer Holzhütte bei einer Gruppe, deren krassestes „Aktionslevel" darin bestand, sich hinzusetzen und ein Protestlied auf die Melodie von „Hejo, spann den Wagen an" zu singen. Ein paar Stunden später hat mich ein Polizist aus dem Dorf gezerrt. Keine Ahnung, was mit diesen Sätzen an den Wänden passiert ist.

Ich weiß zwar nicht viel über Besetzungen, aber zumindest, dass die Dinge dort anders laufen als in der Welt drumherum. Ein leerstehendes Haus wird zum Protestobjekt, eine Wand zeitgleich Poesiealbum, Notizheft, schwarzes Brett und zu etwas, das mit allen Menschen im Haus spricht. Mit denen, die es bewohnen und denen, die es zerstören.

Wenn Sie also vorhaben, bald mal ein Haus zu besetzen, rate ich Ihnen immer einen Edding dabei zu haben. Allein weil man dann etwas alltagsungewöhnliches machen kann – Wände beschmieren, obwohl Sie Gast sind. Weil gleichzeitig niemand Gast ist. (Beiträge von Morsch, Annika Reiß, Aron Boks; Text und Recherche: OE)

Lützerath, Ger. → Lützerath. After the last remaining part of → Hambach Forest could be spared from clearing due to the protests of climate activists, a new → protest camp developed in Lützerath. Located around forty kilometers from the Hambach open-pit mine, Lützerath is one of a series of villages slated for demolition in order to expand lignite mining at the Garzweiler II site—before coal-fired power generation is to be phased out in Germany by 2038.

Couldn't the → blockade of an open-pit mine extension, which had led to success in "Hambi" after years of conflict, succeed a second time in Lützerath? The starting point of the protest camp, which existed between the summer of → 2020 and January 2023, was the farm of Eckardt Heukamp, with its annexes and neighboring buildings, the last of which were located only about 200 meters from the edge of the slope of the Garzweiler II open-pit mine. Heukamp, the last resident of Lützerath who did not want to sell to RWE, was threatened with expropriation. He allowed the climate activists to set up their camp on his property. As a further protest strategy, he sold a meadow to the tax consultant Kurt Claßen, who is also the landowner of the "Meadow Camp" at Hambach Forest, in the hope that this would create another legal hurdle for the → destruction of Lützerath.

The protest camp at Lützerath is characterized by its combination of → tree houses and ground-based structures. Since the space in Lützerath was limited and nearly all the suitable trees

Martin Junkermann: Tagebaugrube und Protestcamp kurz vor der Räumung (Open-pit mine and protest camp shortly before eviction), 4. Januar 2023

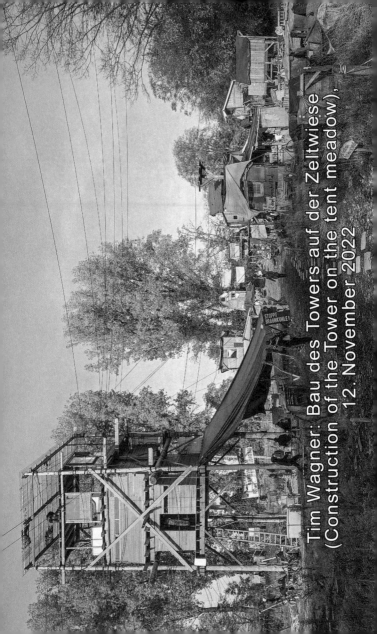

Tim Wagner: Bau des Towers auf der Zeltwiese
(Construction of the Tower on the tent meadow),
12. November 2022

Tim Wagner: Infopoint, 2. November 2021

Tim Wagner: Dreigeteilter Turm, von oben nach unten: „Kobel", „Mittelschicht" und „Pöbel" (Tower divided into three sections, from top to bottom: "shack," "middle class," and "rabble"), 3. April 2022

Oliver Elser: „Schloss" ("Castle"),
30. Mai 2022

Anna-Maria Mayerhofer: „Chaos",
30. Mai 2022

Anna-Maria Mayerhofer:
„Rotkœlchen“, 30. Mai 2022

Thomas Victor: „Rotkœlchen" kurz vor der Räumung ("Rotkœlchen" shortly before eviction), 11. Januar 2023

Anna-Maria Mayerhofer: Zeltwiese mit Tower und „Reihenhaussiedlung" (Tent meadow with Tower and "terraced house settlement"), 8. Januar 2023

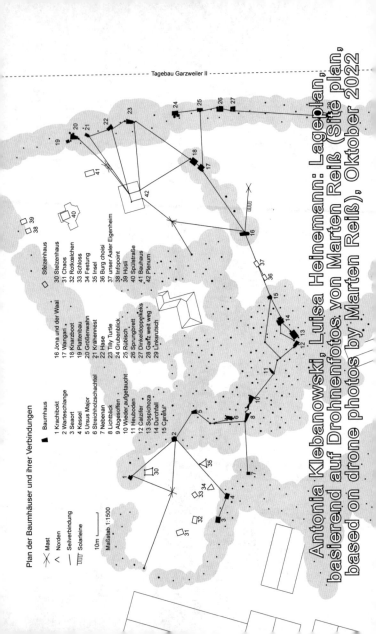

Plan der Baumhäuser und ihrer Verbindungen

◇ Stelzenhaus

✕ Norden
∧ Seilverbindung
— Seilverbindung
〰 Solarleine

■ Baumhaus

1 Krachlbolt
2 Warteschlange
3 Seaort
4 Kessel
5 Ursus Major
6 Streichholzschachtel
7 Nebenan
8 Lichtblick
9 Abgesoffen
10 Wiederaufgetaucht
11 Heuboden
12 Calzifer
13 Sospichoza
14 Durchfall
15 Cgräßul'

16 Jona und der Waal
17 Wangar'
18 Knarzboot
19 Plattenbau
20 Größenwahn
21 Krähennest
22 Hase
23 Tilly Turtle
24 Grubenblick
25 Rübisch
26 Sprungbrett
27 Dinkeldoppelkeks
28 Ganz weit weg
29 Linksrutsch

30 Stelzenhaus
31 Chaos
32 Rotkœlchen
33 Schloss
34 Festung
35 Insel
36 Burg choisi
37 unser Aaler Eigenheim
38 Infopoint
39 Hösli
40 Spülstraße
41 Bauhaus
42 Plenum

10m
Maßstab 1:1500

Tagebau Garzweiler II

Antonia Klebanowski, Luisa Heinemann: Lageplan, basierend auf Drohnenfotos von Marten Reiß (Site plan, based on drone photos by Marten Reiß), Oktober 2022

Tim Wagner: Barrio „Fantasialand" (Barrio „Fantasy Land"), 11. Januar 2023

David Klammer: Camp-Eingang mit Lock-on Device (Camp entrance with lock-on device), 11. Januar 2023

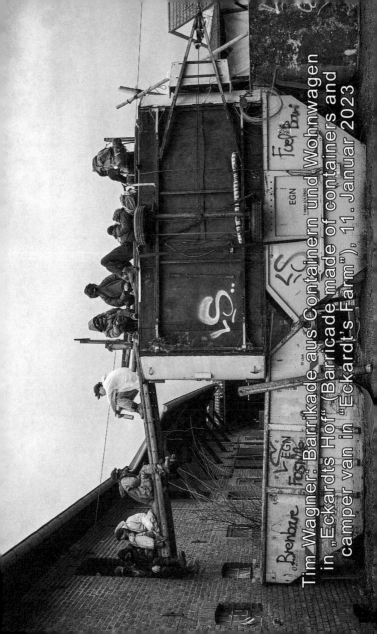
Tim Wagner: Barrikade aus Containern und Wohnwagen in „Eckardts Hof" (Barricade made of containers and camper van in "Eckardt's Farm"), 11. Januar 2023

David Klammer: Barrikade aus herausgelösten Pflastersteinen vor „Eckardts Hof", darüber eine Traverse (A traverse above a barricade made of repurposed cobblestones in front of "Eckardt's Farm"), 11. Januar 2023

Tim Wagner: Tripods und Monopods während der Räumung (Tripods and monopods during eviction), 11. Januar 2023

were quickly occupied by tree houses, a new → *building type* of "delaying architecture" was invented in the form of ground-based structures. These "tree houses without trees," standing on the ground but erected on stilts, were at least 2.5 meters high and had roofs that could be walked on, since for all eviction operations at a height of more than 2.5 meters, the → *police* have to call in special units known as "climbing cops" in the parlance of the activists. Due to the limited availability of these height intervention teams, this strategy is intended to draw out the eviction operation. The time gained through this can be used for solidarity demonstrations or for swaying public opinion through media coverage of a long and likely conflict-ridden eviction (→ *Demonstration*, → *Media*). Countless examples show that violent police interventions can spark feelings of solidarity in people who previously had no connection with a protest movement, helping the movement to grow (→ *Acts of solidarity*, → *Violence*).

It is striking that though there were various densely packed settlement areas for tree houses and ground-based structures in Lützerath (such as the "row house complex," "Fantasy Land" on "Kurt's Meadow," or the "Grove"), these have—according to the impression gained during two visits in May 2022 and January 2023—less internal cohesion than the → *barrios* in Hambach Forest. In January 2023, just two days before the announced eviction date, many of the structures on the ground did not appear to be permanently inhabited at all, but had evidently been built in order to be occupied only in the event of eviction. This assumption is based on the observation that some of the structures had sheets of paper stuck to them asking whether anyone was residing in them permanently and how many people they could accommodate.

The large amount of "delaying architecture" structures, which seemed to have been erected purely for the event of an eviction (according to the hypothesis), probably also had to do with the fact that prior to the eviction, many occupiers were able to find accommodation in the numerous existing buildings in Lützerath. In addition to "Eckardt's Farm," there was also "Paula's Farm," the "Villa," the "Wild 8" (an "area for people under forty—or safe space for young people"), and barns filled with bales of straw (Helten, Wertgen 2022).

The outdoor area was divided into zones, each with special buildings: on a meadow stood the approximately fifteen-meter-high tower (→ *Tower*), the tallest building in Lützerath, under whose vast tarpaulins plenary sessions were held. Next to the Tower, a bicycle workshop was set up, along with the "burning job center" (a kind of information pavilion), a tent with a piano, and several ground-based tiny houses for accommodation. The community kitchen was located in the large sheet-metal barns. Another barn served as a studio or as a skate hall, which was also used for climbing training.

An important contact and anchor point, which also enjoyed legal recognition, was the "protest vigil," comprised of a camper van parked on the road between Lützerath and the sloping edge of the open-pit mine. A construction survey by RWTH Aachen University (Helten and Wertgen 2022) from October 2022 records a variety of small-scale architecture in addition to the twenty-nine tree houses and eleven ground-based structures: a first aid tent, an "awareness kiosk," a bathroom, a garbage station, a COVID isolation room, a Corona test center, a "squat piss toilet," and a community washbasin.

In January 2023, a number of other buildings were added. On Sunday, January 8, the second visit by the team from the protest exhibition took place in Lützerath. This time the aim was to talk with activists to ascertain the circumstances under which a ground-based structure called "Rotkœlchen" could be saved as an exhibit for the show. On this day, barely forty-eight hours before the expected eviction, the scene was dominated by the action of erecting → *barricades* and → *tripods*. Lützerath was virtually turned inside out, with the paved paths between the farms being torn up to build barricade-like fortifications from interlocking concrete pavers. The existing → *traverses*, comprising bridges made of climbing ropes (→ *Ropes*), were supplemented by several tripods inside of which people could be suspended. Making it possible to move from tripod to tripod without touching the ground.

Meanwhile, the police had created an effective system of roads and staging areas around the village so that emergency and evacuation vehicles could move in quickly: a gravel police ring road enabling them to encircle Lützerath.

The eviction was accompanied by great media attention. The number of live reports, features, and special reports probably exceeded the media coverage of the eviction in Hambach Forest. The police operation itself can only be recounted here from the distant perspective of intensive media use. With all due caution in making judgments from the comfort of an external vantage point, what can nevertheless be noted—and was also confirmed by information from activists—is that the eviction was able to be completed far too quickly. It began on Tuesday morning and was largely over by Saturday. The various delaying strategies had proved relatively ineffective in the face of the large police contingent. A → *tunnel*, which was only discovered during the eviction and from which the two activists Pinky and Brain reported via video, caused the longest delay.

When the eviction began, the attempt to save the Rotkœlchen got underway. The ground-based structure was located in Fantasy Land, had a floor space of about six square meters and a height of around five meters. A loan agreement had been made between the activists and the DAM, which was not to be presented to the police until the occupants were ready for the handover. A provisional monument plaque was attached to the Rotkœlchen, with a cell phone number and a request for the police to contact the DAM.

On Wednesday afternoon, January 11,

the phone rang in the architecture museum: the police are now in Fantasy Land, an activist said, and that our loan agreement could delay the eviction. So a request for administrative assistance was sent by fax to the relevant police department in Aachen. On Thursday, the request for administrative assistance is presented to the chief of police of Aachen, whose response is: "Are they kidding me?" (Eberle 2023). A lot of phone calls are made: to activists who are still in the Rotkœlchen and to a freelance journalist who puts a police communications officer in touch with the museum team. Later, the police call back: the Rotkœlchen is now empty, but they do not want to secure it with police tape, adding that the owner—the RWE Group—is now responsible. This is followed by a call to the head of corporate communications at RWE, Stephanie Schunck, who shows no interest in getting involved in the preservation of the ground-based structure. On Friday afternoon, the head of RWE's legal department, Elmar Schweers, writes that he can "at the present moment neither comprehend with whom you were able to sign a possible loan agreement last Sunday, nor whether the persons in question were entitled to dispose of the dwelling you described." At that point, the Rotkœlchen was still standing in the meadow, unharmed, as journalists on site affirmed. Other structures on the ground, however, were immediately destroyed, partly by the police and partly by RWE.

In effect, this meant that the Rotkœlchen campaign had failed. On Saturday afternoon, however, the phone rang again. A group connected with the Tower, which at this point is still occupied, has a request: Could the DAM perhaps try to save the Tower? Although the Tower is even more interesting from a structural point of view due to its many guy wires, it would exceed the scope of the exhibition by any measure, being too large, too complicated, and too expensive to handle for the display in Frankfurt. The desperation in Lützerath is great, every delay of the eviction is a relief. Finally, an agreement is made that the DAM will reach out to the public via social media to call for the rescue of the Rotkælchen and the Tower. Hours later, both are destroyed; a video of the Tower's demolition is viewed 1.2 million times on Twitter (Laquer 2023). On Monday, the following headline appears on dpa: "Architecture museum wanted hut from Lützerath for exhibition." *DLF Kultur* asks for an interview. On Thursday, January 19, *FAZ* editor Jürgen Kaube mocks the Rotkælchen action: "Cultural assets, it was said, should not be demolished. Only dousing them with pea soup, it should be added, is allowed" (Kaube 2023).

On the same day, this time with the support of the police, a relic from the → *Fechenheim Forest* → *occupation* is recovered in Frankfurt: the tip of a monopod is sent to the museum. In the following months, attempts are made to discuss with the activists how their protest device can be shown in the exhibition. It was important to avoid the impression that the museum might be seeking to display the object as kind of trophy, divorcing the object from its original context to showcase it in a museum, without acknowledging the tireless work that went into the occupation.

In an email, one of the occupiers of the Rotkælchen called Morsch recounts his story:

On Thursday morning, a communications cop approached us and wanted to talk to us. The cop wanted to know if the structure we were sitting on was the Rotkælchen. We then pointed out the sign [the monument plaque] and the contact details to him and he said it looked like the Rotkælchen could be left standing. What can I say, half an hour later they kicked in our door and removed the rear facade with a crowbar. We had of course long been above 2.5 m, up on the upper floor, and had nailed up the hatch in between.

We kept pointing out the sign in the window and the statement of the communications cop, but they stubbornly continued to tear it down. When he finally did look at the sign, one cop said

that art is a matter of opinion. It was like talking to a brick wall. At some point, they had apparently had enough, and they rummaged through our stuff on the lower floor and took things with them. But at least they stopped attacking the structure.

In the evening, we bowed out. As a precondition for leaving voluntarily, we demanded to be able to speak to the communication cops again. It took about an hour to get them. When they arrived, we were told that the email or your contact details had been exposed as a fake and that nobody knew which communication cop had spoken to us in the morning. I then passed on the business card [from the DAM], and I think you guys then talked on the phone. Anyway, that went back and forth for quite a long time, and various people were called. The whole thing was also accompanied and supported by a sympathetic journalist. In the end, they said RWE was responsible, but that it looked good for the Rotkælchen. Then we left.

To present further voices from Lützerath, Annika Reiß and Aron Boks were invited to write short texts. They spent two weeks in the protest camp for a *taz* column and reported daily. First to write is Annika Reiß, journalist and climate activist:

How does one occupy a village? A whole village with houses, streets, barns, and fields? I am a long-time climate activist and reported on the occupation of Lützerath as a journalist. Both roles involve dealing with one's surroundings in great detail, either in order to report on them or to organize a successful protest. I have experienced many forest occupations in recent years. Some of the central elements of these occupations—occupied platforms, tree houses, barrios (small "villages" with a few occupied structures), and → banners that are always reminding people of this protest and other ones—were also present in Lützerath. The tree houses, built at a height of five to ten meters, illustrated for me a conflict that often occurred in Lützerath. For some people, they primarily represent a certain attitude toward life. At first glance, the idea of living up high in a small space seems like a cool expression of freedom and of rejecting social conventions, which encourages people to romanticize it. Sure, I wish that were the whole truth, too. Yet occupying a structure at a height is a central element of protest. It is difficult to clear and, from a purely legal standpoint, requires many more safety measures than an eviction on the ground. In reality, this has nothing to do with romance. The small clusters of huts in fields and meadows in Lützerath were almost all built many meters up. During the clearing, people persevered on roofs, traverses, and platforms in the huge hangars and barns. In the rain. For hours.

It is easy to forget the strategic role of how and where you build, how you use the very limited → building materials available for an occupation. It is important to emphasize that life in an occupation is not exclusively exciting and fun, and that as occupiers, we are not simply trying to live out our inner child. That is the conflict. We have to act rationally and we are in a serious, sometimes even dangerous situation. Why else was my heart beating so strongly that I thought people must have been able to hear it as I walked past twenty police vans, police horses, and armored evacuation vehicles and left the village for the last time?

Aron Boks, journalist and author, stayed a few hours more:

I don't know if you are planning to squat anytime soon (→ Squatting), but I would like to tell you about an experience. For more than two weeks, I lived with climate activists in a house in an occupied village. I lived as one of them and wrote a diary there for a newspaper, because I was especially interested in this exciting life there. I only knew occupations from Jörg Fauser's poems or songs by Ton Steine Scherben (→ Music). It was all less romantic. But something that called this to mind was an obligatory quote on a wall in the bathroom in Lützerath: "This is our house." One of a thousand slogans scribbled with other short messages, like "I love the way Lützi lives," or urgent pleas such as "tidy up, you nitwits!" pasted all over the occupied farmhouse, weaving it into a giant notebook.

Every morning I thought about whether I should also write a slogan on this wall, and always put it off till later. It felt strange. Maybe because the wall would be destroyed anyway, I thought, feeling like a guest once more. And that's how it was on the last morning before the eviction. Then an alarm went off and a little later I saw people dressed in black with helmets and shields clubbing other people dressed in black. I saw stones, bottles, more bludgeoning, and god knows what else—actually I could only watch this out of the corner of my eye, because out of sheer fear, I didn't want to defend the house for a single second, and just ran away. I found refuge in a wooden hut with a group whose most striking "action level" was to sit down and sing a protest song to the tune of "Hejo, spann den Wagen an" (Hey Ho, Nobody Home). A few hours later, a policeman dragged me out of the village. I don't know what happened to those sentences on the walls.

I don't know much about squatting, but at least I know that things are different there than in the surrounding world. A vacant house becomes an object of protest, a wall turns into a scrapbook, a notebook, a bulletin board, and something that speaks to all the people in the house—to those who inhabit it and those who demolish it.

So if you plan on occupying a house soon, I advise you to always carry a marker on you. Because then you can do something that's not so common in everyday life: scrawl something on the wall, even though you're a guest. Because at the same time, nobody's a guest. (Contributions by Morsch, Annika Reiß, Aron Boks; text and research: OE)

Madres de Plaza de Mayo, engl. → Madres de Plaza de Mayo. Die → Demonstration der Mütter von verschleppten Angehörigen ist ein Sonderfall der → Platzbesetzung. Sie dauerte zu Beginn, im Jahr → 1977, nur 30

Minuten und es wurden bei den ersten Versammlungen auf dem zentralen Platz von Buenos Aires keinerlei → *Banner* oder → *Protestschilder* mitgeführt. Demonstrationen waren von der argentinischen Militärdiktatur verboten worden. Die Mütter trugen als → *Erkennungszeichnen* lediglich weiße Kopftücher. Die türkischen → *Samstagsmütter (Cumartesi Anneleri)* haben ihren Protest und ihre Trauer angesichts ihrer verschleppten Angehörigen seit 1995 ebenfalls trotz erheblichen staatlichen Repressionen im Stadtraum sichtbar gemacht. (OE)

Madres de Plaza de Mayo, Ger. → *Madres de Plaza de Mayo*. The → *demonstration* by the mothers of kidnapped relatives on a prominent square in Buenos Aires is a special case of a → *public square occupation*. At the beginning, in → *1977*, it lasted for only thirty minutes, and at the first rallies, no → *banners* or → *protest placards* were carried. Demonstrations were forbidden under the Argentinian military regime. The mothers simply wore white scarves as → *identifiers*. The Turkish → *Saturday Mothers (Cumartesi Anneleri)* have conducted their protest similarly since 1995, expressing their mourning for their abducted relatives despite considerable state repression, thus rendering it visible in the urban space. (OE)

Mahnwache, engl. → *Protest vigil*; → *Hambacher Wald*, → *Lützerath*

Mai '68, engl. → *May '68*. Bereits zu Beginn der französischen Studierendenproteste spielte die Architektur eine wesentliche Rolle. Die Unzufriedenheit mit dem Neubau-Campus der Sorbonne in Nanterre, einem westlichen Vorort von Paris, war → *1968* einer der Auslöser für die Studierenden, sich zusammenzuschließen (Frei 2008/2018, S. 10) – was wiederum durch die Hochschulleitung zu unterdrücken versucht wurde. Eine Eskalationsspirale begann, andere Themen kamen hinzu. Die Proteste mündeten in Straßenschlachten und den Bau von → *Barrikaden*. Die Gewerkschaften und viele Anwohner*innen solidarisierten sich (→ *Solidaritätsgeste*). Frankreich geriet für einige Tage in eine Stimmung des revolutionären Umsturzes. Alles schien möglich. Flankiert von den bereits 1967 aufgeflammten Protesten in Berlin, Frankfurt am Main, an US-amerikanischen Universitäten und vielen anderen Orten wurde zum ersten Mal seit dem Ende des Zweiten Weltkriegs der Kapitalismus auf vielstimmige Weise infrage gestellt. (OE)

Maidan, Ger. → *Majdan*. In December → *2013*, an initially small number of protesters occupied the symbolic Maidan Nezalezhnosti (Independence Square) in Kyiv. Over the course of the following weeks, a broad protest movement led by groups of different political orientations evolved around a → *protest camp* with thousands of occupiers (→ *Public square occupation*).

The protests on Maidan and Russia's war against Ukraine are directly linked. A few days after the demonstrators forced Viktor Yanukovych's government to resign, Russia invaded the Crimean Peninsula. Hence many Ukrainians speak of a war that started in 2014 and has further escalated with the attacks on the rest of Ukrainian territory since February 2022. A lively culture of remembrance developed in the wake of the Maidan protests and was supported by many cultural initiatives and → *museums*. Consequently, this case study also explores the question of whether and how a dynamic event of this kind can be represented in an exhibition.

The political scientist Maryna Shevtsova, who refers to herself as an LGBTQI activist, provided her analysis of the Maidan protests:

On December 1, 2013, several hundred people gathered in Kyiv's main square—Maidan Nezalezhnosti (Maidan)—in response to the violent attacks that Ukrainian state security forces had inflicted on anti-government demonstrators in Maidan the night before. To show that their intentions were serious, demonstrators made it known that they would not leave the square until those responsible for the attacks were punished. Alongside this demand, a protest camp emerged that would remain at Maidan until August 9, 2014, more than eight months later, when Kyiv city officials demanded that it be dismantled. [...]

In the everyday speech of Ukrainians, the name "Maidan" has long been used to refer to the territory of Maidan Nezalezhnosti (Independence Square) in the centre of Kyiv. The square was given its current name after the fall of the USSR and with the independence of Ukraine, and it has been used for political collective action ever since. Only thirteen years after Ukraine gained its independence, in 2004 Maidan became a space of collective political agitation [the Orange Revolution]. [...] Demonstrators created a protest camp in central Kyiv, with plans to stay until the government re-ran the presidential elections. [...] In the years that followed, there were some attempts to call for new protests: these included, in April 2010, a "Maidan" against Kharkov's agreement, and, in November 2010, a "Fiscal Maidan." However, such attempts were insignificant in number and did not succeed. [...]

Maidan 2013/2014 started with a small group of student activists reacting to the news that President Yanukovych had withdrawn Ukraine's application to the European Union's Association Agreement. Acting spontaneously, a group of no more than 100 people organised a protest camp in Maidan Square. In establishing the camp, the organisers consciously avoided using any party-specific political symbols; instead, they called themselves "Euromaidan." [...] It was only after peaceful protesters were violently attacked by Ukrainian state security forces during the night of November 30, 2013 that participant numbers increased significantly. According to a poll conducted on December 7, 2013, 70 percent of participants came to Maidan because they were outraged by the violence against protesters, while only 53.5 percent expressed aspirations for Ukraine to join the EU. [...]

Many small private companies and big businesses started to support Maidan, providing money or material resources, food, clothes and medical supplies. [...] Smartphones and widely available internet enabled protesters to communi-cate and share ideas at very low cost. [...] Social media networks were used to mobilise people and to provide the protest camp with material resources. Various online groups were created, such as "Maidan SOS," where volunteers constantly updated lists of desired donations such as food items, clothes and medicines. [...]

A large number of people came during the day for political discussions, while a smaller group of permanent inhabitants maintained the camp. Several protesters joined only for the evenings, after work. At night, the number of people in the camp was significantly smaller, but the participants ensured that there was always someone around for security reasons. While infrastructure networks provided the protesters with their basic needs (heating generators, medicines, food, warm clothes and so on), a number of participants [...] also engaged in the organization of cultural events and public educational programmes. [...] The common concern of the camps' participants was not only to create a home place for the protesters but also to refute negative arguments made by the camps' opponents and to prevent disreputable portrayals in the media. "Housekeeping"—that is, taking care of garbage in the camp and organising cleaning teams—was a crucial task for the protesters. There was also a strict "no alcohol" rule. [...]

The escalation of antagonism between the government and protesters eventually led to armed conflict. Maidan inhabitants' perception of the space changed significantly during the process. [...] When the state attempted to dissolve the camp at Maidan in February 2014 using special security forces, the residents responded by transforming it into an improvised fortress and calling it "Sich." The word Sich refers to a fortified Cossack settlement: a form of self-governed semi-military community that existed in the territory of modern Ukraine and Russia between the 16th and the 18th century. The Sich played an important role in the historical and cultural development of Ukraine and became a sym-

Maidan / Case Study

bol of freedom and independence. As it was winter, people built barricades from stones extracted from the square's pavements, tyres and other available objects and covered them with freezing water. In a constant state of alert, residents created a governance structure inside the camp to oversee the camp's defence. Special groups called Sotnyas were formed, inspired by the Cossacks' detachments. [...]

Many [protesters] referred to the importance of being part of the decision-making process at the camp and were very excited talking about Viche; this is an old Slavic term referring to a general assembly of citizens in ancient and mediaeval Kievan Rus' who gathered to discuss common issues and take political decisions. Viche constituted one of the first forms of direct democracy in the Slavic states. From December 22, 2013, thousands of protesters gathered every Sunday around the stage installed in the middle of the square in a modern version of the Viche. At the start of such gatherings, participants sang the Ukrainian national anthem. [...] Every speaker greeted the people in the square with "Slava Ukrayini!" (Glory to Ukraine), to which people would respond "Geroyam Slava!" (Glory to the heroes), a phrase borrowed from the early 20th-century Congress of Ukrainian Nationalists.

The participants' turn towards nationalist practices, however, created space for right-wing groups to become more visible in the protest camp. Since the members of those groups were mostly fit, well-trained men, their role in the defence of the camp was central and widely appreciated. Yet their presence had some negative implications. It resulted in the emergence of a critique of the "fascist nature" of the camp in the foreign press. [...]. Moreover, the presence of right-wing groups influenced the decision of activists belonging to minorities (in particular, feminist and LGBTI groups) to be more discreet about their identity. [...] While right-wing groups maintained a constant presence at Maidan, their role in

the camp and their importance to the protest were definitely exaggerated by foreign media. Research conducted at Maidan [...] shows that only 6 percent of protest actions at Maidan were instigated by "right-wing" groups. [...] (Shevtsova 2017)

Maidan is used as a blanket term for the specific site of the protest camp as well as the entirety of the protest actions, which went far beyond this area. Starting from the camp, the protesters made several attempts to gain access to the parliament building. The first fights with security personnel occurred at places relatively far away from Maidan. In late January, the situation escalated completely after the authorization of a new catalog of measures designed to suppress the protests. The protesters on Maidan, many of them with a military background, formed defense units, so-called "hundreds." When many of the Maidan protesters with military backgrounds formed battlefield units known as "hundreds," other groups also began to adopt this name, including groups committed solely to peaceful forms of resistance, such as the "Women's Hundred," which organized self-defense and first-aid courses, as well as lectures on feminism.

Days of street fights between the parliament building and Maidan led to the first causalities on the side of the protest movement in late January. In February, government forces advanced on the Maidan camp's → barricades, which the protesters had set on → fire in order to defend themselves. An adjacent building caught fire, probably through arson committed by the government forces. About 100 people died at the protests between December and February.

Together with the Ukrainian architect Sergey Ferley, the Swiss architects Leopold Banchini and Daniel Zamarbide documented the structures that developed during the occupation of Maidan. In 2014, the results from their "Maidan Survey" were shown at the Swiss Architecture Museum in Basel. Sergey Ferley, who, like many other residents of Kyiv, went to Maidan every day during the protests, recounted his impressions of the protest camp during a Zoom conversation in February 2023:

Initially the mood was like at a festival. There was → music, people talked. All my colleagues from the architecture firm I was working for at the time were there. We were full of hope and enjoyed being there. When big → demonstrations or concerts took place, hundreds of thousands of people came to the square. Besides Maidan, the protesters had also occupied several adjoining → streets and squares. In late January, large parts of Kyiv's government district were under "Maidan's control." Barricades had been set up at the borders of the occupied areas and confrontations with the police were an almost daily occurrence. One could sit by the fire in the safety of the protest camp and have a good time or go to the edges of the zones to carry tires, stack sandbags, and throw stones.

The cartographer Dmytro Vortman created precise maps of the "frontlines" of these street fights. During the height of the confrontations in mid-February, he updated them several times a day. When the police tried to evict Maidan, the character of the protest camp changed, and it became a fortress with elaborate defense tactics.

Spectacular barricades made from tires, plywood, reinforcing steel, paving stones, sandbags, and barbed wire were set up at the entrances. On cold days, water was poured over these constructions to further stabilize them with the resulting ice.

People travelled to Kyiv from all over Ukraine to take part in the protests. Many of them found accommodation in the buildings occupied by the protesters (→ Squatting), such as the Hotel Ukraine, the October Palace, and the building of the Kyiv City Council. The buildings around Maidan generally played an important role in the protests: this is where events and press conferences were held and the injured were treated. The Trade Unions House served as the headquarters of the protest until its → destruction through a fire started by police forces on February 18.

Some of the protesters lived in the over 200 tents and huts (→ Building types) set up on Maidan, often together with people from the same region or with similar political views. Besides camping tents and yurts, dark-green military tents equipped with furnaces and → kitchens dominated the scene. Inside the protest camp, barricades made from wooden pallets and tires offered further → protection for the tents and huts and divided the space into smaller zones (→ Settlement structure). Clusters of three to five buildings usually had a communal courtyard with a fireplace. A large stage in the middle of the square served as a meeting and assembly place. Communal kitchens supplied the protesters with warm meals. Tea and snacks were brought to the people working at the barricades and guarding the entrances at regular intervals. Many of those involved in the often very creative installation of the constructions had a military background or worked on building sites. Some welcomed the opportunity to build watchtowers (→ Tower), catapults, and potato cannons (→ Weapons). They'd make a quick sketch on a piece of paper or just jump right in.

Ihor Poshyvailo is the director of the Maidan Museum, a collection of over 4,000 objects and documents resulting from the Maidan Protests. In December 2013, when the movement became a mass event and Poshyvailo was still the deputy director of the Ivan Honchar Museum, the National Center of Folk Culture, he started to collect flyers, posters, photos, sound, and video material as well as objects such as → flags, shields, and helmets. In part, this idea was inspired by American musicologist Linda Norris's blog post, "If I ran a Museum in Kyiv, Right Now." Together with other people from the cultural sphere, Poshyvailo implemented her suggestions to open the doors of museums to protesters, to supply them with hot beverages, to offer places for reflection, and to start a collection of objects and photographs as well as an oral history project as soon as possible (Norris 2013).

In January 2014, the initiative "Maidan Museum" got to work. Two years later, the civilian group was transformed into a state project with the aim of developing a concept for a museum of remembrance, the "National Memorial to the Heavenly Hundred Heroes and Revolution of Dignity Museum." The museum's collection includes Molotov cocktails, painted tents, burned-out → *vehicles* as well as wooden catapults and parts of the metal frame of the "Yolka," Kyiv's Christmas tree that was decorated with protest banners and national flags in 2013.

At an international architecture competition for the Maidan Museum, the design by the Berlin architecture firm Kleihues + Kleihues won first prize. Construction was to start in autumn 2022 but had to be postponed due to the Russian invasion in February 2022. After the Russian attack, the collection was moved to a secret location for fear that it might be destroyed intentionally to erase pro-European remembrance. Since February 2022, Poshyvailo has been involved with HERI (Heritage Emergency Response Initiative), a grassroots organization he founded for the protection of museum collections and the documentation of lost cultural heritage. He also started a collection of objects from the war zones.

In February 2016, Poshyvailo spoke to Laura Weber during a project seminar at Berlin's Humboldt University. They discussed the establishment of the Maidan Museum and the challenges of "rapid response collecting," a collecting strategy first applied by London's Victoria and Albert Museum in 2014.

Laura Weber: You personally took all those helmets, shields, banners, etc. from the Maidan square, while they were still in use. How did people react when you tried to archive their ongoing protest? Isn't there a risk of "freezing" a protest movement by putting it in a museum? Were you confronted with resistance?

Ihor Poshyvailo: [...] Unlike official positions and collecting policies of many Ukrainian museums which were

quite "shy" [...], we started collecting objects and stories immediately, being well aware of the historical value of the events. [...] The people reacted in different ways but mostly with deep understanding and assistance. However, it took a lot of time and effort to approach the activists, to explain our mission and inspire confidence. Many items we simply took from the trash, saving them from destruction. Many objects were also given to us later [...] people saw our initiative and trusted us. In fact, there is no risk of "freezing" the protest movement by preserving its artefacts and putting them into a museum. It's impossible to freeze or imitate any movement at the museum, of course. And this is not our goal anyways. We focused our efforts on preserving some objects to later serve at the exhibitions, to help creating the contextual environment, to [...] keep memories and evoke emotions. [...]

LW: A shield on Maidan is used by the protester to protect his or her body [...]. In a museum its meaning changes dramatically. [...] Aren't you afraid of taking the authentic and genuine meaning from things by artificially reconstructing them in a new [...] [institutional] space?

IP: [...] The shields were given one more connotation by protesters. They didn't use them only to protect themselves (both physically and spiritually), but also to communicate messages. For this, we have a wonderful example in our collection—a plywood shield with a handwritten inscription, saying: "Mum, I will never let you be hurt. I'm here for our Ukraine and for our parents. I will not leave Maidan without victory...." [...] Hence, the exhibition will be rather people- and concept-centered than object-centered. And of course the context will be lavishly provided alongside the objects' authentic and genuine meaning so that the curators and visitors might rediscover and reinterpret them in the most inclusive ways possible. [...]

LW: In his recent lecture on "The Arts of Occupation" held at the Freie Universität of Berlin, W.J.T. Mitchell reflected on the transitional process protest objects undergo when put in a museum. Referring to the installation State Britain by Mark Wallinger displayed in Tate Britain in 2007, Mitchell concludes his talk with the question whether in the museum the political meaning of Brian Haw's occupation protest was destroyed. Transferring a revolution or a protest into the space of memory, which the museum certainly is, was a very discouraging thought to Mitchell. What can, in your understanding, be the protest objects' function in a museum?

IP: [...] It's true, the museums, which in this or that way depend upon the government or private groups, can easily change the political meaning of the exhibiting issues. As David Fleming from The Liverpool Museums argues in his work, all museums are political but not all of them publically admit this. We have similar fears that the government may take over this initiative and quickly and formally appropriate the Maidan Museum. But how objective would the exhibition, the programs, and the concept be in that way? Therefore, from the very beginning we wanted the communities and the protest activists to be engaged in the process as much as possible to advice, control and influence the process. We envision the Maidan Museum as a timeless and inclusive institution which will represent various points of view and be relevant both in form and content to various audiences and generations. (Weber 2016) (Texts by Maryna Shevtsova, Ihor Poshyvailo, Laura Weber; conversation with Sergey Ferley; introduction, research, and editing: AMM)

Majdan, engl. → *Maidan*. In Kyjiw besetzten im Dezember → *2013* zunächst wenige Protestierende den symbolträchtigen Majdan Nesaleschnosti („Platz der Unabhängigen"). In den folgenden Wochen entstand eine breite, von unterschiedlichen politischen Richtungen getragene Protestbewegung, deren Zentrum ein → *Protestcamp* mit tausenden Besetzer*innen bildete (→ *Platzbesetzung*).

Die Proteste auf dem Majdan und der Krieg Russlands gegen die Ukraine ste-

hen in einem direkten Zusammenhang. Wenige Tage nachdem die Demonstrierenden im Februar 2014 den Rücktritt der Regierung von Wiktor Janukowytsch erzwungen hatten, erfolgte die russische Invasion der Halbinsel Krim. Viele Ukrainer*innen sprechen daher von einem Krieg, der seit 2014 besteht und im Zuge dessen die Angriffe auf das übrige Territorium der Ukraine seit Februar 2022 als eine weitere Eskalationsstufe hinzugekommen sind. Infolge der Majdan-Proteste entstand eine lebendige Erinnerungskultur, die u.a. von vielen Kulturinitiativen und → *Museen* getragen wurde. Daher wird in dieser Case Study auch darauf eingegangen, ob und wie sich ein solches dynamisches Geschehen in einer Ausstellung repräsentieren lässt.

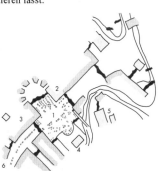

■ Barrikade (Barricade)
▨ Angeeignetes Gebäude (Appropriated building)

Majdan, Februar 2014. 1 Protestcamp, Majdan Nesaleschnosti 2 Haus der Gewerkschaften 3 Hauptpostamt 4 Hotel Ukraine 5 Oktober-Palast 6 Gebäude des Kyjiwer Stadtrates (Maidan, February 2014. 1 Protest camp, Maidan Nezalezhnosti 2 Trade unions building 3 Central Post Office 4 Hotel Ukraine 5 October Palace 6 Kyiv City Council building)

Die Politikwissenschaftlerin Maryna Shevtsova, die sich selbst als LGBTQI-Aktivistin bezeichnet, hat uns ihre Analyse der Majdan-Proteste zur Verfügung gestellt:

Majdan / Case Study

Am 1. Dezember 2013 versammelten sich mehrere hundert Menschen auf dem Hauptplatz von Kyjiw, dem Majdan Nesaleschnosti (Majdan). Sie reagierten damit auf die gewaltsamen Übergriffe der ukrainischen Sicherheitskräfte auf regierungskritische Demonstrant*innen, die sich dort in der Nacht zuvor abgespielt hatten. Um zu zeigen, dass sie es ernst meinten, erklärten die Demonstrant*innen, dass sie den Platz nicht verlassen würden, bis die für die Angriffe Verantwortlichen bestraft worden seien. Gleichzeitig entstand ein Protestcamp, das mehr als acht Monate auf dem Majdan verbleiben sollte, bis schließlich die Kyjiwer Stadtverwaltung am 9. August 2014 seine Auflösung verlangte. [...]

Im alltäglichen Sprachgebrauch der Ukrainer*innen wird der Name „Majdan" seit langem für das Gebiet des Majdan Nesaleschnosti (Unabhängigkeitsplatz) im Zentrum von Kyjiw verwendet. Seinen heutigen Namen erhielt der Platz nach dem Zusammenbruch der UdSSR infolge der Unabhängigkeit der Ukraine. Seither wird er für Demonstrationen und Kundgebungen genutzt. Nur 13 Jahre nach der Neugründung der Ukraine wurde der Majdan im Jahr 2004 zu einem Ort der kollektiven politischen Auseinandersetzung [der Orangenen Revolution]. [...] Die Demonstrant*innen errichteten bereits damals ein Camp im Zentrum Kyjiws, wo sie so lange bleiben wollten, bis die Regierung die Präsidentschaftswahlen wiederholen würde. [...] In den folgenden Jahren gab es einige Versuche, neue Protestbewegungen zu formieren: Im April 2010 wurde ein „Majdan" gegen das Abkommen von Charkow und im November 2010 ein „Fiskalischer Majdan" organisiert. Diese Versuche hatten jedoch nur wenig Zulauf und führten nicht zum Erfolg. [...]

Der Majdan 2013/2014 wurde von einer kleinen Gruppe studentischer Aktivist*innen ausgelöst. Sie kamen zusammen, weil Präsident Janukowytsch ein geplantes Assoziierungsabkommen mit der Europäischen Union zurückgenommen hatte. Spontan organisierte eine Gruppe von ca. 100 Personen ein Protestcamp auf dem Majdan-Platz. Bei der Errichtung des Camps verzichteten die Organisator*innen bewusst auf die Verwendung parteispezifischer politischer Symbole; stattdessen nannten sie sich „Euromajdan". [...] Erst nachdem die friedlichen Demonstrant*innen in der Nacht zum 30. November 2013 von ukrainischen Sicherheitskräften gewaltsam angegriffen wurden, stieg die Teilnehmer*innenzahl des Camps deutlich an. Laut einer am 7. Dezember 2013 durchgeführten Umfrage kamen 70 Prozent der Teilnehmer*innen zum Majdan, weil sie über die Gewalt gegen die Demonstrant*innen empört waren, während nur 53,5 Prozent den Wunsch nach einem EU-Beitritt der Ukraine äußerten. [...]

Viele kleine Privatunternehmen und einige große Firmen begannen, den Majdan zu unterstützen, indem sie Geld oder materielle Ressourcen, Lebensmittel, Kleidung und medizinische Versorgung zur Verfügung stellten. [...] Smartphones und die sehr gute Internetabdeckung ermöglichten es den Demonstrant*innen, auf einfache Weise zu kommunizieren und Ideen auszutauschen. [...] Social-Media-Kanäle wurden genutzt, um Menschen zu mobilisieren und das Protestcamp mit allem Nötigen zu versorgen. Es wurden verschiedene Online-Gruppen gegründet, wie z.B. „Majdan SOS", wo Freiwillige ständig Listen mit benötigten Spenden wie Lebensmitteln, Kleidung und Medikamenten aktualisierten. [...]

Tagsüber kamen zahlreiche Menschen zu politischen Diskussionen, während eine kleinere Gruppe von ständigen Bewohner*innen das Camp auch Nachts betreute. Einige Demonstrant*innen kamen nur abends nach der Arbeit hinzu. Nachts war die Zahl der Menschen im Lager deutlich geringer, aber die Teilnehmer*innen sorgten dafür, dass aus Sicherheitsgründen immer jemand vor Ort war. Während die infrastrukturellen Netzwerke die Demonstrant*innen hinsichtlich ihrer Grundbedürfnisse versorgten (Heizgeneratoren, Medikamente, Lebensmittel, warme Kleidung usw.), engagierten sich einige Teilnehmer*innen [...] auch für die Organisation von

Kulturveranstaltungen und öffentlichen Bildungsprogrammen. [...] Das gemeinsame Anliegen der Teilnehmer*innen des Camps bestand nicht nur darin, eine Heimat für die Demonstrant*innen zu schaffen, sondern auch darin, die Propaganda der Gegner*innen des Camps zu widerlegen und diskreditierenden Beiträgen in den Medien vorzubeugen. Das „Housekeeping", d.h. die Beseitigung des Mülls im Camp und die Organisation von Reinigungsteams, war eine wesentliche Aufgabe für die Besetzer*innen. Außerdem herrschte ein striktes Alkoholverbot. [...]

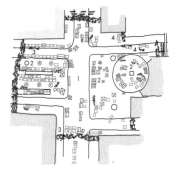

■ Gemeinschaftsbauten (Community buildings)

■ Individuelle Zelte und Hütten (Individual tents and huts)

■ Barrikade (Barricade)

Angeeignetes Gebäude (Appropriated building)

Majdan, Februar 2014. 1 Versammlungsplatz 2 Essensstand 3 Beobachtungsturm 4 Katapulte, Kartoffelkanonen, Rammböcke (Maidan, February 2014. 1 Assembly area 2 Food stand 3 Watchtower 4 Catapults, potato cannons, battering rams)

Die Eskalation zwischen der Regierung und den Protestierenden führte schließlich zu einem bewaffneten Konflikt. Die Inanspruchnahme des Majdan durch die Besetzer*innen änderte sich im Laufe des Prozesses erheblich. [...] Als der Staat im Februar 2014 versuchte, das Camp auf dem Majdan mithilfe von Spezialkräften aufzulösen, reagierten die Protestierenden darauf, indem sie

den Majdan in eine improvisierte Festung umwandelten und das Camp fortan „Sitsch" [ukrainisch: сiч] nannten. Das Wort „Sitsch" bezeichnet eine befestigte Kosakensiedlung, eine Form der selbstverwalteten semimilitärischen Gemeinschaft, die auf dem Gebiet der heutigen Ukraine und Russlands zwischen dem 16. und dem 18. Jahrhundert bestand. Die Kosaken spielten eine wichtige Rolle für die Geschichte und Kultur der Ukraine und wurden zu einem Symbol für Freiheit und Unabhängigkeit. [...] Da es Winter war, errichteten die Menschen [auf dem Majdan] vereiste Barrikaden. Die Pflastersteine der Gehwege sowie Reifen und anderer Müll wurden mit Wasser übergossen, woraufhin alles von einer Eisschicht zusammengebacken wurde. In ständiger Alarmbereitschaft schufen die Bewohner*innen innerhalb des Lagers eine Organisationsstruktur, um die Verteidigung des Camps zu überwachen. In Anlehnung an die Kosakenkommandos wurden spezielle Gruppen gebildet, die Sotnyas [Hundertschaften] genannt wurden. [...]

Viele [Demonstrant*innen] redeten davon, wie bedeutend es sei, Teil des Entscheidungsprozesses im Camp zu sein, und waren sehr enthusiastisch, als sie über die Vitsche sprachen. Vitsche ist ein alter slawischer Begriff, der sich auf eine Vollversammlung von Bürger*innen in der mittelalterlichen Kyjiwer Rus bezieht. Die Vitsche war eine der ersten Formen der direkten Demokratie in den slawischen Staaten. Seit dem 22. Dezember 2013 versammeln sich jeden Sonntag Tausende von Demonstrant*innen vor Ort auf der Bühne in der Mitte des Platzes, die eine moderne Version der Vitsche war. Zu Beginn dieser Versammlungen sangen die Teilnehmer*innen die ukrainische Nationalhymne. [...] Alle Redner*innen begrüßten die Menschen auf dem Platz mit „Slava Ukrayini!" („Ruhm der Ukraine!"), woraufhin die Menschen „Geroyam Slava!" („Ruhm den Helden!") antworteten, ein Ausruf, der vom Kongress der ukrainischen Nationalisten Anfang des zwanzigsten Jahrhunderts übernommen wurde.

Majdan / Case Study

Die Hinwendung der Teilnehmer∗innen zu nationalistischen Praktiken eröffnete jedoch auch rechten Gruppen den Raum, im Protestcamp sichtbarer zu werden. Da es sich bei den Mitgliedern dieser Gruppen zumeist um gut trainierte, erfahrene Männer handelte, spielten sie bei der Verteidigung des Camps eine zentrale Rolle und wurden allgemein geschätzt. Ihre Präsenz hatte jedoch auch einige negative Auswirkungen. Sie führte dazu, dass in der ausländischen Presse der „faschistische Charakter" des Camps angeprangert wurde. [...] Darüber hinaus beeinflusste die Präsenz rechter Gruppen die Entscheidung von Aktivist∗innen aus dem feministischen und LGBTI-Spektrum sich weniger offen zu zeigen. [...] Obwohl rechte Gruppen auf dem Majdan ständig präsent waren, wurde ihre Rolle im Camp und ihre Bedeutung für den Protest von den ausländischen Medien eindeutig übertrieben dargestellt. Die auf dem Majdan durchgeführten Untersuchungen [...] zeigten, dass nur 6 Prozent der Protestaktionen auf dem Majdan von „rechten" Gruppen initiiert wurden. [...] (Shevtsova 2017)

Der Begriff Majdan bezeichnet sowohl den konkreten Platzraum mit dem Protestcamp als auch die gesamten, weit darüber hinausgehenden Protestaktionen. Ausgehend vom Camp versuchten die Protestierenden mehrmals bis zum Parlament durchzudringen. Die Orte, an denen mit den Sicherheitskräften gekämpft wurde, waren zunächst relativ weit vom Majdan entfernt. Ende Januar eskalierte die Situation vollends, nachdem ein neuer Maßnahmenkatalog zur Unterdrückung der Proteste verabschiedet wurde. Als sich auf dem Majdan unter dem Namen der „Hundertschaften" viele Protestierende mit militärischem Hintergrund zu Verteidigungseinheiten zusammenschlossen, benannten sich infolgedessen auch solche Gruppen auf diese Weise, die sich ausschließlich dem friedlichen Widerstand verschrieben haben, etwa die „Frauenhundertschaft", die neben Selbstverteidigungs- und Erste-Hilfe-Kursen auch Vorlesungen über Feminismus organisierte.

Bei tagelangen Straßenschlachten zwischen Parlament und Majdan gab es Ende Januar die ersten Toten auf Seiten der Protestbewegung (→ *Gewalt*). Im Februar rückten die staatlichen Einheiten direkt an die → *Barrikaden* des Majdan-Camps vor, die zur Verteidigung angezündet wurden (→ *Feuer*). Ein angrenzendes Gebäude geriet in Brand, vermutlich durch staatliche Brandstiftung. Bei den Protesten starben zwischen Dezember und Februar etwa 100 Menschen.

Majdan. 1 Barrikade mit Überwachungsturm 2 Feuerstelle 3 Sofa und Tisch aus Paletten 4 Steilwandzelt 5 Steilwandzelt mit Ofen (Maidan. 1 Barricade with surveillance tower 2 Fireplace 3 Sofa and table made of pallets 4 Wall tent 5 Wall tent with oven)

Die Schweizer Architekten Leopold Banchini und Daniel Zamarbide dokumentierten gemeinsam mit dem ukrainischen Architekten Sergey Ferley die baulichen Strukturen, die während der Besetzung auf dem Majdan entstanden sind. Die Ergebnisse ihrer „Maidan Survey" wurden 2014 im Schweizerischen Architekturmuseum in Basel gezeigt. In einem Zoom-Gespräch im Februar 2023 berichtete Sergey Ferley, der ebenso wie viele andere Bewohner∗innen von Kyjiw während der Proteste jeden Tag zum Majdan fuhr, von seinen Eindrücken aus dem Protestcamp:

Am Anfang war die Stimmung wie bei einem Festival. Es gab → Musik, man unterhielt sich. Alle Kolleg∗innen aus dem Architekturbüro, in dem ich damals arbeitete, waren da. Wir waren sehr hoffnungsvoll und genossen es, uns dort aufzuhalten. Wenn große → Demonstrationen oder Konzerte stattfanden, waren hunderttausende Menschen auf dem Platz. Die Protestierenden hatten nicht nur den Maidan besetzt, sondern auch einige angrenzende → Straßen und Plätze. Ende Januar waren große Teile des Regierungsviertels von Kyjiw unter der Kontrolle des „Majdans". An den Grenzen der besetzten Gebiete gab es Barrikaden und es kam fast täglich zu Konfrontationen mit der → Polizei. Man konnte im Protestcamp, wo es sicher war, am Feuer sitzen und eine gute Zeit haben, zur gleichen Zeit konnte man an den Zonenrändern Reifen schleppen, Sandsäcke stapeln und Steine werfen.

Der Kartograf Dmytro Vortman fertigte von den „Frontverläufen" dieser Straßenkämpfe präzise Karten an. In der Hochphase der Auseinandersetzungen Mitte Februar aktualisierte er sie mehrmals täglich. Als dann die Polizei versuchte, die Besetzung auf dem Majdan zu räumen, veränderte sich auch der Charakter des Protestcamps und wurde zu einer Festung mit ausgefeilten Verteidigungstaktiken. Aus Autoreifen, Sperrholz, Bewehrungsstahl, → Pflastersteinen, Sandsäcken und Stacheldraht (→ Baumaterial) wurden an den Zugängen spektakuläre Barrikaden errichtet, die an kalten Tagen mit Wasser übergossen und durch das dabei entstehende Eis zusätzlich stabilisiert wurden.

Um an den Protesten teilzunehmen, reisten Menschen aus der gesamten Ukraine nach Kyjiw. Viele von ihnen kamen in den von Protestierenden besetzten Gebäuden unter (→ Hausbesetzung), etwa dem Hotel Ukraine, dem Oktober-Palast und dem Gebäude des Kyjiwer Stadtrates. Auch sonst spielten die Gebäude rund um den Majdan für die Proteste eine wichtige Rolle: Hier fanden Veranstaltungen und Pressekonferenzen statt; Verletzte wurden versorgt. Das Haus der → Gewerkschaften stellte bis zu seiner → Zerstörung durch einen von Polizeikräften verursachten Brand am 18. Februar eine Art Hauptquartier der Proteste dar.

Einige Protestierende wohnten zudem – häufig zusammen mit Menschen aus derselben Region oder mit ähnlicher politischer Gesinnung – in den über 200 → Zelten und Hütten (→ Bautypen), die auf dem Majdan errichtet wurden. Neben Campingzelten und Jurten handelte es sich dabei größtenteils um dunkelgrüne Militärzelte, die mit Heizöfen und → Küchen ausgestattet waren. Auch innerhalb des Protestcamps gab es Barrikaden aus Holzpaletten und Autoreifen, die den Zelten und Hütten zusätzlich → Schutz boten und dabei den Platz in kleinere Zonen unterteilten (→ Siedlungsstruktur). Cluster aus je drei bis fünf Bauten hatten meist einen gemeinsamen Vorplatz mit Feuerstelle. Eine große Bühne in der Mitte des Platzes war Treffpunkt und Versammlungsort. Gemeinschaftsküchen versorgten die Protestierenden mit warmen Mahlzeiten. Den Menschen, die an den Barrikaden arbeiteten und die Zugänge zum Platz überwachten, wurden regelmäßig Tee und kleine Gerichte vorbeigebracht. Viele, die beim Aufbau der oftmals mit großer Kreativität errichteten Bauten halfen, hatten militärische Erfahrung oder arbeiteten sonst auf Baustellen. Manche freuten sich über die Möglichkeit, Beobachtungstürme (→ Turm), Katapulte und Kartoffelkanonen (→ Waffen) bauen zu dürfen. Sie kritzelten eine schnelle Zeichnung auf ein Blatt Papier oder legten einfach los.

Ihor Poshyvailo ist der Direktor des Majdan-Museums, einer Sammlung von über 4000 Objekten und Dokumenten, die während der Majdan-Proteste entstanden sind. Als im Dezember 2013 die Bewegung Massencharakter annahm, begann er – damals als stellvertretender Direktor des Iwan-Hontschar-Museums, des Ukrainischen Zentrums für Volkskultur – Flugblätter, Poster, Foto-, Ton- und Videomaterial sowie Objekte wie → Fahnen, → Schutzschilde und Helme zu sammeln. Auslöser war u.a. das Blog-Posting „If I Ran a Museum in Kyiv, Right Now" der US-amerikanischen Museumswissenschaftlerin Linda Norris. Ihre Vorschläge, die Türen der Museen für Protestierende zu öffnen,

Oli Zitch: Militärzelte auf einer Zufahrtstraße zum Majdan (Military tents on an access road to Maidan), 15. Februar 2014

Lipefee: Jurten und Zelte zwischen Barrikaden aus Holz, Reifen und Eissäcken (Yurts and tents between barricades made of wood, tires, and ice bags), 2. Februar 2014

Sergei Supinsky: Mehrstufige Barrikade mit Flaggen und Weihnachtsdekoration (Multilayer barricade with flags and Christmas decorations), 3. Januar 2014

Oleksandr Burlaka: Barrikade aus mit Eis gefüllten Plastiksäcken (Barricade made of plastic bags filled with ice, 13. Dezember 2013

Oleksandr Burlaka: Barrikade aus Palettenholz und Sperrmüll (Barricade made of pallet wood and bulky waste), 11. Dezember 2013

Oleksandr Burlaka: Barrikade aus Autoreifen (Barricade made of car tires), 21. Februar 2014

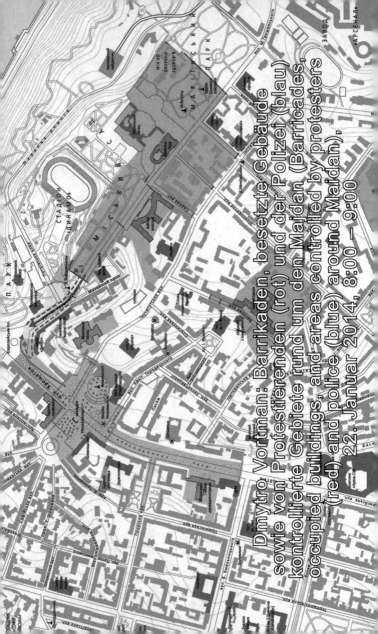

Dmytro Vortman: Barrikaden, besetzte Gebäude sowie von Protestierenden (rot) und der Polizei (blau) kontrollierte Gebiete rund um den Maidan (Barricades, occupied buildings, and areas controlled by protesters (red) and police (blue) around Maidan), 22. Januar 2014, 8:00 – 9:00

Айманна хикари. Polizeikette mit Schutzschilden, dahinter Zelte der Polizei (Police line with protective shields, police tents in the background), 12. Februar 2014

Oleksandr Burlaka: Straßenkämpfe
(Street fights), 19. Februar 2014

Oleksandr Burlaka: In Brand gesetzte Barrikaden auf dem Majdan (Burning barricades on Maidan), 19. Februar 2014

Ivan Bogdan: Ausgebrannte Fahrzeuge und verkohlte Barrikaden nach dem Ende der Proteste (Burned-out vehicles and charred barricades after the end of the protests), 23. Februar 2014

Perboge: Ausgebranntes Haus der Gewerkschaften
(Burned-out trade unions building), 15. Mai 2014

Raphaël Vinot: Barrikade auf dem gereinigten Platz, mehrere Monate nach den Protesten (Barricade on the cleaned-up square, several months after the protests), 8. Juni 2014

sie mit warmen Getränken zu versorgen, Orte zur Reflektion anzubieten sowie rasch mit dem Sammeln von Objekten, Fotografien und einem Oral-History-Projekt zu starten (Norris 2013), setzte Poshyvailo zusammen mit anderen Kulturschaffenden in die Tat um.

Im Januar 2014 nahm die Initiative „Majdan-Museum" ihre Arbeit auf. Zwei Jahre später wurde die zivilgesellschaftliche Gruppe in ein staatliches Projekt umgewandelt, um ein Konzept für ein Museum der Erinnerung zu erarbeiten mit dem Titel „Nationale Gedenkstätte der hundert himmlischen Helden und Heldinnen der Revolution der Würde". Zu den Objekten der Museumssammlung gehören neben Molotowcocktails, bemalten Zelten und ausgebrannten →Fahrzeugen hölzerne Katapulte sowie Teile des Metallgestells der „Yolka", des Weihnachtsbaums von Kyjiw, der 2013 mit Protestbannern und Nationalflaggen behängt wurde.

In einem internationalen Architekturwettbewerb für das Majdan-Museum wurde der Entwurf des Berliner Architekturbüros Kleihues + Kleihues mit einem ersten Preis ausgezeichnet. Der Baubeginn, der ab Herbst 2022 geplant war, musste nach der russischen Invasion im Februar 2022 verschoben werden. Die Sammlung befindet sich derzeit an einem geheimen Ort, da nach dem russischen Angriff befürchtet wurde, dass sie gezielt zerstört werden könnte, um die pro-europäische Erinnerung auszulöschen. Poshyvailo engagiert sich seit Februar 2022 bei der von ihm gegründeten Graswurzelorganisation HERI (Heritage Emergency Response Initiative), die sich dem Schutz von Museumssammlungen und der Dokumentation von Verlusten des kulturellen Erbes verschrieben hat. Er begann außerdem mit dem Aufbau einer Sammlung von Objekten aus den Kriegsgebieten.

Im Februar 2016 sprach Poshyvailo im Rahmen eines Projektseminars der Berliner Humboldt-Universität mit Laura Weber über den Aufbau des Majdan-Museums und die Herausforderungen des *Rapid Response Collecting*, eine 2014 erstmals vom Londoner Victoria and Albert Museum betriebene Sammlungsstrategie:

Laura Weber: Sie persönlich haben all diese Helme, Schilde, Transparente usw. vom Majdan-Platz mitgenommen, als sie noch in Gebrauch waren. Wie haben die Leute reagiert, als Sie versucht haben, ihren laufenden Protest zu „archivieren"? Besteht nicht die Gefahr, dass eine Protestbewegung „eingefroren" wird, wenn man sie in ein Museum stellt? Wurden Sie mit Vorbehalten konfrontiert?

*Ihor Poshyvailo: [...] Im Gegensatz zu den staatlichen Stellen und zu den ukrainischen Museen, die eine ziemlich „schüchterne" Sammlungspolitik hatten [...], begannen wir sofort mit dem Sammeln von Objekten und Geschichten, da wir uns des historischen Wertes der Ereignisse sehr bewusst waren. [...] Die Menschen reagierten auf unterschiedliche Weise, aber meist mit großem Verständnis und Unterstützung. Es hat jedoch viel Zeit und Mühe gekostet, auf die Aktivist*innen zuzugehen, ihnen unseren Auftrag zu erklären und Vertrauen zu schaffen. Viele Gegenstände haben wir einfach aus dem Müll geholt, um sie vor der Zerstörung zu bewahren. Viele Gegenstände wurden uns auch später noch geschenkt [...], denn die Menschen bemerkten unsere Initiative und vertrauten uns. Eigentlich besteht keine Gefahr, die Protestbewegung „einzufrieren", indem man ihre Artefakte konserviert und sie in ein Museum stellt. Es ist natürlich unmöglich, eine Bewegung im Museum zu konservieren oder zu imitieren. Und das ist auch gar nicht unser Ziel. Wir haben uns darauf konzentriert, einige Objekte zu bewahren, um sie später in den Ausstellungen zu zeigen, um das kontextuelle Umfeld zu schaffen, [...] um Erinnerungen zu bewahren und Emotionen zu wecken. [...]*

*LW: Ein Schutzschild auf dem Majdan wird von den Demonstrant*innen benutzt, um ihren Körper zu schützen [...]. In einem Museum ändert sich seine Bedeutung dramatisch. [...] Haben Sie nicht Angst, den Dingen ihre authentische und ursprüngliche Bedeutung zu nehmen, indem Sie sie in einem abge-*

schirmten Raum künstlich rekonstruieren?

IP: [...] Die Schilde wurden von den Demonstrant*innen mit einer weiteren Bedeutung versehen. Sie benutzten sie nicht nur, um sich zu schützen (sowohl physisch als auch geistig), sondern auch, um Botschaften zu vermitteln. Dafür haben wir ein wunderbares Beispiel in unserer Sammlung – ein Sperrholzschild mit einer handschriftlichen Inschrift, die lautet: „Mama, ich werde nie zulassen, dass man dir wehtut. Ich bin für unsere Ukraine und für unsere Eltern da. Ich werde den Majdan nicht ohne Sieg verlassen...". [...] Die Ausstellung wird also eher personen- und konzeptzentriert sein als objektzentriert. Und natürlich wird neben der authentischen und unverfälschten Bedeutung der Objekte auch der Kontext umfassend dargestellt, damit die Besucher*innen und andere Kurator*innen die Objekte auf möglichst umfassende Weise neu entdecken und interpretieren können. [...]

LW: In seinem kürzlich an der Freien Universität Berlin gehaltenen Vortrag über „The Arts of Occupation" reflektierte W.J.T. Mitchell über den Transformationsprozess, den Protestobjekte durchlaufen, wenn sie in ein Museum kommen. Unter Bezugnahme auf die Installation State Britain von Mark Wallinger, die 2007 in der Tate Britain gezeigt wurde, beendete Mitchell seinen Vortrag mit der Frage, ob im Museum die politische Bedeutung der Protestaktion von Brian Haw [der fast zehn Jahre lang auf dem Parliament Square in London ausharrte] zerstört wurde. Eine Revolution oder einen Protest in ein Depot für Erinnerungen zu übertragen, was das Museum ja zweifellos ist, war für Mitchell ein sehr entmutigender Gedanke. Welche Funktion können Ihrer Meinung nach die Protestobjekte in einem Museum haben?

IP: [...] Es stimmt, dass die Museen, die auf die eine oder andere Weise von der Regierung oder privaten Gruppen abhängig sind, die politische Bedeutung der ausgestellten Objekte leicht verfälschen können. Wie David Fleming von den Liverpool Museums argumentiert, sind alle Museen politisch, aber nicht alle geben dies öffentlich zu. Wir haben ähnliche Befürchtungen, dass die Regierung unsere Initiative übernehmen und sich das Majdan-Museum schnell und offiziell aneignen könnte. Aber wie objektiv wären die Ausstellung, die Programme und das Konzept in diesem Fall? Deshalb wollten wir von Anfang an, dass die verschiedenen Bevölkerungsgruppen und die Protestaktivist*innen so weit wie möglich in den Prozess einbezogen werden, um zu beraten, zu kontrollieren und zu beeinflussen. Wir stellen uns das Majdan-Museum als eine zeitgemäße und integrative Einrichtung vor, die verschiedene Standpunkte vertritt und sowohl in Form als auch Inhalt für verschiedene Zielgruppen und Generationen relevant ist. (Weber 2016) (Texte von Maryna Shevtsova, Ihor Poshyvailo, Laura Weber; Gesprächspartner: Sergey Ferley; Einleitung, Recherche und Zusammenfassung: AMM)

Maplewood Mudflats, engl. → *Maplewood Mudflats*. Ende der → *1960er* Jahre siedelte eine Gruppe auf einem 126 Hektar großen Gezeitengebiet im kanadischen Vancouver an. Sie lebten in selbstgebauten Hütten, im Einklang mit der Natur. Die → *Besetzung* hatte das Ziel, den Bau eines Jachthafens und andere städtische Entwicklungspläne zu verhindern, um das ökologisch bedeutende Gebiet und den vielfältigen Lebensraum zu schützen. Die Konstruktion der Hütten war schwebend auf Pfählen oder Holzplattformen, die sich mit dem Wasserstand des Wattenmeeres hoben und senkten. Im Dezember 1971 setzten Behörden die Hütten in Brand, das Hippie-Paradies wurde abrupt beendet (→ *Feuer*). (JD)

Maplewood Mudflats, Ger. → *Maplewood Mudflats*. In the late → *1960s*, a group settled on a 311-acre section of tidal flats in North Vancouver, Canada. They lived in self-built huts in harmony with nature. The purpose of the → *occupation* was to prevent the construction of a yacht harbor and other urban development plans. The huts were constructed to balance on piles or wooden plat-

Masterplan. Tim Wagner: Klimacamp im Rheinland, 24. August 2017 (Master plan. Tim Wagner: Camp for Climate Action in the Rhineland, August 24, 2017)

forms that rose and sank with the water levels of the tidal flats. In 1971, the authorities set → *fire* to the huts, thus putting an abrupt end to this hippie paradise. (JD)

March Revolution, Ger. → *Märzrevolution.* In March → *1848*, the revolutionary fire that had been sparked by the February Revolution in Paris also spread to other Central European countries. In the states of the German Confederation, the protests had a significant impact on the German freedom and national movement and were carried out behind → *barricades* in a range of cities between Berlin and Vienna. Hence many pictures of the barricade fighting feature the black, red, and gold national flags which the German Confederation's parliament had adopted on March 9, 1848 from the Vormärz (Pre-March) movements (→ *Flag*). (SH)

Märzrevolution, engl. → *March Revolution.* Im März → *1848* sprang der durch die → *Februarrevolution* in Paris entfachte revolutionäre Funke auf andere mitteleuropäische Länder über. Insbesondere in den Staaten des Deutschen Bundes bildeten die Proteste, die zwischen Berlin und Wien vielerorts auf den → *Barrikaden* ausgefochten wurden, wichtige Ereignisse der deutschen Freiheits- und Nationalbewegung. Entsprechend wurden auf den Bildern der Barrikadenkämpfe häufig die am 9. März 1848 im Bundestag des deutschen Bundes von den Bewegungen des Vormärz übernommenen schwarz-rot-goldenen Nationalflaggen in den Mittelpunkt gerückt (→ *Fahne*). (SH)

Mask, Ger. → *Maske*; → *Clothing*, → *Identifier*, → *Misappropriation*, → *Protection*

Maske, engl. → *Mask*; → *Erkennungszeichen*, → *Kleidung*, → *Schutz*, → *Zweckentfremdung*

Masterplan, engl. → *Master plan.* → *Protestcamps* entstehen häufig spontan, manchmal sind sie jedoch auch das Ergebnis von professioneller Planung. In Washington, DC, entwarfen vier Architekten für die → *Resurrection City* einen modernistischen Masterplan, der die Siedlung in Wohnviertel und eine Versorgungsachse einteilte (→ *Siedlungsstruktur*). Auch in vielen → *Klimacamps* gibt es von den Gemeinschaftsbereichen getrennte Zeltlager, wo Aktivist*innen zur Ruhe kommen können (→ *Zelt*). Im jährlichen „Klimacamp im Rheinland" sind weiße Steilwandzelte (→ *Bautypen*) mit → *Infrastrukturen* zur Versorgung ringförmig um die Versammlungszelte angeordnet, während Komposttoiletten

Mast

und Stellplätze entlang der Grundstücks-
grenzen aufgereiht sind. (AMM)

Master plan, Ger. → *Masterplan (fig.)*.
→ *Protest camps* often arise spontaneously, although sometimes they are
the result of professional planning. In
Washington, DC, four architects designed a modernist masterplan for
→ *Resurrection City*, dividing the settlement into residential areas and a
"supply axis" (→ *Settlement structure*).
In many of the → *Camps for Climate
Action*, there are tent zones set off from
the communal areas where activists
can rest. White wall tents (→ *Building
types*) with → *infrastructures* providing
utilities are arranged in a ring around
the assembly areas at the "Camp for
Climate Action in the Rhineland," while
compost toilets and tent spaces are located along the edges of the site. (AMM)

May '68, Ger. → *Mai '68*. Architecture
played a key role from the very beginning of the French student protests of
→ *1968*. The dissatisfaction with the
new Sorbonne campus in Nanterre, a
western suburb of Paris, was one of the
factors prompting the students to join
ranks (Frei 2008/2018, p. 10)—which
the university directorate, for its part,
tried to suppress. A spiral of escalation
commenced, and other issues were also
taken on board. The protests culminated
in rioting and the erection of → *barricades*, with the trade unions and many
Parisians also expressing their solidarity (→ *Acts of solidarity*). For a few days,
the mood in France was one of revolutionary upheaval—anything seemed
possible. In the wake of the protests that
had flared up in 1967 in Berlin, Frankfurt, at US universities, and in many
other places, for the first time since the
end of World War II, capitalism was
called into question by a whole raft of
different voices. (OE)

Media, Ger. → *Medien*. In the context
of protest movements since 1789, a wide
variety of media have played a role—
whereby the term media is intended
here to encompass not only the branches of the press, i.e. newspapers, radio,
television, and the corresponding news
sites on the Internet, but also the various
other image, communication, and storage resources that serve to convey the
protests in form and content. During the
French Revolution, for example, agitation graphics played a significant role in
raising awareness and politicizing the
masses. Desired images and caricatures
also reached those parts of the population who could not read the texts of no-
tices and announcements, pamphlets,
and newspapers (Herding, Reichardt
1989, p. 15ff.). In the course of the revolution of → *1848*, there was once again
an enormous upswing in visual political
journalism, favored by the temporary abolition of censorship in the states of the
German Confederation. While numerous
publishers of graphic arts and illustrations satisfied the demand of the less educated classes for sensational news using stencil-colored lithographs in large
numbers, newspapers illustrated with
woodcut reproductions reported on political events in words and pictures to the
more educated bourgeoisie throughout
Europe: in both cases, depictions of barricade fighting (→ *Barricade*, → *Weapons*, → *Violence*) made "from drawings
by specially dispatched 'picture report-
ers'" were popular (Schoch 1998, p. 92).
The costly technical reproduction of the
images, which in the second half of the
19th century increasingly included photographic processes, still usually delayed reporting by several weeks.

The flow of information in today's media is much faster—not least because of
the possibilities of direct transmission
and live streaming. The → *digital media* in particular have opened up entirely new channels of → *communication*
for the protest movements of the 21st
century. Political reporting in the press,
meanwhile, is to a certain extent still a
symbiotic relationship because just as
the protest movements need to get their
messages into the headlines in order to
reach the widest possible public, the
news relies on current and spectacular
events to be of interest to a broad audience. Media presence is all the more
important for protests the further away
they are from urban centers and thus
from public attention—the actions of

environmental protection movements such as Greenpeace in the most remote regions of the world, staged for the cameras, may serve as an example of this. Remote → *building site occupations*, however, also often gain media attention in city centers by way of → *demonstrations*, as in the case of the → *Lobau* protests in front of the Vienna City Hall in 2022 or the expressions of solidarity for → *Lützerath* in various German cities. The reality of the protests as perceived by the participants and the often divergent portrayals of it in the media is a constant topic of debate—especially with regard to the extent of the violence; in which state forces usually play a considerable role, if only because of their marked structural advantage.

Beyond the mass media of the press, protest movements also frequently make use of the characteristic media of countercultural and alternative movements. Since the 1960s, relevant catchwords, slogans, images, and symbols have been disseminated on posters, buttons, stickers, bags, and T-shirts (→ *Identifier*, → *Icon*)—especially in the context of the peace, human rights, and environmental movements. The professional production of these accessories has opened up new market segments for the merchandise industry that are largely independent of the actual protagonists in the protest movements—just as the protest song has done for the music industry (→ *Music*) and protest literature for the book trade (→ *Literaturverzeichnis*). In local and regional protests, on the other hand, homemade media are frequently used; they can range from self-painted → *protest placards* and → *banners* to unusual disguises (→ *Clothing*, → *Costume*) and converted accessories to painted → *vehicles* and elaborately designed show-trucks for demonstrations. The fact that the protesters themselves also function as a medium becomes evident in rehearsed protest shouts and chants, as well as in choreographies in which human bodies—sometimes unclothed (→ *Nakedness*)—are arranged into specific formations, images, or lettering (→ *Body deployment*).

Finally, architecture, too, can in many ways become a medium of protest: in the hope of reaching more people than through printed matter, members of the White Rose in the resistance movement against National Socialism painted building facades and other surfaces with lettering and crossed-out swastikas in Munich in 1943. By contrast, the → *graffiti* written on the facades of buildings during the protests in → *May '68* in Paris, such as "Soyez réalistes demandez l'impossible" ("Be realists, demand the impossible"), gave the revolt an almost poetic expression. In the course of the → *Gezi Park* protests in Istanbul in → *2013*, the then Atatürk Cultural Center on Taksim Square was hung with banners and thus transformed, as it were, into a current protest exhibition (→ *Archive*, → *Museum*). If today's generations are increasingly asking themselves how they can express their protests, then the various → *building types* examined in this dictionary appear as legitimate media of resistance: their architecture manifests itself spatially as symbols of protest (→ *Protest architecture*). (SH)

Medien, engl. → *Media*. Im Umfeld der Protestbewegungen seit 1789 haben die verschiedensten Medien eine Rolle gespielt – wobei der Begriff Medien hier nicht nur die Organe der Presse umfassen soll, also Zeitungen, Radio, Fernsehen und die entsprechenden Nachrichtenseiten im Internet, sondern auch die diversen anderen Bild-, Kommunikations- und Speichermittel, die der Vermittlung der Proteste in Form und Inhalt dienen. Während der Französischen Revolution etwa hatte die Agitationsgrafik einen erheblichen Anteil an der Bewusstseinsbildung und Politisierung der Massen. Wunschbilder und Karikaturen erreichten auch diejenigen Teile der Bevölkerung, welche die Texte der Aushänge und Bekanntmachungen, Flugschriften und Zeitungen nicht lesen konnten (Herding, Reichardt 1989, S. 15 ff.). Im Zuge der Revolution von → *1848* kam es – in den Staaten des Deutschen Bundes durch die vorübergehende Aufhebung der Zensur begünstigt – erneut zu einem enormen Aufschwung der politischen Bildpublizistik. Während zahlreiche Grafik- und Bilderbogenverlage die Nachfrage der weniger gebildeten Schichten nach Sensationsmeldungen mit schablonenkolorierten Lithografien in großer Zahl befriedigten, berichteten mit Holzstichreproduktionen illustrierte Zeitungen dem gebildeteren Bürger*innentum europaweit von den politischen Ereignissen in Wort und Bild: In beiden Fällen beliebt waren Darstellungen der Barrikadenkämpfe (→ *Barrikade*, → *Waffen*, → *Gewalt*), die „nach Zeichnungen von eigens entsandten ‚Bildreportern'" angefertigt wurden (Schoch 1998, S. 92). Die aufwendige technische Reproduktion der Bilder – die in der zweiten Hälfte des 19. Jahrhunderts zunehmend auch fotografische Verfahren berücksichtigte – verzögerte die Berichterstattung noch meist um mehrere Wochen.

Der Informationsfluss heutiger Medien ist – nicht zuletzt durch die Möglichkeiten von Direktübertragung und Live-Streaming – ungleich schneller. Dabei haben vor allem die → *Digitalen Medien* den Protestbewegungen des 21. Jahrhunderts gänzlich neue Kanäle der → *Kommunikation* erschlossen. Bei der politischen Berichterstattung in der Presse handelt es sich indes nach wie vor um eine gewissermaßen symbiotische Beziehung, denn ebenso wie die Protestbewegungen ihre Botschaften in die Schlagzeilen bringen müssen, um eine möglichst große Öffentlichkeit zu erreichen, sind die Nachrichten auf aktuelle und spektakuläre Ereignisse angewiesen, um für ein breites Publikum von Interesse zu sein. Die mediale Präsenz ist für die Proteste dabei umso wichtiger, je weiter entfernt sie von den urbanen Zentren und damit der öffentlichen Aufmerksamkeit stattfinden – die für die Kameras inszenierten Aktionen von Umweltschutzbewegungen wie Greenpeace in den entlegensten Regionen der Erde können dafür als Beispiel dienen. Abgelegene → *Bauplatzbesetzungen* werden aber auch immer wieder medienwirksam durch → *Demonstrationen* in die Innenstädte getragen, etwa bei den → *Lobau*-Protesten vor dem Wiener Rathaus 2022 oder den Solidaritätsbekundungen für → *Lützerath* in verschiedenen deutschen Städten. Die von den Teilnehmenden wahrgenommene Realität der Proteste und die davon oft abweichende Darstellung in den Medien wird stets aufs Neue diskutiert – vor allem, was das Ausmaß der Gewalt betrifft; die Organe der Staatsgewalt haben daran meist einen erheblichen Anteil, schlicht weil sie strukturell im Vorteil sind.

Über die Massenmedien der Presse hinaus bedienen sich die Protestbewegungen häufig auch der charakteristischen Medien der Gegenkultur und der Alternativbewegung. Seit den 1960er Jahren werden einschlägige Schlagworte, Sprüche, Bilder und Symbole auf Plakaten, Buttons, Aufklebern, Taschen und T-Shirts verbreitet (→ *Erkennungszeichen*, → *Ikone*) – vor allem im Rahmen der Friedens-, Menschenrechts- und Umweltbewegungen. Die professionelle Herstellung dieses Zubehörs hat der Warenindustrie neue und von den eigentlichen Akteur*innen der Protestbewegungen größtenteils unabhängige Marktsegmente erschlossen – ebenso wie der Protestsong der Musikbranche (→ *Musik*) und die Protestliteratur dem Buchhandel (→ *Literaturverzeichnis*). Bei lokalen und regionalen Protesten kommen dagegen meist selbstgemachte Medien zum Einsatz; sie können von selbstgemalten → *Protestschildern* und Transparenten über ausgefallene Verkleidungen (→ *Kleidung*, → *Kostüm*) und umfunktionierte Accessoires bis zu bemalten → *Fahrzeugen* und aufwendig gestalteten Show-Trucks für Demonstrationen reichen. Dass die Protestierenden auch selbst als Medium fungieren, wird bei einstudierten Protestrufen und -gesängen deutlich sowie bei Choreografien, bei denen die menschlichen Körper – bisweilen unbekleidet (→ *Nacktheit*) – zu bestimmten Formationen, Bildern oder Schriftzügen arrangiert werden (→ *Körpereinsatz*).

Auf vielfältige Weise kann schließlich auch Architektur zum Medium der Proteste werden: In der Hoffnung, damit mehr Menschen als durch Druckschriften zu erreichen, hatten Mitglieder der Weißen Rose in der Widerstandsbewegung gegen den Nationalsozialismus 1943 in München Hauswände und Mauern mit Schriftzügen und durchgestrichenen Hakenkreuzen bemalt. Die bei den Protesten im → *Mai '68* in Paris an die Hausfassaden geschriebenen → *Graffitis* wie „Soyez réalistes demandez l'impossible" („Seid realistisch, verlangt das Unmögliche") gaben der Revolte dagegen einen geradezu poetischen Ausdruck. Im Zuge der → *Gezi-Park*-Proteste → *2013* in Istanbul wurde das damalige Atatürk-Kulturzentrum am Taksim-Platz mit Transparenten behängt und damit gleichsam in eine aktuelle Protest-Ausstellung verwandelt (→ *Archiv*, → *Museum*). Wenn sich für heutige Generationen zunehmend die Frage stellt, in welcher Form sie ihren Protesten Ausdruck verleihen können, dann erscheinen die diversen in diesem Lexikon untersuchten → *Bautypen* als Medien des Widerstands legitim: Ihre Architektur manifestiert sich räumlich als Zeichen des Protests (→ *Protestarchitektur*). (SH)

Menschenkette, engl. → *Human chain*; → *Baltischer Weg*, → *Demonstration*, → *Greenham Common Friedenscamp*, → *Hongkong-Proteste*, → *Körpereinsatz*

Mirror, Ger. → *Spiegel (fig.)*. Exactly one month after Berkut special forces attacked a peaceful demonstration on → *Maidan* in Kyiv, dozens of women gathered on the square to protest against police violence. They assembled face-to-face with a line of police in order to "hold a mirror up to them." Their → *protest placards* read: "Who and what do you want to protect?" Inspired by the performative → *demonstration* in Ukraine, artist Cannupa Hanska Luger deployed reflective → *protective shields* at the → *Dakota Access Pipeline protests* in order to confront the → *police* with their own reflection. At actions by → *protest organization* Extinction Rebellion as well as Israel-critical protests in the Gaza Strip, by contrast, mirrors were used to dazzle police or soldiers. (AMM)

Misappropriation, Ger. → *Zweckentfremdung (fig.)*. Water bottles become gas masks, images of saints become → *protective shields*, → *vehicles* become → *barricades*, swords become ploughshares, → *cooking pots* become helmets, or → *barriers* are turned into a counter for meals to be distributed (→ *Infrastructure*). One of the fundamental principles of protest design is that things get repurposed. (OE)

Möbel, engl. → *Furniture*, → *Barrikade*, → *Baumaterial*, → *Gezi-Park*, → *Infrastruktur*

Mobile phone, Ger. → *Handy*; → *Digital media*, → *Hong Kong protests*

Molotov cocktail, Ger. → *Molotowcocktail*; → *Fire*, → *Hong Kong protests*, → *Maidan*, → *Weapons*

Molotowcocktail, engl. → *Molotov cocktail*; → *Feuer*, → *Hongkong-Proteste*, → *Majdan*, → *Waffen*

Monday demonstration, Ger. → *Montagsdemonstration*; → *Demonstration*

Monopod, engl. → *Monopod*. Altgriechisch, „Ein-fuß". 1. Kreatur: Fabelwesen mit nur einem Fuß (auch: Skiapod); 2. Fotoausrüstung: Einbeinstativ; 3. Protestarchitektur: Hochsitz an einem bis zu zehn Meter langen Baumstamm, der mit → *Seilen* am Boden abgespannt wird. Monopods sind wie viele → *Türme* Verzögerungsarchitekturen (→ *Bautypen*). Sie sollen die polizeiliche Räumung eines → *Protestcamps* in die Länge ziehen. Anders als → *Tripods*, die auf drei Beinen stehen, sind Monopods auf ihre Abspannungen angewiesen: Würde die → *Polizei* ein Seil lösen oder durchschneiden, fiele der Monopod um und der Mensch, der die Struktur besetzt (→ *Körpereinsatz*), würde verletzt werden. Die Plattform an der Spitze ist über → *Traversen* zusätzlich mit anderen Strukturen, z.B. → *Baumhäusern* verbunden. Wenn sich die Polizei mit einer Hebebühne nähert, können die Besetzer∗innen über die Seilverbindungen wegklettern. In vielen → *Besetzungen*, z.B. in → *Lützerath*, gab es neben Monopods außerdem Highpods und bis zu 40 Meter hohe Skypods. Nach der Räumung im Januar 2023 konnte die Übernahme eines Monopods aus dem → *Fechenheimer Wald* ins Deutsche Architekturmuseum organisiert werden. (AMM)

Mono

Monopod, Ger. → *Monopod.* Ancient Greek for "one foot." 1. Creature: mythical being with only one foot (also: skiapod). 2. Photographic equipment: single-foot tripod. 3. Protest architecture: high seat on a tree trunk up to ten meters long tied to the ground by → *ropes.* Monopods, like many → *towers,* are forms of delaying architecture (→ *Building types*). They are designed to drag out the police clearance of a → *protest camp.* Unlike → *tripods,* which stand on three legs, monopods depend on being anchored by rope: if the → *police* detach or cut one of the ropes, the monopods would crash to the ground and the person perched on the structure would be injured. The platform at the tip is additionally connected by → *traverses* to other structures such as → *tree houses.* If the police approach with a lifting platform, the occupiers can climb off using the rope connections. In many → *occupations,* such as in → *Lützerath,* along with the monopods there were also highpods and skypods that were up to forty meters high. After the site was cleared in January 2023, arrangements were made to secure one of the monopods from the → *Fechenheim Forest* for the Deutsches Architekturmuseum. (AMM)

Montagsdemonstration, engl. → *Monday demonstration*; → *Demonstration*

Movimiento 15M, engl. → *Movimiento 15M.* Die Movimiento 15M (15M-Bewegung, benannt nach dem Starttag am 15. Mai → *2011*) war ein Zusammenschluss zahlreicher Initiativen in Spanien, die sich gegen die Folgen der Schuldenkrise sowie gegen Korruption und die neoliberale Politik einsetzten. Sie machten mit → *Platzbesetzungen* in über 30 spanischen Städten auf soziale, wirtschaftliche und politische Missstände im Land aufmerksam und organisierten → *Hausbesetzungen,* um Menschen vor Zwangsräumungen ihrer Wohnungen zu bewahren.

Das für vier Wochen bestehende → *Protestcamp* auf der Puerta del Sol in Madrid mit über 300 Besetzer∗innen wurde zum Vorbild für weitere Camps in Spanien und auf der ganzen Welt. Die Kunsthistorikerin Julia Ramírez Blanco war Teil des „Documentation and Archive Committee" und widmete der Besetzung und ihrer Architektur ein Kapitel ihrer 2018 veröffentlichten Publikation *Artistic Utopias of Revolt*:

[...] In Madrid wurde zwischen 2007 und 2008 die Hausbesetzer∗innenbewegung (okupa) nach einer zeitweiligen Krise wiederbelebt. Verschiedene selbstverwaltete Autonome Zentren blühten auf, als prächtige, aber verlassene Gebäude in Orte für Konzerte, Workshops und in Treffpunkte einer politisierten Gegenkultur verwandelt wurden. [...] Die Regionalwahlen am 22. Mai [2011] rückten näher, und man spürte ein tiefes Misstrauen gegenüber einer politischen Klasse, die sich von der Bevölkerung entfremdet zu haben schien. [...]

Democracia Real Ya (DRY) [Echte Demokratie jetzt] – eine erst kürzlich gegründete Mobilisierungsplattform – rief für den 15. Mai zu einem landesweiten Protest auf. Während den Angaben der Polizei zufolge an diesem Tag 20 000 Menschen auf die Straße gingen, schätzte die DRY die Zahl auf 50 000. Nachdem es zu den üblichen Zusammenstößen mit der Polizei gekommen war, beschloss eine Gruppe von dreißig bis fünfzig Personen am Abend, auf der Puerta del Sol zu übernachten, wo zuvor die Madrider Demonstration geendet hatte. In der Folge wurde dort ein komplexes Camp errichtet, das in den sozialen Netzwerken schnell den Namen Acampadasol [Camp der Sonne] erhielt.

Diese Form des Protests war nicht ungewöhnlich, sondern Teil eines etablierten Aktionsrepertoires: Ein wichtiger Vorläufer auf lokaler Ebene war das sogenannte Campamento de la Esperanza [Camp der Hoffnung], eine beeindruckende Protestsiedlung, die von Arbeiter∗innen des nicht mehr existierenden Unternehmens Sintel 2001 im Zentrum von Madrid errichtet wurde. Im Jahr 2011 war die Idee, den zentralen Platz der Stadt zu besetzen und ein Protestcamp zu errichten, jedoch direkt von den zahlreichen Revolutionen inspiriert, die in der arabischen Welt gerade begonnen hatten. Insbesondere der Tahrir-Platz in Kairo war zu einer Ikone geworden: Sei-

ne Zelte entsprachen einem für die Wüste typischen Bauelement, das dort – und in Madrid – zur Strukturierung der städtischen Unzufriedenheit umgewidmet wurde. Die Journalistin Olga Rodríguez, die für ein alternatives Mediennehmen über den ägyptischen Aufstand berichtet hatte, spricht davon, wie spanische Aktivist*innen „ein Protestmodell kopierten, das aus einem Camp und der Eroberung eines Platzes bestand". In Madrid wurde Rodríguez in der Nacht des 15. Mai angerufen und gefragt, was die Demonstrant*innen unternommen hätten, um die Nacht auf dem Tahrir-Platz verbringen zu können. Dort, antwortete sie, sei es zunächst darum gegangen, Lebensmittel zu beschaffen und für ein Dach über dem Kopf zu sorgen. In Spanien fragte die kleine Gruppe nach Essensresten in nahegelegenen Restaurants und suchte nach Pappkartons, Schlafsäcken und Decken, um zu schlafen: Es war immer noch kalt. [...]

In der Nacht des 15. Mai fand zugleich eine erste Vollversammlung auf dem Platz statt, die von Straßenlaternen und elektronischen Geräten beleuchtet wurde. Nach einem Organisationskonzept, das den Autonomen Zentren der Hausbesetzer*innen entlehnt war, teilten sich die Aktivist*innen in Arbeitsgruppen und Komitees auf. Davon gab es fünf Stück: Infrastruktur, Lebensmittel, Reinigung, Ausbau und Kommunikation. [...] Der Bau des Camps begann in den frühen Morgenstunden: Während die erste Versammlung stattfand, errichtete eine Gruppe von etwa sieben Punks etwas wie eine Jaima, eine Art Zelt im nordafrikanischen Stil. Sie benutzten vier Müllcontainer, ein Gerüst und eine Baustellenplane und dämmten den Innenraum mit Pappkartons als Isolationsmaterial. Dieses Zelt, das von der Versammlung nicht genehmigt worden war, war der erste Bau auf einem Platz, auf dem das Campen gesetzlich verboten ist. Am nächsten Tag tauchte ein blaues Gartenhäuschen mit einem kleinen Plastikfenster in den Stoffwänden auf. [...] Im Inneren dieser Hütte waren Tische aufgestellt. Einige Hacker*innen kamen herein, stellten ihre Computer auf und

boten in weniger als fünfundvierzig Minuten kostenlosen Internetzugang in der Gegend an. Der Hashtag #spanishrevolution wurde zu einem „Trending Topic" im sozialen Netzwerk Twitter. Die blaue Hütte löste den ersten Konflikt mit der Polizei aus, die ihre Beseitigung forderte. [...]

■ Gemeinschaftliche Zelte (Community tents)
■ Individuelle Zelte (Individual tents)
Angeeignetes Gebäude (Appropriated building)

Movimiento 15M. 1 Protestcamp, Puerta del Sol 2 Baustelle mit Protestbannern 3 Regierungsgebäude 4 Eingang U-Bahn-Station (Movimiento 15M. 1 Protest camp, Puerta del Sol 2 Construction site with protest banners 3 Government building 4 Metro station entrance)

Die Menschen waren für acht Uhr abends zu einer Versammlung aufgerufen worden, aber es dauerte lange, die Vorbereitungen dafür zu treffen. Als mehr als tausend Menschen eintrafen und den Platz zum ersten Mal füllten [...], wurde entschieden, dass es eine „symbolische Vollversammlung" sein sollte. [...] Später blieben etwa 250 Menschen zum Schlafen. In dieser Nacht wurden sie von der Polizei geräumt: Die Behörden entfernten die Jaima und die Hütte und machten tabula rasa. Als die Morgendämmerung des 17. Mai anbrach, war der Platz frei von baulichen Elementen. Die Räumung hatte den Effekt einer Mobilisierung: Im Laufe des Tages wurde die Kundgebung immer größer und bei Einbruch der Dunkelheit war die Puerta del Sol immer noch voll. In dieser Situation der Selbstermächtigung wurden die ersten Grundlagen für das gelegt, was man wirklich als Protestcamp bezeichnen könnte. Kleine Gruppen widmeten sich der Aufgabe, zwischen den Menschen den Raum zu strukturieren. Sie kehrten den Boden mit Pappe, die sie dann auf den Bürger*innensteig klebten, und schufen so eine Art riesigen Teppich, der von Wegen unterbrochen wurde. Die Leute begannen auch, Seile an die Laternenpfähle und das Reiterstandbild zu knüpfen: An diese leichte Konstruktion hängten sie eine Plane, die einen Wetterschutz bilden sollte. [...] Am 19. Mai beschloss die Vollversammlung, das Camp bis nach den Wahlen weiterzuführen, die nur drei Tage später stattfinden sollten. Am 21. Mai wurde auf dem Beet, das die beiden Brunnen auf der Puerta del Sol umgibt, ein Gemüsegarten angelegt. „La plaza echa raíces" [„der Platz schlägt Wurzeln"] war auf einem kleinen Plakat zu lesen, das metaphorisch den Wunsch ausdrückte, bleiben zu wollen. [...]

Im Acampadasol wollte sich die Arbeitsgruppe Infrastruktur nicht als Gruppe von Spezialist*innen aufspielen. Vielmehr wollte sie sich der Aufgabe widmen, die angelieferten Materialien zu verteilen, damit die Menschen ihre Hütten im Geiste des „Do-it-yourself" selbst bauen konnten. Der Selbstbau aktivierte bei den Teilnehmer*innen verschiedene Arten von praktischem Knowhow, z.B. in Bezug auf Elektriker- und Schreinerarbeiten, und es kamen wertvolle Erfahrungen aus dem Umfeld der Hausbesetzer*innen hinzu. Materialien wurden recycelt und sparsam eingesetzt, auf der Straße gefundene Möbel zerlegt und ihre Teile zum Bau neuer Konstruktionen verwendet. Der Überfluss an Kartonplatten hängt mit der zentralen Lage des Platzes zusammen: Große Handelsgeschäfte verursachen eine besondere Art von Müll, der zum größten Teil aus Verpackungsresten besteht. Im Acampadasol wurde Karton als Bauelement, zur Isolierung und als Träger für Plakate verwendet. Die Pappe verlieh dem Ort einen ockerfarbenen Ton, der im Dialog mit dem Blau und Weiß der Planen stand, die mit Seilen an Laternenpfähle gebunden oder von selbstgebauten Säulen gehalten wurden. Die Architekt*innengruppe Zuloark lobte diese Stützen, die aus einer Mischung aus Holz, Besenstielen und sogar einer Toilettenschüssel bestanden und äußerst fantasievoll zusammengefügt waren. Zuloark betonte [...], dass die Säulen eine „doppelte und dreifache Funktion haben, die es ihnen ermöglicht, zu einem Medium für Informationen, Mülleimer und Ruhezonen zu werden". Das blaue Gewebe der Planen, die an den vertikalen Elementen befestigt sind wie Segel an einem Mast, verleiht einer Stadt am Meer ein gewisses maritimes Aussehen: Flatternd im Wind scheinen die Planen manchmal an die Bewegung des Wassers zu erinnern. Darunter wurde eine Atmosphäre der völligen Andersartigkeit geschaffen, die an die Souks der muslimischen Vergangenheit Spaniens erinnert. In der Zone der Zelte tauchten Abschirmungen aus heimeligen Laken auf, die im öffentlichen Raum einen Hauch von Intimität erzeugten. [...]

Auf dem Platz ging der Selbstbau Hand in Hand mit einem System der Selbstverwaltung durch Vollversammlungen, bei denen die Mitarbeit freiwillig war. [...] Mit der Forderung nach einer anderen Gesellschaft begannen die Aktivist*innen, eine kleine Stadt innerhalb der Metropole Madrid zu errichten, die einige Ciudad de Sol [Stadt der Sonne] nannten. [...] Als die Arbeitsgruppen wuchsen, folgten Stände aus Holz und Pappe. [...] Auf Tischen wurden Informationen und Broschüren ausgelegt und Listen mit allem, was benötigt wurde. [...] Während des raschen Wachstums des Camps wurde eine Reihe von Durchgängen freigehalten. Die Unterteilung der Zonen dazwischen erfolgte nach räumlichen Funktionen: Die Schlafbereiche (das eigentliche Camp), der Ruhebereich und der Bereich, der für die täglichen Versammlungen vorgesehen war, waren klar abgegrenzt. Der westliche Abschnitt in der Nähe der Bäckerei Mallorquina wurde immer freigehalten, um im Falle von Problemen den Zugang für Krankenwagen zu ermöglichen. Es scheint, dass eine Gruppe von Feuerwehrleuten bei diesen Sicherheitsüberlegungen eine wichtige Rolle spielte.

Der erste Stadtplan der „Stadt der Sonne" wurde in der Nacht des 17. Mai gezeichnet. Die Kartierung schien zeitgleich mit dem Bau voranzuschreiten, doch ihre Darstellungen waren angesichts der ständigen Erweiterung des Camps schnell wieder veraltet. Die verschiedenen kartografischen Arbeiten sind Dokumente, die seinerzeit der Orientierung in der komplexen räumlichen Struktur der Aktivist*innensiedlung dienten. Heute sind sie Momentaufnahmen, die den beeindruckenden Organisationsgrad der Arbeitsgruppen des Camps zeigen. Verschiedene Arbeitsgruppen beschäftigten sich mit der Logistik und damit, den Platz fortwährend aufzuräumen. Die Arbeitsgruppe Lebensmittel, die sich um die Essensspenden kümmerte, hatte schließlich drei verschiedene Stände auf dem Platz und lagerte überschüssige Verpflegung und Getränke. Außerdem wurden tragbare Toiletten aufgestellt, die Arbeitsgruppe für Infrastruktur und Reinigung wurde gegründet sowie ein Platz für verlorene Gegenstände und eine Recyclingstelle eingerichtet. [...] In kurzen Kursen wurden die Aktivist*innen im Umgang mit Publikumsmedien und in ihrer Rolle als Stellvertreter*innen für die gesamte Besetzungsbewegung geschult. Die Arbeitsgruppe Kommunikation nutzte das Internet intensiv, um mit Texten, Fotos und Videos zu informieren, zu analysieren und zu vermitteln. [...]

Kulturelle Aktivitäten spielten auf der Puerta del Sol eine wichtige Rolle: Zwischen dem 19. und 21. Mai wurde eine Bibliothek mit einem Bereich für Erwachsene und einem Bereich für Kinder eingerichtet. [...] Gleichzeitig wurde eine Arbeitsgruppe für Dokumentation und Archivierung gebildet: Die Geschichte der Platzbesetzung wurde in Echtzeit aufgezeichnet. Im Camp sollte ein System der direkten Demokratie etabliert werden. Wie in den besetzten Autonomen Zentren wurden verschiedene Arbeitsgruppen gebildet, die in einer Vollversammlung zusammenkamen. [...] Diese Art von Vollversammlung fand zweimal am Tag in einem eigens dafür reservierten Bereich statt. Die Leute saßen auf dem Boden rund um die U-Bahn-Station und ließen „Trampelpfade" frei. Jede Versammlung hatte eine Tagesordnung

und die Teilnehmer*innen mussten warten, bis sie an der Reihe waren, um das Wort zu ergreifen. Eine Tonanlage sorgte dafür, dass jede Stimme gehört wurde. Zustimmung, Zweifel und Veto wurden in Gebärdensprache ausgedrückt, damit die Redner*innen nicht unterbrochen wurden. Anfangs war für die Beschlussfassung Einstimmigkeit erforderlich, doch später wurde diese Haltung aufgeweicht und eine Einigung mit einer deutlichen Mehrheit (vier Fünftel) angestrebt, um das System praktikabler zu machen. Auch wenn die Vollversammlungen aufgrund ihrer Größe kaum funktionsfähig waren, verkörperte ihr Diskussionsraum die eigentliche Bedeutung des Platzes als Agora. [...] In gewissem Sinne diente der Platzraum als eine Art „Messe für Aktivismus", auf der jede Gruppe ihren eigenen, selbstgebauten „Messestand" aufstellen konnte, von dem aus sie über ihre Aktivitäten und ihre Sicht der Welt informieren und andere einladen konnte, sich anzuschließen. [...]

Auf der Puerta del Sol kam die Vielfalt sowohl politisch als auch ästhetisch zum Ausdruck. [...] Im Camp war alles von Plakaten übersät: Sie hingen an den Seilen, die die Planen hielten, klebten an den Wänden der umliegenden Gebäude, auf den Tischen der Arbeitsgruppen und an den Wänden ihrer Stände. Eine Architektur der Zeichen nahm auf dem Platz Gestalt an [...]. Die Arbeitsgruppe Grafik und visuelle Künste arbeitete kontinuierlich an der Herstellung von Schildern und symbolhaften Elementen für die Ausstellung auf dem Platz. Während Transparente auf Demonstrationen mobil sind und mit ihren Träger*innen mitwandern, waren die Plakate im Camp der Sonne eher statisch, sie wurden von den Demonstrant*innen angebracht, die ihr Lager auf dem Platz aufgeschlagen hatten, und sie spielten eine grundlegende Rolle bei der Schaffung eines neuen Raumgefühls. [...] Der ständige Vormarsch der Zeichen hatte einen modularen Charakter, bei dem das Kleine überwog: Da alles Große von der Versammlung genehmigt werden musste, fügten die Plakate dem Protestcamp im Wesentlichen kleine Elemente von hori-

Movimiento 15M / Case Study

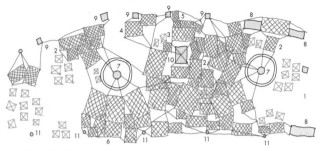

■ Gemeinschaftliche Zelte (Community tents)
■ Individuelle Zelte (Individual tents)

Movimiento 15M. 1 Versammlungsplatz 2 Essensausgabe 3 Arbeitsgruppe Kommunikation
4 Arbeitsgruppe für Rechtliches 5 Arbeitsgruppe Archiv 6 Kinderbetreuung 7 Brunnen
8 Eingang U-Bahn-Station 9 Kiosk 10 Reiterstatue 11 Straßenlaterne (Movimiento 15M.
1 Assembly area 2 Food bank 3 Communication working group 4 Legal affairs working
group 5 Archive working group 6 Childcare 7 Fountain 8 Metro station entrance
9 Kiosk 10 Equestrian statue 11 Streetlamp)

zontalem Wachstum mit verschiedenen Konzentrationspunkten hinzu. [...] Die handgefertigten Banner – und mit ihnen die politischen Slogans – wuchsen rhizomatisch und wurden spontan im Raum platziert, was durchaus von einer Art horror vacui motiviert war. [...]

In der ersten Woche hörte das Camp nicht auf zu wachsen. Die Bewohner*innen des Platzes wurden von einem Gefühl des bevorstehenden sozialen Umsturzes überwältigt. In der Zwischenzeit stellte die Arbeitsgruppe Recht die Telefonnummern an Anwält*innen zur Verfügung, die die Menschen auf ihre Haut schrieben, um sie im Falle einer Räumung und/oder Verhaftung zu benutzen. Diese ersten Momente waren eine Zeit des Staunens. Das Madrider Camp zog fast unverzüglich ähnliche Siedlungen in verschiedenen spanischen Städten nach sich. In der Hauptstadt wuchs die Euphorie. Doch außerhalb des Camps und seiner Umgebung herrschte im Rest der Stadt weiterhin das Regime der alten „Normalität", als ob der Ort der Aktivist*innen in einer anderen Zeit existierte. [...]

Als am 22. Mai die Regionalwahlen stattfanden, schien es, als hätte das aktivistische Ereignis keine Spuren in der parlamentarischen Politik hinterlassen. Die Partido Popular, die am weitesten rechts stehende der etablierten Parteien, gewann mit überwältigender Mehrheit. Viele Menschen hatten sich der Stimme enthalten, und einige hatten in Anspielung auf die Korruption der politischen Klasse Scheiben von Chorizo in den Wahlumschlag gelegt. Darüber hinaus hatte sich die Puerta del Sol merklich geleert. Während die Aktivist*innen in ständiger Angst vor einer Räumung waren, hatten die Behörden nach den polizeilichen Repressionen vom 15. Mai jedoch keinen erneuten Versuch unternommen, das Camp zu entfernen. Nach den Wahlen wurde der Aufbau der Strukturen des Camps in einer Größenordnung fortgesetzt, die weit weniger Menschen umfasste. Die Bewohner*innen der Siedlung waren nun noch enger mit der gegenkulturellen Szene und den Netzwerken voriger aktivistischer Bewegungen verbunden. Mit der Zeit wurden die internen Konflikte immer erbitterter. Diebstähle und aggressives Verhalten nahmen größer werdende Ausmaße an. Die Teilnehmer*innen waren sich wiederum bewusst, dass der Rauswurf von

Personen, deren Verhalten „problematisch" war, gegen ihre eigenen Prinzipien verstieß.

Es wurde vielfach festgestellt, wie viel Energie für die Organisation und Aufrechterhaltung der Besetzung aufgewendet wurde, was zu Lasten der Durchführung von Aktionen ging. Daher diskutierte man darüber, wann und wie man den Platz verlassen sollte, um die soziale Bewegung auf andere Weise weiterzuführen. Nach einer Woche spannungsgeladener Versammlungen, bei denen sich nur wenige Personen gegen diesen Grundtenor aussprachen, beschlossen die Besetzer*innen, die Siedlung aufzulösen. Daraufhin begann man, von Mudanzas 15M [15M-Umsiedlung] zu sprechen. Am 12. Juni 2011 wurden die Materialien des Camps in Kleintransporter verladen und zum größten Teil in verschiedene Autonome Zentren der Hausbesetzer*innen gebracht. Zu diesem Zeitpunkt wurden Plakate, Transparente und andere Gegenstände als Teil des 15M-Archivs gesammelt. Nach der Räumung des Platzes wollte das Acampadasol einen permanenten Informationspunkt und ein ebenerdiges Denkmal auf dem Platz hinterlassen: Neben der Statue von Carlos III. wurde eine Metallplatte mit der Aufschrift „Dormíamos, despertamos. Plaza tomada, 2011" [„Wir schliefen, wir wachten auf, Platz erobert, 2011"] angebracht. Am letzten Tag der Besetzung fand eine Vollversammlung statt, bei der die verschiedenen Arbeitsgruppen und Komitees über ihre Arbeit berichteten. Das Camp hatte insgesamt achtundzwanzig Tage durchgehalten.

Währenddessen war das Acampadasol [...] zu einem globalen Vorbild geworden, und als das Camp in Madrid verschwand, waren bereits ähnliche Siedlungen an vielen anderen Orten auf der ganzen Welt entstanden, was eine neue Welle des Aktivismus auf internationaler Ebene auslöste. Am 17. September 2011 entstand Occupy Wall Street und errichtete sein Camp im Zuccotti Park, ganz in der Nähe der New Yorker Börse, einem der wichtigsten symbolischen Zentren des Kapitalismus.

[...] Das Camp in Madrid hatte das arabische Protestszenario in den Westen übertragen und die Grundlage für eine Art utopische und gegenkulturelle Siedlung geschaffen, in der das gemeinschaftliche Experiment untrennbar mit dem politischen Protest verbunden war. Obwohl die Camps je nach Kontext sehr unterschiedlich waren, hatten sie doch gemeinsame Elemente. Sie alle waren geprägt von der Ästhetik des Provisorischen, dem Überfluss an Worten durch kleine handgefertigte Plakate und der Konstruktion von Raum durch Strukturen aus Holz und Pappe. [...]

Movimiento 15M. 1 Dachkonstruktion aus gespannten Seilen 2 Straßenlaterne 3 Selbstgebaute Stütze, Fundament aus Mülltonne 4 Stand einer Arbeitsgruppe 5 Kuppelzelt (Movimiento 15M. 1 Roof construction made of tensioned ropes 2 Streetlamp 3 Self-made support, rubbish bin as foundation 4 Working group stand 5 Dome tent)

Der öffentliche Raum wurde durch den Bau einer kleinen Metropole innerhalb der großen Metropole in Besitz genommen – eine Art symbolischer Staat, der eine radikale Infragestellung der Funktionsweise der Welt mit sich brachte. Aber diese Protestcamps funktionierten nicht auf Dauer, und sie hätten auch nicht ohne die vom Rest der Stadt bereitgestellten Ressourcen überleben können. Statt „echter" Gemeinschaften waren die Camps eher „performative" Gemeinschaften, es entstand bisweilen der Eindruck, als würde eine Art Theaterstück aufgeführt. Dennoch konnten die Menschen in diesen Räumen die Erfahrung machen, dass eine andere Art *ihr Leben zu leben im Bereich des Möglichen sein könnte. [...]*

Zunächst hatte das Camp kaum Einfluss auf die etablierte Politik. In Spanien entwickelte sich jedoch sehr schnell ein politischer Prozess, der dazu führte, dass bei den folgenden Wahlen ein starker Einfluss zu spüren war. Es war nicht vorhersehbar, dass die Erfahrungen des Protestcamps die Gründung einer neuen politischen Partei namens Podemos [Wir können] im Jahr 2014 anstoßen würden. [...] Die Generation der globalisierungskritischen Aktivist*innen hatte Zulauf durch all jene erhalten, die durch die Camps von 2011 politisiert worden waren, und einige von ihnen hatten beschlossen, fortan die Sprache der Medien zu sprechen und [mit Podemos] in das Spiel der politischen Parteien einzusteigen. (Ramírez Blanco 2018) (Text von Julia Ramírez Blanco; Einleitung und Recherche: AMM)

Movimiento 15M, Ger. → *Movimiento 15M*. The 15M Movement, named after the day on which it started, May 15, → *2011*, was an alliance of countless different initiatives in Spain that took a stand against the impact of the debt crisis, corruption, and neoliberal policies. It drew attention to social, economic, and political grievances in the country through → *public square occupations* in over thirty Spanish cities and also organized → *squatting* campaigns in order to protect people against compulsory eviction from their apartments.

The → *protest camp* on Puerta del Sol in Madrid with over 300 occupiers existed for four weeks and was the role model for other camps in Spain and all around the world. Art historian Julia Ramírez Blanco was a member of the "Documentation and Archive Committee" and dedicated a chapter in her 2018 publication *Artistic Utopias of Revolt* to the occupation and its architecture:

In Madrid, between 2007 and 2008 the squatters' (okupa) movement revived after a period of some crisis: various self-managed social centers flourished, where sumptuous, abandoned buildings were transformed into places for concerts, workshops, and meetings of a politicized counterculture. [...] Regional elections on May 22 were approaching and the atmosphere was one of a profound lack of confidence in a political class that seemed very distant from the population that had voted for it. [...] Democracia Real Ya (DRY) [Real Democracy Now]—a recently created mobilization platform—called for a national protest on May 15. While the police said that 20,000 people took to the streets that day, DRY's figures put the total at 50,000. At night, after the customary clashes with the police, a group of between thirty and fifty people decided to sleep on Puerta del Sol, where the Madrid demonstration had ended and from which in theory people should have dispersed. Soon, a complex camp was set up there, quickly dubbed Acampadasol [Sol Camp] in social networks.

This form of protest was part of an inherited repertoire of action: at the local level, an important precedent was the so-called Campamento de la Esperanza (Camp of Hope), an impressive protest settlement that workers from the defunct Sintel company set up in central Madrid in 2001. However, in 2011, the idea of taking to the central square of a town or city and setting up camp was directly inspired by the series of successive revolutions which had just started to take place in the Arab world. In particular, Cairo's Tahrir Square had become iconic: its tents dovetailed with an element of construction typical of the desert, which now served to structure urban dissidence. The journalist Olga Rodríguez, who had covered the Egyptian uprising for an alternative media outlet, speaks of how Spanish activists "copied a protest model which was the camp and the taking over of a square." In Madrid, during the night of May 15 Rodríguez was telephoned, and asked what had been done by protesters in order to spend the night in Tahrir Square. There, the first thing had been getting hold of food and shelter. In Spain, the small group of people asked for leftovers from nearby restaurants and looked for cardboard boxes, sleeping bags, and blankets in order to sleep: it was still cold. [...]

Olmo Calvo: Dach aus Planen und selbstgebauten Holzstützen bei Regen (Roof made of tarpaulin and self-made wooden supports in the rain), 4. Juni 2011

Julio Albarrán: Puerta del Sol während einer Kundgebung (Puerta del Sol during a rally), 19. Mai 2011

Olmo Calvo: Straßenlaterne, Befestigungspunkt der Dachkonstruktion (Streetlight, anchor point of the roof structure), 6. Juni 2011

Julio Albarrán: Polizeipräsenz auf der Puerta del Sol (Police presence at Puerta del Sol), 19. Mai 2011

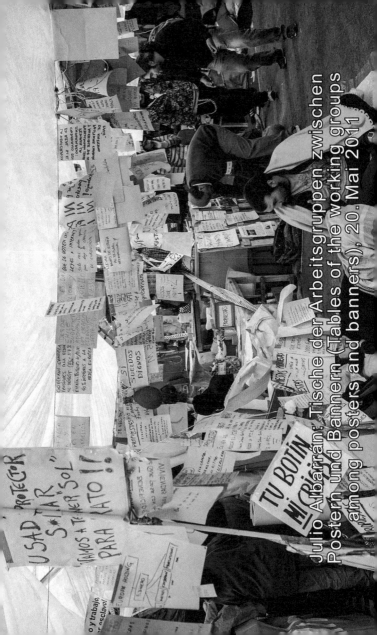

Julio Albarrán: Tische der Arbeitsgruppen zwischen Postern und Bannern (Tables of the working groups among posters and banners), 20. Mai 2011

Julio Albarrán: „Teppich" aus Karton
("Carpet" made of cardboard),
18. Mai 2011

Julio Albarrán: An langen Seilen befestigtes Planendach, darunter Schlafbereiche und abgesteckte Erschließungswege (Tarpaulin roof attached to long ropes, underneath sleeping areas and marked-out paths), 20. Mai 2011

Julio Albarrán: Zelte und Schlafplätze unter freiem Himmel (Tents and open-air sleeping places), 20. Mai 2011

Julio Albarrán: Mit Bannern überhängte Werbung, an einem Baustellengerüst (Advertising covered with banners on construction-site scaffolding), 20. Mai 2011

Movimiento 15M / Case Study

During the night of May 15, an assembly took place, lit by street lamps and electronic devices. Adopting an organizational approach that came from the squatters' social centers, activists divided themselves into working groups and committees. Five committees were set up: Infrastructure, Food, Cleaning, Expansion, and Communication. [...] Building began in the early hours of the morning: While the first assembly was taking place, a group of about seven punks built a kind of jaima, a sort of North African-style tent. They used four rubbish containers, scaffolding, and a building-site canvas, insulating the interior with cardboard boxes. This tent, which had not been approved by the assembly, was the first construction in a square where camping is prohibited by law. The next day, a blue garden hut with a small plastic window in its fabric walls appeared. [...] Inside the hut, tables were arranged. Some hackers came in, set up their computers, and within less than forty-five minutes were providing free Internet access to the area. The hashtag #spanishrevolution became a 'trending topic' on the Twitter social network. The blue hut provoked the first conflict with the police, who demanded its removal. [...]

People had been called to an assembly at eight in the evening, but it took an hour just to make the preparations. When more than a thousand people arrived, filling the square for the first time [...], it was consciously decided to make it a 'symbolic assembly'. [...] Later, some 250 people stayed to sleep. During the night they were evicted by the police: The authorities removed the jaima and the hut, leaving everything in tabula rasa. As dawn rose on May 17, the square was free of constructed elements. The eviction had the effect of issuing a rallying cry: during that day, the event became massive and at nightfall the Puerta del Sol was still full. It was in this context of empowerment when the first foundations were laid of what could really be called the 'camp.' Small groups devoted themselves to clearing a space between the people. They swept the ground with cardboard which they then stuck to the pavement, creating a kind of giant carpet which was broken up to form pathways. People also started to tie ropes to the lamp posts and the equestrian statue: From this lightweight structure they hung the tarpaulin which would create a fabric covering. [...] On May 19, the assembly decided to remain camped out until after the elections, which were to take place just three days later. On May 21, a vegetable garden was planted in the piece of earth which surrounded the two fountains in the Puerta del Sol. "La plaza echa raíces" (The square is putting down roots) could be read on a small poster, which metaphorically expressed a desire to remain. [...]

At the Acampadasol, the Infrastructure Committee did not want to set itself up as a group of specialists. Rather, it sought to dedicate itself to sharing out the materials that arrived so that people could make their own huts in a 'do-it-yourself' spirit. Self-construction activated various kinds of practical know-how from the participants in terms of skills such as electricity and carpentry, and the experience of those who were related to the squatter environment proved fundamental. Here materials were recycled and tended to be modest. Furniture found in the street was taken apart and its pieces used to build other structures. The profusion of cardboard was related to the central location of the square: Big commercial stores create a special kind of rubbish, most of which comprises the remains of packaging. At the Acampadasol, cardboard was used as an element in construction, as insulation, and as the medium for posters. It lent the place an ocher tone that was in dialog with the blue and white of the canvas above, which was tied with rope to lamp posts or held up by homemade pillars. The Zuloark architectural group eulogized these supports—made from a mixture of wood, broom sticks, and even a toilet bowl—which presented extremely imaginative building solutions. Zuloark highlighted [...] that the pillars served a "double and triple function, which *allowed them to become a medium for information, rubbish bins, and rest spaces." Tied to the vertical elements, like sails to a mast, the blue canvas of the awnings lent a certain maritime image to a city without a beach: fluttering in the breeze, at times seeming to evoke the movement of water. Below, an atmosphere of complete otherness was created, recalling the souks of Spain's Muslim past. In the zone of the tents, homely sheets appeared, creating resonances of intimacy in the public space. [...]*

In the square, self-construction went hand in hand with a system of self-government via assemblies, where work was voluntary. [...] Asking for a different society, activists started to build a small town within the metropolis of Madrid which some came to call Ciudad de Sol (City of Sol, or City of the Sun). [...] As the committees proliferated, stalls made of wood and cardboard followed. [...] On tables which served as display counters, information and pamphlets were laid out, along with lists of everything that was needed. [...] Throughout the camp's rapid growth a series of passageways was maintained at all times. Zonal divisions were designated according to spatial functions: The areas for sleeping (the camp itself), the rest area, and the perimeter set aside for daily general assemblies were clearly marked out. The west zone, near the Mallorquina bakery, was always left free to allow access for ambulances in the event of any problems. It seems that a group of firefighters played an important role in these safety considerations.

The first map of the City of Sol was sketched on the night of May 17. Mapping seemed to advance at the same time as construction, but its representations were out of date almost immediately given the camp's constant expansion. The various cartographic efforts are documents that, at the time, served to provide orientation within the complex spatiality of the activist settlement. Today, they serve as snapshots that show the impressive heights of organization reached by the camp committees. Various committees occupied themselves with logistics

and maintaining the space. The Food Committee, which handled donations, ended up having three different stands in the square and stored surplus food and drink. Portable toilets were also set up and the Committee for Infrastructure and Cleaning was established, along with a place for lost objects, and a recycling point. [...] Short courses were given to train activists in how to deal with the conventional media and act as spokespeople. The Communication Committee used the Internet intensively to convoke, disseminate, analyze, and inform through texts, photographs, and videos. [...]

The Puerta del Sol took on a strong cultural dimension: Between May 19-21, a library was created, with a section for adults and a children's area. [...] At the same time, a Documentation and Archive Committee was formed: History was being recorded from inside the very process itself. In the Acampada, self-government sought to follow a system of direct democracy. As in the squatted social centers, various committees were made up of working groups and came together in a general assembly. [...] This type of meeting took place twice a day in a space reserved specifically for the purpose. People sat on the ground around the metro station, leaving free 'pathways.' Each meeting had an agenda, and in order to speak participants had to wait their turn to address the assembly. A sound system enabled everyone's voice to be heard. Approval, doubt, and veto were expressed in sign language so that speakers were not interrupted. At the start, the taking of decisions required unanimity, but eventually this posture was softened to the search for an agreement with a substantial majority (four fifths) in order to make the system more functional. Even though the huge size of the General Assembly meant that they were barely functional, their space for discussion encapsulated the very meaning of the square as an agora. [...] In a certain sense, the square acted as a kind of 'fair' for activism, where each group was able to set up its own self-made 'pavilion' from which it could provide information about its ac-

Movimiento 15M / Case Study

tivities and ways of seeing the world, inviting others to join. [...]

In the Puerta del Sol, heterogeneity was both political and aesthetic. [...] Within the settlement, posters invaded everything: hung from the ropes that held up the awnings, stuck to the walls of surrounding buildings, on the committee tables, on the walls of their stalls. An architecture of signs took shape in the square [...]. The Graphic and Visual Arts Committee worked continuously to produce signs and symbolic elements for display in the square. While banners on demonstrations are mobile, walking along with their bearers, the placards in the Sol camp were more static, placed there by protesters who had set up camp in the square, and they played a fundamental role in creating a new sense of space. [...] The constant advance of signs was of a modular character, in which the small predominated: as anything big had to be approved by the Assembly, the aesthetic elements of the camp essentially added small items of horizontal growth with various points of concentration. [...] The handmade banners (and with them, the concepts they displayed) grew rhizomatically and were placed in the space in a spontaneous way, with a kind of horror vacui. [...]

During the first week, the camp did not stop growing. The square's inhabitants were overwhelmed with a feeling of imminent social change. Meanwhile, the Legal Committee provided the telephone numbers of lawyers, which people wrote on their skin, to use in the event of eviction and/or arrest. These first moments were a period of wonder. Almost immediately the Madrid camp spawned similar settlements in various Spanish cities. In the capital the euphoria grew. Nonetheless, outside the Acampada and its surroundings, the rest of the city continued under the regime of earlier 'normality', as if the activist place inhabited a different temporality. [...]

When the regional elections took place on May 22 it seemed that the activist event had left no mark on parliamentary politics. The Partido Popular, the most right-wing option among the main-stream parties, won an overwhelming majority: many people had abstained from voting, and some had put slices of chorizo in the voting envelope, alluding to the corruption of the political class. On top of all this, the square had emptied noticeably. Despite the constant fear of eviction, after the police repression of May 15 the authorities had not sought to repeat an attempt at removing the Madrid camp. After the elections, the building of the Acampada's structures continued to progress in a space that sheltered far fewer people. Now the settlement's inhabitants were more clearly tied to the countercultural scene and the networks of previous activism. In time, internal conflicts became increasingly bitter, and thefts and aggressive behavior took on greater significance. Again, the participants were aware that to throw out those whose behavior was 'problematic' was against their own principles.

Many people noticed how a large amount of energy was focused on managing the space, to the detriment of carrying out actions. Where previously there had been consensus, the debate started about when and how to leave in order to be able to channel the social movement in another way. After a week of tense assemblies where only a small number of people opposed the general decision, the group decided to dismantle the settlement. People then started to talk of Mudanzas 15M (15M Removals). On June 12, 2011, the materials of the Sol camp were put into vans and most were taken to various squatters' social centers in the city. At this time, there was a big gathering up of posters, banners, and other objects which became part of the 15M Archive. Once the ground had been swept and the area vacated, the Acampadasol wanted to leave a permanent information point in the square along with a ground-level monument: Next to the statue of Carlos III a metal plate was placed, with the text "Dormíamos, despertamos. Plaza tomada, 2011" ("We were sleeping, we awoke. Square taken over, 2011"). On the last day of the settlement, there was a summing-up assembly at which the various commit-tees and working groups gave accounts of their work. The camp had endured for a total of twenty-eight days.

By now, the Acampadasol had [...] be-come a global trigger and when the Ma-drid camp disappeared, there were al-ready similar settlements in many other places across the globe, initiating a new wave of activism at an international level. On September 17, 2011, Occupy Wall Street appeared, siting its dissident camp in Zuccotti Park, very near the New York Stock Exchange, one of cap-italism's main symbolic centers. [...] The Madrid camp had translated the Arab phenomenon to the West, establishing the basis for a kind of utopian and coun-tercultural settlement, where the com-munitarian experiment was insepara-ble from political protest. Although very varied according to their different con-texts, the camps had elements in com-mon. They all included the aesthetic of precariousness, the profusion of words through small handmade posters, and the construction of space through struc-tures of wood and cardboard. [...]

Public space was taken over by build-ing a small metropolis inside the main one—a kind of symbolic State that im-plied a radical questioning of how things function. But the settlements did not function in the long term, nor would they have survived without resources provided by the rest of the city. More than 'real' communities, the camps were performative communities. None-theless, in these spaces, people could experience that another way of living could be possible. [...]

At first, the camp barely influenced institutional politics. However, a very rapid political process unfolded in Spain which ensured that a strong im-pact would be felt in subsequent elec-tions. It was not easy to predict that the experience of the camp would give legitimacy to the creation in 2014 of a new political party, called Podemos [We Can]. [...] The alter-globalization gen-eration of activists had come together with new waves of people who had been politicized by 2011's camps, and some of

them had decided to speak the language of the media and to enter the game of po-litical parties. (Ramírez Blanco 2018) (Text by Julia Ramírez Blanco; intro-duction and research: AMM)

MTST, engl. →*MTST*. Lange Rei-hen mit rechteckigen Hütten aus Plas-tikplanen in verschieden Farben, da-zwischen in regelmäßigen Abständen schmale Gassen und kleine Plätze – ihr auffallend aufgeräumter Grundriss un-terscheidet die Povo-Sem-Medo-Beset-zung von vielen heterogen strukturierten →*Protestcamps* (→*Siedlungsstruktur*). Mit 33 000 Beteiligten und über 12 000 Hütten war sie nicht nur die bekannteste Besetzung der MTST, sondern auch eine der größten in Lateinamerika.

MTST steht für Movimento dos Tra-balhadores Sem Teto ("Bewegung der Arbeiter∗innen ohne Dach"). Seit 1997 organisieren sich bei der MTST in den urbanen Regionen Brasiliens wohnungslose und wohnungssuchende Menschen. Durch die →*Besetzung* von brachliegenden Grundstücken macht die MTST auf Boden- und Immobilienspe-kulation aufmerksam und kämpft für die Nutzbarmachung dieser Flächen als be-zahlbaren Wohnraum.

In einem Zoom-Gespräch im Dezem-ber 2022 schildern die drei MTST-Ak-tivistinnen Andreia Barbosa, Monika Ottermann und Larissa Napoli den ty-pischen Ablauf ihrer Aktionen. Andreia Barbosa ist eine von drei Hauptkoor-dinatorinnen der von MTST durchge-führten Besetzung mit dem Projektna-men "Povo Sem Medo" ("Volk ohne Angst"), die ab → *2017* in São Bernar-do do Campo nahe São Paulo stattfand. Monika Ottermann, eine deutsche Theo-login, lebt in São Bernardo und ist seit 2017 MTST-Aktivistin im Bereich Or-ganisation, Finanzen und Internationa-ler Austausch. Larissa Napoli ist Archi-tektin, die sich seit 2019 als Mitglied im Architektursektor der MTST engagiert.

Das Recht auf Wohnen verknüpft MTST mit einem umfassenden Recht auf Stadt, das alle Bürger∗innenrechte einbeziehet, sowie mit einer alternativen Vorstellung von gemeinschaftlichem Zusammenle-ben unter der aktiven Beteiligung der

Bürger*innen an Gestaltungsprozessen. Die Mutterorganisation der MTST, die Movimento dos Trabalhadores Rurais Sem Terra („Bewegung der Landarbeiter*innen ohne Boden"), kurz MST, macht sich bereits seit den 1980er Jahren für eine Landreform stark. Landlosen Arbeiter*innen in ländlichen Regionen ermöglicht sie durch die Besetzung von bisher ungenutzten Grundstücken Zugang zu Bewirtschaftungsflächen. Rechtliche Grundlage der Besetzungen beider Organisationen sind Artikel 5 und 6 der brasilianischen Verfassung von 1988, die die Sozialfunktion von Landbesitz festschreiben und die Enteignung von Eigentümer*innen ermöglichen, deren Land diese soziale Funktion nicht erfüllt. Besetzungen von nicht genutztem Land sind in Brasilien daher legal und gelten in sozialkritisch eingestellten Kreisen als gängige Strategie, an Wohn- und Produktionsflächen zu gelangen.

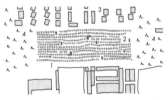

MTST. 1 Protestcamp 2 Versammlungsplatz mit Bühne 3 Wohngebiet 4 Wald (MTST. 1 Protest camp 2 Assembly area with stage 3 Residential area 4 Forest)

Die Besetzungen der MTST werden sorgfältig vorbereitet und folgen festen Abläufen. Organisiert werden sie von den verschiedenen Sektoren der Bewegung. Diese umfassen u.a. die Bereiche Organisation, → Infrastruktur, Finanzen, Rechtliches, Sicherheit, Architektur, → Kommunikation und Bildung. Um in einen der Sektoren aufgenommen zu werden, ist für Menschen, die nicht durch die Teilnahme an einer Besetzung zur MTST kommen, eine einjährige Grundausbildung vorgesehen. Die Hauptorganisation der Besetzungen übernimmt eine kleine Gruppe erfahrener Aktivist*innen, die einen Grund-

stock an Material und Lebensmitteln bereitstellt, die Arbeit der einzelnen Sektoren koordiniert und Versammlungen einberuft. Die Auswahl eines zu besetzenden Grundstücks geschieht im Sektor für Rechtliches, in dem sich hauptsächlich Anwält*innen engagieren. Die Basis der Besetzungen bilden wohnungslose oder wohnungssuchende Arbeiter*innen, die durch ihr aktives Engagement in der Bewegung und eine Art Punktesystem ein Anrecht auf eine Sozialwohnung erlangen können. Denn das Ziel der MTST-Besetzungen besteht nicht darin, auf den besetzten Grundstücken eine Favela, also eine dauerhafte informelle Siedlung entstehen zu lassen, wie es sie in brasilianischen Städten vielerorts gibt, sondern die Besetzung als Druckmittel für die Enteignung der oft verschuldeten Eigentümer*innen und den Bau von Sozialwohnungen auf den Grundstücken zu nutzen. Die Bewegung tritt deshalb, sobald ein Grundstück besetzt wurde, mit Eigentümer*innen und Behörden in Verhandlungen. Diese enden häufig damit, dass das Grundstück zu Staatseigentum wird, den Eigentümer*innen dafür die Grundsteuerschulden auf dem Grundstück erlassen werden und der Staat dort Sozialwohnungen errichtet. Bei erfolgreichen Verhandlungen – die im Schnitt ein Jahr, im Extremfall jedoch bis zu zehn Jahre dauern können – baut die MTST die Besetzung freiwillig ab.

Der genaue Ort bleibt bis zu Beginn der Besetzung geheim, um die Eigentümer*innen nicht vorzuwarnen, denn diese können in den ersten Stunden die sofortige Räumung durch die → Polizei fordern. Zwar ist die Besetzung eines Grundstücks, das seine Sozialfunktion nicht erfüllt, legal, dennoch interpretiert die Polizei das Eindringen ins Grundstück mitunter als Straftat und handelt bei „Gefahr im Verzug" mit der sofortigen Räumung. Bei früheren Besetzungen kam es (teils unter Einsatz von → Gewalt) zu einer zügigen Vertreibung der Besetzer*innen. Um eine schnelle Reaktion der Eigentümer*innen und der Polizei möglichst zu verhindern, erfolgt die Besetzung eines

Geländes daher bei Nacht: Eine Gruppe von bis zu 300 besetzungserfahrenen MTST-Aktivist∗innen kommt mit Bussen, verschafft sich Zugang zum Grundstück und errichtet aus mitgebrachtem → Baumaterial rasch provisorische Zeltbauten sowie eine erste → Küche. Für den Fall, dass die Polizei anrückt, befinden sich Anwält∗innen der MTST auf dem Gelände – leicht zu erkennen an ihren Anzügen und Kunstledermappen. Durch Dokumente können sie gegenüber der Polizei belegen, dass das Grundstück ungenutzt und die Besetzung daher rechtens ist. Dafür sammeln sie im Vorfeld zusammen mit lokalen Aktivist∗innen alle notwendigen Informationen zum Grundstück: zur Vorgeschichte und der aktuellen Nutzung des Geländes, zu geltenden Bebauungsplänen und der Höhe der Grundsteuerschulden.

Für die Bautätigkeit in dieser ersten Nacht bekommen die Besetzer∗innen von der Bewegung drei Bambusstangen, ein 3 Meter langes Stück schwarze Plastikplane und etwas Kordel – ein einheitliches Starterset, das die schnelle Aneignung des Grundstücks ermöglicht. Der Aufbau geschieht spontan und oft wild durcheinander. Sobald es aber hell wird, untersuchen Aktivist∗innen aus dem Architektursektor das oft unübersichtliche Gelände, um es für den Aufbau einer temporären Siedlung zu erschließen. Lange Erkundungsmärsche werden mittlerweile oft durch Drohnenflüge ersetzt, die den Aktivist∗innen Informationen über die Topografie, Bodenbeschaffenheit und Vegetation liefern. Mit Pflöcken und Absperrbändern werden dann zuerst Bereiche für den Versammlungsplatz und die Hauptküche sowie Längs- und Querstraßen abgesteckt. Neben den stark frequentierten Hauptwegen befinden sich zwischen jeder Hüttenreihe schmale Wege, sodass die Sicherheitskräfte der MTST, die durch ihre nächtlichen Kontrollgänge für den → Schutz aller Besetzer∗innen sorgen, zwischen den Hütten durchlaufen können.

Der hohe Organisationsgrad beim Aufbau der Siedlungen entwickelte sich über die Jahre und ist ein Resultat von Erfahrungen aus früheren Besetzungen. Die für MTST-Besetzungen charakteristische Aufteilung des Geländes in dominante Längs- und schmale Quergassen, ein Raster, das an die Avenues und Streets im Straßensystem in New York City erinnert, war anfänglich noch Aufgabe der Hauptkoordinator∗innen. Diese hatten jedoch in der hektischen ersten Nacht zu viele Aufgaben zu bewältigen, sodass diese Tätigkeiten an den 2019 gegründeten Architektursektor ausgelagert wurden. Bei weiter zurückliegenden Besetzungen ergaben sich die Gassen häufig aus Trampelpfaden, entstanden also ohne Planungsabsicht.

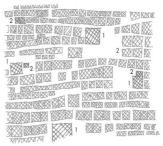

■ Gemeinschaftsbauten (Community buildings)
■ Individuelle Unterkünfte (Individual shelters)

MTST. 1 Gemeinschaftsküche 2 Gemüsegarten (MTST. 1 Community kitchen 2 Vegetable garden)

Während die meisten Aktivist∗innen überall auf dem Gelände die Dreifüße bauen, errichten Mitglieder des Infrastruktursektors am Versammlungsplatz die Gemeinschaftsküche – das Herz jeder MTST-Besetzung. Bei Sonnenaufgang gibt es hier Frühstück – Kaffee, Tee und Brötchen mit Margarine –, ab Mittag dann weitere Mahlzeiten. Auch beginnt so schnell wie möglich der Bau einer größeren Baracke für Sitzungen und die Aufbewahrung von Materialien sowie einer Außenbühne, von der aus bei den Versammlungen gesprochen wird. Nach der ersten Vollversammlung – wer hier spricht, steht meistens noch

*auf einer Obstkiste oder einer kleinen
Anhöhe, damit die Stimme durchdringt
– beginnt die organisierte Errichtung
von Baracken (portugiesisch: „barracos"). Das sind viereckige Hütten aus
Bambusstangen und Plastikplanen mit
einer einheitlichen Grundfläche von
2 × 2 Metern. Sie ersetzen die schnell
errichteten Dreifüße und markieren die
mittelfristigen Ansprüche der Beset-
zer∗innen. 2 × 2 Meter, das ist für die
MTST der minimale Platzbedarf einer
Person. Das Ziel ist, möglichst viele Baracken auf dem Gelände unterzubringen
– eine weitere Strategie, um das Risiko
einer Räumung in den ersten Tagen gering zu halten. Hat die Besetzung einmal eine gewisse Größe und Infrastruktur erreicht, kann sie nur noch durch
einen richterlichen Beschluss geräumt
werden.*

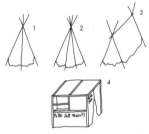

MTST. 1–3 Hütten der ersten Nacht 4 „Barraco" (MTST. 1–3 First-night huts 4 "Barraco")

*Schnell spricht sich in der Stadt her-
um, dass es eine neue MTST-Besetzung
gibt, und viele Menschen aus benachbarten Vierteln oder sogar von weit her
kommen innerhalb weniger Tage zum
Gelände, um sich der Besetzung anzuschließen. Wohnraum ist in den brasilianischen Metropolregionen sehr teuer.
Deshalb ist Wohnungslosigkeit besonders unter Familien verbreitet. Viele leben bei Freund∗innen oder Verwandten,
in Favelas und Risikogebieten und haben die Hoffnung, durch die Beteiligung
an einer Besetzung an eine Wohnung in
einem Sozialwohnungsbau zu gelangen.
Am Eingang des besetzten Areals wer-*

*den ihre Namen und Handynummern
registriert – die Bewegung nutzt Whats-
App-Gruppen zum Austausch und zur
Verbreitung von Informationen –, dann
wird ihnen ein Platz auf dem Gelände
zugewiesen, wo sie ihre Baracke aufbauen können. Material hierfür wird
nicht wie in der ersten Nacht zur Verfügung gestellt, sondern muss selbst
mitgebracht werden. Innerhalb weniger
Tage schießen deshalb die Preise in den
Baumärkten der Umgebung in die Höhe
und beliebte Materialien sind ausver-
kauft. Bambusstangen, Planen und Holz
sind für den Hüttenbau erlaubt, →Zie-
gelsteine dagegen nicht – der Eindruck,
dass hier eine Favela entsteht, soll unter
allen Umständen vermieden werden.*

*Das besetzte Gelände wird in Zonen
eingeteilt: Je 100 bis 300 Besetzer∗in-
nen bilden eine Gruppe. Jede Baracke
bekommt eine Adresse, die sich aus der
Gruppennummer (G1, G2 usw.) und ihrer Position innerhalb der Gruppe zusammensetzt: G2B715 oder G15B34
steht dann in weißer Farbe auf die Hütten geschrieben. In den Gruppen werden eigene kleine Küchen errichtet, die
nach einem Stundenplan betrieben werden und bis zu drei Mahlzeiten am Tag
ausgeben, teils mit Gemüse aus einem
kleinen Gemeinschaftsgarten. Auf dem
Vorplatz der Küchenhütten mit Schutz-
dach und Bänken finden gruppeninter-
ne Versammlungen, Diskussionsrunden
und Kinderbetreuung statt. Die Gruppen wählen im Laufe der Zeit zudem
eine eigene Leitung, die sich um Küche
und Latrine kümmert, die Bewohner∗in-
nen der Gruppe betreut und sich an der
Sitzung aller Gruppenleitungen und
Hauptkoordinator∗innen beteiligt.*

*Bei der Povo-Sem-Medo-Besetzung
registrierten sich innerhalb von sieben
Monaten insgesamt 33 000 Menschen,
darunter 9000 Familien. Dauerhafte
Bewohner∗innen hatte die Besetzung
im Schnitt jedoch nur 350, also rund
1 %. Das liegt an dem Punktesystem,
nach dem die MTST die durch ihre Besetzungen erlangten Sozialwohnungen
vergibt: Die Registrierten bekommen
Punkte für die Beteiligungen an Aktivitäten, zu denen Versammlungen, De-*

Flavio Forner: „barracos" und Gruppenküchen ("barracos" and group kitchens), Povo Sem Medo, 25. November 2017

Mídia Ninja: Provisorische Hütten aus der ersten Nacht, im Hintergrund bereits errichtete Baracken (Provisional huts from the first night, in the background already built "barracos"), Povo Sem Medo, 21. Oktober 2017

Mídia Ninja: Versammlungsplatz mit Hauptküche und Sitzungsbaracke (Assembly square with main kitchen and meeting barrack), Povo Sem Medo, 1. Oktober 2017

Mídia Ninja: 2 × 2 Meter-Baracke (two-by-two-meter barrack), Povo Sem Medo, 1. Oktober 2017

Mídia Ninja: Protestcamp, umgeben von Wohn- und Industrievierteln (Protest camp, surrounded by residential and industrial districts), Povo Sem Medo, 1. Oktober 2017

Mídia Ninja: Lange Gasse zwischen Baracken
(Long alley between barracks), Povo Sem Medo,
1. Oktober 2017

Mídia Ninja: Zusammengestürzte Baracken (Collapsed barracks), Povo Sem Medo, 21. Oktober 2017

monstrationen, Kurse, Gespräche oder die Übernahme von Aufgaben innerhalb des Besetzungslagers zählen, nicht aber für den bloßen Aufenthalt auf dem Gelände. Die wenigen Besetzer∗innen, die in ihren Hütten tatsächlich leben, weil sie keine andere Unterkunftsmöglichkeit haben, bauen ihre Baracken im Laufe der Besetzung aus. Die schwarze, dünne Plane wird durch eine robustere Folie oder durch Spanplatten ersetzt, Familien bewohnen oft drei oder vier der Grundmodulhütten.

Für die meisten Beteiligten der Besetzung haben die Hütten jedoch nach der dynamischen Anfangsphase nur noch symbolischen Wert. Eine Hütte in der MTST-Besetzung zu haben steht für die Entscheidung, sich eine Sozialwohnung erkämpfen zu wollen. Viele Baracken bleiben in einem rudimentären Zustand, manche stürzen nach einer Weile ein. An Wochentagen, wenn viele Besetzer∗innen arbeiten gehen, halten sich in der Siedlung nur wenige Menschen auf. Die Povo-Sem-Medo-Besetzung wurde nach sieben Monaten, am 10. April 2018, abgebaut. Ein Vergleich war ausgehandelt worden: Die MTST bekam vom Bundesstaat vier kleinere Grundstücke zugesprochen, auf denen Sozialwohnungen gebaut werden sollen, nach derzeitigem Stand mit insgesamt etwa 1500 bis 2000 Wohnungen. Das Grundstück der Besetzung selbst blieb leer: Hier möchte der Eigentümer vielleicht irgendwann ein Logistikzentrum errichten. (Gesprächspartnerinnen: Andreia Barbosa, Monika Ottermann, Larissa Napoli; Einleitung, Recherche und Zusammenfassung: AMM)

MTST, Ger. → *MTST*. Long rows of rectangular huts constructed from plastic tarpaulins in different colors, divided by narrow lanes and small squares at regular intervals—the remarkably neat layout distinguishes the Povo Sem Medo occupation from many heterogeneously structured →*protest camps* (→*Settlement structure*). With 33,000 participants and over 12,000 huts, it was not only the MTST's most famous occupation but also one of the biggest in Latin America.

MTST stands for *Movimento dos Trabalhadores Sem Teto* (Homeless Workers' Movement). Since 1997, people without or in search of a home in Brazil's urban regions have been joining forces at the MTST. With the → *occupation* of unused pieces of property, the organization calls attention to land and real estate speculation and fights for the utilization of these sites as affordable living spaces.

In a Zoom conversation in December 2022, the three MTST activists Andreia Barbosa, Monika Ottermann, and Larissa Napoli describe the typical procedure of their actions. Andreia Barbosa is one of the three main coordinators of the MTST's "Povo Sem Medo" (People without Fear) occupation, which began in São Bernardo do Campo near São Paulo in 2017. Monika Ottermann, a German religious studies scholar, lives in Brazil and has been an MTST activist in the field of organization, finances, and international exchange since 2017. Larissa Napoli is an architect and has been involved in the MTST's architectural sector since 2019.

The MTST combines the right to housing with a comprehensive right to the city including all civil rights, and an alternative concept of communal cohabitation that promotes the citizens' active involvement in creative processes. The parent organization of the MTST, the Movimento dos Trabalhadores Rurais Sem Terra (Landless Workers' Movement), MST for short, has been campaigning for land reforms since the 1980s. By occupying unused pieces of property, the organization gives landless workers in rural areas access to farmland. The legal basis for both organizations' occupations is provided by the sections five and six of the Brazilian constitution of 1988, which stipulate the social function of landownership and enable the dispossession of owners whose land does not fulfil said function. Occupations of unused land are therefore legal in Brazil. In critically minded circles, this measure is regarded as a common strategy for obtaining land for housing and production.

The MTST's occupations are planned

meticulously and follow established protocols. They are organized by the movement's different sectors. These include areas such as organization, → infrastructure, finances, legalities, security, architecture, → communication, and education. A year of basic training is required for anyone who wants to be admitted to one of the sectors and has not come to the MTST by participating in an occupation. The main organization of the occupations is undertaken by a small group of experienced activists who provide a basic supply of materials and food, coordinate the work of the individual sectors, and convene assemblies. The legal sector, which is mainly composed of lawyers, chooses a piece of land. Workers without or in search of a home make up the basis of the occupations. Through their active engagement in the movement and a kind of points system, they can achieve the right to a subsidized home. After all, the aim of the MTST is not to build favelas—a type of permanent informal settlement prevalent in many Brazilian cities—but instead to use the occupation as leverage for the dispossession of the often indebted owners and for the construction of subsidized apartments on the properties. Once a piece of land has been occupied, the movement enters into negotiations with the owners and the authorities. These frequently result in the piece of land becoming public property, the cancellation of the owner's property tax debts, and the government's commitment to build subsidized housing. In the event of successful negotiations—which usually take a year but can go on for up to ten years in extreme cases—the MTST removes the occupation voluntarily.

The exact location is not revealed until the beginning of the occupation, so as not to warn the owners who can demand an immediate eviction by the → police within the first hours. While the occupation of land that does not fulfil its social function is legal, the police have been known to interpret trespassing on a property as a criminal offense and to respond with an immediate removal if they see signs of "imminent danger."

Some earlier occupations fell victim to instant evictions (sometimes with the use of → violence). To prevent prompt reactions from the owners and the police, the occupation of an area is carried out at night: a group of up to 300 seasoned MTST occupiers arrives in buses at the site, gains entry, and quickly sets up provisional → tent structures and a first → kitchen using → building materials they bring with them. Easily recognizable by their suits and synthetic leather folders, MTST lawyers are also on the premises in case the police show up. The documents they carry prove that the property is unused, thus making the occupation legal. Prior to the occupation, the lawyers team up with local activists to collect all the necessary information on the property: its history and the current utilization of the area, prevailing development plans, and the amount of the property tax debts.

For this first night of building activities, the occupiers of the movement are equipped with three bamboo poles, a three-meter-long piece of black tarpaulin, and some string—a uniform starter kit for the speedy appropriation of the property. The set-up occurs spontaneously and is often very chaotic. But as soon as it gets light, the activists from the architectural sector explore the unfamiliar premises to plan a temporary settlement. Today, long explorations on foot are often replaced by drone flights which provide the activists with information on the topography, ground conditions, and vegetation. To begin with, the assembly square and the main kitchen as well as the grid of streets are marked off with posts and barrier tapes. In addition to the heavily frequented main routes, narrow paths run between the rows of huts so that the MTST's security forces can pass through on their nightly patrols to ensure the occupiers' → protection.

The high level of organization when establishing the settlements evolved over time and results from the experiences of earlier occupations. The MTST occupations' characteristic division of an area into broad main paths and narrow intersecting ones, a grid that is reminiscent of

MTST / Case Study

New York City's layout with its avenues and streets, was initially left up to the main coordinators. But due to the many tasks they had to deal with during the hectic first night, these activities were delegated to the architectural sector, which was founded in 2019. In earlier occupations, lanes often emerged from well-trodden paths without any planning.

While most activists set up tripods all over the premises, the members of the infrastructure sector establish the main kitchen at the assembly square—the heart of every MTST occupation. At sunrise it provides breakfast—coffee, tea, and rolls with margarine—and further meals from midday onward. The construction of a larger barrack for meetings and storing materials as well as an outdoor stage for speeches during assemblies is also carried out as quickly as possible. After the first assembly—anybody speaking here usually stands on a fruit crate or a small mound to make themselves heard—the organized construction of the barracks (Portuguese: "barracos") begins. These square huts are made from bamboo poles and plastic tarpaulins with a uniform floorspace of two by two meters. They replace the hastily erected tripods and mark the occupiers' medium-term demands. Two by two meters, according to the MTST, is the minimum amount of space a person needs. The aim is to fit as many barracks as possible onto the area—yet another strategy to decrease the risk of eviction during the first days. Once an occupation has attained a certain size and infrastructure, it can only be removed via a court order.

News of a new MTST occupation spreads fast throughout the city, and many people from neighboring districts or even further afield come to the area within a few days to join the action. Living space in Brazil's metropolitan regions is very expensive, which is why homelessness is especially prevalent among families. Many live with friends or relatives, in favelas or risk areas, and hope to gain access to an apartment in a subsidized building by participating in an occupation. After their names and cell phone numbers are registered at the entrance to the occupied area—the movement uses WhatsApp groups to exchange and circulate information—the participants are assigned a place on the premises where they can set up their barracks. As building supplies are only provided during the first night, the occupiers must bring their own material. Consequently, prices in local hardware stores surge and popular materials sell out within days. Bamboo poles, tarpaulins, and wood are permitted for the construction of the huts, → bricks, however, are not—the impression that a favela is developing is to be avoided at all costs.

The occupied property is divided into zones according to groups of 100 to 300 occupiers. Each barrack is given an address made up of the group number (G1, G2, etc.) and its position within the group: the resulting codes, such as G2B715 or G15B34, are painted onto the huts in white. Each group has its own small kitchen which runs according to a timetable and hands out three meals a day, partly with vegetables from a small communal garden. The courtyards in front of the kitchen huts are covered and furnished with benches and are used for group meetings, discussions, and childcare. Over time, the groups elect their own leaders who manage the kitchen and the latrine, take care of the residents in the group, and take part in the General Assemblies with all the group leaders and main coordinators.

Over a period of seven months, a total of 33,000 people, including 9,000 families, registered with the Povo Sem Medo occupation. On average, however, the occupation only had 350 permanent residents, so around 1 percent. This has to do with the points system according to which the MTST allots the apartments achieved through the occupations: those registered receive points for participating in activities, which include assemblies, demonstrations, courses, talks, or taking on tasks within the occupation camp, but not for simply being on the premises. The few occupiers who live in their huts because they have no oth-

Mülltonne. Kurt Weiner: Barrikade vor dem besetzten Haus Kettenhofweg 51, Frankfurt am Main, 29. März 1973 (Garbage can. Kurt Weiner: Barricade outside the squatted house at 51 Kettenhofweg, Frankfurt am Main, March 29, 1973)

er home refine their barracks over the course of the occupation. The thin black tarpaulin is replaced by a sturdier covering or by chipboards, families often inhabit three or four basic-module huts.

For most of the participants in the occupation, however, the huts retain a purely symbolic value after the dynamic initial phase. Having a hut in the MTST occupation represents their decision to fight for a subsidized apartment. Many of the barracks remain rudimentary, some collapse after a while. On weekdays, when many occupiers go off to work, only a few people remain in the settlement. After seven months, on April 10, 2018, the Povo Sem Medo occupation was dismantled. A settlement had been negotiated: the federal state was to give the MTST four small parcels of land for subsidized housing, according to current information, with altogether 1,500 to 2,000 apartments. The site of the occupation itself remained empty: the owner is considering building a logistics center at some point. (Conversation with Andreia Barbosa, Monika Ot-termann, Larissa Napoli; introduction, research, and editing: AMM)

Mülltonne, engl. →*Garbage can.* →*Barrikaden* werden aus urbanem Mobiliar errichtet (→*Baumaterial*). Dazu zählen auch Mülltonnen, die sich wegen ihrer Größe bei gleichzeitiger Beweglichkeit besonders gut dazu eignen, →*Blockaden* zu bilden. Eine Steigerung besteht darin, Mülltonnen in Brand zu stecken; oft als symbolische Handlung: Es wird ein →*Feuer* entfacht, das gefährlich wirkt, doch im Unterschied zu echter Brandstiftung das Schicksal des Mülls, der sowieso verbrannt würde, bloß um einige Stunden vorzieht. Im Pariser →*Mai '68* verwendeten die Studierenden die Deckel von Mülleimern als →*Schutzschilde*. Die Frankfurter Mülltonnenbarrikade entstand kurz nach dem „Blutigen Mittwoch" 1973, einem der Höhe- und Schlusspunkte des →*Frankfurter Häuserkampfs*. (OE)

Museum, engl. →*Museum*. In den letzten Jahren ist ein verstärktes Interesse von Museen zu beobachten, den aktuellen Protestbewegungen nicht nur in Ausstellungen Raum zu geben, sondern wichtige Zeugnisse und Quellen dieser Bewegungen auch direkt in ihre Sammlungen aufzunehmen. Musste das materielle und immaterielle Erbe der Proteste früher erst „historisch" – und damit „museumsreif" – werden, bevor es als Kulturgut bewahrt, erforscht und interpretiert werden konnte, findet die museale Dokumentation heute oft schon statt, noch bevor die Proteste beendet sind. In Wien etwa interessieren sich derzeit mehrere öffentliche Museen – darunter das Haus der Geschichte Österreichs und das Wien Museum (vgl. Nußbaumer, Stuiber 2021) – dafür, Objekte der laufenden Umweltproteste in ihre Sammlungen zu übernehmen. Auch an anderen Orten scheinen Museen, → *Archive* und Bibliotheken heute unmittelbarer auf die verschiedenen Protestbewegungen zu reagieren, um sich an wichtigen und aktuellen Debatten zu beteiligen und dabei sicherzustellen, dass diese auch gut dokumentiert werden. Das war in der Vergangenheit nicht immer der Fall: Einerseits konnten viele Quellen aufgrund ihres ephemeren Charakters im Nachhinein nicht mehr erschlossen werden – selbst Druckerzeugnisse sind in den Protesten meist nur von kurzzeitiger Aktualität, zirkulieren in niedrigen Auflagen und werden kaum je als Pflichtexemplare an die dafür zuständigen offiziellen Stellen abgegeben. Andererseits haben die aus öffentlicher Hand finanzierten, städtischen und staatlichen Institutionen die oft antiautoritär und verfassungswidrig agierenden Protestbewegungen auch immer wieder argwöhnisch, wenn nicht feindselig betrachtet und die Aufnahme von Dokumenten verweigert. So ist es häufig privaten Initiativen und den von den Protestierenden selbst kurzfristig ins Leben gerufenen Archiven zu verdanken, dass wertvolle Aktenbestände, Flugblätter, Zeitschriften, Graue Literatur, Plakate, → *Banner*, → *Protestschilder*, Grafiken, Zeichnungen und Fotos, aber auch audiovisuell bzw. neuerdings auch digital dokumentierte Quellen nicht unwiederbringlich verloren gegangen sind (→ *Kommunikation*, → *Medien*, → *Di-*

gitale Medien). Das autonome Archiv der Sozialen Bewegungen in Hamburg agiert etwa seit 1989 unabhängig von staatlichen Einflüssen und versteht sich als Teil der Protest- und Widerstandsbewegungen, die es dokumentiert. Das 1984 gegründete Hamburger Institut für Sozialforschung, dessen Sammlungsbestand zum Thema „Protest, Widerstand und Utopie in der Bundesrepublik Deutschland" bereits einen Umfang von 2000 Regalmetern erreicht hat – wird dagegen durch eine private Stiftung finanziert. Wenn es politisch opportun erscheint oder es einen breiten gesellschaftlichen Konsens für eine historische Widerstandsbewegung gibt, ist es bisweilen auch im staatlichen Interesse, entsprechende Dokumentationszentren und Museen zu gründen. So gibt es in vielen europäischen Ländern Institutionen, die dem Widerstand gegen die Nationalsozialistische Okkupation während des Zweiten Weltkriegs gewidmet sind – in Österreich beispielsweise das Dokumentationsarchiv des österreichischen Widerstandes in Wien oder in den Niederlanden das Verzetsmuseum in Amsterdam. In einigen Ländern wurden dagegen spezielle Museen gegründet, um an erfolgreiche Aufstände und Revolutionen zu erinnern – etwa das Museo de la Revolución in Havanna auf Kuba oder das National Museum of the Islamic Revolution and Holy Defense in Teheran: Sie dienen oft ganz unverhohlen der staatlichen Legitimation und Propaganda. Einen Spezialfall bilden die Kriminal- und Polizeimuseen, deren Bestände sich zum Teil aus beschlagnahmten Asservaten und strafrechtlich wichtigen Beweisstücken speisen – unter anderem auch aus → *Waffen* und Ausrüstungsgegenständen, die im Rahmen von Protesten zum Einsatz kamen (→ *Gewalt*, → *Kleidung*, → *Schutz*). Nicht zuletzt – und sicher nicht zu Unrecht – sind auch die Museen selbst in den Fokus von Protesten geraten: Im Zuge der → *Occupy*-Bewegung hat sich in den USA der Ableger „Occupy Museums" gebildet, der sich kritisch mit dem Anteil der Museen an der Spekulation am Kunstmarkt und der finanziellen Ausbeutung von Museumsmitarbeiter∗innen auseinandersetzt. Auch wenn die Führungsetagen in diesen Fragen meist ausweichend reagieren, ist doch das generelle Bewusstsein der Museen dafür gestiegen, dass es sich bei den Protestbewegungen (sofern sie nicht das jeweilige Museum selbst betreffen) um gesellschaftsrelevante Ereignisse handelt, die als wertvoller Teil der Kulturgeschichte dokumentiert und erforscht werden müssen (→ *Camp Studies*) und denen – so sie nicht per se gewalttätig und verfassungsfeindlich sind oder auf absurden esoterischen Verschwörungstheorien gründen (→ *Rechte Proteste*) – durch Ausstellungen ein Forum gegeben werden kann: In diesem Sinne versuchen auch das Deutsche Architekturmuseum und das Museum für angewandte Kunst mit ihren Ausstellungen in Frankfurt und Wien ein Publikum zu erreichen, das mit den Bewegungen „auf der → *Straße*" nicht unbedingt konfrontiert war. (SH)

Museum, Ger. → *Museum*. In recent years, there has been an increased interest on the part of museums not only to provide space for current protest movements in exhibitions but also to incorporate important artifacts and sources from these movements directly into their collections. Whereas in the past, the material and immaterial heritage of protests first had to become "historical," and thus "old enough" for the museum, before it could be preserved, researched, and interpreted as a cultural asset, today museum documentation often takes place even before the protests have ended. In Vienna, for example, several public museums, including the Haus der Geschichte Österreichs and the Wien Museum (see Nußbaumer, Stuiber 2021), are currently interested in incorporating objects from the ongoing environmental protests into their collections. Elsewhere, museums, → *archives*, and libraries also seem to be responding more directly to the various protest movements today, engaging in important and topical debates while ensuring that they are well-documented. This has not always been the case in the past: on the one hand, many sources could not be made accessible in retrospect due to their ephemeral nature— even printed materials usually have only short-lived relevance in the protests, circulate in small editions, and are hardly ever given as deposit copies to the relevant official bodies. On the other hand, the publicly funded, municipal, and state institutions have repeatedly viewed the often anti-authoritarian and unconstitutional protest movements with suspicion, if not hostility, and refused to accept documents. Thus, it is often thanks to private initiatives and archives set up in the short term by the protesters themselves that valuable files, leaflets, magazines, gray literature, posters, → *banners*, → *protest placards*, graphics, drawings, and photos, but also audiovisually, or, more recently, digitally documented sources have not been irretrievably lost (→ *Communication*, → *Media*, → *Digital media*). The autonomous Archiv der Sozialen Bewegungen in Hamburg has been operating independently of state influence since about 1989 and sees itself as part of the protest and resistance movements that it documents. By contrast, The Hamburger Institut für Sozialforschung, founded in 1984, whose collection on the subject of "Protest, Resistance, and Utopia in the Federal Republic of Germany" has already reached a size of 2,000 shelf meters, is financed by a private foundation.

If it seems politically opportune or there is a broad social consensus for a historical resistance movement, it is sometimes also in the state's interest to establish corresponding documentation centers and museums. In many European countries, for example, there are institutions dedicated to the resistance to the Nazi occupation during World War II—in Austria, for example, the Documentation Centre of Austrian Resistance in Vienna, or in the Netherlands the Verzetsmuseum in Amsterdam. In some countries, on the other hand, special museums have been founded to commemorate successful uprisings and revolutions—for example, the Museo de la Revolución in Havana, Cuba, or the National Museum of the Islamic Revolution and Holy Defense in Tehran: which often serve quite blatantly to legitimate the state and disseminate propaganda. Crime and police museums are a special case, with their collections partly sourced from court exhibits and criminally important pieces of evidence, including →*weapons* and equipment that were used during protests (→*Violence*, →*Clothing*, →*Protection*). As well as this, these museums are notable for the fact that they have sometimes—and certainly not without good reason—become the focus of protests themselves: in the course of the →*Occupy* movement, for example, an "Occupy Museums" branch has formed in the USA, which critically examines the role of museums in art market speculation and in the financial exploitation of museum employees. Even if the management usually reacts evasively to these questions, there has been an increase in awareness among museums that protest movements (as long as they do not affect the respective museum itself) are socially relevant events that must be documented and researched as a valuable part of cultural history (→*Camp Studies*) and that—as long as they are not inherently violent and anti-constitutional or based on absurd esoteric conspiracy theories (→*Right-wing protests*)—they can be provided with a forum through exhibitions: and it is in this spirit that with their exhibitions in Frankfurt and Vienna, the Deutsches Architekturmuseum and the Museum of Applied Arts are seeking to reach an audience that was not necessarily confronted with the movements "on the →*street*." (SH)

Music, Ger. →*Musik*. In October 2022 the German rapper Ben Salomo, who was born in Israel in 1977, released a cover version of the protest song "Baraye" for the freedom movement in Iran. To show solidarity with the incarcerated Iranian singer Shervin Hajipour who composed the original, he recorded a German version of the song with the title "Ich träume" (I am Dreaming). In the space of just a few days, the song was played on Instagram over a million times. Since the murder of the 22-year-old Kurdish woman Mahsa Amini, a Jewish songwriter's music has been accompanying the central slogan of the protests "Jin, Jiyan, Azadî" (woman, life, freedom) at →*demonstrations* against the theocratic mullah regime on squares in Germany.

Music is an integral part in the formulation of dissent and the formation of protest: the scope of the power of voices and sounds ranges from the songs of the Peasant Wars in the 1520s and the hymns of the slaves deported across the *Black Atlantic* to the songs of the French Revolution and the lyrics of the workers' movement to the sound of the civil rights movement and the global revolts around 1968 to the morning of February 27, 2022, when the Ukrainian singer Andriy Khlyvnyuk stepped onto the street in Kiev and started singing: "Oi u luzi chernova kalyna." The connections forged through music are central. In the process, music has been, and still is, subjected to censorship; melodies or even certain sounds can come under scrutiny. American music channels thus banned the instrumental piece "Rumble" (1958) by the Indigenous guitarist Link Wray: the distorted sound of the electric guitar was feared to enhance subversive forces and to instigate riots and street fights. Can a song, a melody, or a composition achieve more than the production of a fleeting moment of anti-normativity? Perhaps the central element of mass protesting with and through music is the collective realization that the gathering must inevitably disperse at the end of the day. Tones and sounds generate temporary communities without rigid structures, an *anarchitecture*, as the artists in New York in the 1970s called this blend of anarchy and architecture. However, since the late 1960s, rock and pop festivals have generated their own myths of nomadic architecture and antiauthoritarian furniture. Accordingly, Woodstock set the stage for the spontaneous and playful experimentation with alternative lifestyles in 1969. Fascinating images of electrified mud resulted: at the height of the Cold War, ecstatic bodies hurled themselves into the sludge to distorted sounds produced by Jimi Hendrix in a playful celebration of freedom, strong-mindedness—and (unconscious) capitalism. Today, these actions no longer represent the (desired) class war of the students, but rather the self-absorbed hedonism of the future elites. The "Woodstock Nation" also produced an irresistible combination of backward-looking utopia, provided by musicians such as Crosby, Stills, Nash & Young, and the unlimited possibilities of the consumer society. This music transformed the counterculture into folk rock and even worse musical varieties. And thus, forty years on, under the pontificate of Benedict XVI of all people, the Vatican's "handbook of musical resistance" listed David Crosby's solo album *If I Could Only Remember My Name* as their second choice after *Revolver* by the Beatles (Quinlan 2010).

Besides the folk singers' harmonies and melodious chants, a second form of musical protest developed over the course of the 20th century: → *noise*—very much in keeping with the Marxist music historian Günter Mayer, who proposed a distinction between exhausted and new musical material. The interest in noise and droning is linked to the industrial revolution in two ways—on the one hand, through the machines of production, and on the other, through the → *media* of reproduction. After all, it was only through electronic recording techniques that the category of sound came into being. In 1913, the Futurist composer Luigi Russolo noted in his manifesto for sounds and noises of all kinds: "noise evolved with the invention of machines in the 19th century" (Russolo 1913/2000, p. 5). This became apparent in Arseny Avraamov's *Symphony of Sirens*, which featured factory sirens and steam whistles, and was performed by sailors, firemen, and workers in the then Soviet city of Baku on November 7, 1922. This acoustic materiality also defines metal music, which has been produced increasingly in the cities of heavy industry from the United Kingdom to the USA since the onset of deindustrialization.

For fifty years, the pairing of noise and

anger has manifested as direct criticism toward the housing complexes of neoliberalism. Founded in Berlin in 1970, the squatter band Ton Steine Scherben presented themselves as a collective for alternative structures made up of "clay, stones, and shards." Written in an occupied house in 1972, their "Rauch-Haus-Song" (Smoke House Song) provides the slogan for all squats: "Ihr kriegt uns hier nicht raus! Das ist unser Haus!" (You won't get us out! This is our house!; → *Squatting*). Noise and anger blend especially well in the streets. From 1976 onwards, the Sogenanntes Linksradikales Blasorchester (So-Called Radical-Left Brass Orchestra) in Frankfurt tried to push forward the revolutionary movement. And yet, most of the capitalist city centers have been reduced to "Ghost Towns," and musicians have become increasingly resigned, as the antifascist band The Specials lamented in their eponymous hit in 1981 after racist unrest in several British cities. Since bands such as the Einstürzende Neubauten (Imploding New Buildings), there has been a shift from protest to action, with musicians picking up angle grinders, drills, and electric hammers as demolition crews. As the title of the LP *Strategien gegen Architekturen* implies, the aim is to present "strategies against architectures," developing a coarse poetry of protest. (Dietmar Rübel)

Musik, engl. → *Music*. Der Deutsch-Rapper Ben Salomo, geboren 1977 in Israel, veröffentlichte im Oktober 2022 eine Cover-Version des Protestsongs „Baraye" für die Freiheitsbewegung im Iran. Aus Solidarität mit dem inhaftierten iranischen Sänger Shervin Hajipour, der das Original komponiert hat, nahm er eine deutschsprachige Version des Songs unter dem Titel „Ich träume" auf. Das Lied wurde innerhalb weniger Tage über eine Millionen Mal auf Instagram aufgerufen. Seit der Ermordung der 22-jährigen Kurdin Mahsa Amini erklingt, gemeinsam mit dem zentralen Slogan der Proteste „Jin, Jiyan, Azadî" („Frau, Leben, Freiheit"), die Musik eines jüdischen Songwriters auf → *Demonstrationen* gegen das theokratische Mullah-Regime auf Plätzen in Deutschland.

Musik ist fester Bestandteil bei der Formulierung von Gegenstimmen und der Formierung von Protest: Von den Liedern der Bauernkriege in den 1520er Jahren und den Chorälen der über den *Black Atlantic* verschleppten Sklav*innen über die Gesänge der Französischen Revolution und die Texte der Arbeiter*innen-Bewegung zum Sound des *Civil Rights Movement* sowie den globalen Revolten um 1968 bis zum Morgen des 27. Februar 2022, als der ukrainische Sänger Andrij Chlywnjuk in Kyjiw auf die → *Straße* trat und zu singen begann: „Oi u luzi chernova kalyna" – so weit reicht die Kraft der Stimmen und Klänge. Zentral sind die Beziehungsweisen, die durch Musik hergestellt werden. Dabei wurde und wird Musik der Zensur unterworfen; dies kann auch Melodien oder gar einen bestimmten Sound betreffen. So verboten etwa US-amerikanische Musiksender das Instrumentalstück „Rumble" (1958) des indigenen Gitarristen Link Wray: Der übersteuerte Sound der Elektro-Gitarre, so die Angst, würde subversive Kräfte verstärken und zu Aufruhr und Straßenkampf anstacheln.

Kann ein Lied, eine Melodie oder Komposition mehr erreichen als die Herstellung eines kurzen Momentes von Anti-Normativität? Vielleicht ist das zentrale Element einer mit und über Musik protestierenden Masse die kollektive Einsicht, dass sich die Versammlung am Ende eines Tages wieder auflösen muss. Töne und Klänge schaffen temporäre Gemeinschaften und keine festen Strukturen, eben eine *Anarchitecture* – wie Künstler*innen im New York der 1970er Jahre diese Mischung aus Anarchie und Architektur nannten. Allerdings bilden Rock-und-Pop-Festivals seit Ende der 1960er Jahre eigene Mythen von nomadischen Architekturen und antiautoritären Möbeln. Es ging beispielsweise 1969 in Woodstock darum, spontan und spielerisch alternative Lebensformen auszutesten. Dabei entstanden faszinierende Bilder von elektrifiziertem Schlamm: Zum verzerrten Sound eines Jimi Hendrix warfen sich die aufgepeitschten Körper in fluiden Matsch und feierten inmitten des Kalten Krieges spielerisch Freiheit, Eigensinn – und (unbewusst) Kapitalismus. Heute stehen diese Aktionen nicht mehr für den (erträumten) Klassenkampf von Studierenden, sondern für den selbstverliebten Hedonismus der zukünftigen Eliten. Dabei ging aus der „Woodstock Nation" auch eine unwiderstehliche Verbindung aus rückwärtsgewandter Utopie, wie sie etwa Crosby, Stills, Nash & Young anboten, und den grenzenlosen Möglichkeiten der Konsumgesellschaft hervor. Diese Musik konvertierte die Counterculture in Folk Rock oder schlimmere musikalische Spielarten. Und so kam es, dass vierzig Jahre später der Vatikan, ausgerechnet unter dem Pontifikat von Benedikt XVI., nach „Revolver" von den Beatles die Soloplatte von David Crosby „If I Could Only Remember My Name" an zweiter Stelle in seinem „Handbuch des musikalischen Widerstands" auflistet (Quinlan 2010).

Abgesehen von den Harmonien und melodischen Gesängen der Singer-Songwriter*innen entwickelt sich im Laufe des 20. Jahrhunderts eine zweite musikalische Protestform: → *Lärm*. Durchaus im Sinne des marxistischen Musikhistorikers Günter Mayer, der eine Unterscheidung zwischen verbrauchtem und neuem musikalischen Material vorschlägt. Das Interesse an Lärm und Getöse ist in zweierlei Hinsicht mit den industriellen Revolutionen verbunden – einerseits mit den Maschinen der Produktion, andererseits mit den → *Medien* der Reproduktion. Denn mit den elektronischen Aufnahmetechniken entsteht überhaupt erst die Kategorie des Sounds. Der futuristische Komponist Luigi Russolo notierte 1913 zudem in seinem Manifest für Klänge und Lärm aller Art: „Mit der Erfindung der Maschinen im 19. Jahrhundert entstand das Geräusch" (Russolo 1913/2000, S. 5). Eindrücklich wurde dies im *Konzert für Fabriksirenen und Dampfpfeifen*, das Arsenij Avraamov am 7. November 1922 im damals sowjetischen Baku von Matrosen, Feuerwehrleuten und Arbeiter*innen aufführen ließ. Diese akustische Materialität bestimmt auch die Metal Music, die seit der Deindustrialisierung in den Städten der Schwerindustrie von Großbritannien und in den USA verstärkt produziert wird.

Wenn Lärm sich mit Wut verbindet, formiert sich seit fünfzig Jahren gezielt Kritik an den Wohnmaschinen des Neoliberalismus. Die 1970 in Berlin gegründete Hausbesetzer-Band Ton Steine Scherben stellt sich schon im Namen als Genossenschaft für alternative Gebilde vor. 1972 wurde ihr „Rauch-Haus-Song" in einem besetzten Haus geschrieben, der den Slogan aller *Squatted Houses* bereitstellt: „Ihr kriegt uns hier nicht raus! Das ist unser Haus!" (→ *Hausbesetzung*). Lärm und Wut mischen sich besonders gut auf der Straße. Seit 1976 versuchte etwa in Frankfurt am Main das Sogenannte Linksradikale Blasorchester die revolutionären (Sponti-)Kräfte zu forcieren. Trotzdem erscheinen die meisten kapitalistischen Innenstädte seitdem nur noch als „Ghost Town" und die Musiker∗innen resignieren vermehrt, wie es die antifaschistischen The Specials 1981, als es in britischen Städten zu rassistischen Unruhen kam, in ihrem gleichnamigen Hit beklagen. Spätestens mit den Einstürzenden Neubauten schlägt der Protest in Aktion nieder und die Musiker∗innen agieren mit Flex, Bohrmaschine und Elektrohammer als Abbruchunternehmen. Vorgestellt werden, so der Titel einer LP, *Strategien gegen Architekturen*, die eine brachiale Poetik des Protests entfalten. (Dietmar Rübel)

Myanmar-Proteste, engl. → *Myanmar protests*. Als sich im Januar → *2021* das Militär an die Macht putschte und die De-facto-Regierungschefin Aung San Suu Kyi in Gewahrsam nahm, entstand in Myanmar eine breite prodemokratische Bewegung. Die Protestierenden organisierten sich dezentral und trafen sich spontan zu Flashmobs und → *Demonstrationen*. Auf das gewaltsame Vorgehen von → *Polizei* und Militär reagierten sie mit der Errichtung von → *Barrikaden* aus → *Ziegelsteinen*, Bambusstangen und Stacheldraht (→ *Baumaterial*). Gegen Tränengasattacken schützten sie sich mit Regenschirmen und Skibrillen

(→ *Schutz*). Die Ähnlichkeiten zu den → *Hongkong-Protesten* sind kein Zufall: Digitale → *Handbücher* aus Hongkong zirkulierten auf burmesisch. Von den regierungskritischen Protesten in Thailand 2020 übernahmen die Myanmar∗innen u.a. den Dreifingergruß, ursprünglich eine Widerstandsgeste aus dem Film *Tribute von Panem*, der zum → *Erkennungszeichen* der Myanmar-Proteste wurde. Viele Menschen aus Hongkong, Thailand und Taiwan solidarisierten sich mit ihrem Nachbar∗innenland unter den Hashtags #MilkTeaAlliance und #EastAsianSpring (→ *Solidaritätsgeste*). Die myanmarischen Protestierenden teilten Szenen von Polizeigewalt auf → *Digitalen Medien* wie Facebook und Twitter, um auf die Brutalität des Regimes aufmerksam zu machen (→ *Gewalt*). In Yangon, der größten Stadt Myanmars, versuchten sie das Vorankommen der Sicherheitskräfte zu bremsen, indem sie immer wieder den Verkehr lahmlegten (→ *Blockade*). Sie ließen ihre anscheinend kaputten Autos (→ *Fahrzeuge*) auf großen Verkehrsachsen stehen oder banden sich auf Verkehrskreuzungen die Schuhe zu. Auf einen ähnlichen Effekt zielte das Plakatieren des Gesichts von Juntaführer Min Aung Hlaing auf den Asphalt ab: Weil das Militär zögern würden, auf die Portraits zu treten, würde es die Viertel der Protestierenden nur mit Verspätung erreichen. Im September 2021 rief die „Nationale Liga für Demokratie", die Partei von San Suu Kyi, zu einem Volksaufstand auf. Aus der Bewegung entstand ein bewaffneter Widerstand mit hunderten Guerillagruppen (→ *Waffen*, → *Guerillataktiken*). Mindestens 1719 Zivilist∗innen (Stand: März 2022) sind bei den Protesten zu Tode gekommen. (AMM)

Myanmar protests, Ger. → *Myanmar-Proteste*. When in January → *2021* the military seized power through a coup and took the legitimate head of government Aung San Suu Kyi into custody, a broad pro-democracy movement mushroomed in Myanmar. The protesters chose to organize decentrally and met up spontaneously in flash mobs

and → *demonstrations*. They responded to → *police* and military violence
by setting up → *barricades* made of
→ *bricks*, sticks of bamboo, and barbed
wire (→ *Building materials*), and used
umbrellas and ski goggles as → *protection* against tear-gas attacks. It is no
coincidence that there are similarities
to the → *Hong Kong protests*, as digital manuals from Hong Kong were circulating in Burmese (→ *Handbücher /
Online-Manuals*). From the 2020 protests against the Thai government, the
Myanmar protesters adopted, among
other things, the three-finger greeting,
originally a gesture of resistance from
the film *The Hunger Games* and something that became the → *identifier* of the
Myanmar protests. Many people from
Hong Kong, Thailand, and Taiwan expressed their solidarity with the citizens
of Myanmar using the hashtags #Milk-
TeaAlliance and #EastAsianSpring
(→ *Acts of solidarity*). The protesters in
Myanmar shared scenes of police violence on → *digital media* such as Facebook and Twitter to draw attention to the
regime's brutality (→ *Violence*). In Yangon, the country's largest city, they tried
to slow advances by the security forces
by repeatedly bringing traffic to a halt
(→ *Blockade*). They abandoned their
apparently broken-down automobiles
(→ *Vehicles*) in the middle of major traffic arteries or tied their shoes on traffic
crossings. A similar effect was achieved
by gluing posters of the face of junta
leader Min Aung Hlaing to the asphalt:
because members of the military would
hesitate to step on portraits of the general, they would take longer to reach the
protesters' districts. In September 2021,
the "National League for Democracy,"
San Suu Kyi's party, called for a popular uprising. The movement spawned
armed resistance with hundreds of guerrilla groups (→ *Weapons*, → *Guerrilla tactics*). At least 1,719 civilians (as
of March 2022) have been killed in the
protests. (AMM)

Nacktheit, engl. → *Nakedness*. Strategie, durch → *Körpereinsatz* maximale
Schutzlosigkeit ins Spiel zu bringen, um
eine Situation zu deeskalieren („Nack-

tensamstag" → *Startbahn West*). Mit
der Züricher Nacktdemo reagierten die
Jugendlichen auf die vorherigen brutalen Polizeieinsätze (→ *Demonstration*,
→ *Gewalt*, → *Polizei*) mit einer Geste
der asymmetrischen Entschärfung bei
gleichzeitiger Provokation der bürgerlichen Öffentlichkeit (→ *Züri brännt*).
Zum → *Erkennungszeichen* einer Protestbewegung wurde die Nacktheit
durch die Femen-Aktionen, die 2008 in
der Ukraine entstanden. (OE)

Nakedness, Ger. → *Nacktheit (fig.)*.
Strategy of → *body deployment* in
which a maximum lack of bodily protection is used in order to de-escalate a
situation ("Naked Saturday" → *Startbahn West*). The naked → *demonstration* in Zurich, Switzerland, was a way
for young people to respond to brutal
→ *police* tactics (→ *Violence*) with a
gesture of asymmetrical de-escalation
that simultaneously provoked the middle-class public (→ *Zurich youth protests*). Nudity became the → *identifier*
of a protest movement from 2008 onward with the Femen actions that arose
in Ukraine that year. (OE)

Net, Ger. → *Netz*; → *Body deployment*,
→ *Building materials*, → *Claremont
Road*, → *Hambach Forest*, → *Ropes*

Netz, engl. → *Net*; → *Baumaterial*,
→ *Claremont Road*, → *Hambacher Wald*,
→ *Körpereinsatz*, → *Seile*

No Border Camps, engl. → *No Border
camps*. No Border ist ein 1999 gegrün-
detes europäisches Netzwerk, das gegen
Grenzen und Einwanderungskontrollen
kämpft und sich für die Niederlassungs-
freiheit über die Europäische Union hinaus einsetzt. Viele der Mitglieder identifizieren sich selbst als Anarchist∗innen.
Das Netzwerk organisiert, in Zusammenarbeit mit Betroffenen und autonomen migrantischen Gruppen, Aktionen
wie → *Demonstrationen*, Kampagnen
und seit 2002 → *Protestcamps* in verschiedenen europäischen Städten – z.B.
2009 im sogenannten Dschungel von
Calais (Frankreich). Wiederkehrendes
Merkmal der Camps ist ein großes Zir-
kuszelt, das für Zusammenkünfte und
Diskussionen genutzt wird (→ *Zelt*,
→ *Bautypen*). (JD)

No Border camps, Ger. →*No Border Camps*. No Border is a European network founded in 1999 that protests against borders and immigration controls and also advocates freedom of movement beyond the confines of the European Union. Many of the members consider themselves anarchists. Together with people affected and autonomous migrant groups, the network organizes actions such as →*demonstrations*, campaigns, and, since 2002, →*protest camps* in different European cities—e.g. in 2009 in the so-called Jungle of Calais, France. A recurrent feature of the camps is a large circus tent used for assemblies and discussions (→*Tent*, →*Building types*). (JD)

Noise, Ger. →*Lärm*. Just like →*music*, noise can occur on either side of a protest event. Security forces can use noise (or music) to intimidate and disrupt protests. During the →*Maidan* protests in →*2013/2014*, Berkut special forces drummed rhythmically on their shields with batons to emphasize their forbidding appearance acoustically. Low-flying helicopters were used against the →*Gorleben* →*demonstrations* in →*1980* and at Brokdorf in 1981. With a booming loud "playlist from hell," the government of New Zealand tried to disperse demonstrations against the strict COVID-19 rules in front of the parliament in February 2022.

Far more common is the generation of noise on the part of the protesters. →*Cazerolazo* refers to the loud banging of →*cooking pots* and lids, a common form of protest, especially in South America. Many demonstrations add an acoustic dimension to the space actually occupied. In the Canadian trucker protests of →*2022*, the combination of hard-to-clear trucks and the noise level of their piercing horns (→"*Freedom convoy*," →*Vehicles*) was particularly effective. During the chanting of protest slogans at demonstrations, noise and music merge into an acoustic spatial event. (OE)

Nordirlandkonflikt, engl. →*The Troubles*. Gewaltsamer langanhaltender Konflikt zwischen probritischen protestantischen Unionist∗innen und irischen Katholik∗innen. Um die seit →*1969* eskalierenden Spannungen zu verringern, wurden in nordirischen Städten zunächst →*Barrikaden*, später Mauern errichtet, welche die jeweiligen Wohn-

Nacktheit. Nacktdemo in Zürich, 14. Juni 1980 (Nakedness. Naked demonstration in Zurich, Switzerland, June 14, 1980)

gebiete voneinander abgrenzen sollten. Die sogenannten „Friedenslinien" sind teilweise bis zu acht Meter hoch und mehrere Kilometer lang. (JD)

Occupation, Ger. →*Besetzung*, can be found within this book as→*building site occupation*, →*squatting*, or →*public square occupation*.

Occupy Wall Street, engl. →*Occupy Wall Street*. Im Herbst →*2011* wurde für die Dauer von 60 Tagen der Zuccotti Park im Finanzdistrikt von New York City besetzt. Der Protest zielte darauf ab, sich gegen die Auswirkungen der Weltfinanzkrise und gegen die Dominanz von Großunternehmen zur Wehr zu setzen (→*Protestziele*). Das →*Protestcamp* von Occupy Wall Street entstand am Ende eines protestreichen Jahres, das mit dem Arabischen Frühling (→*Tahrir-Platz*) begann und sich in Madrid (→*Movimiento 15M*) und Athen (→*Syntagma-Platz*) fortsetzte. Während aber die vorherigen Protestereignisse jeweils lokale oder regionale Auswirkungen hatten, entstand nach dem Vorbild von Occupy Wall Street eine globale antikapitalistische Bewegung in rund 90 Ländern mit hunderten Camps, die größtenteils sehr viel länger bestanden als die am 15. November 2011 geräumte New Yorker Initialzündung.

„Are you ready for a Tahrir moment? On Sept 17, flood into lower Manhattan, set up tents, kitchens, peaceful barricades and occupy Wall Street", schrieb die Adbusters Media Foundation auf ihrer Website am 13. Juli 2011 (→*Protestorganisationen*), nur wenige Tage nach dem Wiederaufflammen der Proteste auf dem Tahrir-Platz. Als für die →*Demonstration* am 17. September verschiedene Protestorte von der →*Polizei* untersagt wurden, zogen etwa 1000 Protestierende zum Zuccotti Park. Dabei handelt es sich um einen „Privately owned public space", kurz POPS, einen öffentlichen Platz, der sich im Besitz der Immobiliengesellschaft Brookfield Properties befindet. Für die Besetzer∗innen war das von Vorteil, denn die Polizei konnte zwar die angrenzenden Gehwege, nicht aber den Platz selbst kontrollieren. Die

mediale Reaktion (→*Medien*) auf die Proteste war anfangs verhalten. Das änderte sich jedoch am 1. Oktober, als es nach einer Demonstration mit über 700 Festnahmen zu einem starken Anstieg der Unterstützung kam. Wie bei vielen anderen Protestbewegungen sorgte der unverhältnismäßige Polizeieinsatz dafür, dass zuvor Unbeteiligte nun solidarisch Position bezogen (→*Solidaritätsgeste*).

Angeeignetes Gebäude (Appropriated building)

Occupy Wall Street. 1 Camp, Zuccotti Park 2 60 Wall Street Atrium 3 Wall Street 4 Trinity Church 5 Ground Zero

Im Zuccotti Park entstand ein utopischer Mikrokosmos zur Verwirklichung der von vielen Teilnehmer∗innen gewünschten alternativen Politik. In General Assemblies erprobten die Besetzer∗innen Ansätze der direkten Demokratie. Weil in New York die Verwendung von Megafonen und Soundverstärkern im →*öffentlichen Raum* genehmigungspflichtig ist, entwickelten die Protestierenden eine Technik, die es ermöglichte, Informationen allein mit der menschlichen Stimme zu verbreiten: Beim *Human Microphone* wiederholte die gesamte General Assembly im Chor jeweils Satz für Satz die Redebeiträge der Sprecher*innen und machte sie auf diese Weise für alle im Park verständlich (→*Kommunikation*).

Der Zuccotti Park wurde während der Besetzung mit einer neuen →*Infrastruktur* überlagert, wobei seine existierenden Gestaltungselemente wie Stützmauern und Tische integriert wurden, etwa die charakteristischen langen Steinbänke zur Zonierung des Camps (→*Siedlungsstruktur*) oder ein Bankkreis als „heiliger Raum" für Meditationen. Die bunte Vielfalt der Besetzer*innen jenseits von bereits etablierten aktivistischen Strukturen war zwar eine Bereicherung, brachte aber im Alltag viele Herausforderung mit sich: Die Koordinator*innen, die sich um die Organisation des Camps und die Kommunikation mit den Akteur*innen der Stadt kümmerten, verbrachten die Nächte oft zu Hause, während die „normalen" Besetzer*innen, darunter auch Obdachlose, Tag und Nacht im Park lebten und höheren Sicherheitsrisiken ausgesetzt waren (→*Schutz*, →*Körpereinsatz*). Die Gruppen zogen sich in separate Enden des Parks zurück; eine „Uptown" mit Infostand und Versammlungsort und eine „Downtown" mit den Schlafbereichen entstand. Systemkritische Funktionen, etwa die Arbeitsgruppe für Medien und Rechtliches, positionierten die Besetzer*innen im Nordosten des Platzes, der durch einen Niveauunterschied weniger einsehbar war. Die Polizei behielt den Überblick, indem sie zur Überwachung der Proteste einen „Skywatch"-Aussichtsturm nutzte, der normalerweise vom amerikanischen Militär eingesetzt wird (→*Turm*).

Von den Kuppelzelten, die infolge der globalen Verbreitung der Bewegung zum →*Erkennungszeichen* von Occupy wurden, waren im Zuccotti Park anfangs keine zu sehen. Zunächst wollten die Besetzer*innen im Sinne einer radikalen Offenheit auf die privatisierende Wirkung von →*Zelten* verzichten und schliefen stattdessen auf Matratzen und Matten unter freiem Himmel. Außerdem war gemäß der von Brookfield Properties zu Beginn der Besetzung präzisierten Nutzungsrichtlinien des Parks die Errichtung von Zelten untersagt, weswegen die New Yorker Polizei alle zeltähnlichen Strukturen umgehend räumte. Dies änderte sich, als die Polizei ein Sanitätszelt tolerierte, da dort ja nicht übernachtet werden sollte. Die Besetzer*innen hingegen argumentierten, dass Zelte notwendig wären, um weiterhin das Recht auf freie Meinungsäußerung wahrnehmen zu können. Mit dem Kälteeinbruch Ende Oktober stieg dann die Zahl der individuellen Zelte rasant an.

Die Organisation des Zusammenlebens erwies sich langfristig als anstrengend. Viele Besetzer*innen zogen sich nach der anfänglichen Begeisterung mehr und mehr aus der Gemeinschaft zurück und das soziale Miteinander zerfiel zunehmend. Eine Nulltoleranzpolitik gegenüber Gewalt, Missbrauch sowie Drogen und Alkohol führte zusätzlich zu Spannungen in der Gemeinschaft, die sich Hierarchien entschiedene widersetzte, in den General Assemblies aber nur selten konsensuale Entscheidungen treffen konnte. Nach zwei Wochen räumte die Polizei das Protestcamp, offiziell aufgrund intolerabler hygienischer Zustände. 140 Protestierende wurden verhaftet.

Jesse Goldstein, Beka Economopoulos und Jason Jones beteiligten sich an der Besetzung des Zuccotti Parks. Sie engagierten sich in verschiedenen Initiativen und Aktionen in New York, u.a. in der Mieter*innen- und Obdachlosenbewegung und bei Studierendenprotesten. In dem folgenden Gespräch beschreiben sie Occupy Wall Street als →*Protestarchitektur*; der Beitrag trägt den Titel „Goldman Sachs Doesn't Care if You Raise Chickens Unless You're Raising Them in Zuccotti Park" (frei übersetzt: „Goldman Sachs ist es egal, ob Du Dich vom Kapitalismus abwendest, es sein denn, Du machst es im Zuccotti Park").

Jesse Goldstein: Die Besetzung des Zuccotti Parks war ein offenes, niedrigschwelliges Angebot und stand in einem

Occupy Wall Street / Case Study

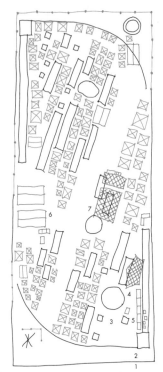

- ■ Gemeinschaftliche Zelte (Community tents)
- ▪ Individuelle Zelte (Individual tents)
- ⊠ Zaun aus Absperrgittern der Polizei (Fence of police barriers)
- ◼ Bestehendes Parkmobiliar (Pre-existing park furniture)

Occupy Wall Street, November 2011.
1 Öffentlicher Raum 2 POPS 3 Versammlungsort 4 Arbeitsgruppe Medien und Rechtliches 5 Bibliothek 6 Sanitätszelt 7 Küche
(Occupy Wall Street, November 2011. 1 Public
space 2 POPS 3 Assembly area 4 Media
and legal working group 5 Library
6 First-aid tent 7 Kitchen)

engen Austausch mit der umgebenden
Stadtstruktur. Es war ein Durchgangs-
raum: Täglich kamen Tourist∗innen und

Besucher∗innen, die sich durch ein Meer
von Zelten und Abdeckplanen bewegten,
die für Hunderte von Protestierenden
ein vorübergehendes Zuhause geworden
waren. Die Leute gingen ein und aus;
ein großer Teil von uns schlief zu Hause und kehrte jeden Tag zurück – fast
so, als würden wir zur Arbeit gehen. Es
gab ein paar nahe gelegene Geschäftsräume, die wir nutzen konnten, wie etwa
eine leere Bankfiliale auf der anderen
Straßenseite. Nur einen kurzen Spaziergang entfernt gab es ein großes öffentliches Atrium in einem Hochhaus, 60
Wall Street, in dem sich Arbeitsgruppen
trafen, wenn sie der Kälte entkommen
wollten. Wesentliche Dinge sind sowohl
innerhalb als auch außerhalb des Zuccotti Parks passiert. Es gab dort zwar
noch nicht mal einen Ort zum scheißen,
aber dafür war eine ganze Stadt aus Bodegas und Delikatessenläden gleich um
die Ecke. Schnell wurde klar, welche von
denen uns freundlich gesinnt waren.

Jason Jones: Mich interessiert am
meisten, wie unsere Besetzung über den
Zuccotti Park hinausgewachsen ist, physisch und symbolisch. Bevor es mit der
Occupy-Bewegung losging, haben wir
viele Demos organisiert, aber die Polizei schien sich nicht viel daraus zu machen. Doch als der Zuccotti Park besetzt
wurde, hat sich daraus schnell eine so
bedrohliche Sache entwickelt, dass sie
für jede∗n von uns zwei Polizist∗innen
geschickt haben, wenn etwas von wei-
tem „nach Occupy gerochen" hat. Occupy wurde zum Symbol. Auch bei der
Architektur geht es um Symbole, darum,
wie ein Gebäude Reichtum oder Macht
zum Ausdruck bringt. Protestarchitektur sollte sich ihrer Symbolik genauso
bewusst sein: Sie muss ein Gefühl von
Großzügigkeit, Stärke und Ernsthaftigkeit vermitteln. Proteste haben ihre eigenen Traditionen, die stets aufs Neue
aktualisiert werden müssen. Sie sind
wirkungsvoll, wenn sie zur Bedrohung
werden.

Beka Economopoulos: Es ist sehr
wichtig, sich daran zu erinnern, dass
Occupy nicht in einem Vakuum entstanden ist. Kurz zuvor gab es die Proteste auf den Plätzen in Tunesien, Spani-

en, Griechenland und Großbritannien. Diese Handzeichen zum Beispiel, mit denen wir uns verständigt haben, waren überall dieselben. Ich denke, dass es bei der Protestarchitektur darum geht, das raumpolitische Vokabular und die Symbole, die unsere Nutzung des Raums bestimmen, neu zu konfigurieren und einzusetzen, um die Ziele der Protestbewegung voranzubringen. Sogar bloße Körper können architektonisch sein, auch ohne weitere Zutaten. In gewisser Weise war die bedeutendste Architektur des Zuccotti Parks der Mix aus den unterschiedlichen Arbeitsgruppen: Occupy Library, Occupy Security, Occupy Sanitation – das alles hatte zu tun mit der Wall Street, die nur wenige Blocks entfernt war. Es war ein Mikrokosmos, der in scharfer Opposition dazu stand, was die Weltfinanzkrise uns allen angetan hatte, sowie zum Neoliberalismus, der den Staat ausgehöhlt hatte.

JG: Absolut. Was Occupy so bedrohlich machte, bestand ganz einfach in der Tatsache, dass wir plötzlich frei waren, alles neu zu denken. Ich war Mitglied der Siebdruckwerkstatt; wir haben auf einem Klapptisch im Park mit allen, die mitmachen wollten, →Kleidung und Poster bedruckt. Wir brauchten bloß einen Antrag in der General Assembly zu stellen, so mit Handzeichen und Human Mic und so weiter, schon wurde ein Großeinkauf finanziert und danach besaßen wir riesige Plastikboxen mit Stoffen und Farben und kistenweise einfarbige T-Shirts und Sweatshirts. Das meiste davon wurde gegenüber vom Zuccotti Park in einer leeren Bankfiliale aufbewahrt, die wir als riesige Bühne und Lager genutzt haben. Wenn wir gedruckt haben, kam immer ein Besetzer mit einem Besen vorbei, um zu plaudern und den Park um uns herum zu fegen. Ich erinnere mich, dass ich dachte, wie stolz er ist, dass er sich um unsere Werkstatt kümmert. In diesem Moment, in dem es eine Krise des Kapitalismus gibt und die Menschen das Gefühl haben, keinen Zugang zu einer sinnvollen Arbeit oder einem sinnvollen Leben zu haben, bestand sein Protest darin, in der Öffentlichkeit einen Besen zu schwingen. Viele der Ar-

beitsgruppen nahmen sehr wenig Raum ein – vielleicht mit Ausnahme von Occupy Food und Occupy Communications. Der Rest von uns begnügte sich mit wenigen Dingen, die jeden Tag leicht auf- und abgebaut werden konnten. Die Occupy-Bibliothek war großartig: einfach nur Bücher in großen Kunststoffkisten mit einem OWS-Stempel auf dem Einband. Sie war nach Genres geordnet – sie brauchte kein Zelt, nicht mal einen Tisch, nur Kisten auf einem Betonsockel links von der Parktreppe; wenn es regnete, wurde alles einfach mit Planen abgedeckt. Ich glaube, der Stempel war der wichtigste Teil; der Stempel machte die Bücher zum Bestandteil der Occupy Library.

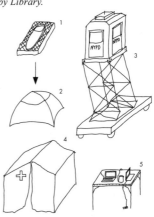

Occupy Wall Street. 1 Matratze 2 Kuppelzelt 3 Überwachungsturm der Polizei 4 Sanitätszelt 5 Medienstation (Occupy Wall Street. 1 Mattress 2 Dome tent 3 Surveillance tower 4 Medical tent 5 Media station)

BE: Das erinnert mich an eine Geschichte. Lange vor Occupy sprach unsere Freundin Jodi Dean auf einer Veranstaltung und sagte: „Goldman Sachs ist es egal, ob Du Dich vom Kapitalismus abwendest." Wir fanden es lustig und haben es sogar auf ein T-Shirt drucken lassen. Damals hatte ich das Gefühl, dass es politisch wäre, ein altes Rennrad zu fahren oder heimlich auf dem Dach einen Garten anzulegen. Warum sollte ich protestieren? Aber der Kapitalismus schafft es, alles zur Ware zu machen – wir entdeckten Werbeplakate für Luxus-Eigentumswohnungen mit einem Kerl auf einem Rennrad. „Radikale Lebensstile" wurden zu einer Möglichkeit, die Immobilienwerte zu steigern. Aber im Zuccotti Park konnten wir uns solche alternativen Lebensmodelle zurückerobern. Als wir das sahen, mussten wir Jodis Satz ergänzen: „Goldman Sachs ist es egal, ob Du Dich vom Kapitalismus abwendest, es sein denn, Du machst es im Zuccotti Park."

JG: Occupy war im maximal dehnbares Konzept. Jede∗r konnte etwas beitragen. Du konntest die Hühner aus deinem Garten in den Zuccotti Park mitbringen. Dein Besen verschwand aus deiner Küche und wanderte in den Zuccotti Park. Das erzeugte eine revolutionäre Stimmung. Alles war denkbar, es war für alles gesorgt. Occupy Food versorgte uns tatsächlich mit einem warmen Buffet, natürlich auch mit Pizza und anderen zufälligen Snacks, die wir aus Müllcontainern gerettet hatten. Durch Projekte wie Food Not Bombs war das bereits gut vorbereitet worden.

JJ: Besetzt was auch immer! Im Zusammenhang einer sozialen Bewegung kann noch das Banalste als Bedrohung wahrgenommen werden. Man konnte seinen Besen in den Zuccotti Park bringen und ihn mit Bedeutung aufladen. Das funktionierte aber auch umgekehrt. Zum Beispiel wurden die Zelte zu einem Symbol. Nach der Räumung des Zuccotti Parks sah man mit einem Mal in jedem Zelt, das nicht in der freien Natur stand, ein potentielles Protestzubehör. Occupy verbreitete sich viral. Wir hatten dazu diese Slogans: „Macht uns fertig, dann werden wir mehr!" – „Räumt uns, dann werden wir mehr!"

BE: Occupy hat die Symbole und Werkzeuge, mit denen wir den Stadtraum nutzten, umgedeutet. Gemeinsam haben wir versucht, die bestehende Ordnung zu destabilisieren. Da gab es zum Beispiel die Absperrnetze, mit denen die Polizei die Demonstrant∗innen ein-

kesseln kann (→ Polizeikessel). Wir besorgten uns dieselben orangefarbenen Netze, beschrifteten sie mit dem Namen Occupy und nutzten sie, um den Raum nach unseren Vorstellungen zu organisieren. Oder es gab diese großen Betonblöcke, die die Polizei einsetzt; wir machten welche, die genauso aussahen, aber aus Schaumstoff, und anstatt „NYPD" stand darauf, in der selben Schriftart: „Occupy: Schutz der Menschen vor den Mächtigen".

JG: Der Zuccotti Park war voller Zelte und Kunststoffplanen, aber tagsüber traten sie total in den Hintergrund, und die leeren Räume zwischen den Zelten wurden durch all die Aktivitäten der Arbeitsgruppen lebendig: die Bibliothek, die Druckerei, die Essensausgabe, Begegnungsräume für das gemeinsame Miteinander. Man konnte sich wie in einem quirligen Stadtzentrum fühlen, da war eine Festivalatmosphäre.

BE: Das stimmt alles, einerseits. Aber ich kann mir auch vorstellen, dass es für einige auch eine herausfordernde und befremdende Erfahrung war; vielleicht hängt es einfach davon ab, über welche Phase von Occupy man spricht. Solche Räume verändern sich mit der Zeit und haben einen Lebenszyklus, der sich entwickelt – zum Guten und zum Schlechten.

JJ: Eine solche Besetzung ist wie ein großer Riss in der bestehenden Ordnung. Menschen können damit experimentieren: Was willst du erreichen? Gemeinsam tauschen wir unsere Ideen aus und die Dinge beginnen zu wachsen. Der konkrete Ort, an dem alles stattfand, war wichtig, um eine andere Gesellschaft zu modellieren. Aber ich denke, dass Occupy überall stattfinden kann. Zuccotti hat funktioniert, aber es war auch unsere größte Einschränkung. Occupy, das waren – einerseits – all die Dinge, aus denen sich das Protestcamp zusammensetzt. Aber zugleich war da eine immaterielle Infrastruktur. Dass wir geräumt wurden war unausweichlich, aber das bedeutete nicht das Ende der Proteste; es war nur eine von einer Million Möglichkeiten. Wie könnten wir weitermachen und zum Beispiel Krankenhäuser

Alex Fradkin: „Skywatch"–Überwachungsturm der Polizei
(„Skywatch" police surveillance tower),
24. September 2011

David Shankbone: Zeltstadt am Tag des ersten Schneefalls (Tent city on the day of the first snowfall), 29. Oktober 2011

David Shankbone: Arbeitsgruppe für Medien (Media working group), 19. September 2011

Working Group Schedule:

MON 10/17	TUES 10/18	10/19	10/20	10/14	10/15	10/16
Kitchen Lunch 11:00 @ Food	Kitchen Lunch 11:00 6:15 - 11:00 @ Cube	Kitchen Lunch 11:00	Kitchen Lunch 11:00 6:15-11:00 @ Cube	Kitchen Lunch 11:00	Kitchen Lunch 11:00	Kitchen Lunch 11:00 6:15-11:00 @ Cube
Media - 11:00	Media - 11:00	Media - 11:00	Media - 11:00	Media - 11:00	Media - 11:00	Media 12 @ Media
Security 12 @ Media	Security 12 @ Media	Security 12 @ Media	Security 12 @ Media	Security 12 @ Media	Security 12 @ Media	Design 11:00 Tri-pod
Community Relations 12:30 @ Media	Community Relations 12:30 @ Media					Speak Easy 1:00 @ Cube
Direct Action 2:00 @ Trinity Park	Direct Action 2:00 @ Trinity Park	Direct Action 2:00 @ Trinity Park	Direct Action 2:00 @ Trinity Park	Direct Action		OWS Think Tank 12-6 (not therapy)
Open Source 3:00	Open Source 3:00					

Occupy Central Park 3pm by RED Sculpture

Lucas, Sam Vill.

Facilitation - 5:30 Training

Media - 5:00

Open Source 7pm

Info 6:00

Safe Spaces 5:1 Study of ...

Interfaith / banter Park

Justice

Political EL Dorado 6pm

Kitchen Dinner Night 11:00
Facilitation 4:00
Minutes + Doc 4:30   Media 5:00
Accountability / Transparency 6:30 @ Sittingman

David Shankbone. Arbeitsgruppe für Presse und Rechtliches unter Dach aus Planen (Press and legal working group under tarpaulin roof), 2. November 2011

John Saeyong Ra: Zuccotti Park hinter Absperrgittern
der Polizei (Zuccotti Park behind police barriers),
12. November 2011

Melvin Félix: Occupy Wall Street-Aktivist*innen im 60 Wall Street Atrium in der Nähe des Zuccotti Parks ("Occupy Wall Street activists at the 60 Wall Street Atrium near Zuccotti Park), 24. Oktober 2011

Occupy Wall Street / Case Study

besetzen? Leerstehende Häuser? Alte Schulen? Wir experimentieren immer noch, auch wenn sich die Namen ändern.

BE: Es ist auch wichtig, den Zuccotti Park als Bühne zu sehen; er war ein Ort der Performance. Die Stufen waren wichtig – sie waren so breit wie der gesamte Park, führten von der Wall Street aus hinein und erzeugten einen Amphitheater-Effekt. Es gab auch einfache Podeste – aus allem, was stabil genug war, um darauf zu stehen (→ Baumaterial). Jede*r konnte hingehen und sprechen. Der Park wurde zum Zentrum für die Unzufriedenen, zu denen in heutigen Spätkapitalismus fast alle von uns zählen. Wir haben wirklich demokratische Versammlungen abgehalten, in denen echt alle zu Wort kamen und gehört wurden. Das war bis zu einem gewissen Grad eine Performance, eine Art von Theaterstück, weil eine Menge Entscheidungen nicht dort, sondern hinter den Kulissen getroffen wurden. Trotzdem war es nicht bloß eine Show. Es fanden echte Begegnungen, ein richtiger Austausch und Arbeitssitzungen statt. Das Ganze spielte sich nicht nur im Bereich des Symbolischen ab.

JJ: Occupy Wall Street bestand nicht allein aus den Menschen, die im Zuccotti Park waren. Die Bewegung bestand auch aus all jenen, die der Kapitalismus aus New York vertrieben hatte und die uns deshalb aus der Ferne unterstützt haben. Oder aus all den Care-Arbeiter*innen, die zu Hause bleiben mussten; oder aus Leuten, die dabei sein wollten, es aber aufgrund der einen oder anderen Form der Prekarität nicht konnten. Auch sie waren Occupy, dafür hat die maximal inklusive Organisationsstruktur des Protests gesorgt.

JG: Da sagst du etwas sehr Wichtiges. Es geht nicht nur um Pizzakartons, Plastikkisten und Zelte. Denn dieses Zeug war hochgradig mit Bedeutung aufgeladen und in ein Netzwerk eingesponnen. Zum Beispiel indem jemand aus dem Mittleren Westen eine Pizzalieferung für den Zuccotti Park bestellt, wodurch ein paar Leute satt werden; oder indem eine Plastikkiste als Podest dient, auf dem jemand seine Stimme er-

hebt. Es sind unendlich viele Beziehungen entstanden, weil wir uns gegen eine mächtige Bedrohung da draußen erhoben haben. Millionen von Leuten hatten das Gefühl: „Oh verdammt, ja, ich denke, ich sollte dort in diesem Park sein, auch wenn ich gerade woanders sein muss." (Gespräch: Jesse Goldstein, Beka Economopoulos, Jason Jones; Interview-Redaktion: SH; Einleitung und Recherche: AMM)

Occupy Wall Street, Ger. → *Occupy Wall Street*. In fall → *2011*, Zuccotti Park in New York City's financial district was occupied for a total of sixty days. The protest was intended to oppose the outcome of the global financial crisis and the dominance of big corporations (→ *Protest goals*). The → *protest camp* organized by Occupy Wall Street arose at the end of a year full of protest, one that had started with the Arab Spring (→ *Tahrir Square*) and had continued in Madrid (→ *Movimiento 15M*) and Athens (→ *Syntagma Square*). Whereas the prior protest movements had local or regional impacts, the Occupy Wall Street model gave rise to a global, anti-capitalist movement in some ninety different countries with hundreds of camps, most of which survived far longer than the initial New York one, which was cleared on November 15, 2011.

"Are you ready for a Tahrir moment? On September 17, flood into lower Manhattan, set up tents, kitchens, peaceful barricades and occupy Wall Street," is what the Adbusters Media Foundation posted on its website on July 13, 2011 (→ *Protest organizations*), only a few days after protests had flared up again on Tahrir Square. When the → *police* then banned various venues for the → *demonstration* on September 17, around 1,000 protesters headed for Zuccotti Park. The latter was a "privately owned public space" or POPS for short, and is owned by Brookfield Properties. This was an advantage for the occupiers, as the police were authorized to patrol the neighboring sidewalks but not the park itself. The → *media* response to the protests was restrained at first. All that changed on October 1, when support surged after a demonstration that led to over 700 arrests. As with many other protest movements, the police's disproportionate use of force prompted many people who had previously not been involved to take a stand in an → *act of solidarity*.

At Zuccotti Park, a utopian microcosm arose in which the alternative politics desired by many of the participants could be realized. In the course of General Assemblies, the occupiers tried out approaches for direct democracy. Because the use of megaphones and sound-amplifying equipment in → *public space* in New York is subject to prior official approval, the protesters developed a technique enabling information to be spread solely through reliance on the human voice: acting as a "human microphone," choir-like, the entire General Assembly repeated the speeches sentence by sentence, enabling everyone in the park to understand it (→ *communication*).

During the occupation, new → *infrastructure* was installed in Zuccotti Park that largely integrated the existing design elements, such as retaining walls and tables; using the characteristic, long stone benches, for example, to zone the camp (→ *Settlement structure*), or converting a circle of benches into a "sacred space" for meditation. The vibrant diversity of the occupiers cut across the established activist structures and was enriching, but also entailed many challenges at the everyday level. The coordinators who handled the organization of the camp and communication with city representatives often spent their nights at home while the "normal" occupiers, including homeless people, lived in the park day and night and were exposed to greater risks to their safety (→ *Protection*, → *Body deployment*). The groups withdrew to opposite ends of the park; an "Uptown" arose on one side, replete with information desk and an assembly venue, and a "Downtown" on the other, with sleeping areas. The occupiers positioned system-critical functions, such as the working group for media and legal matters on the northeast of the square, which, due to a difference in ground level, was less exposed to the eye. The police managed to maintain surveillance by using a "Skywatch" tower to monitor the protests, something normally used by the US Army (→ *tower*).

The dome tents which, in the course of the global spread of the movement, became the → *identifier* of Occupy, were not originally in evidence in Zuccotti Park. Initially, the occupiers sought to act in the spirit of radical openness and get by without the privatizing effect of → *tents*, sleeping instead on mattresses and mats under the open sky. Moreover, in line with the user guidelines for the park, which Brookfield Properties had tightened at the beginning of the occupation, it was forbidden to pitch tents, which is why the New York Police Department immediately cleared all tent-like structures. This changed when the police tolerated a sanitary tent, as no one was supposed to sleep in it. By contrast, the occupiers argued that tents were necessary in order to be able to exercise their right to freedom of expression. The number of individual tents mushroomed when a cold spell set in at the end of October.

Organizing the shared use of the space proved to be very arduous in the long term. After the initial enthusiasm ebbed, many of the occupiers increasingly withdrew from the community and the sense of social togetherness gradually dissolved. Moreover, the zero-tolerance policy on violence, drug, and alcohol abuse led to additional strain within the community which, despite its strict rejection of hierarchies, was rarely able to reach consensus-based decisions in the General Assemblies. After nine weeks, the police cleared the protest camp, officially because of intolerable health and safety conditions. A total of 140 protesters were arrested.

Jesse Goldstein, Beka Economopoulos, and Jason Jones took part in the occupation of Zuccotti Park. They were involved in various initiatives and actions in New York, among others in the tenants' and homeless movement and in student organizing. In the following conversation, they describe Occupy

Occupy Wall Street / Case Study

Wall Street as a form of → *protest architecture*; the section is entitled "Goldman Sachs Doesn't Care if You Raise Chickens Unless You're Raising Them in Zuccotti Park."

Jesse: The occupation of Zuccotti Park was porous and interwoven with the fabric of the city surrounding it. It was a passing through space: tourists and visitors came daily, moving through a sea of tents and tarps that had become a temporary home for hundreds. Occupiers came and went; a large portion of us slept at home and would return each day—almost like it was our chosen job. There were a few nearby corporate places that we used—an empty bank branch across the street, and then a short walk away there was a large public atrium in a skyscraper at 60 Wall Street that working groups met in to get out of the cold. Basic functions happened both within and beyond the park—there were no places to shit in the occupation, but a city full of bodegas and delis a short walk away—and it readily became clear which businesses were friendly to our movement.

Jason: What interests me most is the way that our occupation extended beyond Zuccotti, physically and symbolically. Before Occupy we would have lots of demos, and the police wouldn't seem to care much. But by the time of the occupation in Zuccotti Park, Occupy had become such a threatening signifier that if there was something with "occupy" written on it they would send two cops for every one person. Architecture isn't just about how buildings function. It's also about how they operate as symbols of wealth, power, and authority. Protest architecture has to do the same, I think: create a sense of social wealth, movement power, and popular authority. It is a language that carries from the past, and is iterated on it in the present. It exists when it's recognizable as a threat.

Beka: It's also really important to remember that Occupy didn't exist in a vacuum. Our antecedents were the movement of the squares from Tunisia to Europe to Spain and Greece and the UK. When this global movement came

to NYC, it was recognizable because of the twinkle fingers and a set of things that had been happening overseas. In general, I think protest architecture is about reconfiguring and deploying vocabularies of spatial politics and symbols that govern our use of space in order to advance movement aims. Even bodies assembled without other added materials can be architectural. In some ways, the most significant architecture of Zuccotti Park was a configuration of working groups with distinct roles: Occupy Library, Occupy Security, Occupy Sanitation, all emerging in relation to Wall Street only blocks away. It was a microcosm of society performed in opposition to a post-2008 society in which neoliberalism had hollowed these same institutions out.

Jesse: I agree. What made Occupy threatening had a lot to do with this very simple tactic: anything could be reimagined in its "occupy" alternative. During the occupation I was part of the OWS Screenprinters Guild; we screenprinted clothing and posters on a folding table in the park with anyone who wanted to join. We had large plastic boxes of screens and inks, and boxes and boxes of blank T-shirts and sweatshirts after petitioning the general assembly (twinkle fingers and human mic and all) to fund a major supply purchase. Most of these materials were stored across the street from Zuccotti in an empty bank branch that we were using as a massive staging/storage area. When we were printing, this one occupier would always come by with a broom to chat, sweeping up the park around us. I remember thinking, he is so proud to be taking care of our space. At this moment where there's a crisis of capitalism and a crisis of people not feeling like they have any access to meaningful work or lives, his protest was wielding a broom in public space. A lot of the working groups had a pretty minimal structural presence—maybe except for Occupy Food and Occupy Communications. The rest of us made do with a very mobile setup—easily assembled and disassembled each day. Occupy Library was awesome: just some books in large plastic boxes with an OWS stamp across the binding. It was organized according to genre—there wasn't a tent or a table, just plastic boxes on a concrete ledge to the left of the park stairs; when it rained everything just got covered with tarps. I think the stamp was the most important part; the stamp made the books into Occupy Library.

Beka: That reminds me of a story. Before Occupy, our friend Jodi Dean came to speak at an event, and she said, "Goldman Sachs doesn't care if you raise chickens." We thought that was hysterical; we even made it into a T-shirt. At the time it felt like politics were being located in lifestyle choices like track bikes and rooftop gardens, instead of protest movements. But capitalism can sell these lifestyles right back to us—we would even see billboards for luxury condos with a dude on a track bike—"radical" lifestyles became a way to raise property values. But once Zuccotti happened, we could bring these same alternatives into focus as a collective as opposed to individual performance. As we saw this shift, we had to update Jodi's line: Goldman Sachs doesn't care if you raise chickens unless you're raising them in Zuccotti Park.

Jesse: Occupy was this elastic concept that everyone was invited to append to anything. It took your chickens from your backyard and put them in Zuccotti Park. It took your broom from your kitchen and brought it to Zuccotti Park. That invitation was the threat. Of course, it was substantiated by real →infrastructure—Occupy Food actually fed us with heated chafing plates of prepared foods, of course pizza, and other random snacks liberated from dumpsters—skills that were already well established by projects like Food Not Bombs in our community.

Jason: Occupy chickens! In the context of a social movement even a chicken can become recognizable as a threat. You could bring your broom to Zuccotti Park and charge it with meaning, but this also worked in reverse, where the things that were in the park could charge what's outside. For instance, the tent became

a signifier. After the eviction of the Zuccotti occupation, any tent, anywhere not in a national forest, held symbolic significance as a node of protest. It became like a virus, and even part of the movement's slogan: "Fuck us and we multiply!"; "Evict us and we multiply!"

Beka: Occupy repurposed the symbols and tools that govern the use of space, and by putting them in the hands of protesters, we tried to destabilize the symbolic order. For instance, there were the →kettling nets that the cops use to contain protesters, so we got orange kettling nets, put the Occupy name all over them and used them to hold space on our terms. Or there were those big concrete blocks that the police deploy; we made ones that look identical out of foam, and instead of NYPD on them, they were stenciled with the same NYPD font: "Occupy: Protecting the people from the powerful."

Jesse: Zuccotti Park was full of tents and tarps, but during the day they really receded into the background, and the empty spaces between the tents came alive with all this working group activity; the library, the print shop, the food station, spaces of conviviality and shared life. It could feel like a swarming town center—people milling about, like a festival.

Beka: I think that's probably true. But I can imagine that it was also an intense and alienating space for some; maybe it just depends on what stage of Occupy you're talking about. These spaces shift over time, and have a life course that changes—for better and for worse—as things progress.

Jason: An occupation is like a big gap in the world for people to join and experiment with. What do you want to bring? Collectively, we bounce ideas off each other and things start to grow. The space itself was essential for modeling another society. But I also think it's important to see that Occupy could happen anywhere. Zuccotti worked, but it was also our greatest limitation. You can conceive of Occupy as the physical things that are in the protest encampment, but if you define it more broadly, *it's more like an attitude toward infra-structure. The eviction of our occupation was inevitable, but that didn't mean the end of our movement; it was just one out of a million possibilities. How could we take that basic idea and take over hospitals? Vacant homes? Old schools? We're still effectively experimenting with these same forms, even as names change.*

Beka: It's also important to see Zuccotti Park as a stage; it was a space for performance. The steps in the park were important—the width of the entire park, they led down from Wall Street into the park and created an amphitheater effect. There were simple soap boxes too—made out of whatever seemed sturdy enough to stand on (→ Building materials). Anyone could go and speak. It became a center of gravity for the disaffected, which in the context of late capitalism is almost all of us. There was no other stage like it. We were performing a space of democratic assembly and it felt like anyone could have a voice and be heard. That was true to some extent, even though there was a lot of decision making and politicking present behind the scenes. It wasn't just performance. It was also a space in which real meetings and relationship building and planning happened. It didn't purely live in the realm of the symbolic.

Jason: It's also important to remember that the occupiers weren't just the people in the park. They were all of the people who were displaced or absent from capitalism and who might be supporting from afar. They were the caretakers who couldn't go because they were at home; the folks who wanted to be there but couldn't because of one form of precarity or another. Those are occupiers, and the architecture of the movement allowed for them to feel as though they were also participants.

Jesse: I think you're onto something really important. It's not just about pizza boxes and plastic boxes and tents. These materials were imbued with relations that helped tether the movement together, and to other international movements, and to precarious workers and caregivers in other states who

also feel like they are occupiers. Someone in the Midwest calls in a pizza delivery to Zuccotti; it feeds a few people then the box enables a few more people to add their voice to the park. It's a whole circuit of relations that substantiated the most powerful threat of all: the sense we felt that there were so many people, millions of us, who all felt like, "oh fuck yeah, I think I should be in that park even if I'm not." (Interview: Jesse Goldstein, Beka Economopoulos, Jason Jones; interview editing: SH; introduction and research: AMM)

Öffentlicher Raum, engl. → *Public space*. Meist wird der öffentliche Raum mit der Öffentlichkeit gleichgesetzt: Bei Hannah Arendt und Henri Lefebvre heißt es sinngemäß, dass der physische öffentliche Raum eine wesentliche Voraussetzung dafür ist, dass überhaupt Öffentlichkeit entstehe, also ein öffentlicher Diskurs mit allen Konflikten, → *Demonstrationen* und der produktiven Erfahrung von Unterschieden zwischen den dort auftretenden Akteur*innen (vgl. Arendt 1958; Lefebvre 1968) möglich werde. Doch die Räume, in denen sich Proteste vollziehen, sind keineswegs immer öffentlich. Paradoxe Situationen können entstehen, wenn etwa → *Occupy Wall Street* → *2011* von der üblicherweise als Problem definierten Privatisierung des öffentlichen Raums profitieren konnte. Als „Privately Owned Public Space" (POPS) konnte der Zuccotti Park zunächst nicht durch die → *Polizei* geräumt werden. Bei den Tagebauprotesten im → *Hambacher Wald* ab → *2012* war das durch → *Baumhäuser* besetzte Waldstück eigentumsrechtlich bereits im Besitz des Energiekonzerns RWE. Das Bundeswaldgesetz sowie das Landesforstgesetz regeln jedoch, dass der Wald in Deutschland der Öffentlichkeit grundsätzlich zugänglich ist. Somit konnte um den Wald kein Zaun errichtet werden und das Demonstrationsrecht galt auch auf dem Firmengelände. Öffentliches Eigentum und öffentlicher Raum können einander bedingen, so beispielsweise bei den Protesten gegen den Fluglärm am Frankfurter Flughafen in den Jahren ab 2011. Dort waren die „Montagsdemonstrationen" in der Abflughalle zulässig, da die Betreibergesellschaft Fraport AG mehrheitlich in öffentlichem Besitz ist. Versammlungsfreiheit besteht in Deutschland unter Umständen sogar auf privaten, aber öffentlich zugänglichen Grundstücken, wie 2015 durch das Bundesverfassungsgericht entschieden wurde (Eilantrag zum „Bierdosen-Flashmob für die Freiheit" auf dem privatisierten Nibelungenplatz in Passau). (OE)

Open-pit mine occupations, Ger. →Tagebaubesetzungen; →Camps for Climate Action, →Finger, →Overall, →Protest organizations, →Straw

Opposition, Ger. →Dagegensein. "Even more than the commitment to the social market economy and its democratic dividends, the habit of protest has a firm place in the history of the Federal Republic. And with it, we also stand out worldwide. The issues have changed, and so quickly that biographical breaks within the generation of protesters would have been unavoidable had it not been for the possibility of moving from protest to protest. Protests against remilitarization and nuclear armament are followed by Easter marchers and Emergency Acts opposition, the student movement and neo-Marxism, citizens' initiatives, anti-occupational ban campaigns, the peace movement, the women's movement, self-help groups, and—boasting best results—the environmental movement. New social movements form under the influence of the 'change in values' and take in candidates from the Marxist camps who can only be recognized by their accent. Issues of distribution are supplemented, if not replaced, by issues of risk. Remaining alternative is the motto. Opposition oblige." (Luhmann 1990/2016, p. 159)

Oranienplatz-Camp, engl. →Oranienplatz camp. Im Zuge der →2012 einsetzenden selbstorganisierten Geflüchtetenproteste, noch bevor der Dschungel von Calais entstand, wurde ein →Protestcamp in Berlin errichtet; direkt am zentral in Kreuzberg gelegenen Oranienplatz. Die Forderungen: Abschaffung von Sammelunterkünften, von Ab-

schiebungen sowie die Aussetzung der Residenzpflicht. Parallel besetzten Geflüchtete gemeinsam mit Aktivist∗innen eine benachbarte leerstehende Schule (→Hausbesetzung). Das außenwirksame Camp mit Plenums- und Küchenzelt blieb aber Dreh- und Angelpunkt des Protests. Bis zur polizeilichen Räumung 2014 waren zuletzt bis zu 600 Menschen in →Zelten und der ehemaligen Schule untergebracht. (JD)

Oranienplatz camp, Ger. →Oranienplatz-Camp. In the course of the self-organized refugee protests that had started in →2012, long before the "Calais Jungle," a →protest camp was established in Berlin—right on Oranienplatz, in the middle of Kreuzberg. The demands included the abolition of collective accommodations and deportations, as well as the suspension of regulations forcing people without permanent protection status to remain within a clearly defined region. At the same time, refugees and activists occupied a nearby empty school (→Squatting). However, the publicly effective camp with its plenum and kitchen tent remained the main hub of the protest. Almost 600 people were accommodated in the →tents and the former school until the police evicted the premises in 2014. (JD)

Overall, engl. →Overall. Bei Aktionen der Klimabewegung stehen sich häufig die weißen Overalls der Aktivist∗innen und die schwarzen Uniformen der →Polizei gegenüber – und damit auch die symbolische Farbe der Unschuld im Gegensatz zu staatlicher Militanz. Die Overalls werden zum →Schutz vor äußeren Einflüssen und polizeilicher Identitätsfeststellung getragen (→Kleidung). Darüber hinaus schaffen sie eine visuelle Einheit und drücken Genderneutralität aus. (JD)

Overall, Ger. →Overall (fig.). During actions by the climate movement, the white overalls of the activists often contrast with the black uniforms of the →police—and thus also stage the symbolic color of innocence vs. state militarism. The overalls are worn for →protection against external factors and police ID checks (→Clothing). Further-

Overall. Tim Wagner: Tagebaublockade von Ende Gelände, Lützerath, 31. Oktober 2021
(Overall. Tim Wagner: Open-pit mining blockade by Ende Gelände, Lützerath, October 31, 2021)

more, they create visual unity and have a gender-neutral appearance. (JD)

Paris Commune, Ger. → *Pariser Kommune*. From March 18 to May 28, → *1871*, a spontaneously formed municipal council attempted to install socialist rule in Paris. As there was relatively broad consent to defend the city with armed force, if need be (→ *Violence*, → *Weapons*), 900 → *barricades* were installed, some of which were heavily fortified—mostly in the districts of the workers and the poor. During the so-called "Bloody Week of May," fierce but ultimately futile battles were fought against the troops of the conservative central government. (SH)

Pariser Kommune, engl. → *Paris Commune*. Vom 18. März bis zum 28. Mai → *1871* versuchte ein spontan gebildeter Gemeinderat, Paris sozialistisch zu regieren. Da ein gewisser Konsens bestand, die Stadt notfalls auch mit Waffengewalt zu verteidigen (→ *Waffen*, → *Gewalt*), wurden – zumeist in den Vierteln der Arbeiter*innen und Armen – 900 zum Teil sehr wehrhaft wirkende → *Barrikaden* errichtet. Während der sogenannten „Blutigen Maiwoche" wur-

den erbitterte, aber letztlich erfolglose Kämpfe gegen die Truppen der konservativen Zentralregierung geführt. (SH)

Passport office, Ger. → *Passstelle*; → *Autonomous zone*, → *Gorleben*

Passstelle, engl. → *Passport office*; → *Autonome Zone*, → *Gorleben*

Pearl Roundabout, engl. → *Pearl Roundabout*. Der → *Kreisverkehr* mit der großen Perlenskulptur aus dem Jahr 1982 bildete in Bahrain das Zentrum der etwa einen Monat andauernden Konflikte, die als lokale Reaktion auf die Ereignisse des Arabischen Frühlings in Tunesien und Ägypten begannen. Im Februar → *2011* stieß eine erste → *Großdemonstration* auf brutale Reaktionen auf Seiten der Ordnungskräfte (→ *Gewalt*). Es gab Verletzte und einen ersten Toten. Trotzdem gelang es der Opposition, für vier Wochen ein → *Protestcamp* entstehen zu lassen. Danach wurde der Aufstand mithilfe von Truppen der Nachbarstaaten niedergeschlagen. Unmittelbar nach der Räumung des Camps erfolgte die → *Zerstörung* der Skulptur und die Überschreibung des Kreisverkehrs mit einer Kreuzung als vorbeugende → *Anti-Protestmaßnahme*.

Das Protestsymbol wurde ausgelöscht, vergleichbar mit der Umgestaltung des → *Tahrir-Platzes* in Kairo. (OE)

Pearl Roundabout, Ger. → *Pearl Roundabout*. The → *roundabout* with the large sculpture of a pearl erected in 1982 formed the epicenter in Bahrain of conflicts that persisted for about a month and started as a local response to the events of the Arab Spring in Tunisia and Egypt. In February → *2011*, the first large-scale → *demonstration* encountered a brutal reaction on the part of the authorities (→ *Violence*). People were injured and the first fatalities occurred. The opposition nevertheless succeed in creating a → *protest camp* for four weeks, after which the uprising was quashed with help from troops from neighboring states. Immediately after the camp was cleared, → *destruction* of the sculpture commenced, and the the roundabout was replaced with in intersection as a preventative → *anti-protest measure.* The symbol of protest was erased, comparable to the redesign of Cairo's → *Tahrir Square*. (OE)

Pfahlbau, engl. → *Pile dwellings*. → *Bautypen*, → *Gorleben*, → *Lützerath*, → *Maplewood Mudflats*, → *Turm*

Pflasterstein, engl. → *Cobblestone.* Herausgerissene Pflastersteine gelten in Westeuropa als Inbegriff des politischen Aufstands und der → *Gewalt* auf der → *Straße*, seitdem sie während der dreitägigen Straßenkämpfe der → *Julirevolution* → *1830* in Paris erstmals derart vehement aus dem Boden gerissen, zu → *Barrikaden* aufgetürmt und als → *Waffe* gegen die königlichen Truppen umfunktioniert wurden. Die quaderförmigen, zuvor ordentlich in Reihen verlegten Steine, die in Paris so groß und schwer waren, dass die Revolutionär*innen sie nur aus dem Fenster der Gebäude, aber nicht von der Straße aus auf das Militär werfen konnten, sollen neben Möbeln und Hausrat wie „Hagel" (Anonym 1831, S. 55) vom Himmel geregnet sein. Sie brachten dem Bürgerkönig Louis-Philippe, der nach der Revolution den Thron bestieg, den Spitznamen „Pflasterkönig" (Börne 1832/1964, S. 439) ein. Und bereits ihr

Herausreißen galt als so subversiv, dass der Journalist Ludwig Börne, als sein Verleger ihn hat, Lithografien über die Julirevolution mit Texten zu versehen, entschied, er „möchte gerne etwas dazu beitragen, Deutschland zu *entpflastern*" (Börne 1830/1968, S. 1208). In Frankreich war der Straßenbelag als „Pflaster des Königs", als „pavé du Roi" (Birk 1934/1971, S. 292), bekannt, seitdem Louis XIV. die Heer- und Handelsstraße von Paris nach Orléans damit hatte pflastern lassen. Während die Perfektion der am Boden fest aneinandergefügten Steine, die in Fronarbeit behauen und verlegt worden waren, als „Monument" der königlichen Herrschaft (Patte 1765, S. 9) galt, signalisierten die durch die Luft fliegenden Pflastersteine buchstäblich den Umsturz der etablierten Hierarchien von Oben und Unten.

Der revolutionäre Gebrauch, der seit der Revolution von → *1848* in nahezu ganz Westeuropa verbreitet ist, hat sich den Steinen angelagert und blieb auch dann erhalten, wenn nach den Revolutionen zügig wieder gepflastert wurde, damit, wie Heinrich Heine argwöhnte, „keine äußere Spur der Revolution bleibe" (Heine 1832/1976, S. 110) – und sogar dann, wenn die Steine durch Schotter nach 1968 durch Asphalt ersetzt wurden, um künftige Aufstände zu verhindern, zur „Unterdrückung von Barrikaden" (Archives de Paris), wie die entsprechenden Akten der Pariser Stadtverwaltung betitelt sind. Pflastersteine werden seither von unterschiedlichsten Gruppierungen gezielt aufgesammelt und genutzt: von → *Gelbwesten*, die gegen die Finanzierung der überfälligen Energiewende demonstrieren, von Bewohner*innen der Banlieues, die sich gegen ihre systematische Ausgrenzung und Diskriminierung wehren, bei Protesten gegen die Ergebnisse von französischen Präsident*innenschaftswahlen auf der für linke → *Demonstrationen* berühmten Place de la Bastille und seit den 1980er Jahren am 1. Mai in Berlin-Kreuzberg. Vor allem im → *Mai '68* setzten die protestierenden Studierenden in Paris sie als „historisches Zitat" (Gilcher-Holtey 1995, S. 240) ein, als

Pflasterstein. Atelier Populaire: *La beauté est dans la rue*, Plakat (Siebdruck), Paris, Mai 1968 (Cobblestone. Atelier Populaire: *La beauté est dans la rue*, poster (silkscreen), Paris, May 1968)

Pflasterstein. Jo Schnapp: Fotomontage aus Walter Lewino: *L'imagination au pouvoir. Photographies de Jo Schnapp*, Paris 1968 (Cobblestone. Jo Schnapp: photomontage from Walter Lewino: *L'imagination au pouvoir. Photographies de Jo Schnapp*, Paris 1968)

sie die Sorbonne besetzten, das Straßenpflaster im Quartier latin aufbrachen, die → *Polizei* und die Bereitschaftspolizei mit Pflastersteinen bewarfen und mit Barrikaden aus Pflastersteinen die Straßen blockierten, weil ihr Protest dann aussah wie eine Revolution, auch wenn

Friedrich Engels diese „Rebellion alten Stils" (Engels 1895/1972, S. 519) – die vielleicht erst mit den → *Ziegelstein*-Barrikaden → *2019* in → *Hongkong* erneuert wurde – schon lange zuvor für überholt erklärt hatte. Die Parole „sous les pavés, la plage" („unter dem Pflaster der Strand") der Studierenden versprach einen Urzustand ohne das Pflaster, das auf Schritt und Tritt die einstige königliche Regierungsgewalt in Erinnerung brachte und alle, die darauf liefen, zu Untertan∗innen herabsetzte. Die herausgerissenen und geworfenen Pflastersteine von 1968, die nicht länger die Machtausübung des Königs, sondern die der Revoltierenden sichtbar machten und das Durchbrechen starrer sozialer, politischer und formaler Konventionen, sollten wie in Jo Schnapps Fotomontage aus dem Pariser Mai die Fantasie ankurbeln, dass überhaupt andere Zustände möglich sein könnten: „l'imagination au pouvoir" („die Fantasie an die Macht")! Statt Herrschaft sei dann Schönheit auf der Straße zu finden, wie es auf einem Poster des Atelier Populaire hieß, einem aktivistischen Kollektiv, das in der besetzten Kunsthochschule Plakate produzierte.

Längst sind die Pflastersteine im → *Museum* gelandet. Während Künstler∗innen wie Robert Filliou mit Pflasterstein-Multiples in Kisten nach 1968 die „Fetischisierung der Revolte" (Lebel, Brau, Merlhès 1969, S. 460) markierten oder wie Joseph Beuys versuchten, die den Steinen anhaftenden subversiven Möglichkeiten in den eigenen Multiples zu speichern und durch deren Vertrieb im Kunstversand zu verbreiten, vermögen die mittlerweile in der Regel in Vitrinen präsentierten Dinge im Museum keine Revolution mehr auszulösen. Das gilt auch für all die Pflastersteine, die als persönliche Souvenirs mit nach Hause genommen wurden, in historischen Museen oder als Beweisstücke in den Asservatenkammern der Polizei landeten – diese betreibt vermutlich das geheime Pflastersteinmuseum mit Exemplaren aller wichtigen Straßenschlachten, von dem in urbanen Legenden immer wieder die Rede ist. Der „Zauber" (Sarrans 1832, S. 311) der losen Pflastersteine auf der Straße scheint heute trotzdem noch zu funktionieren. Anders lässt sich kaum erklären, dass anlässlich von angemeldeten Demonstrationen in den → *digitalen Medien* immer wieder gezielt Falschmeldungen mit Fotografien von ordinären Straßenbauarbeiten lanciert werden, verbunden mit Warnungen, „die Linken" hätten sich dort, clever mit Bauzäunen, Baustellenschildern und Absperrband getarnt, bereits im Vorfeld Pflastersteine bereitgelegt. (Kathrin Rottmann)

Pile dwellings, Ger. → *Pfahlbau*; → *Building types*, → *Gorleben*, → *Lützerath*, → *Maplewood Mudflats*, → *Tower*

Plakat, engl. → *Poster*; → *Medien*, → *Protestschild*

Plane, engl. → *Tarpaulin*; → *Baumaterial*, → *Bender*, → *Movimiento 15M*

Platzbesetzung, engl. → *Public square occupation*. Die Platzbesetzung als historisch weit zurückreichende Protestform ist zu unterscheiden von der Platzbewegung. Als Platzbewegungen werden in der Politikwissenschaft die relativ jungen, ab → *2011* sichtbaren politischen Protestströmungen verstanden, die sich von den vorangegangenen „Farbenrevolutionen" unterscheiden (z.B. „Orange Revolution", Ukraine 2004 oder „Grüne Bewegung", Iran 2009; vgl. Kim, Nonhoff 2022). Diese „Farbenrevolutionen" stehen oft im Zusammenhang mit Wahlen oder Wahlfälschungen und die Farbe entspricht der Kampagnenfarbe der unterdrückten Bewerber*innen. Die Platzbewegungen seit dem „Protestjahr 2011" sind aus Platzbesetzungen hervorgegangen und haben im Unterschied zu den „Farbenrevolutionen" oft eine viel weitreichendere Agenda und umfassen meist ein sehr breites, in seinen Zielen uneinheitliches politisches Spektrum (die Beispiele für Platzbewegungen in der Ausstellung *Protest/Architektur* sind → *Movimiento 15M*, → *Occupy Wall Street*, → *Tahrir-Platz* und → *Majdan*). Eine Sonderform der Platzbesetzung ist die → *Gelbwestenbewegung* von → *2018*, die auf → *Kreisverkehren* in ganz Frankreich ihren Anfang nahm, bevor sie zeitweilig auch den symbolisch

hoch aufgeladenen Platz um den Arc de Triomphe in Paris in Besitz nahm. Die Symbolkraft von Plätzen spielt für Platzbesetzungen eine wichtige Rolle. Sie garantiert nicht nur größte Sichtbarkeit und mediale Aufmerksamkeit, sondern ist auch als politisches Zeichen zu werten. Der Sturz der Siegessäule auf der von → *Barrikaden* gesicherten Place Vendôme in Paris im Zuge der → *Pariser Kommune* → *1871* wurde auf unzähligen Grafiken und einigen Fotografien festgehalten (→ *Denkmalsturz*). Die National Mall in Washington, DC, war 1963 das Ziel des „March on Washington for Jobs and Freedom", einem der Höhepunkte der US-Bürger*innenrechtsbewegung. Martin Luther King hielt dort seine „I Have a Dream"-Rede. In unmittelbarer, und dadurch symbolisch hoch aufgeladener Nähe wurde → *1968* die → *Resurrection City* aufgebaut. Die Besetzung des Tian'anmen-Platzes in Peking im Jahr 1989 endete mit einem Massaker, als das chinesische Militär die Proteste der Bevölkerung gewaltsam niederschlug. (OE)

Police, Ger. → *Polizei*. Numerous manifestations of → *protest architecture* can be understood as responses to the rules and strategies of the police or other security forces (→ *Anti-protest measures*). This begins at the symbolic level. When → *demonstrations*, → *blockades*, or → *public square occupations* are restricted by police cordons or → *kettling*, scenes of extremely asymmetrical symbolism often emerge in these confrontation zones: on the one side, the police in full combat and riot gear with helmets and → *protective shields*, on the other, the protesters in plain clothes, unprotected, with linked arms, sometimes sitting, and with full → *body deployment* and a high risk of injury (→ *Violence*). Many elements of → *protest camps* are designed to make it as difficult as possible for the police to clear them (as "delaying architecture")—for example, the → *towers* and the roof of the community house designed for sit-in blockades in → *Gorleben* in → *1980* or, more generally, all kinds of constructions in which protesters use their vulnerability to force the police to be cautious (as in the

Polizeikessel. Dirk Eisermann: Einkesselung von 861 Demonstrant∗innen in Hamburg am 8. Juni 1986 (Kettling. Dirk Eisermann: Kettling of 861 demonstrators in Hamburg, June 8, 1986)

case of activists attaching themselves to a tree as well as in connection with →*tree houses*, →*nakedness*, →*ropes*, →*rappelling*). At protests with counterprotests, the police may take on a protective role, as is the case when there is a need to protect protestors from the aggression of angry bystanders, such as in the controversial roadblocks of Letzte Generation.(→*Protection*, →*Super-gluing*). (OE)

Political plastic, Ger. →*Politische Plastik*. Following the concept of "social sculpture" (*soziale Plastik*) by the artist Joseph Beuys, which is based on the idea that every human being is an artist and can positively influence societal conditions through creative action, the architect and architectural theorist Eyal Weizman coined the term "political plastic." This new buzzword specifically targeted Israel's settlement policy in the border region with the territories claimed by the Palestinians and an "architecture of occupation" dominated by barriers, →*blockades*, exclusion zones, and checkpoints, which Weizman described as "politics in matter" (Weizman 2017, p. 5). When he characterized Is-

raeli construction measures as "elastic" in this context, it was not meant to imply that the architecture was soft and pliable but that houses, containers, →*streets*, and walls were strategically laid out and could change their position, which "responds to and reflects political and military conflicts" (Weizman 2017, p. 7). The architect Anders Rubing has attempted to transfer the notion of "political plastic" to the strategy of →*protest camps*—whereby the term regains some of the positive connotations of Beuys's "social sculpture," but without losing the explicitly political thrust of Weizman's consideration: as could be observed in the example of Occupy LA. The plasticity of the 2011 camp set up in front of Los Angeles City Hall, for instance, lay "in the changing geography, the extension and expansion [...] both adapting and breaking the external boundaries of the site: *simultaneously altering* its density to the number of protesters present" (Rubing 2018, p. 42). (SH)

Politische Plastik, engl. →*Political plastic*. In Anlehnung an das Konzept der „sozialen Plastik" des Künstlers Joseph Beuys, dem der Gedanke zugrunde liegt, dass jeder Mensch ein Künstler sei und durch kreatives Handeln positiv auf die gesellschaftlichen Verhältnisse einwirken könne, hat der Architekt und Architekturtheoretiker Eyal Weizman den Begriff der „politischen Plastik" geprägt. Dieses neue Schlagwort zielte konkret auf die israelische Siedlungspolitik in der Grenzregion zu den von den Palästinenser∗innen beanspruchten Gebieten und eine von Barrieren, → *Blockaden*, Sperrzonen und Kontrollpunkten dominierte „Architektur der Besatzung", die Weizman als „in Material gegossene Politik" bezeichnete (Weizman 2009, S. 11). Wenn er die israelischen Baumaßnahmen dabei als „elastisch" charakterisierte, sollte dies nicht bedeuten, dass die Architektur weich und nachgiebig wäre, sondern dass Häuser, Container, → *Straßen* und Mauern strategisch angelegt werden und ihre Position in „Reaktion auf politische und militärische Konflikte" verändern können (Weizman 2009, S. 14). Der Architekt Anders Rubing hat versucht, den Aspekt der „politischen Plastik" auf die Strategie der → *Protestcamps* zu übertragen – wodurch der Begriff wieder einige der positiven Konnotationen von Beuys' „sozialer Plastik" zurückgewinnt, ohne aber die explizit politische Stoßrichtung von Weizmans Betrachtung einzubüßen: Wie sich am Beispiel von Occupy LA beobachten ließ, lag die Plastizität des 2011 vor dem Rathaus in Los Angeles angelegten Camps etwa „in the changing geography, the extension and expansion [...] both adapting and breaking the external boundaries of the site: *simultaneously altering* its density to the number of protesters present" (Rubing 2018, S. 42). (SH)

Polizei, engl. → *Police*. Zahlreiche Ausprägungen von → *Protestarchitektur* lassen sich als Antworten auf die Regeln und Strategien der Polizei oder anderer Sicherheitskräfte verstehen (→ *Anti-Protestmaßnahmen*). Dies beginnt auf der symbolischen Ebene. Wenn → *Demonstrationen,* → *Blockaden* oder → *Platzbesetzungen* durch Polizeiketten oder einen → *Polizeikessel* begrenzt werden, so entstehen in diesen Konfrontationszonen oft Szenen extrem asymmetrischer Symbolik: hier die Polizei in voller Kampfmontur, in *Riot Gear* mit Helmen und → *Schutzschilden*, dort die Protestierenden in Zivil, schutzlos, untergehakt, manchmal sitzend, voller → *Körpereinsatz* mit hohem Risiko, verletzt zu werden (→ *Gewalt*). Viele Elemente von → *Protestcamps* sind darauf abgestimmt, der Polizei die Räumung maximal zu erschweren („Verzögerungsarchitektur"). So beispielsweise die → *Türme* und das für Sitzblockaden ausgelegte Dach des Gemeinschaftshauses in → *Gorleben* → *1980* oder, ganz allgemein gesagt, alle Arten von Konstruktionen, in denen Protestierende ihre Verletzlichkeit zum Einsatz bringen, um die Seite der Polizei zur Vorsicht zu zwingen (beispielsweise beim Tree-Hugging sowie im Zusammenhang mit → *Baumhaus,* → *Nacktheit,* → *Seilen,* → *Abseilen*). Bei Protesten und Gegenprotesten kann der Polizei eine Schutzfunktion zukommen, ebenso bei der Sicherung von Protestierenden vor der Aggression aufgebrachter Dritter wie bei den umstrittenen Straßenblockaden der Letzten Generation (→ *Schutz,* → *Ankleben*). (OE)

Polizeikessel, engl. → *Kettling*. Lang andauerndes Einkreisen und damit Blockieren von Protestierenden durch die → *Polizei* (→ *Blockade*). Beim „Hamburger Kessel" im Jahr 1986 wurden Personen, die gegen die Verhinderung einer Anti-Atomkraft-Demonstration durch die Polizei protestieren wollten (→ *Demonstration*), durch einen weiteren Polizeieinsatz bis zu 13 Stunden auf offener → *Straße* festgesetzt. Die Maßnahme wurde später vom Verwaltungsgericht Hamburg für rechtswidrig erklärt. Ein etwa fünf Stunden dauernder Polizeikessel gegen ca. 1000 Aktivist∗innen bei den Blockupy-Protesten in Frankfurt am Main im Jahr 2013 hingegen wurde vom Bundesverfassungsgericht als rechtmäßig eingestuft. (OE)

Poster, Ger. → *Plakat*; → *Media,* → *Protest placard*

Pot lid, Ger. → *Topfdeckel*; → *Noise*

Protection, Ger. → *Schutz*. Protest events are associated with risks for all participants, which vary in magnitude depending on the political system, form of action, and → *protest goal*. For activists, a threat to physical and psychological safety can be posed by the state, the → *police*, the military, or from a movement with divergent viewpoints, but so can individuals or groups within the movement, especially for people who belong to a minority due to their gender, sexuality, or ethnicity. In potentially violent encounters (→ *Violence*), protesters often use helmets, → *protective shields*, → *clothing*, goggles, and masks to protect themselves against → *anti-protest measures* such as pepper spray, tear gas, and → *water cannons*, and in dictatorial systems, also against live ammunition, batons, and other → *weapons*. For this purpose, everyday objects such as hard hats, ski goggles, closet doors, and kickboards are usually misappropriated (→ *Misappropriation*, → *Myanmar protests* in → *2021*), materials from bulky waste are recycled or, as at → *Maidan* in Kyiv, even police shields stolen during clashes are used. The police and military also protect themselves during such outbreaks of violence with protective gear, which—as shown, for example, by photos of the Zurich police shields at the → *Zurich youth protests* or the uniform of the Frankfurt police during the protests against → *Startbahn West*, both from → *1980*—has grown in scope and professionalism over the past decades. In contrast, "arming up" often takes place at short notice on the part of the protesters, with knowledge about which protective measure effectively helps against which anti-protest measure being quickly disseminated via social media, sometimes also through manuals (→ *Handbücher / Online-Manuals*).

At the → *Hong Kong protests* in → *2014*, the umbrella initially used to protect against pepper spray and surveillance cameras became the symbol of the movement. It was utilized in artworks (→ *Media*) as well as in combative confrontations, where the "tortoise formation," which was already widespread in ancient Rome—here consisting of several umbrellas interlocked with each other—proved to be particularly effec-

tive. In → *Caracas* in → *2014*, wooden shields were given symbolic value by being painted with pictures of deceased protesters and Christian motifs. Passive armament—that is, the carrying of items that are suitable as pieces of armor—is prohibited in Germany at gatherings. This includes not only respirator masks, body armor, and bullet-proof vests, but also, for example, the straw sacks (→ *Straw*) brought along by climate activists at open-pit → *blockades*, which serve as seat pads during long-lasting actions. At Maidan in Kyiv, protesters used → *cooking pots*, sieves, and metal buckets as protective helmets after the parliament made it a punishable offense to wear "real" helmets.

In contrast to protective gear as a tangible tool for direct confrontations on the → *street*, spatial strategies help to make everyday life in the → *protest camp* safer. To avoid attacks by the police and military as well as people who sympathized with the authorities, activists set up a safe zone protected with → *barricades* in → *Tahrir Square* in → *2011* and carried out access controls. Particularly sensitive amenities, such as childcare, were located in the center of the → *roundabout*. To increase internal security, protesters against the → *Dakota Access Pipeline* in North Dakota in → *2016* also screened new arrivals to the camp for alcohol and drugs. At → *Occupy Wall Street*, despite a zero-tolerance policy against drugs, violence, and abuse, there were allegations of rape and, as a consequence, a women's tent was set up. At the beginning of the occupation, the activists in New York actually wanted to go without → *tents*—in the spirit of radical openness, but also to prevent criminal activities. With the onset of fall, however, the occupiers' need for shelter from snow and rain prevailed. As the number of private tents grew, social cohesion disintegrated. This trend was reinforced by the division of the movement into "protected" and "unprotected" people: the organizers of the occupation retreated to their apartments in the evening, while the camp offered a home primarily to those who did not have an apartment in the city. Activists decided to set up "safe spaces" for women and gender-diverse people not only at Occupy Wall Street: in → *Hambach Forest* there was an "All-Flinta Barrio." At → *Lützerath*, a queer feminist house project developed in "Paula's Farm." During the → *Farmers' protests* in India, men and women slept in clearly separated zones. At the → *Greenham Common Peace Camp*, people even went one step further: from 1982 on, only women were allowed to stay there, and the activists undertook night watches to protect the camp from "vigilantes" who tried to intimidate the protesters by harassing them. Also in the → *MTST* land occupations in São Paulo, the security issue directly affects the layout of the camp. Narrow paths are laid out between the single rows of tents, which are regularly patrolled and checked by safety officers.

In some forms of protest, such as the campaigns of Letzte Generation (→ *Rappelling*, → *Super-gluing*), activists also deliberately put themselves in danger through their → *body deployment*. They demonstratively display their vulnerability and defenselessness; in this way, → *nakedness* can sometimes be used as a weapon. This tactic worked on a large scale in the overthrow of dictator Ferdinand Marcos during the → *EDSA Revolution* in Manila in → *1986*: a "human shield" formed by hundreds of thousands of supporters of the opposition poured into the streets for its protection and blocked the military troops loyal to the regime, causing them to refuse an order from the commander to shoot, which would have led to a high number of civilian casualties. During evictions of protest camps, for example in Lützerath or in → *Dannenrod Forest*, the delaying strategies were often based on the fact that the physical integrity of all participants must be guaranteed at all times according to German constitutional law. When the eviction of Occupy Wall Street took place for health and safety reasons, the police in New York, in contrast, invoked a duty to protect for their part.

In order to protect themselves from legal consequences in confrontations with the police, protesters often create their own photographic and film documentation, which can be used as evidence in court proceedings. In Germany, parties such as DIE LINKE (The Left) also send parliamentary observers to → *civil disobedience* actions, including those of the climate movement, to monitor the work of the police.

In Lützerath and at the Dakota Access Pipeline protests, tips for nonviolent resistance and correct behavior during evictions and arrests were provided in skillshares and workshops. When protesters face repression because of their involvement in protests or certain forms of protest, a particular focus is often placed on identity protection. In → *Hong Kong* in → *2019*, activists attempted to evade police facial-recognition software not only by wearing masks but also by jamming cameras with laser pointers. To disguise their digital identities, they also used one-way passes instead of personalized subway tickets, and used prepaid SIM cards, secure messenger services, and Bluetooth to exchange information. (AMM)

Protective shield, Ger. → *Schutzschild (fig.)*. Shields primarily serve to provide demonstrators with physical → *protection*, in part against → *violent* → *anti-protest measures* such as teargas or truncheons. In addition, they can have a symbolic meaning. During the → *Venezuelan protests* in → 2014, wooden shields were painted with art. These included Christian motifs and images of protesters who had been killed (→ *Misappropriation*). This sparked a certain reluctance among police when it came to beating activists to the ground. (JD)

Protest architecture, Ger. → *Protestarchitektur,* covers those aspects of protest movements that involve space and intervene in space: by which sites are appropriated, blocked, marked, or defended. The means brought to bear range from the bodies of protesters (who occupy spaces or link up in formations) to the strategic production of concrete-built structures. The result are temporary architectural configurations that are as different in terms of expanse and shape as are the protests themselves: ad hoc approaches come up against carefully planned edifices; hand-crafted pieces alternate with engineering and prefabrication; attempts to create a home-like environment contrast with almost military tactics.

If spaces are occupied, settled with camps, and buttressed by barricades, then the demands and objectives take on a material form. Structures become established, new forms of communication evolve, and utopian models for society emerge. The temporal horizon of the protest architecture depends on the success: if the protesters win the day, then the structures and installations have fulfilled their purpose and can be abandoned. If the protests come to nothing, the barricades, tree houses, tents, towers, and huts will sooner or later be cleared away and destroyed. Protest architecture is a race against time. Who will endure the state of emergency away from everyday life for longer—the protesters or those who oppose the protest?

As spatially separated counterworlds within a society, protest events can be considered "heterotopias"—particularly the protest camps that were first emerging as a protest strategy when Michel Foucault coined the aforementioned term in 1967 in line with his concept of "counter-sites." They are "a kind of effectively enacted utopia" (Foucault 1967/1984, p. 3). Their actual architectural realization arises from the overall conditions and the movement's objectives. For its part, the spatial realization impacts on the protests in a kind of feedback loop. Because it simply makes a difference whether people stand on the outskirts of a city on a traffic circle, or instead occupy a central square, a forest, or a piece of private land, whether they gather in one-person or in communal tents, burrow underground or head for the heights.

The political movements since 1830 presented in the exhibition *Protest/Architecture* and in the present volume have not been selected because the team of curators sympathized with them or felt them to be worthy of support, but solely on the basis of their strong spatial elements. Above all, the thirteen case studies demonstrate that in different sociopolitical contexts and using limited resources, people can create experimental if temporary edifices for unusual communities. What is fascinating about all of them is the protesters' energy, passion, and willingness to take risks. In order to describe the research that went beyond the specific cases and brought a wide range of references and linkages to light, we decided that this book needed to take the shape of a lexicon. Indeed, this article is the only one without cross-references, if only because the wealth of connecting links would have rendered it as good as illegible. (OE, JD, SH, AMM)

Protestarchitektur, engl. → *Protest architecture,* umfasst die räumlichen, in den Raum ausgreifenden Aspekte von Protestbewegungen: Orte werden ungeeignet, blockiert, markiert, verteidigt. Die eingesetzten Mittel reichen von den Körpern der Protestierenden – die Räume besetzen oder Formationen bilden – bis zur strategischen Errichtung konkret-baulicher Strukturen. Es entstehen ephemere Architekturen, die in ihrer Ausdehnung und Form so unterschiedlich sind wie die Proteste selbst: Ad-hoc-Ansätze treffen auf planvoll entworfene Konstruktionen, Handwerk auf Ingenieurskunst und Vorfabrikation, das Sich-häuslich-Einrichten auf fast schon militärische Taktiken.

Wenn Räume eingenommen, mit Camps besiedelt und durch Barrikaden befestigt werden, dann materialisieren sich die Forderungen und Ziele. Strukturen werden aufgebaut, neue Kommunikationsformen entstehen, utopische Gesellschaftsmodelle blitzen auf. Der zeitliche Horizont der Protestarchitektur ist vom Erfolg bestimmt: Können die Protestierenden sich durchsetzen, dann haben die Strukturen und Bauwerke ihren Zweck erfüllt und können aufgegeben werden. Scheitern die Proteste, werden die Barrikaden, Baumhäuser, Zelte, Türme und Hütten früher oder später geräumt und zerstört. Protestarchitektur ist ein Wettlauf gegen die Zeit. Wer wird den Ausnahmezustand vom Alltag länger durchhalten: die Protestierenden oder diejenigen, gegen die sich die Proteste richten?

Als räumlich abgegrenzte Gegenwelten innerhalb einer Gesellschaft können Protestereignisse zu den „Heterotopien" gezählt werden. Insbesondere die Protestcamps, die gerade erst dabei waren, sich als Proteststrategie zu etablieren, als Michel Foucault den Begriff 1967 zum ersten Mal verwendete, entsprechen seinem Konzept der „Gegenplatzierungen oder Widerlager". Sie sind „tatsächlich realisierte Utopien" (Foucault 1967/1993, S. 39). Ihre konkrete architektonische Umsetzung ergibt sich aus den Rahmenbedingungen und den Zielen der Bewegung. Die räumliche Realisierung beeinflusst – in einer Art Rückkopplungsschleife – wiederum die Proteste. Denn es macht einen Unterschied, ob Menschen in der Peripherie an Verkehrskreiseln stehen, einen zentralen Platz, einen Wald oder ein Privatgrundstück besetzen, ob sie sich in Einzel- oder Gemeinschaftszelten versammeln, unter der Erde bauen oder in die Höhe gehen.

Die in der Ausstellung *Protest/Architektur* und dieser Publikation vorgestellten politischen Bewegungen seit 1830 wurden nicht danach ausgesucht, ob sie dem Kurator*innen-Team sympathisch oder unterstützenswert erschienen, sondern aufgrund ihrer starken räumlichen Komponenten. Vor allem die 13 Case Studies demonstrieren, dass in unterschiedlichen gesellschaftspolitischen Kontexten aus begrenzten Ressourcen experimentelle Bauten für ungewöhnliche Gemeinschaften auf Zeit entstehen können. Faszinierend ist in allen Fällen die Energie, Leidenschaft und Risikobereitschaft der Protestierenden. Um die darüber hinausreichende Recherche abzubilden, die ein weitverzweigtes Feld an Bezügen und Verweisen hervortreten ließ, wurde für dieses Buch die Form eines Lexikons gewählt. Dabei ist dieser Eintrag der einzige ohne Querverweise – die Fülle der Bezüge hätte den Lesefluss unmöglich gemacht. (OE, JD, SH, AMM)

Protestcamp, engl. → *Protest camp.* Jenen Architekturen, die sich zu Protestcamps entwickeln, haftet meist eine unvorhersehbare Dynamik an, ob sie nun detailliert geplant werden oder eher beiläufig entstehen (→ *Alternative Architektur*). Im Unterschied zu temporären → *Demonstrationen* stellen Protestcamps Räume dar, die auf Dauerhaftigkeit ausgelegt sind. Sie müssen so aufgebaut und ausgestattet sein, dass für das alltäglich Notwendige, das für das Funktionieren einer Protestbewegung gebraucht wird, gesorgt ist. Dazu gehören → *Küchen* und Duschen genauso wie Medienzentren (→ *Medien*).

Protestcamps entwickeln sich unterschiedlich – Vorbilder und Ideen kursieren über Landesgrenzen hinweg. Oft entstehen Ad-hoc-Architekturen, denn die materiellen Möglichkeiten sind begrenzt (→ *Baumaterial*). Vieles wird spontan und aus dem Bauch heraus entwickelt. Dabei werden → *Zelte* häufig zu dem architektonischen → *Erkennungszeichen* von Protestcamps. Die verwendeten Baumaterialien wie Textilien, aber auch alltägliche, funktionale Gegenstände entfalten ein symbolisches Potenzial, indem sie im Kontext des Protestcamps zu kraftvollen Gesten des Widerstands umgedeutet werden. Der Architekt Gregory Cowan, der sich mit der Rolle architektonischer Protestformen beschäftigt, sieht in Zelten bei → *Besetzungen* „eine architektonische Strategie, die nicht nur rein pragmatisch ist. Ideologische Gründe untermauern die Verwendung dieser Art von Konstruktionen" (Cowan, undatiert). Für Cowan sind Zelte aufgrund ihrer offenen, mobilen, temporären und schnell aufstellbaren Beschaffenheit sowohl konzeptionell als auch architektonisch von Bedeutung, da sie einen Gegensatz zur Vorstellung von einem statischen und kleinfamiliär geprägten Zuhause bilden.

Eine frühe Meisterleistung im Bereich der Protestarchitektur war die Initiative von Martin Luther King für ein Protestcamp (später nach seiner Ermordung in → *Resurrection City* umbenannt), das Tausende von armen Menschen nach Washington, DC, die Hauptstadt der

Vereinigten Staaten, bringen sollte, um dort politische Reformen einzufordern. Die 15 Hektar große Resurrection City befand sich auf der National Mall, nur wenige Schritte von Lincoln Memorial entfernt. Sie wurde von professionellen Architekten und Stadtplanern nach dem Vorbild von Armeelagern und Einrichtungen für Wanderarbeiter errichtet. Konkrete Vorlagen waren das Camp der → *Bonus Army* im Jahr → *1932* und die Pfadfinderlager, die seit den frühen 1900er Jahren populär waren (Feigenbaum, Frenzel, McCurdy 2013). Der Bauplatz an der Mall wurde anhand eines Rastersystems in eine Reihe von Unterabschnitten oder „Gemeinschaftseinheiten" unterteilt. Dutzende von Freiwilligen halfen beim Aufbau und Betrieb von Zahn- und Gesundheitszentren sowie von Küchen, die drei Mahlzeiten pro Tag servierten. Außerdem gab es das „Many Races Soul Center", eine „Poor People's University" und das „Coretta Scott King Day Care Center" (Wiebenson 1969).

Dies steht im Gegensatz zu Besetzungen an Orten wie dem → *Gezi-Park* oder in → *Hongkong*, die nicht von der sorgfältigen Vorplanung oder den großen Freiflächen der Resurrection City profitierten und daher stärker von den Grenzen und Möglichkeiten der bestehenden Stadtstruktur bestimmt wurden. „Die hyperdichte, kommerzielle Architektur Hongkongs hat die Protestbewegung sowohl verschärft als auch erleichtert", erklärt der Landschaftsarchitekt Adam Bobbette (Feigenbaum 2015). An städtischen Standorten sind die Protestcamps oft „Gegenstädte in der Stadt", so Bobbette. In nur kurzer Zeit entsteht „eine ganze Welt aus selbstgebauten, schnell organisierten und oft schönen Instrumenten des Protests, der Freizeitgestaltung, des Kultes und der Infrastruktur" (Feigenbaum 2015; → *Infrastruktur*).

Als politische Akte der Inbesitznahme stehen Protestcamps für eine kollektive Rückeroberung der Stadt. Sie stellen sich den Infrastrukturen des Kapitalismus – seinen Superhighways, Einkaufszentren, kommerziellen Zentren und privatisierten Plätzen – entgegen. Statt-

dessen machen sie die Stadt menschlicher. Indem sie die Routinen des Alltags durchbrechen, entstehen neue, intensive zwischenmenschliche Beziehungen. Im Gegensatz zur Zerrissenheit unserer Städte und unserer auf Rollen festgelegten Existenz, bieten sie Strukturen für ein Leben ohne Kommerz. Dabei sind Protestcamps nicht auf städtische Zentren beschränkt. Sie werden auch häufig in ländlichen Gebieten, in alten Wäldern, auf Ackerland, in Kohleminen, an Pipelinetrassen und auf indigenem Land errichtet. Durch Protestcamps wird die Aufmerksamkeit darauf gelenkt, dass dort etwas ausgebeutet, abgebaggert oder unterworfen werden soll.

Dennoch ist es wichtig, Protestcamps nicht übermäßig zu romantisieren. Yelta Köm, Herausgeberin und Koordinatorin des Projekts „Herkes İçin Mimarlık" („Architektur für alle"), stellt fest, dass Occupy Gezi sowohl als gemeinschaftliches Experiment als auch als „Konfliktraum" funktionierte (Feigenbaum 2015). In den Protestcamps müssen die Menschen sich rund um die Uhr zusammenraufen. Auch wenn sie ein gemeinsames Anliegen haben, können die Ideen, Erfahrungen und Ideologien der Protestcamper∗innen aufeinanderprallen. Externe Faktoren verstärken diese Spannungen: Protestcamps sind verletzliche Orte, an denen die Menschen ständig der → *Polizei*, den Medien, dem Wetter und dem Klicken von Touristenkameras ausgesetzt sind.

Die Spontaneität von Protestcamps kann die Architektur auf neue Wege bringen. „Niemand kann ein städtisches Protestcamp auf konventionelle Weise entwerfen", sagt Köm. „Die wichtigsten gestalterischen Herausforderungen werden in jeder einzelnen Situation anders sein" (Feigenbaum 2015). Daraus zu lernen, wie Menschen auf diese Herausforderungen reagieren, kann dazu beitragen, weitere lebendige Protestcamp-Architekturen auf besetzten → *Straßen*, Parks und Plätzen auf der ganzen Welt entstehen zu lassen. (Anna Feigenbaum, Fabian Frenzel, Patrick McCurdy)

Protest camp, Ger. → *Protestcamp*.

From the cunningly planned to the irreverently accidental, there is a chaotic mobility about the architectural forms that comprise protest camps (→ *Alternative architecture*). Distinct from other forms of social activism like → *demonstrations* or marches, protest camps are living spaces. They make visible all of the architectures and objects required for the social reproduction of protest and daily life, from → *kitchens* and showers to → *media* centers. These protest camp architectures, their objects and environments, are a critical part of what makes social movements work the way they do.

Protest camp design dynamics are promiscuous—ideas travel across time and place, between cities, rural areas, and continents. The limited resources and heightened emotional settings of the camps alter the stakes of design, resulting in the creation of ad hoc architectures (→ *Building materials*). → *Tents* are often the central architectural feature of protest camps (→ *Identifier*), acting as set design on the hyper-mediated stage of protest, and are often perceived in this light; there is a tactical element to this artful display. The spectacular aesthetics of protest camps exploit the symbolic potential of textiles and building materials—these are everyday, functional objects transformed into powerful acts of defiance. Architect Gregory Cowan, who studies the role of protest in the built environment, sees the appearance of tents in → *occupations* as "a choice of architectural strategy that is not merely pragmatic. Ideological reasons underpin the uses of these kinds of structure" (Cowan n.d.). For Cowan, the tent's indeterminate, mobile, temporary, and rapidly deployable qualities make it both theoretically and architecturally important as a counterpoint to the idea of home as being static and nuclear, and to buildings as being solid and stately.

One of the earliest and greatest feats in defiant architecture came with Martin Luther King Jr.'s plans for a camp (later named → *Resurrection City* after his murder) that would bring thousands of poor people to Washington, DC, the capital of the United States, to demand change. Locted in the National Mall and just steps away from the Lincoln Memorial, the fifteen-acre Resurrection City was loosely modeled by professional architects and urban planners on army camps and sites for migratory workers, such as the → *Bonus Army* encampment in the 1930s and the scout camps popularized in the early 1900s (Feigenbaum, Frenzel, McCurdy 2013). The Mall was divided into a series of subsections or "community units" using a grid system. Dozens of volunteers helped set up and run dental and healthcare centers, as well as kitchens serving three meals a day, alongside the Many Races Soul Center, the Poor People's University, and the Coretta Scott King Day Care Center (Wiebenson 1969).

This can be contrasted with occupations in places such as → *Gezi Park* and → *Hong Kong,* which did not benefit from the rigorous pre-planning or large open spaces of Resurrection City, and thus were more strongly determined by the limits and possibilities of existing built and natural environments. "Hong Kong's hyper-dense, commercial architecture both exacerbated and facilitated the protest movement," explains landscape architect Adam Bobbette (Feigenbaum 2015). In urban locations, protest camps often manifest what Bobbette refers to as "counter-cities within the city." In just a brief time, they can produce "a world of self-built, rapidly organised and often beautiful tools of protest, leisure, worship and infrastructures" (Feigenbaum 2015; → *Infrastructure*).

As political acts of occupation, protest camps enact a collective refusal to leave, which interferes with and takes back the city. They confront the landscapes of capitalism—its superhighways, shopping malls, commercial centers, and privatized squares—and re-create them as places that are both more human and humane. In redirecting the rhythm and flow of urban movement, these occupations become paths of desire, replacing the enforced paths of our normal lives, and introducing a new intensity to interactions. In contrast to the architectures of our atomized cities and the commuting and commercial routines that dominate our existence, they offer structures that facilitate human connection. Protest camps are not limited to urban centers. They are also frequently erected in rural areas, old-growth forests, farmland, coal mines, pipeline routes, and on unceded Indigenous land. Camp architecture renders such sites visible and, through their construction, can present a direct and physical challenge to sites of development, extraction, and colonialization.

Yet it is important not to overly romanticize protest camps. Yelta Köm, editor and coordinator of the project "Herkes İçin Mimarlık" (Architecture for All), observes that Occupy Gezi acted as both common ground and "a conflict space" (Feigenbaum 2015). At protest camps, people must live and work together twenty-four seven. While they may share a common cause, protest campers' ideas, experiences, and ideologies can both converge and clash. External factors heighten these tensions: protest camps are vulnerable spaces where people are constantly exposed to the → *police*, the media, and the elements, as well as to the clicks of tourists' cameras.

Embracing the spontaneity of protest camps can lead architecture in new directions. "No one can design an urban-based protest camp in conventional ways," says Köm. "The key design challenges will always be different in every individual situation" (Feigenbaum 2015). Examining how people respond to these challenges can help transform imaginative ideas from conceptual designs into intentional practices, enabling vibrant, functional protest camp architectures to be built on occupied → *streets*, parks, and squares around the world. (Anna Feigenbaum, Fabian Frenzel, and Patrick McCurdy)

Protest goals, Ger. → *Protestziele*. Protest movements often only agree on what they are protesting. Common ideas on the organization of a future society are usually not part of this concurrence. Two basic modes of protest goals can be determined: protest directed against a specific injustice, abuse, or law; and protest with the aim of achieving an overall social transformation. In the second case, the protest is usually accompanied by utopian excess. As in: "We don't want a bigger piece of the cake, we want the whole bakery."

In terms of the spatial dimension, there are also two different modes: on the one hand, the temporary use of → *public space*, and on the other hand, the permanent appropriation or → *occupation* of both public and private spaces. Protest goals are articulated as concrete or abstract demands. → "*Lobau* bleibt!" (Lobau stays) or "Weg mit dem §218!" (Abolish Paragraph 218!) serve as examples of concrete demands. Inspired by the "Manifeste des 343 salopes" (Manifesto of the 343 Sluts; *Le Nouvel Observateur* 1971) in France, the action "Wir haben abgetrieben" (We had abortions; *stern* 1971) was more confessional. By contrast, slogans such as "Gegen den Faschismus und das Kapital—der Kampf um Befreiung ist international!" (Against fascism and capital—the fight for liberation is international!) are more abstract. Another variant is the abbreviated diagnosis, as used by the Fridays for Future movement: "Wir sind hier, wir sind laut, weil ihr uns die Zukunft klaut!" (We are here, we are loud, because you are stealing our future!).

Protests have different causes. Therefore, protests typically come together in the form of an alliance. In an alliance, different organizations and individuals agree "against" something. Alliances of this kind are heterogenous, and the abstract goals of these unions can be contrary. This became apparent during the protests against the COVID-19 measures, which brought together libertarians, autonomists, neo-Nazis, all manner of anti-vaxxers, and those affected economically. Left-wing democrats had to justify themselves for affiliating with COVID deniers. Their engagement against the COVID measures became a disaster as right-wing extremism ultimately hijacked the narrative. This led to considerable rifts between previously allied groups. Common ground once shared (such as the peace movement) and many friendships broke apart. However, that was just the peak of a development during which protests against "those at the top" moved away from calls for solidarity and communality to the promotion of exclusion and individualism. This includes protests against climate-protection measures, such as local bans on diesel-powered → *vehicles*, or against the provision of accommodations for refugees. They often lack explicitly political goals and are instead driven by fantasies of empowerment or purging (Charim 2023), which lead to authoritarian revolt. These manifestations are contrasted by demands intended as "concrete utopias" as outlined by Ernst Bloch. A distinction can be made between minoritarian and solidarity-based protests.

Protest movements require perseverance. They cannot expect the protest to yield immediate results. The mid- or long-term effects are equally hard to predict. For some, a protest is only a success when the originally (sometimes abstractly) formulated goals have been achieved. Others primarily want to bring about shifts and changes within the hegemonic structure of the discourse. For still others, drawing public attention to the thematization of an issue is already a success. For marginalized groups, it can be enough to close ranks.

There is widespread contention about which protest tactics are permissible. Some movements proceed from the assumption that a "liberated society" should already be visible in the movement that seeks to bring it about. They believe the idea behind the protest of an alternative society without domination and → *violence* should be manifest in the protest itself. For these groups, the journey is the destination. By contrast, there have been and still are movements that accept a militant approach and violence against inanimate objects, or allow for active resistance against → *police* violence (→ *Destruction*). However, the experiences with the RAF in the 1970s and 1980s in Germany led to a broad consensus regarding the rejection of violence against persons. → *Civil disobedience* is a form of protest that transgresses valid laws without contesting democratic rules of procedure. The violation of rules is viewed as part of the democratic formulation of objectives.

In concrete protest actions, the conflict surrounding the protest goals often has a spatial aspect. → *Blockade* actions, for example, deal with the question of maintaining occupied spaces. In this case, bodies step onto the stage of the protest, and to many protesters their resolute commitment seems more authentic than a click on a social media platform or a protest selfie (see Schönberger 2019). → *Body deployment* is regarded as a token of the earnestness with which the objective is pursued.

In → *sit-ins* and teach-ins, the body plays a central role in time and space. These protest actions primarily have a symbolic quality, since all participants know that a public → *street* cannot and should not be occupied or blocked permanently. The purpose of the concomitant violation of rules is rather to promote the visibility, perception, and representation of the protest. Above all, a violation of rules via physical means signals a certain degree of determination to implement the protest goals in question. The spatial aspect has a slightly different significance when a building is occupied with the aim of appropriating it permanently. In the 1970s to 1990s, the purpose of → *squatting* was to take possession of an appropriated space left empty by speculators or other owners unwilling to rent their property. The balance of political power decided whether the rights of the property owner were asserted using state violence or whether the property had been chosen so cleverly that it conformed with local urban planning objectives. Due to the protesters' readiness to take militant action and so-called *Scherbendemos* (literally shard demonstrations), the political price in Berlin was high, and thus, many squats were "legalized," meaning that the occupation was transformed into a contractual tenancy (→ *Legalization*). In other cities, such as Munich or Freiburg, this was only achieved in isolated cases. And yet, this movement was infectious, especially in the 1980s. Even in Stetten, a village in the Rems Valley in Baden-Württemberg, the local youth managed to obtain a permanent youth center (Kamann, Kögel 1993 and 1994). In the context of counterpropaganda against political protests, activists are often referred to as left-wing extremists and frequently equated with right-wing extremism. The concept of extremism serves the purpose of excluding ideas from the center's intellectual and imaginative realm of possibilities. However, over the course of the past thirty years, this "center" has shifted further and further to the right, so that now even an appeal for human rights can be denounced as left-wing extremist. The suffragettes experienced similar reactions when they campaigned for women's right to vote in the early 20th century. They fought for emancipation in general but also in a specific (feminist) sense. At the time, this seemed decidedly radical and transcended the predominant intellectual realm of possibilities.

Currently the "climate gluers" of the Letzte Generation are regarded as radical. They demand a fundamental social transformation of "fossil capitalism" and thereby question the capitalist mode of production as a whole. At the same time, they use forms of civil disobedience when they glue themselves to roads and interrupt the flow of traffic or carry out fake attacks on artworks in → *museums*.

Their aim is not to suppress and exclude, or even to commit acts of violence against other social groups. And yet, from the perspective of the imaginary "center," their thoughts and actions are "radical." Consequently, the opponents of a changed climate policy try to denounce them as terrorists (Peball, Schönberger 2022). However, it is the radical forms of action that draw attention to the issue of climate goals and climate change. They problematize the "imperial way of life" and hold up a mirror to the majority—not to convince, but to cause discomfort. (Klaus Schönberger)

Protestorganisationen, engl. → *Protest organizations*. Greenpeace, Extinction Rebellion, PETA, Robin Wood oder das Zentrum für Politische Schönheit: Es gibt Organisationen, die den Protest professionalisiert haben. Sie haben teilweise große Mitgliederzahlen und finanzielle Ressourcen. Das ermöglicht ihnen, aufwendige Aktionen durchzuführen, z.B. gigantische → *Banner* in der Arktischen See auszubreiten, sich von hohen Brücken → *abzuseilen* oder einen fahrenden Öltanker mit einer Botschaft zu bemalen. (AMM)

Protestorganisationen. Daniel Bockwoldt: Greenpeace-Aktivist∗innen beschriften russischen Kohlefrachter im Hamburger Hafen, 4. März 2022 (Protest organizations. Daniel Bockwoldt: Greenpeace activists paint a slogan on the hull of a Russian coal freighter in the Port of Hamburg, March 4, 2022)

Protest organizations, Ger. → *Protestorganisationen (fig.)*. Greenpeace, Extinction Rebellion, PETA, Robin Wood, or the Zentrum für Politische Schönheit: There are organizations that have professionalized protest. Many of them have a large number of members, financial resources and rely on a considerable wealth of experience. This enables them to organize elaborate actions, such as unfurling gigantic → *banners* in the Arctic Sea, → *rappelling* from high bridges, or painting a slogan on an oil tanker that is on the move. (AMM)

Protest placard, Ger. → *Protestschild (fig.)*. Unlike a flexible → *banner*, only one person holds a rigid protest placard. Greta Thunberg's protest against the climate crisis started as a one-person action. Protest placards played an important spatial role in the → *Occupy Wall Street protests* and → *Movimiento 15M*. The sea of placards took up a lot of space, and while it can be read as a sign of the movement's strength, it also documents that there was no agreement on central shared demands. Many placards, little unity, maximum openness—Occupy Wall Street eventually sought to develop this into a polyphonic political agenda. (OE)

Protestschild. Anders Hellberg: Greta Thunberg am ersten Tag ihres Schulstreiks, 20. August 2018 (Protest placard. Anders Hellberg: Greta Thunberg on the first day of her school strike, August 20, 2018)

Protestschild, engl. → *Protest placard*. Im Unterschied zu einem flexiblen → *Banner* wird ein starres Protestschild nur von einer Person getragen. Als Ein-Personen-Protest begann Greta Thunbergs Engagement gegen die Klimakrise. Bei den → *Occupy-Wall-Street-*Protesten und der → *Movimiento 15M* spielten Protestschilder eine wichtige räumliche Rolle. Die Vielzahl von Schildern nahm sehr viel Platz ein, was zwar als Zeichen für die Stärke der Bewegung verstanden werden kann, zugleich aber auch dokumentiert, dass keine Einigung auf zentrale gemeinsame Forderungen erzielt werden konnte. Viele Schilder, wenig Einigkeit, maximale Offenheit – daraus versuchte Occupy Wall Street schließlich ein politisches Programm der Vielstimmigkeit zu entwickeln. (OE)

Protestsong, engl. → *Protest song*; → *Musik*

Protest song, Ger. → *Protestsong*; → *Music*

Protest vigil, Ger. → *Mahnwache*; → *Hambach Forest*, → *Lützerath*

Protestziele, engl. → *Protest goals.* Protestbewegungen sind sich zumeist nur darin einig, wogegen sie protestieren. Geteilte Vorstellungen über die Ausgestaltung einer künftigen Gesellschaft gibt es in der Regel keine. Es lassen sich zwei grundlegende Modi von Protestzielen konstatieren: Protest, der sich gegen einen konkreten Missstand, Übergriff oder ein Gesetz richtet, und Protest, der darauf abzielt, die Gesellschaft in toto zu verändern. Im zweiten Fall ist der Protest zumeist mit einem utopischen Überschuss verbunden. Etwa in dem Sinne: „Wir wollen nicht ein größeres Stück vom Kuchen, wir wollen die ganze Bäckerei."

In Bezug auf die räumliche Dimension lassen sich ebenfalls zwei verschiedene Modi unterscheiden: zum einen die temporäre Nutzung des → *öffentlichen Raums* und zum anderen eine dauerhafte Aneignung oder → *Besetzung* öffentlicher wie privater Räume. Protestziele werden als konkrete oder abstrakte Forderungen artikuliert. Konkrete Forderungen waren zum Beispiel: →„*Lobau bleibt!*" oder „Weg mit dem §218!". Bekenntnishafter war die Aktion „Wir haben abgetrieben" (*stern* 1971), die sich das „Manifeste des 343 salopes" (*Le Nouvel Observateur* 1971) in Frankreich zum Vorbild genommen hatte. Abstrakter sind demgegenüber Parolen wie „Gegen den Faschismus und das Kapital – der Kampf um Befreiung ist international!" Es finden sich auch Diagnosen in Kurzform wie bei Fridays for Future: „Wir sind hier, wir sind laut, weil ihr uns die Zukunft klaut!"

Proteste haben unterschiedliche Gründe. Daher ist eine typische Vergemeinschaftungsform von Protest im *Bündnis*. In einem Bündnis verständigen sich unterschiedliche Organisationen und Einzelpersonen „gegen" etwas. Solche Bündnisse sind heterogen und die abstrakten Ziele dieser Zusammenschlüsse können gegenläufig sein. Dies zeigte sich beim Protest gegen die Corona-

Maßnahmen. Hier versammelten sich Libertäre, Autonome, Neonazis, Impfgegner*innen verschiedenster Couleur und ökonomisch Betroffene. Linke Demokrat*innen mussten sich für ihr Zusammengehen mit Coronaleugner*innen rechtfertigen. Ihr Engagement gegen die Corona-Maßnahmen wurde zum Desaster, da am Ende der Rechtsextremismus die Deutungshoheit übernommen hatte. Es kam hierüber zu erheblichen Verwerfungen zwischen einst verbündeten Gruppen. Frühere Gemeinsamkeiten (etwa in der Friedensbewegung) und viele Freundschaften zerbrachen. Das war aber nur die Zuspitzung einer Entwicklung, bei der Proteste gegen „die da oben" nicht mehr Solidarität und Gemeinsinn reklamieren, sondern Ausgrenzung und Individualismus zum Programm erhoben. Hierzu zählen Proteste gegen Klimaschutzmaßnahmen wie kommunale Dieselfahrverbote oder gegen die Bereitstellung von Unterkünften für Geflüchtete. Häufig haben wir es dabei gar nicht mit explizit politischen Zielen zu tun, sondern wir beobachten Ermächtigungs- bzw. Säuberungsfantasien (Charim 2023), die in eine autoritäre Revolte münden. Dem stehen Forderungen, die sich im Sinne von Ernst Bloch als „konkrete Utopien" verstehen, gegenüber. Es lassen sich partikulare und solidarische Proteste unterscheiden.

Protestbewegungen benötigen einen langen Atem. Sie können nicht erwarten, dass Protest unmittelbare Wirkungen zeitigt. Auch die Einschätzung von mittel- oder langfristigen Wirkungen ist kaum prognostizierbar. Für die einen ist ein Protest erst dann erfolgreich, wenn die ursprünglich (bisweilen abstrakt) formulierten Ziele tatsächlich erreicht wurden. Andere wollen vor allem Verschiebungen und Veränderungen in der hegemonialen Diskurshoheit bewirken. Für Dritte ist es bereits ein Erfolg, wenn die Thematisierung eines Sachverhalts in der Öffentlichkeit sichtbar wird. Für marginalisierte Gruppen kann es auch genügen, die eigenen Reihen zu schließen.

Umstritten sind die zulässigen Mittel des Protests. Einige Strömungen gehen davon aus, dass die „Befreite Gesellschaft" bereits auf dem Weg zu ihr sichtbar sein müsse. Die hinter dem Protest stehende Vorstellung einer anderen Gesellschaft ohne Herrschaft und →Gewalt müsse bereits im Protest selbst aufscheinen. Der Weg ist hier das Ziel. Demgegenüber gab und gibt es immer wieder Strömungen, die im militanten Auftreten und Gewalt gegen Sachen akzeptieren oder die aktive Gegenwehr gegen Polizeigewalt einkalkulieren (→Polizei). Nach den Erfahrungen mit der RAF in den 1970er und 1980er Jahren hat sich aber ein breiter Konsens der Ablehnung von Gewalt gegen Personen etabliert. Der →zivile Ungehorsam gilt als Protestform, bei dem es darum geht, die gültigen gesetzlichen Regeln zu überschreiten, ohne dabei demokratische Verfahrensregeln in Abrede zu stellen. Die Regelverletzung wird als Teil der demokratischen Willensbildung angesehen.

In konkreten Protestaktionen hat der Konflikt um die Protestziele häufig einen räumlichen Aspekt. Bei →Blockade-Aktionen geht es beispielsweise um die Frage, inwiefern besetzte Räume gehalten werden müssen. Hier betreten Körper die Protestbühne und ihr entschiedener Einsatz erscheint vielen Protestierenden als authentischer als ein Klick auf einer Social-Media-Plattform oder ein Protest-Selfie (vgl. Schönberger 2019). Der →Körpereinsatz gilt als ein Garant für die Ernsthaftigkeit des Anliegens.

Bei Sitzblockaden oder Teach-ins spielt der Körper die zentrale Rolle in Zeit und Raum. Diesen Protestaktionen kommt vor allem ein symbolischer Gehalt zu. Es ist nämlich allen Beteiligten klar, dass eine →Straße im öffentlichen Raum nicht auf Dauer besetzt werden kann oder soll. Die hiermit einhergehende Regelverletzung dient vielmehr der Sichtbarkeit, Wahrnehmung und der Repräsentation des Protests. Eine Regelverletzung mittels Körpereinsatz signalisiert vor allem eine gewisse Entschlossenheit zur Durchsetzung der jeweiligen Protestziele.

Etwas anders ist der räumliche Aspekt gelagert, wenn das Ziel die dauerhafte Aneignung eines Gebäudes nach der Besetzung ist. → *Hausbesetzungen* in den 1970er bis 1990er Jahren zielten auf eine Inbesitznahme eines angeeigneten Raumes, der von Spekulant*innen oder anderen vermietungsunwilligen Eigentümer*innen leer gelassen wurde. Hier kam es auf die politische Kräfteverhältnisse an, ob der Eigentumstitel mit staatlicher Gewalt durchgesetzt wurde oder ob ein Objekt so intelligent ausgewählt worden war, dass die Besetzung stadtplanerischen Kalkülen entgegenkam. In Berlin war der politische Preis angesichts der Bereitschaft zur Militanz und zu sogenannten „Scherbendemos" hoch und es gelang viele Häuser zu „legalisieren", sprich die Besetzung wurde in ein ordentliches Mietverhältnis umgewandelt (→ *Legalisierung*). Andernorts wie in München oder in Freiburg gelang es nur in Einzelfällen. Doch diese Bewegung war insbesondere in den 1980er Jahren ansteckend. Selbst im württembergischen Stetten im Remstal erstritt die Dorfjugend ein dauerhaftes Jugendzentrum (Kamann, Kögel 1993 und 1994).

Im Rahmen der Gegenpropaganda zu politischen Protesten werden die Akteur*innen häufig als Linksextremist*innen bezeichnet und nicht selten dem Rechtsextremismus gleichgestellt. Der Extremismus-Begriff dient der Ausgrenzung aus dem Möglichkeitsraum des Denkens und der Imagination einer Mitte. De facto ist diese „Mitte" in den letzten 30 Jahren aber stets nach rechts gewandert, sodass bereits die Berufung auf die Menschenrechte als linksextrem denunziert werden kann. Die Suffragetten mussten Ähnliches erfahren, als sie sich Anfang des 20. Jahrhunderts für das Frauenwahlrecht einsetzten. Sie stritten für Emanzipation im Allgemeinen, aber auch in einem spezifisch feministischen Sinne. Das erschien zu dieser Zeit als überaus radikal und überschritt den Möglichkeitsraum des vorherrschenden Denkens.

Als Radikale werden derzeit die „Klimakleber*innen" der Letzten Generation angesehen. Sie fordern eine grundlegende gesellschaftliche Transformation des „fossilen Kapitalismus" und stellen damit die kapitalistische Produktionsweise als Ganzes in Frage. Zugleich bedienen sie sich Aktionsformen des zivilen Ungehorsams, wenn sie sich auf der Straße festkleben und den Verkehrsfluss unterbrechen oder Fake-Angriffe auf Kunstwerke in Museen unternehmen.

Es geht ihnen allerdings nicht um Unterdrückung und Ausgrenzung oder gar um gewalttätiges Handeln gegen andere Bevölkerungsgruppen. Dennoch handeln und denken sie aus der Perspektive der imaginären „Mitte" als „radikal". Die Gegner*innen einer veränderten Klimapolitik versuchen sie demzufolge als Terrorist*innen zu denunzieren (Peball, Schönberger 2022). Die radikalen Aktionsformen aber sind es, die die Frage der Klimaziele und des Klimawandels in unser Bewusstsein rücken. Sie problematisieren die „imperiale Lebensweise" und halten der Mehrheit den Spiegel vor. Dabei geht es nicht ums Überzeugen, sondern ums Unbequemsein. (Klaus Schönberger)

Public space, Ger. → *Öffentlicher Raum*. Public space is usually equated with the public sphere: Hannah Arendt and Henri Lefebvre state that physical public space is an essential prerequisite for the emergence of the public sphere, i.e. public discourse with all its conflicts, → *demonstrations*, and the productive experience of differences between actors (see Arendt 1958; Lefebvre 1968). However, the spaces in which protests take place are by no means always public spaces. Paradoxical situations may arise, as in the case of → *Occupy Wall Street* in → *2011* benefiting from the privatization of public space, which is usually defined as a problem. As a "privately owned public space" (POPS), Zuccotti Park could not initially be cleared by the → *police*. During the open-pit mining protests in the → *Hambach Forest* beginning in → *2012*, the forest area occupied by → *tree houses* was already owned by the energy company RWE in terms of property rights. However, the Federal Forest Act as well as the State

Forest Act state that the forest in Germany must fundamentally be accessible to the public. Thus, no fence could be erected around the forest and the right to demonstrate also applied on the company's property. Public property and public space can be mutually dependent, as was the case, for example, with the protests against aircraft noise at Frankfurt Airport beginning in 2011, where the "Monday demonstrations" in the departures hall were permissible because the operating company Fraport AG is majority publicly owned. Freedom of assembly exists in Germany under certain circumstances, even on private but publicly accessible property, as was decided by the Federal Constitutional Court in 2015 (urgent application regarding the "Bierdosen-Flashmob für die Freiheit" ("Beer Can Flash Mob for Freedom") on the privatized Nibelungenplatz in Passau, Germany). (OE)

Public square occupation, Ger. → *Platzbesetzung*. As a form of protest with a long history, public square occupation is to be distinguished from public square movements (or "square protests"). In political science, public square movements are understood as the relatively recent political protest movements that became visible from → *2011* and that differ from previous "color revolutions" (e.g. the Orange Revolution in Ukraine in 2004 or the Green Movement in Iran in 2009; see Kim, Nonhoff 2022). These "color revolutions" are often related to elections or electoral fraud, with the color corresponding to the campaign color of the oppressed candidates. The public square movements since the "year of protest" in 2011 have emerged from public square occupations and, unlike the "color revolutions," often have a much wider agenda and usually encompass a very broad political spectrum that is disparate in its goals (the examples of public square movements in the *Protest/Architecture* exhibition are → *Movimiento 15M*, → *Occupy Wall Street*, → *Tahrir Square*, and → *Maidan*). A special form of occupation is the → *Yellow Vests movement* of → *2018*, which started on → *round-*

abouts all over France before temporarily also taking possession of the symbolically highly charged square around the Arc de Triomphe in Paris. The symbolic power of plazas plays an important role for public square occupation. Not only does it guarantee the greatest visibility and media attention, but it can also be seen as a political signal. The toppling of the victory column on the Place Vendôme in Paris during the→ *Paris Commune* in → *1871*, despite the fact that it had been secured by → *barricades*, was captured in countless prints and some photographs (→ *Toppling monuments*). The National Mall in Washington, DC, was the destination of the March on Washington for Jobs and Freedom in 1963, one of the highlights of the US civil rights movement. Martin Luther King Jr. gave his "I Have a Dream" speech there. In the immediate and thus symbolically highly charged vicinity, → *Resurrection City* was built in → *1968*. The occupation of Tiananmen Square in Beijing in 1989 ended in a massacre when the Chinese military → *violently* suppressed the protests of the population. (OE)

Pyramid, Ger. → *Pyramide*; → *Building types*, → *Concrete pyramid*, → *Icon*, → *Lobau*

Pyramide, engl. → *Pyramid*; → *Betonpyramide*, → *Bautypen*, → *Ikone*, → *Lobau*

Rappelling, Ger. → *Abseilen (fig.)*. Protest strategy of → *blockades*. Using → *body deployment*, protesters rappel from structures such as highway bridges, incurring significant personal risk in order to block traffic; thus the strategy is comparable with → *super-gluing*. In the case of the BlockIAA protests, the protesters also appropriated the typography of the German autobahn signage to present their message. (OE)

Rechte Proteste, engl. → *Right-wing protests*. Eine der am häufigsten gestellten Fragen bei der Vorbereitung der Ausstellung *Protest/Architektur* war, ob denn auch rechte Proteste behandelt würden? Von Beginn an bestand innerhalb des kuratorischen Teams darüber Einigkeit, dass der Angriff auf das → *Kapitol* in Washington, DC, am

6. Januar → *2021* vorkommen soll. Aber was genau hat dieses Ereignis mit Protestarchitektur zu tun? Zeitweilig wurde erwogen, das Ereignis als → *Hausbesetzung* einzuordnen. Doch obwohl in den USA diskutiert wird, dass die Attacke im Zusammenhang eines geplanten Staatsstreichs stattfand (was letztlich u.a. am Vizepräsidenten scheiterte), war eine dauerhafte Besetzung wohl nicht beabsichtigt. Es handelte sich eher um den Versuch einer → *Blockade*, um die Bestätigung des Wahlergebnisses zu verhindern. Zugleich zielte die Aktion aber auf die maximale Symbolkraft der architektonischen Würde des Gebäudes (das bereits zuvor in etlichen Hollywood-Blockbustern lustvoll zertrümmert wurde): die Eroberung der Herzkammern der amerikanischen Demokratie durch das Überwinden der Sicherheitsbarrieren und die Vertreibung der gewählten Volksvertreter∗innen. Im übertragenen Sinne wurde sogar ein Denkmal gestürzt, denn auch der → *Denkmalsturz* ist eine (zumindest) zeitweilige symbolische Machtübernahme, also ein Kontrollverlust der Ordnungsmacht.

Als rechte Proteste können auch die Corona-Proteste angesehen werden, die oft als „Spaziergang" angesetzt wurden, um nicht als → *Demonstration* zu gelten. In Wien haben sie für drei Wochen ein → *Protestcamp* im Stadtpark hervorgebracht, das im November 2021 von der → *Polizei* aufgelöst wurde.

In der umfangreichen Literatur zu „rechten Räumen" (z.B. Trüby 2021) ist rechte Protestarchitektur auf der Ebene der räumlichen Machtfantasien zu finden. Sogenannte „National befreite Zonen" als rassistische Wahn- und Wunschvorstellungen einer ethnisch reinen → *Autonomen Zone* bilden das rechte Pendant zum linken, anarchistischen Konzept der „T.A.Z." (Temporary Autonomous Zone; vgl. Bey 1991). (OE)

Reclaim the Streets, engl. → *Reclaim the Streets*, ist eine Aktionsform, die → *1995* in Großbritannien entstand, ursprünglich als Reaktion auf das Verbot öffentlicher Technomusik-Events (→ *Musik*). Die zeitlich begrenzte → *Besetzung* von → *Straßen* sollte auf Probleme der durchkommerzialisierten Umwelt aufmerksam machen und Alternativen zum Autoverkehr fördern (→ *Blockade*). In Form von karnevalartigen Festen fand eine kollektive Aneignung von → *öffentlichem Raum* statt (→ *Kostüm*). Die Aktionen waren wie Flashmobs organisiert, d.h. sie wurden den Behörden nicht vorher mitgeteilt. (JD)

Reclaim the Streets, Ger. → *Reclaim the Streets*. The Reclaim the Streets actions developed in Great Britain around → *1995*, initially in response to the ban on public techno music events (→ *Music*). The temporary → *occupation* of → *streets* sought to call attention to the problems resulting from a commercialized environment and to promote alternatives to automobile traffic (→ *Blockade*). The collective appropriation of → *public spaces* took the shape of carnivalesque celebrations (→ *Costume*). The actions were organized like flash mobs, meaning that the authorities were not informed in advance. (JD)

Regenschirm, engl. → *Umbrella*; → *Erkennungszeichen*, → *Hongkong-Proteste*, → *Schutz*

Resurrection City, engl. → *Resurrection City*. Im Mai → *1968* entstand auf der National Mall in Washington, DC, im Rahmen der von Martin Luther King Jr. organisierten Poor People's Campaign ein → *Protestcamp* mit 3000 Menschen. Zwei Wochen dauerte der Aufbau der von vier Architekten entworfenen modernistischen Planstadt. Doch die Bewohner∗innen der Resurrection City entwickelten schnell ihren eigenen Umgang mit den Bauvorgaben der Planer.

Insgesamt 42 Tage lebten die Protestierenden in 650 selbstgebauten A-Frame-Häusern auf einer Wiese parallel zum Lincoln Memorial Reflecting Pool, einem ikonischen Ort der US-Bürger∗innenrechtsbewegung. 1963 hatte dort der „March on Washington for Jobs and Freedom" seinen Höhepunkt. Fünf Jahre später sollte am selben Ort ein offiziell genehmigtes Protestcamp von mehrheitlich Schwarzen Protestierenden aus allen Teilen des Landes der US-Bevölkerung die Lebensverhältnisse der Armen vor Augen führen. Sie forderten ein 30-Milliarden-US-Dollar-Hilfspaket für bessere Bildung, Sozialleistungen und günstigen Wohnraum von der Regierung. Das Camp sowie unzählige Gespräche mit Behörden und → Demonstrationen (u.a. der Solidarity Day March am 19. Juni mit über 50 000 Menschen) bewirkten in der Folge jedoch nur kleine Veränderungen, etwa die Ausgabe von Essensmarken und die Einführung von kostenlosem Schulessen. Im Protestcamp gestaltete sich der Alltag als schwierig: Die Top-down-Organisation der Kampagne führte zu vielen Konflikten. Kriminalität, Vandalismus und Überfälle wurden zum Problem, nachdem das Protestcamp in Dauerregen und Matsch versank und nur noch wenige dort wohnten. Als die sechswöchige Genehmigung am 24. Juni auslief, räumte die → Polizei das Camp.

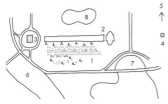

Resurrection City. 1 Camp 2 Reflecting Pool 3 Lincoln Memorial 4 Washington Monument 5 White House 6 Potomac River 7 Tidal Basin 8 Constitution Gardens Pond

Die US-amerikanische Architektin, Architekturhistorikerin und Kuratorin Mabel O. Wilson verfasste 2022 einen Aufsatz über die Resurrection City, in dem sie auf die Motivation und Hintergründe der vier Protestcamp-Architekten einging:

Der Architekt und Planer John Wiebenson und seine Mitarbeiter entwarfen das Camp mit dem ausdrücklichen Ziel, „den Armen zur Sichtbarkeit zu verhelfen, indem sie Repräsentant*innen nach Washington entsenden. Dort werden sie während ihres Aufenthalts unübersehbar für die Kongressabgeordneten und *sind, dank der Presse und des Fernsehens, auch für den Rest des Landes nicht mehr zu ignorieren" (Wiebenson 1969, S. 405). Sie zollten damit dem Lebenswerk und den Zielen des Vordenkers der Poor People's Campaign, Martin Luther King Jr., ihren Respekt, der am 5. April 1968, einen Monat vor dem geplanten Beginn der Aktion, von einem weißen Attentäter ermordet worden war. Ziel der Kampagne war es, das Leben aller armen Amerikaner*innen, nicht nur das der Schwarzen, entscheidend zu verbessern. [...]*

Wiebenson – ein junger weißer Professor, der kurz zuvor an der Gründung der Architekturschule der University of Maryland mitgewirkt hatte – führte eine kleine Gruppe von Planern und Entwerfern an. Zu seinen engagierten Mitarbeitern gehörten Kenneth Jadin, ein weißer Architekturprofessor an einer lokalen, traditionell Schwarzen Universität, der Howard University; Tunney Lee, ein chinesischstämmiger Planer und Architekt aus Washington, DC, der später an die Fakultät für Architektur und Stadtplanung des MIT berufen wurde; und James Goodell, ein weißer Architekt und Stadtplaner, der damals für Urban America Inc. arbeitete, eine gemeinnützige Organisation, die von Architekt*innen, Stadtplaner*innen, Banker*innen und Immobilienentwickler*innen geleitet wurde, die sich für urbane Erneuerungsprogramme einsetzte. Sie alle bildeten die „Arbeitsgruppe Bau". Alle waren in der Hochschullehre tätig, wollten soziale Verbesserungen erreichen und arbeiteten direkt mit Anthony Henry zusammen, einem Schwarzen Soziologen aus Chicago, der den Bau von Resurrection City als Bevollmächtigter des Geldgebers, der Southern Christian Leadership Conference (SCLC), leiten sollte (Wiebenson 1969, S. 406). (Wilson 2022)

John Wiebenson veröffentlichte im November 1969, eineinhalb Jahre nach dem Ende der Resurrection City, einen Baubericht im *Journal of the American Institute of Planners*, in dem er auf die Planungs-, Bau- und Nutzungsphase der Protestsiedlung zurückblickte:

Etwa einen Monat vor dem ursprünglichen Starttermin für den Aufbau von Resurrection City wurde eine Arbeitsgruppe gebildet, die Empfehlungen zu den Gebäuden und ihrer Gruppierung in Nachbar*innenschaften abgeben sollte. Ursprünglich sollte unsere Arbeitsgruppe die Auslastung und Anordnung der gespendeten Zelte ermitteln. Aber wie so viele versprochene Spenden kamen auch die Zelte nie an. Bald wurden wir um immer mehr Ratschläge gebeten, und schließlich halfen einige von uns bei der Planung der Baumaßnahmen oder unterstützten die Organisatoren der Kampagne bei den Verhandlungen mit der Regierung über den Standort. Als „Arbeitsgruppe Bau" arbeiteten wir mit anderen Arbeitsgruppen zusammen, die sich mit Lebensmitteln, Medikamenten, Beschaffung und Lagerung, Dienstleistungen, Transport, Rechtsbeistand und der Beteiligung von Leuten außerhalb der Kampagne befassten. Die meisten Arbeitsgruppenmitglieder stammten aus dem Großraum Washington, und die meisten waren weiße Fachleute, aber es gab auch viele Schwarze Fachkräfte sowie einige arme Menschen aus der Umgebung, die beteiligt waren. [...]

Die Bewohner*innen wurden aus dem ganzen Land rekrutiert, vor allem aber aus dem ländlichen Süden und den großen Städten im Nordosten und Mittleren Westen. Unter ihnen waren Indianer*innen [heute: Native Americans], Weiße, Puertoricaner*innen und US-Bürger*innen mexikanischer Herkunft, aber die meisten waren Schwarze. Niemand wusste, wie viele kommen würden, und die Schätzungen schwankten zwischen 3000 und 5000, gingen einmal sogar hoch bis zu 15 000. [...]

Der Standort für die Siedlung sollte im Großraum Washington liegen, wurde aber erst etwa drei Tage vor Baubeginn festgelegt. [...] Wir richteten unsere Expertise an möglichen Problembereichen aus und erarbeiteten Lösungen unter Berücksichtigung der Aspekte von Sicherheit, Gesundheitsvorsorge und sozialen Bedürfnissen. [...] Als nächstes begannen wir, die Gebäude und die Infrastruktur zu planen. [...]

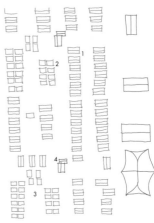

■ Gemeinschaftsbauten (Community buildings)
■ Individuelle Hütten (Individual huts)

Resurrection City. 1 Typ A, A-Frame, 6 × 2,40 m 2 Typ B 3 Nachbarschaft um Innenhof 4 Toiletten (Resurrection City. 1 Type A, A-frame, 6 × 2.40 m 2 Type B 3 Neighborhood around courtyard 4 Toilets)

Die vorrangigen Ziele der Baumaßnahmen waren: (1) Unterbringung und Versorgung der Bewohner*innen kurz nach ihrer Ankunft; (2) strenge Sparsamkeit bei den Materialien; (3) optimale Nutzung aller Arbeitsressourcen; (4) Langlebigkeit; und (5) Schutz vor dem Wetter. Dies führte zu der Überlegung, dass die Unterkünfte aus Bauteilen bestehen sollten, die von Freiwilligen vorgefertigt und von den Bewohner*innen selbst zusammengebaut werden würden. Aufgrund unserer Prognosen entwickelten wir zwei Bautypen – einen für Familien und eine Art Schlafsaal, der fünf oder sechs Personen beherbergen konnte. Einige größere, komplexere Bauten, die nicht so einfach vorgefertigt werden konnten, wurden ebenfalls benötigt und schließlich angemietet: chemische Toiletten, Zelte für Speisesäle und Kühlwagen für die Lagerung von Lebensmitteln. Alle anderen Bauarbeiten fanden vor Ort statt.

Resurrection City / Case Study

Die Evaluierung unserer Überlegungen erfolgte anhand von zwei Kriterien. Zum einen wurden sie mit vergleichbaren Lösungsansätzen verglichen. Da es jedoch nur wenige Vorbilder gab (Armeelager, Lager für Wanderarbeiter u. ä.), wurde ein Stegreif an der Architekturfakultät der Howard University genutzt, um alternative Modelle für den Bau und die Planung zu finden. Darüber hinaus wurden interessierte Architekt*innen aus Washington gebeten, ihre Vorschläge einzureichen. Anschließend wurden Prototypen von Unterkünften gebaut, um Materialien, Nutzung, Bauweise und Haltbarkeit zu testen. [...]

Die endgültigen Unterkünfte hatten einen dreieckigen Querschnitt, mit Boden- und Dachplatten aus Sperrholz auf Latten mit einem Querschnitt von 38 x 89 Millimetern. Am Dachfirst wurde zur Abdeckung eine Kunststoffmembran verwendet. Dadurch kam Licht herein, ohne störende Einblicke zu erlauben, und es entstand ein einfacher wasserdichter Dachabschluss. Die größeren Bauten, die in der Siedlung für verschiedene Servicefunktionen errichtet werden sollten, wurden ebenfalls aus Holzbohlen und Sperrholz entworfen und sollten mit stabilen Böden Schutz vor dem Wetter bieten. [...]

Am 13. Mai wurden die vorfabrizierten Elemente der Wohnbauten mit Lastwagen zum Standort in der Nähe des Lincoln Memorials gebracht. Am Tag zuvor hatten Freiwillige anhand von Plänen, die wir angefertigt hatten, damit begonnen, Markierungen auf das Gras zu malen, um die Baustelle zu kennzeichnen. (Die Markierungen mussten zwei Tage später neu aufgetragen werden, nachdem die Rasenmäher des Parks darübergefahren waren.) Unmittelbar nach dem Pfarrer Abernathy einen feierlichen Spatenstich vorgenommen hatte, rief ein hierfür speziell geschulte „Vorarbeiter*innen" den Armen und örtlichen Freiwilligen, die Unterkünfte aus den ausgelegten Teilen zu bauen. Viele Einheiten wurden in diesen ersten Tagen errichtet. Die meisten Bauarbeiter*innen steigerten ihre Effizienz, indem sie sich zu Teams zusammenschlossen, um eine bestimmte

Aufgabe zu erledigen: Es gab Teams für die Böden und die A-Frame-Wände, für Dachfenster und für Türen. [...]

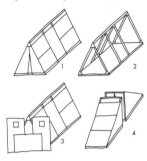

Resurrection City. 1 Typ A mit Vorhang 2 Typ A, Skelett 3 Typ A mit Sperrholzplatten als Türen 4 Typ B (Resurrection City. 1 Type A with curtain 2 Type A, frames 3 Type A with plywood panels as doors 4 Type B)

Während dieser intensiven Bauphase, die sich über die ersten ein bis zwei Wochen hinzog, versuchte die Bau-Arbeitsgruppe mit mindestens einem Mitglied den ganzen Tag über auf der Baustelle präsent zu sein. [...] Die Mitwirkung beim Bauen ermöglichte es den Mitgliedern der Arbeitsgruppe zu sehen, wie die Menschen mit Begeisterung und Stolz ihre eigenen Unterkünfte errichteten. [...] Die Leute aus New York konnten zum Beispiel mit einem Dreierteam alle fünfzehn Minuten eine Unterkunft errichten. [...]

Bei der Ausarbeitung der stadtplanerischen Grundlagen für die Resurrection City bemühte sich die Bau-Arbeitsgruppe darum, Raumangebote, Infrastruktur und Identität auf verschiedenen Ebenen zu schaffen. Die kleinste Einheit war die einzelne Unterkunft, die eine Familie oder, als Schlafsaal, fünf oder sechs Personen beherbergte. Die nächste Größenordnung waren neun Wohneinheiten (etwa fünfzig Personen), die zu einer Nachbar*innenschaft zusammengefasst wurden, die an ein Dusch- und Toilettengebäude grenzte. Gruppen von vier Nachbar*innenschaften (etwa 200

Personen) haben wir mit einem Leitungsgebäude ergänzt (das auch als Lager und zur Versorgung der Gruppe diente). Schließlich war einer Gruppe von etwa 900 Personen ein Speisezelt an der Main Street zugeordnet. Die „Main Street", das zentrale Rückgrat der Gemeinschaft, sollte alle anderen Dienste beherbergen und die verschiedenen Elemente sowohl funktional als auch symbolisch miteinander verbinden. Dieser Plan war nur ein Leitfaden, der angepasst werden sollte, wenn der Standort schließlich endgültig festgelegt würde. [...]

Mehrere [...] Dienstleistungsgebäude, die für die Main Street [...] vorgesehen waren, wurden nie realisiert, [...] was das mögliche Niveau der Aktivitäten reduzierte, trotzdem war die Main Street immer noch der öffentlichste Ort. Da die kommunalen Einrichtungen hier angesiedelt waren und sich die Straße durch die ganze Stadt erstreckte, herrschte hier das größte Verkehrsaufkommen – hauptsächlich durch Fußgänger*innen. Neue Dienstleistungen würden sich natürlich hier ansiedeln. Als ein paar Digger (eine Gruppe aus San Francisco, die kostenlose Waren anbot) ankamen, richteten sie hier ihre Bäckerei ein. [...]

Organisatorische Schwierigkeiten auf der Ebene der Gesamtorganisation waren angesichts der unübersichtlichen politischen Lage wohl unvermeidlich. Von Zeit zu Zeit wurden Bürger*innenversammlungen abgehalten, und es gab Versuche, einen Stadtrat zu bilden. Doch diese Foren hatten keine Entscheidungsgewalt. Wichtige Beschlüsse konnten nur in der Leitungsgruppe der Kampagne getroffen werden – und die ließ sich selten blicken. [...] So wurde die Stadt zu einer losen Ansammlung von Gruppen und Aktivitäten, von denen einige organisiert waren und einige nicht. [...] Auch wenn die Struktur von Resurrection City es nicht ermöglichte, Verbesserungen zu organisieren, hinderte sie Einzelpersonen und kleine Gruppen nicht daran, auf eigene Faust Veränderungen vorzunehmen. [...] Eine Handvoll lokaler Elektriker ließ sich von ihrer Arbeit beurlauben und arbeitete wochenlang an der Verkabelung der Siedlung, nur unterbrochen durch Regen oder zeitweise durch eine eingeschränkte Stromversorgung. [...] Ein geschickter Schreiner kam regelmäßig, um beim Bau zu helfen, bis Material- und Organisationsprobleme den Bau stoppten.

Auf der untersten Ebene, den einzelnen Unterkünften, gab es immer ein starkes Gefühl der Zugehörigkeit. Sie waren das Eigentum ihrer Bewohner*innen, und das ungebetene Eindringen von Außenstehenden wurde heftig missbilligt. Die Menschen bauten Türen ein, die sicherer waren als die vorhandenen Segeltuchtüren. Die Besitzer*innen schrieben meist ihren Namen auf ihre Behausungen. [...] [Ein] Zaun war errichtet worden, um potenzielle Bedrohungen auf Distanz zu halten. [...] Als Probleme zunahmen, kam der Ausbau zum Stillstand, und die Menschen zogen sich aus der Gemeinschaft zurück. Bald verschwanden die Qualitäten, die diese Stadt zu etwas Besonderem machten. [...]

Zu Beginn wollten einige Mitglieder der Organisation, dass die Siedlung eine tatsächliche Zurschaustellung der Probleme der Armen ist. Andere wollten damit zeigen, was in Armutsgebieten durch die Entwicklung wirksamer Lebensmittel-, Wohn-, Medizin- und Ausbildungsprogramme möglich ist. Trotz der medizinischen und zahnmedizinischen Einrichtungen, Ärzt*innen, Ernährungsberatungen, Planer*innen, Verwaltungsangestellten und Sozialarbeiter*innen wurde Resurrection City eher zu einer Veranschaulichung der bestehenden Zustände als der möglichen Alternative.

Der Schluss kam Ende Juni, kaum mehr als sechs Wochen nach dem Beginn. Die Siedlung wurde [von der Polizei] geräumt und ihre Bewohner*innen schwanden. Die Gebäude wurden abgerissen, um sie an einen Bauunternehmer aus Tennessee zu verkaufen. Wo vorher Schlamm war, wurde Gras ausgerollt. Das Gebiet erhielt seinen parkähnlichen Charakter zurück, ein Ort mit Gras, Bäumen und Fahnen, ein Ort für Denkmäler und Gedenkstätten. (Wiebenson 1969)

Resurrection City / Case Study

Mabel O. Wilson bewertet in ihrem bereits oben zitierten Aufsatz die Protestsiedlung aus heutiger Perspektive und führt dabei John Wiebensons Kritik an der Resurrection City einen Schritt weiter:

Resurrection City rückte das Thema Armut zweifellos landesweit in den Fokus. Aber ihre Erfolgsbilanz als Experiment der Selbstverwaltung und des kollektiven Wohnens ist schwerer zu beurteilen. Die Art und Weise, wie die Menschen die Module in Besitz nahmen, indem sie sie umgestalteten, Details veränderten und bemalten, war ein zentraler Bestandteil des Selbsthilfe-Ethos, das die Designer zu fördern hofften. In einer Bilanz des Experiments, die Wiebenson veröffentlichte, wies er jedoch darauf hin, dass die „Unfähigkeit, eine partizipatorische Regierung zu entwickeln, die Unfähigkeit, das Entstehen von Gruppenstrukturen unter den Unorganisierten zu fördern, schnell auf sich ändernde Bedürfnisse zu reagieren und sie zu erfüllen", zu räumlicher Territorialisierung geführt habe, die von einer Vorstellung von Privateigentumsansprüchen durchdrungen war (Wiebenson 1969, S. 411). Aus der Sicht der Bau-Arbeitsgruppe war Resurrection City „zu einem Anschauungsmodell der gegenwärtigen amerikanischen Gemeinschaft" geworden und nicht zu einem Prototyp für eine zukünftige Gemeinschaft. Kritisieren lässt sich, dass die Selbsthilfelösungen für die Unterbringung der Armen – beginnend mit der Aufgabe, die eigene Wohnung zusammenzubauen – in der Tradition des guten alten, von Booker T. Washington vertretenen Liberalismus des „zieh Dich selbst aus dem Sumpf" stand. Diese Haltung hatte schon den Kampf der frisch emanzipierten Sklav*innen für gleiche Teilhabe am gesellschaftlichen Leben unterdrückt, sehr zur Freude der weißen Süd- und Nordstaatler*innen. (Wilson 2022)

Im Dezember 2011 sprachen Tunney Lee, Architekt der Resurrection City, und Lawrence Vale, Professor für Urban Design and Planning am Massachusetts Institute of Technology, über die Planung der Resurrection City und darüber, welche Rolle die Architektur bei der Entwicklung des Protestcamps spielte:

Lawrence Vale: Inwiefern waren Sie [...] beim Entwurf und der Umsetzung der Resurrection City beteiligt?

Tunney Lee: [...] Wir wurden mit all den Dingen beauftragt, die mit der Planung zu tun hatten, mit der Standortsuche und mit der Erstellung einer Liste von Standorten, über die verhandelt werden sollte.

LV: [...] Was waren die wichtigsten Kriterien für die Auswahl der Standorte?

TL: Wir hatten eine ganze Reihe. Eines war natürlich der Platzbedarf. [...] Das zweite Kriterium war die Erreichbarkeit. Wir haben also nach Standorten in der Nähe von öffentlichen Verkehrsmitteln, Autobahnen und Versorgungseinrichtungen gesucht. Und das andere wichtige Kriterium war, wem das Gelände gehört. [...]

LV: Sichtbarkeit scheint bei einem solchen Massenereignis, das als Kampagne für die arme Bevölkerung dient, ziemlich entscheidend zu sein. Die Leute müssen von Beginn an auffallen.

TL: Wir haben eine sehr technische Arbeit geleistet – wir haben eine Karte vorbereitet, auf der einige der möglichen Standorte eingezeichnet waren. [...] Der Wunsch war natürlich ein Ort im prachtvollen Zentrum – an der National Mall oder in der Nähe. [...] Aber es gehörte auch dazu, dass wir den SCLC-Leuten, die die Verhandlungen mit der Bundesregierung führten, den bestmöglichen professionellen Rat geben. Sie wollten gegenüber der Regierung rational und vernünftig auftreten und belegen können, dass wir uns auch alle möglichen Alternativstandorte angesehen haben. [...] Aber nichts geschah, bis King ermordet wurde. Ich weiß nicht, wo wir gelandet wären, wenn das nicht passiert wäre. [...] nachdem King tot war, bekamen wir den Standort. [...]

LV: Was schwebte Ihnen vor, als Sie über die Art und Form einer Siedlung nachdachten, die an einem so berühmten Ort entstehen sollte?

TL: Unser Ansatz war die klassische modernistische Stadtplanung. Da das Gelände lang und schmal ist, haben

Jack Rottier: Resurrection City, Sommer 1968

Thomas O'Halloran: Probeaufbau einer A-Frame-Hütte Typ A, in der Mitte Architekt John Wiebenson (Test construction of an A-frame hut, type A, in the middle architect John Wiebenson), Sommer 1968

Marion S. Trikosko: A-Frame-Hütte, links der Bürgerrechtler Reverend Ralph Abernathy (A-frame hut, civil rights activist Reverend Ralph Abernathy on the left), 22. Mai 1969

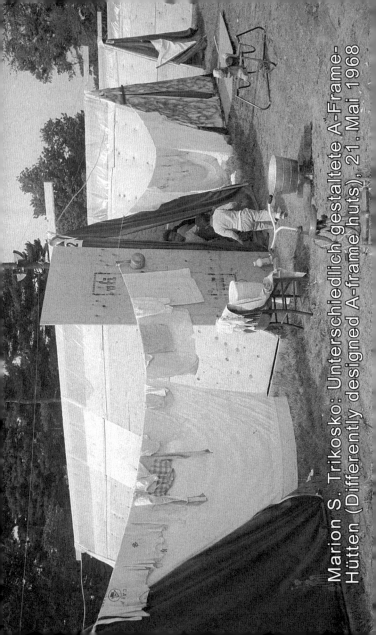

Marion S. Trikosko: Unterschiedlich gestaltete A-Frame-Hütten (Differently designed A-frame huts), 21. Mai 1968

Ken Heinen: Familie in A-Frame-Hütte (Family in A-frame hut), Mai 1968

Robert Houston: Lange Gasse
zwischen Typ-B-Holzhütten (Long
alley between type B wooden huts),
Sommer 1968

Jill Freedman: Erweiterte Variante einer Typ-B-Holzhütte
(Extended variant of a type B wooden hut),
Sommer 1968

Robert Houston: A-Frames und Toilettenhaus nach Sommerregen (A-frames and toilet house after summer rain), Juni 1968

Verwaistes Camp nach der Räumung durch die Polizei
(Deserted camp after eviction by the police),
24. Juni 1968

wir die Wohngebiete in Nachbar∗innen-schafts-Clustern und die kommunalen Einrichtungen entlang eines Rückgrats organisiert, sodass sie für alle zugänglich wurden. [...]

LV: Und wie sieht es mit der Umsetzung aus? [...] Wie viel von Ihrer Gestaltungs-vision zu diesem Ort war tatsächlich bau- und umsetzbar [...]?

TL: Wir hatten ein Grundlayout, von dem wir annahmen, dass es sich ver-ändern würde, wenn die Leute darauf aufbauen. Aber das Ausmaß, in dem die Leute es veränderten, hat uns über-rascht. [...] Auf einigen der frühen Fotos sieht man die ersten Bauten, die fertig-gestellt wurden, bevor die Leute ein-trafen. Sie wurden von einem Team von Freiwilligen gebaut, die die Struktur einfach aufstellten. Die erste Gruppe von Bewohner∗innen, die kam, hat sie sofort umgestaltet. [...] Die Leute bilde-ten größere und vielfältigere Cluster. Sie organisierten Innenhöfe. [...] Das Schöne an diesen Bauten war, dass zwei Perso-nen sie einfach verschieben konnten. [...] Es gab ein paar Familien, die zwei oder drei von ihnen nahmen und eine Nach-bar∗innenschaft zusammenstellten. [...] Aber das Überraschendste war, wie sie sogar mehrstöckige Strukturen aufbau-ten. Das hatten wir nicht erwartet. [...]

LV: Und was die Erwartungen an die saisonale Überlebensfähigkeit angeht, so war die Konstruktion darauf ausge-richtet, den Regen im Frühjahr und die Hitze eines Washingtoner Sommers zu überstehen?

TL: [...] Die zeltartigen Strukturen wa-ren ziemlich gut, sie waren eine natür-liche Art von Regenschutz. Das Problem war der Boden, der völlig aufgeweicht war, obwohl wir anfingen, einen Teil des Sperrholzes zu verwenden, um Stege zu bauen. Am Ende haben die meisten Leute das Siedlungsgelände verlassen. Es wur-de ziemlich ungemütlich.

LV: [...] [Waren] die Entwürfe auch ir-gendwie dafür verantwortlich, zu wel-chem Zeitpunkt die Siedlung beendet wurde? [...]

TL: Nein, das hatte nichts miteinander zu tun. Wir hätten den Sommer problem-los durchziehen können. Es war eindeu-tig die Politik, denn zu dieser Zeit war Kings Ruhm in gewisser Weise am Ver-blassen: einerseits weil er gegen den Vi-etnamkrieg war, auf der anderen Seite auch wegen der zunehmenden Militanz junger Schwarzer Anführer. [...]

LV: [...] Wenn wir all das zusammen-nehmen, warum und wie ging es mit der Resurrection City zu Ende?

TL: Nun, ich denke, die Regenfälle waren der größte Faktor. Die Menschen hatten bereits begonnen, das Camp der Resurrection City zu verlassen, weil es einfach nicht mehr bewohnbar war. Fa-milien mit Kindern ergriffen die Flucht. Zurück blieb die Kriminalität. Sie war die ganze Zeit gegenwärtig, hielt sich jedoch im Zaum, solange die Dinge im Camp noch gut liefen. Aber als alles an-fing auseinanderzufallen, bot das eine Rechtfertigung für die Regierung einzu-greifen. [...]

LV: Wenn Sie darauf zurückblicken, glauben Sie, dass die Gestaltung und Planung des physischen Raums eine Rolle spielte, um die Protestbewegung zu unterstützen?

TL: Das glaube ich nicht – ich den-ke, Planung und Gestaltung sind bloß Hilfsmittel für politische Bewegun-gen. Politische Bewegungen werden von vielen Menschen geformt, und als Bürger∗innen können wir dazu beitra-gen. (Lee, Vale 2013) (Texte von Ma-bel O. Wilson, John Wiebenson, Tunney Lee, Lawrence Vale; Einleitung und Re-cherche: AMM)

Resurrection City, Ger. →Resurrec-tion City. In May →1968 the Poor Peo-ple's Campaign organized by Martin Luther King Jr. led to the establishment of a →protest camp with 3,000 people on the National Mall in Washington, DC. The modernist planned city was de-signed by four architects and took two weeks to set up. However, the inhabi-tants of Resurrection City soon found their own way of handling the planners' building scheme.

For a total of forty-two days, the pro-testers lived in 650 self-built A-frame houses on a lawn parallel to the Lincoln Memorial Reflecting Pool, an iconic site of the American civil rights movement.

This is where the March on Washington for Jobs and Freedom culminated in 1963. Five years later an officially approved protest camp with predominantly Black protesters from all parts of the country would draw the American people's attention to the living conditions of the poor. They demanded a thirty-billion-dollar aid package from the government for better education, social benefits, and affordable housing. However, despite the strong media response to Resurrection City, countless discussions with authorities, and →*demonstrations* (including the Solidarity Day March on June 19 with over 50,000 people), only small changes were made in the aftermath, such as the distribution of food stamps and the introduction of free meals at schools. Everyday life in the protest camp was challenging: the top-down organization of the campaign led to many conflicts. Crime, vandalism, and attacks became a problem after the protest camp was swamped by endless rain and mud and only a few people remained to live there. When the six-week permit ran out on June 24, the →*police* cleared the camp.

In 2022, the American architect, architectural historian, and curator Mabel O. Wilson wrote an essay about Resurrection City in which she explored the four protest camp architects' motivations and backgrounds:

Architect and planner John Wiebenson and his collaborators designed the encampment with the express mission to "make the poor 'visible' by bringing representatives to Washington where, during the life of the City, they would be seen by Congressmen and, via the press and TV, by the rest of the country" (Wiebenson 1969, p. 405). For them, it was a way to honor the humanitarian appeal of the visionary behind the Poor People's Campaign, Rev. Martin Luther King, Jr., who had been murdered by a white assassin on April 5, 1968, the month before the planned start of the event. The goal of the campaign was to vastly improve the lives of all poor Americans, not just Black Americans. [...] Wiebenson—a young white professor who had recently contributed to the formation of the school of architecture at the University of Maryland—spearheaded a small group of planners and urban designers. His dedicated collaborators included Kenneth Jadin, a white architecture professor at a local historically Black university, Howard University; Tunney Lee, a Chinese planner and architect based [in] Washington, DC, who would later join MIT's planning faculty; and James Goodell, a white architect and planner working at the time for Urban America Inc., a nonprofit headed by architects, planners, bankers, and developers dedicated to urban improvement. They formed the "Structures Committee," a group of educators committed to social change, who worked directly with Anthony Henry, a Chicago-based Black sociologist charged with overseeing the construction of Resurrection City for its sponsor, the Southern Christian Leadership Conference (SCLC) (Wiebenson 1969, p. 406). (Wilson 2022)

In November 1969, one and a half years after the end of Resurrection City, John Wiebenson published a construction report in the *Journal of the American Institute of Planners* in which he looked back on the planning, building, and utilization phase of the protest settlement:

About a month before the original starting date for building Resurrection City, a committee was formed to give advice on buildings and community plans. Originally, our committee was to advise on occupancy and layout of donated tents. But, like so many donations, the tents never appeared. We were soon asked for more and more advice, and eventually some of us helped build or helped campaign leaders negotiate with the government for the site. As the "Structures Committee," we worked with other committees for food, medicine, procurement and storage, services, transportation, legal aid, and non-poor involvement. Most committee members came from the Washington area, and most were white professionals, but there were many Black professionals and local poor as well. [...]

Resurrection City / Case Study

Residents were recruited from all over the country, but mostly from the rural South and the large cities of the Northeast and Midwest. [...] There were Indians [Indigenous Americans], whites, Puerto Ricans, and Mexican Americans among them, but most were Blacks. Nobody knew how many would come, and estimates varied between 3,000 and 5,000, once getting as high as 15,000. [...]

The site for the City was to be within the Washington area, but its specific location was not pinned down until about three days before it was to begin. [...] We organized our information in terms of problem areas and problem responses with attention to security, health, and social needs. [...] Next we started developing plans for construction and community systems. [...]

The primary goals of the construction systems were: (1) shelter and services for the residents soon after their arrival; (2) severe economy of materials; (3) full use of all labor resources; (4) durability; and (5) protection from the weather. This suggested that shelter structures should be made of components prefabricated by volunteers and assembled by residents. Because of our population assumptions, we developed two types—one for families and one for dormitories, housing five or six people. Some larger, more complex structures, which could not be easily prefabricated, were also needed, so these were rented—chemical toilets, tents for dining halls, and refrigerated trucks for food storage. All other construction took place at the site.

Testing of designs was carried out on two fronts. First, we checked them against other designs, but since there were few precedents (army camps, migratory worker camps, and the like), we used a sketch problem at Howard University's Department of Architecture to provide alternative models for building and planning. In addition, interested Washington architects were asked to submit their proposals. Next, shelter prototypes were built to test materials, use, methods of construction, and durability. [...]

The final shelter units were triangular in section, with floor and roof panels of plywood on 2 × 4's [Slats with a cross section of 38 × 89 millimeters]. A plastic membrane was used at the ridges to admit light without loss of privacy and to make a simple waterproof joint. The larger structures to be built at the City for service functions were also designed of lumber and plywood and had floors to prevent weather problems. [...]

Shelter unit components were trucked to the site near the Lincoln Memorial on May 13th. The day before, volunteers, using plans we had made, started painting marks on the grass to locate construction. (The marks had to be repainted two days later when park lawnmowers came through.) Then, immediately after Rev. Abernathy drove a ceremonial spike, "foremen" trained by the yard supervisor helped the poor people and local volunteers erect shelters from the laid-out components. Many units were put up during these first few days. Most builders increased their efficiency by forming into teams to accomplish a specific task: there were floor-and-frame teams, skylight teams, and door teams. [...]

During this period of major construction lasting for the first week or two of the City's life, the [Structures] committee tried to have at least one member at the site during the entire day. [...] Helping with construction made it possible for members of the committee to see how people could build their own shelters with enthusiasm and pride. [...] The New York crowd, for example, was able to put up shelters at a rate of about one unit per fifteen minutes per three-man team. [...]

In developing the community plan for Resurrection City, the Structures Committee tried to provide for spaces, services, and identity at several scales. The smallest scale was the single shelter unit that housed one family or, as a dormitory, five or six people. The next scale was nine shelter units (about fifty people) formed into a compound that backed onto a shower and toilet "core." Then, groups of four compounds (about

200 people) were formed with a leader's shack (also used for group storage and supplies) at its entranceway. Finally, a group of about 900 people would share a dining tent at their location on the Main Street. "Main Street," the central community spine, was to hold all other services and to tie the diverse elements together, both functionally and symbolically. This plan was only a guide, to be adapted when the site was finally made known. [...]

Several [...] service buildings scheduled for the Main Street [...] failed to appear, [...] reducing its possible level of activities, but Main Street was still the public place. Because community services were located here, and because it went the length of the City, this was the place of greatest traffic—basically pedestrian. New services would naturally locate here. When a couple of Diggers (a San Francisco group organized to provide free goods) arrived, they put up their bakery here. [...]

Organizational difficulties at the City scale were, with the amorphous political structure, probably unavoidable. Town meetings were held from time to time, and efforts were made to form a City Council. Neither held power; they operated as forums. Major decisions could be made only by Campaign leaders, and they were seldom in the City. [...] Thus, the City became a loose assembly of groups and services, some organized and some not. [...] If the structure of Resurrection City did not make it possible to organize improvements, it did not hinder individuals and small groups from making improvements on their own. [...] A handful of local electricians took leaves of absence from their jobs and worked for weeks at wiring the City, stopped only by rain or, for a while, by limited power service. [...] A skilled carpenter came in regularly to help at building until material and organizational problems stopped construction. [...]

At the smaller scale of an individual shelter unit, there was always a strong sense of possession. Their inhabitants owned them, and uninvited entry by outsiders was strongly resented. People put in doors that could be made more secure than the canvas ones provided. Owners usually wrote their names on their shelters. [...] [A] fence had been put up to keep potential threats at a distance. [...] As problems increased building came to a halt, and people withdrew from the community. Soon, qualities making this a special city disappeared. [...]

At the start, some members of the organization had wanted the City to be an actual demonstration of the problems of the poor. Others had wanted the City to be a demonstration of what could happen in poverty areas through development of real food, housing, medical, and training programs. As it happened, despite medical and dental trailers, doctors, dieticians, planners, administrators, and workers, Resurrection City became more a demonstration of conditions that exist rather than those that could be.

The end came in late June, little more than six weeks after the beginning. The City was emptied [by the police], and its inhabitants dispersed. Its buildings were taken down to be sold to a contractor from Tennessee. Sod was rolled out where mud had been. The area was returned to its park-like character, a place of grass and trees and flags, a place for monuments and memorials. (Wiebenson 1969)

In her essay cited above, Mabel O. Wilson assesses the protest settlement from today's perspective and takes John Wiebenson's criticism of Resurrection City a step further:

Resurrection City certainly gave the issue of poverty a nationwide focus. But its effectiveness as an experiment in self-governance and collective living was harder to gauge. The manner in which people took possession of the modules by transforming arrangements, modifying details, and painting them, was a central part of the self-help ethos the designers hoped to foster. But in a published assessment of their experiment Wiebenson reflected on how an "inability to develop participatory government; inability to encourage growth of group structures among the disorganized; inability to develop rapid response and follow through to changing needs" had created patterns of spatial territorialization associated with private ownership (Wiebenson 1969, p. 411). From the perspective of the Structures Committee, Resurrection City had "become a demonstration model of the current American community" rather than a model for a future one. One critique that can be made relates to how their self-help solution to housing the poor—beginning with the task of assembling your own unit—was in the tradition of the good old-fashioned "pull yourself up by your bootstraps" liberalism espoused by Booker T. Washington, which had quelled the ambitions to equality of newly emancipated slaves, much to the delight of white Southerners and Northerners. (Wilson 2022)

In December 2011, Tunney Lee, one of the architects of Resurrection City, and Lawrence Vale, Professor of Urban Design and Planning at the Massachusetts Institute of Technology, discussed the planning of Resurrection City and the role architecture played in the development of the protest camp:

Lawrence Vale: So [...] how did you [...] get involved in the design and planning of Resurrection City?

Tunney Lee: [...] We were charged with all the things that have to do with planning, do a site search, and come up with a list of sites that would have to be negotiated.

LV: [...] What were the most important criteria for picking the sites?

TL: We had a bunch of them. One obviously was the size. [...] The second criterion was access. So we looked for sites within distance of public transportation, highway, utilities. And then the other important criterion was who owns it. [...]

LV: Visibility seems crucial in a march, to have a poor people's campaign that arrives in Washington—there has to be a priority to being seen once you're there.

TL: We did a very technical job—we prepared a map that showed some of the possible sites. [...] Obviously the first choice was somewhere in the monumental core—the Mall, or other locations.

[...] But part of it is, we needed to give the best professional advice to the SCLC people who were doing the negotiating with the federal government. They wanted to come in as rational and reasonable, and say we've looked at all possible sites. [...] But nothing happened until King was assassinated, I don't know where would we have gotten if that had not happened. [...] And after King was assassinated, we got the site. [...]

LV: What kinds of things were on your minds when thinking about the nature and form of a settlement that ought to take place on that prized site?

TL: Our approach was classic modernist city planning. Because the site was long and narrow, we organized the residential areas into clusters like neighborhoods and communal services along a spine so that they were accessible to all. [...]

LV: And what about the implementation of this? [...] How much of your organizational vision for what the place could be was actually buildable and implementable [...]?

TL: We had a basic layout that we assumed would be altered as people built on it. But the extent of how people altered surprised us. [...] In some of the early photographs, the first batch that was done before people came. It was built by a bunch of volunteers, who just lined up the structure. The first group came and immediately re-organized it. [...] They made more and different clusters. They organized courtyards. [...] The nice thing about these structures was that two people could just move them. [...] There were a couple of families that took two or three of them and put a group of families together. [...] But the most surprising thing was how they made multi-level structures. We never anticipated that. [...]

LV: And in terms of the expectations for seasonal viability, this was prepared to withstand Spring rains and the heat of a Washington Summer as you thought forward?

TL: [...] The tent structures were pretty good, they were a natural kind of rain shelter. The problem was the ground, it became completely soggy, even though we started using some of the plywood to make boardwalks. By the end most people had left. It got pretty miserable.

LV: [...] [Did] the role of the design [have] anything to do with the timing and longevity of the event? [...]

TL: No, there was nothing in the design. We could have gone easily through the Summer. It was clearly the politics, because by that time, King's legacy was really vanishing in a sense, both because he was against the Vietnam war, and the increasing militancy of emerging young Black leaders. [...]

LV: [...] If we put all that together, why did the Resurrection City occupation end when it did and how it did?

TL: Well the rains I think were the biggest factor. People had already started to leave because it just wasn't livable. Families with kids left. What you're left with is some of the criminal elements. They had been always there but they were very well behaved when the thing was going fine. But when things began to fall apart, it gave an excuse for the federal government to move in. [...]

LV: When you look back on this, do you think there was any role for the design and planning of physical space to support this kind of a movement?

TL: I don't think that—I think planning and design are adjuncts to political movements. Political movements are created by many people and as citizens, we participate. (Lee, Vale 2013) (Texts by Mabel O. Wilson, John Wiebenson, Tunney Lee, and Lawrence Vale; introduction and research: AMM)

Rettungsdecke, engl. → *Survival blanket.* Was die schwarz-rot-goldenen Flaggen der 1848er Revolutionen und die roten → *Fahnen* im 20. Jahrhundert waren, das scheinen die Rettungsdecken in den 2010er Jahren zu sein: In ihrer allgemeinen Verbreitung den → *Gelbwesten* verwandt, die ebenfalls in jedem Auto(-verbandskasten) zu finden sind, dienen die Rettungsdecken als Symbol einer eher linken, antirassistischen Grundhaltung und wurden von der Initiative „Die Vielen" ab 2017 als Markenzeichen übernommen: als → *Banner*

ohne explizit ausformulierte Botschaft (→ *Erkennungszeichen*). Zugleich dient die Rettungsdecke bei Besetzungsaktionen wie dem Tree-Hugging im → *Dannenröder Wald* als Kälteschutz, was an den Gebrauch bei Hochleistungssportarten erinnert. Beim Marathonlauf etwa hüllen sich Sportler*innen nach dem Zieleinlauf oft in solche Folien, um nicht auszukühlen. Auch Proteste erfordern Höchstleistungen. (OE)

Rettungsdecke. Gordon Welters: Räumung des Protestcamps im Dannenröder Wald, 5. Dezember 2020 (Survival blanket. Gordon Welters: Clearing the protest camp in Dannenrod Forest, December 5, 2020)

Revolution of 1848, Ger. → *Revolution von 1848;* → *February Revolution / June Days Uprising,* → *March Revolution,* → *Frankfurt September Uprising,* → *Vienna Uprising,* → *Dresden May Uprising*

Revolution von 1848, engl. → *Revolution of 1848;* → *Februarrevolution / Juniaufstand,* → *Märzrevolution,* → *Frankfurter Septemberaufstand,* → *Wiener Oktoberaufstand,* → *Dresdner Maiaufstand*

Right-wing protests, Ger. → *Rechte Proteste.* One of the most frequently asked questions during the preparation of the exhibition *Protest/Architecture* was whether right-wing protests would also be covered? From the beginning, there was agreement within the curatorial team that the → *Capitol attack* in Washington, DC, on January 6, → *2021* should be included. However, what exactly does this event have to do with

Rope

protest architecture? It was temporarily considered to classify the event as → *squatting*. Although there is, indeed, discussion in the US that the attack took place in the context of a planned coup d'état (which ultimately failed due to the vice president, among others), a permanent occupation was probably not intended. Rather, it was an attempt at a → *blockade* in order to prevent the confirmation of the election results. At the same time, however, the action aimed at the maximum symbolic power of the architectural dignity of the building (which had already been lustily smashed in several Hollywood blockbusters): the conquest of the core of American democracy by overcoming the security barriers and expelling the elected representatives of the people. And in a figurative sense, we could even say that it involved toppling a monument, since → *toppling monuments*, also involves a symbolic assumption of power—even if only a temporary one—and a loss of control by regulatory powers.

The COVID-19 protests can also be considered right-wing protests, which in Germany were often scheduled as a "walk" so as not to be considered a → *demonstration*. In Vienna, they spawned a → *protest camp* at the Stadtpark for three weeks, which was broken up by the → *police* in November 2021.

In the extensive literature on "right-wing spaces" (see, for example, Trüby 2021), right-wing protest architecture can be found at the level of spatial fantasies of power. So-called "nationally liberated zones" as racist delusions and wishful thinking with regard to an ethnically pure → *autonomous zone* form the right-wing counterpart to the left-wing, anarchist concept of the "T.A.Z." (Temporary Autonomous Zone; cf. Bey 1991). (OE)

Ropes, Ger. → *Seile*, as → *building materials* are mainly used in lightweight architecture. Sports facilities, exhibition halls, and temporary buildings are often created as membrane and tensile structures, for which the architect Frei Otto has become particularly well known. However, the origin of modern suspended structures lies in the traditional → *tents*, suspension bridges, and sunshade roofs of vernacular architecture. For Otto, the tensile buildings he derived from the forms of nature represented the "natural" solution to the technical and economic challenges facing architecture at the time (Otto 1954). Advantages appear not only in the low material input and the ease with which large spans can be bridged but also in the great flexibility in construction, deconstruction, and in dealing with changing requirements.

For these reasons, tensile structures also play an important role in protest architecture when it comes to the construction of shelters and → *infrastructures*. In Madrid, protesters from → *Movimiento 15M* created a tent roof spanning the entire square, made of blue tarpaulins fixed with ropes to streetlamps and kiosks. At → *Tahrir Square*, protesters erected self-made tents out of ropes and textiles, as well as a huge sunshade roof of white fabric sheets. In a sense, they were able to draw on collective forms of knowledge: textile architecture for shading public squares, streets, and courtyards have a millennia-old tradition in warmer climates. Easy-to-erect rope-and-tarpaulin structures are also used all over the world in temporary architecture for religious and cultural festivals, as well as in makeshift architectures in military and refugee camps. In Spain, the expertise for the erection of tensile structures on the Puerta del Sol came mainly from the local squatter scene, which had adopted many strategies of → *alternative architecture* over the preceding decades.

Ropes gain particular importance when protests shift to the heights, for example in forest occupations: on the one hand because protesters have to secure themselves with ropes when climbing, on the other because ropes and nets are often used here to build shelters and eviction architectures (→ *Building types*). In the → *1994* anti-roads protests at → *Claremont Road*, protesters stretched reinforced transportation nets across the street between the roofs of occupied houses and adjacent trees. The aerial bridges facilitated circulation and distribution of supplies between residential and →tree houses; but most importantly, they delayed eviction by the →police, as protesters were able to move quickly in the nets and repeatedly escape the police officers on lifting platforms.

The use of ropes also has a long tradition in tree occupations. As early as the 1970s and 1980s, activists in Scandinavia, Australia, and the United States used climbing ropes, hammocks, and rope-attached platforms to prolong their stay in the trees and thereby delay deforestation as long as possible. In order to access the trees and move around safely, they used the techniques of sport and industrial climbing, two disciplines that developed in the 1970s in the USA and the UK nearly at the same time as the tree-sitting scene. Especially in the 1990s and 2000s, many tree house settlements built with the help of ropes emerged during protests in the UK, Australia, Canada, the USA, and Germany. International attention was attracted, among others, by the American environmental activist Julia Butterfly Hill, who from 1997 on, lived for two years in a coastal redwood tree in California on two platforms fixed with ropes at a height of sixty meters.

In the late 2010s, tree occupations became more professional, for example in the →Hambach Forest and →Dannenrod Forest. Activists built tree houses up to thirty-five meters high and multi-story tree house towers, which were connected by wooden bridges, nets, and →traverses. The use of ropes to fix the platforms not only protects the trees themselves but also facilitates the dismantling and reuse of many building materials, as well as the reinstallation of damaged structures, for example after storms. Screw attachments, while similarly compatible for trees, cannot be made without the use of expensive tools, unlike rope connections. Ropes are also often used to suspend individual beams or entire structures from higher branches. By constructing a multitude of tra-

verses, all structures in the Hambach Forest were connected to each other at a height of up to twenty-five meters, enabling the activists to move around in the protest camp without touching the ground. Similar to the protests in Claremont Road, there were—partly donated and partly self-made—nets, which delayed eviction by the police but were also used by the activists as as a material depot, sleeping place, or air bridge between different tree houses. Various constructions with rope anchors also hampered police operations at →Lützerath, including →monopods, gigapods, and free-swinging platforms. Simply loosening or cutting the ropes would have endangered the lives of the people occupying the structures, so the occupiers had to be evicted individually using lifting platforms. The same applies to so-called →tensegrity structures—constructions made of rods and cables that are stabilized by tensile forces and whose development was promoted by Richard Buckminster Fuller and Kenneth Snelson, among others. The →towers, which are often several meters high, are now also becoming increasingly popular for →demonstrations and →blockades, for example as part of the →Lobau protests in Austria in 2022.

A wide variety of different types of ropes are used today in tree occupations, which, unlike most other materials, cannot be recycled but must be purchased new for safety reasons and are financed by donations, merchandise sales, or collection campaigns: throw lines for initial access, semi-static climbing ropes for climbing up, round ropes for pulleys, dynamic ropes as cow's tails (safety lines), static polypropylene ropes, so-called "polyprops" for building. The activists learn how to use the ropes and the most important knots, such as the clove hitch and fisherman's knot, offset overhand bend, and Blake's hitch, at skillshares and multi-day action climbing workshops. Here, activists also share their knowledge of climbing techniques, materials, force distribution, and rescue procedures at height. Knot

Rotk

boards, knot nights, and climbing clubs are further low-threshold offers to enable new residents of an occupation and interested visitors to build and use the structures in the forest. (AMM, after a conversation with the activists Ronni and Castroya)

Rotkœlchen → *Lützerath*

Roundabout, Ger. → *Kreisverkehr (fig.).* Countless → *public square occupations* have taken place on rounadbouts. Architect, curator, and founder of Forensic Architecture, Eyal Weizman, exhaustively discussed the interconnections of protests and traffic circles in his book *The Roundabout Revolutions* (Weizman 2015; → *Tahrir Square,* → *Pearl Roundabout,* → *Gezi Park*). (OE)

Sabotage, engl. → *Sabotage;* → *Dakota-Access-Pipeline-Proteste,* → *Gorleben,* → *Guerillataktiken*

Sabotage, Ger. → *Sabotage;* → *Dakota Access Pipeline Protests,* → *Gorleben,* → *Guerrilla tactics*

Samstagsmütter (Cumartesi Anne-leri), engl. → *Saturday Mothers (Cumartesi Anneleri).* Der Versuch, in Istanbul durch eine regelmäßige kurzzeitige → *Platzbesetzung* an verschwundene Familienmitglieder zu erinnern, ist seit dem Beginn der Bewegung im Jahr → *1995* immer wieder staatlichen Repressionen ausgesetzt. Zwischen 1999 und 2009 konnten die Versammlungen daher nicht stattfinden und seit 2018 sind sie erneut verboten. Dies zeigt, welche Wirkung auch in einer digitalen Medienwelt der tatsächliche, leibhafte Protest im → *öffentlichen Raum* haben kann (→ *Digitale Medien*), da ihn die Staatsorgane trotz des friedlichen Charakters der Zusammenkünfte offenbar für zu gefährlich halten; in diesem Falle wegen der Behauptung einer ideologischen Nähe zur prokurdischen, als Terrororganisation eingestuften PKK. (OE)

Sandbag, Ger. → *Sandsack;* → *Maidan*

Sandsack, engl. → *Sandbag;* → *Majdan*

Saturday Mothers (Cumartesi Anneleri), Ger. → *Samstagsmütter (Cumartesi Anneleri).* The attempt to draw attention to relatives who had been "disappeared" by holding a regular, brief → *public square occupation* in Istanbul has sustained repeated state reprisals since the movement started in → *1995.* Between 1999 and 2009, the mothers were therefore not able to gather, and since 2018 they have again been forbidden to do so. This only goes to show what effect actual, physical protest in the → *public space* can have even in a → *digital media* world, because the agencies of the state evidently consider it too dangerous despite its peaceful nature. In this case, the protest was accused of being ideologically affiliated to the pro-Kurdish PKK, which is classified by the state as a terrorist organization. (OE)

Schafschererstreik, engl. → *Shearers' Strike.* Der über vier Monate andauernde Streik richtete sich gegen schlechte Arbeitsbedingungen und niedrige Löhne. → *1891* entstanden im australischen Queensland mehrere nach dem Vorbild von Armeelagern organisierte und mit → *Waffen* gesicherte → *Protestcamps* mit Wohn- und Gemeinschaftszelten, Feuerstellen und sogar einem Bibliothekszelt (→ *Zelt,* → *Infrastruktur*). Im Hauptcamp nahe Barcaldine waren bis zu 1000 Arbeiter, teilweise mit ihren Familien, untergebracht. Das Gelände steht seit 1992 unter → *Denkmalschutz,* nachdem 1989 → *archäologische Untersuchungen* durchgeführt wurden (vgl. Egloff, O'Sullivan, Ramsay 1991). (JD)

Schutz, engl. → *Protection.* Protestereignisse sind für alle Beteiligten mit Risiken verbunden, die je nach politischem System, Aktionsform und → *Protestziel* unterschiedlich groß sind. Für Aktivist*innen kann vom Staat, der → *Polizei,* dem Militär oder einer Bewegung mit divergierenden Ansichten eine Bedrohung der physischen und psychischen Sicherheit ausgehen, jedoch genauso von Personen oder Gruppen innerhalb der Bewegung, insbesondere für Menschen, die aufgrund ihres Geschlechts oder ihrer Hautfarbe einer Minderheit angehören. Bei potenziell gewaltsamen Begegnungen (→ *Gewalt*) verwenden Protestierende oft Helme, spezielle → *Kleidung,* → *Schutzschil-*

de, -brillen und -masken, um sich gegen → *Anti-Protestmaßnahmen* wie Pfefferspray, Tränengas und → *Wasserwerfer*, in diktatorischen Systemen auch gegen scharfe Munition, Schlagstöcke und andere → *Waffen* zu schützen. Hierfür werden meist Alltagsgegenstände wie Bauhelme, Skibrillen, Schranktüren und Schwimmbretter zweckentfremdet (→ *Zweckentfremdung*, → *Myanmar-Proteste* → *2021*), Materialien aus dem Sperrmüll recycelt oder, wie auf dem → *Majdan* in Kyjiw, auch die in Auseinandersetzungen entwendeten Schutzschilde der Polizei genutzt. Auch Polizei und Militär schützen sich bei solchen Gewaltausbrüchen mit einer Schutzausrüstung, die – wie etwa Fotos von den Schilden der Zürcher Polizei bei → *Züri brännt* → *1980* oder die Uniform der Frankfurter Polizei bei den Protesten gegen die → *Startbahn West* → *1980* zeigen – über die letzten Jahrzehnte an Umfang und Professionalität zugewonnen hat. Eine „Aufrüstung" findet auf Seiten der Protestierenden dagegen oft kurzfristig statt, wobei das Wissen darüber, welche Schutzmaßnahme effektiv gegen welche Anti-Protestmaßnahme hilft, schnell über → *soziale Medien*, manchmal auch über → *Handbücher* verbreitet wird.

Bei den → *Hongkong-Protesten von* → *2014* entwickelte sich der zum Schutz vor Pfefferspray und Überwachungskameras verwendete Regenschirm zum Symbol der Bewegung. Er kam in Kunstwerken (→ *Medien*) genauso zum Einsatz wie bei kämpferischen Auseinandersetzungen, wo sich die bereits im alten Rom weit verbreitete „Schildkrötenformation" – hier aus mehreren ineinander verhakten Regenschirmen – als besonders effektiv herausstellte. In → *Caracas* → *2014* bekamen hölzerne Schutzschilde symbolischen Wert, indem sie mit Bildern von verstorbenen Protestierenden und christlichen Motiven bemalt wurden. Die passive Bewaffnung, also das Mitführen von als Schutzwaffen geeigneten Gegenständen ist in Deutschland bei Versammlungen verboten. Darunter fallen nicht nur Atemschutzmasken, Protektoren und

Schutzwesten, sondern z.B. auch die von Klimaaktivist∗innen bei Tagebaublockaden mitgebrachten Strohsäcke (→ *Stroh*), die ihnen bei lange andauernden Aktionen als Sitzunterlage dienen. Auf dem Majdan in Kyjiw verwendeten Protestierende → *Kochtöpfe*, Siebe und Blecheimer als Schutzhelme, nachdem das Parlament u.a. das Tragen „richtiger" Helme unter Strafe gestellt hatte.

Im Unterschied zur Schutzausrüstung als gegenständliches Hilfsmittel für direkte Konfrontationen auf der → *Straße*, helfen räumliche Strategien, den Alltag im → *Protestcamp* sicherer zu gestalten. Zur Vermeidung von Angriffen durch Polizei und Militär sowie Menschen, die sich mit der Staatsgewalt solidarisieren, richteten Aktivist∗innen → *2011* auf dem → *Tahrir-Platz* eine mit → *Barrikaden* geschützte sichere Zone ein und führten Zugangskontrollen durch. Besonders sensible Orte wie für die Betreuung von Kindern befanden sich in der Mitte des → *Kreisverkehrs*. Zur Erhöhung der inneren Sicherheit kontrollierten Protestierende gegen die → *Dakota Access Pipeline* in North Dakota → *2016* Neuankömmlinge im Camp außerdem auf Alkohol und Drogen. Bei → *Occupy Wall Street* kam es trotz einer Nulltoleranz-Politik gegenüber Drogen, Gewalt und Missbrauch zu Vergewaltigungsvorwürfen und als Konsequenz zur Einrichtung eines Frauenzelts. Auf → *Zelte* hatten die Aktivist∗innen in New York zu Beginn der Besetzung eigentlich verzichten wollen – im Sinne radikaler Offenheit, aber eben auch, um kriminellen Aktivitäten vorzubeugen. Mit dem Herbsteinbruch überwog jedoch das Bedürfnis der Besetzer∗innen, sich vor Schnee und Regen zu schützen. Mit ansteigender Zahl der privaten Zelte zerfiel indes das soziale Miteinander. Verstärkt wurde dieser Trend durch die Spaltung der Bewegung in „Geschützte" und „Schutzlose": Die Organisator∗innen der Besetzung zogen sich abends in ihre Wohnungen zurück, während das Camp vor allem jenen ein Zuhause bot, die keine Wohnung in der Stadt besaßen. Zur Einrichtung von „Safe Spaces" für FLINTA∗-Personen entschieden sich Aktivist*innen nicht nur bei Occupy Wall Street: Im → *Hambacher Wald* gab es ein „All-Flinta Barrio". In → *Lützerath* entwickelte sich in „Paulas Hof" ein queerfeministisches Hausprojekt. Bei den Protesten der → *Farmers* in Indien schliefen Frauen und Männer in klar voneinander getrennten Zonen. Im → *Greenham Common Friedenscamp* ging man noch einen Schritt weiter: Ab 1982 waren hier nur Frauen zugelassen, zudem übernahmen die Aktivistinnen Nachtwachen, um das Protestcamp vor „Bürger*innenwehren" zu schützen, die versuchten, die Protestierenden durch Belästigung einzuschüchtern. Auch bei den Grundstücksbesetzungen der → *MTST* in São Paulo wirkt sich die Sicherheitsfrage direkt auf den Grundriss des Camps aus. Zwischen den einzelnen Zeltreihen werden schmale Wege angelegt, die von Sicherheitsbeauftragten regelmäßig abgegangen und kontrolliert werden.

Bei manchen Protestformen, etwa bei den Aktionen der Letzten Generation (→ *Abseilen*, → *Ankleben*), bringen sich Aktivist*innen durch ihren → *Körpereinsatz* auch bewusst in Gefahr. Demonstrativ stellen sie dabei ihre Verletzlichkeit und Schutzlosigkeit zur Schau – auf die Weise kann bisweilen → *Nacktheit* als Waffe eingesetzt werden. Im großen Maßstab funktionierte diese Taktik beim Sturz des Diktators Ferdinand Marcos während der → *EDSA-Revolution* → *1986* in Manila: Ein „menschliches Schild" aus hunderttausenden Unterstützer*innen der oppositionellen Gruppe strömte zu deren Schutz auf die Straße und blockierte die regimetreuen Truppen des Militärs, sodass diese einen Schießbefehl des Befehlshabers verweigerten, der zu einer hohen Anzahl ziviler Opfer geführt hätte. Bei Räumungen von Protestcamps, z.B. in Lützerath oder im → *Dannenröder Wald* beruhten die Verzögerungsstrategien oftmals darauf, dass die körperliche Unversehrtheit aller Beteiligter per deutschem Grundgesetz zu jedem Zeitpunkt gewährleistet sein muss. Als die Räumung von Occupy Wall Street aus hygienischen Grün-

den erfolgte, berief sich die New Yorker Polizei dagegen ihrerseits auf eine Schutzpflicht.

Um sich bei Auseinandersetzungen mit der Polizei vor rechtlichen Konsequenzen zu schützen, erstellen Protestierende häufig eigene fotografische und filmische Dokumentationen, die bei Gerichtsverfahren als Beweise eingesetzt werden können. In Deutschland entsenden Parteien wie DIE LINKE außerdem parlamentarische Beobachter*innen zu Aktionen des → *zivilen Ungehorsams*, u.a. der Klimaschutzbewegung, um die Arbeit der Exekutive zu kontrollieren.

In Lützerath und bei den Protesten gegen die Dakota Access Pipeline wurden in Skillshares und Workshops Tipps für den gewaltfreien Widerstand und das richtige Verhalten bei Räumungen und Verhaftungen gegeben. Wenn Protestierende aufgrund ihrer Mitwirkung bei Protesten oder bestimmten Protestformen mit Repressionen zu rechnen haben, liegt ein besonderer Fokus häufig auf dem Schutz der Identität. In → *Hongkong* versuchten → *2019* die Aktivist*innen der Gesichtserkennungssoftware der Polizei nicht nur durch das Tragen von Masken zu entgehen, sondern auch durch das Stören der Kameras mit Laserpointern. Um ihre digitale Identität zu verschleiern, nutzten sie zudem Einzelfahrscheine statt personalisierter U-Bahntickets, Prepaid-SIM-Karten sowie sichere Messengerdienste und Bluetooth für den Austausch von Informationen. (AMM)

Schutzschild, engl. → *Protective shield*. Schilde dienen in erster Linie dem physischen → *Schutz* von Demonstrierenden vor teils → *gewaltsamen* → *Anti-Protestmaßnahmen*, die z.B. Tränengas oder Schlagstöcke beinhalten. Darüber hinaus können sie auch eine symbolische Bedeutung haben. Während der → *Venezuela-Proteste* → *2014* waren Schilde aus Holz mit Kunstwerken bemalt. Sie zeigten christliche Motive und Bilder von verstorbenen Protestierenden (→ *Zweckentfremdung*). So konnte auch eine gewisse Hemmung erzeugt werden, die Aktivist*innen niederzuknüppeln. (JD)

Schutzschild. Fernando Llano: Menschenbar-
rikade mit christlich-nationalen Motiven des
Künstlers Oscar Olivares in Caracas,
7. Juni 2017 (Protective shield. Fernando
Llano: Human barricade with Christian and national motifs by artist Oscar Olivares in Caracas, June 7, 2017)

Seile, engl. → *Ropes*, werden als → *Baumaterial* vor allem in der Leichtbauar-
chitektur eingesetzt. Sportstätten, Mes-
sehallen und temporäre Bauten werden
oft in Membran- und Seilnetzbauweisen
erstellt – Konstruktionen, für die insbesondere der Architekt Frei Otto berühmt geworden ist. Ihren Ursprung haben die modernen Hängekonstruktionen
allerdings in den traditionellen → *Zelten*, Hängebrücken und Sonnenschutz-
dächern der vernakulären Architektur.
Für Otto stellten die zugbeanspruchten
Bauten, die er aus den Formen der Natur ableitete, seinerzeit die „natürliche"
Lösung für die technischen und wirtschaftlichen Herausforderungen in der
Architektur dar (Otto 1954). Vorteilhaft
erscheint nicht nur der geringe Material-
aufwand und die leichte Überbrückung
großer Spannweiten, sondern auch die
große Flexibilität beim Aufbau, Rückbau sowie im Umgang mit veränderten
Anforderungen.

Aus diesen Gründen spielen Seilkonstruktionen auch in der Protestarchitektur bei der Errichtung von Unterkünften
und → *Infrastrukturen* eine wichtige
Rolle. In Madrid erstellten Protestierende der → *Movimiento 15M* ein den gesamten Platz überspannendes Zeltdach
aus blauen Planen, die mit Seilen an
Straßenlaternen und Kiosken fixiert waren. Auf dem → *Tahrir-Platz* errichteten

Protestierende selbstgebaute Zelte aus
Seilen und Textilien sowie ein riesiges
Sonnenschutzdach aus weißen Stoffbah-
nen. Dabei konnten sie gewissermaßen
auf ein kollektives Know-how zurückgreifen: Textile Architekturen zur Be-
schattung von öffentlichen Plätzen, Straßen und Höfen haben in den wärmeren
Klimazonen eine jahrtausendealte Tradition. Leicht zu errichtende Seil-Planen-
Konstruktionen kommen zudem überall
auf der Welt bei ephemeren Architekturen für religiöse und kulturelle Feste
sowie bei Behelfsbauten im Militär- und
Geflüchtetencamps zum Einsatz. In Spanien kam die Expertise für den Aufbau
der Seilkonstruktionen auf der Puerta
del Sol vor allem aus der lokalen Beset-
zer∗innen-Szene, die sich über die letzten
Jahrzehnte viele Strategien der → *alternativen Architektur* angeeignet hatte.

Seile gewinnen insbesondere dann
eine große Bedeutung, wenn sich Proteste bspw. bei Waldbesetzungen in die
Höhe verlagern: Einerseits weil sich die
Protestierenden beim Klettern mit Seilen absichern müssen, andererseits weil
Seile und Netze hier häufig zum Bau
von Unterkünften und Räumungsarchitekturen (→ *Bautypen*) verwendet werden. Bei den Anti-Roads-Protesten in
der → *Claremont Road* → *1994* spannten Protestierende verstärkte Transport-
Netze quer über die Straße zwischen den
Dächern der besetzten Häuser und den
angrenzenden Bäumen. Die Luftbrü-
cken erleichterten die Zirkulation und
die Verteilung von Vorräten zwischen
Wohn- und → *Baumhäusern*; vor allem
aber verzögerten sie die Räumung durch
die → *Polizei*, denn die Protestierenden
konnten sich in den Netzen schnell fort-
bewegen und den Polizist∗innen auf den
Hebebühnen immer wieder entkommen.

Auch bei Baumbesetzungen hat die
Verwendung von Seilen eine lange Tradition. Bereits in den 1970er und 1980er
Jahren nutzten Aktivist∗innen in Skan-
dinavien, Australien und die USA Kletterseile, Hängematten und mit Seilen
befestigte Plattformen, um ihren Aufenthalt in den Bäumen zu verlängern
und dadurch die Abholzung von Wäldern so lange wie möglich hinauszuzö-

gern. Um die Bäume zu erschließen und sich dort sicher zu bewegen, bedienten sie sich der Techniken des Sport- und Industriekletterns, zweier Sparten, die sich in den 1970er Jahren in den USA und in Großbritannien fast zeitgleich zur Baumbesetzer*innenszene entwickelten. Vor allem in den 1990er und 2000er Jahren entstanden bei Protesten in Großbritannien, Australien, Kanada, den USA und Deutschland viele Baumhaussiedlungen, die mithilfe von Seilen gebaut wurden. Internationale Aufmerksamkeit erregte u.a. die amerikanische Umweltaktivistin Julia Butterfly Hill, die ab 1997 für zwei Jahre einen Küstenmammutbaum in Kalifornien auf zwei in 60 Metern Höhe mit Seilen fixierten Plattformen bewohnte.

Zu einer Professionalisierung von Baumbesetzungen kam es in den späten 2010er Jahren u.a. im → *Hambacher Wald* und → *Dannenröder Wald*. Aktivist*innen bauten dort Baumhäuser in bis zu 35 Metern Höhe und mehrstöckige Baumhaustürme, die über Holzbrücken, Netze und → *Traversen* verbunden wurden. Die Verwendung von Seilen zur Befestigung der Plattformen schützt nicht nur die Bäume selbst, sondern erleichtert auch den Rückbau und die Wiederverwendung vieler Baumaterialien sowie die Neu-Einbindung von beschädigten Strukturen, etwa nach Stürmen. Schraubbefestigungen sind zwar für die Bäume ähnlich verträglich, können jedoch anders als Seilverbindungen nicht ohne den Einsatz teurer Werkzeuge hergestellt werden. Häufig werden zudem einzelne Balken oder ganze Bauwerke mit Seilen von höheren Ästen abgehängt. Durch den Bau einer Vielzahl von Traversen waren im Hambacher Wald sämtliche Strukturen auf einer Höhe von bis zu 25 Metern miteinander verbunden und die Fortbewegung der Aktivist*innen im → *Protestcamp* ohne Bodenkontakt möglich. Vergleichbar mit den Protesten in der Claremont Road gab es dort zudem – teils gespendete, teils selbst geknüpfte – Netze: Sie verzögerten die Räumung durch die Polizei, wurden von den Aktivist*innen aber auch als Materiallager,

Schlafplatz oder Luftbrücke zwischen mehreren Baumhäusern genutzt. Diverse Konstruktionen mit Seilabspannungen erschwerten auch in → *Lützerath* den Einsatz der Polizei, darunter → *Monopods*, Gigapods und frei schwingende Plattformen. Das einfache Lockern oder Durchschneiden der Seile hätte das Leben der Menschen, die die Strukturen besetzt hatten, gefährdet, sodass die Besetzer*innen einzeln mit Hebebühnen evakuiert werden mussten. Ähnliches gilt für die sogenannten → *Tensegrity*-Strukturen – Konstruktionen aus Stäben und Seilen, die durch Zugkräfte stabilisiert werden und deren Entwicklung u.a. von Richard Buckminster Fuller und Kenneth Snelson befördert wurde. Die oft mehrere Meter hohen → *Türme* erfreuen sich inzwischen auch bei → *Demonstrationen* und → *Blockaden* zunehmender Beliebtheit, etwa im Rahmen der → *Lobau*-Proteste in Österreich 2022.

Bei Baumbesetzungen kommt heute eine Vielzahl verschiedener Seilarten zum Einsatz, die im Unterschied zu den meisten anderen Materialien nicht recycelt werden können, sondern aus Sicherheitsgründen neu gekauft werden müssen und durch Spenden, Merchandise-Verkäufe oder Sammelaktionen finanziert werden: Wurfleinen zur Ersterschließung, halbstatische Kletterseile zum Hochklettern, runde Seile für Flaschenzüge, dynamische Seile als *Cowtails* (Sicherheitsleinen), statische Polypropylen-Seile, sogenannte „Polyprops" zum Bau der Strukturen. Den Umgang mit den Seilen und den wichtigsten Knoten, etwa dem Mastwurf-Spierenstich, Sackstich und Blake-Knoten, lernen die Aktivist*innen bei Skillshares und mehrtägigen Aktionsklettertrainings (AKTs). Hier tauschen Aktivist*innen außerdem ihr Wissen über Klettertechniken, Materialien, Kräfteverteilung und Rettungsmaßnahmen in der Höhe aus. Knotenboards, Knotenabende und Kletter-AGs sind weitere niedrigschwellige Angebote, um neuen Bewohner*innen der Besetzung und interessierten Besucher*innen den Bau und die Benutzung der Strukturen im Wald zu ermöglichen. (AMM, nach einem Gespräch mit den Aktivist∗innen Ronni Zepplin und Castroya)

Sekundenkleber, engl. → Superglue; → Ankleben, → Blockade, → Fahrzeuge, → Guerillataktiken, → Hongkong-Proteste, → Körpereinsatz

Semper barricade, Ger. → Semper-Barrikade (fig.). The main barricade at the entrance to Wilsdruffer Gasse at today's Postplatz, with which the insurgents of the → Dresden May Uprising of → 1849 closed off the city center in the direction of Altmarkt, was referred to as the Semper barricade. It was named after Gottfried Semper, who had been a professor of architecture and the chairman of the building school at the Royal Academy of Fine Arts since 1834. In accordance with his specifications, the barricade was so well-reinforced that it proved unconquerable. The revolt only lasted a few days, from May 3 to 9, 1849, and was one of the last insurgencies of the revolutionary years 1848. A year earlier, when the Paris uprising of February 1848 triggered a Europe-wide revolutionary movement (→ February Revolution / June Days Uprising, → March Revolution), Saxony had remained peaceful. Democratic groups seemed to manage to make themselves heard by political means. In the elections of December 1848, democratic and liberal forces reached a majority in both chambers of the Saxon parliament (Förster 1980, p. 53). However, the overall constellation in Saxony remained fragile. In political clubs, discussions continued to focus not only on democratic reforms, but also on transitional avenues to republican forms of government in which the king no longer had a place (Hildebrand 2020, p. 78f.).

Semper reportedly presented himself as a "staunch republican" in the circles he frequented (Pecht 1894, p. 290). He had witnessed the Paris → July Revolution of → 1830 firsthand and regarded himself as a republican ever since. In artistic terms, his political position was informed by an idealized image of Ancient Greek democracy and the cultural heyday it had brought forth, which, he believed, was only possible "under the sun of liberty" (Semper 1834a/2014, p. IX). However, in his capacity as a practicing architect, Semper had little regard for the principle of parliamentary participation, insofar as it gave uneducated "peasants and spice traders" a voice (Semper 1834b).

The Dresden May Uprising happened after the Saxon king pivoted toward Prussia's anti-democratic line and ordered the dissolution of the two Saxon chambers of parliament. The Vaterlandsverein (Fatherland Association), of which Semper was also a member, responded with a public call for a fight for liberty, democracy, and national unity—not without sending final addresses to the king which all remained unanswered (Groß 1980a, p. 59). The start of the uprising was marked by a → demonstration in front of the armory on May 2, during which the guards responded to the stones thrown at them with gunfire, killing eleven demonstrators (Förster 1980, p. 54). By the following morning, over 100 barricades had been erected around the Altmarkt. Among other items, they were made up of thirty-four court carriages, tool wagons, and travel and dress coaches which had been stolen form the royal coach house (Groß 1980b, p. 60; → Building materials, → Barricades, → Vehicles).

Notably, the revolutionaries tried to counter the potentially chaotic tendencies of the riot with orderly structures from the beginning. This professionalization extended to both the political and the military organization—they appointed a provisional government with a seat in the townhall and a military high command—as well as the arrangement of the barricades recorded in the Dresden Barricade Plan: important → streets and squares were secured with "multiple barricades," which formed "successive rows at each new street corner" (Groß 1980c, p. 60). Further battle stations were installed in the adjacent corner buildings. As a member of the "academic department" of the municipal guard (Mallgrave 2001, p. 183), Semper and his company were entrusted

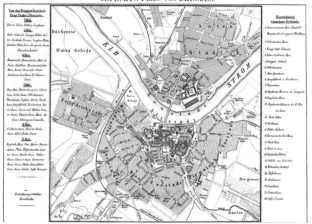

Semper-Barrikade. Friedrich Gustav Waldersee, Carl Birck: *Gefechtsplan von Dresden*, hand-kolorierte Lithografie, Berlin, 1849 (Semper barricade. Friedrich Gustav Waldersee, Carl Birck: *Battle plan of Dresden*, hand-colored lithograph, Berlin, 1849)

Semper-Barrikade. Carl Wilhelm Arldt: *Die große Barrikade am Eingang der Wilsdruffer Gasse bei Engels Restauration*, Lithografie, Dresden, 1849 (Semper barricade. Carl Wilhelm Arldt: *The Great Barricade at the Entrance to Wilsdruffer Gasse next to Engels Restaurant*, lithograph, Dresden, 1849)

with the defense of the main barricade at the entrance to Wilsdruffer Gasse. There he took up position, not only as a citizen rifleman "in full uniform" (Wagner 1911, p. 469), but also as an architect concerned with the construction of the barricade. Richard Wagner, another prominent state-commissioned artist among the revolutionaries, recalled how Semper came to him at the townhall and told him about the "profoundly flawed construction" of the main barricade: "To assuage his artistic conscience as an engineer, I recommended he join the cabinet of the military commission appointed for the defense. He followed my advice with a sense of a duty to be fulfilled; there he was probably given the necessary authorization to oversee the important construction of the defense works at this poorly maintained position" (Wagner 1911, p. 469). A contemporary lithograph (→ *Media*) by Carl Wilhelm Arldt shows the bulwark that extended to the first story of the adjacent building and was subsequently described by the royal troops as "unassailable and resistant even to heavy artillery" (cited in Groß 1980c, p. 60). The barricade did in fact withstand the attacks until the end.

Semper only returned home on the fourth day of the uprising "to rest after many nights of keeping vigil." This he wrote in a letter to his brother after the suppression of the revolt and his flight from Dresden. Besides providing the most authentic report about his participation, this letter also contains an array of elements that characterize the May Uprising as a whole: he talks about a "catastrophe that sucked me into its vortex," but also about his commitment to formal exactitude regarding details and his sense of duty: "Everyone should know what their sense of duty demands from them and act accordingly. Half-heartedness is only too common among our educated classes, who, even when they take a stand, are unwilling to make any sacrifices for it". (Semper 1849). Among other things, the insurgents owe the barricade at Wilsdruffer Gasse to Semper's sense of duty, and his

sacrifice was the abrupt end of a dazzling career in Dresden and the long years of deprivation in exile. The arrest warrant issued against him in 1849 was only withdrawn in 1863. He first returned to Dresden in 1870 for the rebuilding of the court theater (today's "Semperoper"). (Sonja Hildebrand)

Semper-Barrikade, engl. → *Semper barricade*. Als Semper-Barrikade wurde die Hauptbarrikade am Eingang der Wilsdruffer Gasse beim heutigen Postplatz bekannt, mit der die Aufständischen des Dresdner → *Maiaufstands* → *1849* das Stadtzentrum in Richtung Altmarkt abgeriegelt hatten. Ihren Namen verdankt sie Gottfried Semper, der seit 1834 Architekturprofessor und Vorstand der Bauschule an der Königlichen Kunstakademie war. Nach dessen Vorgaben war sie so gut verstärkt worden, dass sie sich als uneinnehmbar erwies. Die nur wenige Tage, vom 3. bis zum 9. Mai 1849 dauernde Revolte war einer der letzten Aufstände der Revolutionsjahre 1848/1849. Im Jahr zuvor, als der Pariser Aufstand vom Februar 1848 eine europaweite revolutionäre Bewegung in Gang gesetzt hatte (→ *Februarrevolution*, → *Märzrevolution*), war es in Sachsen ruhig geblieben. Demokratischen Gruppierungen schien es zu gelingen, sich auf politischem Weg Gehör zu verschaffen. In den Wahlen vom Dezember 1848 erlangten demokratische und liberale Kräfte in beiden Kammern des sächsischen Parlaments die Mehrheit (Förster 1980, S. 53).

Die politische Gesamtkonstellation in Sachsen blieb dennoch fragil. In politischen Clubs wurden weiterhin nicht nur demokratische Reformen diskutiert, sondern auch Wege des Übergangs zu republikanischen Staatsformen, in denen der König keinen Platz mehr haben würde (Hildebrand 2020, S. 78 f.).

Von Semper wird berichtet, dass er in den von ihm besuchten Zirkeln als „entschiedener Republikaner" aufgetreten sei (Pecht 1894, S. 290). Er selbst betrachtete sich seit der Pariser → *Julirevolution* → *1830*, die er als Augenzeuge miterlebt hatte, als Republikaner. Künstlerisch knüpfte sich seine politische Haltung an ein idealisiertes Bild der antiken griechischen Demokratie und der aus ihr hervorgegangenen kulturellen Blüte, die nur „unter der Sonne der Freiheit" möglich gewesen sei (Semper 1834a/2014, S. IX). Als bauender Architekt hielt Semper dann allerdings wenig vom Prinzip parlamentarischer Mitsprache, sofern dieses ungebildeten „Bauern und elenden Gewürtzhändlern" eine Stimme gab (Semper 1834b).

Zum Dresdner Maiaufstand kam es, nachdem der sächsische König auf die anti-demokratische Linie Preußens eingeschwenkt und Ende April die Auflösung der beiden sächsischen Parlamentskammern verfügt hatte. Der Vaterlandsverein, dem auch Semper angehörte, beantwortete dies mit einem öffentlichen Aufruf zum Kampf für Freiheit, Demokratie und nationale Einheit – nicht ohne letzte Adressen an den König zu senden, die aber allesamt unbeantwortet blieben (Groß 1980a, S. 59). Den eigentlichen Beginn des Aufstands markiert eine → *Demonstration* vor dem Zeughaus am 2. Mai, in deren Verlauf Steinwürfe auf die Wachmannschaft mit Gewehrfeuer erwidert wurden, wodurch elf Demonstrierende starben (Förster 1980, S. 54). Bis zum folgenden Morgen wurden daraufhin rings um den Altmarkt über 100 Barrikaden errichtet, für die unter anderem 34 aus dem königlichen Wagenhaus entwendete Hof-, Rüst-, Reise- und Galawagen benutzt wurden (Groß 1980b, S. 60; → *Baumaterial*, → *Barrikade*, → *Fahrzeuge*).

Es fällt auf, dass die Revolutionär*innen von Anfang an versuchten, den potenziell chaotischen Zügen des Aufstands geordnete Strukturen entgegenzusetzen. Diese Professionalisierung betraf sowohl die politische und militärische Organisation – es wurden eine Provisorische Regierung mit Sitz im Rathaus am Altmarkt sowie ein militärisches Oberkommando eingesetzt – als auch die im Dresdner Barrikadenplan überlieferte Anordnung der Barrikaden: Wichtige → *Straßen* und Plätze wurden mit „mehrfachen Barrikaden abgesichert", die „an jeder neuen Straßenecke

hintereinandergelegte Linien" bildeten (Groß 1980c, S. 60). Weitere Gefechtsstellungen wurden in angrenzenden Eckgebäuden eingerichtet.

Semper, der der „akademischen Abteilung" der Kommunalgarde angehörte (Mallgrave 2001, S. 183), wurde mit seiner Kompanie für die Verteidigung der Hauptbarrikade am Eingang der Wilsdruffer Gasse eingeteilt. Dort bezog er seine Stellung nicht nur als „Bürger-Schütze", „in voller Uniform [...] mit dem Bannerhute" (Wagner 1911, S. 469), sondern auch als um die Kon-struktion der Barrikade besorgter Architekt. Richard Wagner, ein weiterer prominenter staatlich bestalter Künstler unter den Revolutionär*innen, erinnert sich, wie Semper ihn im Rathaus aufgesucht und ihm von der „höchst fehlerhaften Construction" der Hauptbarrikade erzählt habe: „Um sein artistisches Gewissen als Ingenieur zu beruhigen, wies ich ihn an, in das Kabinet der für Vertheidigung erannnten militärischen Commission einzutreten. Er folgte meiner Empfehlung wie im Gefühle einer zu erfüllenden Pflicht; vermuthlich erhielt er dort die nötige Autorisation zur Anleitung des wichtigen Baues der Verteidigungsarbeiten auf jenem schlecht verwahrten Punkte" (Wagner 1911, S. 469). Eine zeitgenössische Lithografie (→ *Medien*) von Carl Wilhelm Arldt zeigt das bis zum ersten Geschoss der angrenzenden Gebäude reichende Bollwerk, das später von den königlichen Truppen „als sturmfrei und selbst als widerstandsfähig gegen schweres Geschütz" beschrieben wurde (zit. nach Groß 1980c, S. 60). Tatsächlich konnte die Barrikade bis zuletzt gehalten werden.

Semper selbst kehrte am vierten Tag des Aufstands nach Hause zurück, „um nach vielen durchwachten Nächten einmal auszuruhen." So berichtet er es nach der Niederschlagung des Aufstands und seiner Flucht aus Dresden in einem Brief an seinen Bruder. Dieser Brief ist nicht nur der authentischste Bericht über seine Beteiligung, sondern enthält auch eine Reihe von Elementen, die den Maiaufstand als Ganzes kennzeichnen: Von einer „Catastrophe", die „auch mich in den Strudel mit fortgerissen" hat, ist darin die Rede, aber auch von Sempers Bemühen um formale Korrektheit im Einzelnen und von Pflichtgefühl: „Jeder muss wissen, was sein Pflichtgefühl von ihm fordert und darnach handeln. Halbheit ist ohnedies nur zu sehr bei uns gebildeteren Ständen zu finden, die, wenn schon Parthei nehmend, doch nichts für ihre Parthei opfern mögen." (Semper 1849). Sempers Pflichtgefühl verdankten die Aufständischen unter anderem die Barrikade an der Wilsdruffer Gasse, sein Opfer bestand im abrupten Ende seiner glänzenden Dresdner Karriere und in einem langjährigen und entbehrungsreichen Exil. Der 1849 gegen ihn erlassene Haftbefehl wurde erst 1863 aufgehoben. Semper hatte darum gebeten, ungefährdet nach Hamburg reisen zu können. Nach Dresden kehrte er erstmals 1870 für den Wiederaufbau des Hoftheaters (die heutige „Semperoper") zurück. (Sonja Hildebrand)

Settlement structure, Ger. → *Siedlungsstruktur (fig.)*. Term from urban and spatial research. → *Protest camps* are characterized not only by different → *building types* but also by the density and spatial distribution of buildings and uses—in short: their settlement structure. The morphological study of protest camps through aerial photographs and figure-ground plans, among other methods, not only allows for systematic comparisons between the temporary settlements but can also help to better trace the course of protests. Depending on the location of the camp and the protesters' need for → *protection* (from heat and cold, for example, or attacks by the → *police*), as well as the local building and settlement culture, structures with similar or very different layouts develop in protest camps. When setting up Hut Village 1004 in → *Gorleben*, the activists followed the regionally widespread historical settlement form of the "Wendländischer Rundling," a round village with a central square, though this was already located on the eastern edge of the protest camp after a few days due to a rapid expansion. In the hut village

against → *Startbahn West*, the initial settlement of "Westend" was similarly complemented by a "new quarter." The protest camps in → *Hambach Forest* and → *Dannenrod Forest* can be described as a kind of scattered settlement. Activists live in such camps either in villages often consisting of only a few structures, so-called → *barrios*, or in → *tree houses* standing freely in the forest. → *Public square occupations* in large cities usually have a much denser settlement structure than the forest and meadow camps of the climate and peace movements, such as those to be found at the → *Greenham Common Peace Camp* in → *1981*, in the → *Hainburger Au* in → *1984*, and in → *Fechenheim Forest* in → *2021*. On the Puerta del Sol in the center of Madrid, the activists of → *Movimiento 15M* constructed a complex and dynamic roofscape from → *ropes* and tarpaulins, in which orientation was facilitated by → *site plans*. In the → *MTST* land occupations in São Paulo, only small squares and narrow alleys are left free between long rows of tents. The → *Hong Kong protests'* tent camp in → *2014* on an eight-lane highway in Hong Kong, was reminiscent of a linear city—an urban layout that typically develops along transportation routes. In the street occupations of the → *Farmers' protests* in Delhi in → *2020*, quiet yards were formed by trolleys parked in a quadrangle, while the newly designated → *streets* in the camp saw a never-ending stream of → *vehicles* and pedestrians. Similar settlement patterns emerge in the case of wagon forts, such as in the → *autonomous zone* of → *Zaffaraya*. In contrast, the architect-designed → *Resurrection City* in Washington, DC, was a classic planned city. The elongated wooden huts were regularly arranged in rows or around courtyards and formed clusters as autonomous supply units.

Most protest camps, however, have an irregular settlement structure due to their spontaneous emergence and uncontrolled growth. In the short period of their existence, they often go through a history of settlement in fast-forward, as it were. From the euphoric occupation of Zuccotti Park by → *Occupy Wall Street* to the construction of the first structures and the development of a dense tent city and the eventual eviction of the camp, a mere two months passed. On the → *Maidan* in Kyiv, the protest camp evolved from a visitor-friendly festival site into a fortress with high → *barricades* within a few weeks, following violent clashes with the police. Security fortifications are sometimes also erected by the police during protests: the container settlements erected by security forces to protect their vehicles in the Hambach and Fechenheim Forests were reminiscent of medieval wagon forts set up by wandering peoples and armies to defend their fleets of wagons. (AMM)

Shearers' Strike, Ger. → *Schafschererstreik.* For over four months, the strike protested poor labor conditions and low wages. In → *1891* several → *protest camps* materialized in Queensland, Australia. Organized in the manner of army camps, they were equipped with → *weapons*, residential and communal → *tents*, fireplaces, and even a library tent (→ *Infrastructure*). Up to 1000 workers, some with their families, were accommodated in the main camp near Barcaldine. Following → *archaeological investigations* in 1989, the area was listed on the Queensland Heritage Register in 1992 (see Egloff, O'Sullivan, Ramsay 1991; → *Heritage protection*). (JD)

Siedlungsstruktur, engl. → *Settlement structure*. Begriff aus der Stadt- und Raumforschung. → *Protestcamps* werden nicht nur durch verschiedene → *Bautypen* charakterisiert, sondern auch durch die Dichte und räumliche Verteilung der Bauten und Nutzungen – kurz: ihre Siedlungsstruktur. Die morphologische Untersuchung von Protestcamps u.a. durch Luftbilder und Schwarzpläne ermöglicht nicht nur systematische Vergleiche zwischen den temporären Siedlungen, sondern kann auch dabei helfen, den Verlauf der Proteste besser nachzuvollziehen. Je nach Standort des Camps, Schutzbedürfnis der Protestierenden (→ *Schutz* etwa vor Hitze und Kälte oder Angriffen durch die → *Polizei*) so-

wie lokaler Bau- und Siedlungskultur entwickeln sich in Protestcamps Bebauungen mit ähnlichen oder ganz unterschiedlichen Grundrissen. Beim Aufbau des „Hüttendorfs 1004" in → *Gorleben* orientierten sich die Aktivist∗innen an der regional verbreiteten historischen Siedlungsform des „Wendländischen Rundlings", einem Runddorf mit zentralem Dorfplatz, wobei dieser aufgrund einer schnellen Ausdehnung nach wenigen Tagen schon am östlichen Rand des Protestcamps lag. Auch im Hüttendorf gegen die → *Startbahn West* entstand neben dem „Westend", der anfänglichen Siedlung, ein „Neubauviertel". Die Protestcamps im → *Hambacher Wald* und → *Dannenröder Wald* können als eine Art Streusiedlung bezeichnet werden. Aktivist∗innen leben in solchen Camps entweder in teils nur aus wenigen Strukturen bestehenden Dörfern, sogenannten → *Barrios*, oder in frei im Wald stehenden → *Baumhäusern*.

→ *Platzbesetzungen* in Großstädten haben zumeist eine viel dichtere Siedlungsstruktur als die Wald- und Wiesencamps der Klima- und Friedensbewegungen, wie sie u.a. auch im → *Greenham Common Friedenscamp* → *1981*, in der → *Hainburger Au* → *1984* und im → *Fechenheimer Wald* → *2021* zu finden waren. Auf der Puerta del Sol im Zentrum von Madrid errichteten die Aktivist∗innen von → *Movimiento 15M* aus → *Seilen* und Planen eine komplexe und dynamische Dachlandschaft, in der die Orientierung durch → *Lagepläne* erleichtert wurde. Bei den Grundstücksbesetzungen der → *MTST* in São Paulo werden zwischen den langen Zeltreihen nur kleine Plätze und schmale Gassen freigelassen. Das während der → *Hongkong-Proteste* → *2014* auf einer achtspurigen Highway in Hongkong errichtete Zeltlager erinnerte an eine Bandstadt – eine Stadtanlage, die sich typischerweise entlang von Transportwegen entwickelt. Bei den Straßenbesetzungen der → *Farmers* → *2020* in Delhi wurden durch die im Viereck geparkten Traktorwagen ruhige Höfe gebildet, während auf den neu ausgewiesenen → *Straßen* im Camp ein

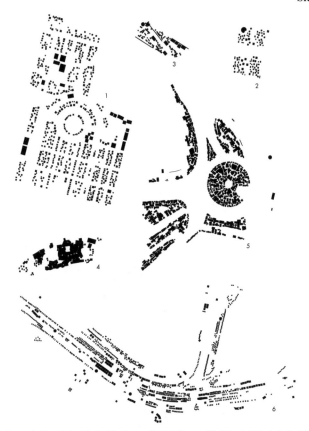

Siedlungsstruktur. 1 Gezi-Park 2 Syntagma-Platz 3 Occupy Wall Street 4 Movimiento 15M 5 Tahrir-Platz 6 Hongkong-Proteste (Settlement structure. 1 Gezi Park 2 Syntagma Square 3 Occupy Wall Street 4 Movimiento 15M 5 Tahrir Square 6 Hong Kong protests)

nicht abreißender Strom von →*Fahrzeugen* und Fußgänger∗innen unterwegs war. Ähnliche Siedlungsstrukturen entstehen bei Wagenburgen, z.B. in der →*Autonomen Zone* →*Zaffaraya.* Die von Architekten geplante →*Resurrection City* in Washington, DC, war dagegen eine klassische Planstadt. Die länglichen Holzhütten waren in Zeilen-

bzw. Hofbauweise regelmäßig angeordnet und bildeten Cluster als autonome Versorgungseinheiten.

Die meisten Protestcamps weisen aufgrund ihrer spontanen Entstehung und ihres unkontrollierten Wachstums allerdings eine unregelmäßige Siedlungsstruktur auf. Häufig durchlaufen sie in der kurzen Zeit ihres Bestehens gleich-

451

Site

sam eine Siedlungsgeschichte im Zeitraffer. Von der euphorischen Besetzung des Zuccotti Parks durch → *Occupy Wall Street* über den Bau erster Strukturen und die Entwicklung einer dichten Zeltstadt bis zur Räumung des Camps vergingen gerade einmal zwei Monate. Auf dem → *Majdan* in Kyjiw entwickelte sich das Protestcamp innerhalb weniger Wochen von einem besucher∗innenfreundlichen Festivalgelände in eine Festung mit hohen → *Barrikaden*, nachdem es zu gewaltsamen Auseinandersetzungen mit der Polizei gekommen war. Sicherheitsfestungen werden bei Protesten teils auch von der Polizei errichtet: Die Containersiedlungen im Hambacher und Fechenheimer Wald, die zum Schutz der Fahrzeuge von Sicherheitskräften aufgebaut wurden, erinnerten an mittelalterliche Wagenburgen, die Wandervölker und Armeen zur Verteidigung ihrer Wagenparks aufstellten. (AMM)

Site plan, Ger. → *Lageplan*. The fact that site plans play a role in protests seems paradoxical at first glance, since the spontaneously organized actions of grassroots movements have little in common with the lengthy building permit procedures in which they are normally used. However, it is precisely at the interface between protests and construction planning that site plans have a vital meaning. For → *Resurrection City* in Washington, DC, architects designed a functionalist → *master plan* before the beginning of the protests, which divided the green spaces on the National Mall, where a protest camp was to be set up, into organizational units and neighborhoods. → *Camps for Climate Action* in Germany are sometimes preceded by long approval processes in which the use of precisely defined areas as resting, supply, or meeting spaces must be agreed upon with the authorities. Sometimes site plans are still drawn during protests, when, as with the → *Movimiento 15M* in Madrid, the → *protest camp* is expanded over time to such an extent that protesters can no longer find their way around it. As an attempt to maintain an overview, they constantly drew new maps, though they quickly

became outdated due to the continuous transformation of the camp. Therefore, additional → *information signs* were produced to help protesters navigate around the square. Both systems—the site plan and the information sign—coexisted, but in the end contributed less to orientation than to documenting the surprisingly complex structure of the settlement. At the protests of → *Occupy Wall Street* and → *Maidan* in Kyiv, site plans of the camps were also drawn by enthusiastic architects in order to record the ephemeral architecture for posterity. The squatters at → *MTST* in São Paulo, on the other hand, pursue a completely different strategy to orient themselves in a confusing occupation: each hut is given an address, which consists of the zone in which it is located and a two- or three-digit number. (AMM)

Sit-in. Bernard Larsson: Sit-in an der FU Berlin (Rudi Dutschke am Mikrophon), 1967 (Sit-in. Bernard Larsson: Sit-in at FU Berlin, student protest leader Rudi Dutschke at the microphone), 1967)

Sit-in, engl. → *Sit-in.* Gängige gewaltfreie Protestform der amerikanischen Bürger∗innenrechtsbewegung, die sich in den 1960er Jahren, insbesondere durch die → *Greensboro Sit-ins*, etablierte und später von der Studierendenbewegung international angewandt wurde; beispielsweise am 19. und 20. April 1967, als Studierende das Foyer des Henry-Ford-Baus der FU Berlin besetzten. Ein Sit-in ist, wie das → *Die-in*, keine → *Blockade*, sondern stört Abläufe bzw. zweckentfremdet einen Raum. (JD)

Sit-in, Ger. → *Sit-in (fig.).* Common, nonviolent form of protest devised by the American civil rights movement in the 1960s, which came to fame especially through the → *Greensboro Sit-ins*. The tactic was later used internationally by the student movement. For example, on April 19 and 20, 1967, students occupied the foyer of the Henry Ford Building at the FU Berlin. Sit-ins, like → *die-ins*, are not a → *blockade*, but disturb the standard procedures or misuse the space. (JD)

Sitzblockade → *Blockade*

Skillshare, engl. → *Skillshare*; → *Hambacher Wald*, → *Schutz*, → *Seile*

Skillshare, Ger. → *Skillshare*; → *Hambach Forest*, → *Protection*, → *Ropes*

Social Media, engl. → *Social media*; → *Digitale Medien*, → *Kommunikation*

Social media, Ger. → *Social Media*; → *Communication*, → *Digital media*

Solaranlage, engl. → *Solar energy system*; → *Gorleben*, → *Infrastruktur*, → *Lützerath*

Solar energy system, Ger. → *Solaranlage*; → *Gorleben*, → *Infrastructure*, → *Lützerath*

Solidaritätsgeste, engl. → *Acts of solidarity.* Die meisten Protestbewegungen erhalten Hilfe aus der Bevölkerung; von Menschen, die nicht selbst auf die → *Straße* gehen, sich nicht aktiv beteiligen. Solche Gesten der Solidarität werden trotzdem immer wieder aufmerksam von Berichterstatter∗innen registriert, wie hier beispielsweise die Unterstützung der Straßenkämpfe in der „Nacht der Barrikaden" des 10./11. Mai 1968 in Paris (→ *Mai '68*, → *Barrikade*, → *Medien*), wiedergegeben in der *Neuen Zürcher* Zeitung am 13. Mai 1968 auf der Titelseite:

„Die Anwohner der Rue Gay-Lussac nahmen für die Studenten Partei. Sie brachten ihnen vor dem Angriff der Polizei Wasser, Biscuits, Schokolade und andere Lebensmittel, warfen nachher Wasser von den Fenstern hinunter, um die Gasschwaden niederzuschlagen, gaben den Studenten nasse Tücher zum Schutz der Gesichter und Atmungsorgane, holten Flüchtende und Verletzte in die Häuser hinein, in einer Solidaritätsbewegung, wie sie in Paris nicht an der Tagesordnung ist" (Frei 2008/2018, S. 18; → *Polizei*, → *Schutz*). (OE)

Spartacist Uprising, Ger. → *Januaraufstand / Spartakusaufstand.* In January → *1919*, Berlin became the site of → *street* fighting, which came to be referred to as the "Spartacist Uprising" (→ *Barricade*). Supporters of the USPD (Independent Social Democratic Party of Germany) and the Communist Party fought against troops loyal to the government. As the provisional government of the German Empire under Friedrich Ebert was made up of social democrats from the MSPD (Majority Social Democratic Party of Germany), this was a confrontation between two left-wing factions. The initial aim was to occupy the government district. However, the protest was redirected to the newspaper district, supposedly by police informants (→ *Police*). Social democratic newspapers had repeatedly published critical or sometimes even hostile reports on the rival communists. The event brought the work of the newspapers to a standstill (see exh. cat. *Berlin in der Revolution 1918/1919* 2018). (JD)

Spaziergang, engl. → *Walking*; → *Demonstration*, → *Rechte Proteste*

Spiegel. Sergei Chuzavkov: Spiegelprotest auf dem Majdan, 30. Dezember 2013 (Mirror. Sergei Chuzavkov: Mirror protest on Maidan, December 30, 2013)

Spiegel, engl. → *Mirror.* Genau einen Monat nachdem die Spezialeinheit Berkut eine friedliche → *Demonstration* auf dem → *Majdan* in Kyjiw angegriffen hatte, versammelten sich Dutzende Frauen∗ auf dem Platz, um gegen Polizeigewalt zu protestieren (→ *Polizei*, → *Gewalt*). Sie stellten sich vor eine Kette von Polizist∗innen, um ihnen „den Spiegel vorzuhalten". „Wen und was wollt Ihr schützen?", stand auf ihren → *Protestschildern*. Inspiriert von der performativen Demonstration in der Ukraine setzte auch der Künstler Cannupa Hanska Luger bei den → *Dakota-Access-Pipeline-Protesten* reflektierende → *Schutzschilde* ein, um die Polizei mit ihrem Spiegelbild zu konfrontieren. Bei Aktionen der → *Protestorganisation* Extinction Rebellion sowie bei israelkritischen Protesten im Gazastreifen wurden Spiegel dagegen verwendet, um Polizeikräfte bzw. Soldat∗innen zu blenden. (AMM)

Squatting, Ger. → *Hausbesetzung*. Squatting means occupying vacant buildings on a long-term basis against the will of their owners. In Europe and North America, a squatter scene closely aligned with anarchist and autonomist movements has existed since the 1970s, which purposely distances itself from social norms while experimenting with enduring forms of alternative communal living and self-governing spaces. In this way, squatting is related to activism for the homeless or those in substandard housing, demands for affordable housing, and protests against speculative vacancies and high rents, or the desire to save buildings from demolition. This kind of protest dwelling is found in both urban and rural areas; it distinguishes itself from temporary, politically motivated takeovers of public facilities such as parliament buildings, radio stations, or electric powerplants.

The anarchist writer and social historian Colin Ward situates the process of urban squatting in the context of examples dating back to the Middle Ages, where people occupied land and built new houses overnight without the permission of the rulers (Ward 2002/2009). A well-known example from the early modern period is represented by the Diggers, who came to prominence in the mid-17th century near the end of the English Civil War. This early Christian communist movement, which rejected the notion of private property, occupied land for several years and erected huts for working the land communally as part of a comprehensive reform. This kind of land grab, however, can also occur under the auspices of those in power. At the same time as the Diggers, European settlers were preparing for the eventual colonization of what would become the United States. Squatted buildings are difficult to track historically because squatters did not always want to make their presence known. A decisive structural change of the modern era began in the 20th century, when public and private property owners decided to leave habitable buildings empty over extended periods rather than rent them out (Ward 1980, p. 109). Squatting takes place worldwide, but the dynamics vary depending on the geographic context because → *infrastructures* that can be squatted do not always exist everywhere. In South Africa, for example, large-scale slums—squatter camps and townships—are emblematic of racial segregation policies; half of the population of Mumbai in India consists of squatters, while Brazil, with its favelas such as Rocinha in Rio de Janeiro, also has large-scale, informal urban structures occupied by the poorest in society.

Squatting took off as a social movement in Europe and North America against the backdrop of the Dutch Provo movement and the aftermath of 1968. The Marxist sociologist and philosopher Henri Lefebvre, for example, had called for the collective "right to the city" in light of urbanization processes such as postwar mass housing construction (Lefebvre 1968/2016). The focus of this kind of activism, which engages with local structures, often involves communal living alongside grassroots democratic or anarchist organizations, as an alternative to the bourgeois nuclear family or the establishment of countercultures. Squatted houses can be integrated into a supra-regional network, while as urban crash pads they can also be in contact with rural communities or other projects (Gordon 2008, p. 61 ff.). Projects such as → *Freetown Christiania* in Copenhagen, founded in → *1971*, have sometimes expanded across larger areas. When such operations are carried out in a publicly visible way, banners, →*graffiti*, or murals are used to communicate political demands and to differentiate these spaces from surrounding areas. In some cases, squatted houses have been transferred to legal housing associations after a successful fight for housing. Squatting is not exclusively a phenomenon of capitalist societies. In socialist and communist countries, squatting was not officially tolerated. Nevertheless, in the GDR for example, there are records of squats in old buildings in Berlin's Prenzlauer Berg district from the 1970s that circumvented the socialist state monopoly (Grashoff 2011). (Petra Lange-Berndt)

Stacheldraht, engl. →*Barbed wire*; →*Anti-Protestmaßnahmen*, →*Barrikade*, →*Baumaterial*

Startbahn West, engl. →*Startbahn West*. Im Flörsheimer Wald südwestlich von Frankfurt am Main entstand ab Mai → *1980* ein →*Protestcamp* gegen den Ausbau des Frankfurter Flughafens. Blockiert wurde der Bauplatz der „Startbahn West". Die in der Region breit verankerten Proteste richteten sich gegen die Rodung von 129 Hektar teils geschütztem Wald und gegen die bereits erhebliche Fluglärmbelastung. Für Teile der Friedensbewegung galt die US-Militärbasis auf dem Frankfurter Flughafen als →*Protestziel*. Das Hüttendorf der Startbahngegner*innen wurde zeitgleich zum Protestcamp in →*Gorleben* errichtet. Während aber im Wendland bereits nach 33 Tagen geräumt wurde, konnte das Hüttendorf mit seinen zu Spitzenzeiten mehr als 60 Bauten für knapp eineinhalb Jahre bestehen bleiben.

Die Planungen zur Erweiterung des verkehrsreichsten deutschen Flughafens um eine dritte Startbahn begannen Anfang der 1960er Jahre. Durch Klagen lokaler Bürger*inneninitiativen, zu denen u.a. die 1965 gegründete „Interessengemeinschaft zur Bekämpfung des Fluglärms e. V." zählte, verzögerte sich der Baubeginn über einen Zeitraum von fast zehn Jahren immer wieder. In den angrenzenden Gemeinden bildeten sich ab Ende der 1970er Jahre parteiübergreifende Bündnisse gegen den Ausbau. In Mörfelden-Walldorf protestierten SPD, CDU, DKP und FDP unter einem gemeinsamen →*Banner*, auch mehrere Pfarrer*innen unterstützten die Bewegung. Ein Jahr nach dem Baubeginn des Hüttendorfs gründete sich die „Arbeitsgemeinschaft Volksbegehren und Volksentscheid – Keine Startbahn West!". Im Herbst 1981 wurde die Waldbesetzung von einem massiven →*Polizeiaufgebot* beendet und kurz danach das Volksbegehren trotz 220 765 gesammelter Unterschriften abgelehnt. Die Proteste dauerten über die Fertigstellung der Startbahn im Jahr 1984 hinaus bis zum November 1987 an, als bei einer →*Demonstration* zum sechsten Jahrestag der Räumung des Hüttendorfs die Polizisten Thorsten Schwalm und Klaus Eichhöfer erschossen wurden. Im Jahr 2011 wurde der Flughafen wieder erweitert, diesmal um eine Landebahn. Nennenswerte Proteste fanden erst statt, nachdem das Ausmaß des ausgeweiteten Fluglärms in der Region spürbar wurde.

Die Bauten des Hüttendorfs sind so gut dokumentiert wie wohl bei keinem anderen Protestcamp. Architekturstudierende der Technischen Hochschule Darmstadt erstellten detaillierte Aufmaßzeichnungen jeder einzelnen Hütte. Der Architekt Ulrich Cremer hat das Seminar am Fachgebiet von Prof. Helmut Striffler betreut und eine Publikation dazu veröffentlicht:

Im September 1979 reicht die Bürgerinitiative (BI) bei der Stadt Flörsheim einen offiziellen Bauantrag zur Errichtung einer Schutzhütte auf dem Gelände der geplanten Startbahn ein. Der Architekt Lotz aus Mörfelden hat die Pläne für eine offene Schutzhütte gefertigt, die Konzeption des 12-Ecks ist aus der Zielsetzung als Versammlungsort entstanden. Der Bauantrag wird abgelehnt. […] Die Bürgerinitiative beschließt, die Hütte dennoch zu errichten und trifft während des Winters alle notwendigen Vorbereitungen. Auf der Grundlage der alten Pläne wird eine geschlossene, bewohnbare Hütte konzipiert, deren Teile vorfabriziert und im Wald versteckt werden. Am 03.05.80 beginnen etwa achtzig BI'ler um sechs Uhr morgens mit dem Bau, mittags steht der Rohbau der Hütte mit elf Metern Durchmesser. Polizei und FAG [Flughafen AG] werden von dieser Aktion völlig überrumpelt. [...]

Startbahn West. 1 Hüttendorf 2 Wald 3 Geplante Startbahn West (Startbahn West. 1 Hut village 2 Forest 3 Planned Runway West)

Die BI-Hütte wird zum ersten Symbol des Widerstandes und bildet das Zentrum des späteren Dorfes. Hier ist die räumliche Mitte der Bewegung, Ort der Diskussion und Informationsvermittlung, Versammlungsort und Ausgangspunkt der Aktionen. Die Hütte wird von Mitgliedern der Bürgerinitiative Tag und Nacht besetzt gehalten und weiter ausgebaut. [...] Als das Dorf entsteht, dient sie als Schlafplatz für die Hüttenbauer, als Vorratslager, Küche und Waschplatz. [...] Im Oktober 1980 eskaliert die Situation; die FAG läßt unter Polizeischutz die ersten sieben Hektar Wald roden. Als Reaktion erfolgt die spontane Errichtung weiterer Hütten. [...]

Für die Funktionsfähigkeit eines unabhängigen, sich selbst versorgenden Gemeinwesens entstehen aus gemeinsamer Anstrengung die Gemeinschaftshütten, die sich in einem Halbkreis um die BI-Hütte gruppieren: das Kinderhaus, die Hüttenkirche, der Funkturm, Brennholzschuppen, Fahrradwerkstatt, Kühlhaus, Vorratshaus und Küche. Zusammen bilden diese Einrichtungen den Kern des Dorfes [...]. Einen äußeren Ring bilden die Wohnhütten, erst halbkreisförmig, später wird der Ring durch das „Neubauviertel" geschlossen, das sich im dichteren, dunkleren Wald im Osten erst entwickelt, als die sonnigeren Plätze des „Westends" schon besetzt sind. [...]

Wie die „Republik Freies Wendland" und die Hütten auf dem Damm der B-8 bei Kelkheim [Hasler 1982] ist das Dorf im Flörsheimer Wald konkret betroffenes Territorium und Symbol für die [...] drohende Zerstörung in einem. [...] Der Verteidigungscharakter des Dorfes äußert sich nicht nur in den Barrikaden, sondern auch in der Baukonzeption der Hütten selbst. [...] Am sichtbarsten wird dies in den Baumhütten. Waren in Gorleben die Türme das schwerste Hindernis für die anrückende Polizei, so bietet sich die Übernahme dieses Prinzips bei dem Standort im Wald hier geradezu an. Bis zu 12 Meter hoch in die Bäume gebaut, an Seilen um oder zwischen Bäumen hängend, demonstrieren sie eine urtümliche Verteidigungsbereitschaft, die in den Meteora-Klöstern ebenso angewendet wurde, wie in den Baumhäusern der Indianer [heute: Indigene]. [...]

Das Leben im Dorf ist hart, Romantik schimmert nur selten durch den Ernst. „Idylle" wird durch Arbeit verhindert. „Hier zu leben bedeutet einen großen Kraftaufwand." Streßerscheinungen treten auf durch den permanenten Lärm startender und landender Flugzeuge, durch die Unterschiedlichkeit der sozialen Zusammensetzung. [...] Horst, der Dorfschreiber [Horst Karasek, s.u., 1981], konstatiert eine Dreistufigkeit in der sozialen Zusammensetzung der Dauerbewohner: die „Dorfakademiker" mit gesicherter Existenz, die „breite Mittelschicht" der Jugendlichen, die Schul-

oder Berufsausbildung unterbrochen und die Beziehung zur bürgerlichen Existenz und Familie gelockert haben, die „Unterschicht", die „Trebegänger", die die Verbindung zur Gesellschaft ganz abgebrochen haben. „[...] Im Dorf sorgen sie dafür, daß der Zündstoff nie ausgeht." [...]

■ Gemeinschaftsbauten (Community buildings)
■ Individuelle Hütten (Individual huts)
■ Verteidigungswall (Defensive wall)

Startbahn West, Oktober 1981. 1 Dorfplatz 2 „Westend" 3 „Neubauviertel" 4 Bl-Hütte 5 Kirche 6 Küche (Startbahn West, October 1981. 1 Village square 2 "Westend" 3 "New district" 4 Bl hut 5 Church 6 Kitchen)

Die Hütten tragen Namen, die Zeugnis geben von ihren Erbauern, von deren politischer Zielsetzung und auch von ganz persönlichen Eigenheiten. [...] „GAF Hütte" steht für Grüne Anarchistische Fraktion und bei der Hütte „Zorngickel" [hessisch für „zorniger Hahn"] verbindet sich Empörung mit Frankfurter Lokalpatriotismus. [...] „Null Bock" als Aufschrift zeugt von der Hoffnungslosigkeit des Bewohners, der „weiß, daß es umsonst ist" und deshalb „keinen Bock" mehr hat, die Hütte endgültig fertigzustellen. Der Name „Villa Kratzberscht" [hessisch für „Kratzbürste"] vermittelt einen Eindruck der Spannungen, die die Frankfurter Bewohnerin „kratzbürstig" werden ließen, „weil das Leben hier nicht so einfach ist." [...]

Möglichst werden natürliche Baustoffe verwandt, Moos wird in die Ritzen zwischen den Baumstämmen der Außenwand gestopft, Stroh als Isolierung verwendet. Die Notwendigkeit, gegen Kälte und Regen auch zu Styropor und Plastikfolie greifen zu müssen, stört viele [...]. [...] Obwohl der einbrechende Winter und die Ungewißheit bei der Einschätzung der politischen Entwicklung zu einer „Funktionalisierung" der Bauten geführt hat, äußert sich hier eine gestalterische Vielfalt; ein sinnlich-ästhetischer Umgang mit dem Material ist spürbar, der Ornament aus der phantasievollen Handhabung der Dinge entstehen läßt. [...] (Cremer 1982)

Vom Hüttendorfbewohner Matthias Feyerabend erscheint in der Architekturzeitschrift ARCH+ im Jahr 1982 ein Bericht über das Leben im Protestcamp:

Alle Fragen, Entscheidungen und Arbeiten des täglichen Lebens im Dorf werden gemeinsam angegangen. Jeden Morgen finden sich ein oder zwei Frühstückholer, die mit dem Auto nach Walldorf zum Einkauf fahren. Das Geld nehmen sie aus der Dorfkasse, die gefüllt wird durch Spenden der Besucher, durch den Verkauf von Aufklebern, Ansteckern und Getränken und durch Beiträge der Dorfbewohner. [...]

Mit gefülltem Magen läßt sich dann gut beratschlagen, was an Arbeit ansteht und wie sie aufgeteilt wird. Brennholz für die Kochherde und Heizöfen muß gesammelt, gesägt und gehackt werden, das Geschirr mal gespült und das Essen gekocht werden, der Müll darf sich nicht im Wald verbreiten, Getränke müssen eingekauft werden, eine neue Klogrube oder eine weitere Barrikade gehört gegraben! Wer informiert die Besucher, wer fährt zur Infoveranstaltung nach Marburg? Der Werkzeugschuppen muß unbedingt aufgeräumt werden, eine Materialspende mit Dachpappe und Bauholz liegt noch im Schlamm rum und nicht zuletzt ist immer noch unklar, wie sich das Dorf am Tag X verhält, dem Tag der Räumung. [...]

Auf den Sitzungen des Waldrats im Dorf und der Widerstandsgruppen in den Orten werden die Formen des ge-

waltfreien, aber aktiven Widerstands durchgesprochen. Maßnahmen zum Selbstschutz wie Helm, Gasschutzbrille und Mundtuch sind genehmigt und erweisen sich als nur zu berechtigt. Steine und Brandsätze werden ausgeschlossen, aber Farbbeutel gegen Wasserwerfer als taktisch sinnvoll eingeschätzt. Gräben und Wälle auf den Waldwegen, die mit im Boden verankerten Baumstämmen verstärkt werden, sollen die staatliche Gewalt aufhalten, damit die alarmierte Unterstützung noch rechtzeitig eintreffen kann. Vorräte an Lebensmitteln und Trinkwasser stehen für die erwartete Belagerung bereit, Spaten, Schaufeln und Handsägen, Wurfanker und Farbbeutel sind im Waldboden vergraben. [...]

Am 5. Oktober [1981] ist es soweit. Für den nächsten Morgen ist ein Polizeieinsatz vorhergesagt. Hunderte von Leuten allen Alters strömen in den Wald und in das Dorf. Sie heben Gräben aus, schütten Wälle auf, verstärken den Verteidigungsring mit spitzen Pfählen und rostigem Draht. [...] Am Dienstagmittag rückt die Polizei in langer Reihe vor. Wie auf einem mittelalterlichen Schlachtengemälde wird eine viertausendköpfige Verteidigermenge belagert von einem waffenstrotzenden Angreifer, ausgerüstet mit Lederkleid, Helm mit Visier, Schutzschild und Schlagstock. Wir sind in unserer Ausrüstung weit unterlegen, aber fühlen uns moralisch hoch überlegen. [...] Das Dorf gräbt sich noch tiefer ein und rückt noch enger zusammen. Die Offenheit verschwindet und macht dem Mißtrauen Platz. Harmlose Besucher werden als Spitzel verdächtigt, der Waldrat verlangt ein Fotografierverbot und angebliche Rufe im dunklen Wald werden zum Anlaß genommen, die Glocken in der Dorfkirche zu läuten und die Bewohner aus dem Schlaf zu reißen. (Feyerabend 1982)

Anfang November 1981 beginnt die Polizei die Räumung des Hüttendorfs, das sie als „logistisches Zentrum" der „Gewalttäter" bezeichnet (*Polizeiliche Maßnahmen* 1984, S. 28; →*Gewalt*). Bereits zuvor wurden zwar „durch das Errichten der Hütten und das Verhalten der sich im Dorf befindlichen Personen [...] zahlreiche gesetzliche Bestimmungen (z.B. Bauordnung, Naturschutzgesetz, Meldegesetz usw.) permanent verletzt", von der lokalen Bauaufsichtsbehörde erhielt die Polizei jedoch keinen Räumungsauftrag. „Die Vollzugspolizei hatte so keine Möglichkeit, eine eigene Zuständigkeit zur Räumung des Hüttendorfes zu begründen" (*Polizeiliche Maßnahmen* 1984, S. 63). In einer internen Dokumentation beschreibt die Polizei den Räumungseinsatz am 2. November 1981:

Startbahn West. 1 BI-Hütte 2 Erdinger-Moos-Hütte 3 Hängebaumhaus „Kuckucksnest" (Startbahn West. 1 BI hut 2 "Erdinger Moos" hut 3 "Cuckoo's nest" suspended tree house)

Gegen 09.00 Uhr drang das SEK mit Unterstützung weiterer Kräfte in das Dorf ein. Die ca. 70 anwesenden Personen waren völlig überrascht. Sie verließen nach Aufforderung fast ausnahmslos und ohne Widerstand zu leisten das Gelände. [...] Erst mit Beginn der polizeilichen Maßnahmen wurde die Alarmierungskette der Startbahngegner ausgelöst. In Mörfelden-Walldorf läuteten die Kirchenglocken und heulten die Sirenen. Daraufhin sammelten sich in den nächsten Stunden mehrere hundert Personen auf dem Baugelände. (*Polizeiliche Maßnahmen* 1984, S. 28)

Am Abend des 2. Novembers und an den darauffolgenden Tagen kam es in den umliegenden Städten und Gemeinden zu teils gewaltsamen Protestaktionen. Im Wald begannen Startbahngegner*innen unterdessen mit dem Bau neuer Protestdörfer. Insgesamt entstanden bis Ende Januar 1982 an fünf Standorten knapp 90 neue Hütten. Der 7. November ging als „Nacktensamstag" in die Startbahngeschichte ein: Bei einer Demonstration mit 40 000 Menschen (max. 25 000 nach Polizeiangaben) waren 60 Personen als Zeichen der Gewaltlosigkeit oberkörperfrei und bekamen daraufhin von der Polizei Zugang zu einem abgesperrten Waldsektor gewährt (→Nacktheit, →Körpereinsatz).

Nicht nur für die Umweltbewegung wurden die Startbahnproteste zu einem Schlüsselereignis, auch die hessische Polizei zog viele Lehren aus den Großeinsätzen. Im internen Einsatzbericht wurde zwar der „Einsatzwille das Engagement aller Einsatzkräfte" gelobt (*Polizeiliche Maßnahmen* 1984, S. 48), jedoch auch in vielen Bereichen Defizite festgestellt: Bei der „verdeckten Aufklärung" im Hüttendorf führte „das taktisch ungeschickte Verhalten von Einsatzkräften" zu Enttarnungen (S. 72). Es gab Probleme bei der Orientierung im Wald, sodass „Suchtrupps" die Polizist*innen „wieder auf den rechten Pfad bringen" mussten (S. 75). Wegen „vereinzelte[r] Klagen über die Eintönigkeit der Kaltverpflegung", gelangte „vermehrt Frischwurst zur Ausgabe" (S. 82). „Sowohl Einsatzanzug als auch Lederjacke sind bei Dauerregen ungeeignet" (S. 83). Trotz des „massiven Einsatzes von CN" [Tränengas] konnten „die geplanten Aktionen selten wirkungsvoll zum Erliegen gebracht werden" (S. 91). Die Wasserwerfer sanken im matschigen Waldboden ein (S. 92).

Der Schriftsteller Horst Karasek zog 1980 mit seiner Schreibmaschine ins Hüttendorf und wurde zum „Dorfschreiber" der Gemeinde:

Ich vertausche meine zentralgeheizte Dachwohnung im Frankfurter Westend mit einer ofengeheizten Erdhütte, anderthalb Meter in den Waldboden eingegraben. [...] An fünf Abenden in der Woche findet der Waldrat statt, an dem Vertreter der Arbeitsgruppen, der

Hütten und der Bürgerinitiativen teilnehmen sollen. Der Waldrat regelt das alltägliche Leben im Dorf und sein Verhältnis zur Umwelt, das davon geprägt ist, alternatives Widerstandsnest zu sein inmitten einer eher kleinbürgerlich gefärbten Landschaft. [...]

Die Darmstädter Hütte ist wohl die schönste am Platz, sie ist aus Baumstämmen gezimmert und mit Moos verfugt. Ein hohes, fein gegliedertes Doppelfenster paßt sich einem Kirchenfenster ähnlich in die Vorderfront ein, ein Giebeldach stülpt sich wie eine tiefgezogene Haube über das Haus. [...] Die Darmstädter Studenten bilden die Avantgarde im Dorf. Sie waren alle schon vor der Platzbesetzung in der Bürgerinitiative aktiv und wissen ganz genau, warum sie in den Wald gekommen sind. Anders als den Bürgern geht es ihnen aber nicht nur darum, sich dem bäumefressenden Moloch Flughafen AG entgegenzustemmen, sondern eine Gegenwelt zu formen, die als ein Gegenmodell zur Warengesellschaft entstehen soll. [...]

Ich habe mich an das Dorfleben gewöhnt. Wie alle Bewohner komme ich aus meiner Winterkleidung kaum noch heraus; morgens wasche ich mir in der BI-Hütte mit dem kalten Grundwasser die Hände und auch mal das Gesicht, rasiere mich nur daheim, und auch zum Zähneputzen komme ich höchst selten. Abends ziehe ich die vermatschten Gummistiefel von den Füßen, hänge die nassen Socken über den Ofen; Hose, Hemd und Pullover lasse ich häufig an, wenn ich mich in den Schlafsack verkrieche. Nicht, daß in der Hütte kalt wäre, ganz im Gegenteil: der Ofen heizt tüchtig ein. [...] Ende November schlägt die Ankündigung, daß Flörsheim seinen Wald an die FAG verkaufen will, wie eine Bombe im Dorf ein. Nach einem Vertragsabschluß stehen die Hütten nicht mehr stillschweigend geduldet auf Flörsheimer Boden, sondern direkt auf FAG-Gelände. [...]

Am Wochenende nach Weihnachten übernehmen Walldorfer Hausfrauen das Regiment. Sie bringen die Küche auf Glanz und stellen die BI-Hütte auf den Kopf. [...] Die Säuberungsaktion

Walter Keber: Aufbau einer Rundhütte (Construction of a round hut), 1981

Walter Keber: IGS-Hütte in der Bauphase (IGS hut in the construction phase), 1981

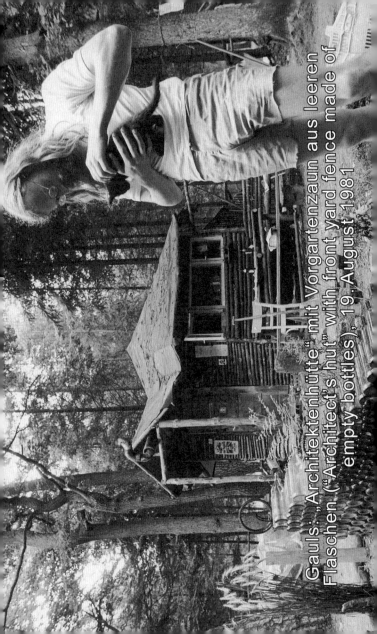

Gauls: „Architektenhütte" mit Vorgartenzaun aus leeren Flaschen. ("Architect's hut" with front yard fence made of empty bottles). 19. August 1981

Dietmar Treber: Erdhaus „Oberurseler Treff" mit Dach aus Erde und Moos (Earth shelter "Oberurseler Treff" with roof made of earth and moss), Oktober 1980

Matthias Feyerabend: Juso-Hütte, ein mit Seilen abgehängtes Baumhaus (Juso hut, a tree house suspended with ropes), Winter 1980

Manfred Prüfer: Ikarus-Hütte, im Hintergrund Carlos Hütte und das Tipi (Icarus hut, in the background Carlo's hut and the tipi), Sommer 1981

Walter Keber: Hüttendorfbewohner*innen zwischen der Darmstädter und Schwarz-Stern Hütte (Hut village residents between the Darmstadt and Schwarz-Stern huts), 1981

Dietmar Treber: Walldorfer Frauen bei der Versorgung mit heißen Getränken (Walldorf women serving hot drinks), Januar 1981

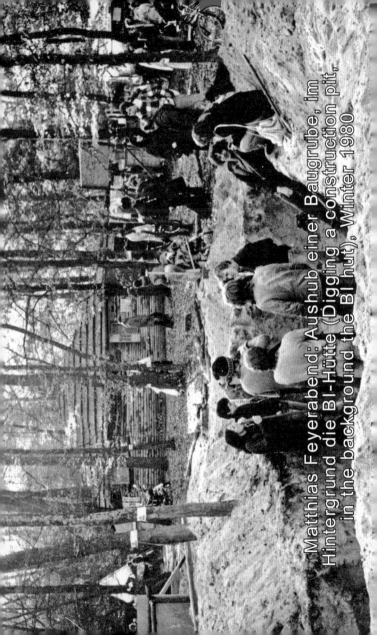

Matthias Feyerabend: Aushub einer Baugrube, im Hintergrund die BI-Hütte (Digging a construction pit, in the background the BI hut), Winter 1980

Walter Keber: Besetzte Bäume und Holzturm (Occupied trees and a wooden tower), Oktober 1981

Wolfgang Eilmes: Besetzter
Holzturm während der Räumung
(Occupied wooden tower during
eviction), Oktober 1981

Walter Keber: Translokation der Hüttenkirche, des einzigen Baus, der bei der Räumung nicht zerstört wurde (Translocation of the village church, the only building not destroyed during eviction), 1986

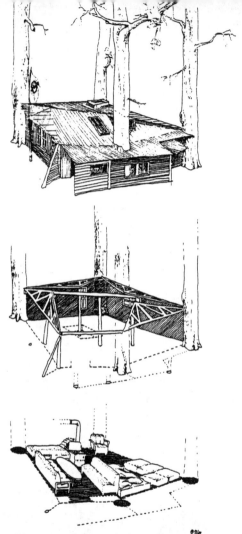

Explosionszeichnung der
Darmstädter Hütte
(Exploded-view drawing of the
Darmstadt hut), 1982

geht natürlich nicht ohne böse Worte über unseren Unrat und unsere Lieder- lichkeit ab. Wir werden bemuttert. [...] Wenn wir uns Kaffee, Tee, Mineralwas- ser oder gar eine Flasche Bier holen, ohne Geld in die Sammelbüchse zu wer- fen, trifft uns ein strafender Blick – und ich greife in die Hosentasche. [...] Wir fühlen uns wie Fremde und Bettler im eigenen Dorf. [...] Am Sonntagnachmit- tag entlädt sich die Spannung zu einem handfesten Krach, die Frauen binden ihre Schürzen ab und schmeißen die Suppenkellen hin. In einer eilig einbe- rufenen Bewohnerversammlung in der Weiterstädter Hütte versuchen die Wall- dorfer und die Waldbewohner, den Streit zu begraben, doch hat der Konflikt tie- fere Ursachen und wird weiterschwelen. [...] (Karasek 1981) (Texte von Ulrich Cremer, Matthias Feyerabend, Horst Karasek; Dokumentation: *Polizeiliche Maßnahmen aus Anlass des Baues der Startbahn 18-West*; Einleitung und Re- cherche: AMM)

Startbahn West, Ger. → *Startbahn West.* In May → *1980*, a → *protest camp* against the expansion of Frankfurt Air- port was set up in the Flörsheim Forest southwest of Frankfurt. The construc- tion site of the Startbahn West (Runway 18 West) was blocked. The protests, widely rooted in the region, were direct- ed against the clearing of 129 hectares of partly protected forest and against al- ready considerable aircraft noise pollu- tion. For parts of the peace movement, the US military base at Frankfurt Air- port was considered a → *protest goal.* The hut village of the runway oppo- nents was set up at the same time as the protest camp in → *Gorleben.* However, while the Wendland camp was evicted after only thirty-three days, the hut vil- lage, with its more than sixty structures at its peak, was able to remain in place for almost a year and a half.

Plans to add a third runway to Germa- ny's busiest airport began in the early 1960s. Due to complaints from local citizens' initiatives, including the "In- teressengemeinschaft zur Bekämpfung des Fluglärms e. V." (Interest Group to Combat Aircraft Noise), founded in

1965, the start of construction was re- peatedly delayed over a period of almost ten years. From the end of the 1970s, cross-party alliances formed in the neighboring municipalities to oppose the expansion. In Mörfelden-Walldorf, the SPD, CDU, DKP, and FDP (social democrats, conservatives, communists, and liberals) protested under a joint → *banner*, and several pastors also sup- ported the movement. One year after the start of construction of the hut vil- lage, the "Arbeitsgemeinschaft Volks- begehren und Volksentscheid—Keine Startbahn West!" (Working Group for a Referendum and Plebiscite—No Start- bahn West!) was founded. In the fall of 1981, the forest occupation was ended by a massive → *police* deployment, and shortly thereafter, the petition for a ref- erendum was rejected, despite 220,765 signatures having been collected. Pro- tests continued beyond the completion of the runway in 1984 up until Novem- ber 1987, when police officers Thorsten Schwalm and Klaus Eichhöfer were shot dead during a → *demonstration* mark- ing the sixth anniversary of the eviction of the hut village. In 2011, the airport was expanded again, this time adding a runway for landings. Notable protests only took place after the extent of the increased aircraft noise became notice- able in the region.

The buildings of the hut village are more well-documented than probably any other protest camp. Architecture students of the Technical Universi- ty of Darmstadt created detailed sur- vey drawings of each hut. The architect Ulrich Cremer supervised the seminar at the department of Professor Helmut Striffler and published a book on it:

In September 1979, the citizens' ini- tiative (Bürgerinitiative, short: BI) sub- mits an official building application to the city of Flörsheim for the erection of a shelter on the site of the planned run- way. The architect Lotz from Mörfelden prepared plans for an open hut; the con- cept of the twelve-corner layout arose from its intended use as a meeting place. The building application is rejected. [...] The citizens' initiative decides to build the hut nevertheless and makes all necessary preparations during the winter. On the basis of the old plans, a closed, habitable hut is designed whose parts are prefabricated and hidden in the forest. On May 3, 1980, about eighty BI members begin construction at six o'clock in the morning, and by noon the shell of the hut, eleven meters in diameter, is in place. The police and FAG [Flughafen AG] are completely taken by surprise by this action. [...]

The BI hut becomes the first symbol of resistance and forms the center of the later village. This forms the spatial center of the movement, the site for discussion and information sharing, as well as serving as a meeting place and starting point for the actions. The hut is occupied day and night by members of the citizens' initiative and is further expanded. [...] When the village comes into being, it serves as a sleeping place for the hut builders, as a supply depot, kitchen, and washing area. [...] In October 1980, the situation escalates; the FAG has the first seven hectares of forest cleared under police protection. In response, more huts are spontaneously built. [...]

For the functioning of an independent, self-sustaining community, the shared huts are created by joint effort and grouped in a semicircle around the BI hut: the children's house, hut church, radio tower, firewood shed, bicycle workshop, cold store, pantry, and kitchen. Together these facilities comprise the core of the village [...]. The residential huts form an outer ring, semicircular at first and later completed by the "new building quarter," which develops in the denser, darker forest in the east only when the sunnier places of the "Westend" are already occupied. [...]

Like the "Free Republic of Wendland" and the huts on the embankment of the B-8 road near Kelkheim [Hasler 1982], the village in the Flörsheim Forest is both a directly affected territory and a symbol for the [...] threatened destruction at the same time. [...] The defensive character of the village is expressed not only in the barricades but also in the construction concept of the huts themselves. [...] This becomes most visible in the tree houses. As in Gorleben, where the towers were the greatest obstacle for the approaching police, the adoption of this principle in the forest location presents itself as an obvious choice. Built up to twelve meters high in the trees, hanging on ropes around or between trees, these tree houses demonstrate a primeval defensive readiness, which was applied in the Meteora monasteries as well as in the tree houses of the Indians [today: Indigenous peoples]. [...]

Life in the village is hard, a sense of romance only rarely shimmers through the seriousness. An "idyll" is prevented by work. "Living here means a great deal of effort." Stress is caused by the permanent noise of planes taking off and landing, by the disparate social composition. [...] Horst, the village scribe [Horst Karasek, see below, 1981], notes a three-tiered social composition of the permanent residents: the "village academics" with a secure livelihood; the "broad middle class" comprising young people who have interrupted school or vocational training and loosened their relationship to bourgeois existence and family; and the "lower class," the "runaways," who have completely broken off their connection to society. " [...] They make sure that there's always a trigger for controversy in the village." [...]

The huts bear names that attest to their builders, their political objectives, and to very personal idiosyncrasies. [...] "GAF Hütte" stands for "Grüne Anarchistische Fraktion" (Green Anarchist Faction) and the "Zorngickel" hut [Hessian for "angry rooster"] combines indignation with Frankfurt-based local patriotism. [...] The label reading "Null Bock" (Can't be bothered) testifies to the hopelessness of the occupant, who "knows that it's all for nothing" and therefore "can't be bothered" to finally finish the hut. The name "Villa Kratzberscht" [Hessian for "Kratzbürste" or "prickly character"] conveys an impression of the tensions that caused the Frankfurt resident to become "prickly" "because life here is not so easy." [...]

474

Natural building materials are used as much as possible; moss is stuffed into the cracks between the tree trunks of an outer wall, straw is used as insulation. The necessity of having to resort to polystyrene and plastic sheeting against the cold and rain bothers many [...]. [...] Although the onset of winter and the uncertainty in the assessment of political developments have led to a "functionalization" of the buildings, a creative diversity is expressed here; a sensually aesthetic approach to materials is discernible, which allows ornamentation to emerge from the imaginative handling of things. [...] (Cremer 1982)

In 1982, the architecture magazine *ARCH+* published a report on life in the protest camp by Matthias Feyerabend, a resident of the hut village:

All everyday questions, decisions, and tasks in the village are tackled together. Every morning, one or two breakfast fetchers can be found who drive to Walldorf by car to go shopping. They take the money from the village treasury, which is filled by donations from visitors, by the sale of stickers, badges, and drinks, and by contributions from the villagers. [...]

With a full stomach, it feels easier to discuss what work needs to be done and how it should be distributed. Firewood for the cooking stoves and heaters needs to be collected, sawed, and chopped; the dishes washed and the food cooked; the garbage should not be spread around the forest. Beverages are to be bought, a new toilet pit or another barricade must be dug! Who is responsible for informing visitors? And for driving to the information event in Marburg? The tool shed has to be tidied up; a material donation consisting of roofing felt and construction timber is still lying around in the mud; and last but not least it is still unclear how the village will behave on D-Day, the day of the eviction. [...]

At the meetings of the forest council in the village and the resistance groups in the towns, the forms of nonviolent but active resistance are talked through. Self-protection measures such as helmets, gas safety goggles, and face masks

are authorized and prove all too justified. Stones and incendiary devices are ruled out, but paint bags for use against water cannons are judged to be tactically useful. Ditches and ramparts on forest paths, reinforced with logs anchored in the ground, are designed to hold off the authorities so that alerted support has time to arrive. Supplies of food and drinking water are kept ready for the expected siege; spades, shovels, and handsaws, grappling hooks and bags of paint, are buried in the forest soil. [...]

On October 5 [1981], the time has come. A police operation is predicted for the next morning. Hundreds of people of all ages pour into the forest and the village. They dig trenches, pile up ramparts, reinforce the defensive ring with pointed stakes and rusty wire. [...] At noon on Tuesday, the police advance in a long line. As in a medieval battle painting, a crowd of 4,000 defenders is besieged by a heavily armed attacker, equipped with leather dress, a visor helmet, protective shield, and baton. We are far inferior in our equipment but feel highly superior in moral terms. [...] The village digs itself in even deeper and moves even closer together. Openness disappears and gives way to mistrust. Harmless visitors are suspected of being informers; the forest council demands a ban on photography; and alleged calls in the dark forest are taken as an excuse to ring the bells in the village church and rouse the inhabitants from their sleep. (Feyerabend 1982)

At the beginning of November 1981, the police start to clear the hut village, which they describe as the "logistical center" of the "perpetrators of violence" (*Polizeiliche Maßnahmen* 1984, p. 28; → *Violence*). Although "numerous legal regulations (e.g. building code, nature conservation law, registration law, etc.) were permanently violated by the erection of the huts and the behavior of the people who were in the village" previously, the police did not receive an eviction order from the local building inspection authority. "The police thus had no possibility of establishing their jurisdiction to evict the hut village" (*Polizei-*

liche Maßnahmen 1984, p. 63). In internal documentation, the police describe the eviction operation on November 2, 1981:

Around 09:00, the SEK (special forces) entered the village with the support of other forces. The approximately seventy people present there were taken by complete surprise. After being asked to do so, they left the premises almost without exception and without offering any resistance. [...] It was only with the start of the police measures that the alarm chain of the runway opponents was triggered. In Mörfelden-Walldorf, the church bells rang and the sirens wailed. As a result, several hundred people gathered at the construction site over the next few hours. (Polizeiliche Maßnahmen 1984, p. 28)

On the evening of November 2 and the following days, there were protests, some of them violent, in the surrounding towns and municipalities. In the meantime, opponents of the runway began building new protest villages in the forest. By the end of January 1982, a total of almost ninety new huts had been built at five locations. November 7 went down in runway history as "Naked Saturday." At a demonstration with 40,000 people (max. 25,000 according to police figures), sixty people were topless in an act of nonviolence and were then granted access to a cordoned-off forest sector by the police (→ *Nakedness,* → *Body deployment*).

The runway protests became a key event not only for the environmental movement but also for the Hessian police, who learned many lessons from the large-scale operations. Although the internal operational report praised the "commitment and dedication of all task forces" (*Polizeiliche Maßnahmen* 1984, p. 48), it also noted deficits in many areas: during "undercover reconnaissance" in the hut village, "the tactically clumsy behavior of task forces" led to their discovery (p. 72). There were problems with orientation in the forest, so that "search teams" had to "bring the police officers back on the right track" (p. 75). Due to "isolated complaints

about the monotony of the cold rations," "more fresh sausage was distributed" (p. 82). "Both the task force uniform and the leather jacket are unsuitable in continuous rain" (p. 83). Despite the "massive use of CN" [tear gas], "the planned actions could rarely be effectively brought to a halt" (p. 91). The water cannon vehicles sank into the muddy forest soil (p. 92).

The writer Horst Karasek moved to the hut village with his typewriter in 1980 and became the "village scribe" of the community:

I am swapping my centrally heated attic apartment in Frankfurt's Westend for a stove-heated earthen hut, buried a meter and a half into the forest soil. [...] Five evenings a week, the forest council is held, which is supposed to be attended by representatives of the working groups, the huts, and the citizens' initiatives. The forest council regulates the daily life in the village and its relationship with the environment, which is characterized as being an alternative nest of resistance in the midst of a primarily petit-bourgeois landscape. [...]

The Darmstadt Hut is probably the most beautiful on the site; it is made of logs and sealed with moss. A high, delicately structured double window fits into the front of the house like a stained-glass window, while a gable roof is pulled over the house like a deep-drawn hood. [...] The Darmstadt students comprise the avant-garde in the village. They were all active in the citizens' initiative before the site's occupation and know exactly why they have come to the forest. Unlike the local citizens, however, they are not only concerned with opposing the tree-devouring juggernaut that is the Flughafen AG but also with creating a village community that is to emerge as a counter-model to consumer society. [...]

I have become accustomed to village life. Like all the residents, I can hardly get out of my winter clothes; in the morning, I wash my hands and sometimes my face with the cold groundwater in the BI hut, shave only at home, and even brush my teeth very rarely. In the evening, I take the muddy rubber boots off my feet, hang the wet socks over the stove; I often leave my pants, shirt, and sweater on when I crawl into my sleeping bag. It's not that it's cold in the hut, quite the opposite: the stove does an excellent job. [...] At the end of November, the announcement that Flörsheim wanted to sell its forest to the FAG hit the village like a bomb. After a contract is signed, the huts will no longer stand tacitly tolerated on Flörsheim soil but directly on FAG land. [...]

On the weekend following Christmas, Walldorf housewives take over the reigns. They spruce up the kitchen and turn the B1 hut upside down. [...] The cleanup of course produces some angry words on their part about our trash and sloppiness. We are being mothered. [...] If we get coffee, tea, mineral water, or even a bottle of beer without throwing money into the collection box, we are met with a punishing look—and I reach into my trouser pocket. [...] We feel like strangers and beggars in our own village. [...] On Sunday afternoon, the tension erupted into a full-blown quarrel, with the women untying their aprons and throwing down their soup ladles. In a hastily called residents' meeting in the Weiterstadt Hut, the Walldorfers and the forest dwellers try to put an end to the dispute, but the conflict has deeper causes and will continue to simmer. [...] (Karasek 1981) (Texts by Ulrich Cremer, Matthias Feyerabend, and Horst Karasek; police report: *Polizeiliche Maßnahmen aus Anlass des Baues der Startbahn 18-West*; introduction and research: AMM)

Sternmarsch, engl. → *Converging protest marches*; → *Demonstration*

Straße, engl. → *Street*. Als im Sommer 2015 Rauchschwaden zwischen den Türmen in Frankfurts Bankenviertel aufstiegen, waren die Aktivist∗innen gerade dabei, die Straßen zu erobern. Viertel und Straßen waren, wie es in Protestbewegungen oft der Fall ist, symbolisch gewählt. Das Herzstück der Aktion war das Viertel um den Neubau der Europäischen Zentralbank (EZB), die als „Krisenverwalterin" stellvertretend für die Sparpolitik der Troika, dem Zusammenschluss von EZB, Internationalem Währungsfond und Europäischer Kommission, stand und zugleich mit ihren Rettungsschirmen für insolvente Banken einen Bruch im Gerüst des Neoliberalismus markierte, der sich doch eigentlich gerade durch seine Unabhängigkeit vom Staat definiert. Die Aktivist∗innen nahmen dies als einen Riss im System wahr, der ihnen die Möglichkeit bot, zwischen den Hochhäusern der Großbanken mitten auf der von ihnen angeeigneten Straße eine andere Gesellschaft jenseits kapitalistischer Logiken aufblitzen zu lassen. So wurden die Eroberung, die → *Besetzung* und die → *Blockade* von Straßen, die sich spätestens mit den linken Gipfelprotesten in Seattle etabliert hatten (→ *Antiglobalisierungs- / WTO-Proteste*), durch die zahlreichen diskursiven Veranstaltungen in den dazugehörigen → *Protestcamps* ergänzt. Die Aktivist∗innen, die aus ganz Europa nach Frankfurt anreisten, um die Krisenpolitik der EU anzuklagen, formierten sich auf der Straße daher als eine Gemeinschaft, die Kritik übte und zugleich für eine bessere Welt einstand – und dafür musste die Straße selbst herhalten, denn „sous les pavés, la plage" („unter dem Pflaster der Strand"), wie es schon im → *Mai '68* in Paris hieß.

Blockupy war, wie es in Protestbewegungen ebenso meist der Fall ist, kein spontanes Vorhaben, sondern ein von langer Hand geplanter Protest, dem langwierige Verhandlungen mit → *Polizei*, Ordnungsamt und Gerichten vorausgingen. Denn Straßen sind in Demokratien im staatlichen Sinne „öffentlich": Sie sind zwar allen Menschen zugänglich und unterliegen mit wenigen Ausnahmen keinem privaten Zugriff, werden aber dennoch regiert, überwacht und nach staatlichen Interessen strukturiert. Straßenproteste in Form von → *Demonstrationen* müssen nach geltendem Recht angemeldet und mit den verantwortlichen staatlichen Akteur∗innen ausgehandelt werden; sie sind deshalb stets die Resultate von Verhandlungsprozessen zwischen denen, die protestieren, und denen, die den

Protest nach staatlichen Gesichtspunkten mitchoreografieren. Dabei ist der Staat zunächst im Vorteil, kann präventiv entscheiden, wer protestieren darf, sei es durch sogenannte Gefährder*innenansprachen oder Platzverweise, die Proteste bei Nichteinhaltung der vereinbarten Einschränkungen sogar verbieten oder sie martialisch begleiten: von vorne mit Wasserwerfern, von oben mit Hubschraubern, von den Seiten mit behelmten Polizist*innen im Spalier oder auf Pferden und durch Sperren an abzweigenden Straßenkreuzungen. Doch je einschränkender der Staat vorrückt, desto dynamischer wird der Protest, sodass sich gerade dann, wenn ersterer besonders drastisch seine Macht demonstriert, dynamische Reaktionen hervorruft – immer in Bewegung und beweglicher Formation, pulsierend, spannungsgeladen, erwartungsvoll, bereit und daher bisweilen nicht kontrollierbar und sogar unregierbar: *ungovernable*, wie die Aktivist*innen diverser Bewegungen es für sich beanspruchen.

Viele Straßenproteste zeichnen sich durch Blockaden aus. So zielten beispielsweise die großen „Dresden Nazifrei"-Demonstrationen darauf ab, die alljährlichen Proteste der Neonaziszene am 13. Februar in Erinnerung an die hier geschichtsrevisionistisch verdrehte Bombardierung Dresdens durch die Alliierten zu blockieren. Auf dieselbe Protestform greifen auch die Klimaaktivist*innen der Letzten Generation zurück, die seit 2022 verstärkt sowohl gewöhnliche Verkehrsstraßen als auch Autobahnen blockierten, mit ihren Körpern als →*Barrikaden* oder durch das →*Ankleben* (→*Körpereinsatz*). Die ausgewählten Straßen stehen erneut symbolisch, in diesem Fall geht es um Autos, den Straßenverkehr als zentralen Verursacher von Emissionen und deshalb auch um die Frage, in welchem öffentlichen Interesse die Straße eigentlich steht: in dem der nächsten Generation und ihrer Zukunft oder der Autolobby und ihren Parteien? Statt auf Bewegung setzen die Aktivist*innen bei Blockaden auf Stillstand, Unterbrechung und Verlangsamung; der Fluss des technisierten Alltags soll verzögert und gestört werden – und die Straßen als das vorgeführt werden, als was sie gebaut wurden: Transport- und Transitwege, die Mobilität vor allem durch jenen Individualverkehr ermöglichen und dadurch Arbeits- und Warenwege möglichst reibungslos gewährleisten. Inwieweit bei solchen eigentlich öffentlichen Orten im „Automobilen Kapitalismus" (vgl. ...ums Ganze! 2021) aus diesem Grund doch privatwirtschaftliche Interessen eine Rolle spielen, hat der Künstler Klaus Staeck bereits 1974 auf einem seiner Plakate zur Debatte gestellt – „For Wider Streets Vote Conservative" persiflierte er die Politik der britischen Konservativen. „Wo der deutsche Staat aufhört und die Automobilindustrie anfängt, lässt sich kaum feststellen", kritisieren Aktivist*innen heute wieder (...ums Ganze! 2021, S. 32). Der Slogan „Whose streets? Our streets!" steht daher zunehmend im Zeichen der Klimabewegung und die Belagerung der Straße ist zum Symbol für den Aufschub der Politik zur Rettung der Welt geworden (→*Protestziele*). (Friederike Sigler)

Straw, Ger. →*Stroh (fig.)*, is not just a popular →*building material* to insulate huts and →*tree houses* (→*Hambacher Forest*), but is also used to sit on at →*blockades*, such as at the blockades of the open-pit mines by →*protest organization* Ende Gelände. To this end, protesters fill vegetable sacks with straw and can then carry them under their arms or attach them to their backpacks. Because the sack of straw can double up as a →*protective shield* (→*protection*) against →*police* truncheons, it has been classified as a passive weapon that is then forbidden at gatherings. (AMM)

Street, Ger. →*Straße*. As billows of smoke rose between the towers of Frankfurt's banking district in the summer of 2015, the activists of the Blockupy alliance were taking over the streets. The districts and streets were chosen for symbolic reasons, as is often the case in protest movements. The heart of the action culminated around the new building of the European Central Bank (ECB), which, as the "crisis manager," represented the austerity policy of the troika, the union between the ECB, the International Monetary Fund, and the European Commission. At the same time, the institution's bailouts for insolvent banks signified a crack in the framework of neoliberalism, which is supposedly defined by its independence from the state. The activists perceived this development as a rupture in the system which allowed them to present a glimpse of an alternative society beyond capitalist logic among the skyscrapers and big banks in the middle of the street they had occupied. In addition to the conquest, → *occupation*, and → *blockade* of streets, an established method since at least the left-wing protests in Seattle (→ *WTO protests / Battle of Seattle*), numerous discursive events took place in the accompanying → *protest camps*. Having travelled to Frankfurt from all over Europe to denounce the crisis management of the EU, the activists came together in the street as a community that expressed criticism, but also advocated for a better world—and, in keeping with the rallying cry of the Paris demonstrations of → *May '68*, "sous les pavés, la plage" (beneath the pavement, the beach), the street served as their platform.

As is also often the case in protest movements, Blockupy was not a spontaneous event, but a protest planned long in advance and preceded by lengthy negotiations with the → *police*, the public order office, and the courts. In democracies, the streets' classification as "public" is defined by the state: while they are open to all people and not subject to private access, apart from a few exceptions, streets are governed, surveilled, and structured according to governmental interests. Prevailing German law stipulates that street protests in the shape of → *demonstrations* are registered and negotiated with the state actors in charge; they are consequently always the results of negotiation processes between the protesters and those micro-choreographing the protest according to aspects determined by the state. The state is initially at an advan-

tage and can decide preemptively who is allowed to protest, whether through so-called warnings to potential troublemakers or expulsions, and can even ban protests if the agreed restrictions are violated or can accompany them with draconian measures: from the front with water cannons, from above with helicopters, from the sides with helmeted police in cordons or on horseback, and with barricades at junctions. However, the more restrictive the state becomes, the more dynamic the protest becomes, so that especially drastic demonstrations of power by the former trigger vigorous reactions in the latter—always in motion and mobile formation, pulsating, charged with tension, expectant, ready, and thus often uncontrollable and even "ungovernable," as activists of diverse movements have said of themselves.

Many street protests are characterized by blockades. The aim of the big "Nazifree" demonstrations in Dresden was to block the annual neo-Nazi rallies on February 13 in remembrance of the Allied bombing of Dresden, in accordance with their disorted historical revisionism. The climate activists of Letzte Generation also use this form of protest. Since 2022, they have blocked an increasing number of regular thoroughfares and highways by using their bodies as → *barricades* (→ *Body deployment*), or by → *super-gluing* themselves to the ground. Once again, the choice of roads is symbolic, in this case, it is about cars, about road traffic as the main cause of emissions, and about the public benefit of the street: Is it to benefit the next generation and their future, or the car lobby and their parties? With their blockades, the activists choose stagnation, interruption, and deceleration over movement; the goal is to delay and disturb the flow of technologized everyday life—and to highlight the purpose of streets as transport and transit routes that primarily enable mobility through individual traffic and thereby ensure smooth paths to the pursuit of work and delivery of goods. As early as 1974, the artist Klaus Staeck addressed the extent to which the interests of the private sector shape these essentially public areas in "automobile capitalism" (see …ums Ganze! 2021)—his poster with the slogan "For Wider Streets Vote Conservative" was a satirical comment on the politics of the British Conservatives. "It is almost impossible to determine where the German state ends and the automobile industry begins," the activists of today criticize (…ums Ganze! 2021, p. 32). Thus, the slogan "Whose streets? Our streets!" has come to represent the climate movement, and the occupation of streets has come to symbolize a suspension of politics for the good of the world (→ *Protest goals*). (Friederike Sigler)

Streik, engl. → *Strike*; → *Blockade*
Strike, Ger. → *Streik*; → *Blockade*

Stroh. Tim Wagner: Aktivist∗innen von Ende Gelände am Tagebau Hambach, 5. November 2017 (Straw. Tim Wagner: Activists from Ende Gelände at the Hambach open-pit mine, November 5, 2017**)**

Stroh, engl. → *Straw*, ist nicht nur ein beliebtes → *Baumaterial* zum Dämmen von Hütten und → *Baumhäusern* (→ *Hambacher Wald*), sondern wird auch als Sitzunterlage bei → *Blockaden*, etwa bei den Tagebaublockaden der → *Protestorganisation* Ende Gelände verwendet. Dafür wird es in Gemüsesäcke gefüllt und unter den Arm oder an den Rucksack geklemmt. Weil der Strohsack auch als → *Schutzschild* (→ *Schutz*) gegen Schlagstöcke der → *Polizei* verwendet werden kann, gilt er als passive Bewaffnung, die bei Versammlungen verboten ist. (AMM)

Superglue, Ger. → *Sekundenkle-* ber; → *Blockade*, → *Body deployment*, → *Guerrilla tactics*, → *Hong Kong protests*, → *Super-gluing*, → *Vehicles*

Super-gluing, Ger. → *Ankleben (fig.)*. Protest form of the 2020s. Like → *rappelling*, super-gluing is a form of → *blockade* in which activists from → *protest organizations* such as Last Generation and Insulate Britain use superglue or expanding foam to stick themselves to busy → *streets*. With the resulting closures, traffic jams, and disruptions to everyday life, the environmental groups draw attention to the climate crisis. Unlike classic → *sit-in* blockades, the stick-on actions require only a few people. However, the extent of the activists' → *body deployment* is considerably greater, even compared to blockades and → *occupations* with → *lock-on devices* because by sticking their hands and feet to the road they risk irreversible damage to their health. For → *protection* against assaults by angry road users (→ *Violence*), the activists only stick themselves on when the → *police* have already arrived. With the first highway blockades of the Last Generation in Germany in January 2022 and the expansion of the stick-on actions to → *museums*, → *vehicles*, and buildings such as airports and oil refineries, a heated media debate broke out about the growing radicalization of the environmental movement. (AMM)

Survival blanket, Ger. → *Rettungsdecke (fig.)*. In the 2010s, survival blankets seem to be what the black, red, and gold → *flags* were to the 1848 Revolutions and the red flags were in the 20th century: similar in their general use to the → *yellow vests* that are likewise to be found in any vehicle, survival blankets serve as a symbol of a more leftist, anti-racist sentiment and were adopted as a hallmark from 2017 onward by the association "Die Vielen," as a → *banner* with no explicitly formulated message. At the same time, the survival blanket functions during occupations, such as the tree-hugging in the → *Dannenrod Forest*, to protect against the cold, possibly with subliminal associations with their use in sports competitions, for example to keep runners warm after crossing a marathon finish line. Protests likewise call for peak performances. (OE)

Symbol, engl. →*Symbol*; →*Denkmalsturz*, →*Erkennungszeichen*, →*Ikone*, →*Kleidung*, →*Kommunikation*, →*Körpereinsatz*, →*Zelt*

Symbol, Ger. →*Symbol*; →*Body deployment*, →*Clothing*, →*Communication*, →*Icon*, →*Identifier*, →*Tent*, →*Toppling monuments*

Syntagma-Platz, engl. →*Syntagma Square*. Ende Mai →*2011* versammelten sich - inspiriert von den Protesten der →*Movimiento 15M* in Madrid - hunderttausende Menschen in Athen, um gegen Arbeitslosigkeit, Korruption und die griechische Sparpolitik zu demonstrieren (→*Demonstration*). Zwei Gruppen besetzten verschiedene Bereiche des Syntagma-Platzes (→*Platzbesetzung*) und drückten ihre Kritik an der Regierung durch unterschiedliche Protesttaktiken aus: Rechts- und linksnationalistische Gruppen organisierten karnevaleske direkte Aktionen auf dem höhergelegenen Abschnitt des Platzes, teils unter Einsatz von →*Gewalt*. Linksalternative Aktivist∗innen errichteten auf dem unteren Teil des Platzes ein →*Protestcamp* und hielten öffentliche Versammlungen ab. Das Camp zu erhalten verbrauchte viele Ressourcen, wodurch sich die Diskussionen in den Versammlungen oft auf organisatorische Fragen verlagerten. Eine breite Öffentlichkeit konnte jedoch über die →*digitalen Medien* erreicht werden. Das Protestcamp wurde während seines zweimonatigen Bestehens mehrmals von der →*Polizei* geräumt. Darauf reagierten die Protestierenden mit dem Bau von →*Barrikaden* aus Pflanzkübeln, Mülltonnen und anderem Stadtmobiliar (→*Baumaterial*). (AMM)

Syntagma Square, Ger. →*Syntagma-Platz*. At the end of May →*2011*, inspired by the protests of →*Movimiento 15M* in Madrid, hundreds of thousands of people gathered in Athens to demonstrate (→*Demonstration*) against unemployment, corruption, and the Greek government's austerity policies. Two groups occupied different areas of Syntagma Square (→*Public square occupation*) and expressed their criticism of the government through various protest tactics: nationalist groups from the left and the right organized carnivalesque direct actions on the higher section of the square, in part using →*Violence*. Left-wing activists set up a →*protest camp* on the lower area of the square and held public assemblies. Maintaining the camp consumed a great deal of resources, meaning that the discussions in the assemblies often centered on organizational issues, while the broader public was reached through →*digital media*. Over the course of its two-month existence, the →*police* cleared the protest camp on several occasions. The protesters responded by erecting →*barricades* consisting of planters, garbage cans, and other street furniture (→*Building materials*). (AMM)

Tagebaubesetzungen, engl. →*Open-pit mine occupations*; →*Finger*, →*Klimacamps*, →*Overall*, →*Protestorganisationen*, →*Stroh*

Tahrir-Platz, engl. →*Tahrir Square*. Von →*2011* bis 2013 war der Tahrir-Platz im Zentrum von Kairo immer wieder ein Schauplatz von Massenprotesten. Zu →*Platzbesetzungen* und der Errichtung von →*Protestcamps* auf dem sonst stark befahrenen →*Kreisverkehr* kam es u.a. im Januar, Juli und November 2011, im Januar 2012 und im Januar 2013. Mit der „Revolution des 25. Januar" fing im Frühjahr 2011 - kurz nach dem Beginn der „Jasminrevolution" in Tunesien - der sogenannte „Arabische Frühling" in Ägypten an. Die Proteste richteten sich gegen das Regime des Präsidenten Muhammad Husni Mubarak und seinen Sicherheitsapparat. Unmittelbarer Auslöser war die Ermordung des Bloggers Khaled Said, der nach der Veröffentlichung eines Videos über Korruption bei der →*Polizei* auf offener Straße zu Tode geprügelt wurde. Die Protestierenden forderten den Rücktritt des Präsidenten, politische Reformen, Meinungsfreiheit und demokratische Wahlen sowie bessere Lebensverhältnisse und mehr soziale Gerechtigkeit. Auf dem Tahrir-Platz hielten sich häufig tausende Menschen in einer sich wandelnden Struktur aus →Zelten und gespannten Planen auf, beim „Marsch der Millionen" am 1. Februar 2011 demonstrierten bis zu 2 Millionen Ägypter∗innen gegen das Mubarak-Regime (→ Demonstration). Immer wieder kam es während der 18-tägigen Revolution zu gewaltsamen Eskalationen mit zahlreichen Toten (→ Gewalt). Trotzdem nahmen viele Besetzer∗innen die „Republik von Tahrir" als einen utopischen Mikrokosmos wahr und feierten den gemeinsamen Protest – oftmals herrschte Festivalstimmung. Es gaben Konzerte (→ Musik) und Straßenhändler∗innen verkauften Essen.

Als Präsident Mubarak am 11. Februar seinen Rücktritt ankündigte, waren zwar die direkten Forderungen der Protestierenden erfüllt, doch langfristig scheiterte die Demokratiebewegung daran, den Protest in ein politisches Programm umzuwandeln. Nach einer kurzen Regierungszeit des Anführers der islamistischen Muslimbruderschaft, Mohammed Mursi, der im Sommer 2012 demokratisch gewählt wurde, putschte sich 2013 das Militär zurück an die Macht. Immer wieder flammten die Proteste auf. Bis heute (Stand 2023) regiert die Militärregierung mit großer Brutalität.

Die Protestbewegung war bei der Revolution im Frühjahr 2011 noch breit gefächert: Studierende, Jugendliche, darunter viele Frauen∗, beteiligten sich; Linke, Bürgerliche, Säkulare, Christ∗innen und Muslim∗innen protestierten gemeinsam. Auch Mitglieder der Muslimbruderschaft kamen zu den Protesten, von diesen fundamentalistisch-religiösen Kräften distanzierte sich aber der Großteil der übrigen Protestierenden. Auf ambivalente Weise unterstützt wurde die Revolution des 25. Januar vom Militär, das nach dem Sturz der Regierung die Macht übernahm. Es sicherte den Protestierenden zwar freie Wahlen zu, ging gegen die neu aufflammenden Proteste jedoch gewaltsam vor. Nach dem Ende der Proteste im Februar 2011 verbündete sich die Muslimbruderschaft mit dem Militär, was viele säkular-liberale Protestierende scharf kritisierten. Spätere Protestwellen waren von der islamistischen Regierung unter Mursi mitorganisiert und von der Polizei infiltriert. Das Momentum der breit verankerten Proteste im Frühjahr 2011 kam nicht mehr zustande.

Der Architekt und Stadtplaner Ahmed Zaazaa war während der Revolution des 25. Januar auf dem Tahrir-Platz. Er verfasste für die Ausstellung Protest/Architektur einen Beitrag mit dem Titel „The Democratic Republic of Tahrir", in dem er die Entstehung der Besetzung und den Verlauf der ersten Protestwelle nachzeichnet:

Über ein ganzes Jahr hinweg wurde die Umgebung des Tahrir-Platzes durch die Proteste – die als „Revolution des 25. Januar" in die Geschichte eingingen – neu geformt, sich angeeignet, wieder in Besitz genommen; sie ist verfallen, hat sich regeneriert, ist geschrumpft und hat sich wieder ausgedehnt. Der Tahrir-Platz ist seit jeher ein Ort der politischen Auseinandersetzung. „Wenn etwas passiert, wird es dort passieren", sagen die Kairoer Bürger∗innen. Zwischen 2001 und 2006 fanden auf dem Platz bereits für die damalige Zeit relativ große Proteste gegen den Irakkrieg oder zur Unterstützung der palästinensischen Intifada statt. Später kam es 2008 zu kleineren Protesten, die von politischen Gruppierungen organisiert wurden, die es ablehnten, dass Gamal Mubarak (der Sohn des damaligen Präsidenten) die Präsidentschaft vererbt wird. All diese Ereignisse luden der Bedeutung des Platzes mit Ideen der Freiheit, des Widerstands und der sozialen Gerechtigkeit auf. Anfang 2011 wurde der Platz zum Ort der Hoffnung, um der immensen Ungerechtigkeiten entgegenzuwirken, die Ägypten während der Regierungszeit Mubaraks erlebt hat.

Am Dienstag, 25. Januar, trafen im Laufe des Nachmittags einige tausend Demonstrant∗innen auf dem Tahrir-Platz ein und reagierten damit auf die Protestaufrufe, die über Facebook (→ Digitale Medien) verbreitet wurden. Um ihre Verachtung für den brutalen Polizeistaat zum Ausdruck zu bringen, beschlossen Tausende von Menschen, ihre Angst vor der staatlichen Gewaltherrschaft beiseite zu schieben und einen Protestmarathon zu starten. Die Zusammenstöße dauerten vom Nachmittag bis Mitternacht an, ehe die Polizei die Demonstrant*innen überwältigte und die volle Kontrolle über den Platz übernahm.

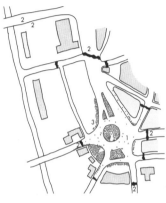

■ Barrikade (Barricade)
Angeeignetes Gebäude (Appropriated building)

Tahrir-Platz, Februar 2011. 1 Protestcamp 2 Konfrontationen mit der Polizei 3 Temporäres Gefängnis (Tahrir Square, February 2011. 1 Protest camp 2 Confrontations with the police 3 Temporary jail)

Doch der darauffolgende Freitag brachte eine neue Entwicklung. Der Freitag ist der ägyptische Sonntag – in Ägypten sind etwa 90 % der Bevölkerung muslimisch. Außerdem findet an diesem Tag das gemeinsame Mittagsgebet statt. Von den verschiedenen Moscheen in Kairo begannen sich Protestmärsche zum Tahrir-Platz zu bewegen. Die Menschen eroberten den Platz und zwangen den Staat, zu fliehen und sich zu verstecken. 18 Tage lang war die „Republik Tahrir", wie die Demonstrant*innen den Platz während der Proteste nannten, ein Knotenpunkt für demokratische Ideen, der sowohl funk-

tionale als auch symbolische Aufgaben erfüllte.

„Der Platz gehört uns", riefen die Menschen, als sie merkten, dass sie die Polizei zum Rückzug zwingen konnten. Auf diese Euphorie folgte sofort eine Frage: „Was kommt als Nächstes?" Die Demonstrant*innen beschlossen, sich schnell zu organisieren und teilten sich in zwei Gruppen auf: Eine Gruppe sicherte die Eingänge (→ Schutz), und die andere Gruppe richtete Übernachtungsmöglichkeiten ein. Politische Parteien stellten Zelte zur Verfügung, die meist in der Mitte des Platzes aufgebaut wurden. Andere Leute bauten behelfsmäßige Strukturen und schufen Dächer aus Laken, wobei sie an vorhandene Strukturen oder Objekte auf dem Platz andockten, beispielsweise an Skulpturen, Beleuchtungsmasten und sogar an Armeepanzern, die vom Militär aufgestellt wurden, um die verschiedenen Akteur*innen (die Bevölkerung und die Polizei) zu trennen. Die Sicherheitsgruppe wurde auf die 14 Eingänge des Platzes verteilt, um als Alarmsystem für nächtliche Angriffe zu agieren. Sie benutzten zerbrochene Platten der bereits verfallenen Gehwege sowie anderen Bauschutt und begannen, an jedem Eingang provisorische → Barrikaden zu errichten.

Diese Eingänge begrenzten den Platz und bildeten einen klar definierten Raum, der viel größer war als der Kreisverkehr selbst. Die erste Nacht verlief friedlich. Die Kälte, der Hunger und die Müdigkeit waren zu diesem Zeitpunkt die größten Feinde. In den nächsten Tagen trafen sich die Demonstrant*innen regelmäßig, um die Logistik der Besetzung zu planen. Neben dem Eingang zum Nil entstanden Reihen von Marktständen. Straßenverkäufer*innen, die Snacks, Getränke und Zigaretten anboten, stellten die Hauptnahrungsquelle bereit – in den ersten Tagen vor allem gebackene Süßkartoffeln. Es wurden Toiletten gebaut und Klempner begannen mit der Installation von Sanitäranlagen. Neben den Haupteingängen des Platzes wurden feste Standorte für die Abfallentsorgung eingerichtet, NGOs stellten schwarze Müllsäcke zur Verfügung.

Tahrir-Platz / Case Study

Die Tage nach dem „Freitag des Zorns" (28. Januar) verliefen relativ sicher. Am Dienstag, dem 2. Februar, griff eine Gruppe regierungstreuer Kräfte den Platz jedoch unerwartet von mehreren Eingängen aus an und konnte das Zentrum des Tahrir-Platzes erreichen. Die Schlacht war grausam und hinterließ Märtyrer*innen und Hunderte von verwundeten Demonstrant*innen. Daher war es unvermeidlich, dass improvisierte Krankenstationen hinzukamen, in denen Ärzt*innen freiwillig zur Verfügung standen. Der Angriff warf zahlreiche Fragen auf, was jenseits der Grenzen des Platzes geschieht, insbesondere da die Angreifer Zivilisten waren. Das Bedürfnis, mit der Außenwelt in Kontakt zu treten, hat dazu geführt, dass an den Wänden eines Gebäudes, das dem Platz zugewandt ist, ein Bereich zum Aufhängen von Tageszeitungen eingerichtet wurde. Die Demonstrant*innen gingen an den Zeitungsreihen entlang, um zu verstehen, wie die → Medien über den Platz berichteten, und stellten fest, dass sie von der Presse dämonisiert und ihre Forderungen umschlagen wurden. Blogger*innen begannen, die Eingänge der Gebäude mit Blick auf den Platz als Räume zum Schreiben zu nutzen. In diesen Eingangshallen gab es Strom, um Laptops und Handys aufzuladen. Andere konnten Elektrizität von den öffentlichen Beleuchtungsmasten in den Straßen abzapfen. An einer dieser Stromquellen installierten politische Parteien eine selbstorganisierte Bühne für wichtige Ankündigungen, zum Anheizen der Sprechchöre und für Musiker*innen. Später wurden noch zwei weitere Bühnen errichtet.

Den Demonstrant*innen gelang es, einige Angreifer als Geiseln zu halten. Ein Lagerraum in einer Baustelle auf dem Platz wurde als Gefängniszelle umfunktioniert, um Angreifer, Spione und verdeckte Provokateure bis zur Übergabe an die Armee festzusetzen. Eine andere Gruppe beschloss, einen Raum als Gedenkstätte für die Märtyrer*innen aus den Anfangstagen der Revolution zu gestalten. Der Erinnerungsort wurde an einer sehr zentralen Stelle auf dem Platz

aufgebaut. Einige Demonstrant*innen sammelten die → Waffen, die → Schutzschilde und die zerrissene Kleidung der Angreifer und richteten ein kleines Museum ein, um die Beute der Schlacht auszustellen (→ Archive).

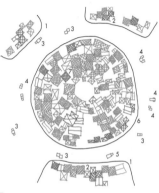

■ Gemeinschaftliche Zelte (Community tents)
■ Individuelle Zelte (Individual tents)

Tahrir-Platz. 1 Bühne 2 Klinik 3 Getränkestand 4 Essensstand 5 Flaggenverkauf 6 Friseur 7 Kindergarten (Tahrir Square. 1 Stage 2 Clinic 3 Drinks stand 4 Food stand 5 Flag vendor 6 Barber shop 7 Childcare)

Nach dem Angriff vom 2. Februar zog der Platz weitere Protestierende an, die sich an der Besetzung beteiligten. Dies führte dazu, dass der Platz noch mehr Angebote und Aktivitäten bereitstellte. Einige Familien brachten ihre Kinder mit. Daher wurde ein Kindergarten in der Mitte des Platzes eingerichtet, dem sichersten Ort, da er am weitesten von den Eingängen entfernt ist. Erzieher*innen meldeten sich freiwillig, um Schichten zu übernehmen, die Kinder zu beaufsichtigen und mit ihnen Kunstaktivitäten durchzuführen. Für die Erwachsenen wurde eine Galerie eingerichtet. Künstler*innen begannen, ihre Kunstwerke und Karikaturen an einer Wand neben den Zeitungen auszustellen.

Für die sich selbst organisierende Gemeinschaft waren der Platz und seine Ressourcen ein gemeinschaftlich zu pflegendes Gut. Die Besetzer∗innen entwickelten ein effizientes Modell, jeden Tag Tausende von Demonstrant∗innen zu beherbergen und zu versorgen. Frauen fühlten sich sicher und die Zahl der sexuellen Belästigungen war verschwindend gering (nach 18 Tagen jedoch wurde die sexuelle Nötigung zu einem Zwangsmittel, das die Polizei einsetzte, um die weiblichen Protestierenden ins Visier zu nehmen, indem sie junge Männer schickte, um sie bei zahlreichen Veranstaltungen anzugreifen). Sogar ein Fundbüro wurde eingerichtet. Es mag romantisch klingen, wenn man die Kämpfe, die Angst und die Ungewissheit bedenkt, die die Demonstrant∗innen während der Proteste erlebt haben müssen, aber die große Solidarität, die sich zwischen verschiedenen Altersgruppen, Religionen, Geschlechtern und Klassen entwickelte, war außergewöhnlich. Alle wussten, dass man sich auf die Person neben einem verlassen können muss, um selbst sicher zu sein.

Am 11. Februar teilten sich die Demonstrant∗innen in zwei Gruppen auf: Eine blieb auf dem Tahrir, die andere marschierte zum fast 10 km entfernten Palast des Präsidenten und forderte seinen Rücktritt. Bei Sonnenuntergang verkündeten die Großbildschirme auf dem Tahrir, dass Mubarak zurückgetreten ist. Die Demonstrant∗innen feierten ausgelassen mit einem Feuerwerk. Fröhliche Sprechchöre wurden angestimmt: „Er ist weg". Am Morgen wachten die Demonstrant∗innen auf und sahen Tausende von Schaulustigen, die diesen entscheidenden Moment der Geschichte miterleben wollten. Sie alle wurden jedoch bald darauf enttäuscht, denn die Aufräumarbeiten auf dem Platz hatten bereits begonnen: Abfälle wurden eingesammelt, aufgerissene → Pflastersteine ausgebessert und die Gehwege gefegt. Zwischen den erschöpften Demonstrant∗innen kam es zu Auseinandersetzungen, da einige vorschlugen, den Platz zu räumen und die Proteste zu beenden, während andere dafür plädierten, die Kontrolle über den Platz zu behalten, bis alle ihre Bedingungen erfüllt

werden. Im Nachhinein betrachtet war es ein großer Fehler, den Platz zu verlassen, denn auf lange Sicht hat sich an der Unterdrückung der ägyptischen Bevölkerung durch einen mächtigen Polizeistaat wenig geändert.

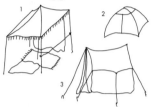

Tahrir-Platz. 1 Zeltgerüst mit Teppichen 2 Kuppelzelt 3 Traditionelles Zelt (Tahrir Square. 1 Tent frame with carpets 2 Dome tent 3 Traditional tent)

Der Tahrir-Platz blieb weiterhin der Schauplatz zahlreicher großer Protestveranstaltungen. Bis Januar 2012 war er nie ganz leer. Im Juli 2011 wurde zum Schutz gegen die Sommerhitze über dem Kreisverkehr ein textiles Zeltdach errichtet (→ Bautypen). Der Erfolg dieser Aktion war begrenzt, da die Luftfeuchtigkeit und der Geruch unter der weißen Plane unerträglich waren, weshalb die Protestierenden es vorzogen, doch in der Sonne zu sitzen. Bei einem anderen Protestcamp im November kam es zu mehreren gewalttätigen Zusammenstößen und die Dynamik auf dem Platz war völlig anders als im Januar/Februar. Die Demonstrant∗innen schliefen kaum und waren in ständige Kämpfe verwickelt. Die Polizei hatte hohe Mauern aus riesigen Betonsteinen errichtet, die den Zugang und die Sicht auf den Platz blockierten. Die Protestierenden sahen nur Tränengaskanister über die Mauern fliegen und warfen Steine zurück, ohne zu wissen, wer auf der anderen Seite steht. Eine ähnliche Besetzung fand im Dezember statt, wurde aber auf die Ostseite des Platzes ausgedehnt, direkt vor dem Amtssitz des Ministerpräsidenten. Bei beiden Besetzungen gab es zahlreiche Tote, meist auf Seiten der Demonstrant∗innen.

Hossam el-Hamalawy: Readymades und selbstgebaute Zelte (Ready-made and self-built tents), 7. Februar 2011

Hossam el-Hamalawy: Barrikade an der Qasr-el-Nil-Brücke (Barricade at the Qasr el Nil Bridge), 3. Februar 2011

Hossam el-Hamalawy: Barrikade am Eingang zum Tahrir-Platz (Barricade at the entrance of Tahrir Square), 11. Februar 2011

Andre Pain: Enge Gasse in einer dichten Siedlung aus Zelten und Planen (Narrow alley in a dense settlement of tents and tarpaulins), 9. Februar 2011

Hossam el-Hamalawy: Protestierende vor Panzern
(Protesters in front of tanks), 7. Februar 2011

Ahmed Abd El-Fatah: Textiles Zeltdach zum Schutz gegen die Julihitze (Textile tent roof for protection against the July heat), 15. Juli 2011

Ahmed Abd El-Fatah: Essensstände und
Straßenverkäufe (Food stalls and street vendors),
15. Juli 2011

Lara Baladi: Protestierende am Rand des überdachten Kreisverkehrs (Protesters on the edge of the covered roundabout), Juli 2011

Ahmed Abd El-Fatah: Juli-Camp, nachdem große Teile des Sonnendachs abgebaut waren (July camp after large parts of the canopy were dismantled), 29. Juli 2011

Ahmed Abd El-Fatah: Protestierende ruhen sich auf ausgebreiteten Bannern aus (Protesters rest on unfurled banners), 29. Juli 2011

Oleh Slobodeniuk: Tahrir-Platz nach der Umgestaltung (Tahrir Square after the redesign), 10. März 2021

Als diese Proteste endeten, änderte sich die Bedeutung des Tahrir-Platzes noch einmal: Zuerst wurde er zu einem beliebten öffentlichen Platz für Menschen aus allen sozialen Schichten. Viele Bürger∗innen von Kairo verbrachten ihre freie Zeit auf dem Platz. Straßenverkäufer∗innen boten Essen und Fahnen zum Kauf an. Diese kurze Zeitspanne war vorbei, als der Platz im Jahr 2021 eine umstrittene Neugestaltung erfuhr, die in Zukunft jegliche Versammlung an diesem Ort verhindern soll. Die Umgestaltung ist als symbolische Rückeroberung des Platzes durch den Staat zu verstehen und wurde offensichtlich von klassischen Schmuckplatzanlagen in Europa beeinflusst. Ein pharaonischer Obelisk wurde vom gegenüberliegenden Flussufer auf den Platz umgesiedelt. Heute ist es verboten, auf dem Tahrir-Platz zu sitzen. Private Polizist∗innen stehen überall herum und passen auf, dass niemand gegen die Regeln verstößt, sich hinsetzt oder andere Tätigkeiten ausübt, als einfach nur weiterzugehen. (Beitrag von Ahmed Zaazaa; Einleitung und Recherche: AMM)

Tahrir Square, Ger. → *Tahrir-Platz*. From → *2011* to 2013, Tahrir Square in downtown Cairo was repeatedly the scene of mass protests. → *Public square occupations*, and → *protest camps* were established on the otherwise busy → *roundabout* in January, July, and November 2011, in January 2012, and in January 2013. With the "January 25 Revolution" in early 2011 (shortly after the beginning of the "Jasmin Revolution" in Tunisia), the so-called "Arab Spring" took root in Egypt. The protests were directed against the regime of President Muhammad Husni Mubarak and his security apparatus, initially triggered by the murder of blogger Khaled Said, who, after posting a video on → *police* corruption, was beaten to death in broad daylight. The protesters called for the president to resign, for political reforms, for freedom of expression, and democratic elections, as well as for better living conditions and more social justice. There were frequently thousands of people lodged on Tahrir Square in an ever-changing structure of → *tents* and tarpaulins, and at the "March of the Millions" on February 1, 2011, up to two million Egyptians marched in protest against the Mubarak regime (→ *Demonstration*). During the eighteen-day-long revolution, the situation repeatedly escalated into violence that resulted in countless deaths (→ *Violence*). Nevertheless, many occupiers perceived the "Republic of Tahrir" as a utopian microcosm, and celebrated the joint protest—which often possessed the atmosphere of a festival, with concerts and street vendors selling food. There were concerts (→ *Music*) and street vendors sold food.

When President Mubarak announced his resignation on February 11, the protesters' immediate demands were met, but in the long term, the democracy movement failed to turn the protest into a comprehensive political agenda. A brief period of government by the leader of the Islamist movement Muslim Brotherhood, Mohammed Mursi, who was democratically elected in summer 2012, was ended by a military coup in 2013, which brought the army back into power. This did not stop recurrent outbreaks of protests. To this day—as of 2023—the extremely brutal military government continues to rule the country.

The protest movement was very broadly based during the first 2011 revolution: students and young people—with many women among them—all took part. Leftists, the middle class, secularists, Christians, and Muslims protested together. Even members of the Muslim Brotherhood attended the protests, though the majority of the other protesters distanced themselves from this religious-fundamentalist faction. The January 25 Revolution was also supported in an ambivalent way by the military, which assumed power after the government was overthrown. While the military assured the protesters there would be free elections, it then responded to the rekindled protests with violence. After the end of the protests in February 2011, the Muslim Brotherhood teamed up with the military, something many of the secular-liberal protesters condemned.

Later waves of protests were co-organized by Mursi's fundamentalist government and infiltrated by the police. The momentum witnessed in the broadly based protests in early 2011 was not to be repeated.

Architect and urban planner Ahmed Zaazaa was on Tahrir Square during the January 25 Revolution. For the *Protest/Architecture* exhibition he has authored a text entitled "The Democratic Republic of Tahrir," in which he describes the occupation of the square and the course of the first wave of protests:

For more than a year, the spatiality of Tahrir Square was shaped, appropriated, and reappropriated by the protests; it decayed, regenerated, shrank, and expanded by the events that went down in history as the "January 25 Revolution." The square has been historically a space for political encounters. "If it happens, it will happen there," was the common understanding among Cairenes. Tahrir has witnessed several protests, clashes, and a few occupations which date back to the beginning of the 20th century, the 1960s, and the beginning of the new millennium. Between 2001 and 2006, what were for the day relatively big protests against the war on Iraq or supporting the Palestinian Intifada took place on the square. Later in 2008, smaller protests started to erupt, mobilized by political movements refusing to allow the presidency to be inherited by Gamal Mubarak (the son of the president back then). All these significant events infused the meaning of the space with ideas about freedom, resistance, and equality. In early 2011, the square was crowned the place of hope to counter the immense injustices that Egypt had experienced during the period of Mubarak's rule.

Starting on Tuesday, January 25, a few thousand protesters arrived at Tahrir square in the course of the afternoon in response to the calls for protest that flooded Facebook (→ Digital media). To express their rejection of police brutality, thousands of individuals decided to embark on a marathon of uncertainty, putting their fear of the state's brutality aside. Clashes were continuous from the afternoon and until midnight, when the police overpowered the protesters and took full control of the space.

However, Friday is Egypt's weekend—Egypt is approximately 90 percent Muslim. Moreover, it is the day Muslims gather for collective prayers at noon. Marches started to rally from the different mosques around Cairo to the square. The people took over the space, forcing the state to flee and hide. For a full eighteen days, the "Republic of Tahrir," a name the protesters gave to the square during the protests, was a node of democratic ideas, fulfilling both functional and symbolic aspects.

"The square is ours," the people started to chant, realizing that they were able to force the police to back down and flee. This euphoria was immediately followed by a question: "What's next?" Protesters decided to quickly organize, splitting into two main groups: one group to secure the entrances, and another group to appropriate the space for sleeping and spending the night (→ Protection). Some political parties provided tents that were mostly erected inside the center of the square. Other people built makeshift structures and created canopies from sheets, reappropriating existing structures or objects in the square, such as statues, lampposts, and even army tanks that were spread around by the military to separate the sides (the people and the police). The security group was distributed across the fourteen entrances to the square, to act as an alarm system for late-night attacks. They used broken tiles from the already dilapidated sidewalks, along with other construction debris, and started to build temporary → barricades at each entrance.

These entrances created borders to the square and formed a well-defined space that was much larger than the traffic circle itself. The first night passed peacefully. At this point, the main enemies were the cold, hunger, and tiredness. During the next few days, the protesters continuously gathered to plan the logistics of the occupation. Linear markets started to appear next to the Nile River entrance. Street vendors selling snacks, drinks, and cigarettes represented the main source of food—mostly baked sweet potato during the first day or two. Toilet spaces were constructed, and plumbers started to install sanitation. There were fixed locations for waste disposal, next to the main entrances of the square, and NGOs provided black waste bags.

The days that followed the "Friday of Rage" (January 28) were relatively safe. However, on Tuesday, February 2, a group of pro-government citizens unexpectedly attacked the square from several entrances and managed to reach the center of the square. The battle was ugly and left behind martyrs and hundreds of wounded protesters. Hence, clinics inevitably started to play a role in the spatial organization of the square, and doctors started to pop up between the protesters' lines, volunteering to help staff the many clinics. The attack raised numerous questions as to what was happening outside the borders of the square, especially since the attackers were civilians. The need to connect with the outside world resulted in a space where daily newspapers could be displayed on the walls of one of the buildings facing the square. Protesters could then walk along the row of papers to understand how the → media were representing "the Square" and soon realized that the media were demonizing and undermining them. Bloggers started to use the entrances of the buildings overlooking the square as spaces for blogging. These entrance halls provided electricity to charge the laptops and mobiles. Others were able to requisition electricity from the public power lines on the lampposts in the streets. At one of these electricity sources, political parties constructed a self-organized stage for important announcements, to fuel chants, and where musicians could sing. A further two stages were constructed later.

The protesters were able to hold a few attackers as hostages. A storage room in a construction site in the square was reused as a jail cell holding-pen for at-

tackers, spies, and infiltrators, until they could be handed over to the army. Another group decided to design a space as a memorial for the martyrs of the early days of the revolution. The memorial was placed in a very prominent location in the square. Some protesters collected the → weapons, → protective shields, and torn clothes of the attackers, and created a small museum to display the spoils of the battle (→ Archive).

After the February 2 attack, the square attracted more protesters wishing to participate in the occupation. This placed a great strain on the space to accommodate even more services and activities. Some families brought their children. Hence, a childcare space was designed in the center of the square, as this was regarded as the most secure space, farthest away from the entrances. Teachers volunteered to take shifts keeping an eye on the children and doing art activities with them. An art gallery was installed for the grown-ups. Artists started to exhibit their artwork and cartoons on a wall next to the newspapers.

For the self-organizing community, the square and its resources were commons. The protesters developed an efficient model that functioned to accommodate and feed hundreds of thousands of protesters every day. Women felt safe and sexual harassment rates were as good as negligible. (After the eighteen days, sexual harassment became a form of pressure that the police used to target the female activists, by sending young men to attack them at numerous events.) Even a lost-and-found desk was set up. While this might sound like romanticizing in light of the struggles, fear, and uncertainty that the protesters must have felt during the protest, however, a quite exceptional solidarity evolved between the different age groups, religions, genders, and classes. Everyone knew that relying on the person next to them was essential as a way of keeping themselves safe.

On February 11, the protesters split into two groups: one remained at Tahrir, the other mached to the presidential palace, nearly ten kilometers away, calling for the resignation of the president. By sunset, the big screens in Tahrir announced that Mubarak was stepping down. The protesters' frenzied celebrations lit the sky with fireworks and happy chanting: "He's left." In the morning, the protesters woke up to thousands of newcomers who wished to witness this decisive moment in history. They were disappointed, as collective efforts had already started to clean the square: waste was picked up, torn up pavement was repaired, sidewalks were swept clean. Arguments started to erupt between exhausted protesters, as some proposed leaving the square and calling an end to it, while others advocated remaining in control until all their conditions were met. In retrospect, leaving the square was a huge mistake, since in the long run, little changed as regards the oppression of the Egyptian population by a powerful police state.

Tahrir Square later witnessed numerous major protest events. It was never completely empty again right through to January 2012. In July 2011, the summer heat led to protesters erecting a textile canopy all over the traffic circle to cover the tents of a new occupation from sunlight (→ Building types). The success proved limited, since the humidity and smell under the white tarpaulin was unbearable and protesters therefore preferred to sit in the sun. Another protest camp in November experienced several violent clashes, and the dynamics in the square were very different. Protesters were rarely able to sleep and became embroiled in continuous fighting. The police had built high walls, using huge concrete bricks that blocked physical and visual access to and from the square. Protesters only saw tear gas canisters flying over the walls and replied by throwing stones in the other direction without knowing who was on the other side. A later similar occupation took place in December but was extended to reach the eastern side of the square, in front of the prime minister's office. Both of these occupations led to numerous deaths, most of the fatalities being protesters.

When the protests ended, the meaning of Tahrir Square changed once again: first, it became a popular public space for people of all social classes. Many Cairenes spent their free time on the square. Street vendors offered food and flags for sale. This short period came to an end in 2021 when the square experienced a controversial makeover designed to prevent any future popular gatherings here. The redesign can be read as the state symbolically reclaiming the square. The implemented design is influenced by classical formal square designs in Europe. A Pharaonic obelisk was relocated from the opposite riverbank. Today, it is forbidden to sit on Tahrir Square. There are private police scattered around the whole area to make sure no one violates the rules by sitting, or by performing any activity other than passing by. (Contribution by Ahmed Zaazaa; introduction and research: AMM)

Tarpaulin, Ger. → Plane; → Bender, → Building materials, → Movimiento 15M

Tear gas, Ger. → Tränengas; → Anti-protest measures

Television set, Ger. → Fernseher (fig.). Alongside electrical appliances such as the → washing machine and the refrigerator, the television set became the emblem of affluent society and the consumer goods industry in the second half of the 20th century. The symbolic destruction of television sets by countercultural artists from the 1960s on (e.g. Fluxus, Ant Farm) was caused by a rejection of the bourgeois lifestyles of the postwar period. At the same time, however, protest movements are still dependent on the mass medium of television (→ Media): the goal of protests was and is usually to attract as much attention as possible and to get into the news (→ Communication). Time and again, television programs themselves have been used for protests, for example when in → 1984 environmental activists used the entertainment program Wetten, dass...? (Wanna bet, that...?) to unveil a banner with the inscription "Don't bet—save the Danube floodplains," drawing attention to the occupation of the → *Hainburger Au* in Austria. In contrast, a veritable television → *barricade* was erected in Zurich in November 1981 on the initiative of the later film director Samir Jamal Aldin: in continuation of the youth unrest that had been going on since → *1980*, activists blocked off Limmatstrasse with an installation of television sets in front of the Autonomous Youth Center they had occupied (→ *Blockade*, → *Zurich youth protests*). Shortly before eight o'clock, the news was switched on on the television sets, essentially reversing the logic of media coverage: before the event could be shown as a street riot on the news, the news broadcast was literally being enacted on the → *street*. (SH)

Tensegrity, engl. → *Tensegrity*. Bei → *Demonstrationen* und Protesten kommen bisweilen sogenannte Tensegrity-Strukturen zum Einsatz: zerlegbare, aber stabile Zugkonstruktionen aus → *Seilen* und Bambusrohren, die leicht zu transportieren sind und schnell aufgebaut werden können. Sie erlauben es einzelnen Aktivist∗innen, sich so hoch über dem Boden einzuhängen, dass die → *Blockade* von Spezialeinheiten geräumt werden muss. Den Aktivist∗innen von Extinction Rebellion gelang es im September 2020 auf diese Weise, die → *Straße* zu den Broxbourne-Druckereien des Medienbarons Rupert Murdoch in Hertfordshire bei London zu blockieren: Nachdem es der britischen → *Polizei* nicht rechtzeitig gelungen war, die Demonstrant∗innen aus den Sitzstangen zu entfernen, mussten Murdochs Samstagszeitungen eingestampft werden – woraufhin die Tensegrity-Strukturen für den renommierten britischen Stirling Prize für herausragende Architektur vorgeschlagen wurden (Harper 2020). (SH)

Tensegrity, Ger. → *Tensegrity (fig.)*. At times, so-called tensegrity structures are deployed at → *demonstrations* and protests: these stable tensioning structures made of → *ropes* and bamboo poles that can be taken apart are easy to transport and can be swiftly assembled. They enable individual activists to suspend themselves so high above the ground

that special forces have to be brought in to clear the → *blockade*. Extinction Rebellion activists used this tactic in September 2020 to block the → *street* to the Broxbourne printworks owned by media tycoon Rupert Murdoch in Hertfordshire, outside London, England. After the British → *police* failed to remove the demonstrators from the seating rods in time, Murdoch's Saturday papers had to be pulped—which led to the tensegrity structures being humorously nominated for the prestigious British Stirling Prize (Harper 2020). (SH)

Tensegrity. Gareth Morris: Aktivist∗innen von Extinction Rebellion blockieren die Zufahrt zu den Broxbourne-Druckereien im englischen Hertfordshire, 5. September 2020 (Tensegrity. Gareth Morris: Activists from Extinction Rebellion block the entrance to the Broxbourne printworks in Hertfordshire, England, September 5, 2020)

Tent, Ger. → *Zelt (fig.)*. A tent can be broadly defined as a textile or a pliable synthetic membrane held in tension, thereby forming a roof and walls, and creating an interior space separated from the outside of that interior space. At sustained protest events such as → *protest camps*, tents often serve as → *infrastructure*, either in a pre-planned sense or as ad hoc solutions.

Tents come in different shapes and sizes, but the material qualities and tension-based tectonics are similar for all tents. Dome-shaped tents from supermarkets or outdoor retailers are con-

Tent

structed with channels in the textile to house poles bent under tension, with the bends suspending the fabric. Two poles support traditional A-frame tents, and tension between perpendicular points in the ground to the top of the poles gives the textile its subsequent shape. Tents can also consist of makeshift textiles stretched between or around objects. The textile can be tensioned to the ground or by the objects, examples being a tarp stretched around bent trees. In traditional Indigenous tent structures, the textile is tensioned around poles in a conical shape, such as the *lavvu* of the Sápmi people, which is formed around a lattice, or a yurt, or as a roof carried by several poles and stretched to the ground like the *bait al shaar*—or Bedouin tent.

In protest spaces, the tent has a symbolic function or a practical infrastructural function, or a combination of both. Symbolic functions include references to traditional use by Indigenous groups. Protest tents can highlight precarity and vulnerability through the tents' makeshift, temporary, and unplanned character or vulnerable exposure to power and violence through their contrast to the solid, hard architecture of the established state or society (→ *Alternative architecture*). As a rudimentary architectural structure, the tent offers → *protection* from the sun, wind, and rain, and delineates the private and the semi-private from the public protest space. When reading the tent as a protest artifact, the performance of the tent goes beyond the basic architectural functionality of separation and protection. The temporary qualities of the tent provide different forms of protest infrastructure, which are shaped by the complex relationships between time, space, vulnerability, legislation, and the human body, as well as being determined by the concrete materiality of the tents themselves. (→ *Building materials*). These relations are best illustrated by way of a number of examples of protest tents from around the globe in the early 2010s.

In London in 2011, during Occupy London, the *Daily Mail* published a picture shot with an infrared camera to show how few tents were inhabited at that moment in time during the protest. The same year, in Melbourne, the → *police* left a protester in her underwear in a park, cutting a modified tent used as an item of clothing from her body (→ *Tent monster*). In Silwan, East Jerusalem, in Palestine/Israel, a tent was repeatedly torn down by the Israeli police and rebuilt by Palestinian anti-settler and anti-demolition protesters. In Oslo, Norway, Palestinian protesters stayed in a tent next to a church throughout an entire winter as a protest and protection against deportation.

Oslo, Melbourne, and London show how the body and the tent are intertwined (→ *Body deployment*). The tent extends the body through time and space, and it extends the area the protest bodies occupy, and prolongs the duration of a protest, as shown in Oslo. Protests depend on bodies and the tent; the tent serves as an extension of the body, but also stands in for the body in the protest space as highlighted by the *Daily Mail's* infrared photos in London. When tents were forbidden in the protest space in Melbourne, it was still possible to bring in tents as a piece of clothing—creating a direct connection to the body as a second skin.

The vulnerability of the tent—but also its flexibility as a component of protest infrastructure—is most strikingly displayed in the examples from Silwan and Melbourne. The vulnerable material is easy to destroy for a police force resorting to violence (→ *Destruction*, → *Violence*). However, the material also allows the tent to change, be re-pitched and redeployed in a protest space, either to highlight the changing protest legislation and violence, as in Melbourne, or to sustain a protest against a violent power, as in Silwan.

The often unclear legal status of tent settlements regularly helps to delay their eviction by authorities. In London and elsewhere, the Occupy movement benefitted from the lack of regulations on tents in publicly and privately owned urban spaces.

Together, these examples underscore how the tent's architectural qualities of vulnerability, flexibility, and ephemerality, along with its ambiguous legal status, its intimate relationship with the human body, and the symbolic value of the structural form of the tent all contribute to making this object a central component of so many protest movements. (Anders Rubing)

Tent Embassy, engl. → *Tent Embassy*. Der Protest startete → *1972* mit lediglich einem Sonnenschirm und einigen → *Protestschildern* gegenüber dem Parlamentsgebäude in Canberra. Damit forderten vier Aborigines mehr Rechte für die indigene Bevölkerung von Australien. Die Aktion weitete sich innerhalb weniger Wochen zu einem → *Protestcamp* mit → *Zelten* aus. Einige Monate später kam es zu gewaltsamen Zusammenstößen von → *Polizei* und Hunderten von Demonstrierenden (→ *Demonstration*, → *Gewalt*). Die Tent Embassy existierte seit 1992 als feste Einrichtung gegenüber dem australischen Parlament. Im Jahr 2022 war sie Teil der documenta auf dem Friedrichsplatz in Kassel. (JD)

Tent Embassy, Ger. → *Tent Embassy*. This protest started in → *1972* with just a parasol and a few → *protest placards* in front of Parliament House in Canberra. The four Aboriginal activists behind this action wanted more rights for Australia's Indigenous people. In the space of just a few weeks, a → *protest camp* with → *tents* evolved. Violent clashes between the police and hundreds of demonstrators ensued a few months later (→ *Demonstration*, → *Violence*). The Tent Embassy has existed as a permanent feature in front of Australia's Parliament House (now the Old Parliament House) since 1992. In 2022, it was displayed at documenta on Kassel's Friedrichsplatz. (JD)

Tent monster, Ger. → *Zeltmonster (fig.)*. After Occupy camps all over the world, such as → *Occupy Wall Street*, had been cleared by the → *police*, some demonstrators imaginatively sought other ways of continuing the → *occupation*. In Melbourne, where tents were banned in the protest camps, activists wore tents as → *clothing* or as → *costumes*. While the police initially simply stood back and watched the tent monsters, they later acted roughly, for example tearing the tent from a woman's body, leaving her standing in her underwear (→ *Violence*). (JD)

The Barricades (Riga), Ger. → *Barrikadentage (Riga)*. After the → *Baltic Way* and before the collapse of the Soviet Union, Lithuania became the site of severe clashes with Soviet forces during "The Barricades" in January → *1991*. Despite the newly introduced policies of *glasnost* (openness) and *perestroika* (restructuring), fourteen people died. Consequently, preventative → *barricades* were set up in Lithuania and the Latvian capital of Riga to protect government buildings from further attacks. (JD)

The Troubles, Ger. → *Nordirlandkonflikt*. A → *violent*, long-lasting conflict between pro-British, Protestant Unionists and Catholic Irish nationalists and republicans, which began to escalate in → *1969*. → *Barricades*, which were eventually replaced with walls, were built to separate the respective residential areas, and thereby, to decrease tension in Northern Irish cities. Some of the so-called "peace lines" are up to eight meters high and several kilometers long. (JD)

Tipi, engl. → *Tipi*; → *Alternative Architektur*, → *Bautypen*, → *Dakota-Access-Pipeline-Proteste*, → *Gorleben*, → *Zelt*

Tipi, Ger. → *Tipi*; → *Alternative architecture*, → *Building types*, → *Dakota Access Pipeline protests*, → *Gorleben*, → *Tent*

Tires, Ger. → *Autoreifen*; → *Barricade*, → *Building materials*, → *Maidan*

Topfdeckel, engl. → *Pot lid*; → *Lärm*

Toppling monuments, Ger. → *Denkmalsturz (fig.)*. With the growing sensitivity towards questions related to the legacies of colonialism and the recognition of historically marginalized cultures, many monuments have been brought down in recent years. In → *2020*, for example, activists from the transnational civil rights movement

Tort

→ *Black Lives Matter* knocked down a monument to the English merchant Edward Colston in Bristol, UK, who had amassed his wealth through the slave trade, and a statue of American president Jefferson Davis in Richmond, USA, who had advocated slavery. However, the → *destruction* of statues and monuments is not a new phenomenon: iconoclasm, including for political purposes, was practiced back in antiquity to make a loss of power and significance symbolically visible or to permanently erase a past rule from memory, in the sense of a *damnatio memoriae*. In modern times, monument toppling has become increasingly associated with revolutions and uprisings. Thus, during the → *Paris Commune* on May 16, → *1871*, the Vendôme Column was toppled: for the Communards, the victory column, erected between 1806 and 1810, and crowned by a statue of Napoleon, embodied the tyranny of the imperial state and the betrayal of revolutionary ideals. In addition to monuments with images of rulers and other insignia of power, buildings have repeatedly been captured, occupied, damaged, and in some cases destroyed, which—like the Bastille in Paris during the French Revolution in 1789 or the Berlin Wall in 1989—were associated with political systems. (A special case is the → *Capitol attack* in → *2021*). Conversely, however, there have also been repeated protests for the preservation of buildings and monuments (→ *Frankfurt Squatting Campaign*, → *Heritage protection*). The redesign of the long-criticized memorial to Karl Lueger, the antisemitic mayor of the city of Vienna from 1897 to 1910, provides an example of a monument toppling that has been carried out within the context of intense public debate: after the temporary overwriting by → *graffiti*, a permanent "artistic contextualization" for the memorial is to be produced in a multi-stage process. (SH)

Torte, engl. → *Cake*; → *Waffen*, → *Protestziele*

Tower, Ger. → *Turm*. Towers are → *building types* that often play a particular role in protests. In → *Hong Kong* in → *2019* and on → *Maidan* in Kyiv in → *2013*, towers were part of the → *protest camps'* fortifications. In these contexts, activists built → *barricades* with high watchtowers to be able to spot attacks by the → *police* early on and repel them efficiently. As forms of "delaying architecture," towers make it more difficult for the police to clear → *occupations* and protest camps, because for structures above a certain height, specially trained forces have to be brought in with their equipment, which makes the operation more protracted and expensive. During protests at → *Claremont Road* in → *1994* against the construction of a new connecting road, activists erected a thirty-meter-high scaffold tower and fixed themselves to the top with → *lock-on devices*. → *Monopods*, which were up to ten meters high, and highpods, some of which protruded above the treetops, were attached to the ground and trees with → *ropes* in → *Fechenheim Forest* and → *Dannenrod Forest*, and—depending on their height and position—had to be cleared with mobile cranes. One- to four-story, multi-functional tower pile dwellings were also used in the → *Hambach Forest* and → *Lützerath* to house activists and as community spaces. In → *Gorleben*, a radio station was installed on the highest tower. Its defense in case of eviction was discussed at length in the protest village and reinforced the division of the movement into a nonviolent and a militant faction. Towers usually receive above-average attention during protests, firstly because they are an eye-catching motif for photos and videos, and are quickly disseminated via the → *media* or → *digital media*. On the other hand, the comparatively laborious eviction of towers often ignites heated discussions about which means should be resorted to, both on the part of the protesters and the police. (AMM)

Tractor, Ger. → *Traktor*; → *Building types*, → *Demonstration*, → *Farmers' protests*, → *Gorleben*, → *Vehicles*

Traktor, engl. → *Tractor*; → *Bautypen*, → *Demonstration*, → *Fahrzeuge*, → *Gorleben*, → *Farmers-Proteste*

Tränengas, engl. → *Tear gas*; → *Anti-Protestmaßnahmen*

Transparent → *Banner*, → *Protestschild*

Traverse, engl. → *Traverse*. Traversen sind im Kontext von Waldbesetzungen zwischen Bäumen oder Häusern gespannte → *Seile*, die zur Aufhängung von Hängematten und Transparenten (→ *Protestschild*), zur Absicherung von Aktivist∗innen und als Luftbrücke zwischen einzelnen Strukturen in Baumhaussiedlungen genutzt werden. Im Fall einer Räumung durch die → *Polizei* können sich Aktivist∗innen in → *Protestcamps* wie im → *Hambacher Wald* und in → *Lützerath* ohne Kontakt zum Boden zwischen Bäumen, → *Baumhäusern* und → *Barrios* hin- und herbewegen. Komfortable Traversen bestehen aus einem Seil für die Füße, dem Walkway, und einem Oberseil, an dem sich die Aktivist∗innen mit einem Karabiner einhängen und festhalten können. Auf einseiligen Traversen, die auch während einer bereits laufenden Räumung noch neu eingerichtet werden können, bewegen sich Aktivist∗innen am Sicherungsseil eingehängt mit einer Rolle oder im Extremfall auch nur mit den Händen. Die mit 300 Metern längste Traverse aus zwei miteinander verflochtenen Seilen überspannte bei den Protesten im → *Dannenröder Wald* einen Fluss und eine Bundesstraße. (AMM)

Traverse, Ger. → *Traverse*. In the context of forest occupations, traverses are → *ropes* stretched between trees or houses, which are used to hang hammocks and banners (→ *Protest placard*), to secure activists, and as air bridges between individual structures in tree house settlements. In the event of an eviction by the → *police*, activists in → *protest camps* such as those in the → *Hambach Forest* and in → *Lützerath* can move between trees, → *tree houses*, and → *barrios* without touching the ground. Comfortable traverses consist of a rope for the feet—the walkway—and a top rope to which activists can hook and hold on to with a carabiner. On single-rope traverses, which can also be set up during an ongoing eviction, activists move around with a pulley or, in extreme cases, using only their hands, while secured to the safety rope. During the protests in the → *Dannenrod Forest*, the longest traverse, consisting of two interwoven ropes, spanned a river and a federal highway, and was 300 meters long. (AMM)

Tree house, Ger. → *Baumhaus*. Tree houses occur as → *building types* in many → *protest camps*, in contexts in which individual trees or forests are to be protected from deforestation for construction projects or for the extraction of raw materials, for example in the → *Hambach Forest* and → *Dannenrod Forest*, in → *Lützerath*, or in protests against the → *Startbahn West*. Furthermore, tree houses play a role in the → *alternative architecture* of countercultures as well as in art. In certain regions, tree houses are also used as regular residential buildings.

For this form of activism, the period around 1970 represents an important point of reference. In 1969, for example, an early tree-sitting took place on the campus of the University of Texas in Austin (the Battle of Waller Creek). Moreover, Lloyd Kahn's seminal 1973 publication *Shelter* mentions tree houses, in addition to domes, → *tents*, or yurts, as suitable architecture for the establishment of a counterculture (Kahn 1973/2013, pp. 94–95; Lange-Berndt 2021). These remote hideouts above the ground promise intimacy as well as a life reminiscent of that in the primitive hut described by Vitruvius, that is, in a house co-determined by living nature (Rykwert 1972). Indeed, they were suitable for these purposes because trees in Europe and North America had long been associated with revolution, a rhetoric of freedom, and protest. Following the French Revolution, they played an important role in civil society. In May 1792 alone, around 60,000 liberty trees were planted in villages and municipalities in France. The aim was to transform the entire republic into a garden; the plants of the royal orangeries, for example, being freed from the "bondage of the boxes." Within this utopia, society was to be converted into an overarching natural order. Trees embodied harmony, so-

Trip

cial concord, and demonstrated political freedom (Harten, Harten 1989, pp. 23ff., 64, 110ff., 113–114). With the advent of Romanticism and the influence of the writings of the philosopher and naturalist Jean-Jacques Rousseau, a variety of tree houses emerged from the 18th century onwards (Henderson, Mornement 2006, p. 30ff.). A key publication in this context is the 1813 novel *The Swiss Family Robinson* by the poet and philosopher Johann David Wyss (Wyss 1813). The book recounts how the Robinson family, stranded on an island near New Guinea after a shipwreck, constructs their house in a tree: with architectural creations such as *L'Île de Robinson* in Paris, the problematic concept of noble savages, who supposedly were "people of nature," unspoiled by civilization and living in paradisiacal innocence, also became established in Europe (Ellingson 2001).

The nests of the "Woodstock Nation" as well as the contemporary activism based on it all draw on these stories in different ways. A life without furniture in a tree promises liberation from the conditioning of civilization as well as a consumerist society. However, this view of industrialized nations may ignore those who were and are dependent on trees in more existential ways. For example, Wyss's narrative, written in times of colonial expansion, also refers to the actual dwellings of the Koiari people living in New Guinea, who used tree houses as guard posts and shelters during attacks (Hackenschmidt 2009, p. 143). Members of the later counterculture did not always critically reflect on these contexts; with some of them seeking to present themselves as a tribal community. Many believed that supposedly primitive peoples had the tendency to sensitively appropriate and reorganize existing resources (Lévi-Strauss 1962/1966).

However, this "Outlaw Nation," which quickly became a → *media* sensation, has also come to embody self-expression in an increasingly global media world. Commercial tree houses, for example, are currently being used as wellness retreats. (Petra Lange-Berndt)

Tripod, engl. → *Tripod*. Konstruktion aus drei langen Stangen, die zusammengebunden und zu einem dreibeinigen → *Turm* aufgestellt werden (→ *Bautypen*). Tripods sind in den 1990er Jahren in England durch → *Reclaim the Streets* bekannt geworden. Wenn sich an der Spitze ein Mensch ankettet, benötigt die → *Polizei* eine Hebebühne, um ihn herunterzubekommen. Der Tripod wird als Räumungsschutz angewandt, wenn statische Alternativen wie Bäume fehlen, z.B. zur effektiven → *Blockade* von → *Straßen*. (JD)

Tripod. Adrian Fisk: Reclaim the Streets, Streatham, London, 1995 (Tripod. Adrian Fisk: Reclaim the Streets, Streatham, London, 1995)

Tripod, Ger. → *Tripod (fig.)*. Construction made of three long poles that are tied together and erected to form a three-legged → *tower* (→ *Building types*). If people chain themselves to the top, the → *police* need a lifting platform to get them down. Used as eviction protection when there is a lack of immobile alternatives such as trees, e.g. to effectively → *blockade* → *streets*. Made popular in England in the 1990s by → *Reclaim the Streets*. (JD)

Truck, engl. → *Truck*; → *Blockade*, → *Fahrzeuge*, → *Farmers-Proteste*, → „*Freedom Convoy*", → *Lärm*

Truck, Ger. → *Truck*; → *Blockade*, → *Farmers' protests*, → "*Freedom convoy*," → *Noise*, → *Vehicles*

Tunnel, engl. → *Tunnel*. Die Ursprünge von Protesttunneln liegen in den 1990er Jahren in England, als britische Anti-Roads-Aktivist∗innen neue Protestformen erprobten (→ *Claremont Road*), die auch heute noch von der Klimabewegung angewandt werden – zuletzt 2023 bei der Räumung von → *Lützerath*. Der Protesttunnel ist eine direkte Reaktion auf die Räumung von Baumbesetzungen und verfolgt eine einfache, aber effektive Taktik: Solange sich Menschen im potenziell einsturzgefährdeten Tunnel aufhalten, dürfen sich den → *Baumhäusern* keine schweren Räumungsgeräte nähern. Gleichzeitig kann der Tunnel nicht geräumt werden, wenn die Lage oberirdisch nicht abgesichert ist, weil sich noch Aktivist∗innen in den Baumhäusern befinden. Ziel ist es, die Räumung so lange wie möglich hinauszuzögern (Siegler 2023). (JD)

Tunnel. Videobotschaft der Tunnelaktivisten von Lützerath, Januar 2023 (Tunnel. Video message from the tunnel activists in Lützerath, January 2023)

Tunnel, Ger. → *Tunnel (fig.)*. The use of protest tunnels dates back to the 1990s in England, when British anti-road activists tried out new forms of protest (→ *Claremont Road*) that are still used by the climate movement today—most recently during the police clearing of the occupation at → *Lützerath* in 2023. The protest tunnel is a direct response to the eviction of tree occupiers and pursues a simple but effective tactic. As long as there are people inside a tunnel that can potentially collapse, no heavy eviction equipment is allowed to approach the → *tree houses*. At the same time, the tunnel cannot be cleared if the situation above ground

is not secured because activists are still in the tree houses. The objective is to delay the eviction for as long as possible (Siegler 2023). (JD)

Turm, engl. → *Tower*. Türme sind → *Bautypen*, die bei Protesten häufig eine besondere Rolle spielen. In → *Hongkong* → *2019* und auf dem → *Majdan* in Kyjiw → *2013* waren Türme Teil der Befestigungsanlagen. Aktivist∗innen bauten hier → *Barrikaden* mit hohen Wachttürmen, um Angriffe der → *Polizei* früh bemerken und abwehren zu können. Als Verzögerungsarchitekturen erschweren Türme die Räumung von → *Besetzungen* und → *Protestcamps* durch die Polizei, weil für Bauten ab einer gewissen Höhe speziell ausgebildete Einsatzkräfte mit ihren Gerätschaften anrücken müssen, was den Einsatz langwieriger und teurer macht. Bei Protesten in der → *Claremont Road* → *1994* gegen den Bau einer neuen Verbindungsstraße errichteten Aktivist∗innen einen 30 Meter hohen Gerüstturm und fixierten sich mit → *Lock-on Devices* an der Spitze. Die bis zu zehn Meter hohen → *Monopods* und die teils über die Baumwipfel hinausragenden Highpods im → *Fechenheimer Wald* und → *Dannenröder Wald* waren mit → *Seilen* an Boden und Bäumen abgespannt und mussten je nach Höhe und Position mit mobilen Kränen geräumt werden. Ein- bis viergeschossige, multifunktionale Turmpfahlbauten wurden im → *Hambacher Wald* und in → *Lützerath* außerdem zur Unterbringung von Aktivist∗innen sowie als Gemeinschaftsräume genutzt. In → *Gorleben* war auf dem höchsten Turm eine Radiostation installiert. Die Verteidigung des Turms im Falle einer Räumung wurde im Protestdorf lange diskutiert und verstärkte die Spaltung der Bewegung in eine gewaltfreie und eine militante Fraktion. Türme erhalten bei Protesten meist überdurchschnittlich viel Aufmerksamkeit, zum einen weil sie ein dankbares Motiv für Fotos und Videos sind und über → *Medien* bzw. → *digitale Medien* schnell verbreitet werden. Zum anderen entzünden sich an der vergleichsweise aufwendigen Räumung von Türmen oft heftige

Umbr

Diskussionen darüber, zu welchen Mitteln gegriffen werden sollte, sowohl auf Seiten der Protestierenden als auch der Polizei. (AMM)

Umbrella, Ger. → *Regenschirm*; → *Hong Kong protests*, → *Identifier*, → *Protection*

Utopia, Ger. → *Utopie*; → *Protest architecture*, → *Protest goals*

Utopie, engl. → *Utopia*; → *Protestarchitektur*, → *Protestziele*

Vehicles, Ger. → *Fahrzeuge (fig.)*, play an important role as moving or stationary objects in very different forms of protest. At → *demonstrations*, cars, parade floats, and trucks fitted with sound systems are simultaneously carriers of messages (→ *Media*) and aids for transporting sound equipment and catering. A protest raft with the inscription "Schiff & Bahn statt Straßenwahn" (Ships & Trains instead of Road Madness) during protests against the construction of the Federal Highway 31 in Breisach in 1996 had a similar role model effect as the bicycle in bicycle demonstrations. Due to the large mass of vehicles, tractor demonstrations (→ *Zwentendorf*, → *Farmers' protests*) and → *flotillas*, boat rallies or "kayaktivists" (activists in kayaks), are particularly effective. In → *blockades* such as the → *"Freedom Convoy"* in Canada in → *2022*, trucks not only disrupt traffic but also attract additional attention through excessive use of their horns (→ *Noise*). Tractors provide farmers in Delhi shelter inside the blockade and supply the movement with transported goods. Wagon forts, too, consist of mobile elements such as camper vans or trailers, which are, however, rarely moved in normal circumstances. During protests in → *public space*, parked cars are not only sprayed with → *graffiti*, damaged (→ *Destruction*), burned (→ *Fire*), or taken in triumphal gestures (→ *G20 summit protests* in Hamburg in → *2017*), they can also serve as → *building materials* for → *barricades*, similar to carriages and wagons during protests in the 19th century (→ *Revolution of 1848*). Activists from the → *protest organization* Extinction Rebellion campaigned against greenwashing in the automotive industry at a car show in Paris in 2022 by sticking themselves to the latest sports cars (→ *Super-gluing*). The → *police* also use vehicles at protests, such as → *water cannons* or the mobile "Skywatch" surveillance tower at → *Occupy Wall Street*. (AMM)

Venezuelan protests, Ger. → *Venezuela-Proteste*. Since → *2014*, there have been numerous protests in Venezuela against President Nicolás Maduro's government (→ *Demonstration*). The demonstrators accused him of corruption, mismanagement, and human rights violations. The Venezuelan capital Caracas became the site of violent, partly fatal clashes (→ *Violence*). Widespread protest symbols included the Venezuelan → *flag* with the seven stars, masks, and → *protective shields* with Christian motifs. (JD)

Venezuela-Proteste, engl. → *Venezuelan Protests*. Seit → *2014* hat es in Venezuela zahlreiche Proteste gegen die Regierung von Präsident Nicolás Maduro gegeben (→ *Demonstration*). Die Demonstrierenden warfen ihm Korruption, Misswirtschaft und Verletzungen der Menschenrechte vor. Es kam zu gewalttätigen, teils tödlichen Auseinandersetzungen in der venezolanischen Hauptstadt Caracas (→ *Gewalt*). Verbreitete Protestsymbole waren die Flagge Venezuelas mit den sieben Sternen (→ *Fahne*), Gesichtsmasken und → *Schutzschilder* mit christlichen Motiven. (JD)

Vienna Uprising, Ger. → *Wiener Oktoberaufstand*. After a promising start on March 13, → *1848*, with student demonstrations for more civil liberties, the imperial troops put a bloody end to the so-called Viennese "October Revolution" half a year later. Likewise, the approximately 160 barricades erected during the revolutionary events in Vienna could not prevent a new period of restoration, and subsequently, the Austrian Empire's neoabsolutist regime. (SH)

Violence, Ger. → *Gewalt*. In one form or another, violence plays a role in almost all protests examined here in connection with their protest architecture. Violent escalations between protesters and security forces often lead to a nascent protest movement gaining more support from the population than was previously foreseeable (→ *Acts of solidarity*). Violence can come from three sides: from the demonstrators, from the representatives of the state "monopoly on the use of force," or from a third party. In this case, the → *police* may have the task of preventing violence between protests and counter-protests.

How, though, is protest architecture shaped by violence? In the case of → *barricades*, this is obvious, since they are supposed to offer → *protection* from violence, while sometimes also enabling counter-violence. Whether barricades should be created at all is a recurring debate within protest movements. In → *Gorleben*, there was a dispute over whether the → *towers* should not merely make eviction more difficult but also be used to throw slurry or paint down on the police (a consensus resolution ultimately opposed this). The → *protest camp* on → *Maidan* in Kyiv, on the other hand, had been expanded into a veritable fortress in anticipation of violent clashes.

Violence is often used as a threat: protests could potentially turn violent, which is why they are stopped in their tracks. Things like → *straw* sacks could serve as → *weapons* and are therefore counted as passive armament and banned in Germany, as are other means of protection against police violence.

Whether a protest proceeds without violence—and if not, who was responsible for an escalation—is one of the most discussed questions of almost every protest movement. The notion of violence is a broad field: Is a → *blockade* already tantamount to violence? And what about actions of → *civil disobedience*? Other countries have different traditions. In France, for example, burning barricades and damaging property are still part of the revolutionary folklore of protests and strikes. Although the state will intervene when such things happen, the social tolerance level there is significantly higher than in many other places, given the history of several successful uprisings (French Revolution of 1789,

→ *July Revolution* of → *1830*, → *March Revolution* of → *1848*). (OE)

Volxküche → *Küche*

Waffen, engl. → *Weapons*. Der professionellen Rüstkammer der Staatsgewalt und der Ordnungskräfte – die von Handschellen, Schlagstöcken und Schutzkleidung (→ *Kleidung*, → *Schutz*) über Pfefferspray, Tränengas und Schusswaffen bis hin zu gepanzerten Einsatzwagen, Wasserwerfern und Hubschraubern (→ *Fahrzeuge*) reicht – steht das improvisierte und technologisch eher einfache Arsenal der Protestierenden gegenüber. Allerdings können auch Pfeil und Bogen, Zwillen, Spieße, Messer, Macheten, Molotowcocktails (→ *Feuer*) und → *Pflastersteine* gefährliche Verletzungen hervorrufen und dem Waffenverbot unterliegen. Wenn die Protestierenden durch ihre Bewaffnung die Bereitschaft zu physischer → *Gewalt* signalisieren (→ *Körpereinsatz*, → *Zerstörung*), wird dies oft als eine über den → *zivilen Ungehorsam* hinausgehende Provokation wahrgenommen, die nicht selten zur Eskalation führt. Bei den Protesten in → *Burundi* → *2015* rüsteten sich die Protestierenden mit selbstgebauten Spielzeugwaffen aus, um auf ihre Wehrlosigkeit gegenüber den mit scharfer Munition operierenden Polizeitruppen hinzuweisen. Über die militärischen Mittel hinaus können aber auch andere – unter Umständen wirksamere – Dinge als Waffen im Kampf für bzw. gegen politische oder religiöse Überzeugungen eingesetzt werden, etwa → *Protestarchitektur*, Protestsongs (→ *Musik*) und die → *Medien* oder Strategien wie → *Blockaden*, → *Besetzungen* und → *Guerillataktiken*: Richtig eingesetzt, kann auch eine Torte die Handlungsfähigkeit des politischen Gegners effektiv beeinträchtigen. (SH)

Wagenburg, engl. → *Wagon fort*; → *Fahrzeuge*, → *Siedlungsstruktur*

Wagon fort, Ger. → *Wagenburg*; → *Settlement structure*, → *Vehicles*

Walking, Ger. → *Spaziergang*; → *Demonstration*, → *Right-wing protests*

Waschmaschine, engl. → *Washing machine*. Nach dem Zweiten Weltkrieg

Wash

Waschmaschine. Giancarlo di Carlo, Bellocchio Carlo, Bruno Caruso: *La protesta dei giovani*, Ausstellung auf der XIV. Triennale di Milano, 30.5.–28.7.1968 (Washing machine. Giancarlo di Carlo, Bellocchio Carlo, and Bruno Caruso: *La protesta dei giovani*, exhibition at XIV Triennale di Milano, May 30–July 28, 1968)

entwickelten sich Waschmaschinen bald zum Inbegriff der Wohlstandsgesellschaft und der Konsumgüterindustrie: Als solcher wurden sie neben einem →*Fernseher* und einem Kühlschrank auf einer →*Barrikade* aus →*Pflastersteinen* inszeniert, die 1968 unter dem Titel *La protesta dei giovani* („Jugendprotest") auf der *Triennale di Milano* zu sehen war. Entsprechend der Zielsetzung der zeitgenössischen Protestbewegungen (→*Protestziele*) sollten die Bestandteile der unter Anleitung des Architekten Giancarlo di Carlo errichteten Installation (→*Baumaterialien*) als Ausdruck der Ablehnung bürgerlicher Werte verstanden werden. (SH)

Washing machine, Ger. →*Waschmaschine (fig.)*. After World War II, washing machines swiftly emerged as the emblem of an affluent society and the consumer goods industry: as such, they were staged alongside a →*Television set* and a fridge on a →*barricade* made of →*cobblestones* that went on show at the 1968 Triennale di Milano with the title *La protesta dei giovani* (Youth Protest). In line with the objectives of con-

temporary protest movements (→*Protest goals*), the components used for the installation, erected under the direction of architect Giancarlo di Carlo (→*Building materials*), were seen as an expression of the rejection of bourgeois values. (SH)

Wasser einfärben, engl. →*Dying water*. Das Einfärben von Seen, Flüssen, Bächen, Kanälen und Brunnen ist eine bei Protesten und →*Demonstrationen* zunehmend gewählte →*Guerillataktik*. In Wien kam sie anlässlich der 16. European Gas Conference im März 2023 zum Einsatz, als der Donaukanal und mehrere Brunnen im Innenstadtbereich im Rahmen einer Protestaktion mit der Chemikalie Uranin grün eingefärbt wurden. Ausgelöst worden waren die Proteste durch das Greenwashing der fortgesetzten Nutzung fossiler Brennstoffe seitens der an der Konferenz teilnehmenden Parteien aus Politik, Finanzwelt und Wirtschaft. (SH)

Wasserwerfer, engl. →*Water cannon*. Spezielle →*Fahrzeuge* der →*Polizei* mit großen Wassertanks, die bei →*Demonstrationen* eingesetzt werden, z.B.

um blockierte → *Straßen* (→ *Blockade*) von Demonstrierenden zu räumen oder brennende → *Barrikaden* zu löschen (→ *Anti-Protestmaßnahmen*). Der erste dokumentierte Einsatz von Wasserwerfern fand 1930 in Berlin statt, als es anlässlich der Kinopremiere des Antikriegsfilms *Im Westen nichts Neues* zu Unruhen kam und infolgedessen ein Demonstrationsverbot erlassen wurde (→ *Rechte Proteste*). (JD)

Wasser einfärben. Aktivist∗innen von Extinction Rebellion färben den Donaukanal im Rahmen einer Protestaktion grün ein, Wien, 23. März 2023 (Dying water. Activists from Extinction Rebellion dye the Danube Canal green as part of a protest action, Vienna, Austria, March 23, 2023)

Wasserwerfer. Georg Pahl: Mercedes-Benz-Wasserwerfer der Berliner Polizei, Wittenbergplatz, Dezember 1930 (Water cannon. Georg Pahl: Mercedes-Benz water cannon used by the Berlin Police Dept., Wittenbergplatz, December 1930)

Watchtower, Ger. → *Beobachtungsturm*; → *Building types*, → *Hong Kong*

protests, → *Maidan*, → *Occupy Wall Street*, → *Tower*

Water cannon, Ger. → *Wasserwerfer (fig.)*. Special → *vehicles* with large water tanks used by the → *police* during → *demonstrations*, e.g., to clear blocked → *streets* of demonstrators or to extinguish burning → *barricades* (→ *Anti-protest measures*). The first documented use of water cannons took place in Berlin in 1930, when riots broke out on the occasion of the cinema premiere of the anti-war film *Im Westen nichts Neues* (All Quiet on the Western Front), which resulted in demonstrations being banned (→ *Right-wing protests*). (JD)

Watts Riots, Ger. → *Watts-Unruhen*. Over the course of six days in August → *1965*, violence escalated during the so-called Watts Riots in Los Angeles, leaving not only 34 dead and over 1,000 people injured in its wake, but also over 600 badly damaged buildings—mainly stores—some of which were entirely burned out (→ *Violence*, → *Fire*, → *Destruction*). The violent rebellion manifested the radicalization within the American civil rights movement of the 1960s and was predominantly a reaction to discriminatory → *police* violence and ongoing racism in everyday life. → *Protest architecture* did not develop in a productive sense, but rather as a symbolic gesture of temporary appropriation, comparable to → *toppling monuments* or → *public square occupations*. (SH)

Watts-Unruhen, engl. → *Watts Riots*. Bei den sogenannten Watts-Unruhen in Los Angeles kam es im August → *1965* zu gewalttätigen Ausschreitungen, die in sechs Tagen nicht nur 34 Todesopfer und über 1000 Verletzte forderten, sondern auch über 600 Gebäude – vor allem Geschäfte – stark beschädigt und zum Teil völlig ausgebrannt zurückließen (→ *Gewalt*, → *Feuer*, → *Zerstörung*). Der gewaltsame Aufstand war Ausdruck einer Radikalisierung innerhalb der amerikanischen Bürger∗innenbewegung der 1960er Jahre und reagierte vor allem auf diskriminierende Polizeigewalt und den fortgesetzten Rassismus im Alltagsleben (→ *Polizei*). → *Protest-*

architektur entstand hier nicht in einem produktiven Sinne, sondern eher als symbolische Geste der kurzzeitigen Aneignung, dem →*Denkmalsturz* oder der →*Platzbesetzung* vergleichbar. (SH)

Weapons, Ger. →*Waffen*. The professional weaponry of state authority and law enforcement forces—ranging from handcuffs, batons, and protective clothing (→*Clothing*, →*Protection*) to pepper spray, tear gas, and firearms, as well as armored emergency vehicles, water cannons, and helicopters (→*Vehicles*)—forms a marked contrast with the improvised and typically technologically simple arsenal of the protesters. However, bows and arrows, slingshots, spears, knives, machetes, Molotov cocktails (→*Fire*), and →*cobblestones* can also cause dangerous injuries and are subject to weapons bans. If protesters indicate their readiness for physical →*violence* by arming themselves (→*Body deployment*, →*Destruction*), this is often perceived as a provocation that goes beyond →*civil disobedience* and frequently leads to escalation. During the →*Burundi protests* in →*2015*, the protesters equipped themselves with homemade toy weapons to indicate their defenselessness in the face of police forces operating with live ammunition. Beyond military means, however, other—possibly more effective—things can be used as weapons in the struggle for or against political or religious beliefs, such as →*protest architecture*, protest songs (→*Music*), and the →*media*, or strategies such as →*blockades*, →*occupations*, and →*guerrilla tactics*: used correctly, even a flung cake can effectively impair a political opponent's ability to act. (SH)

Wiener Oktoberaufstand, engl. →*Vienna Uprising*. Was am 13. März →*1848* mit den →*Demonstrationen* von Studenten für mehr bürgerliche Freiheiten vielversprechend begonnen hatte, endete ein halbes Jahr später mit der blutigen Niederschlagung der sogenannten „Wiener Oktoberrevolution" durch die kaiserlichen Truppen. Auch die rund 160 während der revolutionären Ereignisse in Wien errichteten →*Barrikaden* konnten eine erneute Restauration – und in weiterer Folge den Neoabsolutismus des österreichischen Kaiserhauses – nicht verhindern. (SH)

WTO Protests / Battle of Seattle, Ger. →*Anti-Globalisierungs- / WTO-Proteste*. "N30," as the event is also known, was the first peak in a period of anti-globalization protests, which had been triggered by the World Trade Organization (WTO) Ministerial Conference in Seattle on November 30, →*1999*. The event was characterized by carnivalesque elements such as turtle →*costumes*. Being slow and good-natured, the turtle was an impactful symbol for a peaceful protest. Besides peaceful →*street* occupations, Seattle also became the site of vandalism and street fights (→*Violence*). (JD)

Yellow Vests movement, Ger. →*Gelbwestenbewegung*. The starting point of the "gilets jaunes" was the French government's announcement in →*2018* that it would finance the energy transition by increasing the price of petrol at the pump. For that reason, the protests initially took place at →*roundabouts* on the city limits, as they expected car drivers to express solidarity with them. In other words, it was the first suburban protest movement that was also structured around the social urban/rural divide. Shortly afterwards, major →*demonstrations* took place in Paris with violent rioting (→*Violence*). Thereafter, the attempt failed to take the movement back to the local level of civic councils. (OE)

Yurt, Ger. →*Jurte*; →*Alternative architecture*, →*Building types*, →*Dakota Access Pipeline protests*, →*Lobau*, →*Maidan*, →*Tent*

ZAD Notre-Dame-des-Landes, engl. →*ZAD Notre-Dame-des-Landes*. Die →*Autonome Zone* in der Nähe von Nantes ist die bekannteste *zone à défendre* (deutsch: „zu verteidigende Zone") in Frankreich. Der Begriff ist ein Détournement von *zone d'aménagement différé* (deutsch: „Bauerwartungsgebiet"). Bewohner∗innen eines 1600 Hektar großen Gebiets in Notre-Dame-des-Landes, viele von ihnen Landwirt∗innen, protestierten jahrzehntelang gegen den seit den 1960er Jahren geplanten Bau des Flughafens Grand Ouest. → *2007* kam es zur ersten → *Besetzung* eines Bauernhofs, 2018 gab es knapp 100 selbstverwaltete Projekte auf dem Gelände, darunter landwirtschaftliche Betriebe mit Viehhaltung und Gemüsegärten, eine Bäckerei, eine Brauerei und die Zeitung *ZAD News* (→ *Medien*). Bestehende Gebäude wurden in Selbstbauweise umgebaut, außerdem entstanden viele neue Hütten, sogenannte „Cabanes", die den Einfallsreichtum der „Zadisten" widerspiegeln: verschiedenste Formen, → *Baumaterialien* und experimentelle Konstruktionsprinzipien werden kombiniert. Neben Lehm- und Pfahlbauten gibt es → *Baumhäuser*, Geodome, schwimmende Hütten und bewohnte → *Türme* (→ *Bautypen*). Teils gewaltsame Räumungsversuche der ZAD, u.a. in den Jahren 2012 und 2018, führten zu landesweite Solidaritätsbekundungen (→ *Solidaritätsgeste*). Die Besetzer*innen bauten → *Barrikaden* aus Autoreifen und Holzpaletten, → *blockierten* → *Straßen* mit ihren Traktoren (→ *Fahrzeuge*) und bildeten lange Menschenketten (→ *Körpereinsatz*). 2019 kam es zur → *Legalisierung* einiger Projekte. (AMM)

ZAD Notre-Dame-des-Landes, Ger. → *ZAD Notre-Dame-des-Landes*. The → *Autonomous Zone* close to Nantes is the best-known *zone à défendre* (zone to be defended) in France. The term is a détournement of *zone d'aménagement différé* (zone awaiting construction). Inhabitants of a 1,600-hectare area in Notre-Dame-des-Landes, many of them farmers, protested for decades against the construction of the airport Grand Ouest, which had been planned since the 1960s. In → *2007*, the first → *occupation* of a farmyard was established, and by 2018 there were almost 100 self-governed projects in the area, including agricultural operations with cattle and vegetable gardens, a bakery, a brewery, and the newspaper *ZAD News* (→ *Media*). Existing buildings were converted on the principle of do-it-yourself construction, many new huts, so-called "cabanes," were created, reflecting the in-

ventiveness of the "Zadists": combining all manner of shapes, building materials, and experimental construction methods. There are clay and pile dwellings as well as → *tree houses*, geodomes, floating huts, and inhabited → *towers* (→ *Building types*). Partly violent attempts to evict the ZAD—for example in 2012 and 2018—led to nationwide declarations of solidarity (→ *Acts of solidarity*). The occupiers erected → *barricades* from car tires and wooden pallets, → *blocked* → *streets* with their tractors, (→ *Vehicles*) and formed long human chains (→ *Body deployment*). In 2019, some of the projects were granted legal status (→ *Legalization*). (AMM)

Zaffaraya, engl. → *Zaffaraya*. Die Initiative zum Bau einer linksautonomen Siedlung geht auf die Jugendproteste der Jahre 1980 bis 1982 zurück, als sich nicht nur in Zürich, sondern auch in Basel, Bern und anderen Städten der Schweiz eine Alternativkultur entwickelte (→ *Züri brännt*). Zaffaraya entstand am 31. Juli → *1985* als „Freies Land Zaffaraya" auf dem ehemaligen Gaswerkareal in Bern, darin begrifflich-politisch der „Freien Republik Wendland" verwandt (→ *Gorleben*). Nach einer Räumung, Wiederansiedlung und Verschiebung mit städtischer Hilfe befindet sich die Siedlung heute – ohne offizielle Duldung – in einer Autobahnschleife. (OE)

Zaffaraya, Ger. → *Zaffaraya*. The initiative to build an autonomist settlement dates back to the protests by young people in 1980–82, when a counterculture developed not just in Zurich, but also in Basel, Bern and other Swiss cities (→ *Zurich youth protests*). Zaffaraya arose on July 31, → *1985*, as the "Free Land of Zaffaraya" on the grounds of a former gasworks in Bern. Its name is related conceptually and politically to the "Free Republic of Wendland" (→ *Gorleben*). After being evicted, resettled, and relocated with municipal support, the settlement is now located on a highway junction, though with no official permission. (OE)

Zelt, engl. → *Tent*. Ein Zelt besteht aus Stoff oder einem anderen elastischen

Zelt

Material, das über eine Tragkonstruktion gespannt wird, sodass ein Dach sowie Wände gebildet werden. Es entsteht ein abgegrenzter Innenraum. Bei dauerhaften Protestereignissen wie → *Protestcamps* dienen Zelte oft als → *Infrastruktur*, entweder in geplanter Absicht oder als Ad-hoc-Lösungen.

Zelt. Die umstrittenen Aufnahmen einer Wärmebildkamera zeigen das bei Nacht – vermeintlich – verwaiste Protestcamp vor der St. Paul's Cathedral im Rahmen der Occupy-Bewegung, London, 26. Oktober 2011 (Fotografien im Auftrag der Boulevardzeitung Daily Mail) (Tent. The controversial images made by a thermal imaging camera which showed the (purportedly) vacant protest camp in front of St. Paul's Cathedral in the context of the Occupy movement, London, October 26, 2011 (photographs commissioned by the *Daily Mail* newspaper))

Zelte haben verschiedene Formen und Größen, aber die Materialeigenschaften und die auf Spannung basierende Konstruktion sind bei allen Zelten ähnlich. Bei kuppelförmigen Zelten aus Supermarkt oder Outdoor-Handel sind Tunnelzüge in den Zeltstoff eingenäht, in welche biegsame Stangen gesteckt werden, die beim Aufstellen Bögen bilden, über denen wiederum der Zeltstoff straffgezogen wird. Traditionelle A-Zelte erhalten ihre charakteristische Form durch zwei senkrechte Stangen, die mithilfe von Schnüren und Heringen im Boden unter Zugkraft aufgestellt werden. Zelte können auch aus behelfsmäßigen Textilien bestehen, die zwischen oder um Objekte gespannt werden (→ *Bender*), z.B. aus einer Plane, die um gebogene Bäume drapiert wird. Bei einigen traditionellen indigenen Zeltkonstruktionen werden Textilien kegelförmig um Stangen arrangiert, wie beim *Sápmi Lavvu*; über ein Gitter gelegt, wie bei einer Jurte; oder als Dach über mehrere Stangen bis zum Boden gespannt, wie bei dem *Bayt al Sha'ar*, einem Beduinenzelt.

Bei Protesten hat das Zelt eine symbolische Funktion, einen praktischen, infrastrukturellen Zweck – oder eine Kombination aus beidem. Zu den symbolischen Funktionen zählt die Bezugnahme zur traditionellen Verwendung von Zelten durch indigene Gruppen. Protestzelte können durch ihren provisorischen, flüchtigen und ungeplanten Charakter Prekarität und Verletzlichkeit zum Ausdruck bringen (→ *Alternative Architektur*). Ihre Schutzlosigkeit ist der maximale Kontrast zur üblicherweise beständigen und unverrückbaren Architektur der machtvollen Institutionen von Staat und Gesellschaft. Als elementare architektonische Funktion bietet das Zelt lediglich → *Schutz* vor Sonne, Wind und Regen und grenzt das Private und Halbprivate vom öffentlichen Protestraum ab. Betrachtet man das Zelt als Protestobjekt oder als Protestwerkzeug, so geht die Bedeutung des Zeltes über die grundlegende architektonische Funktion der Abgrenzung und des Schutzes hinaus. Zelte stellen, so flüchtig sie auch sind, auf unterschiedliche Weise Protestinfrastruktur bereit, die von der komplexen Beziehung zwischen Zeit, Raum, Verletzlichkeit, Gesetzgebung und dem menschlichen Körper geformt werden und nicht zuletzt von der konkreten Materialität der Zelte bestimmt sind (→ *Baumaterialien*). Diese Beziehungen lassen sich am besten anhand einiger Beispiele von Protestzelten auf der ganzen Welt zu Beginn der 2010er Jahre veranschaulichen:

In London veröffentlichte die *Daily Mail* 2011 während Occupy London ein mit einer Infrarotkamera aufgenommenes Bild, um zu zeigen, wie wenige Zelte während des Protests überhaupt zum Übernachten genutzt wurden. Im selben Jahr hat die → *Polizei* in Melbourne eine Demonstrantin in Unterwäsche in einem Park zurückgelassen, weil ihr zuvor ein modifiziertes Zelt, das als Kleidungsstück diente, vom Körper geschnitten wurde (→ *Zeltmonster*, → *Körpereinsatz*). In Silwan, einem Ortsteil von Ostjerusalem in Palästina/Israel, wurde ein Zelt wiederholt von der israelischen Polizei abgerissen und von palästinensischen Aktivist∗innen wiederaufgebaut. In Oslo, Norwegen, übernachteten palästinensische Demonstrant∗innen einen Winter lang in einem Zelt neben einer Kirche, um sich durch ihren Protest vor der drohenden Abschiebung zu schützen.

Die Beispiele aus Oslo, Melbourne und London zeigen, wie Körper und Zelte miteinander verwoben sein können. Das Zelt verstetigt den Körper in räumlicher und zeitlicher Hinsicht. Es vergrößert die Fläche, die ein „Protestkörper" einnehmen kann, und verschafft Protesten eine längere Dauer, wie das Beispiel aus Oslo zeigt. Proteste hängen von Körpern und Zelten ab; dabei dient das Zelt als Platzhalter für den Körper im Protestraum, wie die Infrarotfotos der *Daily Mail* in London deutlich machen. Als Zelte bei den Protesten in Melbourne verboten wurden, war es immer noch möglich, sie als Kleidungsstück herumzutragen – und sie auf diese Weise als zweite Haut zu einer direkten Erweiterung des eigenen Körpers zu machen.

Die Verwundbarkeit des Zeltes, aber auch seine Flexibilität als Bestandteil der Protestinfrastruktur wird in den Beispielen Silwan und Melbourne am deutlichsten. Das verletzliche Material ist für eine gewaltbereite Polizei leicht zu zerstören (→ *Gewalt*, → *Zerstörung*). Das textile Material ermöglicht es jedoch auch, das Zelt zu verändern, wieder aufzustellen und im Protestraum neu einzusetzen, entweder um auf eine veränderte Gesetzgebung und auf Gewalt hinzuweisen, wie in Melbourne, oder um einen Protest gegen eine Gewaltmacht zu organisieren, wie in Silwan. Der oft unklare Rechtsstatus von Zeltsiedlungen trägt dazu bei, eine Zwangsräumung durch den Staat hinauszuzögern. In London und anderswo profitierte die Occupy-Bewegung von den fehlenden Regelungen für Zelte in öffentlichen und privaten Stadträumen (→ *Occupy Wall Street*, → *Öffentlicher Raum*).

Die Beispiele zeigen, wie seine architektonischen Eigenschaften von Verletzlichkeit, Flexibilität und Vergänglichkeit zusammen mit dem ungeklärten rechtlichen Status des Zelts, seiner engen Beziehung zum menschlichen Körper und dem symbolischen Wert der Zeltstruktur das Zelt zu einem wesentlichen Bestandteil von Protesten machen können. (Anders Rubing)

Zeltmonster. Videostill, Occupy Melbourne Tent Monsters, 4. Dezember 2011 (Tent monster. Video still, Occupy Melbourne tent monsters, December 4, 2011)

Zeltmonster, engl. → *Tent monster*. Nachdem die → *Protestcamps* nach dem Vorbild von → *Occupy Wall Street* auf der ganzen Welt von der → *Polizei* geräumt werden, erproben die Demonstrierenden anderer Camps erfinderische neue Wege, um die → *Besetzung* fortzusetzen. In Melbourne trugen sie die → *Zelte* als → *Kleidung* oder → *Kostüme*, anstatt in ihnen zu campen, da dies untersagt war. Während die Polizei die Zeltmonster-Parade zunächst nur beobachtete, ging sie später rabiater vor, entfernte beispielsweise gewaltsam das Zelt einer Frau, sodass sie nur noch in Unterwäsche dastand (→ *Gewalt*). (JD)

Zerstörung, engl. → *Destruction*. Proteste und → *Demonstrationen* hinterlassen bisweilen den Eindruck von Zerstörung und Verwüstung. Was in den Nachrichten oft pauschal als Vandalismus bezeichnet wird, kann allerdings völlig verschiedene Ursachen haben. Zu willkürlichen Beschädigungen an Hausfassaden, Schaufenstern, Stadtmobiliar und Fahrzeugen kommt es häufig, wenn sich friedliche Proteste zu gewaltsamen Auseinandersetzungen steigern. Bei bewaffneten Straßenkämpfen (→ *Gewalt*, → *Straße*) haben sich die Protestierenden immer wieder hinter → *Barrikaden* verschanzt (→ *Schutz*), die meist kurzfristig errichtet wurden und aus den verschiedensten, dabei größtenteils zerstörten Gegenständen bestanden. In der Vergangenheit wurde oft auch das Straßenpflaster aufgerissen und zu → *Baumaterial* für die Barrikaden umfunktioniert oder als Wurfgeschoss eingesetzt (→ *Pflasterstein*, → *Waffen*). Die vermeintlich blindwütige und vorwiegend wohl gesetzeswidrige Zerstörung von Dingen – etwa durch das Legen von → *Feuer* – kann indes auch als probates Mittel der Sinnstiftung erscheinen: In einer Gesellschaft, in der kaum etwas so gut geschützt wird wie das Eigentum, kann sie eine beabsichtigte Provokation darstellen. Die Zerstörung von Herrscher∗innenbildern, Hoheitszeichen und Ehrenmälern bildet einen gezielten Angriff auf die Symbole der Macht, der zwangsläufig als Affront betrachtet werden muss. Beim Stürzen von Denkmälern (→ *Denkmalsturz*) und dem Verbrennen von → *Fahnen* handelt es sich um bewusst gewählte und meist mediengerecht inszenierte Strategien (→ *Medien*), die den Protesten eine spezielle Aufmerksamkeit garantieren. (SH)

Ziegelstein, engl. → *Brick*. Im Unterschied zum → *Pflasterstein*, bei dem es sich – zumindest in Europa – gewissermaßen um das allgegenwärtige Urgestein der Protestkultur handelt, wird die Verwendung von Ziegelsteinen als revolutionäres Material vor allem mit den regierungskritischen Protesten in → *Hongkong* → *2019* in Verbindung gebracht. Die Demonstrant∗innen der Demokratiebewegung hatten die → *Straßen* mit Hunderten von kleinen Torbögen blockiert, die jeweils aus drei gewöhnlichen Ziegelsteinen bestanden, zwei davon hochkant mit einem dritten als Dach. In größeren Gruppen bildeten diese knöchelhohen Formationen, für die überwiegend das Pflaster der Gehsteige und Fußgänger∗innenzonen verwendet wurde, wirksame Straßensperren, die den Berufsverkehr stellenweise lahmlegten und die Einsatzfahrzeuge der Polizei verlangsamten. Wenn eine der Strukturen vom Rad eines → *Fahrzeugs* berührt wurde, verkeilte der herabfallende obere Ziegel die beiden anderen und be- bzw. verhinderte die Weiterfahrt. Allerdings wurden die Ziegel in Hongkong durchaus auch – ganz „klassisch" – als Wurfgeschoss verwendet (→ *Waffen*) und zu → *Barrikaden* vermauert. (SH)

Ziviler Ungehorsam, engl. → *Civil disobedience*. „Ziviler Ungehorsam ist ein moralischer *begründeter* Protest, dem nicht nur private Glaubensüberzeugungen oder Eigeninteressen zugrunde liegen dürfen; er ist ein *öffentlicher* Akt, der in der Regel angekündigt ist und von der Polizei in seinem Ablauf kalkuliert werden kann; er schließt die *vorsätzliche Verletzung* einzelner Rechtsnormen ein, ohne den Gehorsam gegenüber der Rechtsordnung im Ganzen zu affizieren, er verlangt die Bereitschaft, für die rechtlichen *Folgen* der Normverletzung *einzustehen*; die Regelverletzung, in der sich ziviler Ungehorsam äußert, hat ausschließlich *symbolischen Charakter* – daraus ergibt sich schon die Begrenzung auf *gewaltfreie* Mittel des Protestes." (Habermas 1983, S. 35)

Züri brännt, engl. → *Zurich youth protests*. Der Slogan „Züri brännt" ist der Titel eines Dokumentarfilms, der von Aktivist∗innen gedreht wurde, während die zugehörigen Ereignisse noch keineswegs abgeschlossen waren. Der Konflikt begann mit den Opernhauskrawallen am 31. Mai → *1980*, als Jugendliche, verstärkt durch Besucher∗innen eines Bob-Marley-Konzerts, dagegen protestierten, dass die Oper saniert, ein Autonomes Jugendzentrum (AJZ) aber keine Unterstützung bekommen sollte. Brutale Polizeieinsätze brachten zahlreiche Gegenstrategien hervor, so etwa die Nacktdemo und die Fernsehbarrikade (→ *Polizei*, → *Nacktheit*, → *Demonstration*, → *Fernseher*). Wenig bekannt

Zweckentfremdung. C. M. Kosemen: Verkaufsstand bei den Gezi-Park-Protesten, Istanbul, Mai 2013 (Misappropriation. C. M. Kosemen: Food stalls at the Gezi Park protests, Istanbul, Turkey, May 2013)

ist, dass zeitweilig ein kleines →*Protestcamp* entstand, von der Lokalpresse „Chaotendorf in der Sihl" genannt. (OE)

Zurich youth protests, Ger. →*Züri brännt*. The slogan "Züri brännt" (Zurich's on fire) is the title of a documentary filmed by activists when the events in question were by no means over. The conflict began with rioting at the Opera House on May 31, →*1980*, when young people, supported by attendees from a Bob Marley concert, protested that while the opera house was being refurbished, the AJZ Autonomous Youth Center was to receive no funding. Brutal police operations triggered numerous counterstrategies, such as the naked demonstration and the TV barricade (→*Police*, →*Nakedness*, →*Demonstration*, →*Television set*). What is less well-known is that at one time, a small →*protest camp* was in place, christened "Chaotendorf in der Sihl" (village of anarchist rabble on the Sihl) in the local press. (OE)

Zweckentfremdung, engl. →*Misappropriation*. Wasserflaschen wer-

den zu Gasmasken, Heiligenbilder zu →*Schutzschilden*, →*Fahrzeuge* zu →*Barrikaden*, Schwerter zu Pflugscharen, →*Kochtöpfe* zu Helmen – oder aus →*Absperrgittern* entsteht ein Ausgabestand für Lebensmittel (→*Infrastruktur*). Es zählt zu den grundlegenden Prinzipien von Protestgestaltung, dass Dinge zweckentfremdet werden. (OE)

Zwentendorf, engl. →*Zwentendorf*. Der Widerstand gegen die Inbetriebnahme des Atomkraftwerks Zwentendorf und gegen den Bau eines Wasserkraftwerks in der →*Hainburger Au* waren die beiden zentralen Protest-Ereignisse der österreichischen Nachkriegsgeschichte. In Wien kommt noch die Besetzung der Arena im Jahr 1976 hinzu, einem alternativen Veranstaltungsort auf einem ehemaligen Schlachthofgelände, obwohl daraus keine mit →*Züri brännt* vergleichbaren Konfrontationen hervorgingen.

Der Zwentendorf-Protest führte zur ersten Volksabstimmung in Österreich nach 1945, die im November →*1978* mit 50,47% zu 49,33% knapp zuguns-

Zwen

ten der AKW-Gegner∗innen ausging.
→ *Protestarchitektur* spielte eine Ne-
benrolle, so etwa als räumliche Dominanz in Gestalt einer → *Blockade* der
Zufahrtswege des fertiggestellten AKW,
weswegen die dort noch fehlenden
Brennstäbe per Hubschrauber eingeflo-
gen werden mussten. Das Bergfeuer mit
dem großen NEIN nahm die heutigen
→ *Lichtprojektionen* vorweg. (OE)

Zwentendorf, Ger. → *Zwentendorf*.
The opposition to the Zwentendorf nuclear power station going into operation
and against the construction of a hydro-
electric power plant in the → *Hainburger Au* were the two central protest events
in postwar Austrian history. In Vienna,
there was also the occupation of the Arena in 1976, an alternative events venue
on the grounds of a former slaughter-
house, although this did not trigger confrontations comparable with the → *Zurich youth protests*.

The Zwentendorf protest led to the first
referendum in Austria after 1945 in November → *1978*, and the tight outcome
revealed 50.47 percent opposing the nuclear power plant and 49.33 percent in
favor. → *Protest architecture* played
a minor role, for example through the
spatial dominance enacted by way of a
→ *blockade* of the access routes to the
completed power plant, which meant
that some of the fuel rods had to be
flown in by helicopter. The configuration of blazing fires on the mountainside
tracing out the word NEIN (no) can be
seen as a precursor to today's → *light
projections*. (OE)

Anhang (Appendix)

Begriffe (Entries)

Abschütten
Abseilen
Absperrgitter
Acampamento Terra Livre, 2019
Acts of solidarity
Adobe hut
A-Frame
Alternative architecture
Alternative Architektur
Angriff
Ankleben
Anti-AMLO-Proteste, 2020
Anti-AMLO protests, 2020
Anti-Globalisierungs- / WTO-Proteste, 1999
Anti-Protestmaßnahmen
Anti-protest measures
Archaeological investigations
Archäologische Untersuchungen
Archiv
Archive
Art
Asphalt
Attack
Authors
Autohupe
Autonome Zone
Autonomous zone
Autoreifen
Autor*innen
Badewanne
Baltic Way, 1989
Baltischer Weg, 1989
Banner
Barbed wire
Barrel
Barricade
Barricade plan
Barrier
Barrikade
Barrikadenplan
Barrikadentage (Riga), 1991
Barrio
Bathtub
Baumaterial
Baumhaus
Bauplatzbesetzung
Bautypen
Bender
Beobachtungsturm
Bergfeuer, 1978
Besetzung

Betonpyramide
Bibliography
Black Lives Matter, 2013–
Blockade
Body deployment
Bonus Army, 1932
Branded Protest
Brick
Bridge
Brücke
Building materials
Building site occupation
Building types
Bürger*innenbesen-Proteste, 2014
Burundi-Proteste, 2015
Burundi protests, 2015
Cake
Camps for Climate Action
Camp Studies
Capitol attack, 2021
Cazerolazo
Children
Civic Broom protests, 2014
Civil disobedience
Claremont Road, 1994
Clothing
Cobblestone
Communication
Concrete pyramid
Converging protest marches
Cooking pot
Costume
Counter-construction
Critical Mass
Dagegensein
Dakota-Access-Pipeline-Proteste, 2016–2017
Dakota Access Pipeline protests, 2016–2017
Dannenröder Wald, 2019–2020
Dannenrod Forest, 2019–2020
Demonstration
Denkmalschutz
Denkmalsturz
Destruction
Die-in
Digitale Medien
Digital media
Dresden May Uprising, 1849
Dresdner Maiaufstand, 1849
Dumping
Dying water
Earth shelter
EDSA-Revolution, 1986

519

Bildrechte (Image credits)

(Ku) = Künstler∗in unbekannt
(artist unknown)
(Fu) = Fotograf∗in unbekannt
(photographer unknown)

(Hu) = Hersteller*in unbekannt
(manufacturer unknown)
(o) = Bild oben (top image)
(u) = Bild unten (bottom image)
(r) = Bild rechts (right image)
(l) = Bild links (left image)

3 Paris Musées / Musée Carnavalet, (Ku) 4 Musée Carnavalet / Musée d'Orsay, Paris 5 Stadtmuseum Berlin 6 Historisches Museum Frankfurt, (Ku) 7 Jüdisches Museum Wien, Inv. Nr. 14182, David Peters 8 Städtische Galerie Dresden – Kunstsammlung, (Ku), Repro: Philipp WL Günther 10 Bibliothèque Historique de la Ville de Paris 11 The Australian Worker's Union of Employees, John Oxley Library, State Library of Queensland 12 bpk, Kunstbibliothek, SMB, Inv.-Nr. WR_A0109_01 13 Harris & Ewing Collection, Library of Congress, (Fu) 14 Farm Security Administration – Office of War Information Photograph Collection, Library of Congress 15 picture alliance / AP Images / Atlanta Journal-Constitution, (Fu) 16 Tony Westman 18 Los Angeles Times Photographic Collection, UCLA Library Digital Collection 19 picture alliance / Associated Press, (Fu) 20 U.S. News & World Report magazine photograph collection, Library of Congress, public domain 21 picture alliance / Reuters, Russell Boyce 22 Institut für Stadtgeschichte Frankfurt am Main, ISG FFM, S7Z Nr. 1971-297, Hans Rempfer 23 picture alliance / Ritzau Scanpix, Mini Wolff 24 Mitchell Library, State Library of New South Wales, courtesy SEARCH Foundation, (Fu) 26 Archivo General de la Nacion, Argentinien, ID: AR-AGN-AGN01-AGAS-Ddf-rg-3099-348581, (Fu) 27 protestwanderweg.at, (Fu) 28 Hans-Hermann Müller 29 ETH-Bibliothek Zürich, Bildarchiv, Com_L30-0048-0024-0002, Patrick Lüthy, CC BY-SA 4.0 30 akg-images, AKG821457, Manfred Prüfer 31 Sarah Booker 33 ullstein bild, Sven Simon 34 Verein für Geschichte der ArbeiterInnenbewegung, Otto Bartel 35 Andreas Blatter (Berner Zeitung) 36 Monina

Allarey Mercado (Hg.): People Power: An Eyewitness History; The Philippine Revolution of 1986, Manila 1986 37 Vladimiras Gulevičius (ELTA) 38 Dobele County Museum, Agris Šiliņš 39 Andrew Wiard, reportphotos.com 40 picture alliance / Reuter, Osman Orsal 42 Adrian Fisk 43 Anna Badcock, Bob Johnston 44 MOHAI, Seattle Post-Intelligencer Collection, 2000.107.19991129.14.30, Paul Joseph Brown 45 Immo Klink 46 Antonio Velázquez 47 Jonathan Rashad 48 Wikipedia: bahrain.viewbook.com, CC BY-SA 3.0 50 Olmo Calvo 51 Flickr: linmtheu, CC BY-SA 2.0 52 Flickr: shankbone (David Shankbone), CC BY 2.0 53 Tim Wagner 54 picture alliance / dpa, Soeren Stache 55 Flickr: Ian Usher, CC BY-NC-SA 2.0 56 picture alliance / Reuters, Gleb Garanich 58 Mariana Vincenti Urdaneta 59 Vicky Chan 60 Sophie Garcia 61 picture alliance / AP Photo, Jerome Delay 62 Scott Heins 63 taz, Jan Kahlcke 64 Flavio Forner 66 picture alliance, BeckerBredel 67 Flickr: Mídia Ninja, CC BY-NC 2.0 68 Flickr: Studio Incendo, CC BY 2.0 69 Tim Wagner 70 Wikipedia: Benjamin Morawek, CC BY-SA 2.0 71 Anna-Maria Mayerhofer 72 cuartoscuro.com, Daniel Augusto 73 picture alliance / EPA-EFE, Rajat Gupta 75 picture alliance / EPA, Jim Lo Scalzo 76 picture alliance / ZUMA-PRESS.com, Aung Kyaw Htet 77 APA / picturedesk.com, Tobias Steinmaurer 78 F.A.Z.-Foto, Lucas Bäuml 79 picture alliance / EPA, Andre Pichette 81 (o) picture-alliance / dpa, DB Publifoto (u) picture alliance / dpa, Matthias Balk 82 Olaf Metzel, Foto: Hans Peter Stiebing 85 (l) Flickr: Stefan Müller (climate stuff), CC BY-NC 2.0 (r) Wikipedia: bahrain.viewbook.com, CC BY-SA 3.0 88 (o, u) Attila Dézsi 96 David Klammer 97 Handbuch der Kommunikationsguerilla, (Fu) 99 Bibliothèque municipale de Lyon, public domain 101 Paris Musées / Musée Carnavalet, public domain 108 Paula Allen 109 picture alliance / Reuters Pictures, Wolfgang Rattay 133 MAK – Museum für angewandte Kunst, Wien 135 Flickr:

magazine photograph collection, Library of Congress **427** DC Public Library, Star Collection, Washington Post **428** Collection of the Smithsonian National Museum of African American History and Culture, Robert Houston **429** Jill Freedman Estate **430** Collection of the Smithsonian National Museum of African American History and Culture, Robert Houston **431** picture alliance / ASSOCIATED PRESS, (Fu) **437** LAIF, Gordon Welters **443** picture alliance / AP Photo, Fernando Llano **446** (o) Sächsische Landesbibliothek – Staats- und Universitätsbibliothek Dresden (SLUB) / Deutsche Fotothek (u) MAK – Museum für angewandte Kunst, Wien **452** bpk / Kunstbibliothek, SMB, Bild-Nr.: 30026586, Bernard Larsson **453** picture alliance / AP Photo, Sergei Chuzavkov **460–461** Walter Keber **462** ullstein bild, Gauls **463** Dietmar Treber **464** Matthias Feyerabend **465** akg-images, AKG821452, Manfred Prüfer **466** Walter Keber **467** Dietmar Treber **468** Matthias Feyerabend **469** Walter Keber **470** picture-alliance / dpa, Wolfgang Eilmes **471** Walter Keber **472** Ursel Brünner, Claus Centner, Andreas, Jörg, in: Cremer 1982, S. 99 **480** Tim Wagner **486–488** Flickr: Hossam el-Hamalawy, CC BY 2.0 **489** picture alliance / dpa, Andre Pain **490** Flickr: Hossam el-Hamalawy, CC BY 2.0 **491–492** Flickr: Ahmed Abd El-Fatah, CC BY-NC-SA 2.0 **493** Lara Baladi **494–495** Flickr: Ahmed Abd El-Fatah, CC BY-NC-SA 2.0 **496** istock, Oleh Slobodeniuk **501** Extinction Rebellion UK, Gareth Morris **506** Adrian Fisk **507** Youtube: LuetziBleibt **510** Triennale Milano – Archivi **511** (o) Extinction Rebellion Österreich, (Fu) (u) Bundesarchiv Bild 102-10865, CC-BY-SA 3.0 **514** Daily Mail, General Trust, London, (Fu) **515** Youtube: TheFreemanSmith **517** C. M. Kosemen **Backcover Var. 1** Tim Wagner / Klimacamp im Rheinland (Camp for Climate Action in the Rhineland), 24. August 2017 **Backcover Var. 2** Hans-Hermann Müller: Freie Republik Wendland (Free Republic of Wend-land), 31. Mai 1980

Alle Zeichnungen, falls nicht anders aufgeführt, von Anna-Maria Mayer-hofer, basierend auf Material von (All illustrations, unless otherwise stated, by Anna-Maria Mayerhofer, based on material from): **142–143** Harp Farmer Pictures **168** Attila Dézsi **191** Aktion Unterholz **217** Umbrella Movement **221** Caroline Wuethrich, Geraldine Borio **263** Fridays For Future Austria **265** Oliver Ressler **283–285** Martin Junker-mann / RWTH Aachen, in: Helten, Wertgen 2022 **313** Dmytro Vortman **315** Leopold Banchini, Daniel Zamarbide, Sergey Ferley **339–342** Movimiento 15M **358–359** Flavio Forner / Mídia Ninja **382** Jonathan Massey, Brett Snyder **418–419** John Wiebenson, in: Wiebenson 1969 **456–457** Technische Hochschule Darmstadt, in: Cremer 1982 **483–484** Ahmed Zaazaa

Kooperationen (Collaborations)

Modellbau (Model Making):
– Technische Universität München, Prof. Dipl.-Ing. Andreas Kretzer, Wahlfach Szenografie, Bachelor Lehrauftrag am Lehrstuhl für Entwerfen und Gestalten, Prof. Uta Graff mit den Studierenden (With the students): Todor Rusev, Selin Uyarlar: Hüttendorf Startbahn West, Frankfurt am Main; Henry Höcherl, Lukas Müller: Euromaidan, Kyiv; Laurie Castella, Mathilde Larose: Lobau bleibt, Wien; Juliana Baumgart, Anggiolina Garcia: Resurrection City, Washington; Tuvanna Gül, Maria Karaivanova: Freie Republik Wendland, Gorleben; Tang Yishui, Xu Xiaoru: Occupy Wall Street, New York; Nini Huang: Movimiento 15M, Madrid
– Hochschule für Technik Stuttgart, Prof. Dipl.-Ing. Andreas Kretzer, Szenografieentwurf, Bachelor und Master, International Master of Interior-Architectural Design mit den Studierenden (With the students): Tanushree Arya, Billur Duru, Sayali Khadse, Annet Thomas: Tahrir Square, Kairo; Gamze

Ceylan, Beyza Günaydin, Christina Krammer, Alexandra Delgado Reboll, Müge Özkan, Nazlican Yesilyurt: Movimiento 15M, Madrid; Revna Elif Çelik, Stefan-Alin Fulop, Iulia-Alexia Hent, Ceren İzgi: Umbrella Movement, Hong Kong
– Rokas Wille, Staatliche Hochschule für Gestaltung Karlsruhe (HfG): 40 Bodenstrukturen, Lützerath (40 ground-based structures, Lützerath)

Fotografie (Photography):
– Staatliche Hochschule für Gestaltung Karlsruhe (HfG), Eisenhart Keimeyer, Werkstattleiter Fotografie, Wahlfach Großbildkamera, Exkursion nach Lützerath 2022

Hängebrücke Hambacher Wald (Hambach Forest Suspension Bridge):
– Stephan Mörsch
– Frodo

Film:
Oliver Hardt, Frankfurt am Main: PROTEST/ARCHITECTURE, 2023
– Written and directed by: Oliver Hardt
– Editing: Sanjeev Hathiramani
– Graphic Design: Christina Kral
– Soundtrack: Albrecht Kunze
– Sound Mix: Antoine Schweitzer
– Motion Graphics: Michael Wagner
– Archive Footage Research and Rights Clearances: Neopol Film, Producer Tonio Kellner, Researchers Antonia Best, Carl Seitz
– Produced by: Oliver Hardt / Signature Films
– Archival Footage: Der Mönch von Lützerath, Martin Lejeune, 2023 / Der Kampf ums Kohledorf, Iván Furlan Cano, Jannis Große, 2022 / Indian Farmer's Protest, Harp Farmer Pictures, 2021 / Lützi bleibt, Isabelle Acker, 2021 / Do Not Split, Anders Hammer, Field of Vision, 2020 / The "Be Water" strategy of Hong Kong's radical protestors, Andy Lo, 2019 / Plantando sonhos, colhendo conquistas (MTST Povo Sem Medo de São Bernardo), 2017 / Euromaidan Rough Cut, Roman Bondarchuk, Kateryna Hornostai, Roman Liubyi, Andriiy Lytvynenko, Olexandr Techyns'kyy, Volodymyr Tykhyi, 2014 / Libre te quiero, Basilio Martín Patino, 2012 / American Autumn: An Occudoc, Dennis Trainor Jr., 2012 / Consensus (Direct Democracy @ Occupy Wall Street), Meerkat Media Collective, 2011 / Fesseln spürt wer sich bewegt, Deutsche Film- und Fernsehakademie Berlin GmbH, Thomas Carlé, 1981 / Der Traum von einer Sache, Roswitha Ziegler, Niels Christian Bolbrinker, Bernd Westphal, Wendländische Filmkooperative, 1981

Dank (Acknowledgments)

Esra Akcan, Cornell University / Volker Albus / APIB, Articulação dos Povos Indígenas do Brasil / Architectures of Order, State Offensive for the Development of Scientific and Economic Excellence (LOEWE) / Paula Argomedo Ruiz de Velasco / David Flöck, Manfred Grohmann, Bollinger+Grohmann / Philipp Brendel, Hamburger Institut für Sozialforschung / Dirk Bühler / Silvia Bühler, Staatsarchiv des Kantons Bern / Juliana Canedo, Technische Universität Berlin / Laura Caroni, Archivo General de la Nación, Buenos Aires / Castroya / Vicky Chan, Avoid Obvious Architects / Markus Dietz, Polizeipräsidium Frankfurt am Main /Orsalia Dimitriou, University of The Arts London / Fiona Dixon, State Library of Queensland / Christian Eibel / Sigurt Elert / Mohamed Elshahed, Cairobserver / Sibylle Fendt / Rolf Engelke, Norbert Saßmannshausen, Frankfurter Archiv der Revolte / Frodo / Sherief Gaber, Mosireen / Marcelo Della Giustina, Technische Universität München / Omar Robert Hamilton / Greta Hansen, Pratt Institute, New York City / Tali Hatuka, Tel Aviv University / Susan

Hecht, Jill Freedman Foundation / Marius Helten, RWTH Aachen / Beate Dannhorn, Nina Gorgus, Dorothee Linnemann, Historisches Museum Frankfurt / Franka Breunig, Matthias Bruhn, Constanze Fischbeck, Eisenhart Keimeyer, Thomas Rustemeyer, Hochschule für Gestaltung Karlsruhe / Carolin Höfler, Technische Hochschule Köln / Christian Hüsen, Kontext Architektur / Birgit Huneke, Gorleben Archiv / Institut für Stadtgeschichte, Frankfurt am Main / Yelta Köm, Bauhaus Universität Weimar / Renata Kovalčiukienė, Lietuvos nacionalinis muziejus (National Museum of Lithuania) / Svenja Kunze, Hamburger Institut für Sozialforschung / Anja Lange, Kriminaltechnische Lehrmittelsammlung des Polizeipräsidiums Frankfurt am Main / Liese Lyon / Leonie Lube / Mira Kapfinger / Otto Kapfinger / Wolfgang Kemp / Ursula Kirschner, Leuphana Universität Lüneburg / Alexander Kluge / Judith Koberstein, Haus der Geschichte Bonn / Andreas Krištof / Marie Haff, Lutz Nitsche, Friederike Tappe-Hornbostel, Kulturstiftung des Bundes / Evita Mača, 1991. gada barikāžu muzejs (Museum of the Barricades of 1991), Riga / Jutta Matysek / Flavia Meireles, Centro Federal de Educação Tecnológica Celso Suckow da Fonseca, Rio de Janeiro / Gideon Mendel / Merle, LobauBleibt / Olaf Metzel / Friederike Meyer / Mik3 / Mike / Morsch / Stephan Mörsch / Heiko Müller-Ripke, Bäuerliche Notgemeinschaft / Monika Ottermann, MTST / Katleen Nagel / Christoph Grill, Henning Schröder, Michael Schrodt, picture alliance / Radieschen / Oleksiy Radynski, Visual Culture Research Center, Kyjiw / Meike Ratering, Hochschule Düsseldorf / Marten Reiß / Oliver Ressler / Samir Jamal Aldin / Aktivist*in „Samstag", Presseteam Lützerath / Dieter Schaarschmidt / Matthias Schmeier / Jonathan Schmidt-Colinet / Christoph Schwarz / Yulia Serdyukova, yutopia films / Deane Simpson, Royal Danish Academy, Kopenhagen / Stefan,

Parents for Future / Stick / Eva Decker, Lars Köppen, Stiftung Günter Zint / Carmen Talhi / Nassim Talhi / Fernanda Tellez Velasco / Lisa Beißwanger, Leonie Lube, Technische Universität Darmstadt / Matthew Thompson, Martin Luther King Memorial Library / Toto / Nayara Benatti, David Sperling, Universidade de São Paulo / Olivia Horsfall Turner, Olivia Stroud, Victoria and Albert Museum / Abigail Wiebenson / Mareike Wiegels / Paula Winkler / Ute Wittich / René Wüthrich, Berner Zeitung / Sarover Zaidi, Jindal School of Art & Architecture / Roswitha Ziegler, Wendländische Filmkooperative / Philip Kurz, Laura Puin, Wüstenrot Stiftung

Unser besonderer Dank gilt den Autor*innen, Gesprächspartner*innen und Fotograf*innen. (Our special thanks go to the authors, conversation partners, and photographers.)

Gefördert durch die

(Funded by the German Federal Cultural Foundation)

Gefördert von

Die Beauftragte der Bundesregierung für Kultur und Medien

(Funded by the Federal Government Commissioner for Culture and the Media)

Teilprojekt zur Architekturvermittlung in Kooperation mit der

(Sub-project on education in collaboration with the Wüstenrot Foundation)

Ausstellung (Exhibition)

Kuratorisches Team DAM + MAK
(Curatorial Team DAM + MAK)

Kurator DAM – Konzeption, Akquise,
Projektleitung (Curator DAM—
Concept, Funding, Curatorial Direction):
Oliver Elser

Kuratorische Assistenz DAM,
Recherche (Curatorial Assistance
DAM, Research):
Anna-Maria Mayerhofer

Wissenschaftliche Volontärin DAM
(Scientific Trainee DAM):
Jennifer Dyck

Kurator MAK (Curator MAK):
Sebastian Hackenschmidt

Assistenz MAK (Assistance MAK):
Judith Huemer

Ausstellungsgestaltung
(Exhibition Design):
Something Fantastic
(Elena Schütz,
Julian Schubert,
Leonard Streich)

Szenografischer Support
(Exhibition Design Assistance):
Vera Gärtner

Team DAM:
– Direktor (Director):
  Peter Cachola Schmal
– Stellvertretende Direktorin
  (Deputy Director):
  Andrea Jürges
– Registrar (Registrar):
  Wolfgang Welker
– Öffentlichkeitsarbeit (Public
  Relations):
  Brita Köhler, Anna Wegmann
– Architekturvermittlung (Education):
  Rebekka Kremershof, Confiyet Aydin
– Papierrestaurierung (Conservator):
  Paula Argomedo
– Bibliothekarin (Librarian):
  Christiane Eulig
– Sekretariat und Verwaltung
  (Administration):
  Inka Plechaty, Nicole Fallert

– Haustechniker (Technicians):
  Daniel Sarvari, Giancarlo Rossano,
  Milan Dejanov
– Kasse (Front Desk):
  Ieva Paegle
– Studentische Mitarbeit
  (Student Assistant):
  Odile Langhammer
– Aufbau (Installation Team):
  Marina Barry, Hans Brückner,
  Caroline Krause, Jörn Schön, Ömer
  Simsek, Gerhard Winkler unter der
  Leitung von (under the direction of)
  Christian Walter

Projektteam MAK
Ausstellung Protest/Architektur
(MAK Project Team Protest/
Architecture exhibition):
– Generaldirektorin und
  wissenschaftliche Geschäftsführerin
  (General Director and Artistic
  Director):
  Lilli Hollein
– Wirtschaftliche Geschäftsführerin
  (Managing Director):
  Teresa Mitterlehner-Marchesani
– Stv. wissenschaftliche
  Geschäftsführerin
  (Deputy Director):
  Martina Kandeler-Fritsch
– Ausstellungsorganisation
  (Exhibition Management):
  Mario Kojetinsky (Head), Alena Volk
– Presse und Öffentlichkeitsarbeit,
  Sponsoring (Public Relations,
  Sponsoring):
  Judith Schwarz-Jungmann
– Kommunikation und Marketing
  (Communications and Marketing):
  Olivia Harrer
– Vermittlung und Outreach
  (Education and Outreach):
  Janina Falkner
– Restaurierung und Werkstätten
  (Conservation and Workshops):
  Anne Biber, Britta Dierig
– Text- und Publikationsmanagement
  (Text and Publication Management):
  Astrid Böhacker, Cornelia Malli